AETERNA PUBLISHING

LECTURES ON DRAMATIC ART AND LITERATURE

BY

AUGUST WILHELM SCHLEGEL

TRANSLATED BY JOHN BLACK

"Were I to pray for a taste which should stand me in stead under every variety of circumstances, and be a source of happiness and cheerfulness to me during life, and a shield against its ills, however things might go amiss and the world frown upon me, it would he a taste for reading.... Give a man this taste, and the means of gratifying it, and you can hardly fail of making him a happy man; unless, indeed, you put into his hands a most perverse selection of Books. You place him in contact with the best society in every period of history,--with the wisest, the wittiest, the tenderest, the bravest, and the purest characters who have adorned humanity. You make him a denizen of all nations, a contemporary of all ages. The world has been created for him."--SIR JOHN HERSCHEL. *Address on the opening of the Eton Library*, 1833.

PREFACE OF THE TRANSLATOR.

The Lectures of A. W. SCHLEGEL on Dramatic Poetry have obtained high celebrity on the Continent, and been much alluded to of late in several publications in this country. The boldness of his attacks on rules which are considered as sacred by the French critics, and on works of which the French nation in general have long been proud, called forth a more than ordinary degree of indignation against his work in France. It was amusing enough to observe the hostility carried on against him in the Parisian Journals. The writers in these Journals found it much easier to condemn M. SCHLEGEL than to refute him: they allowed that what he said was very ingenious, and had a great appearance of truth; but still they said it was not truth. They never, however, as far as I could observe, thought proper to grapple with him, to point out anything unfounded in his premises, or illogical in the conclusions which he drew from them; they generally confined themselves to mere assertions, or to minute and unimportant observations by which the real question was in no manner affected.

In this country the work will no doubt meet with a very different reception. Here we have no want of scholars to appreciate the value of his views of the ancient drama; and it will be no disadvantage to him, in our eyes, that he has been unsparing in his attack on the literature of our enemies. It will hardly fail to astonish us, however, to find a stranger better acquainted with the brightest poetical ornament of this country than any of ourselves; and that the admiration of the English nation for Shakspeare should first obtain a truly enlightened interpreter in a critic of Germany.

It is not for me, however, to enlarge on the merits of a work which has already obtained so high a reputation. I shall better consult my own advantage in giving a short extract from the animated account of M. SCHLEGEL'S Lectures in the late work on Germany by Madame de Stael:--

"W. SCHLEGEL has given a course of Dramatic Literature at Vienna, which comprises every thing remarkable that has been composed for the theatre, from the time of the Grecians to our own days. It is not a barren nomenclature of the works of the various authors: he seizes the spirit of their different sorts of literature with all the imagination of a poet. We are sensible that to produce such consequences extraordinary studies are required: but learning is not perceived in this work, except by his perfect knowledge of the *chefs-d'oeuvre* of composition. In a few pages we reap the fruit of the labour of a whole life; every opinion formed by the author, every epithet given to the writers of whom he speaks, is beautiful and just, concise and animated. He has found the art of treating the finest pieces of poetry as so many wonders of nature, and of painting them in lively colours, which do not injure the justness of the outline; for we cannot repeat too often, that imagination, far from being an enemy to truth, brings it forward more than any other faculty of the mind; and all those who depend upon it as an excuse for indefinite terms or exaggerated expressions, are at least as destitute of poetry as of good sense.

"An analysis of the principles on which both Tragedy and Comedy are founded, is treated in this course with much depth of philosophy. This kind of merit is often found among the German writers; but SCHLEGEL has no equal in the art of inspiring his own admiration; in general, be shows himself attached to a simple taste, sometimes bordering on rusticity; but he deviates from his usual opinions in favour of the inhabitants of the South. Their play on words is not the object of his censure; he detests the affectation which owes its existence to the spirit of society: but that which is excited by the luxury of imagination pleases him, in poetry, as the profusion of colours and perfumes would do in nature. SCHLEGEL, after having acquired a great reputation by his translation of Shakspeare, became also enamoured of Calderon, but with a very different sort of attachment from that with which Shakspeare had inspired him; for while the English author is deep and gloomy in his knowledge of the human heart, the Spanish poet gives himself up with pleasure and delight to the beauty of life, to the sincerity of faith, and to all the brilliancy of those virtues which derive their colouring from the sunshine of the soul.

"I was at Vienna when W. SCHLEGEL gave his public course of Lectures. I expected only good sense and instruction, where the object was merely to convey information: I was astonished to hear a critic as eloquent as an orator, and who, far from falling upon defects, which are the eternal food of mean and little jealousy, sought only the means of reviving a creative genius."

Thus far Madame de Stael. In taking upon me to become the interpreter of a work of this description to my countrymen, I am aware that I have incurred no slight degree of responsibility. How I have executed my task it is not for me to speak, but for the reader to judge. This much, however, I will say,--that I have always endeavoured to discover the true meaning of the author, and that I believe I have seldom mistaken it. Those who are best acquainted with the psychological riches of the German language, will be the most disposed to look on my labour with an eye of indulgence.

AUTHOR'S PREFACE.

From the size of the present work, it will not be expected that it should contain either a course of Dramatic Literature bibliographically complete, or a history of the theatre compiled with antiquarian accuracy. Of books containing dry accounts and lists of names there are already enough. My purpose was to give a general view, and to develope those ideas which ought to guide us in our estimate of the value of the dramatic productions of various ages and nations.

The greatest part of the following Lectures, with the exception of a few observations of a secondary nature, the suggestion of the moment, were delivered orally as they now appear in print. The only alteration consists in a more commodious distribution, and here and there in additions, where the limits of the time prevented me from handling many matters with uniform minuteness. This may afford a compensation for the animation of oral delivery which sometimes throws a veil over deficiencies of expression, and always excites a certain degree of expectation.

I delivered these Lectures, in the spring of 1808, at Vienna, to a brilliant audience of nearly three hundred individuals of both sexes. The inhabitants of Vienna have long been in the habit of refuting the injurious descriptions which many writers of the North of Germany have given of that capital, by the kindest reception of all learned men and artists belonging to these regions, and by the most disinterested zeal for the credit of our national literature, a zeal which a just sensibility has not been able to cool. I found here the cordiality of better times united with that amiable animation of the South, which is often denied to our German seriousness, and the universal diffusion of a keen taste for intellectual amusement. To this circumstance alone I must attribute it that not a few of the men who hold the most important places at court, in the state, and in the army, artists and literary men of merit, women of the choicest social cultivation, paid me not merely an occasional visit, but devoted to me an uninterrupted attention.

With joy I seize this fresh opportunity of laying my gratitude at the feet of the benignant monarch who, in the permission to deliver these Lectures communicated to me by way of distinction immediately from his own hand, gave me an honourable testimony of his gracious confidence, which I as a foreigner who had not the happiness to be born under his sceptre, and merely felt myself bound as a German and a citizen of the world to wish him every blessing and prosperity, could not possibly have merited.

Many enlightened patrons and zealous promoters of everything good and becoming have merited my gratitude for the assistance which they gave to my undertaking, and the encouragement which they afforded me during its execution.

The whole of my auditors rendered my labour extremely agreeable by their indulgence, their attentive participation, and their readiness to distinguish, in a feeling manner, every passage which seemed worthy of their applause.

It was a flattering moment, which I shall never forget, when, in the last hour, after I had called up recollections of the old German renown sacred to every one possessed of true patriotic sentiment, and when the minds of my auditors were thus more solemnly attuned, I was at last obliged to take my leave powerfully agitated by the reflection that our recent relation, founded on a common love for a nobler mental cultivation, would be so soon dissolved, and that I should never again see those together who were then assembled around me. A general emotion was perceptible, excited by so much that I could not say, but respecting which our hearts understood each other. In the mental dominion of thought and poetry, inaccessible to worldly power, the Germans, who are separated in so many ways from each other, still feel their unity: and in this feeling, whose interpreter the writer and orator must be, amidst our clouded prospects we may still cherish the elevating presage of the great and immortal calling of our people, who from time immemorial have remained unmixed in their present habitations.

GENEVA, *February*, 1809.

OBSERVATION PREFIXED TO PART OF THE WORK PRINTED IN 1811.

The declaration in the Preface that these Lectures were, with some additions, printed as they were delivered, is in so far to be corrected, that the additions in the second part are much more considerable than in the first. The restriction, in point of time in the oral delivery, compelled me to leave more gaps in the last half than in the first. The part respecting Shakspeare and the English theatre, in particular, has been, almost altogether re-written. I have been prevented, partly by the want of leisure and partly by the limits of the work, from treating of the Spanish theatre with that fulness which its importance deserves.

MEMOIR OF THE LITERARY LIFE OF AUGUSTUS WILLIAM VON SCHLEGEL

AUGUSTUS WILLIAM VON SCHLEGEL, the author of the following Lectures, was, with his no-less distinguished brother, Frederick, the son of John Adolph Schlegel, a native of Saxony, and descended from a noble family. Holding a high appointment in the Lutheran church, Adolph Schlegel distinguished himself as a religious poet, and was the friend and associate of Rabener, Gellert, and Klopstock. Celebrated for his eloquence in the pulpit, and strictly diligent in the performance of his religious duties, he died in 1792, leaving an example to his children which no doubt had a happy influence on them.

Of these, the seventh, Augustus William, was born in Hanover, September 5th, 1767. In his early childhood, he evinced a genuine susceptibility for all that was good and noble; and this early promise of a generous and virtuous disposition was carefully nurtured by the religious instruction of his mother, an amiable and highly-gifted woman. Of this parent's pious and judicious teaching, Augustus William had to the end of his days a grateful remembrance, and he cherished for her throughout life a sincere and affectionate esteem, whose ardour neither time nor distance could diminish. The filial affection of her favourite son soothed the declining years of his mother, and lightened the anxieties with which the critical and troubled state of the times alarmed her old age. His further education was carried on by a private tutor, who prepared him for the grammar-school at Hanover, where he was distinguished both for his unremitting application, to which he often sacrificed the hours of leisure and recreation, and for the early display of a natural gift for language, which enabled him immediately on the close of his academic career to accept a tutorial appointment, which demanded of its holder a knowledge not only of the classics but also of English and French. He also displayed at a very early age a talent for poetry, and some of his juvenile extempore effusions were remarkable for their easy versification and rhythmical flow. In his eighteenth year he was called upon to deliver in the Lyceum of his native city, the anniversary oration in honour of a royal birthday. His address on this occasion excited an extraordinary sensation both by the graceful elegance of the style and the interest of the matter, written in hexameters. It embraced a short history of poetry in Germany, and was relieved and animated with many judicious and striking illustrations from the earliest Teutonic poets.

He now proceeded to the University of Gottingen as a student of theology.

which science, however, he shortly abandoned for the more congenial one of philology. The propriety of this charge he amply attested by his Essay on the Geography of Homer, which displayed both an intelligent and comprehensive study of this difficult branch of classical archaeology.

At Gottingen he lived in the closest intimacy with Heyne, for whose *Virgil*, in 1788 he completed an index; he also became acquainted with the celebrated Michaelis. It was here too that he formed the friendship of Burger, to whose *Academie der Schonen Redekunste*, he contributed his *Ariadne*, and an essay on *Dante*. The kindred genius of Burger favourably influenced his own mind and tastes, and moved him to make the first known attempt to naturalize the Italian sonnet in Germany.

Towards the end of his university career he combined his own studies with the private instruction of a rich young Englishman, born in the East Indies, and at the close of it accepted the post of tutor to the only son of Herr Muilmann, the celebrated Banker of Amsterdam. In this situation he gained universal respect and esteem, but after three years he quitted it to enter upon a wider sphere of literary activity. On his return to his native country he was elected Professor in the University of Jena. Schlegel's residence in this place, which may truly be called the classic soil of German literature, as it gained him the acquaintance of his eminent contemporaries Schiller and Goethe, marks a decisive epoch in the formation of his intellectual character. At this date he contributed largely to the *Horen*, and also to Schiller's *Musen-Almanach*, and down to 1799 was one of the most fertile writers in the *Allgemeinen Literatur-Zeitung* of Jena. It was here, also, that he commenced his translations of Shakspeare, (9 vols., Berlin, 1797-1810,) which produced a salutary effect on the taste and judgment of his countrymen, and also on Dramatic Art and theatrical representation in Germany. Notwithstanding the favourable reception of this work he subsequently abandoned it, and on the publication of a new edition, in 1825, he cheerfully consigned to Tieck the revision of his own labours, and the completion of the yet untranslated pieces.

Continuing attached to the University of Jena, where the dignity of Professorship was associated with that of Member of the Council, he now commenced a course of lectures on Aesthetics, and joined his brother Frederick in the editorship of the *Athenaeum*, (3 vols., Berlin, 1796-1800,) an Aesthetico-critical journal, intended, while observing a rigorous but an impartial spirit of criticism, to discover and foster every grain of a truly vital development of mind. It was also during his residence at Jena that he published the first edition of his Poems, among which the religious pieces and the Sonnets on Art were greatly admired and had many imitators. To the latter years of his residence at Jena, which may be called the political portion of Schlegel's literary career, belongs the *Gate of Honour for the Stage-President Von-Kotzebue*, (*Ehrenpforte fur den Theater Prasidenten von Kotzebue*, 1800,) an ill-natured and much-censured satire in reply to Kotzebue's attack, entitled the *Hyperborean Ass* (*Hyperboreischen Esee*). At this time he also collected several of his own and brother Frederick's earlier and occasional contributions to various periodicals, and these, together with the hitherto unpublished dissertations on Burger's works, make up the *Characteristiken u Kritiken* (2 vols., Koenigsberg, 1801). Shortly afterwards he undertook with Tieck the editorship of *Musen-Almanack* for 1802. The two brothers were now leading a truly scientific and poetic life, associating and co-operating with many minds of a kindred spirit, who gathered round Tieck and Novalis as their centre.

His marriage with the daughter of Michaelis was not a happy one, and was quickly followed by a separation, upon which Schlegel proceeded to Berlin. In this city, towards the end of 1802, he delivered his *Lectures on the Present State of Literature and the Fine Arts*, which were afterwards printed in the *Europa*, under his brother's editorship. The publication in 1803 of his *Ion*, a drama in imitation of the ancients, but as a composition unmarked by any peculiar display of vigour, led to an interesting argument between himself, Bernhardi, and Schilling. This discussion, which extended from its original subject to Euripides and Dramatic Representation in general, was carried on in the *Journal for the Polite World* (*Zeitung fur die elegante Welt*,) which Schlegel supported by his advice and contributions. In this periodical he also entered the lists in opposition to Kotzebue and Merkel in the *Freimuthige* (*The Liberal*), and the merits of the so-called modern school and its leaders, was the subject of a paper war, waged with the bitterest acrimony of controversy, which did not scruple to employ the sharpest weapons of personal abuse and ridicule.

At this date Schlegel was engaged upon his *Spanish Theatre*, (2 vols., Berlin, 1803-1809). In the execution of this work, much was naturally demanded of the translator of Shakspeare, nor did he disappoint the general expectator, although he had here far greater difficulties to contend with. Not content with merely giving a faithful interpretation of his author's meaning, he laid down and strictly observed the law of adhering rigorously to all the measures, rhythms, and assonances of the original. These two excellent translations, in each of which he has brought to bear both the great command of his own, and a wonderful quickness in catching the spirit of a foreign language, have earned for Schlegel the foremost place among successful and able translators, while his *Flowers of Italian, Spanish, and Portuguese Poetry* (*Blumenstrausse d. Ital. Span. u. Portug. Poesie*, Berlin, 1804), furnish another proof both of his skill in this pursuit and of the extent of his acquaintance with European literature. Moreover, the merit of having by these translations made Shakspeare and Calderon more widely known and better appreciated in Germany would, in default of any other claim, alone entitle him to take high rank in the annals of modern literature.

But a new and more important career was now open to him by his introduction to Madame de Stael. Making a tour in Germany, this distinguished woman arrived at Berlin in 1805, and desirous of acquainting herself more thoroughly with German literature she selected Schlegel to direct her studies of it, and at the same time confided to his charge the completion of her children's education. Quitting Berlin he accompanied this lady on her travels through Italy and France, and afterwards repaired with her to her paternal seat at Coppet, on the Lake of Geneva, which now became for some time his fixed abode. It was here that in 1807 he wrote in French his *Parallel between the Phaedra of Euripides and the Phedre of Racine*, which produced a lively sensation in the literary circles of Paris. This city had peculiar attractions for Schlegel, both in its invaluable literary stores and its re-union of men of letters, among whom his own views and opinions found many enthusiastic admirers and partisans, notwithstanding that in his critical analysis of Racine's *Phedre* he had presumed to attack what Frenchmen deemed the chiefest glory of their literature, and had mortified their national vanity in its most sensitive point.

In the spring of 1808 he visited Vienna, and there read to a brilliant audience his *Lectures on Dramatic Art and Literature*, which, on their publication, were hailed throughout Europe with marked approbation, and which will, unquestionably, transmit his name to the latest posterity. His object in these Lectures is both to take a rapid survey of dramatic productions of different ages and nations, and to develope and determine the general ideas by which their true artistic value must be judged. In his travels with Madame de Stael he was introduced to the present King, then the Crown Prince, of Bavaria, who bestowed on him many marks of his respect and esteem, and about this time he took a part in the *German Museum* (*Deutsche Museum*), of his brother Frederick, contributing some learned and profound dissertations on the *Lay of the Nibelungen*. In 1812, when the subjugated South no longer afforded an asylum to the liberal-minded De Stael, with whose personal fortunes he felt himself inseparably linked by that deep feeling of esteem and friendship which speaks so touchingly and pathetically in some of his later poems, he accompanied that lady on a visit to Stockholm, where he formed the acquaintance of the Crown Prince.

The great political events of this period were not without their effect on

Schlegel's mind, and in 1813 he came forward as a political writer, when his powerful pen was not without its effect in rousing the German mind from the torpor into which it had sunk beneath the victorious military despotism of France. But he was called upon to take a more active part in the measures of these stirring times, and in this year entered the service of the Crown Prince of Sweden, as secretary and counsellor at head quarters. For this Prince he had a great personal regard, and estimated highly both his virtues as a man and his talents as a general. The services he rendered the Swedish Prince were duly appreciated and rewarded, among other marks of distinction by a patent of nobility, in virtue of which he prefixed the "Von" to his paternal name of Schlegel. The Emperor Alexander, of whose religious elevation of character he always spoke with admiration, also honoured him with his intimacy and many tokens of esteem.

Upon the fall of Napoleon he returned to Coppet with Madame de Stael, and in 1815 published a second volume of his *Poetical Works*, (Heildelberg, 1811-1815, 2nd edit., 2 vols., 1820). These are characterized not merely by the brilliancy and purity of the language, but also by the variety and richness of the imagery. Among these the *Arion*, *Pygmalion*, and *Der Heilige Lucas* (St. Luke,) the Sonnets, and the sublime elegy, *Rhine*, dedicated to Madame de Stael, deserve especial mention, and give him a just claim to a poet's crown.

On the death of his friend and patroness in 1819, he accepted the offer of a professor's chair in Bonn, where he married a daughter of Professor Paulus. This union, as short-lived as the first, was followed by a separation in 1820. In his new position of academic tutor, while he diligently promoted the study of the fine arts and sciences, both of the Ancient and the Moderns, he applied himself with peculiar ardour to Oriental literature, and particularly to the Sanscrit. As a fruit of these studies, he published his *Indian Library*, (2 vols., Bonn, 1820-26); he also set up a press for printing the great Sanscrit work, the *Ramajana* (Bonn, 1825). He also edited the Sanscrit text, with a Latin translation, of the Bhagavad-Gita, an episode of the great Indian Epos, the *Mahabharata* (Bonn, 1829). About this period his Oriental studies took, him to France, and afterwards to England, where, in London and in the college libraries of Oxford and Cambridge, and the East India College at Hailesbury, he carefully examined the various collections of Oriental MSS. On his return he was appointed Superintendent of the Museum of Antiquities, and in 1827 delivered at Berlin a course of Lectures on the *Theory and History of the Fine Arts*, (Berlin, 1827). These were followed by his *Criticisms*, (Berlin, 1828), and his *Reflexion sur l'Etude des Langues Asiatiques*, addressed to Sir James Mackintosh. Being accused of a secret leaning to Roman Catholicism, (Kryptocatholicisme,) he ably defended himself in a reply entitled *Explication de quelques Malentendus*, (Berlin, 1828.)

A. W. Von Schlegel, besides being a Member of the Legion of Honour, was invested with the decorations of several other Orders. He wrote French with as much facility as his native language, and many French journals were proud to number him among their contributors. He also assisted Madame de Stael in her celebrated work *De l'Allemagne*, and superintended the publication of her posthumous *Considerations sur la Revolution Francaise*.

After this long career of successful literary activity, A. W. Von Schlegel died at Bonn, 12 May, 1845. His death was thus noticed in the *Athenaeum*:--

"This illustrious writer was, in conjunction with his brother Frederick, as most European readers well know, the founder of the modern romantic school of German literature, and as a critic fought many a hard battle for his faith. The clearness of his insight into poetical and dramatic truth, Englishmen will always be apt to estimate by the fact that it procured for himself and for his countrymen the freedom of Shakspeare's enchanted world, and the taste of all the marvellous things that, like the treasures of Aladdin's garden, are fruit and gem at once upon its immortal boughs:-- Frenchmen will not readily forget that he disparaged Moliere. The merit of Schlegel's dramatic criticism ought not, however, to be thus limited. Englishmen themselves are deeply indebted to him. His Lectures, translated by Black, excited great interest here when first published, some thirty years since, and have worthily taken a permanent place in our libraries."

His collection of books, which was rather extensive, and rich in Oriental, especially Sanscrit literature, was sold by auction in Bonn, December, 1845. It appears by a chronological list prefixed to the catalogue, that reckoning both his separate publications and those contributed to periodicals, his printed works number no fewer than 126. Besides these he left many unpublished manuscripts, which, says the *Athenaeum*, "he bequeathed to the celebrated archaeologist, Welcker, professor at the Royal University of Bonn, with a request that he would cause them to be published."

TABLE OF CONTENTS

DRAMATIC LITERATURE.

LECTURE I.

Introduction--Spirit of True Criticism--Difference of Taste between the Ancients and Moderns--Classical and Romantic Poetry and Art--Division of Dramatic Literature; the Ancients, their Imitators, and the Romantic Poets.

The object of the present series of Lectures will be to combine the theory of Dramatic Art with its history, and to bring before my auditors at once its principles and its models.

It belongs to the general philosophical theory of poetry, and the other fine arts, to establish the fundamental laws of the beautiful. Every art, on the other hand, has its own special theory, designed to teach the limits, the difficulties, and the means by which it must be regulated in its attempt to realize those laws. For this purpose, certain scientific investigations are indispensable to the artist, although they have but little attraction for those whose admiration of art is confined to the enjoyment of the actual productions of distinguished minds. The general theory, on the other hand, seeks to analyze that essential faculty of human nature--the sense of the beautiful, which at once calls the fine arts into existence, and accounts for the satisfaction which arises from the contemplation of them; and also points out the relation which subsists between this and all other sentient and cognizant faculties of man. To the man of thought and speculation, therefore, it is of the highest importance, but by itself alone it is quite inadequate to guide and direct the essays and practice of art.

Now, the history of the fine arts informs us what has been, and the theory teaches what ought to be accomplished by them. But without some intermediate and connecting link, both would remain independent and separate from one and other, and each by itself, inadequate and defective. This connecting link is furnished by criticism, which both elucidates the history of the arts, and makes the theory fruitful. The comparing together, and judging of the existing productions of the human mind, necessarily throws light upon the conditions which are indispensable to the creation of original and masterly works of art.

Ordinarily, indeed, men entertain a very erroneous notion of criticism, and understand by it nothing more than a certain shrewdness in detecting and exposing the faults of a work of art. As I have devoted the greater part of my life to this pursuit, I may be excused if, by way of preface, I seek to lay before my auditors my own ideas of the true genius of criticism.

We see numbers of men, and even whole nations, so fettered by the conventions of education and habits of life, that, even in the appreciation of the fine arts, they cannot shake them off. Nothing to them appears natural, appropriate, or beautiful, which is alien to their own language, manners, and social relations. With this exclusive mode of seeing and feeling, it is no doubt possible to attain, by means of cultivation, to great nicety of discrimination within the narrow circle to which it limits and circumscribes them. But no man can be a true critic or connoisseur without universality of mind, without that flexibility which enables him, by renouncing all personal predilections and blind habits, to adapt himself to the peculiarities of other ages and nations--to feel them, as it were, from their proper central point, and, what ennobles human nature, to recognise and duly appreciate whatever is beautiful and grand under the external accessories which were necessary to its embodying, even though occasionally they may seem to disguise and distort it. There is no monopoly of poetry for particular ages and nations; and consequently that despotism in taste, which would seek to invest with universal authority the rules which at first, perhaps, were but arbitrarily advanced, is but a vain and empty pretension. Poetry, taken in its widest acceptation, as the power of creating what is beautiful, and representing it to the eye or the ear, is a universal gift of Heaven, being shared to a certain extent even by those whom we call barbarians and savages. Internal excellence is alone decisive, and where this exists, we must not allow ourselves to be repelled by the external appearance. Everything must be traced up to the root of human nature: if it has sprung from thence, it has an undoubted worth of its own; but if, without possessing a living germ, it is merely externally attached thereto, it will never thrive nor acquire a proper growth. Many productions which appear at first sight dazzling phenomena in the province of the fine arts, and which as a whole have been honoured with the appellation of works of a golden age, resemble the mimic gardens of children: impatient to witness the work of their hands, they break off here and there branches and flowers, and plant them in the earth; everything at first assumes a noble appearance: the childish gardener struts proudly up and down among his showy beds, till the rootless plants begin to droop, and hang their withered leaves and blossoms, and nothing soon remains but the bare twigs, while the dark forest, on which no art or care was ever bestowed, and which towered up towards heaven long before human remembrance, bears every blast unshaken, and fills the solitary beholder with religious awe.

Let us now apply the idea which we have been developing, of the universality of true criticism, to the history of poetry and the fine arts. This, like the so-called universal history, we generally limit (even though beyond this range there may be much that is both remarkable and worth knowing) to whatever has had a nearer or more remote influence on the present civilisation of Europe: consequently, to the works of the Greeks and Romans, and of those of the modern European nations, who first and chiefly distinguished themselves in art and literature. It is well known that, three centuries and a-half ago, the study of ancient literature received a new life, by the diffusion of the Grecian language (for the Latin never became extinct); the classical authors were brought to light, and rendered universally accessible by means of the press; and the monuments of ancient art were diligently disinterred and preserved. All this powerfully excited the human mind, and formed a decided epoch in the history of human civilisation; its manifold effects have extended to our times, and will yet extend to an incalculable series of ages. But the study of the ancients was forthwith most fatally perverted. The learned, who were chiefly in the possession of this knowledge, and who were incapable of distinguishing themselves by works of their own, claimed for the ancients an unlimited authority, and with great appearance of reason, since they are models in their kind. Maintaining that nothing could be hoped for the human mind but from an imitation of antiquity, in the works of the moderns they only valued what resembled, or seemed to bear a resemblance to, those of the ancients. Everything else they rejected as barbarous and unnatural. With the great poets and artists it was quite otherwise. However strong their enthusiasm for the ancients, and however determined their purpose of entering into competition with them, they were compelled by their independence and originality of mind, to strike out a path of their own, and to impress upon their productions the stamp of their own genius. Such was the case with Dante among the Italians, the father of modern poetry; acknowledging Virgil for his master, he has produced a work which, of all others, most differs from the Aeneid, and in our opinion far excels its pretended model in power, truth, compass, and profundity. It was the same afterwards with Ariosto, who has most unaccountably been compared to Homer, for nothing can be more unlike. So in art with Michael Angelo and Raphael, who had no doubt deeply studied the antique. When we ground our judgment of modern painters merely on their greater or less resemblance to the ancients, we must necessarily be unjust towards them, as Winkelmann undoubtedly has in the case of Raphael. As the poets for the most part had their share of scholarship, it gave rise to a curious struggle between their natural inclination and their imaginary duty. When they sacrificed to the latter, they were praised by the learned; but by yielding to the former, they became the favourites of the people. What preserves the heroic poems of a Tasso and a Camoens to this day alive in the hearts and on the lips of their countrymen, is by no means their imperfect resemblance to Virgil, or even to Homer, but in Tasso the tender feeling of chivalrous love and honour, and in Camoens the glowing inspiration of heroic patriotism.

Those very ages, nations, and ranks, who felt least the want of a poetry of their own, were the most assiduous in their imitation of the ancients; accordingly, its results are but dull school exercises, which at best excite a frigid admiration. But in the fine arts, mere imitation is always fruitless; even what we borrow from others, to assume a true poetical shape, must, as it were, be born again within us. Of what avail is all foreign imitation? Art cannot exist without nature, and man can give nothing to his fellow-men but himself.

Genuine successors and true rivals of the ancients, who, by virtue of congenial talents and cultivation have walked in their path and worked in their spirit, have ever been as rare as their mechanical spiritless copyists are common. Seduced by the form, the great body of critics have been but too indulgent to these servile imitators. These were held up as correct modern classics, while the great truly living and popular poets, whose reputation was a part of their nations' glory, and to whose sublimity it was impossible to be altogether blind, were at best but tolerated as rude and wild natural geniuses. But the unqualified separation of genius and taste on which such a judgment proceeds, is altogether untenable. Genius is the almost unconscious choice of the highest degree of excellence, and, consequently, it is taste in its highest activity.

In this state, nearly, matters continued till a period not far back, when several inquiring minds, chiefly Germans, endeavoured to clear up the misconception, and to give the ancients their due, without being insensible to the merits of the moderns, although of a totally different kind. The apparent contradiction did not intimidate them. The groundwork of human nature is no doubt everywhere the same; but in all our investigations, we may observe that, throughout the whole range of nature, there is no elementary power so simple, but that it is capable of dividing and diverging into opposite directions. The whole play of vital motion hinges on harmony and contrast. Why, then, should not this phenomenon recur on a grander scale in the history of man? In this idea we have perhaps discovered the true key to the ancient and modern history of poetry and the fine arts. Those who adopted it, gave to the peculiar spirit of *modern* art, as contrasted with the *antique* or *classical*, the name of *romantic*. The term is certainly not inappropriate; the word is derived from *romance*--the name originally given to the languages which were formed from the mixture of the Latin and the old Teutonic dialects, in the same manner as modern civilisation is the fruit of the heterogeneous union of the peculiarities of the northern nations and the fragments of antiquity; whereas the civilisation of the ancients was much more of a piece.

The distinction which we have just stated can hardly fail to appear well founded, if it can be shown, so far as our knowledge of antiquity extends, that the same contrast in the labours of the ancients and moderns runs symmetrically, I might almost say systematically, throughout every branch of art--that it is as evident in music and the plastic arts as in poetry. This is a problem which, in its full extent, still remains to be demonstrated, though, on particular portions of it, many excellent observations have been advanced already.

Among the foreign authors who wrote before this school can be said to have been formed in Germany, we may mention Rousseau, who acknowledged the contrast in music, and showed that rhythm and melody were the prevailing principles of ancient, as harmony is that of modern music. In his prejudices against harmony, however, we cannot at all concur. On the subject of the arts of design an ingenious observation was made by Hemsterhuys, that the ancient painters were perhaps too much of sculptors, and the modern sculptors too much of painters. This is the exact point of difference; for, as I shall distinctly show in the sequel, the spirit of ancient art and poetry is *plastic*, but that of the moderns *picturesque*.

By an example taken from another art, that of architecture, I shall endeavour to illustrate what I mean by this contrast. Throughout the Middle Ages there prevailed, and in the latter centuries of that aera was carried to perfection, a style of architecture, which has been called Gothic, but ought really to have been termed old German. When, on the general revival of classical antiquity, the imitation of Grecian architecture became prevalent, and but too frequently without a due regard to the difference of climate and manners or to the purpose of the building, the zealots of this new taste, passing a sweeping sentence of condemnation on the Gothic, reprobated it as tasteless, gloomy, and barbarous. This was in some degree pardonable in the Italians, among whom a love for ancient architecture, cherished by hereditary remains of classical edifices, and the similarity of their climate to that of the Greeks and Romans, might, in some sort, be said to be innate. But we Northerns are not so easily to be talked out of the powerful, solemn impressions which seize upon the mind at entering a Gothic cathedral. We feel, on the contrary, a strong desire to investigate and to justify the source of this impression. A very slight attention will convince us, that the Gothic architecture displays not only an extraordinary degree of mechanical skill, but also a marvellous power of invention; and, on a closer examination, we recognize its profound significance, and perceive that as well as the Grecian it constitutes in itself a complete and finished system.

To the application!--The Pantheon is not more different from Westminster Abbey or the church of St. Stephen at Vienna, than the structure of a tragedy of Sophocles from a drama of Shakspeare. The comparison between these wonderful productions of poetry and architecture might be carried still farther. But does our admiration of the one compel us to depreciate the other? May we not admit that each is great and admirable in its kind, although the one is, and is meant to be, different from the other? The experiment is worth attempting. We will quarrel with no man for his predilection either for the Grecian or the Gothic. The world is wide, and affords room for a great diversity of objects. Narrow and blindly adopted prepossessions will never constitute a genuine critic or connoisseur, who ought, on the contrary, to possess the power of dwelling with liberal impartiality on the most discrepant views, renouncing the while all personal inclinations.

For our present object, the justification, namely, of the grand division which we lay down in the history of art, and according to which we conceive ourselves equally warranted in establishing the same division in dramatic literature, it might be sufficient merely to have stated this contrast between the ancient, or classical, and the romantic. But as there are exclusive admirers of the ancients, who never cease asserting that all deviation from them is merely the whim of a new school of critics, who, expressing themselves in language full of mystery, cautiously avoid conveying their sentiments in a tangible shape, I shall endeavour to explain the origin and spirit of the *romantic*, and then leave the world to judge if the use of the word, and of the idea which it is intended to convey, be thereby justified.

The mental culture of the Greeks was a finished education in the school of Nature. Of a beautiful and noble race, endowed with susceptible senses and a cheerful spirit under a mild sky, they lived and bloomed in the full health of existence; and, favoured by a rare combination of circumstances, accomplished all that the finite nature of man is capable of. The whole of their art and poetry is the expression of a consciousness of this harmony of all their faculties. They invented the poetry of joy.

Their religion was the deification of the powers of nature and of the earthly life: but this worship, which, among other nations, clouded the imagination with hideous shapes, and hardened the heart to cruelty, assumed, among the Greeks, a mild, a grand, and a dignified form. Superstition, too often the tyrant of the human faculties, seemed to have here contributed to their freest development. It cherished the arts by which it was adorned, and its idols became the models of ideal beauty.

But however highly the Greeks may have succeeded in the Beautiful, and even in the Moral, we cannot concede any higher character to their civilisation than that of a refined and ennobled sensuality. Of course this must be understood generally. The conjectures of a few philosophers, and the irradiations of poetical inspiration, constitute an occasional exception. Man can never altogether turn aside his thoughts from infinity, and some obscure recollections will always remind him of the home he has lost; but we are now speaking of the predominant tendency of his endeavours.

Religion is the root of human existence. Were it possible for man to renounce all religion, including that which is unconscious, independent of the will, he would become a mere surface without any internal substance. When this centre is disturbed, the whole system of the mental faculties and feelings takes a new shape.

And this is what has actually taken place in modern Europe through the introduction of Christianity. This sublime and beneficent religion has regenerated the ancient world from its state of exhaustion and debasement; it is the guiding principle in the history of modern nations, and even at this day, when many suppose they have shaken off its authority, they still find themselves much more influenced by it in their views of human affairs than they themselves are aware.

After Christianity, the character of Europe has, since the commencement of the Middle Ages, been chiefly influenced by the Germanic race of northern conquerors, who infused new life and vigour into a degenerated people. The stern nature of the North drives man back within himself; and what is lost in the free sportive development of the senses, must, in noble dispositions, be compensated by earnestness of mind. Hence the honest cordiality with which Christianity was welcomed by all the Teutonic tribes, so that among no other race of men has it penetrated more deeply into the inner man, displayed more powerful effects, or become more interwoven with all human feelings and sensibilities.

The rough, but honest heroism of the northern conquerors, by its admixture with the sentiments of Christianity, gave rise to chivalry, of which the object was, by vows which should be looked upon as sacred, to guard the practice of arms from every rude and ungenerous abuse of force into which it was so likely to sink.

With the virtues of chivalry was associated a new and purer spirit of love, an inspired homage for genuine female worth, which was now revered as the acme of human excellence, and, maintained by religion itself under the image of a virgin mother, infused into all hearts a mysterious sense of the purity of love.

As Christianity did not, like the heathen worship, rest satisfied with certain external acts, but claimed an authority over the whole inward man and the most hidden movement of the heart; the feeling of moral independence took refuge in the domain of honour, a worldly morality, as it were, which subsisting alongside of, was often at variance with that of religion, but yet in so far resembling it that it never calculated consequences, but consecrated unconditionally certain principles of action, which like the articles of faith, were elevated far beyond the investigation of a casuistical reasoning.

Chivalry, love, and honour, together with religion itself, are the subjects of that poetry of nature which poured itself out in the Middle Ages with incredible fulness, and preceded the more artistic cultivation of the romantic spirit. This age had also its mythology, consisting of chivalrous tales and legends; but its wonders and its heroism were the very reverse of those of the ancient mythology.

Several inquirers who, in other respects, entertain the same conception of the peculiarities of the moderns, and trace them to the same source that we do, have placed the essence of the northern poetry in melancholy; and to this, when properly understood, we have nothing to object.

Among the Greeks human nature was in itself all-sufficient; it was conscious of no defects, and aspired to no higher perfection than that which it could actually attain by the exercise of its own energies. We, however, are taught by superior wisdom that man, through a grievous transgression, forfeited the place for which he was originally destined; and that the sole destination of his earthly existence is to struggle to regain his lost position, which, if left to his own strength, he can never accomplish. The old religion of the senses sought no higher possession than outward and perishable blessings; and immortality, so far as it was believed, stood shadow-like in the obscure distance, a faint dream of this sunny waking life. The very reverse of all this is the case with the Christian view: every thing finite and mortal is lost in the contemplation of infinity; life has become shadow and darkness, and the first day of our real existence dawns in the world beyond the grave. Such a religion must waken the vague foreboding, which slumbers in every feeling heart, into a distinct consciousness that the happiness after which we are here striving is unattainable; that no external object can ever entirely fill our souls; and that all earthly enjoyment is but a fleeting and momentary illusion. When the soul, resting as it were under the willows of exile, [Footnote: *Trauerweiden der verbannung*, literally *the weeping willows of banishment*, an allusion, as every reader must know, to the 137th Psalm. Linnaeus, from this Psalm, calls the weeping willow *Salix Babylonica*.--TRANS.] breathes out its longing for its distant home, what else but melancholy can be the key-note of its songs? Hence the poetry of the ancients was the poetry of enjoyment, and ours is that of desire: the former has its foundation in the scene which is present, while the latter hovers betwixt recollection and hope. Let me not be understood as affirming that everything flows in one unvarying strain of wailing and complaint, and that the voice of melancholy is always loudly heard. As the austerity of tragedy was not incompatible with the joyous views of the Greeks, so that romantic poetry whose origin I have been describing, can assume every tone, even that of the liveliest joy; but still it will always, in some indescribable way, bear traces of the source from which it originated. The feeling of the moderns is, upon the whole, more inward, their fancy more incorporeal, and their thoughts more contemplative. In nature, it is true, the boundaries of objects run more into one another, and things are not so distinctly separated as we must exhibit them in order to convey distinct notions of them.

The Grecian ideal of human nature was perfect unison and proportion between all the powers,--a natural harmony. The moderns, on the contrary, have arrived at the consciousness of an internal discord which renders such an ideal impossible; and hence the endeavour of their poetry is to reconcile these two worlds between which we find ourselves divided, and to blend them indissolubly together. The impressions of the senses are to be hallowed, as it were, by a mysterious connexion with higher feelings; and the soul, on the other hand, embodies its forebodings, or indescribable intuitions of infinity, in types and symbols borrowed from the visible world.

In Grecian art and poetry we find an original and unconscious unity of form and matter; in the modern, so far as it has remained true to its own spirit, we observe a keen struggle to unite the two, as being naturally in opposition to each other. The Grecian executed what it proposed in the utmost perfection; but the modern can only do justice to its endeavours after what is infinite by approximation; and, from a certain appearance of imperfection, is in greater danger of not being duly appreciated.

It would lead us too far, if in the separate arts of architecture, music, and painting (for the moderns have never had a sculpture of their own), we should endeavour to point out the distinctions which we have here announced, to show the contrast observable in the character of the same arts among the ancients and moderns, and at the same time to demonstrate the kindred aim of both.

Neither can we here enter into a more particular consideration of the different kinds and forms of romantic poetry in general, but must return to our more immediate subject, which is dramatic art and literature. The division of this, as of the other departments of art, into the antique and the romantic, at once points out to us the course which we have to pursue.

We shall begin with the ancients; then proceed to their imitators, their genuine or supposed successors among the moderns; and lastly, we shall consider those poets of later times, who, either disregarding the classical models, or purposely deviating from them, have struck out a path for themselves.

Of the ancient dramatists, the Greeks alone are of any importance. In this branch of art the Romans were at first mere translators of the Greeks, and afterwards imitators, and not always very successful ones. Besides, of their dramatic labours very little has been preserved. Among modern nations an endeavour to restore the ancient stage, and, where possible, to improve it, has been shown in a very lively manner by the Italians and the French. In other nations, also, attempts of the same kind, more or less earnest, have at times, especially of late, been made in tragedy; for in comedy, the form under which it appears in Plautus and Terence has certainly been more generally prevalent. Of all studied imitations of the ancient tragedy the French is the most brilliant essay, has acquired the greatest renown, and consequently deserves the most attentive consideration. After the French come the modern Italians; viz., Metastasio and Alfieri. The romantic drama, which, strictly speaking, can neither be called tragedy nor comedy in the sense of the ancients, is indigenous only to England and Spain. In both it began to flourish at the same time, somewhat more than two hundred years ago, being brought to perfection by Shakspeare in the former country, and in the latter by Lope de Vega.

The German stage is the last of all, and has been influenced in the greatest variety of ways by all those which preceded it. It will be most appropriate, therefore, to enter upon its consideration last of all. By this course we shall be better enabled to judge of the directions which it has hitherto taken, and to point out the prospects which are still open to it.

When I promise to go through the history of the Greek and Roman, of the Italian and French, and of the English and Spanish theatres, in the few hours which are dedicated to these Lectures, I wish it to be understood that I can only enter into such an account of them as will comprehend their most essential peculiarities under general points of view. Although I confine myself to a single domain of poetry, still the mass of materials comprehended within it is too extensive to be taken in by the eye at once, and this would be the case were I even to limit myself to one of its subordinate departments. We might read ourselves to death with farces. In the ordinary histories of literature the poets of one language, and one description, are enumerated in succession, without any further discrimination, like the Assyrian and Egyptian kings in the old universal histories. There are persons who have an unconquerable passion for the titles of books, and we willingly concede to them the privilege of increasing their number by books on the titles of books. It is much the same thing, however, as in the history of a war to give the name of every soldier who fought in the ranks of the hostile armies. It is usual, however, to speak only of the generals, and those who may have performed actions of distinction. In like manner the battles of the human mind, if I may use the expression, have been won by a few intellectual heroes. The history of the development of art and its various forms may be therefore exhibited in the characters of a number, by no means considerable, of elevated and creative minds.

LECTURE II.

Definition of the Drama--View of the Theatres of all Nations--Theatrical Effect--Importance of the Stage--Principal Species of the Drama.

Before, however, entering upon such a history as we have now described, it will be necessary to examine what is meant by *dramatic*, *theatrical*, *tragic*, and *comic*.

What is dramatic? To many the answer will seem very easy: where various persons are introduced conversing together, and the poet does not speak in his own person. This is, however, merely the first external foundation of the form; and that is dialogue. But the characters may express thoughts and sentiments without operating any change on each other, and so leave the minds of both in exactly the same state in which they were at the commencement; in such a case, however interesting the conversation may be, it cannot be said to possess a dramatic interest. I shall make this clear by alluding to a more tranquil species of dialogue, not adapted for the stage, the philosophic. When, in Plato, Socrates asks the conceited sophist Hippias, what is the meaning of the beautiful, the latter is at once ready with a superficial answer, but is afterwards compelled by the ironical objections of Socrates to give up his former definition, and to grope about him for other ideas, till, ashamed at last and irritated at the superiority of the sage who has convicted him of his ignorance, he is forced to quit the field: this dialogue is not merely philosophically instructive, but arrests the attention like a drama in miniature. And justly, therefore, has this lively movement in the thoughts, this stretch of expectation for the issue, in a word, the dramatic cast of the dialogues of Plato, been always celebrated.

From this we may conceive wherein consists the great charm of dramatic poetry. Action is the true enjoyment of life, nay, life itself. Mere passive enjoyments may lull us into a state of listless complacency, but even then, if possessed of the least internal activity, we cannot avoid being soon wearied. The great bulk of mankind merely from their situation in life, or from their incapacity for extraordinary exertions, are confined within a narrow circle of insignificant operations. Their days flow on in succession under the sleepy rule of custom, their life advances by an insensible progress, and the bursting torrent of the first passions of youth soon settles into a stagnant marsh. From the discontent which this occasions they are compelled to have recourse to all sorts of diversions, which uniformly consist in a species of occupation that may be renounced at pleasure, and though a struggle with difficulties, yet with difficulties that are easily surmounted. But of all diversions the theatre is undoubtedly the most entertaining. Here we may see others act even when we cannot act to any great purpose ourselves. The highest object of human activity is man, and in the drama we see men, measuring their powers with each other, as intellectual and moral beings, either as friends or foes, influencing each other by their opinions, sentiments, and passions, and decisively determining their reciprocal relations and circumstances. The art of the poet accordingly consists in separating from the fable whatever does not essentially belong to it, whatever, in the daily necessities of real life, and the petty occupations to which they give rise, interrupts the progress of important actions, and concentrating within a narrow space a number of events calculated to attract the minds of the hearers and to fill them with attention and expectation. In this manner he gives us a renovated picture of life; a compendium of whatever is moving and progressive in human existence.

But this is not all. Even in a lively oral narration, it is not unusual to introduce persons in conversation with each other, and to give a corresponding variety to the tone and the expression. But the gaps, which these conversations leave in the story, the narrator fills up in his own name with a description of the accompanying circumstances, and other particulars. The dramatic poet must renounce all such expedients; but for this he is richly recompensed in the following invention. He requires each of the characters in his story to be personated by a living individual; that this individual should, in sex, age, and figure, meet as near as may be the prevalent conceptions of his fictitious original, nay, assume his entire personality; that every speech should be delivered in a suitable tone of voice, and accompanied by appropriate action and gesture; and that those external circumstances should be added which are necessary to give the hearers a clear idea of what is going forward. Moreover, these representatives of the creatures of his imagination must appear in the costume belonging to their assumed rank, and to their age and country; partly for the sake of greater resemblance, and partly because, even in dress, there is something characteristic. Lastly, he must see them placed in a locality, which, in some degree, resembles that where, according to his fable, the action took place, because this also contributes to the resemblance: he places them, *i.e.*, on a scene. All this brings us to the idea of the *theatre*. It is evident that the very form of dramatic poetry, that is, the exhibition of an action by dialogue without the aid of narrative, implies the theatre as its necessary complement. We allow that there are dramatic works which were not originally designed for the stage, and not calculated to produce any great effect there, which nevertheless afford great pleasure in the perusal. I am, however, very much inclined to doubt whether they would produce the same strong impression, with which they affect us, upon a person who had never seen or heard a description of a theatre. In reading dramatic works, we are accustomed ourselves to supply the representation.

The invention of dramatic art, and of the theatre, seems a very obvious and natural one. Man has a great disposition to mimicry; when he enters vividly into the situation, sentiments, and passions of others, he involuntarily puts on a resemblance to them in his gestures. Children are perpetually going out of themselves; it is one of their chief amusements to represent those grown people whom they have had an opportunity of observing, or whatever strikes their fancy; and with the happy pliancy of their imagination, they can exhibit all the characteristics of any dignity they may choose to assume, be it that of a father, a schoolmaster, or a king. But one step more was requisite for the invention of the drama, namely, to separate and extract the mimetic elements from the separate parts of social life, and to present them to itself again collectively in one mass; yet in many nations it has not been taken. In the very minute description of ancient Egypt given by Herodotus and other writers, I do not recollect observing the smallest trace of it. The Etruscans, on the contrary, who in many respects resembled the Egyptians, had theatrical representations; and what is singular enough, the Etruscan name for an actor *histrio*, is preserved in living languages even to the present day. The Arabians and Persians, though possessed of a rich poetical literature, are unacquainted with the drama. It was the same with Europe in the Middle Ages. On the introduction of Christianity, the plays handed down from the Greeks and Romans were set aside, partly because they had reference to heathen ideas, and partly because they had degenerated into the most shameless immorality; nor were they again revived till after the lapse of nearly a thousand years. Even in the fourteenth century, in that complete picture which Boccacio gives us of the existing frame of society, we do not find the smallest trace of plays. In place of them they had simply their *conteurs*, *menestriers*, *jongleurs*. On the other hand we are by no means entitled to assume that the invention of the drama was made once for all in the world, to be afterwards borrowed by one people from another. The English circumnavigators tell us, that among the islanders of the South Seas, who in every mental qualification and acquirement are at the lowest grade of civilization, they yet observed a rude drama in which a common incident in life was imitated for the sake of diversion. And to pass to the other extremity of the world, among the Indians, whose social institutions and mental cultivation descend unquestionably from a remote antiquity, plays were known long before they could have experienced any foreign influence. It has lately been made known to Europe that they possess a rich dramatic literature, which goes backward through nearly two thousand years. The only specimen of their plays (nataks) hitherto known to us in the delightful Sakontala, which, notwithstanding the foreign colouring of its native climate, bears in its general structure such a striking resemblance to our own romantic drama, that we might be inclined to suspect we owe this resemblance to the predilection for Shakspeare entertained by the English translator (Sir William Jones), if his fidelity were not attested by other learned orientalists. The drama, indeed, seems to have been a favourite amusement of the Native Princes; and to owe to this circumstance that tone of refined society which prevails in it. Uggargini (Oude?) is specially named as a seat of this art. Under the Mahommedan rulers it naturally fell into decay: the national tongue was strange to them, Persian being the language of the court; and moreover, the mythology which was so intimately interwoven with poetry was irreconcilable with their religious notions. Generally, indeed, we know of no Mahommedan nation that has accomplished any thing in dramatic poetry, or even had any notion of it. The Chinese again have their standing national theatre, standing perhaps in every sense of the word; and I do not doubt, that in the establishment of arbitrary rules, and the delicate observance of insignificant conventionalities, they leave the most correct Europeans very far behind them. When the new European stage sprung up in the fifteenth century, with its allegorical and religious pieces called Moralities and Mysteries, its rise was uninfluenced by the ancient dramatists, who did not come into circulation till some time afterwards. In those rude beginnings lay the germ of the romantic drama as a peculiar invention.

In this wide diffusion of theatrical entertainments, the great difference in dramatic talent which subsists between nations equally distinguished for intellect, is something remarkable; so that theatrical talent would seem to be a peculiar quality, essentially distinct from the poetical gift in general. We do not wonder at the contrast in this respect between the Greeks and the Romans, for the Greeks were altogether a nation of artists, and the Romans a practical people. Among the latter the fine arts were introduced as a corrupting article of luxury, both betokening and accelerating the degeneracy of the times. They carried this luxury so far with respect to the theatre itself, that the perfection in essentials was sacrificed to the accessories of embellishment. Even among the Greeks dramatic talent was far from universal. The theatre was invented in Athens, and in Athens alone was it brought to perfection. The Doric dramas of Epicharmus form only a slight exception to the truth of this remark. All the great creative dramatists of the Greeks were born in Attica, and formed their style in Athens. Widely as the Grecian race was spread, successfully as everywhere almost it cultivated the fine arts, yet beyond the bounds of Attica it was content to admire, without venturing to rival, the productions of the Athenian stage.

Equally remarkable is the difference in this respect between the Spaniards and their neighbours the Portuguese, though related to them both by descent and by language. The Spaniards possess a dramatic literature of inexhaustible wealth; in fertility their dramatists resemble the Greeks, among whom more than a hundred pieces can frequently be assigned by name to a single author. Whatever judgment may be pronounced on them in other respects, the praise of invention has never yet been denied to them; their claim to this has in fact been but too well established, since Italian, French, and English writers have all availed themselves of the ingenious inventions of the Spaniards, and often without acknowledging the source from which they derived them. The Portuguese, on the other hand, while in the other branches of poetry they rival the Spaniards, have in this department accomplished hardly anything, and have never even possessed a national theatre; visited from time to time by strolling players from Spain, they chose rather to listen to a foreign dialect, which, without previous study, they could not perfectly understand, than to invent, or even to translate and imitate, for themselves.

Of the many talents for art and literature displayed by the Italians, the dramatic is by no means pre-eminent, and this defect they seem to have inherited from the Romans, in the same manner as their great talent for mimicry and buffoonery goes back to the most ancient times. The extemporary compositions called *Fabulae Atellanae*, the only original and national form of the Roman drama, in respect of plan, were not perhaps more perfect than the so-called *Commedia dell' Arte*, in which, the parts being fixed and invariable, the dialogue is extemporised by masked actors. In the ancient Saturnalia we have probably the germ of the present carnival, which is entirely an Italian invention. The Opera and the Ballet were also the invention of the Italians: two species of theatrical amusement, in which the dramatic interest is entirely subordinate to music and dancing.

If the German mind has not developed itself in the drama with the same fulness and ease as in other departments of literature, this defect is perhaps to be accounted for by the peculiar character of the nation. The Germans are a speculative people; in other words, they wish to discover by reflection and meditation, the principle of whatever they engage in. On that very account they are not sufficiently practical; for if we wish to act with skill and determination, we must make up our minds that we have somehow or other become masters of our subject, and not be perpetually recurring to an examination of the theory on which it rests; we must, as it were, have settled down and contented ourselves with a certain partial apprehension of the idea. But now in the invention and conduct of a drama the practical spirit must prevail: the dramatic poet is not allowed to dream away under his inspiration, he must take the straightest road to his end; but the Germans are only too apt to lose sight of the object in the course of their way to it. Besides, in the drama the nationality does usually, nay, must show itself in the most marked manner, and the national character of the Germans is modest and retiring: it loves not to make a noisy display of itself; and the noble endeavour to become acquainted with, and to appropriate to itself whatever is excellent in others, is not seldom accompanied with an undervaluing of its own worth. For these reasons the German stage has often, in form and matter, been more than duly affected by foreign influence. Not indeed that the Germans propose to themselves no higher object than the mere passive repetition of the Grecian, the French, the Spanish, or the English theatre; but, as it appears to me, they are in search of a more perfect form, which, excluding all that is merely local or temporary, may combine whatever is truly poetical in all these theatres. In the matter, however, the German national features ought certainly to predominate.

After this rapid sketch of what may be called the map of dramatic literature, we return to the examination of its fundamental ideas. Since, as we have already shown, visible representation is essential to the very form of the drama; a dramatic work may always be regarded from a double point of view,--how far it is *poetical*, and how far it is *theatrical*. The two are by no means inseparable. Let not, however, the expression *poetical* be misunderstood: I am not now speaking of the versification and the ornaments of language; these, when not animated by some higher excellence, are the least effective on the stage; but I speak of the poetry in the spirit and design of a piece; and this may exist in as high a degree when the drama is written in prose as in verse. What is it, then, that makes a drama poetical? The very same, assuredly, that makes other works so. It must in the first place be a connected whole, complete and satisfactory within itself. But this is merely the negative definition of a work of art, by which it is distinguished from the phenomena of nature, which run into each other, and do not possess in themselves a complete and independent existence. To be poetical it is necessary that a composition should be a mirror of ideas, that is, thoughts and feelings which in their character are necessary and eternally true, and soar above this earthly life, and also that it should exhibit them embodied before us. What the ideas are, which in this view are essential to the different departments of the drama, will hereafter be the subject of our investigation. We shall also, on the other hand, show that without them a drama becomes altogether prosaic and empirical, that is to say, patched together by the understanding out of the observations it has gathered from literal reality.

But how does a dramatic work become theatrical, or fitted to appear with advantage on the stage? In single instances it is often difficult to determine whether a work possesses such a property or not. It is indeed frequently the subject of great controversy, especially when the self-love of authors and actors comes into collision; each shifts the blame of failure on the other, and those who advocate the cause of the author appeal to an imaginary perfection of the histrionic art, and complain of the insufficiency of the existing means for its realization. But in general the answer to this question is by no means so difficult. The object proposed is to produce an impression on an assembled multitude, tc rivet their attention, and to excite their interest and sympathy. In this respect the poet's occupation coincides with that of the orator. How then does the latter attain his end? By perspicuity, rapidity, and energy. Whatever exceeds the ordinary measure of patience or comprehension he must diligently avoid. Moreover, when a number of men are assembled together, they mutually distract each other's attention whenever their eyes and ears are not drawn to a common object without and beyond themselves.

Hence the dramatic poet, as well as the orator, must from the very commencement, by strong impressions, transport his hearers out of themselves, and, as it were, take bodily possession of their attention. There is a species of poetry which gently stirs a mind attuned to solitary contemplation, as soft breezes elicit melody from the Aeolian harp. However excellent this poetry may be in itself, without some other accompaniments its tones would be lost on the stage. The melting *harmonica* is not calculated to regulate the march of an army, and kindle its military enthusiasm. For this we must have piercing instruments, but above all a strongly-marked rhythm, to quicken the pulsation and give a more rapid movement to the animal spirits. The grand requisite in a drama is to make this rhythm perceptible in the onward progress of the action. When this has once been effected, the poet may all the sooner halt in his rapid career, and indulge the bent of his own genius. There are points, when the most elaborate and polished style, the most enthusiastic lyrics, the most profound thoughts and remote allusions, the smartest coruscations of wit, and the most dazzling flights of a sportive or ethereal fancy, are all in their place, and when the willing audience, even those who cannot entirely comprehend them, follow the whole with a greedy ear, like music in unison with their feelings. Here the poet's great art lies in availing himself of the effect of contrasts, which enable him at one time to produce calm repose, profound contemplation, and even the self-abandoned indifference of exhaustion, or at another, the most tumultuous emotions, the most violent storm of the passions. With respect to theatrical fitness, however, it must not be forgotten that much must always depend on the capacities and humours of the audience, and, consequently, on the national character in general, and the particular degree of mental culture. Of all kinds of poetry the dramatic is, in a certain sense, the most secular; for, issuing from the stillness of an inspired mind, it yet fears not to exhibit itself in the midst of the noise and tumult of social life. The dramatic poet is, more than any other, obliged to court external favour and loud applause. But of course it is only in appearance that he thus lowers himself to his hearers; while, in reality, he is elevating them to himself.

In thus producing an impression on an assembled multitude the following circumstance deserves to be weighed, in order to ascertain the whole amount of its importance. In ordinary intercourse men exhibit only the outward man to each other. They are withheld by mistrust or indifference from allowing others to look into what passes within them; and to speak with any thing like emotion or agitation of that which is nearest our heart is considered unsuitable to the tone of polished society. The orator and the dramatist find means to break through these barriers of conventional reserve. While they transport their hearers into such lively emotions that the outward signs thereof break forth involuntarily, every man perceives those around him to be affected in the same manner and degree, and those who before were strangers to one another, become in a moment intimately acquainted. The tears which the dramatist or the orator compels them to shed for calumniated innocence or dying heroism, make friends and brothers of them all. Almost inconceivable is the power of a visible communion of numbers to give intensity to those feelings of the heart which usually retire into privacy, or only open themselves to the confidence of friendship. The faith in the validity of such emotions becomes irrefragable from its diffusion; we feel ourselves strong among so many associates, and all hearts and minds flow together in one great and irresistible stream. On this very account the privilege of influencing an assembled crowd is exposed to most dangerous abuses. As one may disinterestedly animate them, for the noblest and best of purposes, so another may entangle them in the deceitful meshes of sophistry, and dazzle them by the glare of a false magnanimity, whose vainglorious crimes may be painted as virtues and even as sacrifices. Beneath the delightful charms of oratory and poetry, the poison steals imperceptibly into ear and heart. Above all others must the comic poet (seeing that his very occupation keeps him always on the slippery brink of this precipice,) take heed, lest he afford an opportunity for the lower and baser parts of human nature to display themselves without restraint. When the sense of shame which ordinarily keeps these baser propensities within the bounds of decency, is once weakened by the sight of others' participation in them, our inherent sympathy with what is vile will soon break out into the most unbridled licentiousness.

The powerful nature of such an engine for either good or bad purposes has in all times justly drawn the attention of the legislature to the drama. Many regulations have been devised by different governments, to render it subservient to their views and to guard against its abuse. The great difficulty is to combine such a degree of freedom as is necessary for the production of works of excellence, with the precautions demanded by the customs and institutions of the different states. In Athens the theatre enjoyed up to its maturity, under the patronage of religion, almost unlimited freedom, and the public morality preserved it for a time from degeneracy. The comedies of Aristophanes, which with our views and habits appear to us so intolerably licentious, and in which the senate and the people itself are unmercifully turned to ridicule, were the seal of Athenian freedom. To meet this abuse, Plato, who lived in the very same Athens, and either witnessed or foresaw the decline of art, proposed the entire banishment of dramatic poets from his ideal republic. Few states, however, have conceived it necessary to subscribe to this severe sentence of condemnation; but few also have thought proper to leave the theatre to itself without any superintendence. In many Christian countries the dramatic art has been honoured by being made subservient to religion, in the popular treatment and exhibition of religious subjects; and in Spain more especially competition in this department has given birth to many works which, neither devotion nor poetry will disown. In other states and under other circumstances this has been thought both objectionable and inexpedient. Wherever, however, the subsequent responsibility of the poet and actor has been thought insufficient, and it has been deemed advisable to submit every piece before its appearance on the stage to a previous censorship, it has been generally found to fail in the very point which is of the greatest importance: namely, the spirit and general impression of a play. From the nature of the dramatic art, the poet must put into the mouths of his characters much of which he does not himself approve, while with respect to his own sentiments he claims to be judged by the spirit and connexion of the whole. It may again happen that a piece is perfectly inoffensive in its single speeches, and defies all censorship, while as a whole it is calculated to produce the most pernicious effect. We have in our own times seen but too many plays favourably received throughout Europe, over-flowing with ebullitions of good-heartedness and traits of magnanimity, and in which, notwithstanding, a keener eye cannot fail to detect the hidden purpose of the writer to sap the foundations of moral principle, and the veneration for whatever ought to be held sacred by man; while all this sentimentality is only to bribe to his purpose the effeminate soft-heartedness of his contemporaries [Footnote: The author it is supposed alludes to Kotzebue.--TRANS.]. On the other hand, if any person were to undertake the moral vindication of poor Aristophanes, who has such a bad name, and whose licentiousness in particular passages, is to our ideas quite intolerable, he will find good grounds for his defence in the general object of his pieces, in which he at least displays the sentiments of a patriotic citizen.

The purport of these observations is to evince the importance of the subject we are considering. The theatre, where many arts are combined to produce a magical effect; where the most lofty and profound poetry has for its interpreter the most finished action, which is at once eloquence and an animated picture; while architecture contributes her splendid decorations, and painting her perspective illusions, and the aid of music is called in to attune the mind, or to heighten by its strains the emotions which already agitate it; the theatre, in short, where the whole of the social and artistic enlightenment, which a nation possesses, the fruit of many centuries of continued exertion, are brought into play within the representation of a few short hours, has an extraordinary charm for every age, sex, and rank, and has ever been the favourite amusement of every cultivated people. Here, princes, statesmen, and generals, behold the great events of past times, similar to those in which they themselves are called upon to act, laid open in their inmost springs and motives; here, too, the philosopher finds subject for profoundest reflection on the nature and constitution of man; with curious eye the artist follows the groups which pass rapidly before him, and from them impresses on his fancy the germ of many a future picture; the susceptible youth opens his heart to every elevating feeling; age becomes young again in recollection; even childhood sits with anxious expectation before the gaudy curtain, which is soon to be drawn up with its rustling sound, and to display to it so many unknown wonders: all alike are diverted, all exhilarated, and all feel themselves for a time raised above the daily cares, the troubles, and the sorrows of life. As the drama, with the arts which are subservient to it, may, from neglect and the mutual contempt of artists and the public, so far degenerate, as to become nothing better than a trivial and stupid amusement, and even a downright waste of time, we conceive that we are attempting something more than a passing entertainment, if we propose to enter on a consideration of the works produced by the most distinguished nations in their most brilliant periods, and to institute an inquiry into the means of ennobling and perfecting so important an art.

LECTURE III.

Essence of Tragedy and Comedy--Earnestness and Sport--How far it is possible to become acquainted with the Ancients without knowing Original Languages--Winkelmann.

The importance of our subject is, I think, fully proved. Let us now enter upon a brief consideration of the two kinds into which all dramatic poetry is divided, the *tragic* and *comic*, and examine the meaning and import of each.

The three principal kinds of poetry in general are the epic, the lyric, and the dramatic. All the other subordinate species are either derived from these, or formed by combination from them. If we would consider these three leading kinds in their purity, we must go back to the forms in which they appeared among the Greeks. For the theory of poetical art is most conveniently illustrated by the history of Grecian poetry; for the latter is well entitled to the appellation of systematical, since it furnishes for every independent idea derived from experience the most distinct and precise manifestation.

It is singular that epic and lyric poetry admit not of any such precise division into two opposite species, as the dramatic does. The ludicrous epopee has, it is true, been styled a peculiar species, but it is only an accidental variety, a mere parody of the epos, and consists in applying its solemn staidness of development, which seems only suitable to great objects, to trifling and insignificant events. In lyric poetry there are only intervals and gradations between the song, the ode, and the elegy, but no proper contrast.

The spirit of epic poetry, as we recognise it in its father, Homer, is clear self-possession. The epos is the calm quiet representation of an action in progress. The poet relates joyful as well as mournful events, but he relates them with equanimity, and considers them as already past, and at a certain remoteness from our minds.

The lyric poem is the musical expression of mental emotions by language. The essence of musical feeling consists in this, that we endeavour with complacency to dwell on, and even to perpetuate in our souls, a joyful or painful emotion. The feeling must consequently be already so far mitigated as not to impel us by the desire of its pleasure or the dread of its pain, to tear ourselves from it, but such as to allow us, unconcerned at the fluctuations of feeling which time produces, to dwell upon and be absorbed in a single moment of existence.

The dramatic poet, as well as the epic, represents external events, but he represents them as real and present. In common with the lyric poet he also claims our mental participation, but not in the same calm composedness; the feeling of joy and sorrow which the dramatist excites is more immediate and vehement. He calls forth all the emotions which the sight of similar deeds and fortunes of living men would elicit, and it is only by the total sum of the impression which he produces that he ultimately resolves these conflicting emotions into a harmonious tone of feeling. As he stands in such close proximity to real life, and endeavours to endue his own imaginary creations with vitality, the equanimity of the epic poet would in him be indifference; he must decidedly take part with one or other of the leading views of human life, and constrain his audience also to participate in the same feeling.

To employ simpler and more intelligible language: the *tragic* and *comic* bear the same relation to one another as *earnest* and *sport*. Every man, from his own experience, is acquainted with both these states of mind; but to determine their essence and their source would demand deep philosophical investigation. Both, indeed, bear the stamp of our common nature; but earnestness belongs more to its moral, and mirth to its animal part. The creatures destitute of reason are incapable either of earnest or of sport. Animals seem indeed at times to labour as if they were earnestly intent upon some aim, and as if they made the present moment subordinate to the future; at other times they seem to sport, that is, they give themselves up without object or purpose to the pleasure of existence: but they do not possess consciousness, which alone can entitle these two conditions to the names of earnest and sport. Man alone, of all the animals with which we are acquainted, is capable of looking back towards the past, and forward into futurity; and he has to purchase the enjoyment of this noble privilege at a dear rate. Earnestness, in the most extensive signification, is the direction of our mental powers to some aim. But as soon as we begin to call ourselves to account for our actions, reason compels us to fix this aim higher and higher, till we come at last to the highest end of our existence: and here that longing for the infinite which is inherent in our being, is baffled by the limits of our finite existence. All that we do, all that we effect, is vain and perishable; death stands everywhere in the back ground, and to it every well or ill-spent moment brings us nearer and closer; and even when a man has been so singularly fortunate as to reach the utmost term of life without any grievous calamity, the inevitable doom still awaits him to leave or to be left by all that is most dear to him on earth. There is no bond of love without a separation, no enjoyment without the grief of losing it. When, however, we contemplate the relations of our existence to the extreme limit of possibilities: when we reflect on its entire dependence on a chain of causes and effects, stretching beyond our ken: when we consider how weak and helpless, and doomed to struggle against the enormous powers of nature, and conflicting appetites, we are cast on the shores of an unknown world, as it were, shipwrecked at our very birth; how we are subject to all kinds of errors and deceptions, any one of which may be our ruin; that in our passions we cherish an enemy in our bosoms; how every moment demands from us, in the name of the most sacred duties, the sacrifice of our dearest inclinations, and how at one blow we may be robbed of all that we have acquired with much toil and difficulty; that with every accession to our stores, the risk of loss is proportionately increased, and we are only the more exposed to the malice of hostile fortune: when we think upon all this, every heart which is not dead to feeling must be overpowered by an inexpressible melancholy, for which there is no other counter-poise than the consciousness of a vocation transcending the limits of this earthly life. This is the tragic tone of mind; and when the thought of the possible issues out of the mind as a living reality, when this tone pervades and animates a visible representation of the most striking instances of violent revolutions in a man's fortunes, either prostrating his mental energies or calling forth the most heroic endurance--then the result is *Tragic Poetry*. We thus see how this kind of poetry has its foundation in our nature, while to a certain extent we have also answered the question, why we are fond of such mournful representations, and even find something consoling and elevating in them? This tone of mind we have described is inseparable from strong feeling; and although poetry cannot remove these internal dissonances, she must at least endeavour to effect an ideal reconciliation of them.

As earnestness, in the highest degree, is the essence of tragic representation; so is sport of the comic. The disposition to mirth is a forgetfulness of all gloomy considerations in the pleasant feeling of present happiness. We are then inclined to view every thing in a sportive light, and to allow nothing to disturb or ruffle our minds. The imperfections and the irregularities of men are no longer an object of dislike and compassion, but serve, by their strange inconsistencies, to entertain the understanding and to amuse the fancy. The comic poet must therefore carefully abstain from whatever is calculated to excite moral indignation at the conduct, or sympathy with the situations of his personages, because this would inevitably bring us back again into earnestness. He must paint their irregularities as springing out of the predominance of the animal part of their nature, and the incidents which befal them as merely ludicrous distresses, which will be attended with no fatal consequences. This is uniformly what takes place in what we call Comedy, in which, however, there is still a mixture of seriousness, as I shall show in the sequel. The oldest comedy of the Greeks was, however, entirely sportive, and in that respect formed the most complete contrast to their tragedy. Not only were the characters and situations of individuals worked up into a comic picture of real life, but the whole frame of society, the constitution, nature, and the gods, were all fantastically painted in the most ridiculous and laughable colours.

When we have formed in this manner a pure idea of the tragic and comic, as exhibited to us in Grecian examples, we shall then be enabled to analyze the various corruptions of both, which the moderns have invented, to discriminate their incongruous additions, and to separate their several ingredients.

In the history of poetry and the fine arts among the Greeks, their development was subject to an invariable law. Everything heterogeneous was first excluded, and then all homogeneous elements were combined, and each being perfected in itself, at last elevated into an independent and harmonious unity. Hence with them each species is confined within its natural boundaries, and the different styles distinctly marked. In beginning, therefore, with the history of the Grecian art and poetry, we are not merely observing the order of time, but also the order of ideas.

In the case of the majority of my hearers, I can hardly presume upon a direct acquaintance with the Greeks, derived from the study of their poetical works in the original language. Translations in prose, or even in verse, in which they are but dressed up again in the modern taste, can afford no true idea of the Grecian drama. True and faithful translations, which endeavour in expression and versification to rise to the height of the original, have as yet been attempted only in Germany. But although our language is extremely flexible, and in many respects resembling the Greek, it is after all a battle with unequal weapons; and stiffness and harshness not unfrequently take the place of the easy sweetness of the Greek. But we are even far from having yet done all that can perhaps be accomplished: I know of no translation of a Greek tragedian deserving of unqualified praise. But even supposing the translation as perfect as possible, and deviating very slightly from the original, the reader who is unacquainted with the other works of the Greeks, will be perpetually disturbed by the foreign nature of the subject, by national peculiarities and numerous allusions (which cannot be understood without some scholarship), and thus unable to comprehend particular parts, he will be prevented from forming a clear idea of the whole. So long as we have to struggle with difficulties it is impossible to have any true enjoyment of a work of art. To feel the ancients as we ought, we must have become in some degree one of themselves, and breathed as it were the Grecian air.

What is the best means of becoming imbued with the spirit of the Greeks, without a knowledge of their language? I answer without hesitation,--the study of the antique; and if this is not always possible through the originals, yet, by means of casts, it is to a certain extent within the power of every man. These models of the human form require no interpretation; their elevated character is imperishable, and will always be recognized through all vicissitudes of time, and in every region under heaven, wherever there exists a noble race of men akin to the Grecian (as the European undoubtedly is), and wherever the unkindness of nature has not degraded the human features too much below the pure standard, and, by habituating them to their own deformity, rendered them insensible to genuine corporeal beauty. Respecting the inimitable perfection of the antique in its few remains of a first-rate character, there is but one voice throughout the whole of civilized Europe; and if ever their merit was called in question, it was in times when the modern arts of design had sunk to the lowest depths of mannerism. Not only all intelligent artists, but all men of any degree of taste, bow with enthusiastic adoration before the masterly productions of ancient sculpture.

The best guide to conduct us to this sanctuary of the beautiful, with deep and thoughtful contemplation, is the History of Art by our immortal Winkelmann. In the description of particular works it no doubt leaves much to be desired; nay, it even abounds in grave errors, but no man has so deeply penetrated into the innermost spirit of Grecian art. Winkelmann transformed himself completely into an ancient, and seemingly lived in his own century, unmoved by its spirit and influences.

The immediate subject of his work is the plastic arts, but it contains also many important hints concerning other branches of Grecian civilisation, and is very useful as a preparation for the understanding of their poetry, and especially their dramatic poetry. As the latter was designed for visible representation before spectators, whose eye must have been as difficult to please on the stage as elsewhere, we have no better means of feeling the whole dignity of their tragic exhibitions, and of giving it a sort of theatrical animation, than to keep these forms of gods and heroes ever present to our fancy. The assertion may appear somewhat strange at present, but I hope in the sequel to demonstrate its justice: it is only before the groups of Niobe or Laocoon that we first enter into the spirit of the tragedies of Sophocles.

We are yet in want of a work in which the entire poetic, artistic, scientific, and social culture of the Greeks should be painted as one grand and harmonious whole, as a true work of nature, prevaded by the most wondrous symmetry and proportion of the parts, and traced through its connected development in the same spirit which Winkelmann has executed in the part which he attempted. An attempt has indeed been made in a popular work, which is in everybody's hands, I mean the *Travels of the Younger Anacharsis*. This book is valuable for its learning, and may be very useful in diffusing a knowledge of antiquities; but, without censuring the error of the dress in which it is exhibited, it betrays more good-will to do justice to the Greeks, than ability to enter deeply into their spirit. In this respect the work is in many points superficial, and even disfigured with modern views. It is not the travels of a young Scythian, but of an old Parisian.

The superior excellence of the Greeks in the fine arts, as I have already said, is the most universally acknowledged. An enthusiasm for their literature is in a great measure confined to the English and Germans, among whom also the study of the Grecian language is the most zealously prosecuted. It is singular that the French critics of all others, they who so zealously acknowledge the remains of the theoretical writings of the ancients on literature, Aristotle, Horace, Quinctilian, &c., as infallible standards of taste, should yet distinguish themselves by the contemptuous and irreverent manner in which they speak of their poetical compositions, and especially of their dramatic literature. Look, for instance, into a book very much read,--La Harpe's *Cours de Litterature*. It contains many acute remarks on the French Theatre; but whoever should think to learn the Greeks from it must be very ill advised: the author was as deficient in a solid knowledge of their literature as in a sense for appreciating it. Voltaire, also, often speaks most unwarrantably on this subject: he elevates or lowers them at the suggestions of his caprice, or according to the purpose of the moment to produce such or such an effect on the mind of the public. I remember too to have read a cursory critique of Metastasio's on the Greek tragedians, in which he treats them like so many school-boys. Racine is much more modest, and cannot be in any manner charged with this sort of presumption: even because he was the best acquainted of all of them with the Greeks. It is easy to see into the motives of these hostile critics. Their national and personal vanity has much to do with the matter; conceiting themselves that they have far surpassed the ancients, they venture to commit such observations to the public, knowing that the works of the ancient poets have come down to us in a dead language, accessible only to the learned, without the animating accompaniment of recitation, music, ideal and truly plastic impersonation, and scenic pomp; all which, in every respect worthy of the poetry, was on the Athenian stage combined in such wonderful harmony, that if only it could be represented to our eye and ear, it would at once strike dumb the whole herd of these noisy and interested critics. The ancient statues require no commentary; they speak for themselves, and everything like competition on the part of a modern artist would be regarded as ridiculous pretension. In respect of the theatre, they lay great stress on the infancy of the art; and because these poets lived two thousand years before us, they conclude that we must have made great progress since. In this way poor Aeschylus especially is got rid of. But in sober truth, if this was the infancy of dramatic art, it was the infancy of a Hercules, who strangled serpents in his cradle.

I have already expressed my opinion on that blind partiality for the ancients, which regards their excellence as a frigid faultlessness, and which exhibits them as models, in such a way as to put a stop to everything like improvement, and reduce us to abandon the exercise of art as altogether fruitless. I, for my part, am disposed to believe that poetry, as the fervid expression of our whole being, must assume new and peculiar forms in different ages. Nevertheless, I cherish an enthusiastic veneration for the Greeks, as a people endowed, by the peculiar favour of Nature, with the most perfect genius for art; in the consciousness of which, they gave to all the nations with which they were acquainted, compared with themselves, the appellation of barbarians,--an appellation in the use of which they were in some degree justified. I would not wish to imitate certain travellers, who, on returning from a country which their readers cannot easily visit, give such exaggerated accounts of it, and relate so many marvels, as to hazard their own character for veracity. I shall rather endeavour to characterize them as they appear to me after sedulous and repeated study, without concealing their defects, and to bring a living picture of the Grecian stage before the eyes of my hearers.

We shall treat first of the Tragedy of the Greeks, then of their *Old* Comedy, and lastly of the *New* Comedy which arose out of it.

The same theatrical accompaniments were common to all the three kinds. We must, therefore, give a short preliminary view of the theatre, its architecture and decorations, that we may have a distinct idea of their representation.

The histrionic art of the ancients had also many peculiarities: the use of masks, for example, although these were quite different in tragedy and comedy; in the former, *ideal*, and in the latter, at least in the Old Comedy, somewhat caricatured.

In tragedy, we shall first consider what constituted its most distinctive peculiarity among the ancients: the ideality of the representation, the prevailing idea of destiny, and the chorus; and we shall lastly treat of their mythology, as the materials of tragic poetry. We shall then proceed to characterize, in the three tragedians of whom alone entire works still remain, the different styles--that is, the necessary epochs in the history of the tragic art.

LECTURE IV.

Structure of the Stage among the Greeks--Their Acting--Use of Masks--False comparison of Ancient Tragedy to the Opera--Tragical Lyric Poetry.

When we hear the word "theatre," we naturally think of what with us bears the same name; and yet nothing can be more different from our theatre, in its entire structure, than that of the Greeks. If in reading the Grecian pieces we associate our own stage with them, the light in which we shall view them must be false in every respect.

The leading authority on this subject, and one, too, whose statements are mathematically accurate, is Vitruvius, who also distinctly points out the great difference between the Greek and Roman theatres. But these and similar passages of the ancient writers have been most incorrectly interpreted by architects unacquainted with the ancient dramatists [Footnote: We have a remarkable instance of this in the pretended ancient theatre of Palladio, at Vicenza. Herculaneum, it is true, had not then been discovered; and it is difficult to understand the ruins of the ancient theatre without having seen a complete one.]; and philologists, in their turn, from ignorance of architecture, have also egregiously erred. The ancient dramatists are still, therefore, greatly in want of that illustration which a right understanding of their scenic arrangements is calculated to throw upon them. In many tragedies I think that I have a tolerably clear notion of the matter; but others, again, present difficulties which are not easily solved. But it is in figuring the representation of Aristophanes' comedies that I find myself most at a loss: the ingenious poet must have brought his wonderful inventions before the eyes of his audience in a manner equally bold and astonishing. Even Barthelemy's description of the Grecian stage is not a little confused, and his subjoined plan extremely incorrect; where he attempts to describe the acting of a play, the *Antigone* or the *Ajax*, for instance, he goes altogether wrong. For this reason the following explanation will appear the less superfluous [Footnote: I am partly indebted for them to the elucidations of a learned architect, M. Genelli, of Berlin, author of the ingenious *Letters on Vitruvius*. We have compared several Greek tragedies with our interpretation of Vitruvius's description, and endeavoured to figure to ourselves the manner in which they were represented; and I afterwards found our ideas confirmed by an examination of the theatre of Herculaneum, and the two very small ones at Pompeii.].

The theatres of the Greeks were quite open above, and their dramas were always acted in day, and beneath the canopy of heaven. The Romans, indeed, at an after period, may have screened the audience, by an awning, from the sun; but luxury was scarcely ever carried so far by the Greeks. Such a state of things appears very uncomfortable to us; but the Greeks had nothing of effeminacy about them; and we must not forget, too, the mildness of their climate. When a storm or a shower came on, the play was of course interrupted, and the spectators sought shelter in the lofty colonnade which ran behind their seats; but they were willing rather to put up with such occasional inconveniences, than, by shutting themselves up in a close and crowded house, entirely to forfeit the sunny brightness of a religious solemnity--for such, in fact, their plays were [Footnote: They carefully made choice of a beautiful situation. The theatre at Tauromenium, at present Taormino, in Sicily, of which the ruins are still visible, was, according to Hunter's description, situated in such a manner that the audience had a view of Etna over the back-ground of the theatre.]. To have covered in the scene itself, and imprisoned gods and heroes in a dark and gloomy apartment, artificially lighted up, would have appeared still more ridiculous to them. An action which so gloriously attested their affinity with heaven, could fitly be exhibited only beneath the free heaven, and, as it were, under the very eyes of the gods, for whom, according to Seneca, the sight of a brave man struggling with adversity is a suitable spectacle. With respect to the supposed inconvenience, which, according to the assertion of many modern critics, hence accrued, compelling the poets always to lay the scene of their pieces out of doors, and consequently often forcing them to violate probability, it was very little felt by Tragedy and the Older Comedy. The Greeks, like many southern nations of the present day, lived much more in the open air than we do, and transacted many things in public places which with us usually take place within doors. Besides, the theatre did not represent the street, but a front area belonging to the house, where the altar stood on which sacrifices were offered to the household gods. Here, therefore, the women, notwithstanding the retired life they led among the Greeks, even those who were unmarried, might appear without any impropriety. Neither was it impossible for them, if necessary, to give a view of the interior of the house; and this was effected, as we shall presently see; by means of the *Encyclema.*

But the principal ground of this practice was that publicity which, according to the republican notion of the Greeks, was essential to all grave and important transactions. This was signified by the presence of the chorus, whose presence during many secret transactions has been judged of according to rules of propriety inapplicable to the country, and so most undeservedly censured.

The theatres of the ancients were, in comparison with the small scale of ours, of colossal magnitude, partly for the sake of containing the whole of the people, with the concourse of strangers who flocked to the festivals, and partly to correspond with the majesty of the dramas represented in them, which required to be seen at a respectful distance. The seats of the spectators were formed by ascending steps which rose round the semicircle of the orchestra, (called by us the pit,) so that all could see with equal convenience. The diminution of effect by distance was counteracted to the eye and ear by artificial contrivances consisting in the employment of masks, and of an apparatus for increasing the loudness of the voice, and of the cothurnus to give additional stature. Vitruvius speaks also of vehicles of sound, distributed throughout the building; but commentators are much at variance with respect to their nature. In general it may be assumed, that the theatres of the ancients were constructed on excellent acoustic principles.

Even the lowest tier of the amphitheatre was raised considerably above the orchestra, and opposite to it was the stage, at an equal degree of elevation. The hollow semicircle of the orchestra was unoccupied by spectators, and was designed for another purpose. However, it was otherwise with the Romans, though indeed the arrangement of their theatres does not at present concern us.

The stage consisted of a strip which stretched from one end of the building to the other, and of which the depth bore little proportion to this breadth. This was called the *logeum*, in Latin *pulpitum*, and the middle of it was the usual place for the persons who spoke. Behind this middle part, the scene went inwards in a quadrangular form, with less depth, however, than breadth. The space thus enclosed was called the *proscenium*. The front of the logeum towards the orchestra was ornamented with pilasters and small statues between them. The stage, erected on a foundation of stonework, was a wooden platform resting on rafters. The surrounding appurtenances of the stage, together with the rooms required for the machinery, were also of wood. The wall of the building, directly opposite to the seats of the spectators, was raised to a level with the uppermost tier.

The scenic decoration was contrived in such a manner, that the principal and nearest object covered the background, and the prospects of distance were given at the two sides; the very reverse of the mode adopted by us. The latter arrangement had also its rules: on the left, was the town to which the palace, temple, or whatever occupied the middle, belonged; on the right, the open country, landscape, mountains, sea-coast, &c. The side-scenes were composed of triangles which turned on a pivot beneath; and in this manner the change of scene was effected. According to an observation on Virgil, by Servius, the change of scene was partly produced by revolving, and partly by withdrawing. The former applies to the lateral decorations, and the latter to the middle of the background. The partition in the middle opened, disappeared at both sides, and exhibited to view a new picture. But all the parts of the scene were not always changed at the same time. In the back or central scene, it is probable, that much which with us is only painted was given bodily. If this represented a palace or temple, there was usually in the proscenium an altar, which in the performance answered a number of purposes.

The decoration was for the most part architectural, but occasionally also a painted landscape, as of Caucasus in the *Prometheus*, or in the *Philoctetes*, of the desert island of Lemnos, and the rocks with its cavern. From a passage of Plato it is clear, that the Greeks carried the illusions of theatrical perspective much farther than, judging from some wretched landscapes discovered in Herculaneum, we should be disposed to allow.

In the back wall of the stage there was one main entrance, and two side doors. It has been maintained, that from them it might be discovered whether an actor played a principal or under part, as in the first case he came in by the main entrance, but in the second, entered from either of the sides. But this should be understood with the proviso, that this must have varied according to the nature of the piece. As the middle scene was generally a palace, in which the principal characters generally of royal descent resided, they naturally came on the stage through the great door, while the servants dwelt in the wings. But besides these three entrances, which were directly opposite to the spectators, and were real doors, with appropriate architectural decorations, there were also four side entrances, to which the name of doors cannot properly apply: two, namely, on the stage on the right and the left, towards the inner angles of the proscenium, and two farther off, in the orchestra, also right and left. The latter were intended properly for the chorus, but were likewise not unfrequently used by the actors, who in such cases ascended to the stage by one or other of the double flight of steps which ran from the orchestra to the middle of the logeum. The entering from the right or the left of itself indicated the place from which the dramatic personages must be supposed to come. The situation of these entrances serves to explain many passages in the ancient dramas, where the persons standing in the middle see some one advancing, long before he approaches them.

Somewhere beneath the seats of the spectators, a flight of stairs was constructed, which was called the Charonic, and by which, unseen by the audience, the shadows of the departed, ascended into the orchestra, and thence to the stage. The furthermost brink of the logeum must sometimes have represented the sea shore. Moreover the Greeks in general skilfully availed themselves even of extra-scenic matters, and made them subservient to the stage effect. Thus, I doubt not, but that in the *Eumenides* the spectators were twice addressed as an assembled people; first, as the Greeks invited by the Pythoness to consult the oracle; and a second time as the Athenian multitude, when Pallas, by the herald, commands silence during the trial about to commence. So too the frequent appeals to heaven were undoubtedly addressed to the real heaven; and when Electra on her first appearance exclaims: "O holy light, and thou air co-expansive with earth!" she probably turned towards the actual sun ascending in the heavens. The whole of this procedure is highly deserving of praise; and though modern critics have censured the mixture of reality and imitation, as destructive of theatrical illusion, this only proves that they have misunderstood the essence of the illusion which a work of art aims at producing. If we are to be truly deceived by a picture, that is, if we are to believe in the reality of the object which we see, we must not perceive its limits, but look at it through an opening; the frame at once declares it for a picture. Now in stage-scenery we cannot avoid the use of architectural contrivances, productive of the same effect on dramatic representation as frames on pictures. It is consequently much better not to attempt to disguise this fact, but leaving this kind of illusion for those cases where it can be advantageously employed, to take it as a permitted licence occasionally to step out of the limits of mere scenic decoration. It was, generally speaking, a principle of the Greeks, with respect to stage imitation, either to require a perfect representation, and where this could not be accomplished, to be satisfied with merely symbolical allusions.

The machinery for the descent of gods through the air, or the withdrawing of men from the earth, was placed aloft behind the walls of the two sides of the scene, and consequently removed from the sight of the spectators. Even in the time of Aeschylus, great use was already made of it, as in the *Prometheus* he not only brings Oceanus through the air on a griffin, but also in a winged chariot introduces the whole choir of ocean nymphs, at least fifteen in number. There were also hollow places beneath the stage into which, when necessary, the personages could disappear, and contrivances for thunder and lightning, for the apparent fall or burning of a house, &c.

To the hindmost wall of the scene an upper story could be added; whenever, for instance, it was wished to represent a tower with a wide prospect, or the like. Behind the great middle entrance there was a space for the Exostra, a machine of a semicircular form, and covered above, which represented the objects contained in it as in a house. This was used for grand strokes of theatrical effect, as we may see from many pieces. On such occasions the folding-doors of the entrance would naturally be open, or the curtain which covered it withdrawn.

A stage curtain, which, we clearly see from a description of Ovid, was not dropped, but drawn upwards, is mentioned both by Greek and Roman writers, and the Latin appellation, *aulaeum*, is even borrowed from the Greeks. I suspect, however, that the curtain was not much used at first on the Attic stage. In the pieces of Aeschylus and Sophocles, the scene is evidently empty at the opening as well as the conclusion, and seems therefore to have required no preparation which needed to be shut out from the view of the spectators. However, in many of the pieces of Euripides, and perhaps also in the *Oedipus Tyrannus*, the stage is filled from the very first, and presents a standing group which could not well have been assembled under the very eyes of the spectators. It must, besides, be remembered, that it was only the comparatively small proscenium, and not the logeum, which was covered by the curtain which disappeared through a narrow opening between two of the boards of the flooring, being wound up on a roller beneath the stage.

The entrances of the chorus were beneath in the orchestra, in which it generally remained, and in which also it performed its solemn dance, moving backwards and forwards during the choral songs. In the front of the orchestra, opposite to the middle of the scene, there was an elevation with steps, resembling an altar, as high as the stage, which was called the *Thymele*. This was the station of the chorus when it did not sing, but merely looked on as an interested spectator of the action. At such times the choragus, or leader of the chorus, took his station on the top of the thymele, to see what was passing on the stage, and to converse with the characters there present. For though the choral song was common to the whole, yet when it took part in the dialogue, one usually spoke for all the rest; and hence we may account for the shifting from *thou* to *ye* in addressing them. The thymele was situated in the very centre of the building; all the measurements were made from it, and the semicircle of the amphitheatre was described round it as the centre. It was, therefore, an excellent contrivance to place the chorus, who were the ideal representatives of the spectators, in the very spot where all the radii converged.

The tragical imitation of the ancients was altogether ideal and rhythmical; and in forming a judgment of it, we must always keep this in view. It was ideal, in so far as it aimed at the highest grace and dignity; and rhythmical, insomuch as the gestures and inflections of voice were more solemnly measured than in real life. As the statuary of the Greeks, setting out, with almost scientific strictness, with the most general conception, sought to embody it again in various general characters which were gradually invested with the charms of life, so that the individual was the last thing to which they descended; in like manner in the mimetic art, they began with the idea (the delineation of persons with heroical grandeur, more than human dignity, and ideal beauty), then passed to character, and made passion the last of all; which, in the collision with the requisitions of either of the others, was forced to give way. Fidelity of representation was less their object than beauty; with us it is exactly the reverse. On this principle, the use of masks, which appears astonishing to us, was not only justifiable, but absolutely essential; far from considering them as a makeshift, the Greeks would certainly, and with justice too, have looked upon it as a makeshift to be obliged to allow a player with vulgar, ignoble, or strongly marked features, to represent an Apollo or a Hercules; nay, rather they would have deemed it downright profanation. How little is it in the power of the most finished actor to change the character of his features! How prejudicial must this be to the expression of passion, as all passion is tinged more or less strongly by the character. Nor is there any need to have recourse to the conjecture that they changed the masks in the different scenes, for the purpose of exhibiting a greater degree of joy or sorrow. I call it conjecture, though Barthelemy, in his *Anacharsis*, considers it a settled point. He cites no authorities, and I do not recollect any. For the expedient would by no means have been sufficient, as the passions often change in the same scene, and this has reduced modern critics to suppose, that the masks exhibited different appearances on the two sides; and that now this, now that side was turned towards the spectators, according to circumstances. Voltaire, in his Essay on the Tragedy of the Ancients and Moderns, prefixed to *Semiramis*, has actually gone this length. Amidst a multitude of supposed improprieties which he heaps together to confound the admirers of ancient tragedy, he urges the following: *Aucune nation* (that is to say, excepting the Greeks) *ne fait paraitre ses acteurs sur des especes d'echasses, le visage couvert d'un masque, qui exprime la douleur d'un cote et la joie de l'autre.* After a conscientious inquiry into the authorities for an assertion so very improbable, and yet so boldly made, I can only find one passage in Quinctilian, lib. xi. cap. 3, and an allusion of Platonius still more vague. (Vide *Aristoph. ed. Kuster, prolegom.* p. x.) Both passages refer only to the new comedy, and only amount to this, that in some characters the eyebrows were dissimilar. As to the intention of this, I shall say a word or two hereafter, when I come to consider the new Greek comedy. Voltaire, however, is without excuse, as the mention of the cothurnus leaves no doubt that he alluded to tragic masks. But his error had probably no such learned origin. In most cases, it would be a fruitless task to trace the source of his mistakes. The whole description of the Greek tragedy, as well as that of the cothurnus in particular, is worthy of the man whose knowledge of antiquity was such, that in his Essay on Tragedy, prefixed to *Brutus*, he boasts of having introduced the

Roman Senate on the stage in *red mantles*. No; the countenance remained from beginning to end the very same, as we may see from the ancient masks cut out in stone. For the expression of passion, the glances of the eye, the motion of the arms and hands, the attitudes, and, lastly, the tones of the voice, remained there. We complain of the loss of the play of the features, without reflecting, that at such a great distance, its effect would have been altogether lost.

We are not now inquiring whether, without the use of masks, it may not be possible to attain a higher degree of separate excellence in the mimetic art. This we would very willingly allow. Cicero, it is true, speaks of the expression, the softness, and delicacy of the acting of Roscius, in the same terms that a modern critic would apply to Garrick or Schroder. But I will not lay any stress on the acting of this celebrated player, the excellence of which has become proverbial, because it appears from a passage in Cicero that he frequently played without a mask, and that this was preferred: by his contemporaries. I doubt, however, whether this was ever the case among the Greeks. But the same writer relates, that actors in general, for the sake of acquiring the most perfect purity and flexibility of voice (and not merely the musical voice, otherwise the example would not have been applicable to the orator), submitted to such a course of uninterrupted exercises, as our modern players, even the French, who of all follow the strictest training, would consider a most intolerable oppression. For the display of dexterity in the mimetic art, without the accompaniment of words, was carried by the ancients in their pantomimes, to a degree of perfection quite unknown to the moderns. In tragedy, however, the great object in the art was the due subordination of every element; the whole was to appear animated by one and the same spirit, and hence, not merely the poetry, but the musical accompaniment, the scenical decoration, and training of the actors, all issued from the poet. The player was a mere instrument in his hands, and his merit consisted in the accuracy with which he filled his part, and by no means in arbitrary bravura, or ostentatious display of his own skill.

As from the nature of their writing materials, they had not a facility of making many copies, the parts were learnt from the repeated recitation of the poet, and the chorus was exercised in the same manner. This was called *teaching a play*. As the poet was also a musician, and for the most part a player likewise, this must have greatly contributed to the perfection of the performance.

We may safely allow that the task of the modern player, who must change his person without concealing it, is much more difficult; but this difficulty affords no just criterion for deciding which of the two the preference must be awarded, as a skilful representation of the noble and the beautiful.

As the features of the player acquired a more decided expression from the mask, as his voice was strengthened by a contrivance attached to the mask, so the cothurnus, consisting of several soles of considerable thickness, as may be seen in the ancient statues of Melpomene, raised his figure considerably above the usual standard. The female parts were also played by men, as the voice and general carriage of women would have been inadequate to the energy of tragic heroines.

The forms of the masks, [Footnote: We have obtained a knowledge of them from the imitations in stone which have come down to us. They display both beauty and variety. That great variety must have taken place in the tragical department (in the comic we can have no doubt about the matter) is evident from the rich store of technical expressions in the Greek language, for every gradation of the age, and character of masks. See the *Onomasticon* of Jul. Pollux. In the marble masks, however, we can neither see the thinness of the mass from which the real masks were executed, the more delicate colouring, nor the exquisite mechanism of the fittings. The abundance of excellent workmen possessed by Athens, in everything which had a reference to the plastic arts, will warrant the conjecture that they were in this respect inimitable. Those who have seen the masks of wax in the grand style, which in some degree contain the whole head, lately contrived at the Roman carnival, may form to themselves a pretty good idea of the theatrical masks of the ancients. They imitate life, even to its movements, in a most masterly manner, and at such a distance as that from which the ancient players were seen, the deception is most perfect. They always contain the white of the eye, as we see it in the ancient masks, and the person covered sees merely through the aperture left for the iris. The ancients must sometimes have gone still farther, and contrived also an iris for the masks, according to the anecdote of the singer Thamyris, who, in a piece which was probably of Sophocles, made his appearance with a black eye. Even accidental circumstances were imitated; for instance, the cheeks of Tyro, streaming blood from the cruel conduct of his stepmother. The head from the mask must no doubt have appeared somewhat large for the rest of the figure; but this disproportion, in tragedy at least, would not be perceived from the elevation of the cothurnus.] and the whole appearance of the tragic figures, we may easily suppose, were sufficiently beautiful and dignified. We should do well to have the ancient sculpture always present to our minds; and the most accurate conception, perhaps, that we can possibly have, is to imagine them so many statues in the grand style endowed with life and motion. But, as in sculpture, they were fond of dispensing as much as possible with dress, for the sake of exhibiting the more essential beauty of the figure; on the stage they would endeavour, from an opposite principle, to clothe as much as they could well do, both from a regard to decency, and because the actual forms of the body would not correspond sufficiently with the beauty of the countenance. They would also exhibit their divinities, which in sculpture we always observe either entirely naked, or only half covered, in a complete dress. They had recourse to a number of means for giving a suitable strength to the forms of the limbs, and thus restoring proportion to the increased height of the player.

The great breadth of the theatre in proportion to its depth must have given to the grouping of the figures the simple and distinct order of the bas-relief. We moderns prefer on the stage, as elsewhere, groups of a picturesque description, with figures more closely crowded together, and partly concealing one another, and partly retiring into the distance; but the ancients were so little fond of foreshortening, that even in their painting they generally avoided it. Their movement kept time with the rhythmus of the declamation, and in this accompaniment the utmost grace and beauty were aimed at. The poetical conception required a certain degree of repose in the action, and the keeping together certain masses, so as to exhibit a succession of *statuesque* situations, and it is not improbable that the player remained for some time motionless in one attitude. But we are not to suppose from this, that the Greeks were contented with a cold and feeble representation of the passions. How could we reconcile such a supposition with the fact, that whole lines of their tragedies are frequently dedicated to inarticulate exclamations of pain, with which we have nothing to correspond in any of our modern languages?

It has been often conjectured that the delivery of their dialogue resembled the modern recitative. For such a conjecture there is no other foundation than the fact that the Greek, like almost all southern languages, was pronounced with a greater musical inflexion than ours of the North. In other respects their tragic declamation must, I conceive, have been altogether unlike recitative, being both much more measured, and also far removed from its studied and artificial modulation.

So, again, the ancient tragedy, because it was accompanied with music and dancing, [Footnote: Even Barthelemy falls into this error in a note to the 70th Chapter of *Anacharsis*.] has also been frequently compared with the opera. But this comparison betrays an utter ignorance of the spirit of classical antiquity. Their dancing and music had nothing but the name in common with ours. In tragedy the primary object was the poetry, and everything else was strictly and truly subordinate to it. But in the opera the poetry is merely an accessory, the means of connecting the different parts together; and it is almost lost amidst its many and more favoured accompaniments. The best prescription for the composition of an opera is, take a rapid poetical sketch and then fill up and colour the outlines by the other arts. This anarchy of the arts, where music, dancing, and decoration are seeking to outvie each other by the profuse display of their most dazzling charms, constitutes the very essence of the opera. What sort of opera-music would it be, which should set the words to a mere rhythmical accompaniment of the simplest modulations? The fantastic magic of the opera consists altogether in the revelry of emulation between the different means, and in the medley of their profusion. This charm would at once be destroyed by any approximation to the severity of the ancient taste in any one point, even in that of the costume; for the contrast would render the variety in all the other departments even the more insupportable. Gay, tinselled, spangled draperies suit best to the opera; and hence many things which have been censured as unnatural, such as exhibiting heroes warbling and trilling in the excess of despondency, are perfectly justifiable. This fairy world is not peopled by real men, but by a singular kind of singing creatures. Neither is it any disadvantage that the opera is brought before us in a language which we do not generally understand; the words are altogether lost in the music, and the language which is most harmonious and musical, and contains the greatest number of open vowels for the airs, and distinct accents for recitative, is therefore the best. It would be as incongruous to attempt to give to the opera the simplicity of the Grecian Tragedy, as it is absurd to think of comparing them together.

In the syllabic composition, which then at least prevailed universally in Grecian music, the solemn choral song, of which we may form to ourselves some idea from our artless national airs, and more especially from our church-tunes, had no other instrumental accompaniment than a single flute, which was such as not in the slightest degree to impair the distinctness of the words. Otherwise it must hare increased the difficulty of the choruses and lyrical songs, which, in general, are the part which *we* find it the hardest to understand of the ancient tragedy, and as it must also have been for contemporary auditors. They abound in the most involved constructions, the most unusual expressions, and the boldest images and recondite allusions. Why then should the poets have lavished such labour and art upon them, if it were all to be lost in the delivery? Such a display of ornament without an object would have been very unlike Grecian ways of thinking.

In the syllabic measures of their tragedies, there generally prevails a highly finished regularity, but by no means a stiff symmetrical uniformity. Besides the infinite variety of the lyrical strophes, which the poet invented for each occasion, they have also a measure to suit the transition in the tone of mind from the dialogue to the lyric, the anapest; and two for the dialogue itself, one of which, by far the most usual, the iambic trimeter, denoted the regular progress of the action, and the other, the trochaic tetrameter, was expressive of the impetuousness of passion. It would lead us too far into the depths of metrical science, were we to venture at present on a more minute account of the structure and significance of these measures. I merely wished to make this remark, as so much has been said of the simplicity of the ancient tragedy, which, no doubt, exists in the general plan, at least in the two oldest poets; whereas in the execution and details the richest variety of poetical ornament is employed. Of course it must be evident that the utmost accuracy in the delivery of the different modes of versification was expected from the player, as the delicacy of the Grecian ear would not excuse, even in an orator, the false quantity of a single syllable.

LECTURE V.

Essence of the Greek Tragedies--Ideality of the Representation--Idea of Fate--Source of the Pleasure derived from Tragical Representations--Import of the Chorus--The materials of Greek Tragedy derived from Mythology-- Comparison with the Plastic Arts.

We come now to the essence of Greek tragedy. That in conception it was ideal, is universally allowed; this, however, must not be understood as implying that all its characters were depicted as morally perfect. In such a case what room could there be for that contrast and collision which the very plot of a drama requires?--They have their weaknesses, errors, and even crimes, but the manners are always elevated above reality, and every person is invested with as high a portion of dignity as was compatible with his part in the action. But this is not all. The ideality of the representation chiefly consisted in the elevation of every thing in it to a higher sphere. Tragic poetry wished to separate the image of humanity which it presented to us, from the level of nature to which man is in reality chained down, like a slave of the soil. How was this to be accomplished? By exhibiting to us an image hovering in the air? But this would have been incompatible with the law of gravitation and with the earthly materials of which our bodies are framed. Frequently, what is praised in art as *ideal* is really nothing more. But this would give us nothing more than airy evanescent shadows incapable of making any durable impression on the mind. The Greeks, however, in their artistic creations, succeeded most perfectly, in combining the ideal with the real, or, to drop school terms, an elevation more than human with all the truth of life, and in investing the manifestation of an idea with energetic corporeity. They did not allow their figures to flit about without consistency in empty space, but they fixed the statue of humanity on the eternal and immovable basis of moral liberty; and that it might stand there unshaken, formed it of stone or brass, or some more massive substance than the bodies of living men, making an impression by its very weight, and from its very elevation and magnificence only the more completely subject to the laws of gravity.

Inward liberty and external necessity are the two poles of the tragic world. It is only by contrast with its opposite that each of these ideas is brought into full manifestation. As the feeling of an internal power of self-determination elevates the man above the unlimited dominion of impulse and the instincts of nature; in a word, absolves him from nature's guardianship, so the necessity, which alongside of her he must recognize, is no mere natural necessity, but one lying beyond the world of sense in the abyss of infinitude; consequently it exhibits itself as the unfathomable power of Destiny. Hence this power extends also to the world of gods: for the Grecian gods are mere powers of nature; and although immeasurably higher than mortal man, yet, compared with infinitude, they are on an equal footing with himself. In Homer and in the tragedians, the gods are introduced in a manner altogether different. In the former their appearance is arbitrary and accidental, and communicate to the epic poem no higher interest than the charm of the wonderful. But in Tragedy the gods either come forward as the servants of destiny, and mediate executors of its decrees; or else approve themselves godlike only by asserting their liberty of action, and entering upon the same struggles with fate which man himself has to encounter.

This is the essence of the tragical in the sense of the ancients. We are accustomed to give to all terrible or sorrowful events the appellation of tragic, and it is certain that such events are selected in preference by Tragedy, though a melancholy conclusion is by no means indispensably necessary; and several ancient tragedies, viz., the *Eumenides*, *Philoctetes*, and in some degree also the *Oedipus Coloneus*, without mentioning many of the pieces of Euripides, have a happy and cheerful termination.

But why does Tragedy select subjects so awfully repugnant to the wishes and the wants of our sensuous nature? This question has often been asked, and seldom satisfactorily answered. Some have said that the pleasure of such representations arises from the comparison we make between the calmness and tranquillity of our own situation, and the storms and perplexities to which the victims of passion are exposed. But when we take a warm interest in the persons of a tragedy, we cease to think of ourselves; and when this is not the case, it is the best of all proofs that we take but a feeble interest in the exhibited story, and that the tragedy has failed in its effect. Others again have had recourse to a supposed feeling for moral improvement, which is gratified by the view of poetical justice in the reward of the good and the punishment of the wicked. But he for whom the aspect of such dreadful examples could really be wholesome, must be conscious of a base feeling of depression, very far removed from genuine morality, and would experience humiliation rather than elevation of mind. Besides, poetical justice is by no means indispensable to a good tragedy; it may end with the suffering of the just and the triumph of the wicked, if only the balance be preserved in the spectator's own consciousness by the prospect of futurity. Little does it mend the matter to say with Aristotle, that the object of tragedy is to purify the passions by pity and terror. In the first place commentators have never been able to agree as to the meaning of this proposition, and have had recourse to the most forced explanations of it. Look, for instance, into the *Dramaturgie* of Lessing. Lessing gives a new explanation of his own, and fancies he has found in Aristotle a poetical Euclid. But mathematical demonstrations are liable to no misconception, and geometrical evidence may well be supposed inapplicable to the theory of the fine arts. Supposing, however, that tragedy does operate this moral cure in us, still she does so by the painful feelings of terror and compassion: and it remains to be proved how it is that we take a pleasure in subjecting ourselves to such an operation.

Others have been pleased to say that we are attracted to theatrical representations from the want of some violent agitation to rouse us out of the torpor of our every-day life. Such a craving does exist; I have already acknowledged the existence of this want, when speaking of the attractions of the drama; but to it we must equally attribute the fights of wild beasts among the Romans, nay, even the combats of the gladiators. But must we, less indurated, and more inclined to tender feelings, require demi-gods and heroes to descend, like so many desperate gladiators, into the bloody arena of the tragic stage, in order to agitate our nerves by the spectacle of their sufferings? No: it is not the sight of suffering which constitutes the charm of a tragedy, or even of the games of the circus, or of the fight of wild beasts. In the latter we see a display of activity, strength, and courage; splendid qualities these, and related to the mental and moral powers of man. The satisfaction, therefore, which we derive from the representation, in a good tragedy, of powerful situations and overwhelming sorrows, must be ascribed either to the feeling of the dignity of human nature, excited in us by such grand instances of it as are therein displayed, or to the trace of a higher order of things, impressed on the apparently irregular course of events, and mysteriously revealed in them; or perhaps to both these causes conjointly.

The true reason, therefore, why tragedy need not shun even the harshest subject is, that a spiritual and invisible power can only be measured by the opposition which it encounters from some external force capable of being appreciated by the senses. The moral freedom of man, therefore, can only be displayed in a conflict with his sensuous impulses: so long as no higher call summons it to action, it is either actually dormant within him, or appears to slumber, since otherwise it does but mechanically fulfil its part as a mere power of nature. It is only amidst difficulties and struggles that the moral part of man's nature avouches itself. If, therefore, we must explain the distinctive aim of tragedy by way of theory, we would give it thus: that to establish the claims of the mind to a divine origin, its earthly existence must be disregarded as vain and insignificant, all sorrows endured and all difficulties overcome. With respect to everything connected with this point, I refer my hearers to the

Section on the Sublime in Kant's *Criticism of the Judgment* (*Kritik der Urtheilskraft*), to the complete perfection of which nothing is wanting but a more definite idea of the tragedy of the ancients, with which he does not seem to have been very well acquainted.

I come now to another peculiarity which distinguishes the tragedy of the ancients from ours, I mean the Chorus. We must consider it as a personified reflection on the action which is going on; the incorporation into the representation itself of the sentiments of the poet, as the spokesman of the whole human race. This is its general poetical character; and that is all that here concerns us, and that character is by no means affected by the circumstance that the Chorus had a local origin in the feasts of Bacchus, and that, moreover, it always retained among the Greeks a peculiar national signification; publicity being, as we have already said, according to their republican notions, essential to the completeness of every important transaction. If in their compositions they reverted to the heroic ages, in which monarchical polity was yet in force, they nevertheless gave a certain republican cast to the families of their heroes, by carrying on the action in presence either of the elders of the people, or of other persons who represented some correspondent rank or position in the social body. This publicity does not, it is true, quite correspond with Homer's picture of the manners of the heroic age; but both costume and mythology were handled by dramatic poetry with the same spirit of independence and conscious liberty.

These thoughts, then, and these modes of feeling led to the introduction of the Chorus, which, in order not to interfere with the appearance of reality which the whole ought to possess, must adjust itself to the ever-varying requisitions of the exhibited stories. Whatever it might be and do in each particular piece, it represented in general, first the common mind of the nation, and then the general sympathy of all mankind. In a word, the Chorus is the ideal spectator. It mitigates the impression of a heart-rending or moving story, while it conveys to the actual spectator a lyrical and musical expression of his own emotions, and elevates him to the region of contemplation.

Modern critics have never known what to make of the Chorus; and this is the less to be wondered at, as Aristotle affords no satisfactory solution of the matter. Its office is better painted by Horace, who ascribes to it a general expression of moral sympathy, exhortation, instruction, and warning. But the critics in question have either believed that its chief object was to prevent the stage from ever being altogether empty, whereas in truth the stage was not at all the proper place for the Chorus; or else they have censured it as a superfluous and cumbersome appendage, expressing their astonishment at the alleged absurdity of carrying on secret transactions in the presence of assembled multitudes. They have also considered it as the principal reason with the Greek tragedians for the strict observance of the unity of place, as it could not be changed without the removal of the Chorus; an act, which could not have been done without some available pretext. Or lastly, they have believed that the Chorus owed its continuance from the first origin of Tragedy merely to accident; and as it is plain that in Euripides, the last of the three great tragic poets, the choral songs have frequently little or no connexion with the fable, and are nothing better than a mere episodical ornament, they therefore conclude that the Greeks had only to take one more step in the progress of dramatic art, to explode the Chorus altogether. To refute these superficial conjectures, it is only necessary to observe that Sophocles wrote a Treatise on the Chorus, in prose, in opposition to the principles of some other poets; and that, far from following blindly the practice which he found established, like an intelligent artist he was able to assign reasons for his own doings.

Modern poets of the first rank have often, since the revival of the study of the ancients, attempted to introduce the Chorus in their own pieces, for the most part without a correct, and always without a vivid idea of its real import. They seem to have forgotten that we have neither suitable singing or dancing, nor, as our theatres are constructed, any convenient place for it. On these accounts it is hardly likely to become naturalized with us.

The Greek tragedy, in its pure and unaltered state, will always for our theatres remain an exotic plant, which we can hardly hope to cultivate with any success, even in the hot-house of learned art and criticism. The Grecian mythology, which furnishes the materials of ancient tragedy, is as foreign to the minds and imaginations of most of the spectators, as its form and manner of representation. But to endeavour to force into that form materials of a wholly different nature, an historical one, for example, to assume that form, must always be a most unprofitable and hopeless attempt.

I have called mythology the chief materials of tragedy. We know, indeed, of two historical tragedies by Grecian authors: the *Capture of Miletus*, of Phrynichus, and the *Persians*, of Aeschylus, a piece which still exists; but these singular exceptions both belong to an epoch when the art had not attained its full maturity, and among so many hundred examples of a different description, only serve to establish more strongly the truth of the rule. The sentence passed by the Athenians on Phrynichus, in which they condemned him to a pecuniary fine because he had painfully agitated them by representing on the stage a contemporary calamity, which with due caution they might, perhaps, have avoided; however hard and arbitrary it may appear in a judicial point of view, displays, however, a correct feeling of the proprieties and limits of art. Oppressed by the consciousness of the proximity and reality of the represented story, the mind cannot retain that repose and self-possession which are necessary for the reception of pure tragical impressions. The heroic fables, on the other hand, came to view at a certain remoteness; and surrounded with a certain halo of the marvellous. The marvellous possesses the advantage that it can, in some measure, be at once believed and disbelieved: believed in so far as it is supported by its connexion with other opinions; disbelieved while we never take such an immediate interest in it as we do in what wears the hue of the every-day life of our own experience. The Grecian mythology was a web of national and local traditions, held in equal honour as a sequence of religion, and as an introduction to history; everywhere preserved in full vitality among the people by ceremonies and monuments, already elaborated for the requirements of art and the higher species of poetry by the diversified manner in which it has been handled, and by the numerous epic or merely mythical poets. The tragedians had only, therefore, to engraft one species of poetry on another. Certain postulates, and those invariably serviceable to the air of dignity and grandeur, and the removing of all meanness of idea, were conceded to them at the very outset. Everything, down to the very errors and weaknesses of that departed race of heroes who claimed their descent from the gods, was ennobled by the sanctity of legend. Those heroes were painted as beings endowed with more than human strength; but, so far from possessing unerring virtue and wisdom, they were even depicted as under the dominion of furious and unbridled passions. It was an age of wild effervescence; the hand of social order had not as yet brought the soil of morality into cultivation, and it yielded at the same time the most beneficent and poisonous productions, with the fresh luxuriant fulness of prolific nature. Here the occurrence of the monstrous and horrible did not necessarily indicate that degradation and corruption out of which alone, under the development of law and order, they could arise, and which, in such a state of things, make them fill us with sentiments of horror and aversion. The guilty beings of the fable are, if we may be allowed the expression, exempt from human jurisdiction, and amenable to a higher tribunal alone. Some, indeed, have advanced the opinion, that the Greeks, as zealous republicans, took a particular pleasure in witnessing the representation of the outrages and consequent calamities of the different royal families, and are almost disposed to consider the ancient tragedy in general as a satire on monarchical government. Such a party-view, however, would have deadened the sympathy of the audience, and consequently destroyed the effect which it was the aim of the tragedy to produce.

Besides, it must be remarked that the royal families, whose crimes and consequent sufferings afforded the most abundant materials for affecting tragical pictures, were the Pelopidae of Mycenae, and the Labdacidae of Thebes, families who had nothing to do with the political history of the Athenians, for whom the pieces were composed. We do not see that the Attic poets ever endeavoured to exhibit the ancient kings of their country in an odious light; on the contrary, they always hold up their national hero, Theseus, for public admiration, as a model of justice and moderation, the champion of the oppressed, the first lawgiver, and even as the founder of liberty. It was also one of their favourite modes of flattering the people, to show to them Athens, even in the heroic ages, as distinguished above all the other states of Greece, for obedience to the laws, for humanity, and acknowledgment of the national rights of the Hellenes. That universal revolution, by which the independent kingdoms of ancient Greece were converted into a community of small free states, had separated the heroic age from the age of social cultivation, by a wide interval, beyond which a few families only attempted to trace their genealogy. This was extremely advantageous for the ideal elevation of the characters of Greek tragedy, as few human things will admit of a very close inspection without betraying some imperfections. To the very different relations of the age in which those heroes lived, the standard of mere civil and domestic morality is not applicable, and to judge of them the feeling must go back to the primary ingredients of human nature. Before the existence of constitutions,--when as yet the notions of law and right were undeveloped,--the sovereigns were their own lawgivers, in a world which as yet was dependent on them; and the fullest scope was thus given to the energetic will, either for good or for evil. Moreover, an age of hereditary kingdom naturally exhibited more striking instances of sudden changes of fortune than the later times of political equality. It was in this respect that the high rank of the principal characters was essential, or at least favourable to tragic impressiveness; and not, as some moderns have pretended, because the changing fortunes of such persons exercise a material influence on the happiness or misery of numbers, and therefore they alone are sufficiently important to interest us in their behalf; nor, again, because internal elevation of sentiment must be clothed with external dignity, to call forth our respect and admiration. The Greek tragedians paint the downfall of kingly houses without any reference to its effects on the condition of the people; they show us the man in the king, and, far from veiling their heroes from our sight by their purple mantles, they allow us to look, through their vain splendour, into a bosom torn and harrowed with grief and passion. That the main essential was not so much the regal dignity as the heroic costume, is evident from those tragedies of the moderns which have been written under different circumstances indeed, but still upon this supposed principle: such, I mean, as under the existence of monarchy have taken their subject from kings and courts. Prom the existing reality they dare not draw, for nothing is less suitable for tragedy than a court and a court life. Wherever, therefore, they do not paint an ideal kingdom, with the manners of some remote age, they invariably fall into stiffness and formality, which are much more fatal to boldness of character, and to depth of pathos, than the monotonous and equable relations of private life.

A few mythological fables alone seem originally marked out for tragedy: such, for example, as the long-continued alternation of crime, revenge, and curses, which we witness in the house of Atreus. When we examine the names of the pieces which are lost, we have great difficulty in conceiving how the mythological fables (such, at least, as they are known to us,) could have furnished sufficient materials for the compass of an entire tragedy. It is true, the poets, in the various editions of the same story, had a great latitude of selection; and this very fluctuation of tradition justified them in going still farther, and making considerable alterations in the circumstances of an event, so that the inventions employed for this purpose in one piece sometimes contradict the story as given by the same poet in another. We must, however, principally explain the prolific capability of mythology, for the purposes of tragedy, by the principle which we observe in operation throughout the history of Grecian mind and art; that, namely, the tendency which predominated for the time, assimilated everything else to itself. As the heroic legend with all its manifold discrepancies was easily developed into the tranquil fulness and light variety of epic poetry, so afterwards it readily responded to the demands which the tragic writers made upon it for earnestness, energy, and compression; and whatever in this sifting process of transformation fell out as inapplicable to tragedy, afforded materials for a sort of half sportive, though still ideal representation, in the subordinate species called the *satirical drama*.

I hope I shall be forgiven, if I attempt to illustrate the above reflections on the essence of Ancient Tragedy, by a comparison borrowed from the plastic arts, which will, I trust, be found somewhat more than a mere fanciful resemblance.

The Homeric epic is, in poetry, what bas-relief is in sculpture, and tragedy the distinct isolated group.

The poetry of Homer, sprung from the soil of legend, is not yet wholly detached from it, even as the figures of a bas-relief adhere to an extraneous backing of the original block. These figures are but slightly raised, and in the epic poem all is painted as past and remote. In bas-relief the figures are usually in profile, and in the epos all are characterized in the simplest manner in relief; they are not grouped together, but follow one another; so Homer's heroes advance, one by one, in succession before us. It has been remarked that the *Iliad* is not definitively closed, but that we are left to suppose something both to precede and to follow it. The bas-relief is equally without limit, and may be continued *ad infinitum*, either from before or behind, on which account the ancients preferred for it such subjects as admitted of an indefinite extension, sacrificial processions, dances, and lines of combatants, &c. Hence they also exhibited bas-reliefs on curved surfaces, such as vases, or the frieze of a rotunda, where, by the curvature, the two ends are withdrawn from our sight, and where, while we advance, one object appears as another disappears. Reading Homer is very much like such a circuit; the present object alone arresting our attention, we lose sight of that which precedes, and do not concern ourselves about what is to follow.

But in the distinct outstanding group, and in Tragedy, sculpture and poetry alike bring before our eyes an independent and definite whole. To distinguish it from natural reality, the former places it on a base as on an ideal ground, detaching from it as much as possible all foreign and accidental accessories, that the eye may rest wholly on the essential objects, the figures themselves. These figures the sculptor works out with their whole body and contour, and as he rejects the illusion of colours, announces by the solidity and uniformity of the mass in which they are constructed, a creation of no perishable existence, but endowed, with a higher power of endurance.

Beauty is the aim of sculpture, and repose is most advantageous for the display of beauty. Repose alone, therefore, is suitable to the single figure. But a number of figures can only be combined together into unity, *i.e., grouped* by an action. The group represents beauty in motion, and its aim is to combine both in the highest degree of perfection. This can be effected even while portraying the most violent bodily or mental anguish, if only the artist finds means so to temper the expression by some trait of manly resistance, calm grandeur, or inherent sweetness, that, with all the most moving truth, the lineaments of beauty shall yet be undefaced. The observation of Winkelmann on this subject is inimitable. He says, that "beauty with the ancients was the tongue on the balance of expression," and in this sense the groups of Niobe and Laocoon are master-pieces; the one in the sublime and severe; the other in the studied and ornamental style.

The comparison with ancient tragedy is the more apposite here, as we know that both Aeschylus and Sophocles produced a Niobe, and that Sophocles was also the author of a Laocoon. In the group of the Laocoon the efforts of the body in enduring, and of the mind in resisting, are balanced in admirable equipoise. The children calling for help, tender objects of compassion, not of admiration, recal our eyes to the father, who seems to be in vain uplifting his eyes to the gods. The wreathed serpents represent to us that inevitable destiny which often involves all the parties of an action in one common ruin. And yet the beauty of proportion, the agreeable flow of the outline, are not lost in this violent struggle; and a representation, the most appalling to the senses, is yet managed with forbearance, while a mild breath of gracefulness is diffused over the whole.

In the group of Niobe there is the same perfect mixture of terror and pity. The upturned looks of the mother, and the mouth half open in supplication, seem yet to accuse the invisible wrath of heaven. The daughter, clinging in the agonies of death to the bosom of her mother, in her childish innocence has no fear but for herself: the innate impulse of self-preservation was never more tenderly and affectingly expressed. On the other hand, can there be a more beautiful image of self-devoting, heroic magnanimity than Niobe, as she bends forward to receive, if possible, in her own body the deadly shaft? Pride and defiance dissolve in the depths of maternal love. The more than earthly dignity of the features are the less marred by the agony, as under the rapid accumulation of blow upon blow she seems, as in the deeply significant fable, already petrifying into the stony torpor. But before this figure, thus *twice* struck into stone, and yet so full of life and soul,--before this stony terminus of the limits of human endurance, the spectator melts into tears.

Amid all the agitating emotions which these groups give rise to, there is still a something in their aspect which attracts the mind and gives rise to manifold contemplation; so the ancient tragedy leads us forward to the highest reflections involved in the very sphere of things it sets before us--reflections on the nature and the inexplicable mystery of man's being.

LECTURE VI.

Progress of the Tragic Art among the Greeks--Various styles of Tragic Art --Aeschylus--Connexion in a Trilogy of Aeschylus--His remaining Works.

Of the inexhaustible stores possessed by the Greeks in the department of tragedy, which the public competition at the Athenian festivals called into being (as the rival poets always contended for a prize), very little indeed has come down to us. We only possess works of three of their numerous tragedians, Aeschylus, Sophocles, and Euripides, and of these but a few in proportion to the whole number of their compositions. The extant dramas are such as were selected by the Alexandrian critics as the foundation for the study of the older Grecian literature, not because they alone were deserving of estimation, but because they afforded the best illustration of the various styles of tragic art. Of each of the two older poets, we have seven pieces remaining; in these, however, we have, according to the testimony of the ancients, several of their most distinguished productions. Of Euripides we have a much greater number, and we might well exchange many of them for other works which are now lost; for example, for the satirical dramas of Achaeus, Aeschylus, and Sophocles, or, for the sake of comparison with Aeschylus, for some of Phrynichus' pieces, or of Agathon's, whom Plato describes as effeminate, but sweet and affecting, and who was a contemporary of Euripides, though somewhat his junior.

Leaving to antiquarians to sift the stories about the waggon of the strolling Thespis, the contests for the prize of a he-goat, from which the name of tragedy is said to be derived, and the lees of wine with which the first improvisatory actors smeared over their visages, from which rude beginnings, it is pretended, Aeschylus, by one gigantic stride, gave to tragedy that dignified form under which it appears in his works, we shall proceed immediately to the consideration of the poets themselves.

The tragic style of Aeschylus (I use the word "style" in the sense it receives in sculpture, and not in the exclusive signification of the manner of writing,) is grand, severe, and not unfrequently hard: that of Sophocles is marked by the most finished symmetry and harmonious gracefulness: that of Euripides is soft and luxuriant; overflowing in his easy copiousness, he often sacrifices the general effect to brilliant passages. The analogies which the undisturbed development of the fine arts among the Greeks everywhere furnishes, will enable us, throughout to compare the epochs of tragic art with those of sculpture. Aeschylus is the

Phidias of Tragedy, Sophocles her Polycletus, and Euripides her Lysippus. Phidias formed sublime images of the gods, but lent them an extrinsic magnificence of material, and surrounded their majestic repose with images of the most violent struggles in strong relief. Polycletus carried his art to perfection of proportion, and hence one of his statues was called the Standard of Beauty. Lysippus distinguished himself by the fire of his works; but in his time Sculpture had deviated from its original destination, and was much more desirous of expressing the charm of motion and life than of adhering to ideality of form.

Aeschylus is to be considered as the creator of Tragedy: in full panoply she sprung from his head, like Pallas from the head of Jupiter. He clad her with dignity, and gave her an appropriate stage; he was the inventor of scenic pomp, and not only instructed the chorus in singing and dancing, but appeared himself as an actor. He was the first that expanded the dialogue, and set limits to the lyrical part of tragedy, which, however, still occupies too much space in his pieces. His characters are sketched with a few bold and strong touches. His plots are simple in the extreme: he did not understand the art of enriching and varying an action, and of giving a measured march and progress to the complication and denouement. Hence his action often stands still; a circumstance which becomes yet more apparent, from the undue extension of his choral songs. But all his poetry evinces a sublime and earnest mind. Terror is his element, and not the softer affections, he holds up a head of Medusa before the petrified spectators. In his handling Destiny appears austere in the extreme; she hovers over the heads of mortals in all her gloomy majesty. The cothurnus of Aeschylus has, as it were, the weight of iron: gigantic figures stalk in upon it. It seems as if it required an effort for him to condescend to paint mere men; he is ever bringing in gods, but especially the Titans, those elder divinities who typify the gloomy powers of primaeval nature, and who had been driven long ago into Tartarus before the presence of a new and better order of things. He endeavours to swell out his language to a gigantic sublimity, corresponding to the vast dimensions of his personages. Hence he abounds in harsh compounds and over-strained epithets, and the lyrical parts of his pieces are often, from their involved construction, extremely obscure. In the singular strangeness of his images and expressions he resembles Dante and Shakspeare. Yet in these images there is no want of that terrific grace which almost all the writers of antiquity commend in Aeschylus.

Aeschylus flourished in the very freshness and vigour of Grecian freedom, and a proud sense of the glorious struggle by which it was won, seems to have animated him and his poetry. He had been an eye-witness of the greatest and most glorious event in the history of Greece, the overthrow and annihilation of the Persian hosts under Darius and Xerxes, and had fought with distinguished bravery in the memorable battles of Marathon and Salamis. In the *Persians* he has, in an indirect manner, sung the triumph which he contributed to obtain, while he paints the downfall of the Persian ascendancy, and the ignominious return of the despot, with difficulty escaping with his life, to his royal residence. The battle of Salamis he describes in the most vivid and glowing colours. Through the whole of this piece, and the *Seven before Thebes*, there gushes forth a warlike vein; the personal inclination of the poet for a soldier's life, shines throughout with the most dazzling lustre. It was well remarked by Gorgias, the sophist, that Mars, instead of Bacchus, had inspired this last drama; for Bacchus, and not Apollo, was the tutelary deity of tragic poets, which, on a first view of the matter, appears somewhat singular, but then we must recollect that Bacchus was not merely the god of wine and joy, but also the god of all higher kinds of inspiration.

Among the remaining pieces of Aeschylus, we have what is highly deserving of our attention--a complete *Trilogy*. The antiquarian account of the trilogies is this: that in the more early times the poet did not contend for the prize with a single piece, but with three, which, however, were not always connected together in their subjects, and that to these was added a fourth,--namely, a *satiric drama*. All were acted in one day, one after another. The idea which, in relation to the tragic art, we must form of the trilogy, is this: a tragedy cannot be indefinitely lengthened and continued, like the Homeric Epos for instance, to which whole rhapsodies have been appended; tragedy is too independent and complete within itself for this; nevertheless, several tragedies may be connected together in one great cycle by means of a common destiny running through the actions of all. Hence the restriction to the number three admits of a satisfactory explanation. It is the thesis, the antithesis, and the synthesis. The advantage of this conjunction was that, by the consideration of the connected fables, a more complete gratification was furnished than could possibly be obtained from a single action. The subjects of the three tragedies might be separated by a wide interval of time, or follow close upon one another.

The three pieces which form the trilogy of Aeschylus, are the *Agamemnon*, the *Choephorae* or, we should call it, *Electra*, and the *Eumenides* or *Furies*. The subject of the first is the murder of Agamemnon by Clytemnestra, on his return from Troy. In the second, Orestes avenges his father by killing his mother: *facto pius et sceleratus eodem*. This deed, although enjoined by the most powerful motives, is, however, repugnant to the natural and moral order of things. Orestes, as a prince, was, it is true, called upon to exercise justice, even on the members of his own family; but we behold him here under the necessity of stealing in disguise into the dwelling of the tyrannical usurper of his throne, and of going to work like an assassin. The memory of his father pleads his excuse; but however much Clytemnestra may have deserved her death, the voice of blood cries from within. This conflict of natural duties is represented in the *Eumenides* in the form of a contention among the gods, some of whom approve of the deed of Orestes, while others persecute him, till at last Divine Wisdom, in the persona of Minerva, balances the opposite claims, establishes peace, and puts an end to the long series of crime and punishment which have desolated the royal house of Atreus.

A considerable interval takes place between the period of the first and second pieces, during which Orestes grows up to manhood. The second and third are connected together immediately in order of time. Upon the murder of his mother, Orestes flees forthwith to Delphi, where we find him at the commencement of the *Eumenides*.

In each of the two first pieces, there is a visible reference to the one which follows. In *Agamemnon*, Cassandra and the chorus, at the close, predict to the haughty Clytemnestra and her paramour, Aegisthus, the punishment which awaits them at the hands of Orestes. In the *Choephorae*, Orestes, upon the execution of the deed of retribution, finds that all peace is gone: the furies of his mother begin to persecute him, and he announces his resolution of taking refuge in Delphi.

The connexion is therefore evident throughout; and we may consider the three pieces, which were connected together even in the representation, as so many acts of one great and entire drama. I mention this as a preliminary justification of the practice of Shakspeare and other modern poets, to connect together in one representation a larger circle of human destinies, as we can produce to the critics who object to this the supposed example of the ancients.

In *Agamemnon*, it was the intention of Aeschylus to exhibit to us a sudden fall from the highest pinnacle of prosperity and renown into the abyss of ruin. The prince, the hero, the general of the combined forces of the Greeks, in the very moment of success and the glorious achievement of the destruction of Troy, the fame of which is to be re-echoed from the mouths of the greatest poets of all ages, in the very act of crossing the threshold of his home, after which he had so long sighed, and amidst the fearless security of preparations for a festival, is butchered, according to the expression of Homer, "like an ox in the stall," slain by his faithless wife, his throne usurped by her worthless seducer, and his children consigned to banishment or to hopeless servitude.

With the view of giving greater effect to this dreadful reverse of fortune, the poet endeavours to throw a greater splendour over the destruction of Troy. He has done this in the first half of the piece in a manner peculiar to himself, which, however singular, must be allowed to be impressive in the extreme, and well fitted to lay fast hold of the imagination. It is of importance to Clytemnestra that she should not be surprised by the sudden arrival of her husband; she has therefore arranged an uninterrupted series of signal fires from Troy to Mycenae, to announce to her that great event. The piece commences with the speech of a watchman, who supplicates the gods for a deliverance from his labours, as for ten long years he has been exposed to the cold dews of night, has witnessed the changeful course of the stars, while looking in vain for the expected signal; at the same time he sighs in secret over the corruption which reigns within the royal house. At this moment he sees the long-wished-for beacon blazing up, and hastens to announce it to his mistress. A chorus of aged persons appears, and in their songs they go through the whole history of the Trojan War, through all its eventful fluctuations of fortune, from its origin, and recount all the prophecies relating to it, and the sacrifice of Iphigenia, by which the sailing of the Greeks was purchased. Clytemnestra explains to the chorus the joyful cause of the sacrifice which she orders; and the herald Talthybius immediately makes his appearance, who, as an eye-witness, relates the drama of the conquered and plundered city, consigned as a prey to the flames, the joy of the victors, and the glory of their leader. With reluctance, as if unwilling to check their congratulatory prayers, he recounts to them the subsequent misfortunes of the Greeks, their dispersion, and the shipwreck suffered by many of them, an immediate symptom of the wrath of the gods. It is obvious how little the unity of time was observed by the poet,--how much, on the contrary, he avails himself of the prerogative of his mental dominion over the powers of nature, to give wings to the circling hours in their course towards the dreadful goal. Agamemnon now arrives, borne in a sort of triumphal car; and seated on another, laden with booty, follows Cassandra, his prisoner of war, and concubine also, according to the customary privilege of heroes. Clytemnestra greets him with hypocritical joy and veneration; she orders her slaves to cover the ground with the most costly embroideries of purple, that it might not be touched by the foot of the conqueror. Agamemnon, with wise moderation, refuses to accept an honour due only to the gods; at last he yields to her solicitations, and enters the palace. The chorus then begins to utter its dark forebodings. Clytemnestra returns to allure, by friendly speeches, Cassandra also to destruction. The latter is silent and unmoved, but the queen is hardly gone, when, seized with prophetic furor, she breaks out into the most confused and obscure lamentations, but presently unfolds her prophecies more distinctly to the chorus; in spirit she beholds all the enormities which have been perpetrated within that house--the repast of Thyestes, which the sun refused to look upon; the ghosts of the mangled children appear to her on the battlements of the palace. She also sees the death which is preparing for her lord; and, though shuddering at the reek of death, as if seized with madness, she rushes into the house to meet her own inevitable doom, while from behind the scene we hear the groans of the dying Agamemnon. The palace opens; Clytemnestra stands beside the body of her king and husband; like an insolent criminal, she not only confesses the deed, but boasts of and justifies it, as a righteous requital for Agamemnon's sacrifice of Iphigenia to his own ambition. Her jealousy of Cassandra, and criminal connexion with the worthless Aegisthus, who does not appear till after the completion of the murder and towards the conclusion of the piece, are motives which she hardly touches on, and throws entirely into the background. This was necessary to preserve the dignity of the subject; for, indeed, Clytemnestra could not with propriety have been portrayed as a frail seduced woman--she must appear with the features of that heroic age, so rich in bloody catastrophes, in which all passions were violent, and men, both in good and evil, surpassed the ordinary standard of later and more degenerated ages. What is more revolting--what proves a deeper degeneracy of human nature, than horrid crimes conceived in the bosom of cowardly effeminacy? If such crimes are to be portrayed by the poet, he must neither seek to palliate them, nor to mitigate our horror and aversion of them. Moreover, by bringing the sacrifice of Iphigenia thus immediately before us, the poet has succeeded in lessening the indignation which otherwise the foul and painful fate of Agamemnon is calculated to awaken. He cannot be pronounced wholly innocent; a former crime recoils on his own head: besides, according to the religious idea of the ancients, an old curse hung over his house. Aegisthus, the author of his destruction, is a son of that very Thyestes on whom his father Atreus took such an unnatural revenge; and this fateful connexion is vividly brought before our minds by the chorus, and more especially by the prophecies of Cassandra.

I pass over the subsequent piece of the *Choephorae* for the present; I shall speak of it when I come to institute a comparison between the manner in which the three poets have handled the same subject.

The fable of the *Eumenides* is, as I have already said, the justification of Orestes, and his absolution from blood-guiltiness: it is a trial, but a trial where the accusers and the defenders and the presiding judges are gods. And the manner in which the subject is treated corresponds with its majesty and importance. The scene itself brought before the eyes of the Greeks all the highest objects of veneration that they acknowledged.

It opens in front of the celebrated temple at Delphi, which occupies the background; the aged Pythia enters in sacerdotal pomp, addresses her prayers to all the gods who at any time presided, or still preside, over the oracle, harangues the assembled people (represented by the actual audience), and goes into the temple to seat herself on the tripod. She returns full of consternation, and describes what she has seen in the temple: a man, stained with blood, supplicating protection, surrounded by sleeping women with snaky hair; she then makes her exit by the same entrance as she came in by. Apollo now appears with Orestes, who is in a traveller's garb, and carries a sword and olive-branch in his hands. He promises him his farther protection, enjoins him to flee to Athens, and commends him to the care of the present but invisible Mercury, to whose safeguard travellers, and especially those who were under the necessity of journeying by stealth, were usually consigned.

Orestes goes off at the side which was supposed to lead to foreign lands; Apollo re-enters his temple, which remains open, and the Furies are seen in the interior, sleeping on the benches. Clytemnestra's ghost now ascends by the charonic stairs, and, passing through the orchestra, appears on the stage. We are not to imagine it a haggard skeleton, but a figure with the appearance of life, though paler, with the wound still open in her breast, and shrouded in ethereal-coloured vestments. She calls on the Furies, in the language of vehement reproach, and then disappears, probably through a trap-door. The Furies awake, and not finding Orestes, they dance in wild commotion round the stage, while they sing the choral song. Apollo again comes out of the temple, and drives them away, as profaning his sanctuary. We may imagine him appearing with the sublime displeasure of the Apollo of the Vatican, with bow and quiver, but also clad with tunic and chlamys.

The scene now changes; but as the Greeks on such occasions were fond of going the shortest way to work, the background probably remained unchanged, and was now supposed to represent the temple of Minerva, on the Areopagus, while the lateral decorations were converted into Athens and its surrounding landscape. Orestes now enters, as from foreign land, and, as a suppliant, embraces the statue of Pallas standing before the temple. The chorus (who, according to the poet's own description, were clothed in black, with purple girdles, and serpents in their hair, in masks having perhaps something of the terrific beauty of Medusa-heads, and marking too their great age on the principles of sculpture) follows close on his steps, but for the rest of the piece remains below in the orchestra. The Furies had at first behaved themselves like beasts of prey, furious at the escape of their booty, but now, hymning with tranquil dignity the high and terrible office they had among mortals, they claim the head of Orestes, as forfeited to them, and devote it with mysterious charms to endless torment. At the intercession of the suppliant, Pallas, the warrior-virgin, appears in a chariot drawn by four horses. She inquires the cause of his invocation, and listens with calm dignity to the mutual complaints of Orestes and his adversaries, and, at the solicitation of the two parties, finally undertakes, after due reflection, the office of umpire. The assembled judges take their seats on the steps of the temple--the herald commands silence among the people by sound of trumpet, just as in a real trial. Apollo advances to advocate the cause of his suppliant, the Furies in vain protest against his interference, and the arguments for and against the deed are debated between them in short speeches. The judges cast their ballots into the urn, Pallas throws in a white one; all is wrought up to the highest pitch of expectation; Orestes, in agony of suspense, exclaims to his protector--

O Phoebus Apollo, how will the cause be decided?

The Furies on the other hand:

O Night, black Mother, seest thou these doings?

Upon counting the black and white pebbles, they are found equal in number, and the accused, therefore, by the decision of Pallas, is acquitted. He breaks out into joyful thanksgiving, while the Furies on the other hand declaim against the overbearing arrogance of these younger gods, who take such liberties with those of Titanic race. Pallas bears their rage with equanimity, addresses them in the language of kindness, and even of veneration; and these so indomitable beings are unable to withstand the charms of her mild eloquence. They promise to bless the land which is under her tutelary protection, while on her part Pallas assigns them a sanctuary in the Attic domain, where they are to be called the *Eumenides*, that is, "the Benevolent Goddesses." The whole ends with a solemn procession round the theatre, with hymns of blessing, while bands of children, women, and old men, in purple robes and with torches in their hands, accompany the Furies in their exit.

Let us now take a retrospective view of the whole trilogy. In the *Agamemnon* we have a predominance of free-will both in the plan and execution of the deed: the principal character is a great criminal, and the piece ends with the revolting impressions produced by the sight of triumphant tyranny and crime. I have already pointed out the allusions it contains to a preceding destiny.

The deed committed in the *Choephorae* is partly enjoined by Apollo as the appointment of fate, and partly originates in natural motives: Orestes' desire of avenging his father, and his brotherly love for the oppressed Electra. It is only after the execution of the deed that the struggle between the most sacred feelings becomes manifest, and here again the sympathies of the spectators are excited without being fully appeased.

From its very commencement, the *Eumenides* stands on the very summit of tragical elevation: all the past is here, as it were, concentrated into a focus. Orestes has become the mere passive instrument of fate; and free agency is transferred to the more elevated sphere of the gods. Pallas is properly the principal character. That opposition between the most sacred relations, which often occurs in life as a problem not to be solved by man, is here represented as a contention in the world of the gods.

And this brings me to the pregnant meaning of the whole. The ancient mythology is in general *symbolical*, although not *allegorical*; for the two are *certainly* distinct. Allegory is the personification of an idea, a poetic story invented solely with such a view; but that is symbolical which, created by the imagination for other purposes, or possessing an independent reality of its own, is at the same time easily susceptible of an emblematical explanation; and even of itself suggests it.

The Titans in general symbolize the dark and mysterious powers of primaeval nature and mind; the younger gods, whatsoever enters more immediately within the circle of consciousness. The former are more nearly allied to original chaos, the latter belong to a world already reduced to order. The Furies denote the dreadful powers of conscience, in so far as it rests on obscure feelings and forebodings, and yields to no principles of reason. In vain Orestes dwells on the just motives which urged him to the deed, the cry of blood still sounds in his ear. Apollo is the god of youth, of the noble ebullition of passionate indignation, of bold and daring action. Accordingly this deed was commanded by him. Pallas is thoughtful wisdom, justice, and moderation, which alone can allay the conflict of reason and passion.

Even the sleep of the Furies in the temple is symbolical; for only in the sanctuary, in the bosom of religion, can the fugitive find rest from the torments of conscience. Scarcely, however, has he ventured forth again into the world, when the image of his murdered mother appears, and again awakes them. The very speech of Clytemnestra betrays its symbolical import, as much as the attributes of the Furies, the serpents, and their sucking of blood. The same may be said of Apollo's aversion for them; in fact, this symbolical character runs through the whole. The equal cogency of the motives for and against the deed is denoted by the equally divided votes of the judges. And if at last a sanctuary within the Athenian territory is offered to the softened Furies, this is as much as to say that reason is not everywhere to enforce its principles against involuntary instinct, that there are in the human mind certain boundaries which are not to be passed, and all contact with which even every person possessed of a true sentiment of reverence will cautiously avoid, if he would preserve peace within.

So much for the deep philosophical meaning which we need not wonder to find in this poet, who, according to the testimony of Cicero, was a Pythagorean. Aeschylus had also political views. Foremost of these was the design of rendering Athens illustrious. Delphi was the religious centre of Greece, and yet how far it is thrown into the shade by him! It can shelter Orestes, indeed, from the first onset of persecution, but not afford him a complete liberation; this is reserved for the land of law and humanity. But, a further, and in truth, his principal object was to recommend as essential to the welfare of Athens the Areopagus [Footnote: I do not find that this aim has ever been expressly ascribed to Aeschylus by any ancient writer. It is, however, too plain to be mistaken, and is revealed especially in the speech of Pallas, beginning with the 680th verse. It agrees, moreover, with the account, that in the very year when the piece was represented, (Olymp. lxxx. 1.) a certain Ephialtes excited the people against the Areopagus, which was the best guardian of the old and more austere constitution, and kept democratic extravagance in check. This Ephialtes was murdered one night by an unknown hand. Aeschylus received the first prize in the theatrical games, but we know that he left Athens immediately afterwards, and passed his remaining years in Sicily. It is possible that, although the theatrical judges did him justice, he might be held in aversion by the populace, and that this induced him, without any express sentence of banishment, to leave his native city. The story of the sight of the terrible chorus of Furies having thrown children into mortal convulsions, and caused women to miscarry, appears to be fabulous. A poet would hardly have been crowned, who had been the occasion of profaning the festival by such occurrences.], an uncorruptible yet mild tribunal, in which the white ballot of Pallas given in favour of the accused is an invention which does honour to the humanity of the Athenians. The poet shows how a portentous series of crimes led to an institution fraught with blessings to humanity.

But it will be asked, are not extrinsic aims of this kind prejudicial to the pure poetical impressions which the composition ought to produce? Most undoubtedly, if pursued in the manner in which other poets, and especially Euripides, have followed them out. But in Aeschylus the aim is subservient to the poetry, rather than the poetry to the aim. He does not lower himself to a circumscribed reality, but, on the contrary, elevates it to a higher sphere, and connects it with the most sublime conceptions.

In the *Oresteia* (for so the trilogy or three connected pieces was called,) we certainly possess one of the sublimest poems that ever was conceived by the imagination of man, and, probably, the ripest and most perfect of all the productions of his genius. The date of the composition of them confirms this supposition: for Aeschylus was at least sixty years of age when he brought these dramas on the stage, the last with which he ever competed for the prize at Athens. But, indeed, every one of his pieces that has come down to us, is remarkable either for displaying some peculiar property of the poet, or, as indicative of the step in art at which he stood at the date of its composition.

I am disposed to consider the *Suppliants* one of his more early works. It probably belonged to a trilogy, and stood between two other tragedies on the same subject, the names of which are still preserved, namely the *Egyptians* and the *Danaidae*. The first, we may suppose, described the flight of the *Danaidae* from Egypt to avoid the detested marriage with their cousins; the second depicts the protection which they sought and obtained in Argos; while the third would contain the murder of the husbands who were forced upon them. We are disposed to view the two first pieces as single acts, introductory to the tragical action which properly commences in the last. But the tragedy of the *Suppliants*, while it is complete in itself, and forms a whole, is yet, when viewed in this position, defective, since it is altogether without reference to or connexion with what precedes and what follows. In the *Suppliants* the chorus not only takes a part in the action, as in the *Eumenides*, but it is even the principal character that attracts and commands our interest. This cast of the tragedy is neither favourable for the display of peculiarity of character, nor the exciting emotion by the play of powerful passions; or, to speak in the language of Grecian art, it is unfavourable both to *ethos* and to *pathos*. The chorus has but one voice and one soul: to have marked the disposition common to fifty young women (for the chorus of *Danaidae* certainly amounted to this number,) by any exclusive peculiarities, would have been absurd in the very nature of things: over and above the common features of humanity such a multitude could only be painted with those common to their sex, their age, and, perhaps, those of their nation. In respect to the last, the intention of Aeschylus is more conspicuous than his success: he lays a great stress on the foreign descent of the *Danaidae*; but this he does but assert of them, without allowing the foreign character to be discovered in their words and discourse. The sentiments, resolutions, and actions of a multitude, and yet manifested with such uniformity, and conceived and executed like the movements of a regular army, have scarcely the appearance of proceeding freely and directly from the inmost being. And, on the other hand, we take a much stronger interest in the situations and fortunes of a single individual with whose whole character we have become intimately acquainted, than in a multitude of uniformly repeated impressions massed as it were together. We have more than reason to doubt whether Aeschylus treated the fable of the third piece in such a way that Hypermnestra, the only one of the *Danaidae* who is allowed to form an exception from the rest, became, with her compassion or her love, the principal object of the dramatic interest: here, again, probably, his chief object was by expressing, in majestic choral songs, the complaints, the wishes, the cares, and supplications of the whole sisterhood, to exhibit a kind of social solemnity of action and suffering.

In the same manner, in the *Seven before Thebes*, the king and the messenger, whose speeches occupy the greatest part of the piece, speak more in virtue of their office than as interpreters of their own personal feelings. The description of the assault with which the city is threatened, and of the seven leaders who, like heaven-storming giants, have sworn its destruction, and who, in the emblems borne on their shields, display their arrogance, is an epic subject clothed in the pomp of tragedy. This long and ascending series of preparation is every way worthy the one agitating moment at which Eteocles, who has hitherto displayed the utmost degree of prudence and firmness, and stationed, at each gate, a patriotic hero to confront each of the insolent foes; when the seventh is described to him as no other than Polynices, the author of the whole threatened calamity, hurried away by the Erinnys of a father's curse, insists on becoming himself his antagonist, and, notwithstanding all the entreaties of the chorus, with the clear consciousness of inevitable death, rushes headlong to the fratricidal strife. War, in itself, is no subject for tragedy, and the poet hurries us rapidly from the ominous preparation to the fatal moment of decision: the city is saved, the two competitors for the throne fall by each other's hands, and the whole is closed by their funeral dirge, sung conjointly by the sisters and a chorus of Theban virgins. It is worthy of remark that Antigone's determination to inter her brother, notwithstanding the prohibition with which Sophocles opens his own piece, which he names after her, is interwoven with the conclusion of this play, a circumstance which, as in the case of the *Choephorae*, immediately connects it with a new and further development of the tragic story.

I wish I could persuade myself that Aeschylus composed the *Persians* to comply with the wish of Hiero, King of Syracuse, who was desirous vividly to realize the great events of the Persian war. Such is the substance of one tradition; but according to another, the piece had been previously exhibited in Athens. We have already alluded to this drama, which, both in point of choice of subject, and the manner of handling it, is undoubtedly the most imperfect of all the tragedies of this poet that we possess. Scarcely has the vision of Atossa raised our expectation in the commencement, when the whole catastrophe immediately opens on us with the arrival of the first messenger, and no further progress is even imaginable. But although not a legitimate drama, we may still consider it as a proud triumphal hymn of liberty, clothed in soft and unceasing lamentations of kindred and subjects over the fallen majesty of the ambitious despot. With great judgment, both here and in the *Seven before Thebes*, the poet describes the issue of the war, not as accidental, which is almost always the case in Homer, but (for in tragedy there is no place for accident,) as the result of overweening infatuation on the one hand, and wise moderation on the other.

The *Prometheus Bound*, held also a middle place between two others--the *Fire-bringing Prometheus* and the *Prometheus Unbound*, if we dare reckon the first, which, without question, was a satiric drama, a part of a trilogy. A considerable fragment of the *Prometheus Unbound* has been preserved to us in a Latin translation by Attius.

The *Prometheus Bound* is the representation of constancy under suffering, and that the never-ending suffering of a god. Exiled in its scene to a naked rock on the shore of the earth-encircling ocean, this drama still embraces the world, the Olympus of the gods, and the earth, the abode of mortals; all as yet scarcely reposing in security above the dread abyss of the dark primaeval powers--the Titans. The idea of a self-devoting divinity has been mysteriously inculcated in many religions, in dim foreboding of the true; here, however, it appears in most fearful contrast to the consolations of Revelation. For Prometheus does not suffer from any understanding with the power which rules the world, but in atonement for his disobedience to that power, and his disobedience consists in nothing but the attempt to give perfection to the human race. He is thus an image of human nature itself; endowed with an unblessed foresight and riveted to a narrow existence, without a friend or ally, and with nothing to oppose to the combined and inexorable powers of nature, but an unshaken will and the consciousness of her own lofty aspirations. The other productions of the Greek Tragedians are so many tragedies; but this I might say is Tragedy herself: her purest spirit revealed with all the annihilating and overpowering force of its first, and as yet unmitigated, austerity.

There is little of external action in this piece. Prometheus merely suffers and resolves from the beginning to the end; and his sufferings and resolutions are always the same. But the poet has, in a masterly manner, contrived to introduce variety and progress into that which in itself was determinately fixed, and has in the objects with which he has surrounded him, given us a scale for the measurement of the matchless power of his sublime Titan. First the silence of Prometheus, while he is chained down under the harsh inspection of *Strength* and *Force*, whose threats serve only to excite a useless compassion in Vulcan, who is nevertheless forced to carry them into execution; then his solitary complainings, the arrival of the womanly tender ocean nymphs, whose kind but disheartening sympathy stimulates him to give freer vent to his feelings, to relate the causes of his fall, and to reveal the future, though with prudent reserve he reveals it only in part; the visit of the ancient Oceanus, a kindred god of the Titanian race, who, under the pretext of a zealous attachment to his cause, counsels submission to Jupiter, and is therefore dismissed with proud contempt; next comes Io, the frenzy-driven wanderer, a victim of the same tyranny as Prometheus himself suffers under: to her he predicts the wanderings to which she is still doomed, and the fate which at last awaits her, which, in some degree, is connected with his own, as from her blood, after the lapse of many ages, his deliverer is to spring; then the appearance of Mercury, as the messenger of the universal tyrant, who, with haughty menaces, commands him to disclose the secret which is to ensure the safety of Jupiter's throne against all the malice of fate and fortune; and, lastly, before Prometheus has well declared his refusal, the yawning of the earth, which, amidst thunder and lightning, storms and earthquake, engulfs both him and the rock to which he is chained in the abyss of the nether world. The triumph of subjection was never perhaps more gloriously celebrated, and we have difficulty in conceiving how the poet in the *Prometheus Unbound* could have sustained himself on the same height of elevation.

In the dramas of Aeschylus we have one of many examples that, in art as well as in nature, gigantic productions precede those that evince regularity of proportion, which again in their turn decline gradually into littleness and insignificance, and that poetry in her earliest appearance attaches itself closely to the sanctities of religion, whatever may be the form which the latter assumes among the various races of men.

A saying of the poet, which has been recorded, proves that he endeavoured to maintain this elevation, and purposely avoided all artificial polish, which might lower him from this godlike sublimity. His brothers urged him to write a new Paean. He answered: "The old one of Tynnichus is the best, and his compared with this, fare as the new statues do beside the old; for the latter, with all their simplicity, are considered divine; while the new, with all the care bestowed on their execution, are indeed admired, but bear much less of the impression of divinity." In religion, as in everything else, he carried his boldness to the utmost limits; and thus he even came to be accused of having in one of his pieces disclosed the Eleusinean mysteries, and was only acquitted on the intercession of his brother Aminias, who bared in sight of the judges the wounds which he had received in the battle of Salamis. He perhaps believed that in the communication of the poetic feeling was contained the initiation into the mysteries, and that nothing was in this way revealed to any one who was not worthy of it.

In Aeschylus the tragic style is as yet imperfect, and not unfrequently runs into either unmixed epic or lyric. It is often abrupt, irregular, and harsh. To compose more regular and skilful tragedies than those of Aeschylus was by no means difficult; but in the more than mortal grandeur which he displayed, it was impossible that he should ever be surpassed; and even Sophocles, his younger and more fortunate rival, did not in this respect equal him. The latter, in speaking of Aeschylus, gave a proof that he was himself a thoughtful artist: "Aeschylus does what is right without knowing it." These few simple words exhaust the whole of what we understand by the phrase, powerful genius working unconsciously.

LECTURE VII.

Life and Political Character of Sophocles--Character of his different Tragedies.

The birth of Sophocles was nearly at an equal distance between that of his predecessor and that of Euripides, so that he was about half a life-time from each: but on this point all the authorities do not coincide. He was, however, during the greatest part of his life the contemporary of both. He frequently contended for the ivy-wreath of tragedy with Aeschylus, and he outlived Euripides, who, however, also attained to a good old age. To speak in the spirit of the ancient religion, it seems that a beneficent Providence wished in this individual to evince to the human race the dignity and blessedness of its lot, by endowing him with every divine gift, with all that can adorn and elevate the mind and the heart, and crowning him with every imaginable blessing of this life. Descended from rich and honourable parents, and born a free citizen of the most enlightened state of Greece;--there were birth, necessary condition, and foundation. Beauty of person and of mind, and the uninterruped enjoyment of both in the utmost perfection, to the extreme term of human existence; a most choice and finished education in gymnastics and the musical arts, the former so important in the development of the bodily powers, and the latter in the communication of harmony; the sweet bloom of youth, and the ripe fruit of age; the possession of and unbroken enjoyment of poetry and art, and the exercise of serene wisdom; love and respect among his fellow citizens, renown abroad, and the countenance and favour of the gods: these are the general features of the life of this pious and virtuous poet. It would seem as if the gods, to whom, and to Bacchus in particular, as the giver of all joy, and the civilizer of the human race, he devoted himself at an early age by the composition of tragical dramas for his festivals, had wished to confer immortality on him, so long did they delay the hour of his death; but as this could not be, they loosened him from life as gently as was possible, that he might imperceptibly change one immortality for another, the long duration of his earthly existence for the imperishable vitality of his name. When a youth of sixteen, he was selected, on account of his beauty, to dance (playing the while, after the Greek manner, on the lyre) at the head of the chorus of youths who, after the battle of Salamis (in which Aeschylus fought, and which he has so nobly described), executed the Paean round the trophy erected on that occasion. Thus then the beautiful season of his youthful bloom coincided with the most glorious epoch of the Athenian people. He held the rank of general as colleague with Pericles and Thucydides, and, when arrived at a more advanced age, was elected to the priesthood of a native hero. In his twenty-fifth year he began to exhibit tragedies; twenty times was he victorious; he often gained the second place, but never was he ranked so low as in the third. In this career he proceeded with increasing success till he had passed his ninetieth year; and some of his greatest works were even the fruit of a still later period. There is a story of an accusation being brought against him by one or more of his elder sons, of having become childish from age, and of being incapable of managing his own affairs. An alleged partiality for a grandson by a second wife is said to have been the motive of the charge. In his defence he contented himself with reading to his judges his *Oedipus at Colonos*, which he had then just composed (or, according to others, only the magnificent chorus in it, wherein he sings the praises of Colonos, his birth-place,) and the astonished judges, without farther consultation, conducted him in triumph to his house. If it be true that the second *Oedipus* was written at so late an age, as from its mature serenity and total freedom from the impetuosity and violence of youth we have good reason to conclude that it actually was, it affords us a pleasing picture of an old age at once amiable and venerable. Although the varying accounts of his death have a fabulous look, they all coincide in this, and alike convey this same purport, that he departed life without a struggle, while employed in his art, or something connected with it, and that, like an old swan of Apollo, he breathed out his life in song. The story also of the Lacedaemonian general, who having entrenched the burying-ground of the poet's ancestors, and being twice warned by Bacchus in a vision to allow Sophocles to be there interred, dispatched a herald to the Athenians on the subject, I consider as true, as well as a number of other circumstances, which serve to set in a strong light the illustrious reverence in which his name was held. In calling him virtuous and pious, I used the words in his own sense; for although his works breathe the real character of ancient grandeur, gracefulness, and simplicity, he, of all the Grecian poets, is also the one whose feelings bear the strongest affinity to the spirit of our religion.

One gift alone was denied to him by nature: a voice attuned to song. He could only call forth and direct the harmonious effusions of other voices; he was therefore compelled to depart from the hitherto established practice for the poet to act a part in his own pieces. Once only did he make his appearance on the stage in the character of the blind singer Thamyris (a very characteristic trait) playing on the cithara.

As Aeschylus, who raised tragic poetry from its rude beginnings to the dignity of the Cothurnus, was his predecessor; the historical relation in which he stood to him enabled Sophocles to profit by the essays of that original master, so that Aeschylus appears as the rough designer, and Sophocles as the finisher and successor. The more artificial construction of Sophocles' dramas is easily perceived: the greater limitation of the chorus in proportion to the dialogue, the smoother polish of the rhythm, and the purer Attic diction, the introduction of a greater number of characters, the richer complication of the fable, the multiplication of incidents, a higher degree of development, the more tranquil dwelling upon all the momenta of the action, and the more striking theatrical effect allowed to decisive ones, the more perfect rounding off of the whole, even considered from a merely external point of view. But he excelled Aeschylus in something still more essential, and proved himself deserving of the good fortune of having such a preceptor, and of being allowed to enter into competition in the same field with him: I mean the harmonious perfection of his mind, which enabled him spontaneously to satisfy every requisition of the laws of beauty, a mind whose free impulse was accompanied by the most clear consciousness. To surpass Aeschylus in boldness of conception was perhaps impossible: I am inclined, however, to believe that is only because of his wisdom and moderation that Sophocles appears less bold, since he always goes to work with the greatest energy, and perhaps with even a more sustained earnestness, like a man who knows the extent of his powers, and is determined, when he does not exceed them, to stand up with the greater confidence for his rights [Footnote: This idea has been so happily expressed by the greatest genius perhaps of the last century, that the translator hopes he will be forgiven for here transcribing the passage: "I can truly say that, poor and unknown as I then was, I had pretty nearly as high an idea of myself and of my works, as I have at this moment, when the public has decided in their favour. It ever was my opinion, that the mistakes and blunders both in a rational and religious point of view, of which we see thousands daily guilty, are owing to their ignorance of themselves. To know myself, had been all along my constant study. I weighed myself alone; I balanced myself with others; I watched every means of information to see how much ground I occupied as a man and as a poet; I studied assiduously nature's design in my formation--where the lights and shades in my character were intended."--*Letter from Burns to Dr. Moore, in Currie's Life.*--TRANS.]. As Aeschylus delights in transporting us to the convulsions of the primary world of the Titans, Sophocles, on the other hand, never avails himself of divine interposition except where it is absolutely necessary; he formed men, according to the general confession of antiquity, better, that is, not more moral and exempt from error, but more beautiful and noble than they really are; and while he took every thing in the most human sense, he was at the same time open to its higher significance. According to all appearance he was also more temperate than Aeschylus in his use of scenic ornaments; displaying perhaps more of taste and chastened beauty, but not attempting the same colossal magnificence.

To characterize the native sweetness and gracefulness so eminent in this poet, the ancients gave him the appellation of the Attic bee. Whoever is thoroughly imbued with the feeling of this peculiarity may flatter himself that a sense for ancient art has arisen within him; for the affected sentimentality of the present day, far from coinciding with the ancients in this opinion, would in the tragedies of Sophocles, both in respect of the representation of bodily sufferings, and in the sentiments and structure, find much that is insupportably austere.

When we consider the great fertility of Sophocles, for according to some he wrote a hundred and thirty pieces (of which, however, seventeen were pronounced spurious by Aristophanes the grammarian), and eighty according to the most moderate account, little, it must be owned, has come down to us, for we have only seven of them. Chance, however, has so far favoured us, that in these seven pieces we find several which were held by the ancients as his greatest works, the *Antigone*, for example, the *Electra*, and the two on the subject of *Oedipus*; and these have also come down to us tolerably free from mutilation and corruption in their text. The *Oedipus Tyrannus*, and the *Philoctetes*, have been generally, but without good reason, preferred by modern critics to all the others: the first on account of the artifice of the plot, in which the dreadful catastrophe, which so powerfully excites the curiosity (a rare case in the Greek tragedies), is inevitably brought about by a succession of connected causes; the latter on account of the masterly display of character, the beautiful contrast observable in those of the three leading personages, and the simple structure of the piece, in which, with so few persons, everything proceeds from the truest and most adequate motives. But the whole of the tragedies of Sophocles are separately resplendent with peculiar excellencies. In *Antigone* we have the purest display of feminine heroism; in *Ajax* the sense of manly honour in its full force; in the *Trachiniae* (or, as we should rather name it, the *Dying Hercules*), the female levity of Dejanira is beautifully atoned for by her death, and the sufferings of Hercules are portrayed with suitable dignity; *Electra* is distinguished by energy and pathos; in *Oedipus Coloneus* there prevails a mild and gentle emotion, and over the whole piece is diffused the sweetest gracefulness. I will not undertake to weigh the respective merits of these pieces against each other: but I own I entertain a singular predilection for the last of them, because it appears to me the most expressive of the personal feelings of the poet himself. As this piece was written for the very purpose of throwing a lustre on Athens, and his own birth-place more particularly, he appears to have laboured on it with a special love and affection.

Ajax and *Antigone* are usually the least understood. We cannot conceive how these pieces should run on so long after what we usually call the catastrophe. On this subject I shall hereafter offer a remark or two.

Of all the fables of ancient mythology in which fate is made to play a conspicuous part, the story of Oedipus is perhaps the most ingenious; but still many others, as, for instance, that of Niobe, which, without any complication of incidents, simply exhibit on a scale of colossal dimensions both of human arrogance, and its impending punishment from the gods, appear to me to be conceived in a grander style. The very intrigue which is involved in that of Oedipus detracts from its loftiness of character. Intrigue in the dramatic sense is a complication arising from the crossing of purposes and events, and this is found in a high degree in the fate of Oedipus, as all that is done by his parents or himself in order to evade the predicted horrors, serves only to bring them on the more surely. But that which gives so grand and terrible a character to this drama, is the circumstance which, however, is for the most part overlooked; that to the very Oedipus who solved the riddle of the Sphinx relating to human life, his own life should remain so long an inextricable riddle, to be so awfully cleared up, when all was irretrievably lost. A striking picture of the arrogant pretension of human wisdom, which is ever right enough in its general principles, but does not enable the possessor to make the proper application to himself.

Notwithstanding the severe conclusion of the first *Oedipus* we are so far reconciled to it by the violence, suspicion, and haughtiness in the character of Oedipus, that our feelings do not absolutely revolt at so horrible a fate. For this end, it was necessary thus far to sacrifice the character of Oedipus, who, however, raises himself in our estimation by his fatherly care and heroic zeal for the welfare of his people, that occasion him, by his honest search for the author of the crime, to accelerate his own destruction. It was also necessary, for the sake of contrast with his future misery, to exhibit him in his treatment of Tiresias and Creon, in all the haughtiness of regal dignity. And, indeed, all his earlier proceedings evince, in some measure, the same suspiciousness and violence of character; the former, in his refusing to be quieted by the assurances of Polybos, when taunted with being a suppositious child, and the latter, in his bloody quarrel with Laius. The latter character he seems to have inherited from both his parents. The arrogant levity of Jocasta, which induces her to deride the oracle as not confirmed by the event, the penalty of which she is so soon afterwards to inflict upon herself, was not indeed inherited by her son; he is, on the contrary, conspicuous throughout for the purity of his intentions; and his care and anxiety to escape from the predicted crime, added naturally to the poignancy of his despair, when he found that he had nevertheless been overtaken by it. Awful indeed is his blindness in not perceiving the truth when it was, as it were, brought directly home to him; as, for instance, when he puts the question to Jocasta, How did Laius look? and she answers he had become gray-haired, otherwise in appearance he was not unlike Oedipus. This is also another feature of her levity, that she should not have been struck with the resemblance to her husband, a circumstance that might have led her to recognize him as her son. Thus a close analysis of the piece will evince the utmost propriety and significance of every portion of it. As, however, it is customary to extol the correctness of Sophocles, and to boast more especially of the strict observance of probability which, prevails throughout this *Oedipus*, I must here remark that this very piece is a proof how, on this subject, the ancient artists followed very different principles from those of modern critics. For, according to our way of thinking, nothing could be more improbable than that Oedipus should, so long, have forborne to inquire into the circumstances of the death of Laius, and that the scars on his feet, and even the name which he bore, should never have excited the curiosity of Jocasta, &c. But the ancients did not produce their works of art for calculating and prosaic understandings; and an improbability which, to be found out, required dissection, and did not exist within the matters of the representation itself, was to them none at all.

The diversity of character of Aeschylus and Sophocles is nowhere more conspicuous than in the *Eumenides* and the *Oedipus Coloneus*, as both these pieces were composed with the same aim. This aim was to glorify Athens as the sacred abode of law and humanity, on whose soil the crimes of the hero families of other countries might, by a higher mediation, be at last propitiated; while an ever-during prosperity was predicted to the Athenian people. The patriotic and liberty-breathing Aeschylus has recourse to a judicial, and the pious Sophocles to a religious, procedure; even the consecration of Oedipus in death. Bent down by the consciousness of inevitable crimes, and lengthened misery, his honour is, as it were, cleared up by the gods themselves, as if desirous of showing that, in the terrible example which they made of him, they had no intention of visiting him in particular, but merely wished to give a solemn lesson to the whole human race. Sophocles, to whom the whole of life was one continued worship of the gods, delighted to throw all possible honour on its last moments as if a more solemn festival; and associated it with emotions very different from what the thought of mortality is in general calculated to excite. That the tortured and exhausted Oedipus should at last find peace and repose in the grove of the Furies, in the very spot from which all other mortals fled with aversion and horror, he whose misfortune consisted in having done a deed at which all men shudder, unconsciously and without warning of any inward feeling; in this there is a profound and mysterious meaning.

Aeschylus has given us in the person of Pallas a more majestic representation of the Attic cultivation, prudence, moderation, mildness, and magnanimity; but Sophocles, who delighted to draw all that is godlike within the sphere of humanity, has, in his Theseus, given a more delicate development of all these same things. Whoever is desirous of gaining an accurate idea of Grecian heroism, as contrasted with the Barbarian, would do well to consider this character with attention.

In Aeschylus, before the victim of persecution can be delivered, and the land can participate in blessings, the infernal horror of the Furies congeals the spectators' blood, and makes his hair stand on end, and the whole rancour of these goddesses of rage is exhausted: after this the transition to their peaceful retreat is the more wonderful; the whole human race seems, as it were, delivered from their power. In Sophocles, however, they do not ever appear, but are kept altogether in the background; and they are never mentioned by their own name, but always alluded to by some softening euphemism. But this very obscurity, so exactly befitting these daughters of night, and the very distance at which they are kept, are calculated to excite a silent horror in which the bodily senses have no part. The clothing the grove of the Furies with all the charms of a southern spring completes the sweetness of the poem; and were I to select from his own tragedies an emblem of the poetry of Sophocles, I should describe it as a sacred grove of the dark goddesses of fate, in which the laurel, the olive, and the vine, are always green, and the song of the nightingale is for ever heard.

Two of the pieces of Sophocles refer, to what in the Greek way of thinking, are the sacred rights of the dead, and the solemn importance of burial; in *Antigone* the whole of the action hinges on this, and in *Ajax* it forms the only satisfactory conclusion of the piece.

The ideal of the female character in *Antigone* is characterized by great austerity, and it is sufficient of itself to put an end to all the seductive representations of Grecian softness, which of late have been so universally current. Her indignation at Ismene's refusal to take part in her daring resolution; the manner in which she afterwards repulses Ismene, when repenting of her former weakness, she begs to be allowed to share her heroic sister's death, borders on harshness; both her silence, and then her invectives against Creon, by which she provokes him to execute his tyrannical threats, display the immovable energy of manly courage. The poet has, however, discovered the secret of painting the loving heart of woman in a single line, when to the assertion of Creon, that Polynices was an enemy to his country, she replies:

My love shall go with thine, but not my hate.

[Footnote: This is the version of Franklin, but it does not convey the meaning of the original, and I am not aware that the English language is sufficiently flexible to admit of an exact translation. The German, which, though far inferior to the Greek in harmony, is little behind in flexibility, has in this respect great advantage over the English; and Schlegel's "*nicht mitzuhassen, mitzulieben bin ich da,*" represents exactly *Outoi synechthein alla symphilein ephyn.*--TRANS.]

Moreover, she puts a constraint on her feelings only so long as by giving vent to them, she might make her firmness of purpose appear equivocal. When, however, she is being led forth to inevitable death, she pours forth her soul in the tenderest and most touching waitings over her hard and untimely fate, and does not hesitate, she, the modest virgin, to mourn the loss of nuptials, and the unenjoyed bliss of marriage. Yet she never in a single syllable betrays any inclination for Haemon, and does not even mention the name of that amiable youth [Footnote: Barthelemy asserts the contrary; but the line to which he refers, according to the more correct manuscripts, and even according to the context, belongs to Ismene.]. After such heroic determination, to have shown that any tie still bound her to existence, would have been a weakness; but to relinquish without one sorrowful regret those common enjoyments with which the gods have enriched this life, would have ill accorded with her devout sanctity of mind.

On a first view the chorus in *Antigone* may appear weak, acceding, as it does, at once, without opposition to the tyrannical commands of Creon, and without even attempting to make the slightest representation in behalf of the young heroine. But to exhibit the determination and the deed of Antigone in their full glory, it was necessary that they should stand out quite alone, and that she should have no stay or support. Moreover, the very submissiveness of the chorus increases our impression of the irresistible nature of the royal commands. So, too, was it necessary for it to mingle with its concluding addresses to Antigone the most painful recollections, that she might drain the full cup of earthly sorrows. The case is very different in *Electra*, where the chorus appropriately takes an interest in the fate of the two principal characters, and encourages them in the execution of their design, as the moral feelings are divided as to its legitimacy, whereas there is no such conflict in Antigone's case, who had nothing to deter her from her purpose but mere external fears.

After the fulfilment of the deed, and the infliction of its penalties, the arrogance of Creon still remains to be corrected, and the death of Antigone to be avenged; nothing less than the destruction of his whole family, and his own despair, could be a sufficient atonement for the sacrifice of a life so costly. We have therefore the king's wife, who had not even been named before, brought at last on the stage, that she may hear the misfortunes of her family, and put an end to her own existence.

To Grecian feelings it would have been impossible to consider the poem as properly concluding with the death of Antigone, without its penal retribution.

The case is the same in Ajax. His arrogance, which was punished with a degrading madness, is atoned for by the deep shame which at length drives him even to self-murder. The persecution of the unfortunate man must not, however, be carried farther; when, therefore, it is in contemplation to dishonour his very corpse by the refusal of interment, even Ulysses interferes. He owes the honours of burial to that Ulysses whom in life he had looked upon as his mortal enemy, and to whom, in the dreadful introductory scene, Pallas shows, in the example of the delirious Ajax, the nothingness of man. Thus Ulysses appears as the personification of moderation, which, if it had been possessed by Ajax, would have prevented his fall.

Self-murder is of frequent occurrence in ancient mythology, at least as adapted to tragedy; but it generally takes place, if not in a state of insanity, yet in a state of agitation, after some sudden calamity which leaves no room for consideration. Such self-murders as those of Jocasta, Haemon, Eurydice, and lastly of Dejanira, appear merely in the light of a subordinate appendage in the tragical pictures of Sophocles; but the suicide of Ajax is a cool determination, a free action, and of sufficient importance to become the principal subject of the piece. It is not the last fatal crisis of a slow mental malady, as is so often the case in these more effeminate modern times; still less is it that more theoretical disgust of life, founded on a conviction of its worthlessness, which induced so many of the later Romans, on Epicurean as well as Stoical principles, to put an end to their existence. It is not through any unmanly despondency that Ajax is unfaithful to his rude heroism. His delirium is over, as well as his first comfortless feelings upon awaking from it; and it is not till after the complete return of consciousness, and when he has had time to measure the depth of the abyss into which, by a divine destiny, his overweening haughtiness has plunged him, when he contemplates his situation, and feels it ruined beyond remedy:--his honour wounded by the refusal of the arms of Achilles; and the outburst of his vindictive rage wasted in his infatuation on defenceless flocks; himself, after a long and reproachless heroic career, a source of amusement to his enemies, an object of derision and abomination to the Greeks, and to his honoured father,--should he thus return to him--a disgrace: after reviewing all this, he decides agreeably to his own motto, "gloriously to live or gloriously to die," that the latter course alone remains open to him. Even the dissimulation,--the first, perhaps, that he ever practised, by which, to prevent the execution of his purpose from being disturbed, he pacifies his comrades, must be considered as the fruit of greatness of soul. He appoints Teucer guardian to his infant boy, the future consolation of his own bereaved parents; and, like Cato, dies not before he has arranged the concerns of all who belong to him. As Antigone in her womanly tenderness, so even he in his wild manner, seems in his last speech to feel the majesty of that light of the sun from which he is departing for ever. His rude courage disdains compassion, and therefore excites it the more powerfully. What a picture of awaking from the tumult of passion, when the tent opens and in the midst of the slaughtered herds he sits on the ground bewailing himself!

As Ajax, in the feeling of inextinguishable shame, forms the violent resolution of throwing away life, Philoctetes, on the other hand, bears its wearisome load during long years of misery with the most enduring patience. If Ajax is honoured by his despair, Philoctetes is equally ennobled by his constancy. When the instinct of self-preservation comes into collision with no moral impulse, it naturally exhibits itself in all its strength. Nature has armed with this instinct whatever is possessed of the breath of life, and the vigour with which every hostile attack on existence is repelled is the strongest proof of its excellence. In the presence, it is true, of that band of men by which he had been abandoned, and if he must depend on their superior power, Philoctetes would no more have wished for life than did Ajax. But he is alone with nature; he quails not before the frightful aspect which she exhibits to him, and still clings even to the maternal bosom of the all-nourishing earth. Exiled on a desert island, tortured by an incurable wound, solitary and helpless as he is, his bow procures him food from the birds of the forest, the rock yields him soothing herbs, the fountain supplies a fresh beverage, his cave affords him a cool shelter in summer, in winter he is warmed by the mid-day sun, or a fire of kindled boughs; even the raging attacks of his pain at length exhaust themselves, and leave him in a refreshing sleep. Alas! it is the artificial refinements, the oppressive burden of a relaxing and deadening superfluity which render man indifferent to the value of life: when it is stripped of all foreign appendages, though borne down with sufferings so that the naked existence alone remains, still will its sweetness flow from the heart at every pulse through all the veins. Miserable man! ten long years has he struggled; and yet he still lives, and clings to life and hope. What force of truth is there in all this! What, however, most moves us in behalf of Philoctetes is, that he, who by an abuse of power had been cast out from society, when it again approaches him is exposed by it to a second and still more dangerous evil, that of falsehood. The anxiety excited in the mind of the spectator lest Philoctetes should be deprived of his last means of subsistence, his bow, would be too painful, did he not from the beginning entertain a suspicion that the open-hearted and straight-forward Neoptolemus will not be able to maintain to the end the character which, so much against his will, he has assumed. Not without reason after this deception does Philoctetes turn away from mankind to those inanimate companions to which the instinctive craving for society had attached him. He calls on the island and its volcanoes to witness this fresh wrong; he believes that his beloved bow feels pain in being taken from him; and at length he takes a melancholy leave of his hospitable cavern, the fountains and the wave-washed cliffs, from which he so often looked in vain upon the ocean: so inclined to love is the uncorrupted mind of man.

Respecting the bodily sufferings of Philoctetes and the manner of representing them, Lessing has in his *Laocoon* declared himself against Winkelmann, and Herder again has in the *Silvae Criticae* (Kritische Walder) contradicted Lessing. Both the two last writers have made many excellent observations on the piece, although we must allow with Herder, that Winkelmann was correct in affirming that the Philoctetes of Sophocles, like Laocoon in the celebrated group, suffers with the suppressed agony of an heroic soul never altogether overcome by his pain.

The *Trachiniae* appears to me so very inferior to the other pieces of Sophocles which have reached us, that I could wish there were some warrant for supposing that this tragedy was composed in the age, indeed, and in the school of Sophocles, perhaps by his son Iophon, and that it was by mistake attributed to the father. There is much both in the structure and plan, and in the style of the piece, calculated to excite suspicion; and many critics have remarked that the introductory soliloquy of Dejanira, which is wholly uncalled-for, is very unlike the general character of Sophocles' prologues: and although this poet's usual rules of art are observed on the whole, yet it is very superficially; no where can we discern in it the profound mind of Sophocles. But as no writer of antiquity appears to have doubted its authenticity, while Cicero even quotes from it the complaint of Hercules, as from an indisputable work of Sophocles, we are compelled to content ourselves with the remark, that in this one instance the tragedian has failed to reach his usual elevation.

This brings us to the consideration of a general question, which, in the examination of the works of Euripides, will still more particularly engage the attention of the critic: how far, namely, the invention and execution of a drama must belong to one man to entitle him to pass for its author. Dramatic literature affords numerous examples of plays composed by several persons conjointly. It is well known that Euripides, in the details and execution of his pieces, availed himself of the assistance of a learned servant, Cephisophon; and he perhaps also consulted with him respecting his plots. It appears, moreover, certain that in Athens schools of dramatic art had at this date been formed; such, indeed, as usually arise when poetical talents are, by public competition, called abundantly and actively into exercise: schools of art which contain scholars of such excellence and of such kindred genius, that the master may confide to them a part of the execution, and even the plan, and yet allow the whole to pass under his name without any disparagement to his fame. Such were the schools of painting of the sixteenth century, and every one knows what a remarkable degree of critical acumen is necessary to discover in many of Raphael's pictures how much really belongs to his own pencil. Sophocles had educated his son Iophon to the tragic art, and might therefore easily receive assistance from him in the actual labour of composition, especially as it was necessary that the tragedies that were to compete for the prize should be ready and got by heart by a certain day. On the other hand, he might also execute occasional passages for works originally designed by the son; and the pieces of this description, in which the hand of the master was perceptible, would be naturally attributed to the more celebrated name.

LECTURE VIII.

Euripides--His Merits and Defects--Decline of Tragic Poetry through him.

When we consider Euripides by himself, without any comparison with his predecessors, when we single out some of his better pieces, and particular passages in others, we cannot refuse to him an extraordinary meed of praise. But on the other hand, when we take him in his connexion with the history of art, when we look at each of his pieces as a whole, and again at the general scope of his labours, as revealed to us in the works which have come down to us, we are forced to censure him severely on many accounts. Of few writers can so much good and evil be said with truth. He was a man of boundless ingenuity and most versatile talents; but he either wanted the lofty earnestness of purpose, or the severe artistic wisdom, which we reverence in Aeschylus and Sophocles, to regulate the luxuriance of his certainly splendid and amiable qualities. His constant aim is to please, he cares not by what means; hence is he so unequal: frequently he has passages of overpowering beauty, but at other times he sinks into downright mediocrity. With all his faults he possesses an admirable ease, and a certain insinuating charm.

These preliminary observations I have judged necessary, since otherwise, on account of what follows, it might be objected to me that I am at variance with myself, having lately, in a short French essay, endeavoured to show the superiority of a piece of Euripides to Racine's imitation of it. There I fixed my attention on a single drama, and that one of the poet's best; but here I consider everything from the most general points of view, and relatively to the highest requisitions of art; and that my enthusiasm for ancient tragedy may not appear blind and extravagant, I must justify it by a keen examination into the traces of its degeneracy and decline.

We may compare perfection in art and poetry to the summit of a steep mountain, on which an uprolled load cannot long maintain its position, but immediately rolls down again the other side irresistibly. It descends according to the laws of gravity with quickness and ease, and one can calmly look on while it is descending; for the mass follows its natural tendency, while the laborious ascent is, in some degree, a painful spectacle. Hence it is, for example, that the paintings which belong to the age of declining art are much more pleasing to the unlearned eye, than those which preceded the period of its perfection. The genuine connoisseur, on the contrary, will hold the pictures of a Zuccheri and others, who gave the tone when the great schools of the sixteenth century were degenerating into empty and superficial mannerism, to be in real and essential worth, far inferior to the works of a Mantegna, Perugino, and their contemporaries. Or let us suppose the perfection of art a focus: at equal distances on either side, the collected rays occupy equal spaces, but on this side they converge towards a common effect; whereas, on the other they diverge, till at last they are totally lost.

We have, besides, a particular reason for censuring without reserve the errors of this poet; the fact, namely, that our own age is infected with the same faults with those which procured for Euripides so much favour, if not esteem, among his contemporaries. In our times we have been doomed to witness a number of plays which, though in matter and form they are far inferior to those of Euripides, bear yet in so far a resemblance to them, that while they seduce the feelings and corrupt the judgment, by means of weakly, and sometimes even tender, emotions, their general tendency is to produce a downright moral licentiousness.

What I shall say on this subject will not, for the most part, possess even the attraction of novelty. Although the moderns, attracted either by the greater affinity of his views with their own sentiments, or led astray by an ill-understood opinion of Aristotle, have not unfrequently preferred Euripides to his two predecessors, and have unquestionably read, admired, and imitated him much more; it admits of being shown, however, that many of the ancients, and some even of the contemporaries of Euripides, held the same opinion of him as myself. In *Anacharsis* we find this mixture of praise and censure at least alluded to, though the author softens everything for the sake of his object of showing the productions of the Greeks, in every department, under the most favourable light.

We possess some cutting sayings of Sophocles respecting Euripides, though he was so far from being actuated by anything like the jealousy of authorship, that he mourned his death, and, in a piece which he exhibited shortly after, he did not allow his actors the usual ornament of the wreath. The charge which Plato brings against the tragic poets, as tending to give men entirely up to the dominion of the passions, and to render them effeminate, by putting extravagant lamentations in the mouths of their heroes, may, I think, be justly referred to Euripides alone; for, with respect to his predecessors, the injustice of it would have been universally apparent. The derisive attacks of Aristophanes are well known, though not sufficiently understood and appreciated. Aristotle bestows on him many a severe censure, and when he calls Euripides "the most tragic poet," he by no means ascribes to him the greatest perfection in the tragic art in general, but merely alludes to the moving effect which is produced by unfortunate catastrophes; for he immediately adds, "although he does not well arrange the rest." Lastly, the Scholiast on Euripides contains many concise and stringent criticisms on particular pieces, among which perhaps are preserved the opinions of Alexandrian critics--those critics who reckoned among them that Aristarchus, who, for the solidity and acuteness of his critical powers, has had his name transmitted to posterity as the proverbial designation of a judge of art.

In Euripides we find the essence of the ancient tragedy no longer pure and unmixed; its characteristical features are already in part defaced. We have already placed this essence in the prevailing idea of Destiny, in the Ideality of the composition, and in the significance of the Chorus.

Euripides inherited, it is true, the idea of Destiny from his predecessors, and the belief of it was inculcated in him by the tragic usage; but yet in him fate is seldom the invisible spirit of the whole composition, the fundamental thought of the tragic world. We have seen that this idea may be exhibited under severer or milder aspects; that the midnight terrors of destiny may, in the courses of a whole trilogy, brighten into indications of a wise and beneficent Providence. Euripides, however, has drawn it down from the region of the infinite; and with him inevitable necessity not unfrequently degenerates into the caprice of chance. Accordingly, he can no longer apply it to its proper purpose, namely, by contrast with it, to heighten the moral liberty of man. How few of his pieces turn upon a steadfast resistance to the decrees of fate, or an equally heroic submission to them! His characters generally suffer because they must, and not because they will.

The mutual subordination, between character and passion and ideal elevation, which we find observed in the same order in Sophocles, and in the sculpture of Greece, Euripides has completely reversed. Passion with him is the first thing; his next care is for character, and when these endeavours leave him still further scope, he occasionally seeks to lay on a touch of grandeur and dignity, but more frequently a display of amiableness.

It has been already admitted that the persons in tragedy ought not to be all alike faultless, as there would then be no opposition among them, and consequently no room for a complication of plot. But (as Aristotle observes) Euripides has, without any necessity, frequently painted his characters in the blackest colours, as, for example, his Menelaus in *Orestes*. The traditions indeed, sanctioned by popular belief, warranted him in attributing great crimes to many of the old heroes, but he has also palmed upon them many base and paltry traits of his own arbitrary invention. It was by no means the object of Euripides to represent the race of heroes as towering in their majestic stature above the men of his own age; he rather endeavours to fill up, or to build over the chasm that yawned between his contemporaries and that wondrous olden world, and to come upon the gods and heroes in their undress, a surprise of which no greatness, it is said, can stand the test. He introduces his spectators to a sort of familiar acquaintance with them; he does not draw the supernatural and fabulous into the circle of humanity (a proceeding which we praised in Sophocles), but within the limits of the imperfect individuality. This is the meaning of Sophocles, when he said that "he drew men such as they ought to be, Euripides such as they are." Not that his own personages are always represented as irreproachable models; his expression referred merely to ideal elevation and sweetness of character and manners. It seems as if Euripides took a pleasure in being able perpetually to remind his spectators--"See! those beings were men, subject to the very same weaknesses, acting from the same motives as yourselves, and even as the meanest among you." Accordingly, he takes delight in depicting the defects and moral failings of his characters; nay, he often makes them disclose them for themselves in the most *naive* confession. They are frequently not merely undignified, but they even boast of their imperfections as that which ought to be.

The Chorus with him is for the most part an unessential ornament; its songs are frequently wholly episodical, without reference to the action, and more distinguished for brilliancy than for sublimity and true inspiration. "The Chorus," says Aristotle, "must be considered as one of the actors, and as a part of the whole; it must co-operate in the action--not as Euripides, but as Sophocles manages it." The older comedians enjoyed the privilege of allowing the Chorus occasionally to address the spectators in its own name; this was called a Parabasis, and, as I shall afterwards show, was in accordance with the spirit of comedy. Although the practice is by no means tragical, it was, however, according to Julius Pollux, frequently adopted by Euripides in his tragedies, who so far forgot himself on some of these occasions, that in the *Danaidae*, for instance, the chorus, which consisted of females, made use of grammatical inflections which belonged only to the male sex.

This poet has thus at once destroyed the internal essence of tragedy, and sinned against the laws of beauty and proportion in its external structure. He generally sacrifices the whole to the parts, and in these again he is more ambitious of foreign attractions, than of genuine poetic beauty.

In the accompanying music, he adopted all the innovations invented by Timotheus, and chose those melodies which were most in unison with the effeminacy of his own poetry. He proceeded in the same manner with his metres; his versification is luxuriant, and runs into anomaly. The same diluted and effeminate character would, on a more profound investigation, be unquestionably found in the rhythms of his choral songs likewise.

On all occasions he lays on, even to overloading, those merely corporeal charms which Winkelmann calls a "flattery of the gross external senses;" whatever is exciting, striking--in a word, all that produces a vivid effect, though without true worth for the mind and the feelings. He labours for effect to a degree which cannot be allowed even to the dramatic poet. For example, he hardly ever omits an opportunity of throwing his characters into a sudden and useless terror; his old men are everlastingly bemoaning the infirmities of age, and, in particular, are made to crawl with trembling limbs, and sighing at the fatigue, up the ascent from the orchestra to the stage, which frequently represented the slope of a hill. He is always endeavouring to move, and for the sake of emotion, he not only violates probability, but even sacrifices the coherence of the piece. He is strong in his pictures of misfortune; but he often claims our compassion not for inward agony of the soul, nor for pain which the sufferer endures with manly fortitude, but for mere bodily wretchedness. He is fond of reducing his heroes to the condition of beggars, of making them suffer hunger and want, and bringing them on the stage with all the outward signs of it, and clad in rags and tatters, for which Aristophanes, in his *Acharnians*, has so humorously taken him to task.

Euripides was a frequenter of the schools of the philosophers (he had been a scholar of Anaxagoras, and not, as many have erroneously stated, of Socrates, with whom he was only connected by social intercourse): and accordingly he indulges his vanity in introducing philosophical doctrines on all occasions; in my opinion, in a very imperfect manner, as we should not be able to understand these doctrines from his statements of them, if we were not previously acquainted with them. He thinks it too vulgar a thing to believe in the gods after the simple manner of the people, and he therefore seizes every opportunity of interspersing something of the allegorical interpretation of them, and carefully gives his spectators to understand that the sincerity of his own belief was very problematical. We may distinguish in him a twofold character: the *poet*, whose productions were consecrated to a religious solemnity, who stood under the protection of religion and who, therefore, on his part, was bound to honour it; and the *sophist*, with his philosophical *dicta*, who endeavoured to insinuate his sceptical opinions and doubts into the fabulous marvels of religion, from which he derived the subjects of his pieces. But while he is shaking the ground-works of religion, he at the same time acts the moralist; and, for the sake of popularity, he applies to the heroic life and the heroic ages maxims which could only apply to the social relations of his own times. He throws out a multitude of moral apophthegms, many of which he often repeats, and which are mostly trite, and not seldom fundamentally false. With all this parade of morality, the aim of his pieces, the general impression which they are calculated to produce is sometimes extremely immoral. A pleasant anecdote is told of his having put into the mouth of Bellerophon a silly eulogium on wealth, in which he declares it to be preferable to all domestic happiness, and ends with observing, "If Aphrodite (who bore the epithet *golden*) be indeed glittering as gold, she well deserves the love of Mortals:" which so offended the spectators, that they raised a great outcry, and would have stoned both actor and poet, out Euripides sprang forward, and called out, "Wait only till the end--he will be requited accordingly!" In like manner he defended himself against the objection that his Ixion expressed himself in too disgusting and abominable language, by observing that the piece concluded with his being broken on the wheel. But even this plea that the represented villany is requited by the final retribution of poetical justice, is not available in defence of all his tragedies. In some the wicked escape altogether untouched. Lying and other infamous practices are openly protected, especially when he can manage to palm them upon a supposed noble motive. He has also perfectly at command the seductive sophistry of the passions, which can lend a plausible appearance to everything. The following verse in justification of perjury, and in which the *reservatio mentalis* of the casuists seems to be substantially expressed, is well known:

The tongue swore, but the mind was unsworn.

Taken in its context, this verse, on account of which he was so often ridiculed by Aristophanes, may, indeed, be justified; but the formula is, nevertheless, bad, on account of the possible abuse of its application. Another verse of Euripides: "For a kingdom it is worth while to commit injustice, but in other cases it is well to be just," was frequently in the mouth of Caesar, with the like intention of making a bad use of it.

Euripides was frequently condemned even by the ancients for his seductive invitations to the enjoyment of sensual love. Every one must be disgusted when Hecuba, in order to induce Agamemnon to punish Polymestor, reminds him of the pleasures which he has enjoyed in the arms of Cassandra, his captive, and, therefore, by the laws of the heroic ages his concubine: she would purchase revenge for a murdered son with the acknowledged and permitted degradation of a living daughter. He was the first to make the unbridled passion of a Medea, and the unnatural love of a Phaedra, the main subject of his dramas, whereas from the manners of the ancients, we may easily conceive why love, which among them was much less dignified by tender feelings than among ourselves, should hold only a subordinate place in the older tragedies. With all the importance which he has assigned to his female characters, he is notorious for his hatred of women; and it is impossible to deny that he abounds in passages descanting on the frailties of the female sex, and the superior excellence of the male; together with many maxims of household wisdom: with all which he was evidently endeavouring to pay court to the men, who formed, if not the whole, certainly the most considerable portion of his audience. A cutting saying and an epigram of Sophocles, on this subject, have been preserved, in which he accounts for the (pretended) misogyny of Euripides by his experience of their seductibility in the course of his own illicit amours. In the manner in which women are painted by Euripides, we may observe, upon the whole, much sensibility even for the more noble graces of female modesty, but no genuine esteem.

The substantial freedom in treating the fables, which was one of the prerogatives of the tragic art, is frequently carried by Euripides to the extreme of licence. It is well known, that the fables of Hyginus, which differ so essentially from those generally received, were partly extracted from his pieces. As he frequently rejected all the incidents which were generally known, and to which the people were accustomed, Le was reduced to the necessity of explaining in a prologue the situation of things in his drama, and the course which they were to take. Lessing, in his *Dramaturgie*, has hazarded the singular opinion that it is a proof of an advance in the dramatic art, that Euripides should have trusted wholly to the effect of situations, without calculating on the excitement of curiosity. For my part I cannot see why, amidst the impressions which a dramatic poem produces, the uncertainty of expectation should not be allowed a legitimate place. The objection that a piece will only please in this respect for the first time, because on an acquaintance with it we know the result beforehand, may be easily answered: if the representation be truly energetic, it will always rivet the attention of the spectator in such a manner that he will forget what he already knew, and be again excited to the same stretch of expectation. Moreover, these prologues give to the openings of Euripides' plays a very uniform and monotonous appearance: nothing can have a more awkward effect than for a person to come forward and say, I am so and so; this and that has already happened, and what is next to come is as follows. It resembles the labels in the mouths of the figures in old paintings, which nothing but the great simplicity of style in ancient times can excuse. But then all the rest ought to correspond, which is by no means the case with Euripides, whose characters always speak in the newest mode of the day. Both in his prologues and denouements he is very lavish of unmeaning appearances of the gods, who are only elevated above men by the machine in which they are suspended, and who might certainly well be spared.

The practice of the earlier tragedians, to combine all in large masses, and to exhibit repose and motion in distinctly-marked contrast, was carried by him to an unwarrantable extreme. If for the sake of giving animation to the dialogue his predecessors occasionally employed an alternation of single-line speeches, in which question and answer, objection and retort, fly about like arrows from side to side, Euripides makes so immoderate and arbitrary use of this poetical device that very frequently one-half of his lines might be left out without detriment to the sense. At another time he pours himself out in endless speeches, where he sets himself to shew off his rhetorical powers in ingenious arguments, or in pathetic appeals. Many of his scenes have altogether the appearance of a lawsuit, where two persons, as the parties in the litigation, (with sometimes a third for a judge,) do not confine themselves to the matter in hand, but expatiate in a wide field, accusing their adversaries or defending themselves with all the adroitness of practised advocates, and not unfrequently with all the windings and subterfuges of pettifogging sycophants. In this way the poet endeavoured to make his poetry entertaining to the Athenians, by its resemblance to their favourite daily occupation of conducting, deciding, or at least listening to lawsuits. On this account Quinctilian expressly recommends him to the young orator, and with great justice, as capable of furnishing him with more instruction than the older tragedians. But such a recommendation it is evident is little to his credit; for eloquence may, no doubt, have its place in the drama when it is consistent with the character and the object of the supposed speaker, yet to allow rhetoric to usurp the place of the simple and spontaneous expression of the feelings, is anything but poetical.

The style of Euripides is upon the whole too loose, although he has many happy images and ingenious turns: he has neither the dignity and energy of Aeschylus, nor the chaste sweetness of Sophocles. In his expressions he frequently affects the singular and the uncommon, but presently relapses into the ordinary; the tone of the discourse often sounds very familiar, and descends from the elevation of the cothurnus to the level ground. In this respect, as well as in the attempt (which frequently borders only too closely on the ludicrous,) to paint certain characteristic peculiarities, (for instance, the awkward carriage of the Bacchus-stricken Pentheus in his female attire, the gluttony of Hercules, and his boisterous demands on the hospitality of Admetus,) Euripides was a precursor of the new comedy, to which he had an evident inclination, as he frequently paints, under the names of the heroic ages, the men and manners of his own times. Hence Menander expressed a most marked admiration for him, and proclaimed himself his scholar; and we have a fragment of Philemon, which displays such an extravagant admiration, that it hardly appears to have been seriously meant. "If the dead," he either himself says, or makes one of his characters to say, "had indeed any sensation, as some people think they have, I would hang myself for the sake of seeing Euripides."--With this adoration of the later comic authors, the opinion of Aristophanes, his contemporary, forms a striking contrast. Aristophanes persecutes him bitterly and unceasingly; he seems almost ordained to be his perpetual scourge, that none of his moral or poetical extravagances might go unpunished. Although as a comic poet Aristophanes is, generally speaking, in the relation of a parodist to the tragedians, yet he never attacks Sophocles, and even where he lays hold of Aeschylus, on that side of his character which certainly may excite a smile, his reverence for him is still visible, and he takes every opportunity of contrasting his gigantic grandeur with the petty refinements of Euripides. With infinite cleverness and inexhaustible flow of wit, he has exposed the sophistical subtilty, the rhetorical and philosophical pretensions, the immoral and seductive effeminacy, and the excitations to undisguised sensuality of Euripides. As, however, modern critics have generally looked upon Aristophanes as no better than a writer of extravagant and libellous farces, and had no notion of eliciting the serious truths which he veiled beneath his merry disguises, it is no wonder if they have paid but little attention to his opinion.

But with all this we must never forget that Euripides was still a Greek, and the contemporary of many of the greatest names of Greece in politics, philosophy, history, and the fine arts. If, when compared with his predecessors, he must rank far below them, he appears in his turn great when placed by the side of many of the moderns. He has a particular strength in portraying the aberrations of a soul diseased, misguided, and franticly abandoned to its passions. He is admirable where the subject calls chiefly for emotion, and makes no higher requisitions; and he is still more so where pathos and moral beauty are united. Few of his pieces are without passages of the most ravishing beauty. It is by no means my intention to deny him the possession of the most astonishing talents; I have only stated that these talents were not united with a mind in which the austerity of moral principles, and the sanctity of religious feelings, were held in the highest honour.

LECTURE IX.

Comparison between the *Choephorae* of Aeschylus, the *Electra* of Sophocles and that of Euripides.

The relation in which Euripides stood to his two great predecessors, may be set in the clearest light by a comparison between their three pieces which we fortunately still possess, on the same subject, namely, the avenging murder of Clytemnestra by her son Orestes.

The scene of the *Choephorae of Aeschylus* is laid in front of the royal palace; the tomb of Agamemnon appears on the stage. Orestes appears at the sepulchre, with his faithful Pylades, and opens the play (which is unfortunately somewhat mutilated at the commencement,) with a prayer to Mercury, and with an invocation to his father, in which he promises to avenge him, and to whom he consecrates a lock of his hair. He sees a female train in mourning weeds issuing from the palace, to bring a libation to the grave; and, as he thinks he recognises his sister among them, he steps aside with Pylades in order to observe them unperceived. The chorus, which consists of captive Trojan virgins, in a speech, accompanied with mournful gestures, reveals the occasion of their coming, namely, a fearful dream of Clytemnestra; it adds its own dark forebodings of an impending retribution of the bloody crime, and bewails its lot in being obliged to serve unrighteous masters. Electra demands of the chorus whether she shall fulfil the commission of her hostile mother, or pour out their offerings in silence; and then, in compliance with their advice, she also offers up a prayer to the subterranean Mercury and to the soul of her father, in her own name and that of the absent Orestes, that he may appear as the avenger. While pouring out the offering she joins the chorus in lamentations for the departed hero. Presently, finding a lock of hair resembling her own in colour, and seeing footsteps near the grave she conjectures that her brother has been there, and when she is almost frantic with joy at the thought, Orestes steps forward and discovers himself. He completely overcomes her doubts by exhibiting a garment woven by her own hand: they give themselves up to their joy; he addresses a prayer to Jupiter, and makes known how Apollo, under the most dreadful threats of persecution by his father's Furies, has called on him to destroy the authors of his death in the same manner as they had destroyed him, namely, by guile and cunning. Now follow odes of the chorus and Electra; partly consisting of prayers to her father's shade and the subterranean divinities, and partly recapitulating all the motives for the deed, especially those derived from the death of Agamemnon. Orestes inquires into the vision which induced Clytemnestra to offer the libation, and is informed that she dreamt that she had given her breast to a dragon in her son's cradle, and suckled it with her blood. He hereupon resolves to become this dragon, and announces his intention of stealing into the house, disguised as a stranger, and attacking both her and Aegisthus by surprise. With this view he withdraws along with Pylades. The subject of the next choral hymn is the boundless audacity of mankind in general, and especially of women in the gratification of their unlawful passions, which it confirms by terrible examples from mythic story, and descants upon the avenging justice which is sure to overtake them at last. Orestes, in the guise of a stranger, returns with Pylades, and desires admission into the palace. Clytemnestra comes out, and being informed by him of the death of Orestes, at which tidings Electra assumes a feigned grief, she invites him to enter and partake of their hospitality. After a short prayer of the chorus, the nurse comes and mourns for her foster-child; the chorus inspires her with a hope that he yet lives, and advises her to contrive to bring Aegisthus, for whom Clytemnestra has sent her, not with, but without his body guard. As the critical moment draws near, the chorus proffers prayers to Jupiter and Mercury for the success of the plot. Aegisthus enters into conversation with the messenger: he can hardly allow himself to believe the joyful news of the death of Orestes, and hastens into the house for the purpose of ascertaining the truth, from whence, after a short prayer of the chorus, we hear the cries of the murdered. A servant rushes out, and to warn Clytemnestra gives the alarm at the door of the women's apartment. She hears it, comes forward, and calls for an axe to defend herself; but as Orestes instantaneously rushes on her with the bloody sword, her courage fails her, and, most affectingly, she holds up to him the breast at which she had suckled him. Hesitating in his purpose, he asks the counsel of Pylades, who in a few lines exhorts him by the most cogent reasons to persist; after a brief dialogue of accusation and defence, he pursues her into the house to slay her beside the body of Aegisthus. In a solemn ode the chorus exults in the consummated retribution. The doors of the palace are thrown open, and disclose in the chamber the two dead bodies laid side by side on one bed. Orestes orders the servants to unfold the garment in whose capacious folds his father was muffled when he was slain, that it may be seen by all; the chorus recognise on it the stains of blood, and mourn afresh the murder of Agamemnon. Orestes, feeling his mind already becoming confused, seizes the first moment to justify his acts, and having declared his intention of repairing to Delphi to purify himself from his blood-guiltiness, flies in terror from the furies of his mother, whom the chorus does not perceive, but conceives to be a mere phantom of his imagination, but who, nevertheless, will no longer allow him any repose. The chorus concludes with a reflection on the scene of murder thrice-repeated in the royal palace since the repast of Thyestes.

The scene of the *Electra of Sophocles* is also laid before the palace, but does not contain the grave of Agamemnon. At break of day Pylades, Orestes, and the guardian slave who had been his preserver on that bloody day, enter the stage as just arriving from a foreign country. The keeper who acts as his guide commences with a description of his native city, and he is answered by Orestes, who recounts the commission given him by Apollo, and the manner in which he intends to carry it into execution, after which the young man puts up a prayer to his domestic gods and to the house of his fathers. Electra is heard complaining within; Orestes is desirous of greeting her without delay, but the old man leads him away to offer a sacrifice at the grave of his father. Electra then appears, and pours out her sorrow in a pathetic address to heaven, and in a prayer to the infernal deities her unconquerable desire of revenge. The chorus, which consists of native virgins, endeavours to console her; and, interchanging hymn and speech with the chorus, Electra discloses her unabatable sorrow, the contumely and oppression under which she suffers, and her hopelessness occasioned by the many delays of Orestes, notwithstanding her frequent exhortations; and she turns a deaf ear to all the grounds of consolation which the chorus can suggest. Chrysothemis, Clytemnestra's younger, more submissive, and favourite daughter, approaches with an offering which she is to carry to the grave of her father. Their difference of sentiment leads to an altercation between the two sisters, during which Chrysothemis informs Electra that Aegisthus, now absent in the country, has determined to adopt the most severe measures with her, whom, however, she sets at defiance. She then learns from her sister that Clytemnestra has had a dream that Agamemnon had come to life again, and had planted his sceptre in the floor of the house, and it had grown up into a tree that overshadowed the whole land; that, alarmed at this vision, she had commissioned Chrysothemis to carry an oblation to his grave. Electra counsels her not to execute the commands of her wicked mother, but to put up a prayer for herself and her sister, and for the return of Orestes as the avenger of his father; she then adds to the oblation her own girdle and a lock of her hair. Chrysothemis goes off, promising obedience to her wishes. The chorus augurs from the dream, that retribution is at hand, and traces back the crimes committed in this house to the primal sin of Pelops. Clytemnestra rebukes her daughter, with whom, however, probably under the influence of the dream, she is milder than usual; she defends her murder of Agamemnon, Electra condemns her for it, but without violent altercation. Upon this Clytemnestra, standing at the altar in front of the house, proffers a prayer to Apollo for health and long life, and a secret one for the death of her son. The guardian of Orestes arrives, and, in the character of a messenger from a Phocian friend, announces the death of Orestes, and minutely enumerates all the circumstances which attended his being killed in a chariot-race at the Pythian games. Clytemnestra, although visited for a moment with a mother's feelings, can scarce conceal her triumphant joy, and invites the messenger to partake of the hospitality of her house. Electra, in touching speeches and hymns, gives herself up to grief; the chorus in vain endeavours to console her. Chrysothemis returns from the grave, full of joy in the assurance that Orestes is near; for she has found his lock of hair, his drink-offering and wreaths of flowers. This serves but to renew the despair of Electra, who recounts to her sister the gloomy tidings which have just arrived, and exhorts her, now that all other hope is at an end, to join with her in the daring deed of putting Aegisthus to death: a proposal which Chrysothemis, not possessing the necessary courage, rejects as foolish, and after a violent altercation she re-enters the house. The chorus bewails Electra, now left utterly desolate. Orestes returns with Pylades and several servants bearing an urn with the pretended ashes of the deceased youth. Electra begs it of them, and laments over it in the most affecting language, which agitates Orestes to such a degree that he can no longer conceal himself; after some preparation he discloses himself to her, and confirms the announcement by producing the seal-ring of their father. She gives vent in speech and song to her unbounded joy, till the old attendant of Orestes comes out and reprimands them both for their want of consideration. Electra with some difficulty recognizes in him the faithful servant to whom she had entrusted the care of Orestes, and expresses her gratitude to him. At the suggestion of the old man, Orestes and Pylades accompany him with all speed into the house, in order to surprise Clytemnestra while she is still alone. Electra offers up a prayer to Apollo in their behalf; the choral ode announces the moment of retribution. From within the house is heard the shrieks of the affrighted Clytemnestra, her short prayer, her cry of agony under the death-blow. Electra from without stimulates Orestes to complete the deed, and he comes out with bloody hands. Warned however by the chorus of the approach of Aegisthus, he hastily re-enters the house in order to take him by surprise. Aegisthus inquires into the story of Orestes' death, and from the ambiguous language of Electra is led to believe that his corpse is in the palace. He commands all the gates to be thrown open, immediately, for the purpose of convincing those of the people who yielded reluctant obedience to his sovereignty, that they had no longer any hopes in Orestes. The middle entrance opens, and discloses in the interior of the palace a body lying on the bed, but closely covered over: Orestes stands beside the body, and invites Aegisthus to uncover it; he suddenly beholds the bloody corpse of Clytemnestra, and concludes himself lost and without hope. He requests to be allowed to speak, but this is prevented by Electra. Orestes constrains him to enter the house, that he may kill him on the very spot where his own father had been murdered.

The scene of the *Electra of Euripides* is not in Mycenae, in the open country, but on the borders of Argolis, and before a solitary and miserable cottage. The owner, an old peasant, comes out and in a prologue tells the audience how matters stand in the royal house, with this addition, however, to the incidents related in the two plays already considered, that not content to treat Electra with ignominy, and to leave her in a state of celibacy, they had forced her to marry beneath her rank, and to accept of himself for a husband: the motives he assigns for this proceeding are singular enough; he declares, however, that he has too much respect for her to reduce her to the humiliation of becoming in reality his wife.--They live therefore in virgin wedlock. Electra comes forth before it is yet daybreak bearing upon her head, which is close shorn in servile fashion, a pitcher to fetch water: her husband entreats her not to trouble herself with such unaccustomed labours, but she will not be withheld from the discharge of her household duties; and the two depart, he to his work in the field and she upon her errand. Orestes now enters with Pylades, and, in a speech to him, states that he has already sacrificed at his father's grave, but that not daring to enter the city, he wishes to find his sister, who, he is aware, is married and dwells somewhere near on the frontiers, that he may learn from her the posture of affairs. He sees Electra approach with the water-pitcher, and retires. She breaks out into an ode bewailing her own fate and that of her father. Hereupon the chorus, consisting of rustic virgins, makes its appearance, and exhorts her to take a part in a festival of Juno, which she, however, depressed in spirit, pointing to her tattered garments, declines. The chorus offer to supply her with festal ornaments, but she still refuses. She perceives Orestes and Pylades in their hiding-place, takes them for robbers, and hastens to escape into the house; when Orestes steps forward and prevents her, she imagines he intends to murder her; he removes her fears, and gives her assurances that her brother is still alive. On this he inquires into her situation, and the spectators are again treated with a repetition of all the circumstances. Orestes still forbears to disclose himself, and promising merely to carry any message from Electra to her brother, testifies, as a stranger, his sympathy in her situation. The chorus seizes this opportunity of gratifying its curiosity about the fatal events of the city; and Electra, after describing her own misery, depicts the wantonness and arrogance of her mother and Aegisthus, who, she says, leaps in contempt upon Agamemnon's grave, and throws stones at it. The peasant returns from his work, and thinks it rather indecorous in his wife to be gossiping with young men, but when he hears that they have brought news of Orestes, he invites them in a friendly manner into his house. Orestes, on witnessing the behaviour of the worthy man, makes the reflection that the most estimable people are frequently to be found in low stations, and in lowly garb. Electra upbraids her husband for inviting them, knowing as he must that they had nothing in the house to entertain them with; he is of opinion that the strangers will be satisfied with what he has, that a good housewife can always make the most of things, and that they have at least enough for one day. She dispatches him to Orestes' old keeper and preserver who lives hard by them, to bid him come and bring something with him to entertain the strangers, and the peasant departs muttering wise saws about riches and moderation. The chorus bursting out into an ode on the expedition of the Greeks against Troy, describes at great length the figures wrought on the shield which Achilles received from Thetis, and concludes with expressing a wish that Clytemnestra may be punished for her wickedness.

The old guardian, who with no small difficulty ascends the hill towards the house, brings Electra a lamb, a cheese, and a skin of wine; he then begins to weep, not failing of course to wipe his eyes with his tattered garments. In reply to the questions of Electra he states, that at the grave of Agamemnon he found traces of an oblation and a lock of hair; from which circumstance he conjectured that Orestes had been there. We have then an allusion to the means which Aeschylus had employed to bring about the recognition, namely, the resemblance of the hair, the prints of feet, as well as the homespun-robe, with a condemnation of them as insufficient and absurd. The probability of this part of the drama of Aeschylus may, perhaps, admit of being cleared up, at all events one is ready to overlook it; but an express reference like this to another author's treatment of the same subject, is the most annoying interruption and the most fatal to genuine poetry that can possibly be conceived. The guests come out; the old man attentively considers Orestes, recognizes him, and convinces Electra that he is her brother by a scar on his eyebrow, which he received from a fall (this is the superb invention, which he substitutes for that of Aeschylus), Orestes and Electra embrace during a short choral ode, and abandon themselves to their joy. In a long dialogue, Orestes, the old slave, and Electra, form their plans. The old man informs them that Aegisthus is at present in the country sacrificing to the Nymphs, and Orestes resolves to steal there as a guest, and to fall on him by surprise. Clytemnestra, from a dread of unpleasant remarks, has not accompanied him; and Electra undertakes to entice her mother to them by a false message of her being in child-bed. The brother and sister now join in prayers to the gods and their father's shade, for a successful issue of their designs. Electra declares that she will put an end to her existence if they should miscarry, and, for that purpose, she will keep a sword in readiness. The old tutor departs with Orestes to conduct him to Aegisthus, and to repair afterwards to Clytemnestra. The chorus sings of the Golden Ram, which Thyestes, by the assistance of the faithless wife of Atreus, was enabled to carry off from him, and the repast furnished with the flesh of his own children, with which he was punished in return; at the sight of which the sun turned aside from his course; a circumstance, however, which the chorus very sapiently adds, that it was very much inclined to call in question. From a distance is heard a noise of tumult and groans; Electra fears that her brother has been overcome, and is on the point of killing herself. But at the moment a messenger arrives, who gives a long-winded account of the death of Aegisthus, and interlards it with many a joke. Amidst the rejoicings of the chorus, Electra fetches a wreath and crowns her brother, who holds in his hands the head of Aegisthus by the hair. This head she upbraids in a long speech with its follies and crimes, and among other things says to it, it is never well to marry a woman with whom one has previously lived in illicit intercourse; that it is an unseemly thing when a woman obtains the mastery in a family, &c. Clytemnestra is now seen approaching; Orestes begins to have scruples of conscience as to his purpose of murdering a mother, and the authority of the oracle, but yields to the persuasions of Electra, and agrees to do the deed within the house. The queen arrives, drawn in a chariot sumptuously hung with tapestry, and surrounded by Trojan slaves; Electra makes an offer to assist her in alighting, which, however, is declined. Clytemnestra then alleges the sacrifice of Iphigenia as a justification of her own conduct towards Agamemnon, and calls even upon her daughter to state her reasons in condemnation, that an opportunity may be given to the latter of delivering a subtle, captious harangue, in which, among other things, she reproaches her mother with having, during the absence of Agamemnon, sat before her mirror, and studied her toilette too much. With all this Clytemnestra is not provoked, even though her daughter does not hesitate to declare her intention of putting her to death if ever it should be in her power; she makes inquiries about her daughter's supposed confinement, and enters the hut to prepare the necessary sacrifice of purification. Electra accompanies her with a sarcastic speech. On this the chorus begins an ode on retribution: the shrieks of the murdered woman are heard within the house, and the brother and sister come out stained with her blood. They are full of repentance and despair at the deed which they have committed; increase their remorse by repeating the pitiable words and gestures of their dying parent. Orestes determines on flight into foreign lands, while Electra asks, "Who will now take me in marriage?" Castor and Pollux, their uncles, appear in the air, abuse Apollo on account of his oracle, command Orestes, in order to save himself from the Furies, to submit to the sentence of the Areopagus, and conclude with predicting a number of events which are yet to happen to him. They then enjoin a marriage between Electra and Pylades; who are to take her first husband with them to Phocis, and there richly to provide for him. After a further outburst of sorrow, the brother and sister take leave of one another for life, and the piece concludes.

We easily perceive that Aeschylus has viewed the subject in its most terrible aspect, and drawn it within that domain of the gloomy divinities, whose recesses he so loves to haunt. The grave of Agamemnon is the murky gloom from which retributive vengeance issues; his discontented shade, the soul of the whole poem. The obvious external defect, that the action lingers too long at the same point, without any sensible progress, appears, on reflection, a true internal perfection: it is the stillness of expectation before a deep storm or an earthquake. It is true the prayers are repeated, but their very accumulation heightens the impression of a great unheard-of purpose, for which human powers and motives by themselves are insufficient. In the murder of Clytemnestra, and her heart-rending appeals, the poet, without disguising her guilt, has gone to the very verge of what was allowable in awakening our sympathy with her sufferings. The crime which is to be punished is kept in view from the very first by the grave, and, at the conclusion, it is brought still nearer to our minds by the unfolding the fatal garment: thus, Agamemnon non, after being fully avenged, is, as it were, murdered again before the mental eye. The flight of Orestes betrays no undignified weakness or repentance; it is merely the inevitable tribute which he must pay to offended nature.

It is only necessary to notice in general terms the admirable management of the subject by Sophocles. What a beautiful introduction has he made to precede the queen's mission to the grave, with which Aeschylus begins at once! With what polished ornament has he embellished it throughout, for example, with the description of the games! With what nice judgment does he husband the pathos of Electra; first, general lamentations, then hopes derived from the dream, their annihilation by the news of Orestes' death, the new hopes suggested by Chrysothemis only to be rejected, and lastly her mourning over the urn. Electra's heroism is finely set off by the contrast with her more submissive sister. The poet has given quite a new turn to the subject by making Electra the chief object of interest. A noble pair has the poet here given us; the sister endued with unshaken constancy in true and noble sentiments, and the invincible heroism of endurance; the brother prompt and vigorous in all the energy of youth. To this he skilfully opposes circumspection and experience in the old man, while the fact that Sophocles as well as Aeschylus has left Pylades silent, is a proof how carefully ancient art disdained all unnecessary surplusage.

But what more especially characterizes the tragedy of Sophocles, is the heavenly serenity beside a subject so terrific, the fresh air of life and youth which breathes through the whole. The bright divinity of Apollo, who enjoined the deed, seems to shed his influence over it; even the break of day, in the opening scene, is significant. The grave and the world of shadows, are kept in the background: what in Aeschylus is effected by the spirit of the murdered monarch, proceeds here from the heart of the still living Electra, which is endowed with an equal capacity for inextinguishable hatred or ardent love. The disposition to avoid everything dark and ominous, is remarkable even in the very first speech of Orestes, where he says he feels no concern at being thought dead, so long as he knows himself to be alive, and in the full enjoyment of health and strength. He is not beset with misgivings or stings of conscience either before or after the deed, so that the determination is more steadily maintained by Sophocles than in Aeschylus; and the appalling scene with Aegisthus, and the reserving him for an ignominious death to the very close of the piece, is more austere and solemn than anything in the older drama. Clytemnestra's dreams furnish the most striking token of the relation which the two poets bear to each other: both are equally appropriate, significant, and ominous; that of Aeschylus is grander, but appalling to the senses; that of Sophocles, in its very tearfulness, majestically beautiful.

The piece of Euripides is a singular example of poetic, or rather unpoetic obliquity; we should never have done were we to attempt to point out all its absurdities and contradictions. Why, for instance, does Orestes fruitlessly torment his sister by maintaining his incognito so long? The poet too, makes it a light matter to throw aside whatever stands in his way, as in the case of the peasant, of whom, after his departure to summon the old keeper, we have no farther account. Partly for the sake of appearing original, and partly from an idea that to make Orestes kill the king and queen in the middle of their capital would be inconsistent with probability, Euripides has involved himself in still greater improbabilities. Whatever there is of the tragical in his drama is not his own, but belongs either to the fable, to his predecessors, or to tradition. In his hands, at least, it has ceased to be tragedy, but is lowered into "a family picture," in the modern signification of the word. The effect attempted to be produced by the poverty of Electra is pitiful in the extreme; the poet has betrayed his secret in the complacent display which she makes of her misery. All the preparations for the crowning act are marked by levity, and a want of internal conviction: it is a gratuitous torture of our feelings to make Aegisthus display a good-natured hospitality, and Clytemnestra a maternal sympathy with her daughter, merely to excite our compassion in their behalf; the deed is no sooner executed, but its effect is obliterated by the most despicable repentance, a repentance which arises from no moral feeling, but from a merely animal revulsion. I shall say nothing of his abuse of the oracle of Delphi. As it destroys the very basis of the whole drama, I cannot see why Euripides should have written it, except to provide a fortunate marriage for Electra, and to reward the peasant for his continency. I could wish that the wedding of Pylades had been celebrated on the stage, and that a good round sum of money had been paid to the peasant on the spot; then everything would have ended to the satisfaction of the spectators as in an ordinary comedy.

Not, however, to be unjust, I must admit that the *Electra* is perhaps the very worst of Euripides' pieces. Was it the rage for novelty which led him here into such faults? He was truly to be pitied for having been preceded in the treatment of this same subject by two such men as Sophocles and Aeschylus. But what compelled him to measure his powers with theirs, and to write an *Electra* at all?

LECTURE X.

Character of the remaining Works of Euripides--The Satirical Drama--Alexandrian Tragic Poets.

Of the plays of Euripides, which have come down to us in great number, we can only give a very short and general account.

On the score of beautiful morality, there is none of them, perhaps, so deserving of praise as the *Alcestis*. Her resolution to die, and the farewell which she takes of her husband and children, are depicted with the most overpowering pathos. The poet's forbearance, in not allowing the heroine to speak on her return from the infernal world, lest he might draw aside the mysterious veil which shrouds the condition of the dead, is deserving of high praise. Admetus, it is true, and more especially his father, sink too much in our esteem from their selfish love of life; and Hercules appears, at first, blunt even to rudeness, afterwards more noble and worthy of himself, and at last jovial, when, for the sake of the joke, he introduces to Admetus his veiled wife as a new bride.

Iphigenia in Aulis is a subject peculiarly suited to the tastes and powers of Euripides; the object here is to excite a tender emotion for the innocent and child-like simplicity of the heroine: but Iphigenia is still very far from being an Antigone. Aristotle has already remarked that the character is not well sustained throughout. "Iphigenia imploring," he says, "has no resemblance to Iphigenia afterwards yielding herself up a willing sacrifice."

Ion is also one of his most delightful pieces, on account of the picture of innocence and priestly sanctity in the boy whose name it bears. In the course of the plot, it is true, there are not a few improbabilities, makeshifts, and repetitions; and the catastrophe, produced by a falsehood, in which both gods and men unite against Xuthus, can hardly be satisfactory to our feelings.

As delineations of female passion, and of the aberrations of a mind diseased, *Phaedra* and *Medea* have been justly praised. The play in which the former is introduced dazzles us by the sublime and beautiful heroism of *Hippolytus*; and it is also deserving of the highest commendation on account of the observance of propriety and moral strictness, in so critical a subject. This, however, is not so much the merit of the poet himself as of the delicacy of his contemporaries; for the *Hippolytus* which we possess, according to the scholiast, is an improvement upon an earlier one, in which there was much that was offensive and reprehensible. [Footnote: The learned and acute Brunck, without citing any authority, or the coincidence of fragments in corroboration, says that Seneca in his *Hippolytus*, followed the plan of the earlier play of Euripides, called the *Veiled Hippolytus*. How far this is mere conjecture I cannot say, but at any rate I should be inclined to doubt whether Euripides, even in the censured drama, admitted the scene of the declaration of love, which Racine, however in his *Phaedra*. has not hesitated to adopt from Seneca.]

The opening of the *Medea* is admirable; her desperate situation is, by the conversation between her nurse and the keeper of her children, and her own wailings behind the scene, depicted with most touching effect. As soon, however, as she makes her appearance, the poet takes care to cool our emotion by the number of general and commonplace reflections which he puts into her mouth. Lower does she sink in the scene with Aegeus, where, meditating a terrible revenge on Jason, she first secures a place of refuge, and seems almost on the point of bespeaking a new connection. This is very unlike the daring criminal who has reduced the powers of nature to minister to her ungovernable passions, and speeds from land to land like a desolating meteor;--the Medea who, abandoned by all the world, was still sufficient for herself. Nothing but a wish to humour Athenian antiquities could have induced Euripides to adopt this cold interpolation of his story. With this exception he has, in the most vivid colours, painted, in one and the same person, the mighty enchantress, and the woman weak only from the social position of her sex. As it is, we are keenly affected by the struggles of maternal tenderness in the midst of her preparations for the cruel deed. Moreover, she announces her deadly purpose much too soon and too distinctly, instead of brooding awhile over the first confused, dark suggestion of it. When she does put it in execution, her thirst of revenge on Jason might, we should have thought, have been sufficiently slaked by the horrible death of his young wife and her father; and the new motive, namely, that Jason, as she pretends, would infallibly murder the children, and therefore she must anticipate him, will by no means bear examination. For she could as easily have saved the living children with herself, as have carried off their dead bodies in the dragon-chariot. Still this may, perhaps, be justified by the perturbation of mind into which she was plunged by the crime she had perpetrated.

Perhaps it was such pictures of universal sorrow, of the fall of flourishing families and states from the greatest glory to the lowest misery, nay, to entire annihilation, as Euripides has sketched in the *Troades*, that gained for him, from Aristotle, the title of *the most tragic of poets*. The concluding scene, where the captive ladies, allotted as slaves to different masters, leave Troy in flames behind them, and proceed towards the ships, is truly grand. It is impossible, however, for a piece to have less action, in the energetical sense of the word: it is a series of situations and events, which have no other connexion than that of a common origin in the capture of Troy, but in no respect have they a common aim. The accumulation of helpless suffering, against which the will and sentiment even are not allowed to revolt, at last wearies us, and exhausts our compassion. The greater the struggle to avert a calamity, the deeper the impression it makes when it bursts forth after all. But when so little concern is shown, as is here the case with Astyanax, for the speech of Talthybius prevents even the slightest attempt to save him, the spectator soon acquiesces in the result. In this way Euripides frequently fails. In the ceaseless demands which this play makes on our compassion, the pathos is not duly economized and brought to a climax: for instance, Andromache's lament over her living son is much more heart-rending than that of Hecuba for her dead one. The effect of the latter is, however, aided by the sight of the little corpse lying on Hector's shield. Indeed, in the composition of this piece the poet has evidently reckoned much on ocular effect: thus, for the sake of contrast with the captive ladies, Helen appears splendidly dressed, Andromache is mounted on a car laden with spoils; and I doubt not but that at the conclusion the entire scene was in flames. The trial of Helen painfully interrupts the train of our sympathies, by an idle altercation which ends in nothing; for in spite of the accusations of Hecuba, Menelaus abides by the resolution which he had previously formed. The defence of Helen is about as entertaining as Isocrates' sophistical eulogium of her.

Euripides was not content with making Hecuba roll in the dust with covered head, and whine a whole piece through; he has also introduced her in another tragedy which bears her name, as the standing representative of suffering and woe. The two actions of this piece, the sacrifice of Polyxena, and the revenge on Polymestor, on account of the murder of Polydorus, have nothing in common with each other but their connexion with Hecuba. The first half possesses great beauties of that particular kind in which Euripides is pre-eminently successful: pictures of tender youth, female innocence, and noble resignation to an early and violent death. A human sacrifice, that triumph of barbarian superstition, is represented as executed, suffered, and looked upon, with that Hellenism of feeling which so early effected the abolition of such sacrifices among the Greeks. But the second half most revoltingly effaces these soft impressions. It is made up of the revengeful artifices of Hecuba, the blind avarice of Polymestor, and the paltry policy of Agamemnon, who, not daring himself to call the Thracian king to account, nevertheless beguiles him into the hands of the captive women. Neither is it very consistent that Hecuba, advanced in years, bereft of strength, and overwhelmed with sorrow, should nevertheless display so much presence of mind in the execution of revenge, and such a command of tongue in her accusation and derision of Polymestor.

We have another example of two distinct and separate actions in the same tragedy, the *Mad Hercules*. The first is the distress of his family during his absence, and their deliverance by his return; the second, his remorse at having in a sudden frenzy murdered his wife and children. The one action follows, but by no means arises out of the other.

The *Phoenissae* is rich in tragic incidents, in the common acceptation of the word: the son of Creon, to save his native city, precipitates himself from the walls; Eteocles and Polynices perish by each other's hands; over their dead bodies Jocasta falls by her own hand; the Argives who hare made war upon Thebes are destroyed in battle; Polynices remains uninterred; and lastly, Oedipus and Antigone are driven into exile. After this enumeration of the incidents, the Scholiast aptly notices the arbitrary manner in which the poet has proceeded, "This drama," says he, "is beautiful in theatrical effect, even because it is full of incidents totally foreign to the proper action. Antigone looking down from the walls has nothing to do with the action, and Polynices enters the town under the safe-conduct of a truce, without any effect being thereby produced. After all the rest the banished Oedipus and a wordy ode are tacked on, being equally to no purpose." This is a severe criticism, but it is just.

Not more lenient is the Scholiast on *Orestes*: "This piece," he says, "is one of those which produce a great effect on the stage, but with respect to characters it is extremely bad; for, with the exception of Pylades, all the rest are good for nothing." Moreover, "Its catastrophe is more suitable to comedy than tragedy." This drama begins, indeed, in the most agitating manner. Orestes, after the murder of his mother, is represented lying on his bed, afflicted with anguish of soul and madness; Electra sits at his feet, and she and the chorus remain in trembling expectation of his awaking. Afterwards, however, everything takes a perverse turn, and ends with the most violent strokes of stage effect.

The *Iphigenia in Tauris*, in which the fate of Orestes is still further followed out, is less wild and extravagant, but in the representation both of character or passion, it seldom rises above mediocrity. The mutual recognition between brother and sister, after such adventures and actions, as that Iphigenia, who had herself once trembled before the bloody altar, was on the point of devoting her brother to a similar fate, produces no more than a transient emotion. The flight of Orestes and his sister is not highly calculated to excite our interest: the artifice by which Iphigenia brings it about is readily credited by Thoas, who does not attempt to make any opposition till both are safe, and then he is appeased by one of the ordinary divine interpositions. This device has been so used and abused by Euripides, that in nine out of his eighteen tragedies, a divinity descends to unravel the complicated knot.

In *Andromache* Orestes makes his appearance for the fourth time. The Scholiast, in whose opinion we may, we think, generally recognize the sentiments of the most important of ancient critics, declares this to be a very second-rate play, in which single scenes alone are deserving of any praise. Of those on which Racine has based his free imitations, this is unquestionably the very worst, and therefore the French critics have an easy game to play in their endeavours to depreciate the Grecian predecessor, from whom Racine has in fact derived little more than the first suggestion of his tragedy.

The *Bacchae* represents the infectious and tumultuous enthusiasm of the worship of Bacchus, with great sensuous power and vividness of conception. The obstinate unbelief of Pentheus, his infatuation, and terrible punishment by the hands of his own mother, form a bold picture. The effect on the stage must have been extraordinary. Imagine, only, a chorus with flying and dishevelled hair and dress, tambourines, cymbals, &c., in their hands, like the Bacchants we see on bas-reliefs, bursting impetuously into the orchestra, and executing their inspired dances amidst tumultuous music,--a circumstance, altogether unusual, as the choral odes were generally sung and danced at a solemn step, and with no other accompaniment than a flute. Here the luxuriance of ornament, which Euripides everywhere affects, was for once appropriate. When, therefore, several of the modern critics assign to this piece a very low rank, they seem to me not to know what they themselves would wish. In the composition of this piece, I cannot help admiring a harmony and unity, which we seldom meet with in Euripides, as well as abstinence from every foreign matter, so that all the motives and effects flow from one source, and concur towards a common end. After the *Hippolytus*, I should be inclined to assign to this play the first place among all the extant works of Euripides.

The *Heraclidae* and the *Supplices* are mere *occasional* tragedies, *i.e.*, owing their existence to some temporary incident or excitement, and they must have been indebted for their success to nothing else but their flattery of the Athenians. They celebrate two ancient heroic deeds of Athens, on which the panegyrists, amongst the rest Isocrates, who always mixed up the fabulous with the historical, lay astonishing stress: the protection they are said to have afforded to the children of Hercules, the ancestors of the Lacedaemonian kings, from the persecution of Eurystheus, and their going to war with Thebes on behalf of Adrastus, king of Argos, and forcing the Thebans to give the rites of burial to the Seven Chieftains and their host. The *Supplices* was, as we know, represented during the Peloponnesian war, after the conclusion of a treaty between the Argives and the Lacedaemonians; and was intended to remind the Argives of their ancient obligation to Athens, and to show how little they could hope to prosper in the war against the Athenians. The *Heraclidae* was undoubtedly written with a similar view in respect to Lacedaemon. Of the two pieces, however, which are both cast in the same mould, the Female Suppliants, so called from the mothers of the fallen heroes, is by far the richest in poetical merit; the *Heraclidae* appears, as it were, but a faint impression of the other. In the former piece, it is true, Theseus appears at first in a somewhat unamiable light, upbraiding, as he does, the unfortunate Adrastus with his errors at such great length, and perhaps with so little justice, before he condescends to assist him; again the disputation between Theseus and the Argive herald, as to the superiority of a monarchical or a democratical constitution, ought in justice to be banished from the stage to the rhetorical schools; while the moral eulogium of Adrastus over the fallen heroes is, at least, very much out of place. I am convinced that Euripides was here drawing the characters of particular Athenian generals, who had fallen in some battle or other. But even in this case the passage cannot be justified in a dramatic point of view; however, without such an object, it would have been silly and ridiculous in describing those heroes of the age of Hercules, (a Capaneus, for instance, who set even heaven itself at defiance,) to have launched out into the praise of their civic virtues. How apt Euripides was to wander from his subject in allusions to perfectly extraneous matters, and sometimes even to himself, we may see from a speech of Adrastus, who most impertinently is made to say, "It is not fair that the poet, while he delights others with his works, should himself suffer inconvenience." However, the funeral lamentations and the swan-like song of Evadne are affectingly beautiful, although she is so unexpectedly introduced into the drama. Literally, indeed, may we say of her, that she jumps into the play, for without even being mentioned before she suddenly appears first of all on the rock, from which she throws herself on the burning pile of Capaneus.

The *Heraclidae* is a very poor piece; its conclusion is singularly bald. We hear nothing more of the self-sacrifice of Macaria, after it is over: as the determination seems to have cost herself no struggle, it makes as little impression upon others. The Athenian king, Demophon, does not return again; neither does Iolaus, the companion of Hercules and guardian of his children, whose youth is so wonderfully renewed. Hyllus, the noble-minded Heraclide, never even makes his appearance; and nobody at last remains but Alcmene, who keeps up a bitter altercation with Eurystheus. Euripides seems to have taken a particular pleasure in drawing such implacable and rancorous old women: twice has he exhibited Hecuba in this light, pitting her against Helen and Polymestor. In general, we may observe the constant recurrence of the same artifice and motives is a sure symptom of mannerism. We have in the works of this poet three instances of women offered in sacrifice, which are moving from their perfect resignation: Iphigenia, Polyxena, and Macaria; the voluntary deaths of Alceste and Evadne belong in some sort also to this class. Suppliants are in like manner a favourite subject with him, because they oppress the spectator with apprehension lest they should be torn by force from the sanctuary of the altar. I have already noticed his lavish introduction of deities towards the conclusion.

The merriest of all tragedies is *Helen*, a marvellous drama, full of wonderful adventures and appearances, which are evidently better suited to comedy. The invention on which it is founded is, that Helen remained concealed in Egypt (so far went the assertion of the Aegyptian priests), while Paris carried off an airy phantom in her likeness, for which the Greeks and Trojans fought for ten long years. By this contrivance the virtue of the heroine is saved, and Menelaus, (to make good the ridicule of Aristophanes on the beggary of Euripides' heroes,) appears in rags as a beggar, and in nowise dissatisfied with his condition. But this manner of improving mythology bears a resemblance to the *Tales of the Thousand and One Nights*.

Modern philologists have dedicated voluminous treatises, to prove the spuriousness of *Rhesus*, the subject of which is taken from the eleventh book of the Iliad. Their opinion is, that the piece contains such a number of improbabilities and contradictions, that it is altogether unworthy of Euripides. But this is by no means a legitimate conclusion. Do not the faults which they censure unavoidably follow from the selection of an intractable subject, so very inconvenient as a nightly enterprise? The question respecting the genuineness of any work, turns not so much on its merits or demerits, as rather on the resemblance of its style and peculiarities to those of the pretended author. The few words of the Scholiast amount to a very different opinion: "Some have considered this drama to be spurious, and not the work of Euripides, because it bears many traces of the style of Sophocles. But it is inscribed in the *Didascaliae* as his, and its accuracy with respect to the phenomena of the starry heaven betrays the hand of Euripides." I think I understand what is here meant by the style of Sophocles, but it is rather in detached scenes, than in the general plan, that I at all discern it. Hence, if the piece is to be taken from Euripides, I should be disposed to attribute it to some eclectic imitator, but one of the school of Sophocles rather than of that of Euripides, and who lived only a little later than both. This I infer from the familiarity of many of the scenes, for tragedy at this time was fast sinking into the domestic tragedy, whereas, at a still later period, the Alexandrian age, it fell into an opposite error of bombast.

The *Cyclops* is a satiric drama. This is a mixed and lower species of tragic poetry, as we have already in passing asserted. The want of some relaxation for the mind, after the engrossing severity of tragedy, appears to have given rise to the satiric drama, as indeed to the after-piece in general. The satiric drama never possessed an independent existence; it was thrown in by way of an appendage to several tragedies, and to judge from that we know of it, was always considerably shorter than the others. In external form it resembled Tragedy, and the materials were in like manner mythological. The distinctive mark was a chorus consisting of satyrs, who accompanied with lively songs, gestures, and movements, such heroic adventures as were of a more cheerful hue, (many in the *Odyssey* for instance; for here, also, as in many other respects, the germ is to be found in Homer,) or, at least, could be made to wear such an appearance. The proximate cause of this species of drama was derived from the festivals of Bacchus, where satyr-masks was a common disguise. In mythological stories with which Bacchus had no concern, these constant attendants of his were, no doubt, in some sort arbitrarily introduced, but still not without a degree of propriety. As nature, in her original freedom, appeared to the fancy of the Greeks to teem everywhere with wonderful productions, they could with propriety people with these sylvan beings the wild landscapes, remote from polished cities, where the scene was usually laid, and enliven them with their wild animal frolics. The composition of demi-god with demi-beast formed an amusing contrast. We have an example in the *Cyclops* of the manner in which the poets proceeded in such subjects. It is not unentertaining, though the subject-matter is for the most part contained in the *Odyssey*; only the pranks of Silenus and his band are occasionally a little coarse. We must confess that, in our eyes, the great merit of this piece is its rarity, being the only extant specimen of its class which we possess. In the satiric dramas Aeschylus must, without doubt, have displayed more boldness and meaning in his mirth; as, for instance, when he introduced Prometheus bringing down fire from heaven to rude and stupid man; while Sophocles, to judge from the few fragments we have, must have been more elegant and moral, as when he introduced the goddesses contending for the prize of beauty, or Nausicaa offering protection to the shipwrecked Ulysses. It is a striking feature of the easy unconstrained character of life among the Greeks, of its gladsome joyousness of disposition, which knew nothing of a starched and stately dignity, but artist-like admired aptness and gracefulness, even in the most insignificant trifles, that in this drama called *Nausicaa*, or "*The Washerwomen*," in which, after Homer, the princess at the end of the washing, amuses herself at a game of ball with her maids, Sophocles himself played at ball, and by his grace in this exercise acquired much applause. The great poet, the respected Athenian citizen, the man who had already perhaps been a General, appeared publicly in woman's clothes, and as, on account of the feebleness of his voice, he could not play the leading part of Nausicaa, took perhaps the mute under part of a maid, for the sake of giving to the representation of his piece the slight ornament of bodily agility.

The history of ancient tragedy ends with Euripides, although there were a number of still later tragedians; Agathon, for instance, whom Aristophanes describes as fragrant with ointment and crowned with flowers, and in whose mouth Plato, in his *Symposium*, puts a discourse in the taste of the sophist Gorgias, full of the most exquisite ornaments and empty tautological antitheses. He was the first to abandon mythology, as furnishing the natural materials of tragedy, and occasionally wrote pieces with purely fictitious names, (this is worthy of notice, as forming a transition towards the new comedy,) one of which was called the *Flower*, and was probably therefore neither seriously affecting nor terrible, but in the style of the idyl, and pleasing.

The Alexandrian scholars, among their other lucubrations, attempted also the composition of tragedies; but if we are to judge of them from the only piece which has come down to us, the *Alexandra* of Lycophron, which consists of an endless monologue, full of prophecy, and overladen with obscure mythology, these productions of a subtle dilettantism must have been extremely inanimate and untheatrical, and every way devoid of interest. The creative powers of the Greeks were, in this department, so completely exhausted, that they were forced to content themselves with the repetition of the works of their ancient masters.

LECTURE XI.

The Old Comedy proved to be completely a contrast to Tragedy-- Parody-- Ideality of Comedy the reverse of that of Tragedy--Mirthful Caprice-- Allegoric and Political Signification--The Chorus and its Parabases.

We now leave Tragic Poetry to occupy ourselves with an entirely opposite species, the *Old* Comedy. Striking as this diversity is, we shall, however, commence with pointing out a certain symmetry in the contrast and certain relations between them, which have a tendency to exhibit the essential character of both in a clearer light. In forming a judgment of the Old Comedy, we must banish every idea of what is called Comedy by the moderns, and what went by the same name among the Greeks themselves at a later period. These two species of Comedy differ from each other, not only in accidental peculiarities, (such as the introduction in the old of real names and characters,) but essentially and diametrically. We must also guard against entertaining such a notion of the Old Comedy as would lead us to regard it as the rude beginnings of the more finished and cultivated comedy of a subsequent age [Footnote: This is the purport of the section of Barthelemy in the *Anacharsis* on the Old Comedy: one of the poorest and most erroneous parts of his work. With the pitiful presumption of ignorance, Voltaire pronounced a sweeping condemnation of Aristophanes, (in other places, and in his *Philosophical Dictionary* under Art. *Athee*), and the modern French critics have for the most part followed his example. We may, however, find the foundation of all the erroneous opinions of the moderns on this subject, and the same prosaical mode of viewing it, in Plutarch's parallel between Aristophanes and Menander.], an idea which many, from the unbridled licentiousness of the old comic writers, have been led to entertain. On the contrary the former is the genuine *poetic* species; but the New Comedy, as I shall show in due course, is its decline into prose and reality.

We shall form the best idea of the Old Comedy, by considering it as the direct opposite of Tragedy. This was probably the meaning of the assertion of Socrates, which is given by Plato towards the end of his *Symposium*. He tells us that, after the other guests were dispersed or had fallen asleep, Socrates was left awake with Aristophanes and Agathon, and that while he drank with them out of a large cup, he forced them to confess, however unwillingly, that it is the business of one and the same man to be equally master of tragic and comic composition, and that the tragic poet is, in virtue of his art, comic poet also. This was not only repugnant to the general opinion, which wholly separated the two kinds of talent, but also to all experience, inasmuch as no tragic poet had ever attempted to shine in Comedy, nor conversely; his remark, therefore, can only have been meant to apply to the inmost essence of the things. Thus at another time, the Platonic Socrates says, on the subject of comic imitation: "All opposites can be fully understood only by and through each other; consequently we can only know what is serious by knowing also what is laughable and ludicrous." If the divine Plato by working out that dialogue had been pleased to communicate his own, or his master's thoughts, respecting these two kinds of poetry, we should have been spared the necessity of the following investigation.

One aspect of the relation of comic to tragic poetry may be comprehended under the idea of *parody*. This parody, however, is one infinitely more powerful than that of the mock heroic poem, as the subject parodied, by means of scenic representation, acquired quite another kind of reality and presence in the mind, from what the epopee did, which relating the transactions of a distant age, retired, as it were, with them into the remote olden time. The comic parody was brought out when the thing parodied was fresh in recollection, and as the representation took place on the same stage where the spectators were accustomed to see its serious original, this circumstance must have greatly contributed to heighten the effect of it. Moreover, not merely single scenes, but the very form of tragic composition was parodied, and doubtless the parody extended not only to the poetry, but also to the music and dancing, to the acting itself, and the scenic decoration. Nay, even where the drama trod in the footsteps of the plastic arts, it was still the subject of comic parody, as the ideal figures of deities were evidently transformed into caricatures [Footnote: As an example of this, I may allude to the well-known vase-figures, where Mercury and Jupiter, about to ascend by a ladder into Alcmene's chamber, are represented as comic masks.]. Now the more immediately the productions of all these arts fall within the observance of the external senses, and, above, all the more the Greeks, in their popular festivals, religious ceremonies, and solemn processions, were accustomed to, and familiar with, the noble style which was the native element of tragic representation, so much the more irresistibly ludicrous must have been the effect of that general parody of the arts, which it was the object of Comedy to exhibit.

But this idea does not exhaust the essential character of Comedy; for parody always supposes a reference to the subject which is parodied, and a necessary dependence on it. The Old Comedy, however, as a species of poetry, is as independent and original as Tragedy itself; it stands on the same elevation with it, that is, it extends just as far beyond the limits of reality into the domains of free creative fancy.

Tragedy is the highest earnestness of poetry; Comedy altogether sportive. Now earnestness, as I observed in the Introduction, consists in the direction of the mental powers to an aim or purpose, and the limitation of their activity to that object. Its opposite, therefore, consists in the apparent want of aim, and freedom from all restraint in the exercise of the mental powers; and it is therefore the more perfect, the more unreservedly it goes to work, and the more lively the appearance there is of purposeless fun and unrestrained caprice. Wit and raillery may be employed in a sportive manner, but they are also both of them compatible with the severest earnestness, as is proved by the example of the later Roman satires and the ancient Iambic poetry of the Greeks, where these means were employed for the expression of indignation and hatred.

The New Comedy, it is true, represents what is amusing in character, and in the contrast of situations and combinations; and it is the more comic the more it is distinguished by a want of aim: cross purposes, mistakes, the vain efforts of ridiculous passion, and especially if all this ends at last in nothing; but still, with all this mirth, the form of the representation itself is serious, and regularly tied down to a certain aim. In the Old Comedy the form was sportive, and a seeming aimlessness reigned throughout; the whole poem was one big jest, which again contained within itself a world of separate jests, of which each occupied its own place, without appearing to trouble itself about the rest. In tragedy, if I may be allowed to make my meaning plain by a comparison, the monarchical constitution prevails, but a monarchy without despotism, such as it was in the heroic times of the Greeks: everything yields a willing obedience to the dignity of the heroic sceptre. Comedy, on the other hand, is the democracy of poetry, and is more inclined even to the confusion of anarchy than to any circumscription of the general liberty of its mental powers and purposes, and even of its separate thoughts, sallies, and allusions.

Whatever is dignified, noble, and grand in human nature, admits only of a serious and earnest representation; for whoever attempts to represent it, feels himself, as it were, in the presence of a superior being, and is consequently awed and restrained by it. The comic poet, therefore, must divest his characters of all such qualities; he must place himself without the sphere of them; nay, even deny altogether their existence, and form an ideal of human nature the direct opposite of that of the tragedians, namely, as the odious and base. But as the tragic ideal is not a collective model of all possible virtues, so neither does this converse ideality consist in an aggregation, nowhere to be found in real life, of all moral enormities and marks of degeneracy, but rather in a dependence on the animal part of human nature, in that want of freedom and independence, that want of coherence, those inconsistencies of the inward man, in which all folly and infatuation originate.

The earnest ideal consists of the unity and harmonious blending of the sensual man with the mental, such as may be most clearly recognised in Sculpture, where the perfection of form is merely a symbol of mental perfection and the loftiest moral ideas, and where the body is wholly pervaded by soul, and spiritualized even to a glorious transfiguration. The merry or ludicrous ideal, on the other hand, consists in the perfect harmony and unison of the higher part of our nature with the animal as the ruling principle. Reason and understanding are represented as the voluntary slaves of the senses. Hence we shall find that the very principle of Comedy necessarily occasioned that which in Aristophanes has given so much offence; namely, his frequent allusions to the base necessities of the body, the wanton pictures of animal desire, which, in spite of all the restraints imposed on it by morality and decency, is always breaking loose before one can be aware of it. If we reflect a moment, we shall find that even in the present day, on our own stage, the infallible and inexhaustible source of the ludicrous is the same ungovernable impulses of sensuality in collision with higher duties; or cowardice, childish vanity, loquacity, gulosity, laziness, &c. Hence, in the weakness of old age, amorousness is the more laughable, as it is plain that it is not mere animal instinct, but that reason has only served to extend the dominion of the senses beyond their proper limits. In drunkenness, too, the real man places himself, in some degree, in the condition of the comic ideal.

The fact that the Old Comedy introduced living characters on the stage, by name and with all circumstantiality, must not mislead us to infer that they actually did represent certain definite individuals. For such historical characters in the Old Comedy have always an allegorical signification, and represent a class; and as their features were caricatures in the masks, so, in like manner, were their characters in the representation. But still this constant allusion to a proximate reality, which not only allowed the poet, in the character of the chorus, to converse with the public in a general way, but also to point the finger at certain individual spectators, was essential to this species of poetry. As Tragedy delights in harmonious unity, Comedy flourishes in a chaotic exuberance; it seeks out the most motley contrasts, and the unceasing play of cross purposes. It works up, therefore, the most singular, unheard-of, and even impossible incidents, with allusions to the well-known and special circumstances of the immediate locality and time.

The comic poet, as well as the tragic, transports his characters into an ideal element: not, however, into a world subjected to necessity, but one where the caprice of inventive wit rules without check or restraint, and where all the laws of reality are suspended. He is at liberty, therefore, to invent an action as arbitrary and fantastic as possible; it may even be unconnected and unreal, if only it be calculated to place a circle of comic incidents and characters in the most glaring light. In this last respect, the work should, nay, must, have a leading aim, or it will otherwise be in want of *keeping*; and in this view also the comedies of Aristophanes may be considered as perfectly systematical. But then, to preserve the comic inspiration, this aim must be made a matter of diversion, and be concealed beneath a medley of all sorts of out-of-the-way matters. Comedy at its first commencement, namely, under the hands of its Doric founder, Epicharmus, borrowed its materials chiefly from the mythical world. Even in its maturity, to judge from the titles of many lost plays of Aristophanes and his contemporaries, it does not seem to have renounced this choice altogether, as at a later period, in the interval between the old and new comedy, it returned, for particular reasons, with a natural predilection to mythology. But as the contrast between the matter and form is here in its proper place, and nothing can be more thoroughly opposite to the ludicrous form of exhibition than the most important and serious concerns of men, public life and the state naturally became the peculiar subject-matter of the Old Comedy. It is, therefore, altogether political; and private and family life, beyond which the new never soars, was only introduced occasionally and indirectly, in so far as it might have a reference to public life. The Chorus is therefore essential to it, as being in some sort a representation of the public: it must by no means be considered as a mere accidental property, to be accounted for by the local origin of the Old Comedy; we may assign its existence to a more substantial reason--its necessity for a complete parody of the tragic form. It contributes also to the expression of that festal gladness of which Comedy was the most unrestrained effusion, for in all the national and religious festivals of the Greeks, choral songs, accompanied by dancing, were performed. The comic chorus transforms itself occasionally into such an expression of public joy, as, for instance, when the women who celebrate the Thesmophoriae in the piece that bears that name, in the midst of the most amusing drolleries, begin to chant their melodious hymn, just as in a real festival, in honour of the presiding gods. At these times we meet with such a display of sublime lyric poetry, that the passages may be transplanted into tragedy without any change or alteration whatever. There is, however, this deviation from the tragic model, that there are frequently, in the same comedy, several choruses which sometimes are present together, singing in response, or at other times come on alternately and drop off, without the least general reference to each other. The most remarkable peculiarity, however, of the comic chorus is the *Parabasis*, an address to the spectators by the chorus, in the name, and as the representative of the poet, but having no connexion with the subject of the piece. Sometimes he enlarges on his own merits, and ridicules the pretensions of his rivals; at other times, availing himself of his right as an Athenian citizen, to speak on public affairs in every assembly of the people, he brings forward serious or ludicrous motions for the common good. The Parabasis must, strictly speaking, be considered as incongruous with the essence of dramatic representation; for in the drama the poet should always be behind his dramatic personages, who again ought to speak and act as if they were alone, and to take no perceptible notice of the spectators. Such intermixtures, therefore, destroy all tragic impression, but to the comic tone these intentional interruptions or intermezzos are welcome, even though they be in themselves more serious than the subject of the representation, because we are at such times unwilling to submit to the constraint of a mental occupation which must perforce be kept up, for then it would assume the appearance of a task or obligation. The Parabasis may partly have owed its invention to the circumstance of the comic poets not having such ample materials as the tragic, for filling up the intervals of the action when the stage was empty, by sympathising and enthusiastic odes. But it is, moreover, consistent with the essence of the Old Comedy, where not merely the subject, but the whole manner of treating it was sportive and jocular. The unlimited dominion of mirth and fun manifests itself even in this, that the dramatic form itself is not seriously adhered to, and that its laws are often suspended; just as in a droll disguise the masquerader sometimes ventures to lay aside the mask. The practice of throwing out allusions and hints to the pit is retained even in the comedy of the present day, and is often found to be attended with great success; although unconditionally reprobated by many critics. I shall afterwards examine how far, and in what departments of comedy, these allusions are admissible.

To sum up in a few words the aim and object of Tragedy and Comedy, we may observe, that as Tragedy, by painful emotions, elevates us to the most dignified views of humanity, being, in the words of Plato, "the imitation of the most beautiful and most excellent life;" Comedy, on the other hand, by its jocose and depreciatory view of all things, calls forth the most petulant hilarity.

LECTURE XII.

Aristophanes--His Character as an Artist--Description and Character of his remaining Works--A Scene, translated from the *Acharnae,* by way of Appendix.

Of the Old Comedy but one writer has come down to us, and we cannot, therefore, in forming an estimate of his merits, enforce it by a comparison with other masters. Aristophanes had many predecessors, *Magnes*, *Cratinus*, *Crates,* and others; he was indeed one of the latest of this school, for he outlived the Old Comedy. We have no reason, however, to believe that we witness in him its decline, as we do that of Tragedy in the case of the last tragedian; in all probability the Old Comedy was still rising in perfection, and he himself one of its most finished authors. It was very different with the Old Comedy and with Tragedy; the latter died a natural, and the former a violent death. Tragedy ceased to exist, because that species of poetry seemed to be exhausted, because it was abandoned, and because no one was now able to rise to the pitch of its elevation. Comedy was deprived by the hand of power of that unrestrained freedom which was necessary to its existence. Horace, in a few words, informs us of this catastrophe: "After these (Thespis and Aeschylus) followed the Old Comedy, not without great merit; but its freedom degenerated into licentiousness, and into a violence which deserved to be checked by law. The law was enacted, and the Chorus sunk into disgraceful silence as soon as it was deprived of the right to injure." [Footnote:

Successit vetus his comedia, non sine multa
Laude, sed in vitium libertas excidit, et vim
Dignam lege regi: lex est accepta: chorusque
Turpiter obticuit, sublato jure nocendi.] Towards the end of the Peloponnesian war, when a few individuals, in violation of the constitution, had assumed the supreme authority in Athens, a law was enacted, giving every person attacked by comic poets a remedy by law. Moreover, the introduction of real persons on the stage, or the use of such masks as bore a resemblance to their features, &c., was prohibited. This gave rise to what is called the *Middle Comedy*. The form still continued much the same; and the representation, if not perfectly allegorical, was nevertheless a parody. But the essence was taken away, and this species must have become insipid when it could no longer be seasoned by the salt of personal ridicule. Its whole attraction consisted in idealizing jocularly the reality that came nearest home to every one of the spectators, that is, in representing it under the light of the most preposterous perversity; and how was it possible now to lash even the

general mismanagement of the state-affairs, if no offence was to be given to individuals? I cannot, therefore, agree with Horace in his opinion that the abuse gave rise to the restriction. The Old Comedy flourished together with Athenian liberty; and both were oppressed under the same circumstances, and by the same persons. So far were the calumnies of Aristophanes from having been the occasion of the death of Socrates, as, without a knowledge of history, many persons have thought proper to assert (for the *Clouds* were composed a great number of years before), that it was the very same revolutionary despotism that reduced to silence alike the sportive censure of Aristophanes, and also punished with death the graver animadversions of the incorruptible Socrates. Neither do we see that the persecuting jokes of Aristophanes were in any way detrimental to Euripides: the free people of Athens beheld alike with admiration the tragedies of the one, and their parody by the other, represented on the same stage; they allowed every variety of talent to flourish undisturbed in the enjoyment of equal rights. Never did a sovereign, for such was the Athenian people, listen more good-humouredly to the most unwelcome truths, and even allow itself to be openly laughed at. And even if the abuses in the public administration were not by these means corrected, still it was a grand point that this unsparing exposure of them was tolerated. Besides, Aristophanes always shows himself a zealous patriot; the powerful demagogues whom he attacks are the same persons that the grave Thucydides describes as so pernicious. In the midst of civil war, which destroyed for ever the prosperity of Greece, he was ever counselling peace, and everywhere recommended the simplicity and austerity of the ancient manners. So much for the political import of the Old Comedy.

But Aristophanes, I hear it said, was an immoral buffoon. Yes, among other things, he was that also; and we are by no means disposed to justify the man who, with such great talents, could yet sink so very low, whether it was to gratify his own coarse propensities, or from a supposed necessity of winning the favour of the populace, that he might be able to tell them bold and unpleasant truths. We know at least that he boasts of having been much more sparing than his rivals in the use of obscene jests, to gain the laughter of the mob, and of having, in this respect, carried his art to perfection. Not to be unjust towards him, we must judge of all that appears so repulsive to us, not by modern ideas, but by the opinions of his own age and nation. On certain subjects the morals of the ancients were very different from ours, and of a much freer character. This arose from the very nature of their religion, which was a real worship of Nature, and had sanctioned many public customs grossly injurious to decency. Besides, from the very retired manner in which the women lived, [Footnote: This brings us to the consideration of the question so much agitated by antiquaries, whether the Grecian women were present at the representation of plays in general, and more especially of comedies. With respect to tragedy, I think the question must be answered in the affirmative, since the story about the *Eumenides* of Aeschylus could not have been invented with any degree of propriety, had women never visited the theatre. Moreover, there is a passage in Plato (*De Leg.*, lib. ii. p. 658, D.), in which he mentions the predilection educated women evince for tragical composition. Lastly, Julius Pollux, among the technical expressions belonging to the theatre, mentions the Greek word for a *spectatress*. But in the case of the old comedy, I should be inclined to think that they were not present. However, its indecency alone does not appear to be a decisive proof. Even in the religious festivals the eyes of the women must have been exposed to sights of gross indecency. But in the numerous addresses of Aristophanes to the spectators, even where he distinguishes them according to their respective ages and otherwise, we never observe any mention of spectatresses, and the poet would hardly have omitted the opportunity which this afforded him for some witticism or joke. The only passage with which I am acquainted, whence any conclusion may be drawn in favour of the presence of women, is *Pax*, v. 963-967. But still it remains doubtful, and I recommend it to the consideration of the critic.--AUTHOR.], while the men were almost constantly together, the language of conversation contracted a certain coarseness, as is always the case under similar circumstances. In modern Europe, since the origin of chivalry, women have given the tone to social life, and to the respectful homage which we yield to them, we owe the prevalence of a nobler morality in conversation, in the fine arts, and in poetry. Besides, the ancient comic writers, who took the world as they found it, had before their eyes a very great degree of corruption of morals.

The most honourable testimony in favour of Aristophanes is that of the sage Plato, who in an epigram says, that the Graces chose his soul for their abode, who was constantly reading him, and transmitted the *Clouds*, (this very play, in which, with the meshes of the sophists, philosophy itself, and even his master Socrates, was attacked), to Dionysius the elder, with the remark, that from it he would be best able to understand the state of things at Athens. He could hardly mean merely that the play was a proof of the unbridled democratic freedom which prevailed in Athens; but must have intended it as an acknowledgment of the poet's profound knowledge of the world, and his insight into the whole machinery of the civil constitution. Plato has also admirably characterised him in his *Symposium*, where he puts into his mouth a speech on love, which Aristophanes, far from every thing like high enthusiasm, considers merely in a sensual view. His description of it is, however, equally bold and ingenious.

We might apply to the pieces of Aristophanes the motto of a pleasant and acute adventurer in Goethe: "Mad, but clever." In them we are best enabled to conceive why the Dramatic Art in general was consecrated to Bacchus: it is the intoxication of poetry, the Bacchanalia of fun. This faculty will at times assert its rights as well as others; and hence several nations have set apart certain festivals, such as Saturnalia, Carnivals, &c., in which the people may give themselves altogether up to frolicsome follies, that when once the fit is over, they may for the rest of the year remain quiet, and apply themselves to serious business. The Old Comedy is a general masquerade of the world, during which much passes that is not authorised by the ordinary rules of propriety; but during which much also that is diverting, witty, and even instructive, is manifested, which would never be heard of without this momentary breaking up of the barricades of precision.

However vulgar and even corrupt Aristophanes may have been in his own personal propensities, and however offensive his jokes are to good manners and good taste, we cannot deny to him, both in the general plan and execution of his poems, the praise of carefulness, and the masterly skill of a finished artist. His language is extremely polished, the purest Atticism reigns in it throughout, and with the greatest dexterity he adapts it to every tone, from the most familiar dialogue up to the high elevation of the Dithyrambic ode. We cannot doubt that he would have been eminently successful in grave poetry, when we see how at times with capricious wantonness he lavishes it only to destroy at the next moment the impression he has made. The elegant choice of the language becomes only the more attractive from the contrast in which it is occasionally displayed by him; for he not only indulges at times in the rudest expressions of the people, the different dialects, and even in the broken Greek of barbarians, but he extends the same arbitrary power which he exercised over nature and human affairs, to language itself, and by composition, allusion to names of persons, or imitation of particular sounds, coins the strangest words imaginable. The structure of his versification is not less artificial than that of the tragedians; he uses the same forms, but differently modified: his object is ease and variety, instead of gravity and dignity; but amidst all this apparent irregularity, he still adheres with great accuracy to the laws of metrical composition. As Aristophanes, in the exercise of his separate but infinitely varied and versatile art, appears to me to have displayed the richest development of almost every poetical talent, so also whenever I read his works I am no less astonished at the extraordinary capacity of his hearers, which the very nature of them presupposes. We might, indeed, expect from the citizens of a popular government an intimate acquaintance with the history and constitution of their country, with public events and transactions, with the personal circumstance of all their contemporaries of any note or consequence. But besides all this, Aristophanes required of his auditory a cultivated poetical taste; to understand his parodies, they must have almost every word of the tragical master-pieces by heart. And what quickness of perception was requisite to catch, in passing the lightest and most covert irony, the most unexpected sallies and strangest allusions, which are frequently denoted by the mere twisting of a syllable! We may boldly affirm, that notwithstanding all the explanations which have come down to us--notwithstanding the accumulation of learning which has been spent upon it, one-half of the wit of Aristophanes is altogether lost to the moderns. Nothing but the incredible acuteness and vivacity of the Athenian intellect could make it conceivable that these comedies which, with all their farcical drolleries, do, nevertheless, all the while bear upon the most grave interests of human life, could ever have formed a source of popular amusement. We may envy the poet who could reckon on so clever and accomplished a public; but this was in truth a very dangerous advantage. Spectators whose understandings were so quick, would not be easily pleased. Thus Aristophanes complains of the too fastidious taste of the Athenians, with whom the most admired of his predecessors were immediately out of favour as soon as the slightest trace of a falling off in their mental powers was perceivable. On the other hand, he allows that the other Greeks could not bear the slightest comparison with them in a knowledge of the Dramatic Art. Even genius in this department strove to excel at Athens, and here, too, the competition was confined within the narrow period of a few festivals, during which the people always expected to see something new, of which there was always a plentiful supply. The prizes (on which all depended, there being no other means of gaining publicity) were distributed after a single representation. We may easily imagine, therefore, the state of perfection to which this would be carried under the directing care of the poet. If we also take into consideration the high state of the co-operating arts, the utmost distinctness of delivery (both in speaking and singing,) of the most finished poetry, as well as the magnificence and vast size of the theatre, we shall then have some idea of a theatrical treat, the like of which has never since been offered to the world.

Although, among the remaining works of Aristophanes, we have several of his earliest pieces, they all bear the stamp of equal maturity. He had, in fact, been long labouring in silence to perfect himself in the exercise of an art which he conceived to be of all others the most difficult; nay, from diffidence in his own power, (or, to use his own words, like a young girl who consigns to the care of others the child of her secret love,) he even brought out his earliest pieces under others' names. He appeared for the first time without this disguise with the *Knights*, and here he displayed the undaunted resolution of a comedian, by an open assault on popular opinion. His object was nothing less than the overthrow of Cleon, who, after the death of Pericles, was at the head of all state affairs, a promoter of war, and a worthless man of very ordinary abilities, but at the same time the idol of an infatuated people. The only opponents of Cleon were the rich proprietors, who constituted the class of horsemen or knights: these Aristophanes in the strongest manner made of his party, by forming the chorus of them. He had the prudence never to name Cleon, though he portrayed him in such a way that it was impossible to mistake him. Yet such was the dread entertained of Cleon and his faction, that no mask-maker would venture to execute his likeness: the poet, therefore, resolved to act the part himself, merely painting his face. We may easily imagine the storms and tumults which this representation must have excited among the assembled crowd; however, the bold and well-concerted efforts of the poet were crowned with success: his piece gained the prize. He was proud of this feat of theatrical heroism, and often alludes with a feeling of satisfaction to the Herculean valour with which he first combated the mighty monster. No one of his plays, perhaps, is more historical and political; and its rhetorical power in exciting our indignation is almost irresistible: it is a true dramatic Philippic. However, in point of amusement and invention, it does not appear to me the most fortunate. The thought of the serious danger which he was incurring may possibly have disposed him to a more serious tone than was suitable to comedy, or stung, perhaps, by the persecution he had already suffered from Cleon, he may, perhaps, have vented his rage in too Archilochean a style. When the storm of cutting invective has somewhat spent itself, we have then several droll scenes, such us that where the two demagogues, the leather-dealer (that is, Cleon) and the sausage-seller, vie with each other by adulation, by oracle-quoting, and by dainty tit-bits, to gain the favour of Demos, a personification of the people, who has become childish through age, a scene humorous in the highest degree; and the piece ends with a triumphal rejoicing, which may almost be said to be affecting, when the scene changes from the Pnyx, the place where the people assembled, to the majestic Propylaea, when Demos, who has been wonderfully restored to a second youth, comes forward in the garb of an ancient Athenian, and shows that with his youthful vigour, he has also recovered the olden sentiments of the days of Marathon.

With the exception of this attack on Cleon, and with the exception also of the attacks on Euripides, whom he seems to have pursued with the most unrelenting perseverance, the other pieces of Aristophanes are not so exclusively pointed against individuals. They have always a general, and for the most part a very important aim, which the poet, with all his turnings, digressions, and odd medleys, never loses sight of. The *Peace*, the *Acharnae*, and the *Lysistrata*, with many turns, still all recommend peace; and one object of the *Ecclesiazusae*, or *Women in Parliament,*, of the *Thesmophoriazusae, or Women keeping the Festival of the Thesmophoriae*, and of *Lysistrata*, is to throw ridicule on the relations and the manners of the female sex. In the *Clouds* he laughs at the metaphysics of the Sophists, in the *Wasps* at the mania of the Athenians for hearing and determining law-suits; the subject of the *Frogs* is the decline of the tragic art, and *Plutus* is an allegory on the unjust distribution of wealth. The *Birds* are, of all his pieces, the one of which the aim is the least apparent, and it is on that very account one of the most diverting.

Peace begins in the most spirited and lively manner; the peace-loving Trygaeus rides on a dung-beetle to heaven in the manner of Bellerophon; War, a desolating giant, with his comrade Riot, alone, in place of all the other gods, inhabits Olympus, and there pounds the cities of men in a great mortar, making use of the most celebrated generals for pestles. The Goddess Peace lies buried in a deep well, out of which she is hauled up by ropes, through the united exertions of all the states of Greece: all these ingenious and fanciful inventions are calculated to produce the most ludicrous effect. Afterwards, however, the play is not sustained at an equal elevation; nothing remains but to sacrifice, and to carouse in honour of the recovered Goddess of Peace, when the importunate visits of such persons as found their advantage in war form, indeed, an entertainment pleasant enough, but by no means correspondent to the expectations which the commencement gives rise to. We have, in this piece, an additional example to prove that the ancient comic writers not only changed the decoration during the intervals, when the stage was empty, but also while an actor was in sight. The scene changes from Attica to Olympus, while Trygaeus is suspended in the air on his beetle, and calls anxiously to the director of the machinery to take care that he does not break his neck. His descent into the orchestra afterwards denotes his return to the earth. It was possible to overlook the liberties taken by the tragedians, according as their subject might require it, with the Unities of Place and Time, on which such ridiculous stress has been laid by many of the moderns, but the bold manner in which the old comic writer subjects these mere externalities to his sportive caprice is so striking, that it must enforce itself on the most short-sighted observers: and yet in all the treatises on the constitution of the Greek stage, due respect has never yet been paid to it.

The *Acharnians*, an earlier piece, [Footnote: The Didascaliae place it in the year before the *Knights*. It is therefore, the earliest of the extant pieces of Aristophanes, and the only one of those which he brought out under a borrowed name, that has come down to us.] appears to me to possess a much higher excellence than *Peace*, on account of the continual progress of the story, and the increasing drollery, which at last ends in a downright Bacchanalian uproar. Dikaiopolis, the honest citizen, enraged at the base artifices by which the people are deluded, and by which they are induced to reject all proposals for peace, sends an embassy to Lacedaemon, and concludes a separate treaty for himself and his family. He then retires to the country, and, in spite of all assaults, encloses a piece of ground before his house, within which there is a peaceful market for the people of the neighbouring states, while the rest of the country is suffering from the calamities of war. The blessings of peace are represented most temptingly to hungry stomachs: the fat Boeotian brings his delicious eels and poultry for sale, and nothing is thought of but feasting and carousing. Lamachus, the celebrated general, who lives on the other side, is, in consequence of a sudden inroad of the enemy, called away to defend the frontiers; Dikaiopolis, on the other hand, is invited by his neighbours to a feast, where every one brings his own scot. Preparations military and preparations culinary are now carried on with equal industry and alacrity; here they seize the lance, there the spit; here the armour rings, there the wine-flagon; there they are feathering helmets, here they are plucking thrushes. Shortly afterwards Lamachus returns, supported by two of his comrades, with a broken head and a lame foot, and from the other side Dikaiopolis is brought in drunk, and led by two good-natured damsels. The lamentations of the one are perpetually mimicked and ridiculed in the rejoicings of the other; and with this contrast, which is carried to the very utmost limit, the play ends.

Lysistrata is in such bad repute, that we must mention it lightly and rapidly, just as we would tread over hot embers. According to the story of the poet, the women have taken it into their heads to compel their husbands, by a severe resolution, to make peace. Under the direction of a clever leader they organize a conspiracy for this purpose throughout all Greece, and at the same time gain possession in Athens of the fortified Acropolis. The terrible plight the men are reduced to by this separation gives rise to the most laughable scenes; plenipotentiaries appear from the two hostile powers, and peace is speedily concluded under the management of the sage Lysistrata. Notwithstanding the mad indecencies which are contained in the piece, its purpose, when stript of these, is upon the whole very innocent: the longing for the enjoyment of domestic joys, so often interrupted by the absence of the husbands, is to be the means of putting an end to the calamitous war by which Greece had so long been torn in pieces. In particular, the honest bluntness of the Lacedaemonians is inimitably portrayed.

The *Ecclesiazusae* is in like manner a picture of woman's ascendency, but one much more depraved than the former. In the dress of men the women steal into the public assembly, and by means of the majority of voices which they have thus surreptitiously obtained, they decree a new constitution, in which there is to be a community of goods and of women. This is a satire on the ideal republics of the philosophers, with similar laws; Protagoras had projected such before Plato. The comedy appears to me to labour under the very same fault as the *Peace*: the introduction, the secret assembly of the women, their rehearsal of their parts as men, the description of the popular assembly, are all handled in the most masterly manner; but towards the middle the action stands still. Nothing remains but the representation of the perplexities and confusion which arise from the different communities, especially the community of women, and from the prescribed equality of rights in love both for the old and ugly, and for the young and beautiful. These perplexities are pleasant enough, but they turn too much on a repetition of the same joke. Generally speaking, the old allegorical comedy is in its progress exposed to the danger of sinking. When we begin with turning the world upside down, the most wonderful incidents follow one another as a matter of course, but they are apt to appear petty and insignificant when compared with the decisive strokes of fun in the commencement.

The *Thesmophoriazusae* has a proper intrigue, a knot which is not loosed till the conclusion, and in this possesses therefore a great advantage. Euripides, on account of the well-known hatred of women displayed in his tragedies, is accused and condemned at the festival of the Thesmophoriae, at which women only were admitted. After a fruitless attempt to induce the effeminate poet Agathon to undertake the hazardous experiment, Euripides prevails on his brother-in-law, Mnesilochus, who was somewhat advanced in years, to disguise himself as a woman, that under this assumed appearance he may plead his cause. The manner in which he does this gives rise to suspicions, and he is discovered to be a man; he flies to the altar for refuge, and to secure himself still more from the impending danger, he snatches a child from the arms of one of the women, and threatens to kill it if they do not let him alone. As he attempts to strangle it, it turns out to be a leather wine-flask wrapped up like a child. Euripides now appears in a number of different shapes to save his friend: at one time he is Menelaus, who finds Helen again in Egypt; at another time he is Echo, helping the chained Andromeda to pour out her lamentations, and immediately after he appears as Perseus, about to release her from the rock. At length he succeeds in rescuing Mnesilochus, who is fastened to a sort of pillory, by assuming the character of a procuress, and enticing away the officer of justice who has charge of him, a simple barbarian, by the charms of a female flute-player. These parodied scenes, composed almost entirely in the very words of the tragedies, are inimitable. Whenever Euripides is introduced, we may always, generally speaking, lay our account with having the most ingenious and apposite ridicule; it seems as if the mind of Aristophanes possessed a peculiar and specific power of giving a comic turn to the poetry of this tragedian.

The *Clouds* is well known, but yet, for the most part, has not been duly understood or appreciated. Its object is to show that the fondness for philosophical subtleties had led to a neglect of warlike exercises, that speculation only served to shake the foundations of religion and morals, and that by the arts of sophistry, every duty was rendered doubtful, and the worse cause frequently came off victorious. The Clouds themselves, as the chorus of the piece (for the poet converts these substances into persons, and dresses them out strangely enough), are an allegory on the metaphysical speculations which do not rest on the ground of experience, but float about without any definite shape or body, in the region of possibilities. We may observe in general that it is one of the peculiarities of the wit of Aristophanes to take a metaphor literally, and to exhibit it in this light before the eyes of the spectators. Of a man addicted to unintelligible reveries, it is a common way of speaking to say that he is up in the clouds, and accordingly Socrates makes his first appearance actually descending from the air in a basket. Whether this applies exactly to him is another question; but we have reason to believe that the philosophy of Socrates was very ideal, and that it was by no means so limited to popular and practical matters as Xenophon would have us believe. But why has Aristophanes personified the sophistical metaphysics by the venerable Socrates, who was himself a determined opponent of the Sophists? There was probably some personal grudge at the bottom of this, and we do not attempt to justify it; but the choice of the name by no means diminishes the merit of the picture itself. Aristophanes declares this play to be the most elaborate of all his works: but in such expressions we are not always to take him exactly at his word. On all occasions, and without the least hesitation, he lavishes upon himself the most extravagant praises; and this must be considered a feature of the licence of comedy. However, the *Clouds* was unfavourably received, and twice unsuccessfully competed for the prize.

The *Frogs*, as we have already said, has for its subject the decline of Tragic Art. Euripides was dead, as well as Sophocles and Agathon, and none but poets of the second rank were now remaining. Bacchus misses Euripides, and determines to bring him back from the infernal world. In this he imitates Hercules, but although furnished with that hero's lion-skin and club, in sentiments he is very unlike him, and as a dastardly voluptuary affords us much matter for laughter. Here we have a characteristic specimen of the audacity of Aristophanes: he does not even spare the patron of his own art, in whose honour this very play was exhibited. It was thought that the gods understood a joke as well, if not better, than men. Bacchus rows himself over the Acherusian lake, where the frogs merrily greet him with their melodious croakings. The proper chorus, however, consists of the shades of those initiated in the Eleusinian mysteries, and odes of surpassing beauty are put in their mouths. Aeschylus had hitherto occupied the tragic throne in the world below, but

Euripides wants to eject him. Pluto presides, but appoints Bacchus to determine this great controversy; the two poets, the sublimely wrathful Aeschylus, and the subtle and conceited Euripides, stand opposite each other and deliver specimens of their poetical powers; they sing, they declaim against each other, and in all their peculiar traits are characterised in masterly style. At last a balance is brought, on which each lays a verse; but notwithstanding all the efforts of Euripides to produce ponderous lines, those of Aeschylus always make the scale of his rival to kick the beam. At last the latter becomes impatient of the contest, and proposes that Euripides himself, with all his works, his wife, children, Cephisophon and all, shall get into one scale, and he will only lay against them in the other two verses. Bacchus in the mean time has become a convert to the merits of Aeschylus, and although he had sworn to Euripides that he would take him back with him from the lower world, he dismisses him with a parody of one of his own verses in *Hippolytus*:

My tongue hath sworn, I however make choice of Aeschylus.

Aeschylus consequently returns to the living world, and resigns the tragic throne in his absence to Sophocles.

The observation on the changes of place, which I made when mentioning *Peace*, may be here repeated. The scene is first at Thebes, of which both Bacchus and Hercules were natives; afterwards the stage is changed, without its ever being left by Bacchus, to the nether shore of the Acherusian lake, which must have been represented by the sunken space of the orchestra, and it was not till Bacchus landed at the other end of the logeum that the scenery represented the infernal world, with the palace of Pluto in the back-ground. This is not a mere conjecture, it is expressly stated by the old scholiast.

The *Wasps* is, in my opinion, the feeblest of Aristophanes' plays. The subject is too limited, the folly it ridicules appears a disease of too singular a description, without a sufficient universality of application, and the action is too much drawn out. The poet himself speaks this time in very modest language of his means of entertainment, and does not even promise us immoderate laughter.

On the other hand, the *Birds* transports us by one of the boldest and richest inventions into the kingdom of the fantastically wonderful, and delights us with a display of the gayest hilarity: it is a joyous-winged and gay-plumed creation. I cannot concur with the old critic in thinking that we have in this work a universal and undisguised satire on the corruptions of the Athenian state, and of all human society. It seems rather a harmless display of merry pranks, which hit alike at gods and men without any particular object in view. Whatever was remarkable about birds in natural history, in mythology, in the doctrine of divination, in the fables of Aesop, or even in proverbial expressions, has been ingeniously drawn to his purpose by the poet; who even goes back to cosmogony, and shows that at first the raven-winged Night laid a wind-egg, out of which the lovely Eros, with golden pinions (without doubt a bird), soared aloft, and thereupon gave birth to all things. Two fugitives of the human race fall into the domain of the birds, who resolve to revenge themselves on them for the numerous cruelties which they have suffered: the two men contrive to save themselves by proving the pre-eminency of the birds over all other creatures, and they advise them to collect all their scattered powers into one immense state; the wondrous city, Cloud-cuckootown, is then built above the earth; all sorts of unbidden guests, priests, poets, soothsayers, geometers, lawyers, sycophants, wish to nestle in the new state, but are driven out; new gods are appointed, naturally enough, after the image of the birds, as those of men bore a resemblance to man. Olympus is walled up against the old gods, so that no odour of sacrifices can reach them; in their emergency, they send an embassy, consisting of the voracious Hercules, Neptune, who swears according to the common formula, by Neptune, and a Thracian god, who is not very familiar with Greek, but speaks a sort of mixed jargon; they are, however, under the necessity of submitting to any conditions they can get, and the sovereignty of the world is left to the birds. However much all this resembles a mere farcical fairy tale, it may be said, however, to have a philosophical signification, in thus taking a sort of bird's-eye view of all things, seeing that most of our ideas are only true in a human point of view.

The old critics were of opinion that Cratinus was powerful in that biting satire which makes its attack without disguise, but that he was deficient in a pleasant humour, also that he wanted the skill to develope a striking subject to the best advantage, and to fill up his pieces with the necessary details. Eupolis they tell us was agreeable in his jokes, and ingenious in covert allusions, so that he never needed the assistance of parabases to say whatever he wished, but that he was deficient in satiric power. But Aristophanes, they add, by a happy medium, united the excellencies of both, and that in him we have satire and pleasantry combined in due proportion and attractive manner. From these statements I conceive myself justified in assuming that among the pieces of Aristophanes, the *Knights* is the most in the style of Cratinus, and the *Birds* in that of Eupolis; and that he had their respective manners in view when he composed these pieces. For although he boasts of his independent originality, and of his never borrowing anything from others, it was hardly possible that among such distinguished contemporary artists, all reciprocal influence should be excluded. If this opinion be well founded, we have to lament the loss of the works of Cratinus, perhaps principally on account of the light they would have thrown on the manners of the times, and the knowledge they might have afforded of the Athenian constitution, while the loss of the works of Eupolis is to be regretted, chiefly for the comic form in which they were delivered.

Plutus was one of the earlier pieces of the poet, but as we have it, it is one of his last works; for the first piece was afterwards recast by him. In its essence it belongs to the Old Comedy, but in the sparingness of personal satire, and in the mild tone which prevails throughout, we may trace an approximation to the Middle Comedy. The Old Comedy indeed had not yet received its death-blow from a formal enactment, but even at this date Aristophanes may have deemed it prudent to avoid a full exercise of the democratic privilege of comedy. It has even been said (perhaps without any foundation, as the circumstance has been denied by others) that Alcibiades ordered Eupolis to be drowned on account of a piece which he had aimed at him. Dangers of this description would repress the most ardent zeal of authorship: it is but fair that those who seek to afford pleasure to their fellow-citizens should at least be secure of their life.

APPENDIX TO THE TWELFTH LECTURE.

As we do not, so far as I know, possess as yet a satisfactory poetical translation of Aristophanes, and as the whole works of this author must, for many reasons, ever remain untranslatable, I have been induced to lay before my readers the scene in the *Acharnians* where Euripides makes his appearance; not that this play does not contain many other scenes of equal, if not superior merit, but because it relates to the character of this tragedian as an artist, and is both free from indecency, and, moreover, easily understood.

The Acharnians, country-people of Attica, who have greatly suffered from the enemy, are highly enraged at Dikaiopolis for concluding a peace with the Lacedaemonians, and determine to stone him. He undertakes to speak in defence of the Lacedaemonians, standing the while behind a block, as he is to lose his head if he does not succeed in convincing them. In this ticklish predicament, he calls on Euripides, to lend him the tattered garments in which that poet's heroes were in the habit of exciting commiseration. We must suppose the house of the tragic poet to occupy the middle of the back scene.

DIKAIOPOLIS.
'Tis time I pluck up all my courage then,
And pay a visit to Euripides.
Boy, boy!

CEPHISOPHON.
Who's there?

DIKAIOPOLIS.
Is Euripides within?

CEPHISOPHON.
Within, and not within: Can'st fathom that?

DIKAIOPOLIS.
How within, yet not within?

CEPHISOPHON.
'Tis true, old fellow.
His mind is out collecting dainty verses, [1]
And not within. But he's himself aloft
Writing a tragedy.

DIKAIOPOLIS.
Happy Euripides,
Whose servant here can give such witty answers.
Call him.

CEPHISOPHON.
It may not be.

DIKAIOPOLIS.
I say, you must though--
For hence I will not budge, but knock the door down.
Euripides, Euripides, my darling! [2]
Hear me, at least, if deaf to all besides.
'Tis Dikaiopolis of Chollis calls you.

EURIPIDES.
I have not time.

DIKAIOPOLIS.
At least roll round. [3]

EURIPIDES.
I can't. [4]

DIKAIOPOLIS.
You must.

EURIPIDES.
Well, I'll roll round. Come down I can't; I'm busy.

DIKAIOPOLIS.
Euripides!

EURIPIDES.
What would'st thou with thy bawling.

DIKAIOPOLIS
What! you compose aloft and not below.
No wonder if your muse's bantlings halt.
Again, those rags and cloak right tragical,
The very garb for sketching beggars in!
But sweet Euripides, a boon, I pray thee.
Give me the moving rags of some old play;
I've a long speech to make before the Chorus,
And if I falter, why the forfeit's death.

EURIPIDES.
What rags will suit you? Those in which old Oeneus,
That hapless wight, went through his bitter conflict?

DIKAIOPOLIS.
Not Oeneus, no,--but one still sorrier.

EURIPIDES.
Those of blind Phoenix?

DIKAIOPOLIS.
No, not Phoenix either;
But another, more wretched still than Phoenix

EURIPIDES.
Whose sorry tatters can the fellow want?
'Tis Philoctetes' sure! You mean that beggar.

DIKAIOPOLIS.
No; but a person still more beggarly.

EURIPIDES.
I have it. You want the sorry garments
Bellerophon, the lame man, used to wear.

DIKAIOPOLIS.
No,--not Bellerophon. Though the man I mean
Was lame, importunate, and bold of speech.

EURIPIDES.
I know, 'Tis Telephus the Mysian.

DIKAIOPOLIS.
Right.
Yes, Telephus: lend me his rags I pray you.

EURIPIDES.
Ho, boy! Give him the rags of Telephus.
There lie they; just upon Thyestes' rags,
And under those of Ino.

CEPHISOPHON.
Here! take them.

DIKAIOPOLIS (*putting them on*).
Now Jove! who lookest on, and see'st through all, [5]
Your blessing, while thus wretchedly I garb me.
Pr'ythee, Euripides, a further boon,
It goes, I think, together with these rags:
The little Mysian bonnet for my head;
"For sooth to-day I must put on the beggar,
And be still what I am, and yet not seem so." [6]
The audience here may know me who I am,
But like poor fools the chorus stand unwitting,
While I trick them with my flowers of rhetoric.

EURIPIDES.
A rare device, i'faith! Take it and welcome.

DIKAIOPOLIS.
"For thee. my blessing; for Telephus, my thoughts." [7]
'Tis well; already, words flow thick and fast.
Oh! I had near forgot--A beggar's staff, I pray.

EURIPIDES.
Here, take one, and thyself too from these doors.

DIKAIOPOLIS.
(*Aside.*) See'st thou, my soul,--he'd drive thee from his door
Still lacking many things. Become at once

A supple, oily beggar. (*Aloud.*) Good Euripides,
Lend me a basket, pray;--though the bottom's
Scorch'd, 'twill do.

EURIPIDES.
Poor wretch! A basket? What's thy need on't?

DIKAIOPOLIS.
No need beyond the simple wish to have it.

EURIPIDES.
You're getting troublesome. Come pack--be off.

DIKAIOPOLIS.
(*Aside.*) Faugh! Faugh!
(*Aloud.*) May heaven prosper thee as--thy good mother. [8]

EURIPIDES.
Be off, I say!

DIKAIOPOLIS.
Not till thou grant'st my prayer.
Only a little cup with broken rim.

EURIPIDES.
Take it and go; for know you're quite a plague.

DIKAIOPOLIS.
(*Aside.*) Knows he how great a pest he is himself?
(*Aloud.*) But, my Euripides! my sweet! one thing more:
Give me a cracked pipkin stopped with sponge.

EURIPIDES.
The man would rob me of a tragedy complete.
There--take it, and begone.

DIKAIOPOLIS.
Well! I am going.
Yet what to do? One thing I lack, whose want
Undoes me. Good, sweet Euripides!
Grant me but this, I'll ask no more, but go--
Some cabbage-leaves--a few just in my basket!

EURIPIDES.
You'll ruin me. See there! A whole play's gone!

DIKAIOPOLIS (*seemingly going off*).
Nothing more now. I'm really off. I am, I own,
A bore, wanting in tact to please the great.
Woe's me! Was ever such a wretch? Alas!
I have forgot the very chiefest thing of all.
Hear me, Euripides, my dear! my darling.
Choicest ills betide me! if e'er I ask
Aught more than this; but one--this one alone:
Throw me a pot-herb from thy mother's stock.

EURIPIDES.
The fellow would insult me--shut the door.
(*The Encyclema revolves, and Euripides and Cephisophon retire.*)

DIKAIOPOLIS.
Soul of me, thou must go without a pot-herb!
Wist thou what conflict thou must soon contend in
To proffer speech and full defence for Sparta?
Forward, my soul! the barriers are before thee.
What, dost loiter? hast not imbibed Euripides?
And yet I blame thee not. Courage, sad heart!
And forward, though it be to lay thy head
Upon the block. Rouse thee, and speak thy mind.
Forward there! forward again! bravely heart, bravely.

NOTES

[1] The Greek diminutive *epullia* is here correctly expressed by the German *verschen*, but versicle would not be tolerated in English.--TRANS.

[2] Euripidion--in the German Euripidelein.--TRANS.

[3] A technical expression from the Encyclema, which was thrust out.

[4] Euripides appears in the upper story; but as in an altana, or sitting to an open gallery.

[5] Alluding to the holes in the mantle which he holds up to the light.

[6] These lines are from Euripides' tragedy of *Telephus*.

[7] An allusion (which a few lines lower is again repeated) to his mother as a poor retailer of vegetables.

[8] See previous footnote.

LECTURE XIII.

Whether the Middle Comedy was a distinct species--Origin of the New Comedy--A mixed species--Its prosaic character--Whether versification is essential to Comedy--Subordinate kinds--Pieces of Character, and of Intrigue--The Comic of observation, of self-consciousness, and arbitrary Comic--Morality of Comedy--Plautus and Terence as imitators of the Greeks here cited and characterised for want of the Originals--Moral and social aim of the Attic Comedy--Statues of two Comic Authors.

Ancient critics assume the existence of a *Middle Comedy*, between the *Old* and the *New*. Its distinguishing characteristics are variously described: by some its peculiarity is made to consist in the abstinence from personal satire and introduction of real characters, and by others in the abolition of the chorus. But the introduction of real persons under their true names was never an indispensable requisite. Indeed, in several, even of Aristophanes' plays, we find characters in no respect historical, but altogether fictitious, but bearing significant names, after the manner of the New Comedy; while personal satire is only occasionally employed. This right of personal satire was no doubt, as I have already shown, essential to the Old Comedy, and the loss of it incapacitated the poets from throwing ridicule on public actions and affairs of state. When accordingly they confined themselves to private life, the chorus ceased at once to have any significance. However, accidental circumstances accelerated its abolition. To dress and train the choristers was an expensive undertaking; now, as Comedy with the forfeiture of its political privileges lost also its festal dignity, and was degraded into a mere amusement, the poet no longer found any rich patrons willing to take upon themselves the expense of furnishing the chorus.

Platonius mentions a further characteristic of the Middle Comedy. On account, he says, of the danger of alluding to public affairs, the comic writers had turned all their satire against serious poetry, whether epic or tragic, and sought to expose its absurdities and contradictions. As a specimen of this kind he gives the *Aeolosikon*, one of Aristophanes' latest works. This description coincides with the idea of parody, which we placed foremost in our account of the Old Comedy. Platonius adduces also another instance in the *Ulysses* of Cratinus, a burlesque of the *Odyssey*. But, in order of time, no play of Cratinus could belong to the Middle Comedy; for his death is mentioned by Aristophanes in his *Peace*. And as to the drama of Eupolis, in which he described what we call an Utopia, or Lubberly Land, what else was it but a parody of the poetical legends of the golden age? But in Aristophanes, not to mention his parodies of so many tragic scenes, are not the Heaven-journey of Trygaeus, and the Hell-journey of Bacchus, ludicrous imitations of the deeds of Bellerophon and Hercules, sung in epic and tragic poetry? In vain therefore should we seek in this restriction to parody any distinctive peculiarity of the so-called Middle Comedy. Frolicsome caprice, and allegorical significance of composition are, poetically considered, the only essential criteria of the Old Comedy. In this class, therefore, we shall rank every work where we find these qualities, in whatever times, and under whatever circumstances, it may have been composed.

As the New Comedy arose out of a mere negation, the abolition, viz., of the old political freedom, we may easily conceive that there would be an interval of fluctuating, and tentative efforts to supply its place, before a new comic form could be developed and fully established. Hence there may have been many kinds of the Middle Comedy, many intermediate gradations, between the Old and the New; and this is the opinion of some men of learning. And, indeed, historically considered, there appears good grounds for such a view; but in an artistic point of view, a transition does not itself constitute a species.

We proceed therefore at once to the New Comedy, or that species of poetry which with us receives the appellation of Comedy. We shall, I think, form a more correct notion of it, if we consider it in its historical connexion, and from a regard to its various ingredients explain it to be a mixed and modified species, than we should were we to term it an original and pure species, as those do who either do not concern themselves at all with the Old Comedy, or else regard it as nothing better than a mere rude commencement. Hence, the infinite importance of Aristophanes, as we have in him a kind of poetry of which there is no other example to be found in the world.

The New Comedy may, in certain respects, be described as the Old, tamed down; but in productions of genius, tameness is not generally considered a merit. The loss incurred by the prohibition of an unrestricted freedom of satire the new comic writers endeavoured to compensate by a mixture of earnestness borrowed from tragedy, both in the form of representation and the general structure, and also in the impressions which they laboured to produce. We have seen how, in its last epoch, tragic poetry descended from its ideal elevation, and came nearer to common reality, both in the characters and in the tone of the dialogue, but more especially in its endeavour to convey practical instruction respecting the conduct of civil and domestic life in all their several requirements. This utilitarian turn in Euripides was the subject of Aristophanes' ironical commendation

[Footnote: The *Frogs*, v. 971-991.]. Euripides was the precursor of the New Comedy; and all the poets of this species particularly admired him, and acknowledged him as their master.--The similarity of tone and spirit is even so great between them, that moral maxims of Euripides have been ascribed to Menander, and others of Menander to Euripides. On the other hand, among the fragments of Menander, we find topics of consolation which frequently rise to the height of the true tragic tone.

New Comedy, therefore, is a mixture of earnestness and mirth. [Footnote: The original here is not susceptible of an exact translation into English. Though the German language has this great advantage, that there are few ideas which may not be expressed in it in words of Teutonic origin, yet words derived from Greek and Latin are also occasionally used indiscriminately with the Teutonic synonymes, for the sake of variety or otherwise. Thus the generic word *spiel* (play), is formed into *lustspiel* (comedy), *trauerspiel* (tragedy), *sing-spiel* (opera), *schauspiel* (drama); but the Germans also use *tragoedie, komoedie,* opera and drama. In the text, the author proposes, for the sake of distinction, to give the name of *lustspiel* to the New Comedy, to distinguish it from the old; but having only the single term comedy in English, I must, in translating *lustspiel*, make use of the two words, *New Comedy*.--TRANS.] The poet no longer turns poetry and the world into ridicule, he no longer abandons himself to an enthusiasm of fun, but seeks the sportive element in the objects themselves; he depicts in human characters and situations whatever occasions mirth, in a word, what is pleasant and laughable. But the ridiculous must no longer come forward as the pure creation of his own fancy, but must be verisimilar, that is, seem to be real. Hence we must consider anew the above described *comic ideal* of human nature under the restrictions which this law of composition imposes, and determine accordingly the different kinds and gradations of the Comic.

The highest tragic earnestness, as I have already shown, runs ever into the infinite; and the subject of Tragedy (properly speaking) is the struggle between the outward finite existence, and the inward infinite aspirations. The subdued earnestness of the New Comedy, on the other hand, remains always within the sphere of experience. The place of Destiny is supplied by Chance, for the latter is the empirical conception of the former, as being that which lies beyond our power or control. And accordingly we actually find among the fragments of the Comic writers as many expressions about Chance, as we do in the tragedians about Destiny. To unconditional necessity, moral liberty could alone be opposed; as for Chance, every one must use his wits, and turn it to his own profit as he best can. On this account, the whole moral of the New Comedy, just like that of the Fable, is nothing more than a theory of prudence. In this sense, an ancient critic has, with inimitable brevity, given us the whole sum of the matter: that Tragedy is a running away from, or making an end of, life; Comedy its regulation.

The idea of the Old Comedy is a fantastic illusion, a pleasant dream, which at last, with the exception of the general effect, all ends in nothing. The New Comedy, on the other hand, is earnest in its form. It rejects every thing of a contradictory nature, which might have the effect of destroying the impressions of reality. It endeavours after strict coherence, and has, in common with Tragedy, a formal complication and denouement of plot. Like Tragedy, too, it connects together its incidents, as cause and effect, only that it adopts the law of existence as it manifests itself in experience, without any such reference as Tragedy assumes to an idea. As the latter endeavours to satisfy our feelings at the close, in like manner the New Comedy endeavours to provide, at least, an apparent point of rest for the understanding. This, I may remark in passing, is by no means an easy task for the comic writer: he must contrive at last skilfully and naturally to get rid of the contradictions which with their complication and intricacy have diverted us during the course of the action; if he really smooths them all off by making his fools become rational, or by reforming or punishing his villains, then there is an end at once of everything like a pleasant and comical impression.

Such were the comic and tragic ingredients of the New Comedy, or Comedy in general. There is yet a third, however, which in itself is neither comic nor tragic, in short, not even poetic. I allude to its portrait-like truthfulness. The ideal and caricature, both in the plastic arts and in dramatic poetry, lay claim to no other truth than that which lies in their significance: their individual beings even are not intended to appear real. Tragedy moves in an ideal, and the Old Comedy in a fanciful or fantastical world. As the creative power of the fancy was circumscribed in the New Comedy, it became necessary to afford some equivalent to the understanding, and this was furnished by the probability of the subjects represented, of which it was to be the judge. I do not mean the calculation of the rarity or frequency of the represented incidents (for without the liberty of depicting singularities, even while keeping within the limits of every-day life, comic amusement would be impossible), but all that is here meant is the individual truth of the picture. The New Comedy must be a true picture of the manners of the day, and its tone must be local and national; and even if we should see comedies of other times, and other nations, brought upon the stage, we shall still be able to trace and be pleased with this resemblance. By portrait-like truthfulness I do not mean that the comic characters must be altogether individual. The most striking features of different individuals of a class may be combined together in a certain completeness, provided they are clothed with a sufficient degree of peculiarity to have an individual life, and are not represented as examples of any partial and incomplete conception. But in so far as Comedy depicts the constitution of social and domestic life in general, it is a portrait; from this prosaic side it must be variously modified, according to time and place, while the comic motives, in respect of their poetical principle, are always the same.

The ancients themselves acknowledged the New Comedy to be a faithful picture of life. Full of this idea, the grammarian Aristophanes exclaimed in a somewhat affected, though highly ingenious turn of expression: "O life and Menander! which of you copied the other?" Horace informs us that "some doubted whether Comedy be a poem; because neither in its subject nor in its language is there the same impressive elevation which distinguished from ordinary discourse by the versification." But it was urged by others, that Comedy occasionally elevates her tone; for instance, when an angry father reproaches a son for his extravagance. This answer, however, is rejected by Horace as insufficient. "Would Pomponius," says he, with a sarcastic application, "hear milder reproaches if his father were living?" To answer the doubt, we must examine wherein Comedy goes beyond individual reality. In the first place it is a simulated whole, composed of congruous parts, agreeably to the scale of art. Moreover, the subject represented is handled according to the laws of theatrical exhibition; everything foreign and incongruous is kept out, while all that is essential to the matter in hand is hurried on with swifter progress than in real life; over the whole, viz., the situations and characters, a certain clearness and distinctness of appearance is thrown, which the vague and indeterminate outlines of reality seldom possess. Thus the form constitutes the poetic element of Comedy, while its prosaic principle lies in the matter, in the required assimilation to something individual and external.

We may now fitly proceed to the consideration of the much mooted question, whether versification be essential to Comedy, and whether a comedy written in prose is an imperfect production. This question has been frequently answered in the affirmative on the authority of the ancients, who, it is true, had no theatrical works in prose; this, however, may have arisen from accidental circumstances, for example, the great extent of their stage, in which verse, from its more emphatic delivery, must have been better heard than prose. Moreover, these critics forget that the Mimes of Sophron, so much admired by Plato, were written in prose. And what were these Mimes? If we may judge of them from the statement that some of the Idylls of Theocritus were imitations of them in hexameters, they were pictures of real life, in which every appearance of poetry was studiously avoided. This consists in the coherence and connexion of a drama, which certainly is not found in these pieces; they are merely so many detached scenes, in which one thing succeeds another by chance, and without preparation, as the particular hour of any working-day or holiday brought it about. The want of dramatic interest was supplied by the mimic element, that is, by the most accurate representation of individual peculiarities in action and language, which arose from nationality as modified by local circumstances, and from sex, age, rank, occupations, and so forth.

Even in versified Comedy, the language must, in the choice of words and phrases, differ in no respect, or at least in no perceptible degree, from that of ordinary life; the licences of poetical expression, which are indispensable in other departments of poetry, are here inadmissible. Not only must the versification not interfere with the common, unconstrained, and even careless tone of conversation, but it must also seem to be itself unpremeditated. It must not by its lofty tone elevate the characters as in Tragedy, where, along with the unusual sublimity of the language, it becomes as it were a mental Cothurnus. In Comedy the verse must serve merely to give greater lightness, spirit, and elegance to the dialogue. Whether, therefore, a particular comedy ought to be versified or not, must depend on the consideration whether it would be more suitable to the subject in hand to give to the dialogue this perfection of form, or to adopt into the comic imitation all rhetorical and grammatical errors, and even physical imperfections of speech. The frequent production, however, of prose comedies in modern times has not been owing so much to this cause as to the ease and convenience of the author, and in some degree also of the player. I would, however, recommend to my countrymen, the Germans, the diligent use of verse, and even of rhyme, in Comedy; for as our national Comedy is yet to be formed, the whole composition, by the greater strictness of the form, would gain in keeping and appearance, and we should be enabled at the very outset to guard against many important errors. We have not yet attained such a mastery in this matter as will allow us to abandon ourselves to an agreeable negligence.

As we have pronounced the New Comedy to be a mixed species, formed out of comic and tragic, poetic and prosaic elements, it is evident that this species may comprise several subordinate kinds, according to the preponderance of one or other of the ingredients. If the poet plays in a sportive humour with his own inventions, the result is a farce; if he confines himself to the ludicrous in situations and characters, carefully avoiding all admixture of serious matter, we have a pure comedy (*lustspiel*); in proportion as earnestness prevails in the scope of the whole composition, and in the sympathy and moral judgment it gives rise to, the piece becomes what is called Instructive or Sentimental Comedy; and there is only another step to the familiar or domestic tragedy. Great stress has often been laid on the two last mentioned species as inventions entirely new, and of great importance, and peculiar theories have been devised for them, &c. In the lacrymose drama of Diderot, which was afterwards so much decried, the failure consisted altogether in that which was new; the affectation of nature, the pedantry of the domestic relations, and the lavish use of pathos. Did we still possess the whole of the comic literature of the Greeks, we should, without doubt, find in it the models of all these species, with this difference, however, that the clear head of the Greeks assuredly never allowed them to fall into a chilling monotony, but that they arrayed and tempered all in due proportion. Have not we, even among the few pieces that remain to us, the *Captives* of Plautus, which may be called a pathetic drama, the *Step-Mother* of Terence, a true family picture; while the *Amphitryo* borders on the fantastic boldness of the Old Comedy, and the *Twin-Brothers* (*Menaechmi*) is a wild piece of intrigue? Do we not find in all Terence's plays serious, impassioned, and touching passages? We have only to call to mind the first scene of the *Heautontimorumenos*. From our point of view we hope in short to find a due place for all things. We see here no distinct species, but merely gradations in the tone of the composition, which are marked by transitions more or less perceptible.

Neither can we allow the common division into *Plays of Character* and *Plays of Intrigue*, to pass without limitation. A good comedy ought always to be both, otherwise it will be deficient either in body or animation. Sometimes, however, the one and sometimes the other will, no doubt, preponderate. The development of the comic characters requires situations to place them in strong contrast, and these again can result from nothing but that crossing of purposes and events, which, as I have already shown, constitutes intrigue in the dramatic sense. Every one knows the meaning of intriguing in common life; namely, the leading others by cunning and dissimulation, to further, without their knowledge and against their will, our own hidden designs. In the drama both these significations coincide, for the cunning of the one becomes a cross-purpose for the other.

When the characters are only slightly sketched, so far merely as is necessary to account for the actions of the characters in this or that case; when also the incidents are so accumulated, that little room is left for display of character; when the plot is so wrought up, that the motley tangle of misunderstandings and embarrassments seems every moment on the point of being loosened, and yet the knot is only drawn tighter and tighter: such a composition may well be called a Play of Intrigue. The French critics have made it fashionable to consider this kind of play much below the so-called Play of Character, perhaps because they look too exclusively to how much of a play may be retained by us and carried home. It is true, the Piece of Intrigue, in some degree, ends at last in nothing: but why should it not be occasionally allowable to divert oneself ingeniously, without any ulterior object? Certainly, a good comedy of this description requires much inventive wit: besides the entertainment which we derive from the display of such acuteness and ingenuity, the wonderful tricks and contrivances which are practised possess a great charm for the fancy, as the success of many a Spanish piece proves.

To the Play of Intrigue it is objected, that it deviates from the natural course of things, that it is improbable. We may admit the former without however admitting the latter. The poet, no doubt, exhibits before us what is unexpected, extraordinary, and singular, even to incredibility; and often he even sets out with a great improbability, as, for example, the resemblance between two persons, or a disguise which is not seen through; afterwards, however, all the incidents must have the appearance of truth, and all the circumstances by means of which the affair takes so marvellous a turn, must be satisfactorily explained. As in respect to the events which take place, the poet gives us but a light play of wit, we are the more strict with him respecting the *how* by which they are brought about.

In the comedies which aim more at delineation of character, the dramatic personages must be skilfully grouped so as to throw light on each other's character. This, however, is very apt to degenerate into too systematic a method, each character being regularly matched with its symmetrical opposite, and thereby an unnatural appearance is given to the whole. Nor are those comedies deserving of much praise, in which the rest of the characters are introduced only, as it were, to allow the principal one to go through all his different probations; especially when that character consists of nothing but an opinion, or a habit (for instance, *L'Optimiste*, *Le Distrait*), as if an individual could thus be made up entirely of one single peculiarity, and must not rather be on all sides variously modified and affected.

What was the sportive ideal of human nature in the Old Comedy I have already shown. Now as the New Comedy had to give to its representation a resemblance to a definite reality, it could not indulge in such studied and arbitrary exaggeration as the old did. It was, therefore, obliged to seek for other sources of comic amusement, which lie nearer the province of earnestness, and these it found in a more accurate and thorough delineation of character.

In the characters of the New Comedy, either the *Comic of Observation* or the *Self-Conscious* and *Confessed Comic*, will be found to prevail. The former constitutes the more refined, or what is called High Comedy, and the latter Low Comedy or Farce.

But to explain myself more distinctly: there are laughable peculiarities, follies, and obliquities, of which the possessor himself is unconscious, or which, if he does at all perceive them, he studiously endeavours to conceal, as being calculated to injure him in the opinion of others. Such persons consequently do not give themselves out for what they actually are; their secret escapes from them unwittingly, or against their will. Rightly, therefore, to portray such characters, the poet must lend us his own peculiar talent for observation, that we may fully understand them. His art consists in making the character appear through slight hints and stolen glimpses, and in so placing the spectator, that whatever delicacy of observation it may require, he can hardly fail to see through them.

There are other moral defects, which are beheld by their possessor with a certain degree of satisfaction, and which he even makes it a principle not to get rid of, but to cherish and preserve. Of this kind is all that, without selfish pretensions, or hostile inclinations, merely originates in the preponderance of the animal being. This may, without doubt, be united to a high degree of intellect, and when such a person applies his mental powers to the consideration of his own character, laughs at himself, confesses his failings or endeavours to reconcile others to them, by setting them in a droll light, we have then an instance of the *Self-Conscious* Comic This species always supposes a certain inward duality of character, and the superior half, which rallies and laughs at the other, has in its tone and occupation a near affinity to the comic poet himself. He occasionally delivers over his functions entirely to this representative, allowing him studiously to overcharge the picture which he draws of himself, and to enter into a tacit understanding with the spectators, that he and they are to turn the other characters into ridicule. We have in this way the *Comedy of Caprice*, which generally produces a powerful effect, however much critics may depreciate it. In it the spirit of the Old Comedy is still at work. The privileged merry-maker, who, under different names, has appeared on almost all stages, whose part is at one time a display of shrewd wit, and at another of coarse clownishness, has inherited something of the licentious enthusiasm, but without the rights and privileges of the free and unrestrained writers of the Old Comedy. Could there be a stronger proof that the Old Comedy, which we have described as the original species, was not a mere Grecian peculiarity, but had its root and principle in the very nature of things?

To keep the spectators in a mirthful tone of mind Comedy must hold them as much as possible aloof from all moral appreciation of its personages, and from all deep interest in their fortunes, for in both these cases an entrance will infallibly be given to seriousness. How then does the poet avoid agitating the moral feeling, when the actions he represents are of such a nature as must give rise sometimes to disgust and contempt, and sometimes to esteem and love? By always keeping within the province of the understanding, he contrasts men with men as mere physical beings, just to measure on each other their powers, of course their mental powers as well as others, nay, even more especially. In this respect Comedy bears a very near affinity to Fable: in the Fable we have animals endowed with reason, and in Comedy we have men serving their animal propensities with their understanding. By animal propensities I mean sensuality, or, in a still more general sense, self-love. As heroism and self-sacrifice raise the character to a tragic elevation, so the true comic personages are complete egotists. This must, however, be understood with due limitation: we do not mean that Comedy never portrays the social instincts, only that it invariably represents them as originating in the natural endeavour after our own happiness. Whenever the poet goes beyond this, he leaves the comic tone. It is not his purpose to direct our feelings to a sense of the dignity or meanness, the innocence or corruption, the goodness or baseness of the acting personages; but to show us whether they act stupidly or wisely, adroitly or clumsily, with silliness or ability.

Examples will place the matter in the clearest light. We possess an involuntary and immediate veneration for truth, and this belongs to the innermost emotions of the moral sense. A malignant lie, which threatens mischievous consequences, fills us with the highest indignation, and belongs to Tragedy. Why then are cunning and deceit admitted to be excellent as comic motives, so long as they are used with no malicious purpose, but merely to promote our self-love, to extricate one's-self from a dilemma, or to gain some particular object, and from which no dangerous consequences are to be dreaded? It is because the deceiver having already withdrawn from the sphere of morality, truth and untruth are in themselves indifferent to him, and are only considered in the light of means; and so we entertain ourselves merely with observing how great an expenditure of sharpness and ready-wittedness is necessary to serve the turn of a character so little exalted. Still more amusing is it when the deceiver is caught in his own snare; for instance, when he is to keep up a lie, but has a bad memory. On the other hand, the mistake of the deceived party, when not seriously dangerous, is a comic situation, and the more so in proportion as this error of the understanding arises from previous abuse of the mental powers, from vanity, folly, or obliquity. But above all when deceit and error cross one another, and are by that means multiplied, the comic situations produced are particularly excellent. For instance, two men meet with the intention of deceiving one another; each however is forewarned and on his guard, and so both go away deceived only in respect to the success of their deception. Or again, one wishes to deceive another, but unwittingly tells him the truth; the other person, however, being suspicious, falls into the snare, merely from being over-much, on his guard. We might in this way compose a sort of comic grammar, which should show how the separate motives are to be entangled one with another, with continually increasing effect, up to the most artificial complication. It might also point out how that tangle of misunderstanding which constitutes a Comedy of Intrigue is by no means so contemptible a part of the comic art, as the advocates of the fine-spun Comedy of Character are pleased to assert.

Aristotle describes the laughable as an imperfection, an impropriety which is not productive of any essential harm. Excellently said! for from the moment that we entertain a real compassion for the characters, all mirthful feeling is at an end. Comic misfortune must not go beyond an embarrassment, which is to be set right at last, or at most, a deserved humiliation. Of this description are corporeal means of education applied to grown people, which our finer, or at least more fastidious age, will not tolerate on the stage, although Moliere, Holberg, and other masters, have frequently availed themselves of them. The comic effect arises from our having herein a pretty obvious demonstration of the mind's dependence on external things: we have, as it were, motives assuming a palpable form. In Comedy these chastisements hold the same place that violent deaths, met with heroic magnanimity, do in Tragedy. Here the resolution remains unshaken amid all the terrors of annihilation; the man perishes but his principles survive; there the corporeal existence remains, but the sentiments suffer an instantaneous change.

As then Comedy must place the spectator in a point of view altogether different from that of moral appreciation, with what right can moral instruction be demanded of Comedy, with what ground can it be expected? When we examine more closely the moral apophthegms of the Greek comic writers, we find that they are all of them maxims of experience. It is not, however, from experience that we gain a knowledge of our duties, of which conscience gives us an immediate conviction; experience can only enlighten us with respect to what is profitable or detrimental. The instruction of Comedy does not turn on the dignity of the object proposed but on the sufficiency of the means employed. It is, as has been already said, the doctrine of prudence; the morality of consequences and not of motives. Morality, in its genuine acceptation, is essentially allied to the spirit of Tragedy.

Many philosophers have on this account reproached Comedy with immorality, and among others, Rousseau, with much eloquence, in his *Epistle on the Drama*. The aspect of the actual course of things in the world is, no doubt, far from edifying; it is not, however, held up in Comedy as a model for imitation, but as a warning and admonition. In the doctrine of morals there is an applied or practical part: it may be called the Art of Living. Whoever has no knowledge of the world is perpetually in danger of making a wrong application of moral principles to individual cases, and, so with the very best intentions in the world, may occasion much mischief both to himself and others. Comedy is intended to sharpen our powers of discrimination, both of persons and situations; to make us shrewder; and this is its true and only possible morality.

So much for the determination of the general idea, which must serve as our clue in the examination of the merits of the individual poets.

LECTURE XIV.

Plautus and Terence as Imitators of the Greeks, here examined and characterized in the absence of the Originals they copied--Motives of the Athenian Comedy from Manners and Society--Portrait-Statues of two Comedians.

On the little of the New Comedy of the Greeks that has reached us, either in fragments or through the medium of Roman imitations, all I have to say may be comprised in a few words.

In this department Greek literature was extremely rich: the mere list of the comic writers whose works are lost, and of the names of their works, so far as they are known to us, makes of itself no inconsiderable dictionary. Although the New Comedy developed itself and flourished only in the short interval between the end of the Peloponnesian war and the first successors of Alexander the Great, yet the stock of pieces amounted to thousands; but time has made such havoc in this superabundance of talented and ingenious works, that nothing remains in the original but a number of detached fragments, of which many are so disfigured as to be unintelligible, and, in the Latin, about twenty translations or recasts of Greek originals by Plautus, and six by Terence. Here is a fitting task for the redintegrative labours of criticism, to put together all the fragmentary traces which we possess, in order to form from them something like a just estimate and character of what is lost. The chief requisites in an undertaking of this kind, I will take upon myself to point out. The fragments and moral maxims of the comic writers are, in their versification and language, distinguished by extreme purity, elegance, and accuracy; moreover, the tone of society which speaks in them breathes a certain Attic grace. The Latin comic poets, on the other hand, are negligent in their versification; they trouble themselves very little about syllabic quantity, and the very idea of it is almost lost amidst their many metrical licences. Their language also, at least that of Plautus, is deficient in cultivation and polish. Several learned Romans, and Varro among others, have, it is true, highly praised the style of this poet, but then we must make the due distinction between philological and poetical approbation. Plautus and Terence were among the most ancient Roman writers, and belonged to an age when a book-language had hardly yet an existence, and when every phrase was caught up fresh from the life. This *naive* simplicity had its peculiar charms for the later Romans of the age of learned cultivation: it was, however, rather the gift of nature than the fruit of poetical art. Horace set himself against this excessive partiality, and asserted that Plautus and the other comic poets threw off their pieces negligently, and wrote them in the utmost haste, that they might be the sooner paid for them. We may safely affirm, therefore, that in the graces and elegances of execution, the Greek poets have always lost in the Latin imitations. These we must, in imagination, retranslate into the finished elegance which we perceive in the Greek fragments. Moreover, Plautus and Terence made many changes in the general plan, and these could hardly be improvements. The former at times omitted whole scenes and characters, and the latter made additions, and occasionally ran two plays into one. Was this done with an artistic design, and were they actually desirous of excelling their Grecian predecessors in the structure of their pieces? I doubt it. Plautus was perpetually running out into diffuseness, and he was obliged to remedy in some other way the lengthening which this gave to the original; the imitations of Terence, on the other hand, from his lack of invention, turned out somewhat meagre, and he filled up the gaps with materials borrowed from other pieces. Even his contemporaries reproached him with having falsified or corrupted a number of Greek pieces, for the purpose of making out of them a few Latin ones.

Plautus and Terence are generally mentioned as writers in every respect original. In Romans this was perhaps pardonable: they possessed but little of the true poetic spirit, and their poetical literature owed its origin, for the most part, first to translation, then to free imitation, and finally to appropriation and new modelling, of the Greek. With them, therefore, a particular sort of adaptation passed for originality. Thus we find, from Terence's apologetic prologues, that they had so lowered the notion of plagiarism, that he was accused of it, because he had made use of matter which had been already adapted from the Greek. As we cannot, therefore, consider these writers in the light of creative artists, and since consequently they are only important to us in so far as we may by their means become acquainted with the shape of the Greek New Comedy, I will here insert the few remarks I have to make on their character and differences, and then return to the Greek writers of the New Comedy.

Among the Greeks, poets and artists were at all times held in honour and estimation; among the Romans, on the contrary, polite literature was at first cultivated by men of the lowest rank, by needy foreigners, and even by slaves. Plautus and Terence, who closely followed each other in time, and whose lifetime belongs to the last years of the second Punic war, and to the interval between the second and third, were of the lowest rank: the former, at best a poor day labourer, and the latter, a Carthaginian slave, and afterwards a freed man. Their fortunes, however, were very different. Plautus, when he was not employed in writing comedies, was fain to hire himself out to do the work of a beast of burthen in a mill; Terence was domesticated with the elder Scipio and his bosom friend Laelius, who deigned to admit him to such familiarity, that he fell under the honourable imputation of being assisted in the composition of his pieces by these noble Romans, and it was even said that they allowed their own labours to pass under his name. The habits of their lives are perceptible in their respective modes of writing: the bold, coarse style of Plautus, and his famous jests, betray his intercourse with the vulgar; in that of Terence, we discern the traces of good society. They are further distinguished by their choice of matter. Plautus generally inclines to the farcical, to overwrought, and often disgusting drollery; Terence prefers the more delicate shades of characterization, and, avoiding everything like exaggeration, approaches the seriously instructive and sentimental kind. Some of the pieces of Plautus are taken from Diphilus and Philemon, but there is reason to believe that he added a considerable degree of coarseness to his originals; from whom he derived the others is unknown, unless, perhaps, the assertion of Horace, "It is said that Plautus took for his model the Sicilian Epicharmus," will warrant the conjecture that he borrowed the *Amphitryo*, a piece which is quite different in kind from all his others, and which he himself calls a Tragi-comedy, from that old Doric comedian, who we know employed himself chiefly on mythological subjects. Among the pieces of Terence, whose copies, with the exception of certain changes of the plan and structure, are probably much more faithful in detail than those of the other, we find two from Apollodorus, and the rest from Menander. Julius Caesar has honoured Terence with some verses, in which he calls him a half Menander, praising the smoothness of his style, and only lamenting that he has lost a certain comic vigour which marked his original.

This naturally brings us back to the Grecian masters. Diphilus, Philemon, Apollodorus, and Menander, are certainly four of the most celebrated names among them. The palm, for elegance, delicacy, and sweetness, is with one voice given to Menander, although Philemon frequently carried off the prize before him, probably because he studied more the taste of the multitude, or because he availed himself of adscititious means of popularity. This was at least insinuated by Menander, who when he met his rival one day said to him, "Pray, Philemon, dost thou not blush when thou gainest a victory over me?"

Menander flourished after the times of Alexander the Great, and was the contemporary of Demetrius Phalereus. He was instructed in philosophy by Theophrastus, but his own opinions inclined him to that of Epicurus, and he boasted in an epigram, "that if Themistocles freed his country from slavery, Epicurus freed it from irrationality." He was fond of the choicest sensual enjoyments: Phaedrus, in an unfinished tale, describes him to us as even in his exterior, an effeminate voluptuary; and his amour with the courtesan Glycera is notorious. The Epicurean philosophy, which placed the supreme happiness of life in the benevolent affections, but neither spurred men on to heroic action, nor excited any sense of it in the mind, could hardly fail to be well received among the Greeks, after the loss of their old and glorious freedom: with their cheerful mild way of thinking, it was admirably calculated to console them. It is perhaps the most suitable for the comic poet, as the stoical philosophy is for the tragedian. The object of the comedian is merely to produce mitigated impressions, and by no means to excite a strong indignation at human frailties. On the other hand, we may easily comprehend why the Greeks conceived a passion for the New Comedy at the very period when they lost their freedom, as it diverted them from sympathy with the course of human affairs in general, and with political events, and absorbed their attention wholly in domestic and personal concerns.

The Grecian theatre was originally formed for higher walks of the drama; and we do not attempt to dissemble the inconveniences and disadvantages which its structure must have occasioned to Comedy. The frame was too large, and the picture could not fill it. The Greek stage was open to the heavens, and it exhibited little or nothing of the interior of the houses [Footnote: To serve this purpose recourse was had to the encyclema, which, no doubt, in the commencement of the *Clouds*, exhibited Strepsiades and his son sleeping on their beds. Moreover, Julius Pollux mentions among the decorations of New Comedy, a sort of tent, hut, or shed, adjoining to the middle edifice, with a doorway, originally a stable, but afterwards applicable to many purposes. In the *Sempstresses* of Antiphanes, it represented a sort of workshop. Here, or in the encyclema, entertainments were given, which in the old comedies sometimes took place before the eyes of the spectators. With the southern habits of the ancients, it was not, perhaps, so unnatural to feast with open doors, as it would be in the north of Europe. But no modern commentator has yet, so far as I know, endeavoured to illustrate in a proper manner the theatrical arrangement of the plays of Plautus and Terence. [See the Fourth Lecture, &c., and the Appendix on the Scenic Arrangement of the Greek Theatre.]]. The New Comedy was therefore under the necessity of placing its scene in the street. This gave rise to many inconveniences; thus people frequently come out of their houses to tell their secrets to one another in public. It is true, the poets were thus also saved the necessity of changing the scene, by supposing that the families concerned in the action lived in the same neighbourhood. It may be urged in their justification, that the Greeks, like all other southern nations, lived a good deal out of their small private houses, in the open air. The chief disadvantage with which this construction of the stage was attended, was the limitation of the female parts. With that due observance of custom which the essence of the New Comedy required, the exclusion of unmarried women and young maidens in general was an inevitable consequence of the retired life of the female sex in Greece. None appear but aged matrons, female slaves, or girls of light reputation. Hence, besides the loss of many agreeable situations, arose this further inconvenience, that frequently the whole piece turns on a marriage with, or a passion for, a young woman, who is never once seen.

Athens, where the fictitious, as well as the actual, scene was generally placed, was the centre of a small territory, and in no wise to be compared with our capital cities, either in extent or population. Republican equality admitted of no marked distinction of ranks; there was no proper nobility: all were alike citizens, richer or poorer, and for the most part had no other occupation than the management of their several properties. Hence the Attic New Comedy could not well admit of the contrasts arising from diversity of tone and mental culture; it generally moves within a sort of middle rank, and has something citizen-like, nay, if I may so say, something of the manners of a small town about it, which is not at all to the taste of those who would have comedy to portray the manners of a court, and the refinement or corruption of monarchical capitals.

With respect to the intercourse between the two sexes, the Greeks knew nothing of the gallantry of modern Europe, nor the union of love with enthusiastic veneration. All was sensual passion or marriage. The latter was, by the constitution and manners of the Greeks, much more a matter of duty, or an affair of convenience, than of inclination. The laws were strict only in one point, the preservation of the pure national extraction of the children, which alone was legitimate. The right of citizenship was a great prerogative, and the more valuable the smaller the number of citizens, which was not allowed to increase beyond a certain point. Hence marriages with foreign women were invalid. The society of a wife, whom, in most cases, the husband had not even seen before his marriage with her, and who passed her whole life within the walls of her house, could not afford him much entertainment; this was sought among women who had forfeited all title to strict respect, and who were generally foreigners without property, or freed slaves, and the like. With women of this description the easy morality of the Greeks allowed of the greatest license, especially to young unmarried men. The ancient writers, therefore, of the New Comedy paint this mode of life with much less disguise than we think decorous. Their comedies, like all comedies in the world, frequently end with marriages (it seems this catastrophe brings seriousness along with it); but the marriage is often entered upon merely as a means of propitiating a father incensed at the irregularities of some illicit amour. It sometimes happens, however, that the amour is changed into a lawful marriage by means of a discovery that the supposed foreigner or slave is by birth an Athenian citizen. It is worthy of remark, that the fruitful mind of the very poet who carried the Old Comedy to perfection, put forth also the first germ of the New. *Cocalus*, the last piece which Aristophanes composed, contained a seduction, a recognition, and all the leading circumstances which were afterwards employed by Menander in his comic pieces.

From what has been said, it is easy to overlook the whole round of characters; nay, they are so few, and so perpetually recur, that they may be almost all enumerated. The austere and stingy, or the mild easy father, the latter not unfrequently under the dominion of his wife, and making common cause with his son against her; the housewife either loving and sensible, or scolding and domineering, and presuming on the accession she has brought to the family property; the young man giddy and extravagant, but frank and amiable, who even in a passion sensual at its commencement is capable of true attachment; the girl of light character, either thoroughly depraved, vain, cunning, and selfish, or still good-hearted and susceptible of better feelings; the simple and clownish, and the cunning slave who assists his young master in cheating his old father, and by all manner of knavish tricks procures him money for the gratification of his passions; (*as this character plays a principal part, I shall shortly make some further observations on it*;) the flatterer or accommodating parasite, who, for the sake of a good meal, is ready to say or do any thing that may be required of him the sycophant, a man whose business it was to set quietly disposed people by the ears, and stir up law-suits, for the conduct of which he offered his services; the gasconading soldier, returned from foreign service, generally cowardly and simple, but who assumes airs and boasts of his exploits abroad; and lastly, a servant or pretended mother, who preaches very indifferent morals to the young girl entrusted to her care; and the slave-dealer, who speculates on the extravagant passions of young people, and regards nothing but his own pecuniary advantage. The two last characters, with their revolting coarseness, are, to our feelings, a real blot in the Greek Comedy; but its very subject-matter rendered it impossible for it to dispense with them.

The knavish servant is generally also the buffoon, who takes pleasure in avowing, and even exaggerating, his own sensuality and want of principle, and who jokes at the expense of the other characters, and occasionally even addresses the pit. This is the origin of the comic servants of the moderns, but I am inclined to doubt whether, with our manners, there is propriety and truth in introducing such characters. The Greek servant was a slave, subject for life to the arbitrary caprice of his master, and frequently the victim of the most severe treatment. A man, who, thus deprived by the constitution of society of all his natural rights, makes trick and artifice his trade may well be pardoned: he is in a state of war with his oppressors, and cunning is his natural weapon. But in our times, a servant, who is free to choose his situation and his master, is a good-for-nothing scoundrel if he assists the son to deceive the father. With respect, on the other hand, to the open avowal of fondness of good eating and drinking which is employed to give a comic stamp to servants and persons in a low rank of life, it may still be used without impropriety: of those to whom life has granted but few privileges it does not require much; and they may boldly own the vulgarity of their inclinations, without giving any shock to our moral feelings. The better the condition of servants in real life, the less adapted are they for the stage; and this at least redounds to the praise of our more humane age, that in our "family picture" tales we meet with servants who are right worthy characters, better fitted to excite our sympathy than our derision.

The repetition of the same characters was as it were acknowledged by the Greek comic writers, by their frequent use of the same names, and those too in part expressive of character. In this they did better than many comic poets of modern times, who, for the sake of novelty of character, torture themselves to attain complete individuality, by which efforts no other effect generally is produced than that of diverting our attention from the main business of the piece, and dissipating it on accessory circumstances. And then after all they imperceptibly fall back again into the old well-known character. It is better to delineate the characters at first with a certain breadth, and to leave the actor room to touch them up more accurately, and to add the nicer and more personal traits, according to the requirements of each composition. In this respect the use of masks admits of justification; which, like many other peculiarities of the ancient theatre, (such as the acting in the open air,) were still retained, though originally designed for other departments of the drama, and though they seem a greater incongruity in the New Comedy than in the Old, and in Tragedy. But certainly it was unsuitable to the spirit of the New, that, while in other respects the representation approached nature with a more exact, nay, illusive resemblance, the masks deviated more from it than in the Old, being overcharged in the features, and almost to caricature. However singular this may appear, it is too expressly and formally attested to admit of a doubt. [Footnote: See Platonius, in *Aristoph. cur. Kuster*, p. xi.] As they were prohibited from bringing portraits of real persons on the stage they were, after the loss of their freedom, very careful lest they should accidentally stumble upon any resemblance, and especially to any of their Macedonian rulers; and in this way they endeavoured to secure themselves against the danger. Yet the exaggeration in question was hardly without its meaning. Accordingly we find it stated, that an unsymmetrical profile, with one eyebrow drawn up and the other down, denoted an idle, inquisitive, and intermeddling busy-body, [Footnote: See *Jul. Pollux*, in the section of comic masks. Compare Platonius as above, and Quinctilian, 1. xi. c. 3. The supposed wonderful discovery of Voltaire respecting tragic masks, which I mentioned in the fourth Lecture, will hardly be forgotten.] and we may in fact remark that men, who are in the habit of looking at things with anxious exact observation, are apt to acquire distortions of this kind.

Among other peculiarities the masks in comedy have this advantage, that from the unavoidable repetition of the same characters the spectator knew at once what he had to expect. I once witnessed at Weimar a representation of the *Adelphi* of Terence, entirely in ancient costume, which, under the direction of Goethe, furnished us a truly Attic evening. The actors used partial masks, cleverly fitted to the real countenance, [Footnote: This also was not unknown to the ancients, as it proved by many comic masks having in the place of the mouth a circular opening of considerable width, through which the mouth and the adjoining features were allowed to appear; and which, with their distorted movements, must have produced a highly ludicrous effect, from the contrast in the fixed distortion of the rest of the countenance.] and notwithstanding the smallness of the theatre, I did not find that they were in any way prejudicial to vivacity. The mask was peculiarly favourable for the jokes of the roguish slave: his uncouth physiognomy, as well as his apparel, stamped him at once as a man of a peculiar race, (as in truth the slaves were, partly even by extraction,) and he might therefore well be allowed to act and speak differently from the rest of the characters.

Out of the limited range of their civil and domestic life, and out of the simple theme of the characters above mentioned, the invention of the Greek comic writers contrived to extract an inexhaustible multitude of variations, and yet, what is deserving of high praise, even in that on which they grounded their development and catastrophe, they ever remained true to their national customs.

The circumstances of which they availed themselves for this purpose were generally the following:--Greece consisted of a number of small separate states, lying round about Athens on the coast and islands. Navigation was frequent, piracy not unusual, which, moreover, was directed against human beings in order to supply the slave-market. Thus, even free-born children might be kidnapped. Not unfrequently, too, they were exposed by their own parents, in virtue of their legal rights, and being unexpectedly saved from destruction, were afterwards restored to their families. All this prepared a ground-work for the recognitions in Greek Comedy between parents and children, brothers and sisters, &c., which as a means of bringing about the denouement, was borrowed by the comic from the tragic writers. The complicated intrigue is carried on within the represented action, but the singular and improbable accident on which it is founded, is removed to a distance both of time and place, so that the comedy, though taken from every-day life, has still, in some degree, a marvellous romantic back-ground.

The Greek Comic writers were acquainted with Comedy in all its extent, and employed themselves with equal diligence on all its varieties, the Farce, the Play of Intrigue, and the various kinds of the Play of Character, from caricature to the nicest delicacy of delineation, and even the serious or sentimental drama. They possessed moreover a most enchanting species, of which, however, no examples are now remaining. From the titles of their pieces, and other indications, it appears they sometimes introduced historical personages, as for instance the poetess Sappho, with Alcaeus's and Anacreon's love for her, or her own passion for Phaon; the story of her leap from the Leucadian rock owes, perhaps, its origin, solely to the invention of the comic writers. To judge from their subject-matter, these comedies must have approached to our romantic drama; and the mixture of beautiful passion with the tranquil grace of the ordinary comic representation must undoubtedly have been very attractive.

In the above observations I have, I conceive, given a faithful picture of the Greek Comedy. I have not attempted to disguise either its defects or its limitation. The ancient Tragedy and the Old Comedy are inimitable, unapproachable, and stand alone in the whole range of the history of art. But in the New Comedy we may venture to measure our strength with the Greeks, and even attempt to surpass them. Whenever we descend from the Olympus of true poetry to the common earth, in other words, when once we mix the prose of a definite reality with the ideal creations of fancy, the success of productions is no longer determined by the genius alone, and a feeling for art, but the more or less favourable nature of circumstances. The figures of the gods of the Grecian sculptors stand before us as the perfect models for all ages. The noble occupation of giving an ideal perfection to the human form having once been entered upon by the fancy, all that is left even to an equal degree of inspiration is but to make a repetition of the same attempts. In the execution, however, of personal and individual resemblances, the modern statuary is the rival of the ancient: but this is no pure creation of art; observation must here come in: and whatever degree of science, profundity, and taste may be displayed in the execution, the artist is still tied down to the object which is actually before him.

In the admirable portrait-statues of two of the most celebrated comic writers, Menander and Posidippus (in the Vatican), the physiognomy of the Greek New Comedy appears to me to be almost visibly and personally expressed! Clad in the most simple dress, and holding a roll in their hands, they are sitting in arm-chairs with all the ease and self-possession which mark the conscious superiority of the master; and in that maturity of age which befits the undisturbed impartial observation which is requisite for Comedy, but yet hale and active, and free from all symptoms of decay. We recognise in them that corporeal vigour, which testifies at once to equal soundness both of mind and of temper; no lofty enthusiasm, but at the same time nothing of folly or extravagance; rather does a sage seriousness dwell on a brow wrinkled indeed, though not with care, but with the exercise of thought; while in the quick-searching eye, and in the mouth half curling into a smile, we have the unmistakable indications of a light playful irony.

LECTURE XV.

Roman Theatre--Native kinds: Atellane Fables, Mimes, Comoedia Togata-- Greek Tragedy transplanted to Rome--Tragic Authors of a former Epoch, and of the Augustan Age--Idea of a National Roman Tragedy--Causes of the want of success of the Romans in Tragedy–Seneca.

The examination of the nature of the Drama in general, as well as the consideration of the Greek theatre, which was as peculiar in its origin as in its maturity it was actually perfect, have hitherto alone occupied our attention. Our notice of the dramatic literature of most of the other nations, which principally call for consideration, must be marked with greater brevity; and yet, we are not afraid that we shall be accused in either case of either disproportionate length or conciseness.

And first, with respect to the Romans, whose theatre is in every way immediately attached to that of the Greeks, we have only, as it were, to notice one great gap, which partly arises from their own want of creative powers in this department, and partly from the loss, with the exception of a few fragments, of all that they did produce in it. The only works which have descended to us from the good classical times are those of Plautus and Terence, whom I have already characterised as *copyists* of the Greeks.

Poetry in general had no native growth in Rome; it was first artificially cultivated along with other luxuries in those later times when the original character of Rome was being fast extinguished under an imitation of foreign manners. In the Latin we have an example of a language modelled into poetical expression, altogether after foreign grammatical and metrical forms. This imitation of the Greek was not accomplished easily and without force: the Graecising was carried even to the length of a clumsy intermixture of the two languages. Gradually only was the poetical style smoothed and softened, and in Catullus we still perceive the last traces of its early harshness, which, however, are not without a certain rugged charm. Those constructions, and especially those compounds which were too much at variance with the internal structure of the Latin, and failed to become agreeable to the Roman ear, were in time rejected, and at length, in the age of Augustus, the poets succeeded in producing the most agreeable combination of the peculiarities, native and borrowed. Hardly, however, had the desired equilibrium been attained when a pause ensued; all free development was checked, and the poetical style, notwithstanding a seeming advance to greater boldness and learning, was irrevocably confined within the round of already sanctioned modes of expression. Thus the language of Latin poetry flourished only within the short interval which elapsed between the period of its unfinished state and its second death; and as to the spirit also of poetry, it too fared no better.

To the invention of theatrical amusements the Romans were not led from any desire to enliven the leisure of their festivals with such exhibitions as withdraw the mind from the cares and concerns of life; but in their despondency under a desolating pestilence, against which all remedies seemed unavailing, they had recourse to the theatre, as a means of appeasing the anger of the gods, having previously been only acquainted with the exercises of the gymnasium and the games of the circus. The *histriones*, however, whom for this purpose they summoned from Etruria, were merely dancers, who probably did not attempt any pantomimic dances, but endeavoured to delight their audience by the agility of their movements. Their oldest spoken plays, the *Fabulae Atellanae*, the Romans borrowed from the Osci, the aboriginal inhabitants of Italy. With these *saturae*, (so called because first they were improvisatory farces, without dramatic connexion; *satura* signifying a medley, or mixture of every thing,) they were satisfied till Livius Andronicus, somewhat more than five hundred years after the foundation of Home, began to imitate the Greeks; and the regular compositions of Tragedy and the New Comedy (the Old it was impossible to transplant) were then, for the first time, introduced into Rome.

Thus the Romans owed the first idea of a play to the Etruscans, of the effusions of a sportive humour to the Oscans, and of a higher class of dramatic works to the Greeks. They displayed, however, more originality in the comic than in the tragic department. The Oscans, whose language soon ceasing to be spoken, survived only in these farces, were at least so near akin to the Romans, that their dialect was immediately understood by a Roman audience: for how else could the Romans have derived any amusement from the *Atellanae*? So completely did they domesticate this species of drama that Roman youths, of noble families, enamoured of this entertainment, used to exhibit it on their festivals; on which account even the players who acted in the Atellane fables for money enjoyed peculiar privileges, being exempt from the infamy and exclusion from the tribes which attached to all other theatrical artists, and were also excused from military service.

The Romans had, besides, their own *Mimes*. The foreign name of these little pieces would lead us to conclude that they bore a great affinity to the Greek *Mimes*; they differed, however, from them considerably in form; we know also that the manners portrayed in them had a local truth, and that the subject-matter was not derived from Greek compositions.

It is peculiar to Italy, that from the earliest times its people have displayed a native talent for a merry, amusing, though very rude buffoonery, in extemporary speeches and songs, with accompanying appropriate gestures; though it has seldom been coupled with true dramatic taste. This latter assertion will be fully justified when we shall have examined all that has been accomplished in the higher walks of the Drama in that country, down to the most recent times. The former might be easily substantiated by a number of circumstances, which, however, would lead us too far from our object into the history of the Saturnalia and similar customs, Even of the wit which prevails in the dialogues of the *Pasquino* and the *Marforio* and of their apposite and popular ridicule on passing events, many traces are to be found even in the times of the Emperors, however little disposed they were to be indulgent to such liberties. But what is more immediately connected with our present purpose is the conjecture--that in these *Mimes* and *Atellane Fables* we have perhaps the first germ of the *Commedia dell' arte*, the improvisatory farce with standing masks. A striking affinity between the latter and the *Atellanae* consists in the employment of dialects to produce a ludicrous effect. But how would Harlequin and Pulcinello be astonished were they to be told that they descended in a direct line from the buffoons of the ancient Romans, and even from the Oscans!--With what drollery would they requite the labours of the antiquarian who should trace their glorious pedigree to such a root! From the figures on Greek vases, we know that the grotesque masks of the Old Comedy bore a dress very much resembling theirs: long trousers, and a doublet with sleeves, articles of dress which the Greeks, as well as the Romans, never used except on the stage. Even in the present day *Zanni* is one of the names of Harlequin; and *Sannio* in the Latin farces was a buffoon, who, according to the accounts of ancient writers, had a shaven head, and a dress patched together of gay parti-coloured pieces. The exact resemblance of the figure of Pulcinello is said to have been found among the frescoes of Pompeii. If he came originally from Atella, he is still mostly to be met with in the old land of his nativity. The objection that these traditions could not well have been preserved during the cessation for so many centuries of all theatrical amusements, will be easily got over when we recollect the licences annually enjoyed at the Carnival, and the Feasts of Fools in the middle ages.

The Greek Mimes were dialogues in prose, and not destined for the stage; the Roman were in verse, were acted, and often delivered extempore. The most celebrated authors of this kind were Laberius and Syrus, contemporaries of Julius Caesar. The latter when dictator, by an imperial request, compelled Laberius, a Roman knight, to appear publicly in his own

Mimes, although the scenic employment was branded with the loss of civil rights. Laberius complained of this in a prologue, which is still extant, and in which the painful feeling of annihilated self-respect is nobly and affectingly expressed. We cannot well conceive how, in such a state of mind, he could be capable of making ludicrous jokes, nor how, with so bitter an example of despotic degradation [Footnote: What humiliation Caesar would have inwardly felt, could he have foreseen that, within a few generations, Nero, his successor in absolute authority, out of a lust for self-degradation, would expose himself frequently to infamy in the same manner as he, the first despot, had exposed a Roman of the middle rank, not without exciting a general feeling of indignation.] before their eyes, the spectators could take any delight in them. Caesar, on his part, kept his engagement: he gave Laberius a considerable sum of money, and invested him anew with the equestrian rank, which, however, could not re-instate him in the opinion of his fellow-citizens. On the other hand, he took his revenge for the prologue and other allusions by bestowing the prize on Syrus, the slave, and afterward the freedman and scholar of Laberius in the mimetic art. Of the Mimes of Syrus we have still extant a number of sentences, which, in matter and elegant conciseness of expression, are deserving of a place by the side of Menander's. Some of them even go beyond the moral horizon of serious Comedy, and assume an almost stoical elevation. How was the transition from low farce to such elevation effected? And how could such maxims be at all introduced, without the same important involution of human relations as that which is exhibited in perfect Comedy? At all events, they are calculated to give us a very favourable idea of the Mimes. Horace, indeed, speaks slightingly of the literary merit of Laberius' Mimes, either on account of the arbitrary nature of their composition, or of the negligent manner in which they were worked out. However, we ought not to allow our own opinion to be too much influenced against him by this critical poet; for, from motives which are easy to understand, he lays much greater stress on the careful use of the file, than on original boldness and fertility of invention. A single entire Mime, which time unfortunately has denied us, would have thrown more light on this question than all the confused notices of grammarians, and all the conjectures of modern scholars.

The regular Comedy of the Romans was, for the most part, *palliata*, that is, it appeared in a Grecian costume, and represented Grecian manners. This is the case with all the comedies of Plautus and Terence. But they had also a *comoedia togata*; so called from the Roman dress which was usually worn in it. Afranius is celebrated as the principal writer in this walk. Of these comedies we have no remains whatever, and the notices of them are so scanty, that we can-not even determine with certainty whether the togatae were original comedies of an entirely new invention, or merely Greek comedies recast with Roman manners. The latter case is the more probable, as Afranius lived in a period when Roman genius had not yet ventured to try a flight of original invention; although, on the other hand, it is not easy to conceive how the Attic comedies could, without great violence and constraint, have been adapted to local circumstances so entirely different. The tenor of Roman life was, in general, earnest and grave, although in private society they had no small turn for wit and joviality. The diversity of ranks among the Romans, politically, was very strongly marked, and the opulence of private individuals was frequently almost kingly; their women lived much more in society, and acted a much more important part than the Grecian women did, and from this independence they fully participated in the overwhelming tide of corruption which accompanied external refinement. The differences being so essential, an original Roman comedy would have been a remarkable phenomenon, and would have enabled us to see these conquerors of the world in an aspect altogether new. That, however, this was not accomplished by the *comoedia togata*, is proved by the indifferent manner in which it is mentioned by the ancients. Quinctilian does not scruple to say, that the Latin literature limps most in comedy; this is his expression, word for word.

With respect to Tragedy, we must, in the first place, remark, that the Grecian theatre was not introduced into Rome without considerable changes in its arrangement. The chorus, for instance, had no longer a place in the orchestra, where the most distinguished spectators, the knights and senators, now sat; but it remained on the stage itself. Here, then, was the very disadvantage which we alleged in objection to the modern attempts to introduce the chorus. Other deviations from the Grecian mode of representation were also sanctioned, which can hardly be considered as improvements. At the very first introduction of the regular drama, Livius Andronicus, a Greek by birth, and the first tragic poet and actor of Rome, in his monodies (lyrical pieces which were sung by a single person, and not by the whole chorus), separated the song from the mimetic dancing, the latter only remaining to the actor, in whose stead a boy, standing beside the flute-player, accompanied him with his voice. Among the Greeks, in better times, the tragic singing, and the accompanying rhythmical gestures, were so simple, that a single person was able to do at the same time ample justice to both. The Romans, however, it would seem, preferred separate excellence to harmonious unity. Hence arose, at an after period, their fondness for pantomime, of which the art was carried to the greatest perfection in the time of Augustus. Prom the names of the most celebrated of the performers, Pylades, Bathyllus, &c., it would appear that it was Greeks that practised this mute eloquence in Rome; and the lyric pieces which were expressed by their dances were also delivered in Greek. Lastly, Roscius frequently played without a mask, and in this respect probably he did not stand alone; but, as far as we know, there never was any instance of it among the Greeks. The alteration in question might be favourable to the more brilliant display of his own skill, and the Romans, who were pleased with it, showed here also that they had a higher relish for the disproportionate and prominent talents of a virtuoso, than for the harmonious impression of a work of art considered as a whole.

In the tragic literature of the Romans, two epochs are to be distinguished: the first that of Livius Andronicus, Naevius, Ennius, and also Pacuvius and Attius, who both flourished somewhat later than Plautus and Terence; and the second, the refined epoch of the Augustan age. The former produced none but translators and remodellers of Greek works, but it is probable that they succeeded better in Tragedy than in Comedy. Elevation of expression is usually somewhat awkward in a language as yet imperfectly cultivated, but still its height may be attained by perseverance; but to hit off the negligent grace of social wit requires natural humour and refinement Here, however, (as well as in the case of Plautus and Terence,) we do not possess a single fragment of any work whose Greek original is extant, to enable us to judge of the accuracy and general felicity of the copy; but a speech of considerable length from Attius' *Prometheus Unbound*, is in no respect unworthy of--Aeschylus, and the versification, also, is much more careful [Footnote: In what metres could these tragedians have translated the Greek choral odes? Horace declares the imitation, in Latin, of Pindar, whose lyrical productions bear great resemblance to those of Tragedy, altogether impracticable. Probably they never ventured into the labyrinths of the choral strophes, which were neither calculated for the language nor for the ear of the Romans. Beyond the anapest, the tragedies of Seneca never ascend higher than a sophic or choriambic verse, which, when monotonously repeated, is very disagreeable to the ear.] than that of the Latin comic writers generally. This earlier style was carried to perfection by Pacuvius and Attius, whose pieces alone kept their place on the stage, and seem to have had many admirers down to the times of Cicero, and even still later. Horace directs his jealous criticism against these, as well as all the other old poets.

It was the ambition of the contemporaries of Augustus, to measure their powers with the Greeks in a more original manner; but their labours were not attended with equal success in every department. The number of amateurs who attempted to shine in Tragedy was particularly great; and works of this kind by the Emperor himself even are mentioned. Hence there is much in favour of the conjecture that Horace wrote his epistle to the Pisos, chiefly with the view of deterring these young men from so dangerous a career, being, in all probability, infected by the universal passion, without possessing the requisite talents. One of the most renowned tragic poets of this age was the famous Asinius Pollio, a man of a violently impassioned disposition, as Pliny informs us, and who was fond of whatever bore the same character in works of fine art. It was he who brought with him from Rhodes, and erected at Rome, the well-known group of the Farnese Bull. If his tragedies bore the same relation to those of Sophocles, which this bold, wild, but somewhat overwrought group does to the calm sublimity of the Niobe, we have every reason to regret their loss. But Pollio's political influence might easily blind his contemporaries to the true value of his poetical labours. Ovid, who tried so many departments of poetry, also attempted Tragedy, and was the author of a *Medea*. To judge from the wordy and commonplace displays of passion in his *Heroides*, we might expect from him, in Tragedy, at most, a caricature of Euripides. Quinctilian, however, asserts that he proved here, for once, what he might have done, had he chosen to restrain himself instead of yielding to his natural propensity to diffuseness.

This, and all the other tragic attempts of the Augustan age, have perished. We cannot estimate with certainty the magnitude of the loss which we have here suffered, but from all appearances it is not extraordinarily great.--First of all the Grecian Tragedy had in Rome to struggle with all the disadvantages of a plant removed to a foreign soil; the Roman religion was in some degree akin to that of the Greeks, (though by no means so completely identical with it as many people suppose,) but at all events the heroic mythology of Greece was first introduced into Rome by the poets, and was in no wise interwoven with the national recollections, as was the case in so many ways with those of Greece. The ideal of a genuine Roman Tragedy floats before me dimly indeed, and in the background of ages, and with all the indistinctness which must surround an entity, which never issued out of the womb of possibility into reality. It would be altogether different in form and significance from that of the Greeks, and, in the old Roman sense, religious and patriotic. All truly creative poetry must proceed from the inward life of a people, and from religion, the root of that life. The spirit of the Roman religion was however originally, and before the substance of it was sacrificed to foreign ornament, quite different from that of the Grecian. The latter was yielding and flexible to the hand of art, the former immutable beneath the rigorous jealousy of priestcraft. The Roman faith, and the customs founded on it, were more serious, more moral, and pious, displaying more insight into nature, and more magical and mysterious, than the Greek religion, at least than that part of it which was extrinsecal to the mysteries. As the Greek Tragedy represented the struggle of the free man with destiny, a true Roman Tragedy would exhibit the subjection of human motives to the holy and binding force of *religion*, and its visible presence in all earthly things. But this spirit had been long extinct, before the want of a cultivated poetry was first felt by them. The Patricians, originally an Etruscan sacerdotal school, had become mere secular statesmen and warriors, who regarded their hereditary priesthood in no other light than that of a political form. Their sacred books, their *Vedas*, were become unintelligible to them, not so much from obsoleteness of character, as because they no longer possessed the higher knowledge which was the key to that sanctuary. What the heroic tales of the Latins might have become under an earlier development, as well as their peculiar colouring, we may still see, from some traces in Virgil, Propertius, and Ovid, although even these poets did but handle them as matters of antiquity.

Moreover, desirous as the Romans were of becoming thorough Hellenists, they wanted for it that milder humanity which is so distinctly traceable in Grecian history, poetry, and art, even in the time of Homer. Prom the most austere virtue, which buried every personal inclination, as Curtius did his life, in the bosom of father-land, they passed with fearful rapidity to a state of corruption, by avarice and luxury, equally without example. Never in their character did they belie the legend that their first founder was suckled, not at the breast of woman, but of a ravening she-wolf. They were the tragedians of the world's history, who exhibited many a deep tragedy of kings led in chains and pining in dungeons; they were the iron necessity of all other nations; universal destroyers for the sake of raising at last, out of the ruins, the mausoleum of their own dignity and freedom, in the midst of the monotonous solitude of an obsequious world. To them, it was not given to excite emotion by the tempered accents of mental suffering, and to touch with a light and delicate hand every note in the scale of feeling. They naturally sought also in Tragedy, by overleaping all intervening gradations, to reach at once the extreme, whether in the stoicism of heroic fortitude, or in the monstrous fury of criminal desire. Of all their ancient greatness nothing remained to them but the contempt of pain and death whenever an extravagant enjoyment of life must finally be exchanged for them. This seal, therefore, of their former grandeur they accordingly impressed on their tragic heroes with a self-satisfied and ostentatious profusion.

Finally, even in the age of cultivated literature, the dramatic poets were still in want of a poetical public among a people fond, even to a degree of madness, of shows and spectacles. In the triumphal processions, the fights of gladiators, and of wild beasts, all the magnificence of the world, all the renders of every clime, were brought before the eye of the spectator, who was glutted with the most violent scenes of blood. On nerves so steeled what effect could the more refined gradations of tragic pathos produce? It was the ambition of the powerful to exhibit to the people in one day, on stages erected for the purpose, and immediately afterwards destroyed, the enormous spoils of foreign or civil war. The relation which Pliny gives of the architectural decoration of the stage erected by Scaurus, borders on the incredible. When magnificence could be carried no farther, they endeavoured to surprise by the novelty of mechanical contrivances. Thus, a Roman, at his father's funeral solemnity, caused two theatres to be constructed, with their backs resting against each other, and made moveable on a single pivot, so that at the end of the play they were wheeled round with all the spectators within them, and formed into one circus, in which gladiator combats were exhibited. In the gratification of the eye that of the ear was altogether lost; rope-dancers and white elephants were preferred to every kind of dramatic entertainment; the embroidered purple robe of the actor was applauded, as we are told by Horace, and so far was the great body of the spectators from being attentive and quiet, that he compares their noise to that of the roar of the ocean, or of a mountain forest in a storm.

Only one sample of the tragical talent of the Romans has come down to us, from which, however, it would be unjust to form a judgment of the productions of better times; I allude to the ten tragedies which pass under Seneca's name. Their claim to this title appears very doubtful; perhaps it is founded merely on a circumstance which would lead rather to a different conclusion; that, namely, in one of them, the *Octavia*, Seneca himself appears among the dramatic personages. The opinions of the learned are very much divided on the subject; some ascribe them partly to Seneca the philosopher, and partly to his father the rhetorician; others, again, assume the existence of a Seneca, a tragedian, a different person from both. It is generally allowed that the several pieces are neither all from the same hand, nor were of the same age. For the honour of the Roman taste, one would be disposed to consider them the productions of a very late period of antiquity: but Quinctilian quotes a verse from the *Medea* of Seneca, which is found in the play of that name in our collection, and therefore no doubt can be raised against the authenticity of this piece, though it seems to be in no way pre-eminent above the rest. [Footnote: The author of this *Medea* makes the heroine strangle her children before the eyes of the people, notwithstanding the admonition of Horace, who probably had some similar example of the Roman theatre before his eyes; for a Greek would hardly have committed this error The Roman tragedians must have had a particular rage for novelty and effect to seek them in such atrocities.]
We find also in Lucan, a contemporary of Nero, a similar display of bombast, which distorts everything great into nonsense. The state of constant outrage in which Rome was kept by a series of blood-thirsty tyrants, gave an unnatural character even to eloquence and poetry.
The same effect has been observed in similar periods of modern history. Under the wise and mild government of a Vespasian and a Titus, and more especially of a Trajan, the Romans returned to a purer taste. But whatever period may have given birth to the tragedies of Seneca, they are beyond description bombastic and frigid, unnatural both in character and action, revolting from their violation of propriety, and so destitute of

theatrical effect, that I believe they were never meant to leave the rhetorical schools for the stage. With the old tragedies, those sublime creations of the poetical genius of the Greeks, these have nothing in common, but the name, the outward form, and the mythological materials; and yet they seem to have been composed with the obvious purpose of surpassing them; in which attempt they succeed as much as a hollow hyperbole would in competition with a most fervent truth. Every tragical common-place is worried out to the last gasp; all is phrase; and even the most common remark is forced and stilted. A total poverty of sentiment is dressed out with wit and acuteness. There is fancy in them, or at least a phantom of it; for they contain an example of the misapplication of every mental faculty. The authors have found out the secret of being diffuse, even to wearisomeness, and at the same time so epigrammatically laconic, as to be often obscure and unintelligible. Their characters are neither ideal nor real beings, but misshapen gigantic puppets, who are set in motion at one time by the string of an unnatural heroism, and at another by that of a passion equally unnatural, which no guilt nor enormity can appal.

In a history, therefore, of Dramatic Art, I should altogether have passed over the tragedies of Seneca, if, from a blind prejudice for everything which has come down to us from antiquity, they had not been often imitated in modern times. They were more early and more generally known than the Greek tragedies. Not only scholars, without a feeling for art, have judged favourably of them, nay, preferred them to the Greek tragedies, but even poets have accounted them worth studying. The influence of Seneca on Corneille's idea of tragedy cannot be mistaken; Racine too, in his *Phaedra*, has condescended to borrow a good deal from him, and among other things, nearly the whole scene of the declaration of love; as may be seen in Brumoy's enumeration.

LECTURE XVI.

The Italians--Pastoral Dramas of Tasso and Guarini--Small progress in Tragedy--Metastasio and Alfieri--Character of both--Comedies of Ariosto, Aretin, Porta--Improvisatore Masks--Goldoni--Gozzi–Latest state.

Leaving now the productions of Classical Antiquity, we proceed to the dramatic literature of the moderns. With respect to the order most convenient for treating our present subject, it may be doubtful whether it is better to consider, *seriatim*, what each nation has accomplished in this domain, or to pass continually from one to another, in the train of their reciprocal but fluctuating influences. Thus, for instance, the Italian theatre, at its first revival, exercised originally an influence on the French, to be, however, greatly influenced in its turn by the latter. So, too, the French, before their stage attained its full maturity, borrowed still more from the Spaniards than from the Italians; in later times, Voltaire attempted to enlarge their theatrical circle, on the model of the English; the attempt, however, was productive of no great effect, even because everything had already been immutably fixed, in conformity with their ideas of imitation of the ancients, and their taste in art. The English and Spanish stages are nearly independent of all the rest, and also of each other; on those of other countries, however, they have exercised a great influence, but experienced very little in return. But, to avoid the perplexity and confusion which would attend such a plan, it will be advisable to treat the several literatures separately, pointing out, at the same time, whatever effects foreign influence may have produced. This course is also rendered necessary, by the circumstance that among modern nations the principle of imitation of the ancients has in some prevailed, without check or modification; while in others, the romantic spirit predominated, or at least an originality altogether independent of classical models The former is the case with the Italians and French, and the latter with the English and Spaniards.

I have already indicated, in passing, how even before the eruption of the northern conquerors had put an end to everything like art, the diffusion of Christianity led to the abolition of plays, which, both with Greeks and Romans, had become extremely corrupt. After the long sleep of the dramatic and theatrical spirit in the middle ages, which, however uninfluenced by the classical models, began to awake again in the Mysteries and Moralities, the first attempt to imitate the ancients in the theatre, as well as in the other arts and departments of poetry, was made by the

Italians. The *Sophonisba* of Trissino, which belongs to the beginning of the sixteenth century, is generally named as the first regular tragedy. This literary curiosity I cannot boast of having read, but from other sources I know the author to be a spiritless pedant. Those even of the learned, who are most zealous for the imitation of the ancients, pronounce it a dull laboured work, without a breath of true poetical spirit; we may therefore, without further examination, safely appeal to their judgment upon it. It is singular, that while all ancient forms, even the Chorus, are scrupulously retained, the province of mythology is abandoned for that of Roman history.

The pastoral dramas of Tasso and Guarini (which belong to the middle of the sixteenth century), whose subjects, though for the most part not tragical, are yet noble, not to say ideal, may be considered to form an epoch in the history of dramatic poetry. They are furnished with choruses of the most ravishing beauty, which, however, are but so many lyrical voices floating in the air; they do not appear as personages, and still less are they introduced with due regard to probability as constant witnesses of the represented actions. These compositions were, there is no doubt, designed for the theatre; and they were represented at Ferrara and at Turin with great pomp, and we may presume with eminent taste. This fact, however, serves to give us an idea of the infantine state of the theatre at that time; although, as a whole, they have each their plot and catastrophe, the action nevertheless stands still in some scenes. Their popularity, therefore, would lead us to conclude that the spectators, little accustomed to theatrical amusements, were consequently not difficult to please, and patiently followed the progress of a beautiful poem, even though deficient in dramatic development. The *Pastor Fido*, in particular, is an inimitable production; original and yet classical; romantic in the spirit of the love which it portrays; in its form impressed with the grand but simple stamp of classical antiquity; and uniting with the sweet triflings of poetry, the high and chaste beauty of feeling. No poet has succeeded so well as Guarini in combining the peculiarities of the modern and antique. He displays a profound feeling of the essence of Ancient Tragedy; for the idea of fate pervades the subject-matter, and the principal characters may be said to be ideal: he has also introduced caricatures, and on that account called the composition a Tragi-Comedy; but it is not from the vulgarity of their manners that they are caricatures, as from their over-lofty sentiments, just as in Ancient Tragedy the subordinate personages ever are invested with more or less of the general dignity.

The great importance of this work, however, belongs rather to the History of Poetry in general; on Dramatic Poetry it had no effect, as in truth it was not calculated to produce any.

I then return to what may properly be called the Tragedy of the Italians. After the *Sophonisba*, and a few pieces of the same period, which Calsabigi calls the first tragic lispings of Italy, a number of works of the sixteenth, seventeenth, and eighteenth centuries are cited; but of these none made, or at any rate maintained any considerable reputation. Although all these writers, in intention at least, laboured, to follow the rules of Aristotle, their tragical abortions are thus described by Calsabigi, a critic entirely devoted to the French system:--"Distorted, complicated, improbable plots, ill-understood scenic regulations, useless personages, double plots, inconsistent characters, gigantic or childish thoughts, feeble verses, affected phrases, the poetry neither harmonious nor natural; all this decked out with ill-timed descriptions and similes, or idle philosophical and political disquisitions; in every scene some silly amour, with all the trite insipidity of common-place sentimentality; of true tragic energy, of the struggle of conflicting passions, of overpowering theatrical catastrophes, not the slightest trace." Amongst the lumber of this forgotten literature we cannot stop to rummage, and we shall therefore proceed immediately to the consideration of the *Merope* of Maffei, which appeared in the beginning of the eighteenth century. Its success in Italy, on its first publication, was great; and in other countries, owing to the competition of Voltaire, it also obtained an extraordinary reputation. The object of both Maffei and Voltaire was, from Hyginus' account of its contents, to restore in some measure a lost piece of Euripides, which the ancients highly commended. Voltaire, pretending to eulogize, has given a rival's criticism of Maffei's *Merope*; there is also a lengthened criticism on it in the *Dramaturgie* of Lessing, as clever as it is impartial. He pronounces it, notwithstanding its purity and simplicity of taste, the work of a learned antiquary, rather than of a mind naturally adapted for, and practised in the dramatic art. We must therefore judge accordingly of the previous state of the drama in the country where such a work could arrive at so great an estimation.

After Maffei came Metastasio and Alfieri; the first before the middle, and the other in the latter half of the eighteenth century. I here include the musical dramas of Metastasio, because they aim in general at a serious and pathetic effect, because they lay claim to ideality of conception, and because in their external form there is a partial observance of what is considered as belonging to the regularity of a tragedy. Both these poets, though totally differing in their aim, were nevertheless influenced in common by the productions of the French stage. Both, it is true, declared themselves too decidedly against the authority of this school to be considered properly as belonging to it; they assure us that, in order to preserve their own originality, they purposely avoided reading the French models. But this very precaution appears somewhat suspicious: whoever feels himself perfectly firm and secure in his own independence, may without hesitation study the works of his predecessors; he will thus be able to derive from them many an improvement in his art, and yet stamp on his own productions a peculiar character. But there is nothing on this head that I can urge in support of these poets: if it be really true that they never, or at least not before the completion of their works, perused the works of French tragedians, some invisible influence must have diffused itself through the atmosphere, which, without their being conscious of it, determined them. This is at once conceivable from the great estimation which, since the time of Louis XIV, French Tragedy has enjoyed, not only with the learned, but also with the great world throughout Europe; from the new-modelling of several foreign theatres to the fashion of the French; from the prevailing spirit of criticism, with which negative correctness was everything, and in which France gave the tone to the literature of other countries. The affinity is in both undeniable, but, from the intermixture of the musical element in Metastasio, it is less striking than in Alfieri. I trace it in the total absence of the romantic spirit; in a certain fanciless insipidity of composition; in the manner of handling mythological and historical materials, which is neither properly mythological nor historical; lastly, in the aim to produce a tragic purity, which degenerates into monotony. The unities of both place and time have been uniformly observed by Alfieri; the latter only could be respected by Metastasio, as change of scene is necessary to the opera poet. Alfieri affords in general no food for the eyes. In his plots he aimed at the antique simplicity, while Metastasio, in his rich intrigues, followed Spanish models, and in particular borrowed largely from Calderon. [Footnote: This is expressly asserted by the learned Spaniard Arteaga, in his Italian work on the *History of the Opera*.] Yet the harmonious ideality of the ancients was as foreign to the one, as the other was destitute of the charm of the romantic poets, which arises from the indissoluble mixture of elements apparently incongruous.

Even before Metastasio, Apostolo Zeno had, as it is called, purified the opera, a phrase which, in the sense of modern critics, often means emptying a thing of all its substance and vigour. He formed it on the model of Tragedy, and more especially of French Tragedy; and a too faithful, or rather too slavish approximation to this model, is the very cause why he left so little room for musical development, on which account his pieces were immediately driven from the stage of the opera by those of his more expert successor. It is in general an artistic mistake for one species to attempt, at evident disadvantage, that which another more perfectly accomplishes, and in the attempt, to sacrifice its own peculiar excellencies. It originates in a chilling idea of regularity, once for all established for every kind alike, instead of ascertaining the spirit and peculiar laws of each distinct species.

Metastasio quickly threw Zeno into the shade, since, with the same object in view, he displayed greater flexibility in accommodating himself to the requisitions of the musician. The merits which have gained for him the reputation of a classic among the Italians of the present day, and which, in some degree, have made him with them what Racine is with the French, are generally the perfect purity, clearness, elegance, and sweetness of his language, and, in particular, the soft melody and the extreme loveliness of his songs. Perhaps no poet ever possessed in a greater degree the talent of briefly bringing together all the essential features of a pathetic situation; the songs with which the characters make their exit, are almost always the purest concentrated musical extract of their state of mind. But, at the same time, we must own that all his delineations of passion are general: his pathos is purified, not only from all characteristic, as well as from all contemplative matter; and, consequently, the poetic representation, unencumbered thereby, proceeds with a light and easy motion, leaving to the musician the care of a richer and fuller development. Metastasio is musical throughout; but, to follow up the simile, we may observe, that of poetical music, melody is the only part that he possesses, being deficient in harmonious compass, and in the mysterious effects of counterpoint. Or, to express myself in different terms, he is musical, but in no respect picturesque. His melodies are light and pleasant, but they are constantly repeated with little or no variation: when we have read a few of his pieces, we know them all; and the composition as a whole is always without significance. His heroes, like those of Corneille, are gallant; his heroines tender, like those of Racine; but this has been too severely censured by many, without a due consideration of the requirements of the Opera. To me he appears censurable only for the selection of subjects, whose very seriousness could not without great incongruity be united with such triflings. Had Metastasio not adopted great historical names--had he borrowed his subject-matter more frequently from mythology, or from still more fanciful fictions--had he made always the same happy choice as that in his *Achilles in Scyros*, where, from the nature of the story, the Heroic is interwoven with the Idyllic, we might then have pardoned him if he invariably depicts his personages as in love. Then should we, if only we ourselves understood what ought to be expected from an opera, willingly have permitted him to indulge in feats of fancy still more venturesome. By his tragical pretensions he has injured himself: his powers were inadequate to support them, and the seductive movingness at which he aimed was irreconcileable with overpowering energy. I have heard a celebrated Italian poet assert that his countrymen were moved to tears by Metastasio. We cannot get over such a national testimony as this, except by throwing it back on the nation itself as a symptom of its own moral temperament. It appears to me undeniable, that a certain melting softness in the sentiments, and the expression of them, rendered Metastasio the delight of his contemporaries. He has lines which, from their dignity and vigorous compression, are perfectly suited to Tragedy, and yet we perceive in them an indescribable something, which seems to show that they were designed for the flexible throat of a soprano singer.

The astonishing success of Metastasio throughout all Europe, and especially at courts, must also in a great measure be attributed to his being a court poet, not merely by profession, but also by the style in which he composed, and which was in every respect that of the tragedians of the era of Louis XIV. A brilliant surface without depth; prosaic sentiments and thoughts decked out with a choice poetical language; a courtly moderation throughout, whether in the display of passion, or in the exhibition of misfortune and crime; observance of the proprieties, and an apparent morality, for in these dramas voluptuousness is but breathed, never named, and the heart is always in every mouth; all these properties could not fail to recommend such tragical miniatures to the world of fashion. There is an unsparing pomp of noble sentiments, but withal most strangely associated with atrocious baseness. Not unfrequently does an injured fair one dispatch a despised lover to stab the faithless one from behind. In almost every piece there is a crafty knave who plays the traitor, for whom, however, there is ready prepared some royal magnanimity, to make all right at the last. The facility with which base treachery is thus taken into favour, as if it were nothing more than an amiable weakness, would have been extremely revolting, if there had been anything serious in this array of tragical incidents. But the poisoned cup is always seasonably dashed from the lips; the dagger either drops, or is forced from the murderous hand, before the deadly blow can be struck; or if injury is inflicted, it is never more than a slight scratch; and some subterranean exit is always at hand to furnish the means of flight from the dungeon or other imminent peril. The dread of ridicule, that conscience of all poets who write for the world of fashion, is very visible in the care with which he avoids all bolder flights as yet unsanctioned by precedent, and abstains from everything supernatural, because such a public carries not with it, even to the fantastic stage of the opera, a belief in wonders. Yet this fear has not always served as a sure guide to Metastasio: besides such an extravagant use of the "aside," as often to appear ludicrous, the subordinate love-stories frequently assume the appearance of being a parody on the others. Here the Abbe, thoroughly acquainted with the various gradations of Cicisbeism, its pains and its pleasures, at once betrays himself. To the favoured lover there is generally opposed an importunate one, who presses his suit without return, the *soffione* among the *cicisbei*; the former loves in silence, and frequently finds no opportunity till the end of the piece, of offering his little word of declaration; we might call him the *patito*. This unintermitting love-chase is not confined to the male parts, but extended also to the female, that everywhere the most varied and brilliant contrasts may offer themselves.

A few only of the operas of Metastasio still keep possession of the stage, owing to the change of musical taste, which demands a different arrangement of the text. Metastasio seldom has choruses, and his airs are almost always for a single voice: with these the scenes uniformly close, and with them the singer never fails to make his exit. It appears as if, proud of having played off this highest triumph of feeling, he left the spectators to their astonishment at witnessing the chirping of the passions in the recitatives rising at last in the air, to the fuller nightingale tones. At present we require in an opera more frequent duos and trios, and a crashing finale. In fact, the most difficult problem for the opera poet is to reduce the mingled voices of conflicting passions in one pervading harmony, without destroying any one of them: a problem, however, which is generally solved by both poet and musician in a very arbitrary manner.

Alfieri, a hold and proud man, disdained to please by such meretricious means as those of which Metastasio had availed himself: he was highly indignant at the lax immorality of his countrymen, and the degeneracy of his contemporaries in general. This indignation stimulated him to the exhibition of a manly strength of mind, of stoical principles and free opinions, and on the other hand, led him to depict the horrors and enormities of despotism. This enthusiasm, however, was by far more political and moral than poetical, and we must praise his tragedies rather as the actions of the man than as the works of the poet. From his great disinclination to pursue the same path with Metastasio, he naturally fell into the opposite extreme: I might not unaptly call him a Metastasio reversed. If the muse of the latter he a love-sick nymph, Alfieri's muse is an Amazon. He gave her a Spartan education; he aimed at being the Cato of the theatre; but he forgot that, though the tragic poet may himself he a stoic, tragic poetry itself, if it would move and agitate us, must never be stoical. His language is so barren of imagery, that his characters seem altogether devoid of fancy; it is broken and harsh: he wished to steel it anew, and in the process it not only lost its splendour, but became brittle and inflexible. Not only is he not musical, but positively anti-musical; he tortures our feelings by the harshest dissonances, without any softening or solution. Tragedy is intended by its elevating sentiments in some degree to emancipate our minds from the sensual despotism of the body; but really to do this, it must not attempt to strip this dangerous gift of heaven of its charms: but rather it must point out to us the sublime majesty of our existence, though surrounded on all sides by dangerous abysses. When we read the tragedies of Alfieri, the world looms upon us dark and repulsive. A style of composition which exhibits the ordinary course of human affairs in a gloomy and troublous light, and whose extraordinary catastrophes are horrible, resembles a climate where the perpetual fogs of a northern winter should be joined with the fiery tempests of the torrid zone. Profound and delicate delineation of character is as little to be looked for in Alfieri as in Metastasio: he does but exhibit the opposite but equally partial view of human nature. His characters also are cast in the mould of naked general notions, and he frequently paints the extremes of black and white, side by side, and in unrelieved contrast. His villains for the most part betray all their deformity, in their outward conduct; this might, perhaps, be allowed to pass, although indeed such a picture will hardly enable us to recognise them in real life; but his virtuous persons are not amiable, and this is a defect open to much graver censure. Of all seductive graces, and even of all subordinate charms and ornaments, (as if the degree in which nature herself had denied them to this caustic genius had not been sufficient,) he studiously divested himself, because as he thought it would best advance his more earnest moral aim, forgetting, however, that the poet has no other means of swaying the minds of men than the fascinations of his art.

From the tragedy of the Greeks, with which he did not become acquainted until the end of his career, he was separated by a wide chasm; and I cannot consider his pieces as an improvement on the French tragedy. Their structure is more simple, the dialogue in some cases less conventional; he has also got rid of confidants, and this has been highly extolled as a difficulty overcome, and an improvement on the French system; he had the same aversion to chamberlains and court ladies in poetry as in real life. But in captivating and brilliant eloquence, his pieces bear no comparison with the better French tragedies; they also display much less skill in the plot, its gradual march, preparations, and transitions. Compare, for instance, the *Britannicus* of Racine with the *Octavia* of Alfieri. Both drew their materials from Tacitus: but which of them has shown the more perfect understanding 01 this profound master of the human heart? Racine appears here before us as a man who was thoroughly acquainted with all the corruptions of a court, and had beheld ancient Rome under the Emperors, reflected in this mirror of observation. On the other hand, if Alfieri did not expressly assure us that his Octavia was a daughter of Tacitus, we should be inclined to believe that it was modelled on that of the pretended Seneca. The colours with which he paints his tyrants are borrowed from the rhetorical exercises of the school. Who can recognise, in his blustering and raging Nero, the man who, as Tacitus says, seemed formed by nature "to veil hatred with caresses?"--the cowardly Sybarite, fantastically vain till the very last moment of his existence, cruel at first, from fear, and afterwards from inordinate lust.

If Alfieri has, in this case, been untrue to Tacitus, in the *Conspiracy of the Pazzi* he has equally failed in his attempt to translate Macchiavel into the language of poetry. In this and other pieces from modern history, the *Filippo* for instance, and the *Don Garcia*, he has by no means hit the spirit and tone of modern times, nor even of his own nation: his ideas of the tragic style were opposed to the observance of everything like a local and determinate costume. On the other hand it is astonishing to observe the subjects which he has borrowed from the tragic cycles of the Greeks, such as the *Orestiad*, for instance, losing under his hands all their heroic magnificence, and assuming a modern, not to say a vulgar air. He has succeeded best in painting the public life of the Roman republic; and it is a great merit in the *Virginia* that the action takes place in the forum, and in part before the eyes of the people. In other pieces, while the Unity of Place is strictly observed, the scene chosen is for the most part so invisible and indeterminate, that one would fain imagine it is some out-of-the-way corner, where nobody comes but persons involved in painful and disagreeable transactions. Again, the stripping his kings and heroes, for the sake of simplicity, of all their external retinue, produces the impression that the world is actually depopulated around them. This stage-solitude is very striking in *Saul*, where the scene is laid before two armies in battle-array, on the point of a decisive engagement. And yet, in other respects this piece is favourably distinguished from the rest, by a certain Oriental splendour, and the lyrical sublimity in which the troubled mind of Saul gives utterance to itself. *Myrrha* is a perilous attempt to treat with propriety a subject equally revolting to the senses and the feelings. The Spaniard Arteaga has criticised this tragedy and the *Filippo* with great severity but with great truth.

I reserve for my notice of the present condition of the Italian theatre all that I have to remark on the successors of Alfieri, and go back in order of time in order to give a short sketch of the history of Comedy.

In this department the Italians began with an imitation of the ancients, which was not sufficiently attentive to the difference of times and manners, and translations of Plautus and Terence were usually represented in their earliest theatres; they soon fell, however, into the most singular extravagancies. We have comedies of Ariosto and Macchiavelli--those of the former are in rhymeless verse, *versi sdruccioli*, and those of the latter in prose. Such men could produce nothing which did not bear traces of their genius. But Ariosto in the structure of his pieces kept too close to the stories of the ancients, and, therefore, did not exhibit any true living picture of the manners of his own times. In

Macchiavelli this is only the case in his *Clitia*, an imitation of Plautus; the *Mandragola*, and another comedy, which is without a name, are sufficiently Florentine; but, unfortunately, they are not of a very edifying description. A simple deceived husband, and a hypocritical and pandering monk, form the principal parts. Tales, in the style of the free and merry tales of Boccacio, are boldly and bluntly, I cannot say, dramatised: for with respect to theatrical effect they are altogether inartificial, but given in the form of dialogue. As *Mimes*, that is, as pictures of the language of ordinary life with all its idioms, these productions are much to be commended. In one point they resemble the Latin comic poets; they are not deficient in indecency. This was, indeed, their general tone. The comedies of Pietro Aretino are merely remarkable for their shameless immodesty. It almost seems as if these writers, deeming the spirit of refined love inconsistent with the essence of Comedy, had exhausted the very lees of the sensual amours of Greek Comedy.

At a still earlier period, in the beginning, namely, of the sixteenth century, an unsuccessful attempt had been made in the *Virginia* of Accolti to dramatise a serious novel, as a middle species between Comedy and Tragedy, and to adorn it with poetical splendour. Its subject is the same story on which Shakspeare's *All's Well that Ends Well*, is founded. I have never had an opportunity of reading it, but the unfavourable report of a literary man disposes me to think favourably of it. [Footnote: Bouterwek's *Geschichte der Poesie und Beredsamkeit.--Ersten Band*, s. 334, &c.] According to his description, it resembles the older pieces of the Spanish stage before it had attained to maturity of form, and in common with them it employs the stanza for its metre. The attempts at romantic drama have always failed in Italy; whereas in Spain, on the contrary, all endeavours to model the theatre according to the rules of the ancients, and latterly of the French, have from the difference of national taste uniformly been abortive.

We have a comedy of Tasso's, *Gli Intrichi d'Amore*, which ought rather to be called a lengthy romance in the form of dialogue. So many and such wonderful events are crowded together within the narrow limit of five acts, that one incident treads closely upon the heels of another, without being in the least accounted for by human motives, so as to give to the whole an insupportable hardness. Criminal designs are portrayed with indifference, and the merriment is made to consist in the manner in which some accident or other invariably frustrates their consequences. We cannot here recognise the Tasso whose nice sense of love, chivalry, and honour speaks so delightfully in the *Jerusalem Delivered*, and on this ground it has even been doubted whether this work be really his. The richness of invention, if we may give this name to a rude accumulation of incidents, is so great, that the attention is painfully tortured in the endeavour to keep clear and disentangled the many and diversely crossing threads.

We have of this date a multitude of Italian comedies on a similar plan, only with less order and connexion, and whoso aim apparently is to delight by means of indecency. A parasite and procuress are standing characters in all. Among the comic poets of this class, Giambatista Porta deserves to be distinguished. His plots, it is true, are like the rest, imitations of Plautus and Terence, or dramatised tales; but, throughout the love-dialogues, on which he seems to have laboured with peculiar fondness, there breathes a tender feeling which rises even from the midst of the rudeness of the old Italian Comedy, and its generally uncongenial materials.

In the seventeenth century, when the Spanish theatre flourished in all its glory, the Italians seem to have borrowed frequently from it; but not without misemploying and disfiguring whatever they so acquired. The neglect of the regular stage increased with the all-absorbing passion for the opera, and with the growing taste of the multitude for improvisatory farces with standing masks. The latter are not in themselves to be despised: they serve to fix, as it were, so many central points of the national character in the comic exhibition, by the external peculiarities of speech, dress, &c. Their constant recurrence does not by any means preclude the greatest possible diversity in the plot of the pieces, even as in chess, with a small number of men, of which each has his fixed movement, an endless number of combinations is possible. But as to extemporary playing, it no doubt readily degenerates into insipidity; and this may have been the case even in Italy, notwithstanding the great fund of drollery and fantastic wit, and a peculiar felicity in farcical gesticulation, which the Italians possess.

About the middle of the last century, Goldoni appeared as the reformer of Italian Comedy, and his success was so great, that he remained almost exclusively in possession of the comic stage. He is certainly not deficient in theatrical skill; but, as the event has proved, he is wanting in that solidity, that depth of characterization, that novelty and richness of invention, which are necessary to ensure a lasting reputation. His pictures of manners are true, but not sufficiently elevated above the range of every-day life; he has exhausted the surface of life; and as there is little progression in his dramas, and every thing turns usually on the same point, this adds to the impression of shallowness and ennui, as characteristic of the existing state of society. Willingly would he have abolished masks altogether, but he could hardly have compensated for them out of his own resources; however, he retained only a few of them, as Harlequin, Brighella, and Pantaloon, and limited their parts. And yet he fell again into a great uniformity of character, which, indeed, he partly confesses in his repeated use of the same names: for instance, his Beatrice is always a lively, and his Rosaura a feeling young maiden; and as for any farther distinction, it is not to be found in him.

The excessive admiration of Goldoni, and the injury sustained thereby by the masked comedy, for which the company of Sacchi in Venice possessed the highest talents, gave rise to the dramas of Gozzi. They are fairy tales in a dramatic form, in which, however, along side of the wonderful, versified, and more serious part, he employed the whole of the masks, and allowed them full and unrestrained development of their peculiarities. They, if ever any were, are pieces for effect, of great boldness of plot, still more fantastic than romantic; even though Gozzi was the first among the comic poets of Italy to show any true feeling for honour and love. The execution does not betoken either care or skill, but is sketchily dashed off. With all his whimsical boldness he is still quite a popular writer; the principal motives are detailed with the most unambiguous perspicuity, all the touches are coarse and vigorous: he says, he knows well that his countrymen are fond of *robust* situations. After his imagination had revelled to satiety among Oriental tales, he took to re-modelling Spanish plays, and particularly those of Calderon; but here he is, in my opinion, less deserving of praise. By him the ethereal and delicately-tinted poetry of the Spaniard is uniformly vulgarised, and deepened with the most glaring colours; while the weight of his masks draws the aerial tissue to the ground, for the humorous introduction of the *gracioso* in the Spanish is of far finer texture. On the other hand, the wonderful extravagance of the masked parts serves as an admirable contrast to the wild marvels of fairy tale. Thus the character of these pieces was, in the serious part, as well as in the accompanying drollery, equally removed from natural truth. Here Gozzi had fallen almost accidentally on a fund of whose value he was not, perhaps, fully aware: his prosaical, and for the most part improvisatory, masks, forming altogether of themselves the irony on the poetical part. What I here mean by irony, I shall explain more fully when I come to the justification of the mixture of the tragic and comic in the romantic drama of Shakspeare and Calderon. At present I shall only observe, that it is a sort of confession interwoven into the representation itself, and more or less distinctly expressed, of its overcharged one-sidedness in matters of fancy and feeling, and by means of which the equipoise is again restored. The Italians were not, however, conscious of this, and Gozzi did not find any followers to carry his rude sketches to a higher degree of perfection. Instead of combining like him, only with greater refinement, the charms of wonderful poetry with exhilarating mirth; instead of comparing Gozzi with the foreign masters of the romantic drama, whom he resembles notwithstanding his great disparity, and from the unconscious affinity between them in spirit and plan, drawing the conclusion that the principle common to both was founded in nature;

the Italians contented themselves with considering the pieces of Gozzi as the wild offspring of an extravagant imagination, and with banishing them from the stage. The comedy with masks is held in contempt by all who pretend to any degree of refinement, as if they were too wise for it, and is abandoned to the vulgar, in the Sunday representations at the theatres and in the puppet-shows. Although this contempt must have had an injurious influence on the masks, preventing, as it does, any actor of talent from devoting himself to them, so that there are no examples now of the spirit and wit with which they were formerly filled up, still the *Commedia dell' Arte* is the only one in Italy where we can meet with original and truly theatrical entertainment. [Footnote: A few years ago, I saw in Milan an excellent Truffaldin or Harlequin, and here and there in obscure theatres, and even in puppet-shows, admirable representations of the old traditional jokes of the country. [Unfortunately, on my last visit to Milan, my friend was no longer to be met with. Under the French rule, Harlequin's merry occupation had been proscribed in the Great Theatres, from a care, it was alleged, for the dignity of man. The Puppet-theatre of Gerolamo still flourishes, however but a stranger finds it difficult to follow the jokes of the Piedmontese and Milan Masks.--LAST EDITION.]]

In Tragedy the Italians generally imitate Alfieri, who, although it is the prevailing fashion to admire him, is too bold and manly a thinker to be tolerated on the stage. They have produced some single pieces of merit, but the principles of tragic art which Alfieri followed are altogether false, and in the bawling and heartless declamation of their actors, this tragic poetry, stripped with stoical severity of all the charms of grouping, of musical harmony, and of every tender emotion, is represented with the most deadening uniformity and monotony. As all the rich rewards are reserved for the singers, it is only natural that their players, who are only introduced as a sort of stop-gaps between singing and dancing, should, for the most part, not even possess the very elements of their art, viz., pure pronunciation, and practised memory. They seem to have no idea that their parts can be got by heart, and hence, in an Italian theatre, we hear every piece as it were twice over; the prompter speaking as loud as a good player elsewhere, and the actors in order to be distinguished from him bawling most insufferably. It is exceedingly amusing to see the prompter, when, from the general forgetfulness, a scene threatens to fall into confusion, labouring away, and stretching out his head like a serpent from his hole, hurrying through the dialogue before the different speakers. Of all the actors in the world, I conceive those of Paris to have their parts best by heart; in this, as well as in the knowledge of versification, the Germans are far inferior to them.

One of their living poets, Giovanni Pindemonti, has endeavoured to introduce greater extent, variety, and nature into his historical plays, but he has been severely handled by their critics for descending from the height of the cothurnus to attain that truth of circumstance without which it is impossible for this species of drama to exist; perhaps also for deviating from the strict observation of the traditional rules, so blindly worshipped by them. If the Italian verse be in fact so fastidious as not to consort with many historical peculiarities, modern names and titles for instance, let them write partly in prose, and call the production not a tragedy, but an historical drama. It seems in general to be assumed as an undoubted principle, that the *verso sciolto*, or rhymeless line, of eleven syllables, is alone fit for the drama, but this does not seem to me to be by any means proved. This verse, in variety and metrical signification, is greatly inferior to the English and German rhymeless iambic, from its uniform feminine termination, and from there being merely an accentuation in Italian, without any syllabic measure. Moreover, from the frequent transition of the sense from verse to verse, according to every possible division, the lines flow into one another without its being possible for the ear to separate them. Alfieri imagined that he had found out the genuine dramatic manner of treating this verse correspondent to the form of his own dialogue, which consists of simply detached periods, or rather of propositions entirely unperiodical and abruptly terminated. It is possible that he carried into his works a personal peculiarity, for he is said to have been extremely laconic; he was also, as he himself relates, influenced by the example of Seneca: but how different a lesson might he have learned from the Greeks! We do not, it is true, in conversation, connect our language so closely as in an oratorical harangue, but the opposite extreme is equally unnatural. Even in our common discourses, we observe a certain continuity, we give a development both to arguments and objections, and in an instant passion will animate us to fulness of expression, to a flow of eloquence, and even to lyrical sublimity. The ideal dialogue of Tragedy may therefore find in actual conversation all the various tones and turns of poetry, with the exception of epic repose. The metre therefore of Metastasio, and before him, of Tasso and Guarini, in their pastoral dramas, seems to me much more agreeable and suitable than the monotonous verse of eleven syllables: they intermingle with it verses of seven syllables, and occasionally, after a number of blank lines, introduce a pair of rhymes, and even insert a rhyme in the middle of a verse. From this the transition to more measured strophes, either in *ottave rime*, or in direct lyrical metres, would be easy. Rhyme, and the connexion which it forms, have nothing in them inconsistent with the essence of dramatic dialogue, and the objection to change of measure in the drama rests merely on a chilling idea of regularity.

No suitable versification for Comedy has yet been invented in Italy. The *verso sciolto*, it is well known, does not answer; it is not sufficiently familiar. The verse of twelve syllables, with a *sdrucciolo* termination selected by Ariosto, is much better, resembling the trimeter of the ancients, but is still somewhat monotonous. It has been, however, but little cultivated. The Martellian verse, a bad imitation of the Alexandrine, is a downright torture to the ear. Chiari, and occasionally Goldoni, came at last to use it, and Gozzi by way of derision. It still remains therefore to the prejudice of a more elegant style of prose.

Of Comedy, the modern Italians have nothing worth the name. What they have, are nothing but pictures of manners still more dull and superficial than those of Goldoni, without drollery, or invention, and from their every-day commonplace, downright disagreeable. They have, on the other hand, acquired a true relish for the sentimental drama and familiar tragedy; they frequent with great partiality the representation of popular German pieces of this description, and even produce the strangest and oddest imitations of them. Long accustomed to operas and ballets, as their favourite entertainments, wherein nothing is ever attempted beyond a beautiful air or an elegant movement, the public seems altogether to have lost all sense of dramatic connexion: they are perfectly satisfied with seeing the same evening two acts from different operas, or even the last act of an opera before the first.

We believe, therefore, that we are not going too far if we affirm, that both dramatic poetry and the histrionic art are in a lamentable state of decline in Italy, that not even the first foundations of a true national theatre have yet been laid, and that there is no prospect of it, till the prevailing ideas on the subject shall have undergone a total change.

Calsabigi attributes the cause of this state to the want of permanent companies of players, and of a capital. In this last reason there is certainly some foundation: in England, Spain, and France, a national system of dramatic art has been developed and established; in Italy and Germany, where there are only capitals of separate states, but no general metropolis, great difficulties are opposed to the improvement of the theatre. Calsabigi could not adduce the obstacles arising from a false theory, for he was himself under their influence.

LECTURE XVII.

Antiquities of the French Stage--Influence of Aristotle and the Imitation of the Ancients--Investigation of the Three Unities--What is Unity of Action?--Unity of Time--Was it observed by the Greeks?--Unity of Place as connected with it.

We now proceed to the Dramatic Literature of France. We have no intention of dwelling at length on the first beginnings of Tragedy in this country, and therefore leave to French critics the task of depreciating the antiquities of their own literature, which, with the mere view of adding to the glory of the later age of Richelieu and Louis XIV., they so zealously enter upon. Their language, it is true, was at this time first cultivated, from an indescribable waste of tastelessness and barbarity, while the harmonious diction of the Italian and Spanish poetry, which had long before spontaneously developed itself in the most beautiful luxuriance, was rapidly degenerating. Hence we are not to be astonished if the French lay such great stress on negative excellences, and so carefully endeavour to avoid everything like impropriety, and that from dread of relapse into rudeness this has ever since been the general object of their critical labours. When La Harpe says of the tragedies of Corneille, that "their tone rises above flatness, only to fall into the opposite extreme of affectation," judging from the proofs which he adduces, we see no reason to differ from him. The publication recently of Legouve's *Death of Henry the Fourth*, has led to the reprinting of a contemporary piece on the same subject, which is not only written in a ludicrous style, but in the general plan and distribution of the subject, with its prologue spoken by Satan, and its chorus of pages, with its endless monologues and want of progress and action, betrays the infancy of the dramatic art; not a naive infancy, full of hope and promise, but one disfigured by the most pedantic bombast and absurdity. For a character of the earlier tragical attempts of the French in the last half of the sixteenth and the first thirty or forty years of the seventeenth century, we refer to Fontenelle, La Harpe, and the *Melanges Litteraires* of Suard and Andre. We shall confine ourselves to the characteristics of three of their most celebrated tragic poets, Corneille, Racine, and Voltaire, who, it would seem, have given an immutable shape to their tragic stage. Our chief object, however, is an examination of the *system of tragic art* practically followed by these poets, and by them, in part, but by the French critics universally, considered as alone entitled to any authority, and every deviation from it viewed as an offence against good taste. If only the system be in itself the right one, we shall be compelled to allow that its execution is masterly, perhaps not to be surpassed. But the great question here is: how far the French tragedy is in spirit and inward essence related to the Greek, and whether it deserves to be considered as an improvement upon it?

Of the earlier attempts it is only necessary for us to observe, that the endeavour to imitate the ancients showed itself from the very earliest period in France. Moreover, they considered it the surest method of succeeding in this endeavour to observe the outward regularity of form, of which their notion was derived from Aristotle, and especially from Seneca, rather than from any intimate acquaintance with the Greek models themselves. In the first tragedies that were represented, the *Cleopatra*, and *Dido* of Jodelle, a prologue and chorus were introduced; Jean de la Peruse translated the *Medea* of Seneca; and Garnier's pieces are all taken from the Greek tragedies or from Seneca, but in the execution they bear a much closer resemblance to the latter. The writers of that day, moreover, modelled themselves diligently on the *Sophonisbe* of Trissino, in good confidence of its classic form. Whoever is acquainted with the procedure of true genius, how it is impelled by an almost unconscious and immediate contemplation of great and important truths, and in no wise by convictions obtained mediately, and by circuitous deductions, will be on that ground alone extremely suspicious of all activity in art which originates in an abstract theory. But Corneille did not, like an antiquary, execute his dramas as so many learned school exercises, on the model of the ancients. Seneca, it is true, led him astray, but he knew and loved the Spanish theatre, and it had a great influence on his mind. The first of his pieces, with which, according to general admission, the classical aera of French tragedy commences, and which is certainly one of his best, the *Cid*, is well known to have been borrowed from the Spanish. It violates in a great degree the unity of place, if not also that of time, and it is animated throughout by the spirit of chivalrous love and honour. But the opinion of his contemporaries, that a tragedy must be framed in strict accordance with the rules of Aristotle, was so universally predominant, that it bore down all opposition. Almost at the close of his dramatic career, Corneille began to entertain scruples of conscience, and in a separate treatise endeavoured to prove that, although in the composition of his pieces he had never even thought of Aristotle, they were yet all accurately written according to his rules. This was no easy task, and he was obliged to have recourse to all manner of forced explanations. If he had been able to establish his case satisfactorily, it would but lead to the inference that the rules of Aristotle must be very loose and indeterminate, if works so dissimilar in spirit and form, as the tragedies of the Greeks and those of Corneille are yet equally true to them.

It is quite otherwise with Racine: of all the French poets he was, without doubt, the one who was best acquainted with the ancients; and not merely did he study them as a scholar, he felt them also as a poet. He found, however, the practice of the theatre already firmly established, and he did not, for the sake of approaching these models, undertake to deviate from it. He contented himself, therefore, with appropriating the separate beauties of the Greek poets; but, whether from deference to the taste of his age, or from inclination, he remained faithful to the prevailing gallantry so alien to the spirit of Greek tragedy, and, for the most part, made it the foundation of the complication of his plots.

Such, nearly, was the state of the French theatre before the appearance of Voltaire. His knowledge of the Greeks was very limited, although he now and then spoke of them with enthusiasm, in order, on other occasions, to rank them below the more modern masters of his own nation, including himself still, he always felt himself bound to preach up the grand severity and simplicity of the Greeks as essential to Tragedy. He censured the deviations of his predecessors therefrom as mistakes, and insisted on purifying and at the same time enlarging the stage, as, in his opinion, from the constraint of court manners, it had been almost straitened to the dimensions of an antechamber. He at first spoke of Shakspeare's bursts of genius, and borrowed many things from this poet, at that time altogether unknown to his countrymen; he insisted, too, on greater depth in the delineation of passion--on a stronger theatrical effect; he called for a scene more majestically ornamented; and, lastly, he frequently endeavoured to give to his pieces a political or philosophical interest altogether foreign to poetry. His labours hare unquestionably been of utility to the French stage, although in language and versification (which in the classification of dramatic excellences ought only to hold a secondary place, though in France they alone almost decide the fate of a piece), he is, by most critics, considered inferior to his predecessors, or at least to Racine. It is now the fashion to attack this idol of a bygone generation on every point, and with the most unrelenting and partial hostility. His innovations on the stage are therefore cried down as so many literary heresies, even by watchmen of the critical Zion, who seem to think that the age of Louis XIV. has left nothing for all succeeding time, to the end of the world, but a passive admiration of its perfections, without a presumptuous thought of making improvements of its own. For authority is avowed with so little disguise as the first principle of the French critics, that this expression of literary heresy is quite current with them.

In so far as we have to raise a doubt of the unconditional authority of the rules followed by the old French tragic authors, of the pretended affinity between the spirit of their works and the spirit of the Greek tragedians, and of the indispensableness of many supposed proprieties, we find an ally in Voltaire. But in many other points he has, without examination, nay even unconsciously, adopted the maxims of his predecessors, and followed their practice. He is alike implicated with them in many opinions, which are perhaps founded more on national peculiarities than on human nature and the essence of tragic poetry in general. On this account we may include him in a common examination with them; for we are here concerned not with the execution of particular parts, but with the general principles of tragic art which reveal themselves in the shape of the works.

The consideration of the dramatic regularity for which these critics contend brings us back to the so-called Three Unities of Aristotle. We shall therefore examine the doctrine delivered by the Greek philosopher on this subject: how far the Greek tragedians knew or observed these rules; whether the French poets have in reality overcome the difficulty of observing them without the sacrifice of freedom and probability, or merely dexterously avoided it; and finally, whether the merit of this observance is actually so great and essential as it has been deemed, and does not rather entail the sacrifice of still more essential beauties.

There is, however, another aspect of French Tragedy from which it cannot appeal to the authority of the ancients: this is, the tying of poetry to a number of merely conventional proprieties. On this subject the French are far less clear than on that of the rules; for nations are not usually more capable of knowing and appreciating themselves than individuals are. It is, however, intimately connected with the spirit of French poetry in general, nay, rather of their whole literature and the very language itself. All this, in France, has been formed under the guardianship of society, and, in its progressive development, has uniformly been guided and determined by it--the guardianship of a society which zealously imitated the tone of the capital, which again took its direction from the reigning modes of a brilliant court. If, as there is indeed no difficulty in proving, such be really the case, we may easily conceive why French literature, of and since the age of Louis XIV., has been, and still is, so well received in the upper ranks of society and the fashionable world throughout Europe, whereas the body of the people, everywhere true to their own customs and manners, have never shown anything like a cordial liking for it. In this way, even in foreign countries, it again in some measure finds the place of its birth.

The far-famed Three Unities, which have given rise to a whole Iliad of critical wars, are the Unities of Action, Time, and Place.

The validity of the first is universally allowed, but the difficulty is to agree about its true meaning; and, I may add, that it is no easy matter to come to an understanding on the subject.

The Unities of Time and of Place are considered by some quite a subordinate matter, while others lay the greatest stress upon them, and affirm that out of the pale of them there is no safety for the dramatic poet. In France this zeal is not confined merely to the learned world, but seems to be shared by the whole nation in common. Every Frenchman who has sucked in his Boileau with his mother's milk, considers himself a born champion of the Dramatic Unities, much in the same way that the kings of England since Henry VIII. are hereditary Defenders of the Faith.

It is amusing enough to see Aristotle driven perforce to lend his name to these three Unities, whereas the only one of which he speaks with any degree of fulness is the first, the Unity of Action. With respect to the Unity of Time he merely throws out a vague hint; while of the Unity of Place he says not a syllable.

I do not, therefore, find myself in a polemical relation to Aristotle, for I by no means contest the Unity of Action properly understood: I only claim a greater latitude with respect to place and time for many species of the drama, nay, hold it essential to them. In order, however, that we may view the matter in its true light, I must first say a few words on the *Poetics* of Aristotle, those few pages which have given rise to such voluminous commentaries.

It is well established that this treatise is merely a fragment, for it does not even touch upon many important matters. Several scholars have even been of opinion, that it is not a fragment of the true original, but of an abridgment which some one had made for his own improvement. On one point all philological critics are unanimous: namely, that the text is very much corrupted, and they have endeavoured to restore it by conjectural emendations. Its great obscurity is either expressly complained of by commentators, or substantiated by the fact, that all in turn reject the interpretations of their predecessors, while they cannot approve their own to those who succeed them.

Very different is it with the *Rhetoric* of Aristotle. It is undoubtedly genuine, perfect, and easily understood. But how does he there consider the oratorical art? As a sister of Logic: for as this produces conviction by its syllogism, so must Rhetoric in a kindred manner operate persuasion. This is about the same as to consider architecture simply as the art of building solidly and conveniently. This is, certainly, the first requisite, but a great deal more is still necessary before we can consider it as one of the fine arts. What we require of architecture is, that it should combine these essential objects of an edifice with beauty of plan and harmony of proportion, and give to the whole a correspondent impression. Now when we see how Aristotle, without allowing for imagination or feeling, has viewed oratory only on that side which is accessible to the understanding, and is subservient to an external aim, can it surprise us if that he has still less fathomed the mystery of poetry, that art which is absolved from every other aim but its own unconditional one of creating the beautiful by free invention and clothing it in suitable language?--Already have I had the hardihood to maintain this heresy, and hitherto I have seen no reason for retracting my opinion. Lessing thought otherwise. But what if Lessing, with his acute analytical criticism, split exactly on the same rock? This species of criticism is completely victorious when it exposes the contradictions for the understanding in works composed exclusively with the understanding; but it could hardly rise to the idea of a work of art created by the true genius.

The philosophical theory of the fine arts collectively was, as a distinct science, little cultivated among the ancients; of technical works on the several arts individually, in which the means of execution were alone considered, they had no lack. Were I to select a guide from among the ancient philosophers, it should undoubtedly be Plato, who acquired the idea of the beautiful not by dissection, which never can give it, but by intuitive inspiration, and in whose works the germs of a genuine Philosophy of Art, are every where scattered.

Let us now hear what Aristotle says on the Unity of Action.

"We affirm that Tragedy is the imitation of a perfect and entire action which has a certain magnitude: for there may be a whole without any magnitude whatever. Now a whole is what has a beginning, middle, and end. A beginning is that which is not necessarily after some other thing, but that which from its nature has something after it, or arising out of it. An end, on the other hand, is that which from its nature is after something else, either necessarily, or usually, but after which there is nothing, A middle, what is itself after some other thing, and after which also there is something. Hence poems which are properly composed must neither begin nor end accidentally, but according to the principles above laid down."

Strictly speaking, it is a contradiction in terms to say that a whole, which has parts, can be without magnitude. But Aristotle goes on to state, in explanation, that by "magnitude" as a requisition of beauty, he means, a certain measure which is neither so small as to preclude us from distinguishing its parts, nor so extensive as to prevent us from taking the whole in at one view. This is, therefore, merely an external definition of the beautiful, derived from experience, and founded on the quality of our organs of sense and our powers of comprehension. However, his application of it to the drama is remarkable. "It must have an extension, but such as may easily be taken in by the memory. The determination of the length according to the wants of the representation, does not come within the province of Art. With respect to the essence of the thing, the composition will be the more beautiful the more extensive it is without prejudice to its comprehensibility." This assertion would be highly favourable for the compositions of Shakspeare and of other romantic poets, who have included in one picture a more extensive circle of life, characters, and events, than is to be found in the simple Greek tragedy, if only we could show that they have given it the necessary unity, and such a magnitude as can be clearly taken in at a view, and this we have no hesitation in affirming to be actually the case.

In another place Aristotle requires the same unity of action from the epic as from the dramatic poet; he repeats the preceding definitions, and says that the poet must not resemble the historian, who relates contemporary events, although they have no bearing on one another. Here we have still a more express demand of that connexion of cause and effect between the represented events, which before, in his explanation of the parts of a whole, was at most implied. He admits, however, that the epic poet may take in a much greater number of events connected with one main action, since the narrative form enables him to describe many things as going on at the same time; on the other hand, the dramatic poet cannot represent several simultaneous actions, but only so much as is going on upon the stage, and the part which the persons who appear there take in one action. But what if a different construction of the scene, and a more skilful theatric perspective, should enable the dramatic poet, duly and without confusion, although in a more compressed space, to develope a fable not inferior in extent to the epic poem? Where would be the objection, if the only obstacle were the supposed impossibility?

This is nearly all that is to be found in the *Poetics* of Aristotle on Unity of Action. A short investigation will serve to show how very much these anatomical ideas, which have been stamped as rules, are below the essential requisites of poetry.

Unity of Action is required. What is action? Most critics pass over this point, as if it were self-evident In the higher, proper signification, action is an activity dependent on the will of man. Its unity will consist in the direction towards a single end; and to its completeness belongs all that lies between the first determination and the execution of the deed.

This idea of action is applicable to many tragedies of the ancients (for instance, Orestes' murder of his mother, Oedipus' determination to discover and punish the murderer of Laius), but by no means to all; still less does it apply to the greater part of modern tragedies, at least if the action is to be sought in the principal characters. What comes to pass through them, and proceeds with them, has frequently no more connexion with a voluntary determination, than a ship's striking on a rock in a storm. But further, in the term action, as understood by the ancients, we must include the resolution to bear the consequences of the deed with heroic magnanimity, and the execution of this determination will belong to its completion. The pious resolve of Antigone to perform the last duties to her unburied brother is soon executed and without difficulty; but genuineness, on which alone rests its claim to be a fit subject for a tragedy, is only subsequently proved when, without repentance, and without any symptoms of weakness, she suffers death as its penalty. And to take an example from quite a different sphere, is not Shakspeare's *Julius Caesar*, as respects the action, constructed on the same principle? Brutus is the hero of the piece; the completion of his great resolve does not consist in the mere assassination of Caesar (an action ambiguous in itself, and of which the motives might have been ambition and jealousy), but in this, that he proves himself the pure champion of Roman liberty, by the calm sacrifice of his amiable life.

Farther, there could be no complication of the plot without opposition, and this arises mostly out of the contradictory motives and views of the acting personages. If, therefore, we limit the notion of an action to the determination and the deed, then we shall, in most cases, have two or three actions in a single tragedy. Which now is the principal action? Every person thinks his own the most important, for every man is his own central point. Creon's determination to maintain his kingly authority, by punishing the burial of Polynices with death, is equally fixed with Antigone's determination, equally important, and, as we see at the end, not less dangerous, as it draws after it the ruin of his whole house. It may be perhaps urged that the merely negative determination is to be considered simply as the complement of the affirmative. But what if each determines on something not exactly opposite, but altogether different? In the *Andromache* of Bacine, Orestes wishes to move Hermione to return his love; Hermione is resolved to compel Pyrrhus to marry her, or she will be revenged on him; Pyrrhus wishes to be rid of Hermione, and to be united to Andromache; Andromache is desirous of saving her son, and at the same time remaining true to the memory of her husband. Yet nobody ever questioned the unity of this piece, as the whole has a common connexion, and ends with one common catastrophe. But which of the actions of the four persons is the main action? In strength of passion, their endeavours are pretty nearly equal--in all the whole happiness of life is at stake; the action of Andromache has, however, the advantage in moral dignity, and

Racine was therefore perfectly right in naming the piece after her.

We see here a new condition in the notion of action, namely, the reference to the idea of moral liberty, by which alone man is considered as the original author of his own resolutions. For, considered within the province of experience, the resolution, as the beginning of action, is not a cause merely, but is also an effect of antecedent motives. It was in this reference to a higher idea, that we previously found the *unity* and *wholeness* of Tragedy in the sense of the ancients; namely, its absolute beginning is the assertion of Free-will, and the acknowledgment of Necessity its absolute end. But we consider ourselves justified in affirming that Aristotle was altogether a stranger to this view; he nowhere speaks of the idea of Destiny as essential to Tragedy. In fact, we must not expect from him a strict idea of action as a resolution and deed. He says somewhere--"The extent of a tragedy is always sufficiently great, if, by a series of probable or necessary consequences, a reverse from adversity to prosperity, or from happiness to misery, is brought about." It is evident, therefore, that he, like all the moderns, understood by *action* something merely that takes place. This action, according to him, must have beginning, middle, and end, and consequently consist of a plurality of connected events. But where are the limits of this plurality? Is not the concatenation of causes and effects, backwards and forwards, without end? and may we then, with equal propriety, begin and break off wherever we please? In this province, can there be either beginning or end, corresponding to Aristotle's very accurate definition of these notions? Completeness would therefore be altogether impossible. If, however, for the unity of a plurality of events nothing more is requisite than casual connexion, then this rule is indefinite in the extreme, and the unity admits of being narrowed or enlarged at pleasure. For every series of incidents or actions, which are occasioned by each other, however much it be prolonged, may always be comprehended under a single point of view, and denoted by a single name. When Calderon in a single drama describes the conversion of Peru to Christianity, from its very beginning (that is, from the discovery of the country) down to its completion, and when nothing actually occurs in the piece which had not some influence on that event, does he not give us as much Unity in the above sense as the simplest Greek tragedy, which, however, the champions of Aristotle's rules will by no means allow?

Corneille was well aware of the difficulty of a proper definition of unity, as applicable to an inevitable plurality of subordinate actions; and in this way did he endeavour to get rid of it. "I assume," says he, "that in Comedy, Unity of Action consists in Unity of the Intrigue; that is, of the obstacles raised to the designs of the principal persons; and in Tragedy, in the unity of the danger, whether the hero sinks under, or extricates himself from it. By this, however, I do not mean to assert that several dangers in Tragedy, and several intrigues or obstacles in Comedy, may not be allowable, provided only that the personage falls necessarily from one into the other; for then the escape from the first danger does not make the action complete, for it draws a second after it, as also the clearing up of one intrigue does not place the acting persons at their ease, because it involves them in another."

In the first place the difference here assumed between tragic and comic Unity is altogether unessential. For the manner of putting the play together is not influenced by the circumstance, that the incidents in Tragedy are more serious, as affecting person and life; the embarrassment of the characters in Comedy when they cannot accomplish their design and intrigues, may equally be termed a danger. Corneille, like most others, refers all to the idea of connexion between cause and effect. No doubt when the principal persons, either by marriage or death, are set at rest, the drama comes to a close; but if nothing more is necessary to its Unity than the uninterrupted progress of an opposition, which serves to keep up the dramatic movement, simplicity will then come but poorly off: for, without violating this rule of Unity, we may go on to an almost endless accumulation of events, as in the *Thousand and One Nights*, where the thread of the story is never once broken.

De la Motte, a French author, who wrote against the Unities in general, would substitute for Unity of action, the *Unity of interest*. If the term be not confined to the interest in the destinies of some single personage, but is taken to mean in general the direction which the mind takes at the sight of an event, this explanation, so understood, seems most satisfactory and very near the truth.

But we should derive but little advantage from groping about empirically with the commentators on Aristotle. The idea of *One* and *Whole* is in no way whatever derived from experience, but arises out of the primary and spontaneous activity of the human mind. To account for the manner in which we in general arrive at this idea, and come to think of one and a whole, would require nothing short of a system of metaphysics.

The external sense perceives in objects only an indefinite plurality of distinguishable parts; the judgment, by which we comprehend these into an entire and perfect unity, is in all cases founded on a reference to a higher sphere of ideas. Thus, for example, the mechanical unity of a watch consists in its aim of measuring time; this aim, however, exists only for the understanding, and is neither visible to the eye, nor palpable to the touch: the organic unity of a plant or an animal consists in the idea of life; but the inward intuition of life, which, in itself uncorporeal, nevertheless manifests itself through the medium of the corporeal world, is brought by us to the observation of the individual living object, otherwise we could not obtain it from that object.

The separate parts of a work of art, and (to return to the question before us,) the separate parts, consequently, of a tragedy, must not be taken in by the eye and ear alone, but also comprehended by the understanding. Collectively, however, they are all subservient to one common aim, namely, to produce a joint impression on the mind. Here, therefore, as in the above examples, the Unity lies in a higher sphere, in the feeling or in the reference to ideas. This is all one; for the feeling, so far as it is not merely sensual and passive, is our sense, our organ for the Infinite, which forms itself into ideas for us.

Far, therefore, from rejecting the law of a perfect Unity in Tragedy as unnecessary, I require a deeper, more intrinsic, and more mysterious unity than that with which most critics are satisfied. This Unity I find in the tragical compositions of Shakspeare, in as great perfection as in those of Aeschylus and Sophocles; while, on the contrary, I do not find it in many of those tragedies which nevertheless are lauded as correct by the critics of the dissecting school.

Logical coherence, the causal connexion, I hold to be equally essential to Tragedy and every serious drama, because all the mental powers act and react upon each other, and if the Understanding be compelled to take a leap, Imagination and Feeling do not follow the composition with equal alacrity. But unfortunately the champions of what is called regularity have applied this rule with a degree of petty subtlety, which can have no other effect than that of cramping the poet, and rendering true excellence impossible.

We must not suppose that the order of sequences in a tragedy resembles a slender thread, of which we are every moment in anxious dread lest it should snap. This simile is by no means applicable, for it is admitted that a plurality of subordinate actions and interests is inevitable; but rather let us suppose it a mighty stream, which in its impetuous course overcomes many obstructions, and loses itself at last in the repose of the ocean. It springs perhaps from different sources, and certainly receives into itself other rivers, which hasten towards it from opposite regions. Why should not the poet be allowed to carry on several, and, for a while, independent streams of human passions and endeavours, down to the moment of their raging junction, if only he can place the spectator on an eminence from whence he may overlook the whole of their course? And if this great and swollen body of waters again divide into several branches, and pour itself into the sea by several mouths, is it not still one and the same stream?

So much for the Unity of Action. With respect to the Unity of Time, we find in Aristotle no more than the following passage: "Moreover, the Epos is distinguished from Tragedy by its length: for the latter seeks as far as possible to circumscribe itself within one revolution of the sun, or to exceed it but little; the Epos is unlimited in point of time, and in that respect differs from Tragedy. At first, however, the case was in this respect alike in tragedies and epic poems."

We may in the first place observe that Aristotle is not giving a precept here, but only making historical mention of a peculiarity which he observed in the Grecian examples before him. But what if the Greek tragedians had particular reasons for circumscribing themselves within this extent of time, which with the constitution of our theatres no longer exist? We shall immediately see that this was really the case.

Corneille with great reason finds the rule extremely inconvenient; he therefore prefers the more lenient interpretation, and says, "he would not scruple to extend the duration of the action even to thirty hours." Others, however, most rigorously insist on the principle that the action should not occupy a longer period than that of its representation, that is to say, from two to three hours.--The dramatic poet must, according to them, be punctual to his hour. In the main, the latter plead a sounder cause than the more lenient critics. For the only ground of the rule is the observation of a probability which they suppose to be necessary for illusion, namely, that the actual time and that of the representation should be the same. If once a discrepancy be allowed, such as the difference between two hours and thirty, we may upon the same principle go much farther. This idea of illusion has occasioned great errors in the theory of art. By this term there has often been understood the unwittingly erroneous belief that the represented action is reality. In that case the terrors of Tragedy would be a true torture to us, they would be like an Alpine load on the fancy. No, the theatrical as well as every other poetical illusion, is a waking dream, to which we voluntarily surrender ourselves. To produce it, the poet and actors must powerfully agitate the mind, and the probabilities of calculation do not in the least contribute towards it. This demand of literal deception, pushed to the extreme, would make all poetic form impossible; for we know well that the mythological and historical persons did not speak our language, that impassioned grief does not express itself in verse, &c. What an unpoetical spectator were he who, instead of following the incidents with his sympathy, should, like a gaoler, with watch or hour-glass in hand, count out to the heroes of the tragedy, the minutes which they still have to live and act! Is our soul then a piece of clock-work, that tells the hours and minutes with infallible accuracy? Has it not rather very different measures of time for agreeable occupation and for wearisomeness? In the one case, under an easy and varied activity, the hours fly apace; in the other, while we feel all our mental powers clogged and impeded, they are stretched out to an immeasurable length. Thus it is during the present, but in memory quite the reverse: the interval of dull and empty uniformity vanishes in a moment; while that which marks an abundance of varied impressions grows and widens in the same proportion. Our body is subjected to external astronomical time, because the organical operations are regulated by it; but our mind has its own ideal time, which is no other but the consciousness of the progressive development of our beings. In this measure of time the intervals of an indifferent inactivity pass for nothing, and two important moments, though they lie years apart, link themselves immediately to each other. Thus, when we have been intensely engaged with any matter before we fell asleep, we often resume the very same train of thought the instant we awake and the intervening dreams vanish into their unsubstantial obscurity. It is the same with dramatic exhibition: our imagination overleaps with ease the times which are presupposed and intimated, but which are omitted because nothing important takes place in them; it dwells solely on the decisive moments placed before it, by the compression of which the poet gives wings to the lazy course of days and hours.

But, it will be objected, the ancient tragedians at least observed the Unity of Time. This expression is by no means precise; it should at least be the identity of the imaginary with the material time. But even then it does not apply to the ancients: what they observe is nothing but the *seeming* continuity of time. It is of importance to attend to this distinction--the seeming; for they unquestionably allow much more to take place during the choral songs than could really happen within their actual duration. Thus the *Agamemnon* of Aeschylus comprises the whole interval, from the destruction of Troy to his arrival in Mycenae, which, it is plain, must have consisted of a very considerable number of days; in the *Trachiniae* of Sophocles, during the course of the play, the voyage from Thessaly to Euboea is thrice performed; and again, in the *Supplices* of Euripides, during a single choral one, the *entire* march of an army from Athens to Thebes is supposed to take place, a battle to be fought, and the General to return victorious. So far were the Greeks from this sort of minute and painful calculations! They had, however, a particular reason for observing the seeming continuity of time in the constant presence of the Chorus. When the Chorus leaves the stage, the continuous progress is interrupted; of this we have a striking instance in the *Eumenides* of Aeschylus, where the whole interval is omitted which was necessary to allow Orestes to proceed from Delphi to Athens. Moreover, between the three pieces of a trilogy, which were acted consecutively, and were intended to constitute a whole, there were saps of time as considerable as those between the three acts of many a Spanish drama.

The moderns have, in the division of their plays into acts, which, properly speaking, were unknown to Greek Tragedy, a convenient means of extending the period of representation without any ill effect. For the poet may fairly reckon so far on the spectator's imagination as to presume that during the entire suspension of the representation, he will readily conceive a much longer interval to have elapsed than that which is measured by the rhythmical time of the music between the acts; otherwise to make it appear the more natural to him, it might be as well to invite him to come and see the next act to-morrow. The division into acts had its origin with the New Comedy, in consequence of the exclusion of the chorus. Horace prescribes the condition of a regular play, that it should have neither more nor less than five acts. The rule is so unessential, that Wieland thought Horace was here laughing at the young Pisos in urging a precept like this with such solemnity of tone as if it were really of importance. If in the ancient Tragedy we may mark it as the conclusion of an act wherever the stage remains empty, and the chorus is left alone to proceed with its dance and ode, we shall often have fewer than five acts, but often also more than five. As an observation that in a representation, between two or three hours long, such a number of rests are necessary for the attention, it may be allowed to pass. But, considered in any other light, I should like to hear a reason for it, grounded on the nature of Dramatic Poetry, why a drama must have so many and only so many divisions. But the world is governed by prescription and tradition: a smaller number of acts has been tolerated; to transgress the consecrated number of five [Footnote: Three unities, five acts: why not seven persons? These rules seem to proceed according to odd numbers.] is still considered a dangerous and atrocious profanation.

As a general rule, the division into acts seems to me erroneous, when, as is so often the case in modern plays, nothing takes place in the intervals between them, and when the persons at the beginning of the new act are exhibited in exactly the same situation as at the close of the foregoing one. And yet this stand-still has given much less offence than the assumption of a considerable interval, or of incidents omitted in the representation, because the former is merely a negative error.

The romantic poets take the liberty even of changing the scene during the course of an act. As the stage is always previously left empty, these also are such interruptions of the continuity, as would warrant them in the assumption of as many intervals. If we stumble at this, but admit the propriety of a division into acts, we have only to consider these changes of scene in the light of a greater number of short acts. But then, it will perhaps be objected, this is but justifying one error by another, the violation of the Unity of Time by the violation of the Unity of Place: we shall, therefore, proceed to examine more at length how far the last-mentioned rule is indispensable.

In vain, as we have already said, shall we look to Aristotle for any opinion on this subject. It is asserted that the rule was observed by the ancients. Not always, only generally. Of seven plays by Aeschylus, and the same number by Sophocles, there are two, the *Eumenides* and the *Ajax*, in which the scene is changed. That they generally retain the same scene follows naturally from the constant presence of the chorus, which must be got rid of by some suitable device before there can be a change of place. And then, again, it must not be forgotten, that their scene represented a much wider extent than in most cases ours does; not a mere room, but the open space before several buildings: and the disclosing the interior of a house by means of the encyclema, may be considered in the same light as the drawing a back curtain on our stage.

The objection to the change of scene is founded on the same erroneous idea of illusion which we have already discussed. To transfer the action to another place would, it is urged, dispel the illusion. But now if we are in reality to consider the imaginary for the actual place, then must stage decoration and scenery be altogether different from what it now is. [Footnote: It is calculated merely for a single point of view: seen from every other point, the broken lines betray the imperfection of the imitation. Even as to the architectural import, so little attention do the audience in general pay to these niceties, that they are not even shocked when the actors enter and disappear through a wall without a door, between the side scenes.] Johnson, a critic who, in general, is an advocate for the strict rules, very justly observes, that if our imagination once goes the length of transporting us eighteen hundred years back to Alexandria, in order to figure to ourselves the story of Antony and Cleopatra as actually taking place before us, the next step, of transporting ourselves from Alexandria to Rome, is easier. The capability of our mind to fly in thought, with the rapidity of lightning, through the immensity of time and space, is well known and acknowledged in common life; and shall poetry, whose very purpose it is to add all manner of wings to our mind, and which has at command all the magic of genuine illusion, that is, of a lively and enrapturing fiction, be alone compelled to renounce this universal prerogative?

Voltaire wishes to derive the Unity of Place and Time from the Unity of Action, but his reasoning is shallow in the extreme. "For the same reason," says he, "the Unity of Place is essential, because no one action can go on in several places at once." But still, as we have already seen, several persons necessarily take part in the one principal action, since it consists of a plurality of subordinate actions, and what should hinder these from proceeding in different places at the same time? Is not the same war frequently carried on simultaneously in Europe and India; and must not the historian recount alike in his narrative the events which take place on both these scenes?

"The Unity of Time," he adds, "is naturally connected with the two first. If the poet represents a conspiracy, and extends the action to fourteen days, he must account to me for all that takes place in these fourteen days." Yes, for all that belongs to the matter in hand; all the rest, being extraneous to it, he passes over in silence, as every good storyteller would, and no person ever thinks of the omission. "If, therefore, he places before me the events of fourteen days, this gives at least fourteen different actions, however small they may be." No doubt, if the poet were so unskilful as to wind off the fourteen days one after another with visible precision; if day and night are just so often to come and go and the characters to go to bed and get up again just so many times. But the clever poet thrusts into the background all the intervals which are connected with no perceptible progress in the action, and in his picture annihilates all the pauses of absolute stand-still, and contrives, though with a rapid touch, to convey an accurate idea of the period supposed to have elapsed. But why is the privilege of adopting a much wider space between the two extremes of the piece than the material time of the representation important to the dramatist, and even indispensable to him in many subjects? The example of a conspiracy given by Voltaire comes in here very opportunely.

A conspiracy plotted and executed in two hours is, in the first place, an incredible thing. Moreover, with reference to the characters of the personages of the piece, such a plot is very different from one in which the conceived purpose, however dangerous, is silently persevered in by all the parties for a considerable time. Though the poet does not admit this lapse of time into his exhibition immediately, in the midst of the characters, as in a mirror, he gives us as it were a perspective view of it. In this sort of perspective Shakspeare is the greatest master I know: a single word frequently opens to view an almost interminable vista of antecedent states of mind. Confined within the narrow limits of time, the poet is in many subjects obliged to mutilate the action, by beginning close to the last decisive stroke, or else he is under the necessity of unsuitably hurrying on its progress: on either supposition he must reduce within petty dimensions the grand picture of a strong purpose, which is no momentary ebullition, but a firm resolve undauntedly maintained in the midst of all external vicissitudes, till the time is ripe for its execution. It is no longer what Shakspeare has so often painted, and what he has described in the following lines:--

Between the acting of a dreadful thing,
And the first motion, all the interim is
Like a phantasma, or a hideous dream:
The genius, and the mortal instruments,
Are then in council; and the state of man,
Like to a little kingdom, suffers then
The nature of an insurrection.

But why are the Greek and romantic poets so different in their practice with respect to place and time? The spirit of our criticism will not allow us to follow the practice of many critics, who so summarily pronounce the latter to be barbarians. On the contrary, we conceive that they lived in very cultivated times, and were themselves highly cultivated men. As to the ancients, besides the structure of their stage, which, as we have already said, led naturally to the seeming continuity of time and to the absence of change of scene, their observance of this practice was also favoured by the nature of the materials on which the Grecian dramatist had to work. These materials were mythology, and, consequently, a fiction, which, under the handling of preceding poets, had collected into continuous and perspicuous masses, what in reality was detached and scattered about in various ways. Moreover, the heroic age which they painted was at once extremely simple in its manners, and marvellous in its incidents; and hence everything of itself went straight to the mark of a tragic resolution.

But the principal cause of the difference lies in the plastic spirit of the antique, and the picturesque spirit of the romantic poetry. Sculpture directs our attention exclusively to the group which it sets before us, it divests it as far as possible from all external accompaniments, and where they cannot be dispensed with, it indicates them as slightly as possible. Painting, on the other hand, delights in exhibiting, along with the principal figures, all the details of the surrounding locality and all secondary circumstances, and to open a prospect into a boundless distance in the background; and light and shade with perspective are its peculiar charms. Hence the Dramatic, and especially the Tragic Art, of the ancients, annihilates in some measure the external circumstances of space and time; while, by their changes, the romantic drama adorns its more varied pictures. Or, to express myself in other terms, the principle of the antique poetry is ideal; that of the romantic is mystical: the former subjects space and time to the internal free-agency of the mind; the latter honours these incomprehensible essences as supernatural powers, in which there is somewhat of indwelling divinity.

LECTURE XVIII.

Mischief resulting to the French Stage from too narrow Interpretation of the Rules of Unity--Influence of these rules on French Tragedy--Manner of treating Mythological and Historical Materials--Idea of Tragical Dignity-- Observation of Conventional Rules--False System of Expositions.

I come now to the influence which the above rules of Unity, strictly interpreted and received as inviolable, have, with other conventional rules, exercised on the shape of French tragedy.

With the stage of a wholly different structure, with materials for the most part dissimilar, and handled in an opposite spirit, they were still desirous of retaining the rules of the ancient Tragedy, so far as they are to be learnt from Aristotle.

They prescribed the same simplicity of action as the Grecian Tragedy observed, and yet rejected the lyrical part, which is a protracted development of the present moment, and consequently a stand-still of the action. This part could not, it is true, be retained, since we no longer possess the ancient music, which was subservient to the poetry, instead of overbearing it as ours does. If we deduct from the Greek Tragedies the choral odes, and the lyrical pieces which are occasionally put into the mouths of individuals, they will be found nearly one-half shorter than an ordinary French tragedy. Voltaire, in his prefaces, frequently complains of the great difficulty in procuring materials for five long acts. How now have the gaps arising from the omission of the lyrical parts been filled up? By intrigue. While with the Greeks the action, measured by a few great moments, rolls on uninterruptedly to its issue, the French have introduced many secondary characters almost exclusively with the view that their opposite purposes may give rise to a multitude of impeding incidents, to keep up our attention, or rather our curiosity, to the close. There was now an end therefore of everything like simplicity; still they flattered themselves that they had, by means of an artificial coherence, preserved at least a unity for the understanding.

Intrigue is not, in itself, a Tragical motive; to Comedy, it is essential, as we have already shown. Comedy, even at its close, must often be satisfied with mere suppositions for the understanding; but this is by no means the poetic side of this demi-prosaic species of the Drama. Although the French Tragedy endeavours in the details of execution to rise by earnestness, dignity, and pathos, as high as possible above Comedy, in its general structure and composition, it still bears, in my opinion, but too close an affinity to it. In many French tragedies I find indeed a Unity for the Understanding, but the Feeling is left unsatisfied. Out of a complication of painful and violent situations we do, it is true, arrive at last, happily or unhappily, at a state of repose; but in the represented course of affairs there is no secret and mysterious revelation of a higher order of things; there is no allusion to any consolatory thoughts of heaven, whether in the dignity of human nature successfully maintained in its conflicts with fate, or in the guidance of an over-ruling providence. To such a tranquillizing feeling the so-called poetical justice is partly unnecessary, and partly also, so very questionably and obliquely is it usually administered, very insufficient. But even poetical justice (which I cannot help considering as a made-up example of a doctrine false in itself, and one, moreover, which by no means tends to the excitation of truly moral feelings) has not unfrequently been altogether neglected by the French tragedians.

The use of intrigue is certainly well calculated to effect the all-desired short duration of an important action. For the intriguer is ever expeditious, and loses no time in attaining to his object. But the mighty course of human destinies proceeds, like the change of seasons, with measured pace: great designs ripen slowly; stealthily and hesitatingly the dark suggestions of deadly malice quit the abysses of the mind for the light of day; and, as Horace, with equal truth and beauty observes, "the flying criminal is only limpingly followed by penal retribution."
[Footnote:
 Raro antecedentem scelestum
 Deseruit pede paena claudo.--TRANS.] Let only the attempt be made, for instance, to bring within the narrow frame of the Unity of Time Shakspeare's gigantic picture of Macbeth's murder of Duncan, his tyrannical usurpation and final fall; let as many as may be of the events which the great dramatist successively exhibits before us in such dread array be placed anterior to the opening of the piece, and made the subject of an after recital, and it will be seen how thereby the story loses all its sublime significance. This drama does, it is true, embrace a considerable period of time: but does its rapid progress leave us leisure to calculate this? We see, as it were, the Fates weaving their dark web on the whistling loom of time; and we are drawn irresistibly on by the storm and whirlwind of events, which hurries on the hero to the first atrocious deed, and from it to innumerable crimes to secure its fruits with fluctuating fortunes and perils, to his final fall on the field of battle. Such a tragic exhibition resembles a comet's course, which, hardly visible at first, and revealing itself only to the astronomic eye, appears at a nebulous distance in the heavens, but soon soars with unheard-of and

accelerating rapidity towards the central point of our system, scattering dismay among the nations of the earth, till, in a moment, when least expected, with its portentous tail it overspreads the half of the firmament with resplendent flame.

For the sake of the prescribed Unity of Time the French poets must fain renounce all those artistic effects which proceed from the gradually accelerated growth of any object in the mind, or in the external world, through the march of time, while of all that in a drama is calculated to fascinate the eye they were through their wretched arrangement of stage-scenery deprived in a great measure by the Unity of Place. Accidental circumstances might in truth enforce a closer observance of this rule, or even render it indispensable. From a remark of Corneille's [Footnote: In his *Premier Discours sur la Poesie Dramatique* he says: "Une chanson a quelquefois bonne grace; et dans les pieces de machines cet ornement est redevenu necessaire pour remplir les oreilles du spectateur, *pendant que les machines descendent*."] we are led to conjecture that stage-machinery in France was in his time extremely clumsy and imperfect. It was moreover the general custom for a number of distinguished spectators to have seats on both sides of the stage itself, which hardly left a breadth of ten paces for the free movements of the actors. Regnard, in *Le Distrait*, gives us an amusing description of the noise and disorder these fashionable *petit-maitres* in his day kept up in this privileged place, how chattering and laughing behind the backs of the actors they disturbed the spectators, and drew away attention from the play to themselves as the prominent objects of the stage. This evil practice continued even down to Voltaire's time, who has the merit of having by his zealous opposition to it obtained at last its complete abolition, on the appearance of his *Semiramis*. How could they have ventured to make a change of scene in presence of such an unpoetical chorus as this, totally unconnected with the piece, and yet thrust into the very middle of the representation? In the *Cid*, the scene of the action manifestly changes several times in the course of the same act, and yet in the representation the material scene was never changed. In the English and Spanish plays of the same date the case was generally the same; certain signs, however, were agreed on which served to denote the change of place, and the docile imagination of the spectators followed the poet whithersoever he chose. But in France, the young men of quality who sat on the stage lay in wait to discover something to laugh at; and as all theatrical effect requires a certain distance, and when viewed too closely appears ludicrous, all attempt at it was, in such a state of things, necessarily abandoned, and the poet confined himself principally to the dialogue between a few characters, the stage being subjected to all the formalities of an antechamber.

And in truth, for the most part, the scene did actually represent an antechamber, or at least a hall in the interior of a palace. As the action of the Greek tragedies is always carried on in open places surrounded by the abode or symbols of majesty, so the French poets have modified their mythological materials, from a consideration of the scene, to the manners of modern courts. In a princely palace no strong emotion, no breach of social etiquette is allowable; and as in a tragedy affairs cannot always proceed with pure courtesy, every bolder deed, therefore, every act of violence, every thing startling and calculated strongly to impress the senses, as transacted behind the scenes, and related merely by confidants or other messengers. And yet as Horace, centuries ago remarked, whatever is communicated to the ear excites the mind far more feebly than what is exhibited to the trusty eye, and the spectator informs himself of. What he recommends to be withdrawn from observation is only the incredible and the revoltingly cruel. The dramatic effect of the visible may, it is true, be liable to great abuse; and it is possible for a theatre to degenerate into a noisy arena of mere bodily events, to which words and gestures may be but superfluous appendages. But surely the opposite extreme of allowing to the eye no conviction of its own, and always referring to something absent, is deserving of equal reprobation. In many French tragedies the spectator might well entertain a feeling that great actions were actually taking place, but that he had chosen a bad place to be witness of them. It is certain that the obvious impression of a drama is greatly impaired when the effects, which the spectators behold, proceed from invisible and distant causes. The converse procedure of this is preferable,--to exhibit the cause itself, and to allow the effect to be simply recounted. Voltaire was aware of the injury which theatrical effect sustained from the established practice of the tragic stage in France; he frequently insisted on the necessity of richer scenical decorations; and he himself in his pieces, and others after his example, have ventured to represent many things to the eye, which before would have been considered as unsuitable, not to say, ridiculous. But notwithstanding this attempt, and the still earlier one of Racine in his *Athalie*, the eye is now more out of favour than ever with the fashionable critics. Wherever any thing is allowed to be seen, or an action is performed bodily before them, they scent a melodrama; and the idea that Tragedy, if its purity, or rather its bald insipidity, was not watchfully guarded, would be gradually amalgamated with this species of play, (of which a word hereafter,) haunts them as a horrible phantom.

Voltaire himself has indulged in various infractions of the Unity of Time; nevertheless he has not dared directly to attack the rule itself as unessential. He did but wish to see a greater latitude given to its interpretation. It would, he thought, be sufficient if the action took place within the circuit of a palace or even of a town, though in a different part of them. In order however, to avoid a change of scene, he would have it so contrived as at once to comprise the several localities. Here he betrays very confused ideas, both of architecture and perspective. He refers to Palladio's theatre at Vicenza, which he could hardly have ever seen: for his account of this theatre, which, as we have already observed, is itself a misconception of the structure of the ancient stage, appears to be altogether founded on descriptions which clearly he did not understand. In the *Semiramis*, the play in which he first attempted to carry into practice his principles on this subject, he has fallen into a singular error. Instead of allowing the persons to proceed to various places, he has actually brought the places to the persons. The scene in the third act is a cabinet; this cabinet, to use Voltaire's own words, gives way (without--let it be remembered--the queen leaving it), to a grand saloon magnificently furnished. The Mausoleum of Ninus too, which stood at first in an open place before the palace, and opposite to the temple of the Magi, has also found means to steal to the side of the throne in the centre of this hall. After yielding his spirit to the light of day, to the terror of many beholders, and again receiving it back, it repairs in the following act to its old place, where it probably had left its obelisks behind. In the fifth act we see that the tomb is extremely spacious, and provided with subterraneous passages. What a noise would the French critics make were a foreigner to commit such ridiculous blunders. In *Brutus* we have another example of this running about of the scene with the persons. Before the opening of the first act we have a long and particular description of the scenic arrangement: the Senate is assembled between the Capitoline temple and the house of the Consuls, in the open air. Afterwards, on the rising of the assembly, Arons and Albin alone remain behind, and of them it is now said: *qui sont supposes etre entres de la salle d'audience dans un autre appartement de la maison de Brutus*. What is the poet's meaning here? Is the scene changed without being empty, or does he trust so far to the imagination of his spectators, as to require them against the evidence of their senses, to take for a chamber a scene which is ornamented in quite a different style? And how does that which in the first description is a public place become afterwards a hall of audience? In this scenic arrangement there must be either legerdemain or a bad memory.

With respect to the Unity of Place, we may in general observe that it is often very unsatisfactorily observed, even in comedy, by the French poets, as well as by all who follow the same system of rules. The scene is not, it is true, changed, but things which do not usually happen in the same place are made to follow each other. What can be more improbable than that people should confide their secrets to one another in a place where they know their enemies are close at hand? or that plots against a sovereign should be hatched in his own antechamber? Great importance is attached to the principle that the stage should never in the course of an act remain empty. This is called binding the scenes. But frequently the rule is observed in appearance only, since the personages of the preceding scene go out at one door the very moment that those of the next enter at another. Moreover, they must not make their entrance or exit without a motive distinctly announced: to ensure this particular pains are taken; the confidants are despatched on missions, and equals also are expressly, and sometimes not even courteously, told to go out of the way. With all these endeavours, the determinations of the places where things take place are often so vague and contradictory, that in many pieces, as a German writer [Footnote: Joh. Elias Schlegel, in his *Gedanken zur Aufnahme des Danischen Theatres*.] has well said, we ought to insert under the list of the *dramatis personae*--"The scene is on the theatre."

These inconveniences arise almost inevitably from an anxious observance of the Greek rules, under a total change of circumstances. To avoid the pretended improbability which would lie in springing from one time and one place to another, they have often involved themselves in real and grave improbabilities. A thousand times have we reason to repeat the observation of the Academy, in their criticism on the *Cid*, respecting the crowding together so many events in the period of twenty-four hours: "From the fear of sinning against the rules of art, the poet has rather chosen to sin against the rules of nature." But this imaginary contradiction between art and nature could only be suggested by a low and narrow range of artistic ideas.

I come now to a more important point, namely, to the handling of the subject-matter unsuitably to its nature and quality. The Greek tragedians, with a few exceptions, selected their subjects from the national mythology. The French tragedians borrow theirs sometimes from the ancient mythology, but much more frequently from the history of almost every age and nation, and their mode of treating mythological and historical subjects respectively, is but too often not properly mythological, and not properly historical. I will explain myself more distinctly. The poet who selects an ancient mythological fable, that is, a fable connected by hallowing tradition with the religious belief of the Greeks, should transport both himself and his spectators into the spirit of antiquity; he should keep ever before our minds the simple manners of the heroic ages, with which alone such violent passions and actions are consistent and credible; his personages should preserve that near resemblance to the gods which, from their descent, and the frequency of their immediate intercourse with them, the ancients believed them to possess; the marvellous in the Greek religion should not be purposely avoided or understated, but the imagination of the spectators should be required to surrender itself fully to the belief of it. Instead of this, however, the

French poets have given to their mythological heroes and heroines the refinement of the fashionable world, and the court manners of the present day; they have, because those heroes were princes ("shepherds of the people," Homer calls them), accounted for their situations and views by the motives of a calculating policy, and violated, in every point, not merely archaeological costume, but all the costume of character. In *Phaedra*, this princess is, upon the supposed death of Theseus, to be declared regent during the minority of her son. How was this compatible with the relations of the Grecian women of that day? It brings us down to the times of a Cleopatra. Hermione remains alone, without the protection of a brother or a father, at the court of Pyrrhus, nay, even in his palace, and yet she is not married to him. With the ancients, and not merely in the Homeric age, marriage consisted simply in the bride being received into the bridegroom's house. But whatever justification of Hermione's situation may be found in the practice of European courts, it is not the less repugnant to female dignity, and the more indecorous, as Hermione is in love with the unwilling Pyrrhus, and uses every influence to incline him to marriage. What would the Greeks have thought of this bold and indecent courtship? No doubt it would appear equally offensive to a French audience, if Andromache were exhibited to them in the situation in which she appears in Euripides, where, as a captive, her person is enjoyed by the conqueror of her country. But when the ways of thinking of two nations are so totally different, why should there be so painful an effort to polish a subject founded on the manners of the one, with the manners of the other? What is allowed to remain after this polishing process will always exhibit a striking incongruity with that which is new-modelled, and to change the whole is either impossible, or in nowise preferable to a new invention. The Grecian tragedians certainly allowed themselves a great latitude in changing the circumstances of their myths, but the alterations were always consistent with the general and prevalent notions of the heroic age. On the other hand, they always left the characters as they received them from tradition and an earlier fiction, by means of which the cunning of Ulysses, the wisdom of Nestor, and the wrath of Achilles, had almost become proverbial. Horace particularly insists on the rule. But how unlike is the Achilles of Racine's *Iphigenia* to the Achilles of Homer! The gallantry ascribed to him is not merely a sin against Homer, but it renders the whole story improbable. Are human sacrifices conceivable among a people whose chiefs and heroes are so susceptible of the tenderest emotions? In vain recourse is had to the powerful influences of religion: history teaches that a cruel religion invariably becomes milder with the softening manners of a people.

In these new exhibitions of ancient fables, the marvellous has been studiously rejected as alien to our belief. But when we are once brought from a world in which it was a part of the very order of things, into a

world entirely prosaical and historically settled, then whatever marvel the poet may exhibit must, from the insulated state in which it stands, appear only so much the more incredible. In Homer, and in the Greek tragedians, everything takes place in the presence of the gods, and when they become visible, or manifest themselves in some wonderful operation, we are in no degree astonished. On the other hand, all the labour and art of the modern poets, all the eloquence of their narratives, cannot reconcile our minds to these exhibitions. Examples are superfluous, the thing is so universally known. Yet I cannot help cursorily remarking how singularly Racine, cautious as he generally is, has on an occasion of this kind involved himself in an inconsistency. Respecting the origin of the fable of Theseus descending into the world below to carry off Proserpine for his friend Pirithous, he adopts the historical explanation of Plutarch, that he was the prisoner of a Thracian king, whose wife he endeavoured to carry off for his friend. On this he grounds the report of the death of Theseus, which, at the opening of the play, was current. And yet he allows Phaedra [Footnote:
  Je l'aime, non point tel que l'ont vu les enfers,
  Volage adorateur de mille objets divers,
  Qui va du dieu des morts deshonorer la couche.] to mention the fabulous tradition as an earlier achievement of the hero. How many women then did Theseus wish to carry off for Pirithous? Pradon manages this much better: when Theseus is asked by a confidant if he really had been in the world below, he answers, how could any sensible man possibly believe so silly a tale! he merely availed himself of the credulity of the people, and gave out this report from political motives.

So much with respect to the manner of handling mythological materials. With respect to the historical, in the first place, the same objection applies, namely, that the French manners of the day are substituted to those which properly belong to the several persons, and that the characters do not sufficiently bear the colour of their age and nation. But to this we must add another detrimental circumstance. A mythological subject is in its nature poetical, and ever ready to take a new poetical shape. In the French Tragedy, as in the Greek, an equable and pervading dignity is required, and the French language is even much more fastidious in this respect, as very many things cannot be at all mentioned in French poetry. But in history we are on a prosaic domain, and the truth of the picture requires conditions, circumstances, and features, which cannot be given without a greater or less descent from the elevation of the tragical cothurnus; such as has been made without hesitation by Shakspeare, the most perfect of historical dramatists. The French tragedians, however, could not bring their minds to submit to this, and hence their works are frequently deficient in those circumstances which give life and truth to a picture; and when an obstinate prosaical circumstance must after all be mentioned, they avail themselves of laboured and artificial circumlocutions.

Respecting the tragic dignity of historical subjects, peculiar principles have prevailed. Corneille was in the best way of the world when he brought his *Cid* on the stage, a story of the middle ages, which belonged to a kindred people, characterized by chivalrous love and honour, and in which the principal characters are not even of princely rank. Had this example been followed, a number of prejudices respecting the tragic Ceremonial would have disappeared of themselves; Tragedy from its greater verisimilitude, and being most readily intelligible, and deriving its motives from still current modes of thinking and acting, would have come more home to the heart: the very nature of the subjects would alone have turned them from the stiff observation of the rules of the ancients, which they did not understand, as indeed Corneille never deviated so far from these rules as, in the train, no doubt, of his Spanish model, he does in this very piece; in one word, the French Tragedy would have become national and truly romantic. But I know not what malignant star was in the ascendant: notwithstanding the extraordinary success of his *Cid*, Corneille did not go one step further, and the attempt which he made found no imitators. In the time of Louis XIV. it was considered as a matter established beyond dispute, that the French, nay generally the modern European history was not adapted for the purposes of tragedy. They had recourse therefore to the ancient universal history: besides the Romans and Grecians, they frequently hunted about among the Assyrians, Babylonians, Persians, and Egyptians, for events which, however obscure they might often be, they could dress out for the tragic stage. Racine, according to his own confession, made a hazardous attempt with the Turks. it was successful, and since that time the necessary tragical dignity has been allowed to this barbarous people, among whom the customs and habits of the rudest despotism and the most abject slavery are often united in the same person, and nothing is known of love, but the most luxurious sensuality; while, on the other hand, it has been refused to the Europeans, notwithstanding that their religion, their sense of honour, and their respect for the female sex, plead so powerfully in their behalf. But it was merely modern, and more particularly French names that, as untragical and unpoetical, could not, for a moment, be tolerated; for the heroes of antiquity are with them Frenchmen in everything but the name; and antiquity was merely a thin veil beneath which the modern French character might be distinctly recognized. Racine's Alexander is certainly not the Alexander of history; but if under this name we imagine to ourselves the great Conde, the whole will appear tolerably natural. And who does not suppose that Louis XIV. and the Duchess de la Valliere are represented under the names Titus and Berenice? The poet has himself flatteringly alluded to his sovereign. Voltaire's expression is somewhat strong, when he says that in reading the tragedies which succeeded those of Racine we might fancy ourselves perusing the romances of Mademoiselle Scuderi, which paint citizens of Paris under the names of heroes of antiquity. He alluded herein more particularly to Crebillon. Corneille and Racine, however, deeply tainted as they were with the way of thinking of their own nation, were still at times penetrated with the spirit of true objective exhibition. Corneille gives us a masterly picture of the Spaniards in the *Cid*; and this is conceivable enough, for he drew his materials from the fountain-head. With the exception of the original sin of gallantry, he succeeded also pretty well with the Romans: of one part of their character, at least, he had a tolerable conception, their predominating patriotism, and unbending pride of liberty, and the magnanimity of their political sentiments. All this, it is true, is nearly the same as we find it in Lucan, varnished over with a certain inflation and self-conscious pomp. The simple republican austerity, and their religious submissiveness, was beyond his reach. Racine has admirably painted the corruptions of the Romans of the Empire, and the first timid outbreaks of Nero's tyranny. It is true, as he himself gratefully acknowledges, he had in this Tacitus for a predecessor, but still it is a great merit so ably to translate history into poetry. He had also a just perception of the general spirit of Hebrew history; here he was guided by religious reverence, which, in greater or less degree, the poet ought always to bring with him to his subject. He was less successful with the Turks: Bajazet makes love quite in the style of an European; the bloodthirsty policy of Eastern despotism is well portrayed, it is true, in the Vizier: but the whole resembles Turkey upside down, where the women, instead of being slaves, have contrived to get possession of the government, which thereupon assumes so revolting an appearance as to incline us to believe the Turks are, after all, not much to blame in keeping their women under lock and key. Neither has Voltaire, in my opinion, succeeded much better in his *Mahomet* and *Zaire*; throughout we miss the glowing colouring of Oriental fancy. Voltaire has, however, this great merit, that as he insisted on treating subjects with more historical truth, he made it also the object of his own endeavours; and farther, that he again raised to the dignity of the tragical stage the chivalrous and Christian characters of modern Europe, which since the time of the *Cid* had been altogether excluded from it. His *Lusignan* and *Nerestan* are among his most truthful, affecting, and noble creations; his *Tancred*, although as a whole the invention is deficient in keeping, will always, like his namesake in Tasso, win every heart. *Alzire*, in a historical point of view, is highly eminent. It is singular enough that Voltaire, in his restless search after tragic materials, has actually travelled the whole world over; for as in *Alzire* he exhibits the American tribes of the other hemisphere, in his *Dschingiskan* he brings Chinese on the stage, from the farthest extremity of ours, who, however, from the faithful observation of their costume, have almost the stamp of comic or grotesque figures.

Unfortunately Voltaire came too late with his projected reformation of the theatre: much had been already ruined by the trammels within which French Tragedy had been so long confined; and the prejudice which gave such disproportionate importance to the observance of external rules and proprieties was, at it appears, established firmly and irrevocably.

Next to the rules regarding the external mechanism, which without examination they had adopted from the ancients, the prevailing national ideas of social propriety were the principal hindrances which impeded the French poets in the exercise of their talents, and in many cases put it altogether out of their power to reach the highest tragical effect. The problem which the dramatic poet has to solve is to combine poetic form with nature and truth, and consequently nothing ought to be included in the former which is inadmissible by the latter. French Tragedy, from the time of Richelieu, developed itself under the favour and protection of the court; and even its scene had (as already observed) the appearance of an antechamber. In such an atmosphere the spectators might impress the poet with the idea that courtesy is one of the original and essential ingredients of human nature. But in Tragedy men are either matched with men in fearful strife, or set in close struggle with misfortune; we can, therefore, exact from them only an ideal dignity, for from the nice observance of social punctilios they are absolved by their situation. So long as they possess sufficient presence of mind not to violate them, so long as they do not appear completely overpowered by their grief and mental agony, the deepest emotion is not as yet reached. The poet may indeed be allowed to take that care for his persons which Caesar, after his death-blow, had for himself, and make them fall with decorum. He must not exhibit human nature in all its repulsive nakedness. The most heart-rending and dreadful pictures must still be invested with beauty, and endued with a dignity higher than the common reality. This miracle is effected by poetry: it has its indescribable sighs, its immediate accents of the deepest agony, in which there still runs a something melodious. It is only a certain full-dressed and formal beauty, which is incompatible with the greatest truth of expression. And yet it is exactly this beauty that is demanded in the style of a French tragedy. No doubt something too is to be ascribed to the quality of their language and versification. The French language is wholly incapable of many bold flights, it has little poetical freedom, and it carries into poetry all the grammatical stiffness of prose. This their poets have often acknowledged and lamented. Besides, the Alexandrine with its couplets, with its hemistichs of equal length, is a very symmetrical and monotonous species of verse, and far better adapted for the expression of antithetical maxims, than for the musical delineation of passion with its unequal, abrupt, and erratic course of thoughts. But the main cause lies in a national feature, in the social endeavour never to forget themselves in presence of others, and always to exhibit themselves to the greatest possible advantage. It has been often remarked, that in French Tragedy the poet is always too easily seen through the discourses of the different personages, that he communicates to them his awn presence of mind, his cool reflections on their situation, and his desire to shine on all occasions. When most of their tragical speeches are closely examined, they are seldom found to be such as the persons speaking or acting by themselves without restraint would deliver; something or other is generally discovered in them which betrays a reference to the spectator more or less perceptible. Before, however, our compassion can be powerfully excited, we must be familiar with the persons; but how is this possible if we are always to see them under the yoke of their designs and endeavours, or, what is worse, of an unnatural and assumed grandeur of character? We must overhear them in their unguarded moments, when they imagine themselves alone, and throw aside all care and reserve.

Eloquence may and ought to have a place in Tragedy, but in so far as it is in some measure artificial in its method and preparation, it can only be in character when the speaker is sufficiently master of himself; for, for overpowering passion, an unconscious and involuntary eloquence is alone suitable. The truly inspired orator forgets himself in the subject of his eloquence. We call it rhetoric when he thinks less of his subject than of himself, and of the art in which he flatters himself he has obtained a mastery. Rhetoric, and rhetoric in a court dress, prevails but too much in many French tragedies, especially in those of Corneille, instead of the suggestions of a noble, but simple and artless nature; Racine and Voltaire, however, have come much nearer to the true conception of a mind carried away by its sufferings. Whenever the tragic hero is able to express his pain in antitheses and ingenious allusions, we may safely reserve our pity. This sort of conventional dignity is, as it were, a coat of mail, which prevents the pain from reaching the inmost heart. On account of their retaining this festal pomp in situations where the most complete self-forgetfulness would be natural, Schiller has wittily enough compared the heroes in French Tragedy to the kings in old engravings who lie in bed, crown, sceptre, robes and all.

This social refinement prevails through the whole of French literature and art. Social refinement sharpens, no doubt, the sense for the ludicrous, and even on that account, when it is carried to a fastidious excess, it is the death of every thing like enthusiasm. For all enthusiasm, all poetry, has a ludicrous aspect for the unfeeling. When, therefore, such a way of thinking has once become universal in a nation, a certain negative criticism will be associated with it. A thousand different things must be avoided, and in attending to these, the highest object of all, that which ought properly to be accomplished, is lost sight of. The fear of ridicule is the conscience of French poets; it has clipt their wings, and impaired their flight. For it is exactly in the most serious kind of poetry that this fear must torment them the most; for extremes run into one another, and whenever pathos fails it gives rise to laughter and parody. It is amusing to witness Voltaire's extreme agony when he was threatened with a parody of his *Semiramis* on the Italian theatre. In a petition to the queen, this man, whose whole life had been passed in turning every thing great and venerable into ridicule, urges his situation as one of the servants of the king's household, as a ground for obtaining from high authority the prohibition of a very innocent and allowable amusement. As French wits have indulged themselves in turning every thing in the world into ridicule, and more especially the mental productions of other nations, they will also allow us on our part to divert ourselves at the expense of their tragic writers, if with all their care they have now and then split upon the rock of which they were most in dread. Lessing has, with the most irresistible and victorious wit, pointed out the ludicrous nature of the very plans of *Rodogune*, *Semiramis*, *Merope*, and *Zaire*. But both in this respect and with regard to single laughable turns, a rich harvest might yet be gathered. [Footnote: A few examples of the latter will be sufficient. The lines with which Theseus in the *Oedipus* of Corneille opens his part, are deserving of one of the first places:

Quelque ravage affreux qu'etale ici la peste
L'absence aux vrais amans est encore plus funeste.

The following from his *Otho* are equally well known:

Dis moi donc, lorsqu' Othon s'est offert a Camille,
A-t-il paru contraint? a-t-elle ete facile?
Son hommage aupres d'elle a-t-il eu plein effet?
Comment l'a-t-elle pris, et comment l'a-t-il fait?

Where it is almost inconceivable, that the poet could have failed to see the application which might be made of the passage, especially as he allows the confidant to answer, *J'ai tout vu.* That *Attila* should treat the kings who are dependent on him like good-for-nothing fellows:

Ils ne sont pas venus, nos deux rois; qu'on leur die
Qu'ils se font trop attendre, et qu' Attila s'ennuie
Qu'alors que je les mande ils doivent se hater:

may in one view appear very serious and true; but nevertheless it appears exceedingly droll to us from the turn of expression, and especially from its being the opening of the piece. Generally speaking, with respect to the ludicrous, Corneille lived in a state of great innocence; since his time the world has become a great deal more witty. Hence, after making al allowances for what he cannot justly be blamed for, what, namely, arises merely from his language having become obsolete, we shall still find an ample field remaining for our ridicule. Among the numerous plays which are not reckoned among his master-pieces, we have only to turn up any one at random to light upon numerous passages susceptible of a ludicrous application. Racine, from the refinement and moderation which were natural to him, was much better guarded against this danger; but yet, here and there, expressions of the same kind escape from him. Among these we may include the whole of the speech in which Theramenes exhorts his pupil Hippolytus to yield himself up to love. The ludicrous can hardly be carried farther than it is in these lines:

Craint-on de s'egarer sur les traces d'Hercule?
Quels courages Venus n'a-t-elle pas domtes?
Vous meme, *ou seriez vous*, vous qui la combattez,
Si toujours Antiope, a ses loix opposee,
D'une *pudique* ardeur n'eut brule pour Thesee?

In *Berenice*, Antiochus receives his confidant, whom he had sent to announce his visit to the Queen, with the words: *Arsace, entrerons-nous?* This humble patience in an antechamber would appear even undignified in Comedy, but it appears too pitiful even for a second-rate tragical hero. Antiochus says afterwards to the queen:

Je me suis tu cinq ans
Madame, et vais encore me taire plus long-tems--

And to give an immediate proof of his intention by his conduct, he repeats after this no less than fifty verses in a breath.

When Orosman says to Zaire, whom he pretends to love with European tenderness,

Je sais que notre loi, favorable aux plaisirs
Ouvre un champ sans limite *a nos vastes desirs*:

his language is still more indecorous than laughable. But the answer of Zaire to her confidante, who thereupon reminded her that she is a Christian, is highly comic:

Ah! que dis-tu? pourquoi rappeler mes ennuis?

Upon the whole, however, Voltaire is much more upon his guard against the ludicrous than his predecessors: this was perfectly natural, for in his time the rage of turning every thing into ridicule was most prevalent. We may boldly affirm that in our days a single verse of the same kind as hundreds in Corneille would inevitably ruin any play.] But the war which Lessing carried on against the French stage was much more merciless, perhaps, than we, in the present day, should be justified in waging. At the time when he published his *Dramaturgie*, we Germans had scarcely any but French tragedies upon our stages, and the extravagant predilection for them as classical models had not then been combated. At present the national taste has declared itself so decidedly against them, that we have nothing to fear of an illusion in that quarter.

It is farther said that the French dramatists have to do with a public not only extremely fastidious in its dislike of any low intermixture, and highly susceptible of the ludicrous, but also extremely impatient. We will allow them the full enjoyment of this self-flattery: for we have no doubt that their real meaning is, that this impatience is a proof of quickness of apprehension and sharpness of wit. It is susceptible, however, of another interpretation: superficial knowledge, and more especially intrinsic emptiness of mind, invariably display themselves in fretful impatience. But however this may be, the disposition in question has had both a favourable and an unfavourable influence on the structure of their pieces. Favourable, in so far as it has compelled them to lop off every superfluity, to go directly to the main business, to be perspicuous, to study compression, to endeavour to turn every moment to the utmost advantage. All these are good theatrical proprieties, and have been the means of recommending the French tragedies as models of perfection to those who in the examination of works of art, measure everything by the dry test of the understanding, rather than listen to the voice of imagination and feeling. It has been unfavourable, in so far as even motion, rapidity, and a continued stretch of expectation, become at length monotonous and wearisome. It is like a music from which the *piano* should be altogether excluded, and in which even the difference between *forte* and *fortissimo* should, from the mistaken emulation of the performers, be rendered indistinguishable. I find too few resting-places in their tragedies similar to those in the ancient tragedies where the lyric parts come in. There are moments in human life which are dedicated by every religious mind to self-meditation, and when, with the view turned towards the past and the future, it keeps as it were holiday. This sacredness of the moment is not, I think, sufficiently reverenced: the actors and spectators alike are incessantly hurried on to something that is to follow; and we shall find very few scenes indeed, where a mere state, independent of its causal connexion, is represented developing itself. The question with them is always *what* happens, and only too seldom *how* happens it. And yet this is the main point, if an impression is to be made on the witnesses of human events. Hence every thing like silent effect is almost entirely excluded from their domain of dramatic art. The only leisure which remains for the actor for his silent pantomime is during the delivery of the long discourses addressed to him, when, however, it more frequently serves to embarrass him than assists him in the development of his part. They are satisfied if the web of the intrigue keeps uninterruptedly in advance of their own quickness of tact, and if in the speeches and answers the shuttle flies diligently backwards and forwards to the end.

Generally speaking, impatience is by no means a good disposition for the reception of the beautiful. Even dramatic poetry, the most animated production of art, has its contemplative side, and where this is neglected, the representation, from its very rapidity and animation, engenders only a deafening tumult in our mind, instead of that inward music which ought to accompany it.

The existence of many technical imperfections in their tragedy has been admitted even by French critics themselves; the confidants, for instance. Every hero and heroine regularly drags some one along with them, a gentleman in waiting or a court lady. In not a few pieces, we may count three or four of these merely passive hearers, who sometimes open their lips to tell something to their patron which he must have known better himself, or who on occasion are dispatched hither and thither on messages. The confidants in the Greek tragedies, either old guardian-slaves and nurses, or servants, have always peculiar characteristical destinations, and the ancient tragedians felt so little the want of communications between a hero and his confidant, to make us acquainted with the hero's state of mind and views, that they even introduce as a mute personage so important and proverbially famous a friend as a Pylades. But whatever ridicule was cast on the confidants, and however great the reproach of being reduced to make use of them, no attempt was ever made till the time of Alfieri to get rid of them.

The expositions or statements of the preliminary situation of things are another nuisance. They generally consist of choicely turned disclosures to the confidants, delivered in a happy moment of leisure. That very public whose impatience keeps the poets and players under such strict discipline, has, however, patience enough to listen to the prolix unfolding of what ought to be sensibly developed before their eyes. It is allowed that an exposition is seldom unexceptionable; that in their speeches the persons generally begin farther back than they naturally ought, and that they tell one another what they must both have known before, &c. If the affair is complicated, these expositions are generally extremely tedious: those of Heraclius and Rodogune absolutely make the head giddy. Chaulieu says of Crebillon's *Rhadamiste*, "The piece would be perfectly clear were it not for the exposition." To me it seems that their whole system of expositions, both in Tragedy and in High Comedy, is exceedingly erroneous. Nothing can be more ill-judged than to begin at once to instruct us without any dramatic movement. At the first drawing up of the curtain the spectator's attention is almost unavoidably distracted by external circumstances, his interest has not yet been excited; and this is precisely the time chosen by the poet to exact from him an earnest of undivided attention to a dry explanation,--a demand which he can hardly be supposed ready to meet. It will perhaps be urged that the same thing was done by the Greek poets. But with them the subject was for the most part extremely simple, and already known to the spectators; and their expositions, with the exception of the unskilful prologues of Euripides, have not the didactic particularising tone of the French, but are full of life and motion. How admirable again are the expositions of Shakspeare and Calderon! At the very outset they lay hold of the imagination; and when they have once gained the spectator's interest and sympathy they then bring forward the information necessary for the full understanding of the implied transactions. This means is, it is true, denied to the French tragic poets, who, if at all, are only very sparingly allowed the use of any thing calculated to make an impression on the senses, any thing like corporeal action; and who, therefore, for the sake of a gradual heightening of the impression are obliged to reserve to the last acts the little which is within their power.

To sum up all my previous observations in a few words: the French have endeavoured to form their tragedy according to a strict idea; but instead of this they have set up merely an abstract notion. They require tragical dignity and grandeur, tragical situations, passions, and pathos, altogether simple and pure, and without any foreign appendages. Stript thus of their proper investiture, they lose much in truth, profundity, and character; and the whole composition is deprived of the living charm of variety, of the magic of picturesque situations, and of all those ravishing effects which a light but preparatory matter, when left to itself, often produces on the mind by its marvellous and spontaneous growth. With respect to the theory of the tragic art, they are yet at the very same point that they were in the art of gardening before the time of Lenotre. All merit consisted, in their judgment, in extorting a triumph from nature by means of art. They had no other idea of regularity than the measured symmetry of straight alleys, clipped edges, &c. Vain would have been the attempt to make those who laid out such gardens to comprehend that there could be any plan, any hidden order, in an English park, and demonstrate to them that a succession of landscapes, which from their gradation, their alternation, and their opposition, give effect to each other, did all aim at exciting in us a certain mental impression.

The rooted and lasting prejudices of a whole nation are seldom accidental, but are connected with some general want of intrinsic capacities, from which even the eminent minds who read the rest are not exempted. We are not, therefore, to consider such prejudices merely as causes; we must also consider them at the same time as important effects. We allow that the narrow system of rules, that a dissecting criticism of the understanding, has shackled the efforts of the French tragedians; still, however, it remains doubtful whether of their own inclination they would ever have made choice of more comprehensive designs, and, if so, in what way they would have filled them up. The most distinguished among them have certainly not been deficient in means and talents. In a particular examination of their different productions we cannot show them any favour; but, on a general view, they are more deserving of pity than censure; and when, under such unfavourable circumstances, they yet produce what is excellent, they are doubly entitled to our admiration, although we can by no means admit the justice of the common-place observation, that the overcoming of difficulty is a source of pleasure, nor find anything meritorious in a work of art merely because it is artificially composed. As for the claim which the French advance to set themselves up, in spite of all their one-sidedness and inadequacy of view, as the lawgivers of taste, it must be rejected with becoming indignation.

LECTURE XIX.

Use at first made of the Spanish Theatre by the French--General Character of Corneille, Racine, and Voltaire--Review of the principal Works of Corneille and of Racine--Thomas Corneille and Crebillon.

I have briefly noticed all that was necessary to mention of the antiquities of the French stage. The duties of the poet were gradually more rigorously laid down, under a belief in the authority of the ancients, and the infallibility of Aristotle. By their own inclination, however, the poets were led to the Spanish theatre, as long as the Dramatic Art in France, under a native education, had not attained its full maturity. They not only imitated the Spaniards, but, from this mine of ingenious invention, even borrowed largely and directly. I do not merely allude to the earlier times under Richelieu; this state of things continued through the whole of the first half of the age of Louis XIV.; and Racine is perhaps the oldest poet who seems to have been altogether unacquainted with the Spaniards, or at least who was in no manner influenced by them. The comedies of Corneille are nearly all taken from Spanish pieces; and of his celebrated works, the *Cid* and *Don Sancho of Aragon* are also Spanish. The only piece of Rotrou which still keeps its place on the theatre, *Wenceslas*, is borrowed from Francisco de Roxas: Moliere's unfinished *Princess of Etis* is from Moreto, his *Don Garcia of Navarre* from an unknown author, and the *Festin de Pierre* carries its origin in its front: [Footnote: And betrays at the same time Moliere's ignorance of Spanish. For if he had possessed even a tolerable knowledge of it, how could he have translated *El Convidado de Piedra* (the Stone Guest) into the *Stone Feast*, which has no meaning here, and could only be applicable to the Feasts of Midas?] we have only to look at the works of Thomas Corneille to be at once convinced that, with the exception of a few, they are all Spanish; as also are the earlier labours of Quinault, namely, his comedies and tragi-comedies. The right of drawing without scruple from this source was so universal, that the French imitators, when they borrowed without the least disguise, did not even give themselves the trouble of naming the author of the original, and assigning to the true owner a part of the applause which they might earn. In the *Cid* alone the text of the Spanish poet is frequently cited, and that only because Corneille's claim to originality had been called in question.

We should certainly derive much instruction from a discovery of the prototypes, when they are not among the more celebrated, or already known by their titles, and thereupon instituting a comparison between them and their copies. We must, however, go very differently to work from Voltaire in *Heraclius*, in which, as Garcia de la Huerta [Footnote: In the introduction to his Theatro Hespanol.] has incontestably proved, he displays both great ignorance and studied and disgusting perversions. If the most of these imitations give little pleasure to France in the present day, this decision is noways against the originals, which must always have suffered considerably from the recast. The national characters of the French and Spanish are totally different; and consequently also the spirit of their language and poetry. The most temperate and restrained character belongs to the French; the Spaniard, though in the remotest West, displays, what his history may easily account for, an Oriental vein, which luxuriates in a profusion of bold images and sallies of wit. When we strip their dramas of these rich and splendid ornaments, when, for the glowing colours of their romance and the musical variations of the rhymed strophes in which they are composed, we compel them to assume the monotony of the Alexandrine, and submit to the fetters of external regularities, while the character and situations are allowed to remain essentially the same, there can no longer be any harmony between the subject and its mode of treatment, and it loses that truth which it may still retain within the domain of fancy.

The charm of the Spanish poetry consists, generally speaking, in the union of a sublime and enthusiastic earnestness of feeling, which peculiarly descends from the North, with the lovely breath of the South, and the dazzling pomp of the East. Corneille possessed an affinity to the Spanish spirit but only in the first point; he might be taken for a Spaniard educated in Normandy. It is much to be regretted that he had not, after the composition of the *Cid*, employed himself without depending on foreign models, upon subjects which would have allowed him to follow altogether his feeling for chivalrous honour and fidelity. But on the other hand he took himself to the Roman history; and the severe patriotism of the older, and the ambitious policy of the later Romans, supplied the place of chivalry, and in some measure assumed its garb. It was by no means so much his object to excite our terror and compassion as our admiration for the characters and astonishment at the situations of his heroes. He hardly ever affects us; and is seldom capable of agitating our minds. And here I may indeed observe, that such is his partiality for exciting our wonder and admiration, that, not contented with exacting it for the heroism of virtue, he claims it also for the heroism of vice, by the boldness, strength of soul, presence of mind, and elevation above all human weakness, with which he endows his criminals of both sexes. Nay, often his characters express themselves in the language of ostentatious pride, without our being well able to see what they have to be proud of: they are merely proud of their pride. We cannot often say that we take an interest in them: they either appear, from the great resources which they possess within themselves, to stand in no need of our compassion, or else they are undeserving of it. He has delineated the conflict of passions and motives; but for the most part not immediately as such, but as already metamorphosed into a contest of principles. It is in love that he has been found coldest; and this was because he could not prevail on himself to paint it as an amiable weakness, although he everywhere introduced it, even where most unsuitable, either out of a condescension to the taste of the age or a private inclination for chivalry, where love always appears as the ornament of valour, as the checquered favour waving at the lance, or the elegant ribbon-knot to the sword. Seldom does he paint love as a power which imperceptibly steals upon us, and gains at last an involuntary and irresistible dominion over us; but as an homage freely chosen at first, to the exclusion of duty, but afterwards maintaining its place along with it. This is the case at least in his better pieces; for in his later works love is frequently compelled to give way to ambition; and these two springs of action mutually weaken each other. His females are generally not sufficiently feminine; and the love which they inspire is with them not the last object, but merely a means to something beyond. They drive their lovers into great dangers, and sometimes also to great crimes; and the men too often appear to disadvantage, while they allow themselves to become mere instruments in the hands of women, or to be dispatched by them on heroic errands, as it were, for the sake of winning the prize of love held out to them. Such women as Emilia in *Cinna and Rodogune*, must surely be unsusceptible of love. But if in his principal characters, Corneille, by exaggerating the energetic and underrating the passive part of our nature, has departed from truth; if his heroes display too much volition and too little feeling, he is still much more unnatural in his situations. He has, in defiance of all probability, pointed them in such a way that we might with great propriety give them the name of tragical antitheses, and it becomes almost natural if the personages express themselves in a series of epigrammatical maxims. He is fond of exhibiting perfectly symmetrical oppositions. His eloquence is often admirable from its strength and compression; but it sometimes degenerates into bombast, and exhausts itself in superfluous accumulations. The later Romans, Seneca the philosopher, and Lucan, were considered by him too much in the light of models; and unfortunately he possessed also a vein of Seneca the tragedian. From this wearisome pomp of declamation, a few simple words interspersed here and there, have been often made the subject of extravagant praise. [Footnote: For instance, the *Qu'il mourut* of the old Horatius; the *Soyons amis, Cinna*: also the *Moi* of Medea, which, we may observe in passing, is borrowed from Seneca.] If they stood alone they would certainly be entitled to praise; but they are immediately followed by long harangues which destroy their effect. When the Spartan mother, on delivering the shield to her son, used the well-known words, "This, or on this!" she certainly made no farther addition to them. Corneille was peculiarly well qualified to portray ambition and the lust of power, a passion which stifles all other human feelings, and never properly erects its throne till the mind has become a cold and dreary wilderness. His youth was passed in the last civil wars, and he still saw around him remains of the feudal independence. I will not pretend to decide how much this may have influenced him, but it is undeniable that the sense which he often showed of the great importance of political questions was altogether lost in the following age, and did not make its appearance again before Voltaire. However he, like the rest of the poets of his time, paid his tribute of flattery to Louis the Fourteenth, in verses which are now forgotten.

Racine, who for all but an entire century has been unhesitatingly proclaimed the favourite poet of the French nation, was by no means during his lifetime in so enviable a situation, and, notwithstanding many an instance of brilliant success, could not rest as yet in the pleasing and undisturbed possession of his fame. His merit in giving the last polish to the French language, his unrivalled excellence both of expression and versification, were not then allowed; on the stage he had rivals, of whom some were undeservedly preferred before him. On the one hand, the exclusive admirers of Corneille, with Madame Sevigne at their head, made a formal party against him; on the other hand, Pradon, a younger candidate for the honours of the Tragic Muse, endeavoured to wrest the victory from him, and actually succeeded, not merely, it would appear, in gaining over the crowd, but the very court itself, notwithstanding the zeal with which he was opposed by Boileau. The chagrin to which this gave rise, unfortunately interrupted his theatrical career at the very period when his mind had reached its full maturity: a mistaken piety afterwards prevented him from resuming his theatrical occupations, and it required all the influence of Madame Maintenon to induce him to employ his talent upon religious subjects for a particular occasion. It is probable that but for this interruption, he would have carried his art still higher: for in the works which we have of him, we trace a gradually advancing improvement. He is a poet in every way worthy of our love: he possessed a delicate susceptibility for all the tenderer emotions, and great sweetness in expressing them. His moderation, which never allowed him to transgress the bounds of propriety, must not be estimated too highly: for he did not possess strength of character in any eminent degree, nay, there are even marks of weakness perceptible in him, which, it is said, he also exhibited in private life. He has also paid his homage to the sugared gallantry of his age, where it merely serves as a show of love to connect together the intrigue; but he has often also succeeded completely in the delineation of a more genuine love, especially in his female characters; and many of his love-scenes breathe a tender voluptuousness, which, from the veil of reserve and modesty thrown over it, steals only the more seductively into the soul. The inconsistencies of unsuccessful passion, the wanderings of a mind diseased, and a prey to irresistible desire, he has portrayed more touchingly and truthfully than any French poet before him, or even perhaps after him. Generally speaking, he was more inclined to the elegiac and the idyllic, than to the heroic. I will not say that he would never have elevated himself to more serious and dignified conceptions than are to be found in his *Britannicus* and *Mithridate*; but here we must distinguish between that which his subject suggested, and what he painted with a peculiar fondness, and wherein he is not so much the dramatic artist as the spokesman of his own feelings. At the same time, it ought not to be forgotten that Racine composed most of his pieces when very young, and that this may possibly have influenced his choice. He seldom disgusts us, like Corneille and Voltaire, with the undisguised repulsiveness of unnecessary crimes; he has, however, often veiled much that in reality is harsh, base, and mean, beneath the forms of politeness and courtesy. I cannot allow the plans of his pieces to be, as the French critics insist, unexceptionable; those which he borrowed from ancient mythology are, in my opinion, the most liable to objection; but still I believe, that with the rules and observations which he took for his guide, he could hardly in most cases have extricated himself from his difficulties more cautiously and with greater propriety than he has actually done. Whatever may be the defects of his productions separately considered, when we compare him with others, and view him in connexion with the French literature in general, we can hardly bestow upon him too high a meed of praise.

A new aera of French Tragedy begins with Voltaire, whose first appearance, in his early youth, as a writer for the theatre, followed close upon the age of Louis the Fourteenth. I have already, in a general way, alluded to the changes and enlargements which he projected, and partly carried into execution. Corneille and Racine led a true artist's life: they were dramatic poets with their whole soul; their desire, as authors, was confined to that object alone, and all their studies were directed to the stage. Voltaire, on the contrary, wished to shine in every possible department; a restless vanity permitted him not to be satisfied with the pursuit of perfection in any single walk of literature; and from the variety of subjects on which his mind was employed, it was impossible for him to avoid shallowness and immaturity of ideas. To form a correct idea of his relation to his two predecessors in the tragic art, we must institute a comparison between the characteristic features of the preceding classical age and of that in which he gave the tone. In the time of Louis the Fourteenth, a certain traditionary code of opinions on all the most important concerns of humanity reigned in full force and unquestioned; and even in poetry, the object was not so much to enrich as to form the mind, by a liberal and noble entertainment. But now, at length, the want of original thinking began to be felt; however, it unfortunately happened, that bold presumption hurried far in advance of profound inquiry, and hence the spread of public immorality was quick followed by a dangerous scoffing scepticism, which shook to the foundation every religious and moral conviction, and the very principles of society itself. Voltaire was by turns philosopher, rhetorician, sophist, and buffoon. The want of singleness, which more or less characterised all his views, was irreconcileable with a complete freedom of prejudice even as an artist in his career. As he saw the public longing for information, which was rather tolerated by the favour of the great than authorised and formally approved of and dispensed by appropriate public institutions, he did not fail to meet their want, and to deliver, in beautiful verses, on the stage, what no man durst yet preach from the pulpit or the professor's chair. He made use of poetry as a means to accomplish ends foreign and extrinsecal to it; and this has often polluted the artistic purity of his compositions. Thus, the end of his *Mahomet* was to portray the dangers of fanaticism, or rather, laying aside all circumlocution, of a belief in revelation. For this purpose, he has most unjustifiably disfigured a great historical character, revoltingly loaded him with the most crying enormities, with which he racks and tortures our feelings. Universally known, as he was, to be the bitter enemy of Christianity, he bethought himself of a new triumph for his vanity; in *Zaire* and *Alzire*, he had recourse to Christian sentiments to excite emotion: and here, for once, his versatile heart, which, indeed, in its momentary ebullitions, was not unsusceptible of good feelings, shamed the rooted malice of his understanding; he actually succeeded, and these affecting and religious passages cry out loudly against the slanderous levity of his petulant misrepresentations. In England he had acquired a knowledge of a free constitution, and became an enthusiastic admirer of liberty. Corneille had introduced the Roman republicanism and general politics into his works, for the sake of their poetical energy. Voltaire again exhibited them under a poetical form, because of the political effect he thought them calculated to produce on popular opinion. As he fancied he was better acquainted with the Greeks than his predecessors, and as he had obtained a slight knowledge of the English theatre and Shakspeare, which, before him, were for France, quite an unknown land, he wished in like manner to use them to his own advantage.--He insisted on the earnestness, the severity, and the simplicity of the Greek dramatic representation; and actually in so far approached them, as to exclude love from various subjects to which it did not properly belong. He was desirous of reviving the majesty of the Grecian scenery; and here his endeavours had this good effect, that in theatrical representation the eye was no longer so miserably neglected as it had been. He borrowed from Shakspeare, as he thought, bold strokes of theatrical effect; but here he was the least successful; when, in imitation of that great master, he ventured in *Semiramis* to call up a ghost from the lower world, he fell into innumerable absurdities. In a word he was perpetually making experiments with dramatic art, availing himself of some new device for effect. Hence some of his works seem to have stopt short half way between studies and finished productions; there is a trace of something unfixed and unfinished in his whole mental formation. Corneille and Racine, within the limits which they set themselves, are much more perfect; they are altogether that which they are, and we have no glimpses in their works of any supposed higher object beyond them. Voltaire's pretensions are much more extensive than his means. Corneille has expressed the maxims of heroism with greater sublimity, and Racine the natural emotions with a sweeter gracefulness; while Voltaire, it must be allowed, has employed the moral motives with greater effect, and displayed a more intimate acquaintance with the primary and fundamental principles of the human mind. Hence, in some of his pieces, he is more deeply affecting than either of the other two.

The first and last only of these three great masters of the French tragic stage can be said to be fruitful writers; and, even these can hardly be accounted so, if compared with the Greeks. That Racine was not more prolific, was owing partly to accidental circumstances. He enjoys this advantage, however, that with the exception of his first youthful attempts, the whole of his pieces have kept possession of the stage, and the public estimation. But many of Corneille's and Voltaire's, even such as were popular at first, have been since withdrawn from the stage, and at present are not even so much as read. Accordingly, selections only from their works, under the title of *Chef-d'oeuvres*, are now generally published. It is remarkable, that few only of the many French attempts in Tragedy have been successful. La Harpe reckons up nearly a thousand tragedies which have been acted or printed since the death of Racine; and of these not more than thirty, besides those of Voltaire, have kept possession of the stage. Notwithstanding, therefore, the great competition in this department, the tragic treasures of the French are far from ample. Still we do not feel ourselves called upon to give a full account even of these; and still farther is it from our purpose to enter into a circumstantial and anatomical investigation of separate pieces. All that our limits will allow us is, with a rapid pen, to sketch the character and relative value of the principal works of those three masters, and a few others specially deserving of mention.

Corneille brilliantly opened his career of fame with the *Cid*, of which, indeed, the execution alone is his own: in the plan he appears to have closely followed his Spanish original. As the *Cid* of Guillen de Castro has never fallen into my hands, it has been out of my power to institute an accurate comparison between the two works. But if we may judge from the specimens produced, the Spanish piece seems written with far greater simplicity; and the subject owes to Corneille its rhetorical pomp of ornament. On the other hand, we are ignorant how much he has left out and sacrificed. All the French critics are agreed in thinking the part of the Infanta superfluous. They cannot see that by making a princess forget her elevated rank, and entertain a passion for Rodrigo, the Spanish poet thereby distinguished him as the flower of noble and amiable knights; and, on the other hand, furnished a strong justification of Chimene's love, which so many powerful motives could not overcome. It is true, that to be attractive in themselves, and duly to aid the general effect, the Infanta's passion required to be set forth more musically, and Rodrigo's achievements against the Moors more especially, *i. e.*, with greater vividness of detail: and probably they were so in the Spanish original. The rapturous applause, which, on its first appearance, universally welcomed a piece like this, which, without the admixture of any ignoble incentive, founded its attraction altogether on the represented conflict between the purest feelings of love, honour, and filial duty, is a strong proof that the romantic spirit was not yet extinct among spectators who were still open to such natural impressions. This was entirely misunderstood by the learned; with the Academy at their head, they affirmed that this subject (one of the most beautiful that ever fell to the lot of a poet) was unfit for Tragedy; incapable of entering historically into the spirit of another age, they made up improbabilities and improprieties for their censure. [Footnote: Scuderi speaks even of Chimene as a monster, and off-hand dismisses the whole, as "*ce mechant combat de l'amour et de l'honneur*." Excellent! Surely he understood the romantic!] The *Cid* is not certainly a tragedy in the sense of the ancients; and, at first, the poet himself called it a Tragi-comedy. Would that this had been the only occasion in which the authority of Aristotle has been applied to subjects which do not belong to his jurisdiction!

The Horatii has been censured for want of unity; the murder of the sister and the acquittal of the victorious Roman is said to be a second action, independent of the combat of the Horatii and Curiatii. Corneille himself was talked into a belief of it. He appears, however, to me fully justified in what he has done. If the murder of Camilla had not made a part of the piece, the female characters in the first act would have been superfluous; and without the triumph of patriotism over family ties, the combat could not have been an action, but merely an event destitute of all tragic complication. But the real defect, in my opinion, is Corneille representing a public act which decided the fate of two states, as taking place altogether *infra privates parietes*, and stripping it of every visible pomp of circumstance. Hence the great flatness of the fifth act. What a different impression would have been produced had Horatius, in presence of the king and people, been solemnly condemned, in obedience to the stern mandate of the law, and afterwards saved through the tears and lamentations of his father, just as Livy describes it. Moreover, the poet, not satisfied with making, as the history does, one sister of the Horatii in love with one of the Curiatii, has thought proper to invent the marriage of a sister of the Curiatii with one of the Horatii: and as in the former the love of country yields to personal inclination, in the latter personal inclination yields to love of country. This gives rise to a great improbability: for is it likely that men would have been selected for the combat who, with a well-known family connexion of this kind, would have had the most powerful inducements to spare one another? Besides, the conqueror's murder of his sister cannot be rendered even poetically tolerable, except by supposing him in all the boiling impetuosity of ungovernable youth. Horatius, already a husband, would have shown a wiser and milder forbearance towards his unfortunate sister's language; else were he a ferocious savage.

Cinna is commonly ranked much higher than *The Horatii*; although, as to purity of sentiment, there is here a perceptible falling off from that ideal sphere in which the action of the two preceding pieces moves. All is diversely complicated and diseased. Cinna's republicanism is merely the cloak of another passion: he is a tool in the hands of Emilia, who, on her part, constantly sacrifices her pretended love to her passion of revenge. The magnanimity of Augustus is ambiguous: it appears rather the caution of a tyrant grown timid through age. The conspiracy is, with a splendid narration, thrust into the background; it does not excite in us that gloomy apprehension which so theatrical an object ought to do. Emilia, the soul of the piece, is called by the witty Balzac, when commending the work, "an adorable fury." Yet the Furies themselves could be appeased by purifications and expiations: but Emilia's heart is inaccessible to the softening influences of benevolence and generosity; the adoration of so unfeminine a creature is hardly pardonable even in a lover. Hence she has no better adorers than Cinna and Maximus, two great villains, whose repentance comes too late to be thought sincere.

Here we have the first specimen of that Machiavellism of motives, which subsequently disfigured the poetry of Corneille, and which is not only repulsive, but also for the most part both clumsy and unsuitable. He flattered himself, that in knowledge of men and the world, in an acquaintance with courts and politics, he surpassed the most shrewd and clear-sighted observers. With a mind naturally alive to honour, he yet conceived the design of taking in hand the "doctrine of the murderous Machiavel;" and displays, broadly and didactically, all the knowledge which he had acquired of these arts. He had no suspicion that a remorseless and selfish policy goes always smoothly to work, and dexterously disguises itself. Had he been really capable of anything of the kind, he might have taken a lesson from Richelieu.

Of the remaining pieces in which Corneille has painted the Roman love of liberty and conquest, the *Death of Pompey* is the most eminent. It is full, however, of a grandeur which is more dazzling than genuine; and, indeed, we could expect nothing else from a cento of Lucan's hyperbolical antitheses. These bravuras of rhetoric are strung together on the thread of a clumsy plot. The intrigues of Ptolemy, and the ambitious coquetry of his sister Cleopatra, have a petty and miserable appearance alongside of the picture of the fate of the great Pompey, the vengeance-breathing sorrow of his wife, and the magnanimous compassion of Caesar. Scarcely has the conqueror paid the last honours to the reluctant shade of his rival, when he does homage at the feet of the beautiful queen; he is not only in love, but sighingly and ardently in love. Cleopatra, on her part, according to the poet's own expression, is desirous, by her love-ogling, to gain the sceptre of her brother. Caesar certainly made love, in his own way, to a number of women: but these cynical loves, if represented with anything like truth, would be most unfit for the stage. Who can refrain from laughing, when Rome, in the speech of Caesar, implores the *chaste* love of Cleopatra for young Caesar?

In *Sertorius*, a much later work, Corneille has contrived to make the great Pompey appear little, and the hero ridiculous. Sertorius on one occasion exclaims--

Que c'est un sort cruel d'aimer par politique!

This admits of being applied to all the personages of the piece. In love they are not in the least; but they allow a pretended love to be subservient to political ends. Sertorius, a hardy and hoary veteran, acts the lover with the Spanish Queen, Viriata; he brings forward, however, pretext after pretext, and offers himself the while to Aristia; as Viriata presses him to marry her on the spot, he begs anxiously for a short delay; Viriata, along with her other elegant phrases, says roundly, that she neither knows love nor hatred; Aristia, the repudiated wife of Pompey, says to him, "Take me back again, or I will marry another;" Pompey beseeches her to wait only till the death of Sylla, whom he dare not offend: after this there is no need to mention the low scoundrel Perpenna. The tendency to this frigidity of soul was perceptible in Corneille, even at an early period of his career; but in the works of his old age it increased to an incredible degree.

In *Polyeucte*, Christian sentiments are not unworthily expressed; yet we find in it more *superstitious reverence* than *fervent enthusiasm* for religion: the wonders of grace are rather *affirmed*, than embraced by a mysterious illumination. Both the tone and the situations in the first acts, incline greatly, as Voltaire observes, to comedy. A woman who, in obedience to her father, has married against her inclinations, and who declares both to her lover (who returns when too late) and to her husband, that "she still retains her first love, but that she will keep within the bounds of virtue;" a vulgar and selfish father, who is sorry that he has not chosen for his son-in-law the first suitor, now become the favourite of the Emperor; all this promises no very high tragical determinations. The divided heart of Paulina is in nature, and consequently does not detract from the interest of the piece. It is generally agreed that her situation, and the character of Severus, constitute the principal charm of this drama. But the practical magnanimity of this Roman, in conquering his passion, throws Polyeucte's self-renunciation, which appears to cost him nothing, quite into the shade. From this a conclusion has been partly drawn, that martyrdom is, in general, an unfavourable subject for Tragedy. But nothing can be more unjust than this inference. The cheerfulness with which martyrs embraced pain and death did not proceed from want of feeling, but from the heroism of the highest love: they must previously, in struggles painful beyond expression, have obtained the victory over every earthly tie; and by the exhibition of these struggles, of these sufferings of our mortal nature, while the seraph soars on its flight to heaven, the poet may awaken in us the most fervent emotion. In *Polyeucte*, however, the means employed to bring about the catastrophe, namely, the dull and low artifice of Felix, by which the endeavours of Severus to save his rival are made rather to contribute to his destruction, are inexpressibly contemptible.

How much Corneille delighted in the symmetrical and nicely balanced play of intrigue, we may see at once from his having pronounced *Rodogune* his favourite work. I shall content myself with referring to Lessing, who has exposed pleasantly enough the ridiculous appearance which the two distressed princes cut, between a mother who says, "He who murders his mistress I will name heir to my throne," and a mistress who says, "He who murders his mother shall be my husband." The best and shortest way of going to work would have been to have locked up the two furies together. As for Voltaire, he is always recurring to the fifth act, which he declares to be one of the noblest productions of the French stage. This singular way of judging works of art by piecemeal, which would praise the parts in distinction from the whole, without which it is impossible for the parts to exist, is altogether foreign to our way of thinking.

With respect to *Heraclius*, Voltaire gives himself the unnecessary trouble of showing that Calderon did not imitate Corneille; and, on the other hand, he labours, with little success, to give a negative to the question whether the latter had the Spanish author before him, and availed himself of his labours. Corneille, it is true, gives out the whole as his own invention; but we must not forget, that only when hard pressed did he acknowledge how much he owed to the author of the Spanish *Cid.* The chief circumstance of the plot, namely, the uncertainty of the tyrant Phocas as to which of the two youths is his own son, or the son of his murdered predecessor, bears great resemblance to an incident in a drama of Calderon's, and nothing of the kind is to be found in history; in other respects the plot is, it is true, altogether different. However this may be, in Calderon the ingenious boldness of an extravagant invention is always preserved in due keeping by a deeper magic colouring of the poetry; whereas in Corneille, after our head has become giddy in endeavouring to disentangle a complicated and ill-contrived intrigue, we are recompensed by a succession of mere tragical epigrams, without the slightest recreation for the fancy.

Nicomedes is a political comedy, the dryness of which is hardly in any degree relieved by the ironical tone which runs through the speeches of the hero.

This is nearly all of Corneille's that now appears on the stage. His later works are, without exception, merely treatises or reasons of state in certain difficult conjunctures, dressed out in a pompous dialogical form. We might as well make a tragedy out of a game at chess.

Those who have the patience to wade through the forgotten pieces of Corneille will perceive with astonishment that they are constructed on the same principles, and, with the exception of occasional negligences of style, executed with as much expenditure of what he considered art, as his admired productions. For example, *Attila* bears in its plot a striking resemblance to *Rodogune*. In his own judgments on his works, it is impossible not to be struck with the unessential nature of things on which he lays stress; all along he seems quite unconcerned about that which is certainly the highest object of tragical composition, the laying open the depths of the mind and the destiny of man. For the unfavourable reception which he has so frequently to confess, his self-love can always find some excuse, some trifling circumstance to which the fate of his piece was to be attributed.

In the two first youthful attempts of Racine, nothing deserves to be remarked, but the flexibility with which he accommodated himself to the limits fixed by Corneille to the career which he had opened. In the *Andromache* he first broke loose from them and became himself. He gave utterance to the inward struggles and inconsistencies of passion, with a truth and an energy which had never before been witnessed on the French stage. The fidelity of Andromache to the memory of her husband, and her maternal tenderness, are affectingly beautiful: even the proud Hermione carries us along with her in her wild aberrations. Her aversion to Orestes, after he had made himself the instrument of her revenge, and her awaking from her blind fury to utter helplesssness and despair, may almost be called tragically grand. The male parts, as is generally the case with Racine, are not to advantageously drawn. The constantly repeated threat of Pyrrhus to deliver up Astyanax to death, if Andromache should not listen to him, with his gallant protestations, resembles the arts of an executioner, who applies the torture to his victim with the most courtly phrases. It is difficult to think of Orestes, after his horrible deed, as a light-hearted and patient lover. Not the least mention is made of the murder of his mother; he seems to have completely forgotten it the whole piece through; whence, then, do the Furies come all at once at the end? This is a singular contradiction. In short, the way in which the whole is connected together bears too great a resemblance to certain sports of children, where one always runs before and tries to surprise the other.

In *Britannicus*, I have already praised the historical fidelity of the picture. Nero, Agrippina, Narcissus, and Burrhus, are so accurately sketched, and finished with such light touches and such delicate colouring, that, in respect to character, it yields, perhaps, to no French tragedy whatever. Racine has here possessed the art of giving us to understand much that is left unsaid, and enabling us to look forward into futurity. I will only notice one inconsistency which has escaped the poet. He would paint to us the cruel voluptuary, whom education has only in appearance tamed, breaking loose from the restraints of discipline and virtue. And yet, at the close of the fourth act, Narcissus speaks as if he had even then exhibited himself before the people as a player and a charioteer. But it was not until he had been hardened by the commission of grave crimes that he sunk to this ignominy. To represent the perfect Nero, that is, the flattering and cowardly tyrant, in the same person with the vain and fantastical being who, as poet, singer, player, and almost as juggler, was desirous of admiration, and in the agony of death even recited verses from Homer, was compatible only with a mixed drama, in which tragical dignity is not required throughout.

To *Berenice*, composed in honour of a virtuous princess, the French critics generally seem to me extremely unjust. It is an idyllic tragedy, no doubt; but it is full of mental tenderness. No one was better skilled than Racine in throwing a veil of dignity over female weakness.--Who doubts that Berenice has long yielded to Titus every proof of her tenderness, however carefully it may be veiled over? She is like a Magdalena of Guido, who languishingly repents of her repentance. The chief error of the piece is the tiresome part of Antiochus.

On the first representation of *Bajazet*, Corneille, it seems was heard to say, "These Turks are very much Frenchified." The censure, as is well known, attaches principally to the parts of *Bajazet* and *Atalide*. The old Grand Vizier is certainly Turkish enough; and were a Sultana ever to become the Sultan, she would perhaps throw the handkerchief in the same Sultanic manner as the disgusting Roxane. I have already observed that Turkey, in its naked rudeness, hardly admits of representation before a cultivated public. Racine felt this, and merely refined the forms without changing the main incidents. The mutes and the strangling were motives which in a seraglio could hardly be dispensed with; and so he gives, on several occasions, very elegant circumlocutory descriptions of strangling. This is, however, inconsistent; when people are so familiar with the idea of a thing, they usually call it also by its true name.

The intrigue of *Mithridate*, as Voltaire has remarked, bears great resemblance to that of the *Miser* of Moliere. Two brothers are rivals for the bride of their father, who cunningly extorts from her the name of her favoured lover, by feigning a wish to renounce in his favour. The confusion of both sons, when they learn that their father, whom they had believed dead, is still alive, and will speedily make his appearance, is in reality exceedingly comic. The one calls out: *Qu'avons nous fait?* This is just the alarm of school-boys, conscious of some impropriety, on the unexpected entrance of their master. The political scene, where Mithridates consults his sons respecting his grand project of conquering Rome, and in which Racine successfully competes with Corneille, is no doubt logically interwoven in the general plan; but still it is unsuitable to the tone of the whole, and the impression which it is intended to produce. All the interest is centred in Monime: she is one of Racine's most amiable creations, and excites in us a tender commiseration.

On no work of this poet will the sentence of German readers differ more from that of the French critics and their whole public, than on the *Iphigenie*.--Voltaire declares it the tragedy of all times and all nations, which approaches as near to perfection as human essays can; and in this opinion he is universally followed by his countrymen. But we see in it only a modernised Greek tragedy, of which the manners are inconsistent with the mythological traditions, its simplicity destroyed by the intriguing Eriphile, and in which the amorous Achilles, however brave in other respects his behaviour may be, is altogether insupportable. La Harpe affirms that the Achilles of Racine is even more Homeric than that of Euripides. What shall we say to this? Before acquiescing in the sentences of such critics, we must first forget the Greeks.

Respecting *Phedre* I may express myself with the greater brevity, as I have already dedicated a separate Treatise to that tragedy. However much Racine may have borrowed from Euripides and Seneca, and however he may have spoiled the former without improving the latter, still it is a great advance from the affected mannerism of his age to a more genuine tragic style. When we compare it with the *Phaedra* of Pradon, which was so well received by his contemporaries for no other reason than because no trace whatever of antiquity was discernible in it, but every thing reduced to the scale of a modern miniature portrait for a toilette, we must entertain a higher admiration of the poet who had so strong a feeling for the excellence of the ancient poets, and the courage to attach himself to them, and dared, in an age of vitiated and unnatural taste, to display so much purity and unaffected simplicity. If Racine actually said, that the only difference between his *Phaedra* and that of Pradon was, that he knew how to write, he did himself the most crying injustice, and must have allowed himself to be blinded by the miserable doctrine of his friend Boileau, which made the essence of poetry to consist in diction and versification, instead of the display of imagination and fancy.

Racine's last two pieces belong, as is well known, to a very different epoch of his life: they were both written at the same instigation; but are extremely dissimilar to each other. *Esther* scarcely deserves the name of a tragedy; written for the entertainment of well-bred young women in a pious seminary, it does not rise much higher than its purpose. It had, however, an astonishing success. The invitation to the representations in St. Cyr was looked upon as a court favour; flattery and scandal delighted to discover allusions throughout the piece; Ahasuerus was said to represent Louis XIV; Esther, Madame de Maintenon; the proud Vasti, who is only incidentally alluded to, Madame de Montespan; and Haman, the Minister Louvois. This is certainly rather a profane application of the sacred history, if we can suppose the poet to have had any such object in view. In *Athalie*, however, the poet exhibited himself for the last time, before taking leave of poetry and the world, in his whole strength. It is not only his most finished work, but, I have no hesitation in declaring it to be, of all French tragedies the one which, free from all mannerism, approaches the nearest to the grand style of the Greeks. The chorus is conceived fully in the ancient sense, though introduced in a different manner in order to suit our music, and the different arrangement of our theatre. The scene has all the majesty of a public action. Expectation, emotion, and keen agitation succeed each other, and continually rise with the progress of the drama: with a severe abstinence from all foreign matter, there is still a display of the richest variety, sometimes of sweetness, but more frequently of majesty and grandeur. The inspiration of the prophet elevates the fancy to flights of more than usual boldness. Its import is exactly what that of a religious drama ought to be: on earth, the struggle between good and evil; and in heaven the wakeful eye of providence beaming, from unapproachable glory, rays of constancy and resolution. All is animated by one breath--the poet's pious enthusiasm, of whose sincerity neither his life nor the work itself allow us a moment to doubt. This is the very point in which so many French works of art with their great pretensions are, nevertheless, deficient: their authors were not inspired by a fervent love of their subject, but by the desire of external effect: and hence the vanity of the artist is continually breaking forth to throw a damp over our feelings.

The unfortunate fate of this piece is well known. Scruples of conscience as to the propriety of all theatrical representations (which appear to be exclusively entertained by the Gallican church, for both in Italy and Spain men of religion and piety have thought very differently on this subject,) prevented the representation in St. Cyr; it appeared in print, and was universally abused and reprobated; and this reprobation of it long survived its author. So incapable of every thing serious was the puerile taste of the age.

Among the poets of this period, the younger Corneille deserves to be mentioned, who did not seek, like his brother, to excite astonishment by pictures of heroism so much as to win the favour of the spectators by "those tendernesses which," to use the words of Pradon, "are so agreeable." Of his numerous tragedies, two, only the *Comte d'Essex* and *Ariadne*, keep possession of the stage; the rest are consigned to oblivion. The latter of the two, composed after the model of *Berenice*, is a tragedy of which the catastrophe may, properly speaking, be said to consist in a swoon. The situation of the resigned and enamoured Ariadne, who, after all her sacrifices, sees herself abandoned by Theseus and betrayed by her own sister, is expressed with great truth of feeling. Whenever an actress of an engaging figure, and with a sweet voice, appears in this character, she is sure to excite our interest. The other parts, the cold and deceitful Theseus, the intriguing Phaedra, who continues to the last her deception of her confiding sister, the pandering Pirithbus, and King Oenarus, who instantly offers himself in the place of the faithless lover, are all pitiful in the extreme, and frequently even laughable. Moreover, the desert rocks of Naxos are here smoothed down to modern drawing-rooms; and the princes who people them, with all the observances of politeness seek to out-wit each other, or to beguile the unfortunate princess, who alone has anything like pretensions to nature.

Crebillon, in point of time, comes between Racine and Voltaire, though he was also the rival of the latter. A numerous party wished to set him, when far advanced in years, on a par with, nay, even to rank him far higher than, Voltaire. Nothing, however, but the bitterest rancour of party, or the utmost depravity of taste, or, what is most probable, the two together, could have led them to such signal injustice. Far from having contributed to the purification of the tragic art, he evidently attached himself, not to the better, but the more affected authors of the age of Louis the Fourteenth. In his total ignorance of the ancients, he has the arrogance to rank himself above them. His favourite books were the antiquated romances of a Calprenede, and others of a similar stamp: from these he derived his extravagant and ill-connected plots. One of the means to which he everywhere has recourse, is the unconscious or intentional disguise of the principal characters under other names; the first example of which was given in the *Heraclius*. Thus, in Crebillon's *Electra*, Orestes does not become known to himself before the middle of the piece. The brother and sister, and a son and daughter of Aegisthus, are almost exclusively occupied with their double amours, which neither contribute to, nor injure, the main action; and Clytemnestra is killed by a blow from Orestes, which, without knowing her, he unintentionally and involuntarily inflicts. He abounds in extravagances of every kind; of such, for instance, as the shameless impudence of Semiramis, in persisting in her love after she has learnt that its object is her own son. A few empty ravings and common-place displays of terror, have gained for Crebillon the appellation of *the terrible*, which affords us a standard for judging of the barbarous and affected taste of the age, and the infinite distance from nature and truth to which it had fallen. It is pretty much the same as, in painting, to give the appellation of the majestic to Coypel.

LECTURE XX.

Voltaire--Tragedies on Greek Subjects: *Oedipe*, *Merope*, *Oreste*--Tragedies on Roman Subjects: *Brute*, *Mort de Cesar*, *Catiline*, *Le Triumvirat*--Earlier Pieces: *Zaire*, *Alzire*, *Mahomet*, *Semiramis*, and *Tancred*.

To Voltaire, from his first entrance on his dramatic career, we must give credit both for a conviction that higher and more extensive efforts remained to be made, and for the zeal necessary to accomplish all that was yet undone. How far he was successful, and how much he was himself blinded by the very national prejudices against which he contended, is another question. For the more easy review of his works, it will be useful to class together the pieces in which he handled mythological materials, and those which he derived from the Roman history.

His earliest tragedy, *Oedipe*, is a mixture of adherence to the Greeks [Footnote: His admiration of them seems to have been more derived from foreign influence than from personal study. In his letter to the Duchess of Maine, prefixed to *Oreste*, he relates how, in his early youth, he had access to a noble house where it was a custom to read Sophocles, and to make extemporary translations from him, and where there were men who acknowledged the superiority of the Greek Theatre over the French. In vain, in the present day, should we seek for such men in France, among people of any distinction, so universally is the study of the classics depreciated.] (with the proviso, however, as may be supposed, of improving on them,) and of compliance with the prevailing manner. The best feature of this work Voltaire owed to Sophocles, whom he nevertheless slanders in his preface; and in comparison with whose catastrophe his own is flat in the extreme. Not a little, however, was borrowed from the frigid *Oedipus* of Corneille; and more especially the love of Philoctetus for Jocaste, which may be said to correspond nearly with that of Theseus and Dirce in Corneille. Voltaire alleged in his defence the tyranny of the players, from which a young and unknown writer cannot emancipate himself. We may notice the frequent allusions to priestcraft, superstition, &c., which even at that early period betray the future direction of his mind.

The *Merope*, a work of his ripest years, was intended as a perfect revival of Greek tragedy, an undertaking of so great difficulty, and so long announced with every note of preparation. Its real merit is the exclusion of the customary love-scenes (of which, however, Racine had already given an example in the *Athalie*); for in other respects

German readers hardly need to be told how much is not conceived in the true Grecian spirit. Moreover the confidants are also entirely after the old traditional cut. The other defects of the piece have been circumstantially, and, I might almost say, too severely, censured by Lessing. The tragedy of *Merope*, if well acted, can hardly fail of being received with a certain degree of favour. This is owing to the nature of its subject. The passionate love of a mother, who, in dread of losing her only treasure, and threatened with cruel oppression, still supports her trials with heroic constancy, and at last triumphs over them, is altogether a picture of such truth and beauty, that the sympathy it awakens is beneficent, and remains pure from every painful ingredient. Still we must not forget that the piece belongs only in a very small measure to Voltaire. How much he has borrowed from Maffei, and changed--not always for the better--has been already pointed out by Lessing.

Of all remodellings of Greek tragedies, *Oreste*, the latest, appears the farthest from the antique simplicity and severity, although it is free from any mixture of love-making, and all mere confidants are excluded. That Orestes should undertake to destroy Aegisthus is nowise singular, and seems scarcely to merit such marked notice in the tragical annals of the world. It is the case which Aristotle lays down as the most indifferent, where one enemy knowingly attacks the other. And in Voltaire's play neither Orestes nor Electra have anything beyond this in view: Clytemnestra is to be spared; no oracle consigns to her own son the execution of the punishment due to her guilt. But even the deed in question can hardly be said to be executed by Orestes himself: he goes to Aegisthus, and falls, simply enough it must be owned, into the net, and is only saved by an insurrection of the people. According to the ancients, the oracle had commanded him to attack the criminals with cunning, as they had so attacked Agamemnon. This was a just retaliation: to fall in open conflict would have been too honourable a death for Aegisthus. Voltaire has added, of his own invention, that he was also prohibited by the oracle from making himself known to his sister; and when carried away by fraternal love, he breaks this injunction, he is blinded by the Furies, and involuntarily perpetrates the deed of matricide. These certainly are singular ideas to assign to the gods, and a most unexampled punishment for a slight, nay, even a noble crime. The accidental and unintentional stabbing of Clytemnestra was borrowed from Crebillon. A French writer will hardly venture to represent this subject with mythological truth; to describe, for instance, the murder as intentional, and executed by the command of the gods. If Clytemnestra were depicted not as rejoicing in the success of her crime, but repentant and softened by maternal love, then, it is true, her death would no longer be supportable. But how does this apply to so premeditated a crime? By such a transition to littleness the whole profound significance of the dreadful example is lost.

As the French are in general better acquainted with the Romans than the Greeks, we might expect the Roman pieces of Voltaire to be more consistent, in a political point of view, with historical truth, than his Greek pieces are with the symbolical original of mythology. This is, however, the case only in *Brutus*, the earliest of them, and the only one which can be said to be sensibly planned. Voltaire sketched this tragedy in England; he had there learned from *Julius Caesar* the effect which the publicity of Republican transactions is capable of producing on the stage, and he wished therefore to hold something like a middle course between Corneille and Shakspeare. The first act opens majestically; the catastrophe is brief but striking, and throughout the principles of genuine freedom are pronounced with a grave and noble eloquence. Brutus himself, his son Titus, the ambassador of the king, and the chief of the conspirators, are admirably depicted. I am by no means disposed to censure the introduction of love into this play. The passion of Titus for a daughter of Tarquin, which constitutes the knot, is not improbable, and in its tone harmonizes with the manners which are depicted. Still less am I disposed to agree with La Harpe, when he says that Tullia, to afford a fitting counterpoise to the republican virtues, ought to utter proud and heroic sentiments, like Emilia in *Cinna*. By what means can a noble youth be more easily seduced than by female tenderness and modesty? It is not, generally speaking, natural that a being like Emilia should ever inspire love.

The *Mort de Cesar* is a mutilated tragedy: it ends with the speech of Antony over the dead body of Caesar, borrowed from Shakspeare; that is to say, it has no conclusion. And what a patched and bungling thing is it in all its parts! How coarse-spun and hurried is the conspiracy! How stupid Caesar must have been, to allow the conspirators to brave him before his face without suspecting their design! That Brutus, although he knew Caesar to be his father, nay, immediately after this fact had come to his knowledge, should lay murderous hands on him, is cruel, and, at the same time, most un-Roman. History affords us many examples of fathers in Rome who condemned their own sons to death for crimes of state; the law gave fathers an unlimited power of life and death over their children in their own houses. But the murder of a father, though perpetrated in the cause of liberty, would, in the eyes of the Romans, have stamped the parricide an unnatural monster. The inconsistencies which here arise from the attempt to observe the unity of place, are obvious to the least discerning eye. The scene is laid in the Capitol; here the conspiracy is hatched in the clear light of day, and Caesar the while goes in and out among them. But the persons, themselves, do not seem to know rightly where they are; for Caesar on one occasion exclaims, "*Courons au Capitole!*"

The same improprieties are repeated in *Catiline*, which is but a little better than the preceding piece. From Voltaire's sentiments respecting the dramatic exhibition of a conspiracy, which I quoted in the foregoing Lecture, we might well conclude that he had not himself a right understanding on this head, were it not quite evident that the French system rendered a true representation of such transactions all but impossible, not only by the required observance of the Unities of Place and Time, but also on account of a demand for dignity of poetical expression, such as is quite incompatible with the accurate mention of particular circumstances, on which, however, in this case depends the truthfulness of the whole. The machinations of a conspiracy, and the endeavours to frustrate them, are like the underground mine and counter-mine, with which the besiegers and the besieged endeavour to blow up each other.--Something must be done to enable the spectators to comprehend the art of the miners. If Catiline and his adherents had employed no more art and dissimulation, and Cicero no more determined wisdom, than Voltaire has given them, the one could not have endangered Rome, and the other could not have saved it. The piece turns always on the same point; they all declaim against each other, but no one acts; and at the conclusion, the affair is decided as if by accident, by the blind chance of war. When we read the simple relation of Sallust, it has the appearance of the genuine poetry of the matter, and Voltaire's work by the side of it looks like a piece of school rhetoric. Ben Jonson has treated the subject with a very different insight into the true connexion of human affairs; and Voltaire might have learned a great deal from the man in traducing whom he did not spare even falsehood.

The *Triumvirat* belongs to the acknowledged unsuccessful essays of his old age. It consists of endless declamations on the subject of proscription, which are poorly supported by a mere show of action. Here we find the Triumvirs quietly sitting in their tents on an island in the small river Rhenus, while storms, earthquakes, and volcanoes rage around them; and Julia and the young Pompeius, although they are travelling on terra firma, are depicted as if they had been just shipwrecked on the strand; besides a number of other absurdities. Voltaire, probably by way of apology for the poor success which the piece had on its representation, says, "This piece is perhaps in the English taste."--Heaven forbid!

We return to the earlier tragedies of Voltaire, in which he brought on the stage subjects never before attempted, and on which his fame as a dramatic poet principally rests: *Zaire*, *Alzire*, *Mahomet*, *Semiramis*, and *Tancred*.

Zaire is considered in France as the triumph of tragic poetry in the representation of lore and jealousy. We will not assert with Lessing, that Voltaire was acquainted only with the *legal* style of love. He often expresses feeling with a fiery energy, if not with that familiar truth and *naivete* in which an unreserved heart lays itself open. But I see no trace of an oriental colouring in Zaire's cast of feeling: educated in the seraglio, she should cling to the object of her passion with all the fervour of a maiden of a glowing imagination, rioting, as it were, in the fragrant perfumes of the East. Her fanciless love dwells solely in the heart; and again how is this conceivable with such a character! Orosman, on his part, lays claim indeed to European tenderness of feeling; but in him the Tartar is merely varnished over, and he has frequent relapses into the ungovernable fury and despotic habits of his race. The poet ought at least to have given a credibility to the magnanimity which he ascribes to him, by investing him with a celebrated historical name, such as that of the Saracen monarch Saladin, well known for his nobleness and liberality of sentiment. But all our sympathy inclines to the oppressed Christian and chivalrous side, and the glorious names to which it is appropriated. What can be more affecting than the royal martyr Lusignan, the upright and pious Nerestan, who, though in the fire of youth, has no heart for deeds of bloody enterprise except to redeem the associates of his faith? The scenes in which these two characters appear are uniformly excellent, and more particularly the whole of the second act. The idea of connecting the discovery of a daughter with her conversion can never be sufficiently praised. But, in my opinion, the great effect of this act is injurious to the rest of the piece. Does any person seriously wish the union of Zaire with Orosman, except lady spectators flattered with the homage which is paid to beauty, or those of the male part of the audience who are still entangled in the follies of youth? Who else can go along with the poet, when Zaire's love for the Sultan, so ill-justified by his acts, balances in her soul the voice of blood, and the most sacred claims of filial duty, honour, and religion?

It was a praiseworthy daring (such singular prejudices then prevailed in France) to exhibit French heroes in *Zaire*. In *Alzire* Voltaire went still farther, and treated a subject in modern history never yet touched by his countrymen. In the former piece he contrasted the chivalrous and Saracenic way of thinking; in this we have Spaniards opposed to Peruvians. The difference between the old and new world has given rise to descriptions of a truly poetical nature. Though the action is a pure invention, I recognise in this piece more historical and more of what we may call symbolical truth, than in most French tragedies. Zamor is a representation of the savage in his free, and Monteze in his subdued state; Guzman, of the arrogance of the conqueror; and Alvarez, of the mild influence of Christianity. Alzire remains between these conflicting elements in an affecting struggle betwixt attachment to her country, its manners, and the first choice of her heart, on the one part, and new ties of honour and duty on the other. All the human motives speak in favour of Alzire's love, which were against the passion of Zaire. The last scene, where the dying Guzman is dragged in, is beneficently overpowering. The noble lines on the difference of their religions, by which Zamor is converted by Guzman, are borrowed from an event in history: they are the words of the Duke of Guise to a Huguenot who wished to kill him; but the glory of the poet is not therefore less in applying them as he has done. In short, notwithstanding the improbabilities in the plot, which are easily discovered, and have often been censured, *Alzire* appears to be the most fortunate attempt, and the most finished of all Voltaire's compositions.

In *Mahomet*, want of true singleness of purpose has fearfully avenged itself on the artist. He may affirm as much as he pleases that his aim was directed solely against fanaticism; there can be no doubt that he wished to overthrow the belief in revelation altogether, and that for that object he considered every means allowable. We have thus a work which is productive of effect; but an alarmingly painful effect, equally repugnant to humanity, philosophy, and religious feeling. The Mahomet of Voltaire makes two innocent young persons, a brother and sister, who, with a childlike reverence, adore him as a messenger from God, unconsciously murder their own father, and this from the motives of an incestuous love in which, by his allowance, they had also become unknowingly entangled; the brother, after he has blindly executed his horrible mission, he rewards with poison, and the sister he reserves for the gratification of his own vile lust. This tissue of atrocities, this cold-blooded delight in wickedness, exceeds perhaps the measure of human nature; but, at all events, it exceeds the bounds of poetic exhibition, even though such a monster should ever have appeared in the course of ages. But, overlooking this, what a disfigurement, nay, distortion, of history! He has stripped her, too, of her wonderful charms; not a trace of oriental colouring is to be found. Mahomet was a false prophet, but one certainly under the inspiration of enthusiasm, otherwise he would never by his doctrine have revolutionized the half of the world. What an absurdity to make him merely a cool deceiver! One alone of the many sublime maxims of the Koran would be sufficient to annihilate the whole of these incongruous inventions.

Semiramis is a motley patchwork of the French manner and mistaken imitations. It has something of *Hamlet*, and something of *Clytemnestra* and *Orestes*; but nothing of any of them as it ought to be. The passion for an unknown son is borrowed from the *Semiramis* of Crebillon. The appearance of Ninus is a mixture of the Ghost in *Hamlet* and the shadow of Darius in Aeschylus. That it is superfluous has been admitted even by the French critics. Lessing, with his raillery, has scared away the Ghost. With a great many faults common to ordinary ghost-scenes, it has this peculiar one, that its speeches are dreadfully bombastic. Notwithstanding the great zeal displayed by Voltaire against subordinate love intrigues in tragedy, he has, however, contrived to exhibit two pairs of lovers, the *partie carree* as it is called, in this play, which was to be the foundation of an entirely new species.

Since the *Cid*, no French tragedy had appeared of which the plot was founded on such pure motives of honour and love without any ignoble intermixtures, and so completely consecrated to the exhibition of chivalrous sentiments, as *Tancred.* Amenaide, though honour and life are at stake, disdains to exculpate herself by a declaration which would endanger her lover; and Tancred, though justified in esteeming her faith less, defends her in single combat, and, in despair, is about to seek a hero's death, when the unfortunate mistake is cleared up. So far the piece is irreproachable, and deserving of the greatest praise. But it is weakened by other imperfections. It is of great detriment to its perspicuity, that we are not at the very first allowed to hear the letter without superscription which occasions all the embarrassment, and that it is not sent off before our eyes. The political disquisitions in the first act are extremely tedious; Tancred does not appear till the third act, though his presence is impatiently looked for, to give animation to the scene. The furious imprecations of Amenaide, at the conclusion, are not in harmony with the deep but soft emotion with which we are overpowered by the reconciliation of the two lovers, whose hearts, after so long a mutual misunderstanding, are reunited in the moment of separation by death.

In the earlier piece of the *Orphelin de la Chine*, it might be considered pardonable if Voltaire represented the great Dschingis-kan in love. This drama ought to be entitled *The Conquest of China*, with the conversion of the cruel Khan of Tartary, &c. Its whole interest is concentrated in two children, who are never once seen. The Chinese are represented as the most wise and virtuous of mankind, and they overflow with philosophical maxims. As Corneille, in his old age, made one and all of his characters politicians, Voltaire in like manner furnished his out with philosophy, and availed himself of them to preach up his favourite opinions. He was not deterred by the example of Corneille, when the power of representing the passions was extinct, from publishing a host of weak and faulty productions.

Since the time of Voltaire the constitution of the French stage has remained nearly the same. No genius has yet arisen sufficiently mighty to advance the art a step farther, and victoriously to refute, by success, their time-strengthened prejudices. Many attempts have been made, but they generally follow in the track of previous essays, without surpassing them. The endeavour to introduce more historical extent into dramatic composition is frustrated by the traditional limitations and restraints. The attacks, both theoretical and practical, which have been made in France itself on the prevailing system of rules, will be most suitably noticed and observed upon when we come to review the present condition of the French stage, after considering their Comedy and the other secondary kinds of dramatic works, since in these attempts have been made either to found new species, or arbitrarily to overturn the classification hitherto established.

LECTURE XXI.

French Comedy--Moliere--Criticism of his Works--Scarron, Beursault, Regnard; Comedies in the Time of the Regency; Marivaux and Destouches; Piron and Gresset--Later Attempts--The Heroic Opera: Quinault--Operettes and Vaudevilles--Diderot's attempted Change of the Theatre--The Weeping Drama--Beaumarchais--Melo-Dramas--Merits and Defects of the Histrionic Art.

The same system of rules and proprieties, which, as I have endeavoured to show, must inevitably have a narrowing influence on Tragedy, has, in France, been applied to Comedy much more advantageously. For this mixed species of composition has, as already seen, an unpoetical side; and some degree of artificial constraint, if not altogether essential to Comedy, is certainly beneficial to it; for if it is treated with too negligent a latitude, it runs a risk, in respect of general structure, of falling into shapelessness, and in the representation of individual peculiarities, of sinking into every-day common-place. In the French, as well as in the Greek, it happens that the same syllabic measure is used in Tragedy and Comedy, which, on a first view, may appear singular. But if the Alexandrine did not appear to us peculiarly adapted to the free imitative expression of pathos, on the other hand, it must be owned that a comical effect is produced by the application of so symmetrical a measure to the familiar turns of dialogue. Moreover, the grammatical conscientiousness of French poetry, which is so greatly injurious in other species of the drama, is fully suited to Comedy, where the versification is not purchased at the expense of resemblance to the language of conversation, where it is not intended to elevate the dialogue by sublimity and dignity above real life, but merely to communicate to it greater ease and lightness. Hence the opinion of the French, who hold a comedy in verse in much higher estimation than a comedy in prose, seems to me to admit fairly of a justification.

I endeavoured to show that the Unities of Place and Time are inconsistent with the essence of many tragical subjects, because a comprehensive action is frequently carried on in distant places at the same time, and because great determinations can only be slowly prepared. This is not the case in Comedy: here Intrigue ought to prevail, the active spirit of which quickly hurries towards its object; and hence the unity of time may here be almost naturally observed. The domestic and social circles in which Comedy moves are usually assembled in one place, and, consequently, the poet is not under the necessity of sending our imagination abroad: only it might perhaps have been as well not to interpret the unity of place so very strictly as not to allow the transition from one room to another, or to different houses of the same town. The choice of the street for the scene, a practice in which the Latin comic writers were frequently followed in the earlier times of Modern Comedy, is quite irreconcileable with our way of living, and the more deserving of censure, as in the case of the ancients it was an inconvenience which arose from the construction of their theatre.

According to French critics, and the opinion which has become prevalent through them, Moliere alone, of all their comic writers, is classical; and all that has been done since his time is merely estimated as it approximates more or less to this supposed pattern of an excellence which can never be surpassed, nor even equalled. Hence we shall first proceed to characterize this founder of the French Comedy, and then give a short sketch of its subsequent progress.

Moliere has produced works in so many departments, and of such different value, that we are hardly able to recognize the same author in all of them; and yet it is usual, when speaking of his peculiarities and merits, and the advance which he gave to his art, to throw the whole of his labours into one mass together.

Born and educated in an inferior rank of life, he enjoyed the advantage of learning by direct experience the modes of living among the industrious portion of the community--the so-called *Bourgeois* class--and of acquiring the talent of imitating low modes of expression. At an after period, when Louis XIV. took him into his service, he had opportunities, though from a subordinate station, of narrowly observing the court. He was an actor, and, it would appear, of peculiar power in overcharged and farcical comic parts; so little was he possessed with prejudices of personal dignity, that he renounced all the conditions by which it was accompanied, and was ever ready to deal out, or to receive the blows which were then so frequent on the stage. Nay, his mimetic zeal went so far, that, actually sick, he acted and drew his last breath in representing his *Imaginary Invalid* (*Le Malade Imaginaire*), and became, in the truest sense, a martyr to the laughter of others. His business was to invent all manner of pleasant entertainments for the court, and to provoke "the greatest monarch of the world" to laughter, by way of relaxation from his state affairs or warlike undertakings. One would think, on the triumphant return from a glorious campaign, this might have been accomplished with more refinement than by the representation of the disgusting state of an imaginary invalid. But Louis XIV. was not so fastidious; he was very well content with the buffoon whom he protected, and even occasionally exhibited his own elevated person in the dances of his ballets. This external position of Moliere was the cause why many of his labours had their origin as mere occasional pieces in the commands of the court. And, accordingly, they bear the stamp of that origin. Without travelling out of France, he had opportunities of becoming acquainted with the *lazzis* of the Italian comic masks on the Italian theatre at Paris, where improvisatory dialogues were intermixed with scenes written in French: in the Spanish comedies he studied the ingenious complications of intrigue: Plautus and Terence taught him the salt of the Attic wit, the genuine tone of comic maxims, and the nicer shades of character. All this he employed, with more or less success, in the exigency of the moment, and also in order to deck out his drama in a sprightly and variegated dress, made use of all manner of means, however foreign to his art: such as the allegorical opening scenes of the opera prologues, musical intermezzos, in which he even introduced Italian and Spanish national music, with texts in their own language; ballets, at one time sumptuous and at another grotesque; and even sometimes mere vaulting and capering. He knew how to turn everything to profit: the censure passed upon his pieces, the defects of rival actors imitated to the life by himself and his company, and even the embarrassment in not being able to produce a theatrical entertainment as quickly as it was required by the king,--all became for him a matter for amusement. The pieces he borrowed from the Spanish, his pastorals and tragi-comedies, calculated merely to please the eye, and also three or four of his earlier comedies, which are even versified, and consequently carefully laboured, the critics give up without more ado. But even in the farces, with or without ballets, and intermezzos, in which the overcharged, and frequently the self-conscious and arbitrary comic of buffoonery prevails, Moliere has exhibited an inexhaustible store of excellent humour, scattered capital jokes with a lavish hand, and drawn the most amusing caricatures with a bold and vigorous pencil. All this, however, had been often done before his time; and I cannot see how, in this department, he can stand alone, as a creative and altogether original artist: for example, is Plautus' braggadocio soldier less meritorious in grotesque characterization than the *Bourgeois Gentilhomme*? We shall immediately examine briefly whether Moliere has actually improved the pieces which he borrowed, in whole or in part, from Plautus and Terence. When we bear in mind that in these Latin authors we have only a faint and faded copy of the new Attic Comedy, we shall then be enabled to judge whether he would have been able to surpass its masters had they come down to us. Many of his shifts and inventions, I am induced to suspect, are borrowed; and I am convinced that we should soon discover the sources, were we to search into the antiquities of farcical literature [Footnote: The learned Tiranoschi (*Storia della Letteratura Italiana*, Lib. III. S 25) attests this in very strong language: "Moliere," says he, "has made so much use of the Italian comic writers, that were we to take from him all that he has taken from others, the volumes of his comedies would be very much reduced in bulk."]. Others are so obvious, and have so often been both used and abused, that they may in some measure be considered as the common stock of Comedy. Such is the scene in the *Malade Imaginaire*, where the wife's love is put to the test by the supposed death of the husband--an old joke, which our Hans Sachs has handled drolly enough. [Footnote: I know not whether it has been already remarked, that the idea on which the *Mariage Force* is founded is borrowed from Rabelais; who makes Panurge enter upon the very same consultation as to his future marriage, and receive from Pantagruel just such a sceptical answer as Sganarelle does from the second philosopher.] We have an avowal of Moliere's, which plainly shows he entertained no very great scruples of conscience on the sin of plagiarism. In the undignified relations amidst which he lived, and in which every thing was so much calculated for dazzling show, that his very name did not legally belong to him, we see less reason to wonder at all this.

And even when in his farcical pieces Moliere did not lean on foreign invention, he still appropriated the comic manners of other countries, and more particularly the buffoonery of Italy. He wished to introduce a sort of masked character without masks, who should constantly recur with the same name. They did not, however, succeed in becoming properly domiciliated in France; because the flexible national character of the French, which so nimbly imitates every varying mode of the day, is incompatible with that odd originality of exterior to which in other nations, where all are not modelled alike by the prevailing social tone, humorsome and singular individuals carelessly give themselves up. As the Sganarelles, Mascarilles, Scapins, and Crispins, must be allowed to retain their uniform, that every thing like consistency may not be lost, they have become completely obsolete on the stage. The French taste is, generally speaking, little inclined to the self-conscious and arbitrary comic, with its droll exaggerations, even because these kinds of the comic speak more to the fancy than the understanding. We do not mean to censure this, nor to quarrel about the respective merits of the different species. The low estimation in which the former are held may perhaps contribute the more to the success of the comic of observation, And, in fact, the French comic writers have here displayed a great deal of refinement and ingenuity: in this lies the great merit of Moliere, and it is certainly very eminent. Only, we would ask, whether it is of such a description as to justify the French critics, on account of some half a dozen of so-called regular comedies of Moliere, in holding in such infinite contempt as they do all the rich stores of refined and characteristic delineation which other nations possess, and in setting up Moliere as the unrivalled Genius of Comedy.

If the praise bestowed by the French on their tragic writers be, both from national vanity and from ignorance of the mental productions of other nations, exceedingly extravagant; so their praises of Moliere are out of all proportion with their subject. Voltaire calls him the Father of Genuine Comedy; and this may be true enough with respect to France. According to La Harpe, Comedy and Moliere are synonymous terms; he is the first of all moral philosophers, his works are the school of the world. Chamfort terms him the most amiable teacher of humanity since Socrates; and is of opinion that Julius Caesar who called Terence a half Menander, would have called Menander a half Moliere.--I doubt this.

The kind of moral which we may in general expect from Comedy I have already shown: it is an applied doctrine of ethics, the art of life. In this respect the higher comedies of Moliere contain many admirable observations happily expressed, which are still in the present day applicable; others are tainted with the narrowness of his own private opinions, or of the opinions which were prevalent in his age. In this sense Menander was also a philosophical comic writer; and we may boldly place the moral maxims which remain of his by the side at least of those of Moliere. But no comedy is constructed of mere apophthegms. The poet must be a moralist, but his personages cannot always be moralizing. And here Moliere appears to me to have exceeded the bounds of propriety: he gives us in lengthened disquisitions the *pro* and *con* of the character exhibited by him; nay, he allows these to consist, in part, of principles which the persons themselves defend against the attacks of others. Now this leaves nothing to conjecture; and yet the highest refinement and delicacy of the comic of observation consists in this, that the characters disclose themselves unconsciously by traits which involuntarily escape from them. To this species of comic element, the way in which Oronte introduces his sonnet, Orgon listens to the accounts respecting Tartuffe and his wife, and Vadius and Trissotin fall by the ears, undoubtedly belongs; but the endless disquisitions of Alceste and Philinte as to the manner in which we ought to behave amid the falsity and corruption of the world do not in the slightest respect belong to it. They are serious, and yet they cannot satisfy us as exhausting the subject; and as dialogues which at the end leave the characters precisely at the same point as at the beginning, they are devoid in the necessary dramatic movement. Such argumentative disquisitions which lead to nothing are frequent in all the most admired pieces of Moliere, and nowhere more than in the *Misanthrope*. Hence the action, which is also poorly invented, is found to drag heavily; for, with the exception of a few scenes of a more sprightly description, it consists altogether of discourses formally introduced and supported, while the stagnation is only partially concealed by the art employed on the details of versification and expression. In a word, these pieces are too didactic, too expressly instructive; whereas in Comedy the spectator should only be instructed incidentally, and, as it were, without its appearing to have been intended.

Before we proceed to consider more particularly the productions which properly belong to the poet himself, and are acknowledged as masterpieces, we shall offer a few observations on his imitations of the Latin comic writers.

The most celebrated is the *Avare*. The manuscripts of the *Aulularia* of Plautus are unfortunately mutilated towards the end; but yet we find enough in them to excite our admiration. From this play Moliere has merely borrowed a few scenes and jokes, for his plot is altogether different. In Plautus it is extremely simple: his Miser has found a treasure, which he anxiously watches and conceals. The suit of a rich bachelor for his daughter excites a suspicion that his wealth is known. The preparations for the wedding bring strange servants and cooks into his house; he considers his pot of gold no longer secure, and conceals it out of doors, which gives an opportunity to a slave of his daughter's chosen lover, sent to glean tidings of her and her marriage, to steal it. Without doubt the thief must afterwards have been obliged to make restitution, otherwise the piece would end in too melancholy a manner, with the lamentations and imprecations of the old man. The knot of the love intrigue is easily untied: the young man, who had anticipated the rights of the marriage state, is the nephew of the bridegroom, who willingly renounces in his favour. All the incidents serve merely to lead the miser, by a gradually heightening series of agitations and alarms, to display and expose his miserable passion. Moliere, on the other hand, without attaining this object, puts a complicated machine in motion. Here we have a lover of the daughter, who, disguised as a servant, flatters the avarice of the old man; a prodigal son, who courts the bride of his father; intriguing servants; an usurer; and after all a discovery at the end. The love intrigue is spun out in a very clumsy and every-day sort of manner; and it has the effect of making us at different times lose sight altogether of Harpagon. Several scenes of a good comic description are merely subordinate, and do not, in a true artistic method, arise necessarily out of the thing itself. Moliere has accumulated, as it were, all kinds of avarice in one person; and yet the miser who buries his treasures and he who lends on usury can hardly be the same. Harpagon starves his coach-horses: but why has he any? This would apply better to a man who, with a disproportionate income, strives to keep up a certain appearance of rank. Comic characterization would soon be at an end were there really only one universal character of the miser. The most important deviation of Moliere from Plautus is, that while the one paints merely a person who watches over his treasure, the other makes his miser in love. The love of an old man is in itself an object of ridicule; the anxiety of a miser is no less so. We may easily see that when we unite with avarice, which separates a man from others and withdraws him within himself, the sympathetic and liberal passion of love, the union must give rise to the most harsh contrasts. Avarice, however, is usually a very good preservative against falling in love. Where then is the more refined characterization; and as such a wonderful noise is made about it, where shall we here find the more valuable moral instruction?--in Plautus or in Moliere? A miser and a superannuated lover may both be present at the representation of Harpagon, and both return from the theatre satisfied with themselves, while the miser says to himself, "I am at least not in love;" and the lover, "Well, at all events I am not a miser." High Comedy represents those follies which, however striking they may be, are reconcilable with the ordinary course of things; whatever forms a singular exception, and is only conceivable amid an utter perversion of ideas, belongs to the arbitrary exaggeration of farce. Hence since (and it was undoubtedly the case long before) the time of Moliere, the enamoured and avaricious old man has been the peculiar common-place of the Italian masked comedy and *opera buffa*, to which in truth it certainly belongs. Moliere has treated the main incident, the theft of the chest of gold, with an uncommon want of skill. At the very beginning Harpagon, in a scene borrowed from Plautus, is fidgetty with suspicions lest a slave should have discovered his treasure. After this he forgets it; for four whole acts there is not a word about it, and the spectator drops, as it were, from the clouds when the servant all at once brings in the stolen coffer; for we have no information as to the way in which he fell upon the treasure which had been so carefully concealed. Now this is really to begin again, not truly to work out. But Plautus has here shown a great deal of ingenuity: the excessive anxiety of the old man for his pot of gold, and all that he does to save it, are the very cause of its loss. The subterraneous treasure is always invisibly present; it is, as it were, the evil spirit which drives its keeper to madness. In all this we have, an impressive moral of a very different kind. In Harpagon's soliloquy, after the theft, the modern poet has introduced the most incredible exaggerations. The calling on the pit to discover the theft, which, when well acted, produces so great an effect, is a trait of the old comedy of Aristophanes, and may serve to give us some idea of its powers of entertainment.

The *Amphitryon* is hardly anything more than a free imitation of the Latin original. The whole plan and order of the scenes is retained. The waiting-woman, or wife of Sosia, is the invention of Moliere. The parody of the story of the master's marriage in that of the servant is ingenious, and gives rise to the most amusing investigations on the part of Sosia to find out whether, during his absence a domestic blessing may not have also been conferred on him as well as on Amphitryon. The revolting coarseness of the old mythological story is refined as much as it possibly could without injury to its spirit and boldness; and in general the execution is extremely elegant. The uncertainty of the personages respecting their own identity and duplication is founded on a sort of comic metaphysics: Sosia's reflections on his two *egos*, which have cudgelled each other, may in reality furnish materials for thinking to our philosophers of the present day.

The most unsuccessful of Moliere's imitations of the ancients is that of the *Phormio* in the *Fourberies de Scapin*. The whole plot is borrowed from Terence, and, by the addition of a second invention, been adapted, well or ill, or rather tortured, to a consistency with modern manners. The poet has indeed gone very hurriedly to work with his plot, which he has most negligently patched together. The tricks of Scapin, for the sake of which he has spoiled the plot, occupy the foremost place: but we may well ask whether they deserve it? The Grecian Phormio, a man who, for the sake of feasting with young companions, lends himself to all sorts of hazardous tricks, is an interesting and modest knave; Scapin directly the reverse. He had no cause to boast so much of his tricks: they are so stupidly planned that in justice they ought not to have succeeded. Even supposing the two old men to be obtuse and brainless in the extreme, we can hardly conceive how they could so easily fall into such a clumsy and obvious snare as he lays for them. It is also disgustingly improbable that Zerbinette, who as a gipsy ought to have known how to conceal knavish tricks, should run out into the street and tell the first stranger that she meets, who happens to be none other than Geronte himself, the deceit practised upon him by Scapin. The farce of the sack into which Scapin makes Geronte to crawl, then bears him off, and cudgels him as if by the hand of strangers, is altogether a most inappropriate excrescence. Boileau was therefore well warranted in reproaching Moliere with having shamelessly allied Terence to Taburin, (the merry-andrew of a mountebank). In reality, Moliere has here for once borrowed, not, as he frequently did, from the Italian masks, but from the Pagliasses of the rope-dancers and vaulters.

We must not forget that the *Rogueries of Scapin* is one of the latest works of the poet. This and several others of the same period, as *Monsieur de Pourceaugnac*, *La Comtesse d'Escarbagnas*, and even his last, the *Malade Imaginaire*, sufficiently prove that the maturity of his mind as an artist did not keep pace with the progress of years, otherwise he would have been disgusted with such loose productions. They serve, moreover, to show that frequently he brought forth pieces with great levity and haste, even when he had full leisure to think of posterity. If he occasionally subjected himself to stricter rules, we owe it more to his ambition, and his desire to be numbered among the classical writers of the golden age, than to any internal and growing aspiration after the highest excellence.

The high claims already mentioned, which the French critics make in behalf of their favourite, are principally founded on the *Ecole des Femmes*, *Tartuffe*, *Le Misanthrope*, and *Les Femmes Savantes*; pieces which are certainly finished with great care and diligence. Now, of these, we must expressly state in the outset, that we leave the separate beauties of language and versification altogether to the decision of native critics. These merits can only be subordinate requisites; and the undue stress which is laid in France on the manner in which a piece is written and versified has, in our opinion, been both in Tragedy and Comedy injurious to the development of other and more essential requisites of the dramatic art. We shall confine our exceptions to the general spirit and plan of these comedies.

L'Ecole des Femmes, the earliest of them, seems to me also the most excellent; it is the one in which there is the greatest display of vivacious humour, rapidity, and comic vigour. As to the invention: a man arrived at an age unsuitable for wedlock, purposely educating a young girl in ignorance and simplicity, that he may keep her faithful to himself, while everything turns out the very reverse of his wishes, was not a new one: a short while before Moliere it had been employed by Scarron, who borrowed it from a Spanish novel. Still, it was a lucky thought in him to adapt this subject to the stage, and the execution of it is most masterly. Here we have a real and very interesting plot; no creeping investigations which do not carry forward the plot; all the matter is of one piece, without foreign levers and accidental intermixtures, with the exception of the catastrophe, which is brought about somewhat arbitrarily, by means of a scene of recognition. The *naive* confessions and innocent devices of Agnes are full of sweetness; they, together with the unguarded confidence reposed by the young lover in his unknown rival, and the stifled rage of the old man against both, form a series of comic scenes of the most amusing, and at the same time of the most refined description.

As an example how little the violation of certain probabilities diminishes our pleasure, we may remark that Moliere, with respect to the choice of scene, has here indulged in very great liberties. We will not inquire how Arnolph frequently happens to converse with Agnes in the street or in an open place, while he keeps her at the same time so carefully locked up. But if Horace does not know Arnolph to be the intended husband of his mistress, and betrays everything to him, this can only be allowable from Arnolph's passing with her by another name. Horace ought therefore to look for Arnolph in his own house in a remote quarter, and not before the door of his mistress, where yet he always finds him, without entertaining any suspicion from that circumstance. Why do the French critics set such a high value on similar probabilities in the dramatic art, when they must be compelled to admit that their best masters have not always observed them?

Tartuffe is an exact picture of hypocritical piety held up for universal warning; it is an excellent serious satire, but with the exception of separate scenes it is not a comedy. It is generally admitted that the catastrophe is bad, as it is brought about by a foreign means. It is bad, too, because the danger which Orgon runs of being driven from his house and thrown into prison is by no means such an embarrassment as his blind confidence actually merited. Here the serious purpose of the work is openly disclosed, and the eulogium of the king is a dedication by which the poet, even in the piece itself, humbly recommends himself to the protection of his majesty against the persecutions which he dreaded.

In the *Femmes Savantes* raillery has also the upper hand of mirth; the action is insignificant and not in the least degree attractive; and the catastrophe, after the manner of Moliere, is arbitrarily brought about by foreign means. Yet these technical imperfections might well be excused for the sake of its satirical merit. But in this respect the composition, from the limited nature of its views, is anything but equal throughout. We are not to expect from the comic poet that he should always give us, along with the exhibition of a folly, a representation also of the opposite way of wisdom; in this way he would announce his object of instructing us with too much of method. But two opposite follies admit of being exhibited together in an equally ludicrous light. Moliere has here ridiculed the affectation of a false taste, and the vain-gloriousness of empty knowledge. Proud in their own ignorance and contempt for all higher enlightenment, these characters certainly deserve the ridicule bestowed on them; but that which in this comedy is portrayed as the correct way of wisdom falls nearly into the same error. All the reasonable persons of the piece, the father and his brother, the lover and the daughter, nay, even the ungrammatical maid, are all proud of what they are not, have not, and know not, and even what they do not seek to be, to have, or to know. Chyrsale's limited view of the destination of the female sex, Clitander's opinion on the inutility of learning, and the sentiments elsewhere advanced respecting the measure of cultivation and knowledge which is suitable to a man of rank, were all intended to convey Moliere's own opinions himself on these subjects. We may here trace in him a certain vein of valet-de-chambre morality, which also makes its appearance on many other points. We can easily conceive how his education and situation should lead him to entertain such ideas; but they are hardly such as entitle him to read lectures on human society. That, at the end, Trissotin should be ignominiously made to commit an act of low selfishness is odious; for we know that a learned man then alive was satirized under this character, and that his name was very slightly disguised. The vanity of an author is, on the whole, a preservative against this weakness: there are many more lucrative careers than that of authorship for selfishness without a feeling of honour.

The *Misanthrope*, which, as is well known, was at first coldly received, is still less amusing than the two preceding pieces: the action is less rapid, or rather there is none at all; and there is a great want of coherence between the meagre incidents which give only an apparent life to the dramatic movement,--the quarrel with Oronte respecting the sonnet, and its adjustment; the decision of the law-suit which is ever being brought forward; the unmasking of Celimene through the vanity of the two Marquisses, and the jealousy of Arsinoe. Besides all this, the general plot is not even probable. It is framed with a view to exhibit the thorough delineation of a character; but a character discloses itself much more in its relations with others than immediately. How comes Alceste to have chosen Philinte for a friend, a man whose principles were directly the reverse of his own? How comes he also to be enamoured of a coquette, who has nothing amiable in her character, and who entertains us merely by her scandal? We might well say of this Celimene, without exaggeration, that there is not one good point in her whole composition. In a character like that of Alceste, love is not a fleeting sensual impulse, but a serious feeling arising from a want of a sincere mental union. His dislike of flattering falsehood and malicious scandal, which always characterise the conversation of Celimene, breaks forth so incessantly, that, we feel, the first moment he heard her open her lips ought to have driven him for ever from her society. Finally, the subject is ambiguous, and that is its greatest fault. The limits within which Alceste is in the right and beyond which he is in the wrong, it would be no easy matter to fix, and I am afraid the poet himself did not here see very clearly what he would be at. Philinte, however, with his illusory justification of the way of the world, and his phlegmatic resignation, he paints throughout as the intelligent and amiable man. As against the elegant Celimene, Alceste is most decidedly in the right, and only in the wrong in the inconceivable weakness of his conduct towards her. He is in the right in his complaints of the corruption of the social constitution; the facts, at least, which he adduces, are disputed by nobody. He is in the wrong, however, in delivering his sentiments with so much violence, and at an unseasonable time; but as he cannot prevail on himself to assume the dissimulation which is necessary to be well received in the world, he is perfectly in the right in preferring solitude to society. Rousseau has already censured the ambiguity of the piece, by which what is deserving of approbation seems to be turned into ridicule. His opinion was not altogether unprejudiced; for his own character, and his behaviour towards the world, had a striking similarity to that of Alceste; and, moreover, he mistakes the essence of dramatic composition, and founds his condemnation on examples of an accidentally false direction.

So far with respect to the famed moral philosophy of Moliere in his pretended master-piece. From what has been stated, I consider myself warranted to assert, in opposition to the prevailing opinion, that Moliere succeeded best with the coarse and homely comic, and that both his talents and his inclination, if unforced, would have determined him altogether to the composition of farces such as he continued to write even to the very end of his life. He seems always to have whipped himself up as it were to his more serious pieces in verse: we discover something of constraint in both plot and execution. His friend Boileau probably communicated to him his view of a correct mirth, of a grave and decorous laughter; and so Moliere determined, after the carnival of his farces, to accommodate himself occasionally to the spare diet of the regular taste, and to unite what in their own nature are irreconcileable, namely, dignity and drollery. However, we find even in his prosaic pieces traces of that didactical and satirical vein which is peculiarly alien to Comedy; for example, in his constant attacks on physicians and lawyers, in his disquisitions upon the true correct tone of society, &c., the intention of which is actually to censure, to refute, to instruct, and not merely to afford entertainment.

The classical reputation of Moliere still preserves his pieces on the stage, [Footnote: If they were not already in possession of the stage, the indecency of a number of the scenes would cause many of them to be rejected, as the public of the present day, though probably not less corrupt than that of the author's times, is passionately fond of throwing over every thing a cloak of morality. When a piece of Moliere is acted, the head theatre of Paris is generally a downright solitude, if no particular circumstance brings the spectators together. Since these Lectures were held, *George Dandin* has been hissed at Paris, to the great grief of the watchmen of the critical Sion. This was probably not on account of mere indecency. Whatever may be said in defence of the morality of the piece, the privileges of the higher classes are offensively favoured in it; and it concludes with the shameless triumph of arrogance and depravity over plain honesty.] although in tone and manners they are altogether obsolete. This is a danger to which the comic poet is inevitably exposed from that side of his composition which does not rest on a poetical foundation, but is determined by the prose of external reality. The originals of the individual portraits of Moliere have long since disappeared. The comic poet who lays claim to immortality must, in the delineation of character and the disposition of his plan, rest principally on such motives as are always intelligible, being taken not from the manners of any particular age, but drawn from human nature itself.

In addition to Moliere we have to notice but a few older or contemporary comedians. Of Corneille, who from the imitation of Spanish comedies acquired a name before he was known as a tragic author, only one piece keeps possession of the stage, *Le Menteur*, from Lope de Vega; and even this evinces, in our opinion, no comic talent. The poet, accustomed to stilts, moves awkwardly in a species of the drama the first requisites of which are ease and sweetness. Scarron, who only understood burlesque, has displayed this talent or knack in several comedies taken from the Spanish, of which two, *Jodelle*, or the *Servant turned Master*, and *Don Japhet of Armenia*, have till within these few years been occasionally acted as carnival farces, and have always been very successful. The plot of the *Jodelle*, which belongs to Don Francisco de Roxas, is excellent; the style and the additions of Scarron have not been able altogether to disfigure it. All that is coarse, nauseous, and repugnant to taste, belongs to the French writer of the age of Louis XIV., who in his day was not without celebrity; for the Spanish work is throughout characterized by a spirit of tenderness. The burlesque tone, which in many languages may be tolerated, has been properly rejected by the French, for whenever it is not guided by judgment and taste, it sinks to disgusting vulgarity. *Don Japhet* represents in a still ruder manner the mystification of a coarse fool. The original belongs to the kind which the Spaniards call *Comedias de Figuron*: it also has undoubtedly been spoiled by Scarron, The worst of the matter is, that his exaggerations are trifling without being amusing.

Racine hit upon a very different plan of imitation from that which was then followed, in his *Plaideurs*, of which the idea is derived from Aristophanes. The piece in this respect stands alone. The action is merely a light piece of legerdemain; but the follies which it portrays belong to a circle, and, with the imitations of the officers of court and advocates, form a complete whole. Many lines are at once witty sallies and characteristic traits; and some of the jokes have that apparently aimless drollery, which genuine comic inspiration can alone inspire. Racine would have become a dangerous rival of Moliere, if he had continued to exercise the talent which he has here displayed.

Some of the comedies of a younger contemporary and rival of Moliere, Boursault, have still kept possession of the stage; they are all of the secondary description, which the French call *pieces a tiroir*, and of which Moliere gave the first example in *Le Facheux*. This kind, from the accidental succession of the scenes, which are strung together on some one common occasion, bear in so far a resemblance to the *Mimes* of the ancients; they are intended also to resemble them in the accurate imitation of individual peculiarities. These subjects are particularly favourable for the display of the Mimic art in the more limited signification of the word, as the same player always appears in a different disguise, and assumes a new character. It is advisable not to extend such pieces beyond a single act, as the want of dramatic movement, and the uniformity of the occasion through all the different changes, are very apt to excite impatience. But Boursault's pieces, which otherwise are not without merit, are tediously spun out to five acts. The idea of exhibiting Aesop, a slave-born sage, and deformed in person, in possession of court favour, was original and happy. But in the two pieces, *Aesop in the City*, and *Aesop at Court*, the fables which are tacked to every important scene are drowned in diffuse morals; besides, they are quite distinct from the dialogue, instead of being interwoven with it, like the fable of Menenius Agrippa in Shakespeare; and modern manners do not suit with this childish mode of instruction. In the *Mercure Galant* all sorts of out-of-the-way beings bring their petitions to the writer of a weekly paper. This thought and many of the most entertaining details have, if I am not mistaken, been borrowed by a popular German author without acknowledgment.

A considerable time elapsed after the death of Moliere before the appearance of Regnard, to whom in France the second place in Comedy is usually assigned. He was a sort of adventurer who, after roaming a long time up and down the world, fell to the trade of a dramatic writer, and divided himself betwixt the composition of regular comedies in verse, and the Italian theatre, which still continued to flourish under Gherardi, and for which he sketched the French scenes. The *Joueur*, his first play, is justly preferred to the others. The author was acquainted with this passion, and a gamester's life, from his own experience: it is a picture after nature, with features strongly drawn, but without exaggeration; and the plot and accessory circumstances, with the exception of a pair of caricatures which might well have been dispensed with, are all appropriate and in character. The *Distrait* possesses not only the faults of the methodical pieces of character which I have already censured, but it is not even a peculiar character at all; the mistakes occasioned by the unfortunate habit of being absent in thought are all alike, and admit of no heightening: they might therefore have filled up an after-piece, but, certainly did not merit the distinction of being spun out into a comedy of five acts. Regnard has done little more than dramatize a series of anecdotes which La Bruyere had assembled together under the name of a certain character. The execution of the *Legataire Universel* shows more comic talent; but from the error of the general plan, arising out of a want of moral feeling, this talent is completely thrown away. La Harpe declares this piece the *chef-d'oeuvre* of comic pleasantry. It is, in fact, such a subject for pleasantry as would move a stone to pity,--as enlivening as the grin of a death's head. What a subject for mirth: a feeble old man in the very arms of death, teased by young profligates for his property, has a false will imposed on him while he is lying insensible, as is believed, on his death-bed! If it be true that these scenes have always given rise to much laughter on the French stage, it only proves the spectators to possess the same unfeeling levity which disgusts us in the author. We have elsewhere shown that, with an apparent indifference, a moral reserve is essential to the comic poet, since the impressions which he would wish to produce are inevitably destroyed whenever disgust or compassion is excited.

Legrand the actor, a contemporary of Regnard, was one of the first comic poets who gained celebrity for after-pieces in verse, a species of composition in which the French have since produced a number of elegant trifles. He has not, however, risen to any thing like the same height of posthumous fame as Regnard: La Harpe dismisses him with very little ceremony. Yet we should be disposed to rank him very high as an artist, even if he had composed nothing else than the *King of Lubberland* (*Le Roi de Cocagne*), a sprightly farce in the marvellous style, overflowing with what is very rare in France, a native fanciful wit, animated by the most lively mirth, which although carried the length of the most frolicsome giddiness, sports on and round all subjects with the utmost harmlessness. We might call it an elegant and ingenious piece of madness; an example of the manner in which the play of Aristophanes, or rather that of Eupolis, [Footnote: See page 167.] who had also dramatised the tale *of Lubberland*, might be brought on our stage without exciting disgust, and without personal satire. And yet Legrand was, certainly, unacquainted with the Old Comedy, and his own genius (we scruple not to use the expression) led him to the invention. The execution is as careful as in a regular comedy; but to this title in the French opinion it can have no pretensions, because of the wonderful world which it represents, of several of the decorations, and of the music here and there introduced. The French critics show themselves in general indifferent, or rather unjust towards every suggestion of genuine fancy. Before they can feel respect for a work it must present a certain appearance of labour and effort. Among a giddy and light-minded people, they have appropriated to themselves the post of honour of pedantry: they confound the levity of jocularity, which is quite compatible with profundity in art, with the levity of shallowness, which (as a natural gift or natural defect,) is so frequent among their countrymen.

The eighteenth century produced in France a number of comic writers of the second and third rank, but no distinguished genius capable of advancing the art a step farther; in consequence of which the belief in Moliere's unapproachable excellence has become still more firmly riveted. As we have not space at present to go through all these separate productions, we shall premise a few observations on the general spirit of French Comedy before entering on the consideration of the writers whom we have not yet mentioned.

The want of easy progress, and over-lengthy disquisitions in stationary dialogue, have characterized more or less every writer since the time of Moliere, on whose regular pieces also the conventional rules applicable to Tragedy have had an indisputable influence. French Comedy in verse has its tirades as well as Tragedy. Besides, there was another circumstance, the introduction of a certain degree of stiff etiquette. The Comedy of other nations has generally, from motives which we can be at no loss in understanding, descended into the circle of the lower classes: but the French Comedy is usually confined to the upper ranks of society. Here, then, we trace the influence of the court as the central point of the whole national vanity. Those spectators who in reality had no access to the great world, were flattered by being surrounded on the stage with marquises and chevaliers, and while the poet satirized the fashionable follies, they endeavoured to snatch something of that privileged tone which was so much the object of envy. Society rubs off the salient angles of character; its only amusement consists in the pursuit of the ridiculous, and on the other hand it trains us in the faculty of being upon our guard against the observations of others. The natural, cordial, and jovial comic of the inferior classes is thrown aside, and instead of it another description (the fruit of polished society, and bearing in its insipidity the stamp of so purposeless a way of living) is adopted. The object of these comedies is no longer life but society, that perpetual negotiation between conflicting vanities which never ends in a sincere treaty of peace: the embroidered dress, the hat under the arm, and the sword by the side, essentially belong to them, and the whole of their characterization is limited to painting the folly of the men and the coquetry of the women. The insipid uniformity of these pictures was unfortunately too often seasoned by the corruption of moral principles which, more especially after the age of Louis XIV., it became, under the Regency of Louis XV., the fashion openly to avow. In this period the favourite of the women, the *homme a bonnes fortunes*, who in the tone of satiety boasts of the multitude of his conquests too easily won, was not a character invented by the comic writers, but a portrait accurately taken from real life, as is proved by the numerous memoirs of the last century, even down to those of a Besenval. We are disgusted with the unveiled sensuality of the love intrigues of the Greek Comedy: but the Greeks would have found much more disgusting the love intrigues of the French Comedy, entered into with married women, merely from giddy vanity. Limits have been fixed by nature herself to sensual excess; but when vanity assumes the part of a sensuality already deadened and enervated, it gives birth to the most hollow corruption. And even if, in the constant ridicule of marriage by the petit-maitres, and in their moral scepticism especially with regard to female virtue, it was the intention of the poets to ridicule a prevailing depravity, the picture is not on that account the less immoral. The great or fashionable world, which in point of numbers is the little world, and yet considers itself alone of importance, can hardly be improved by it; and for the other classes the example is but too seductive, from the brilliancy with which the characters are surrounded. But in so far as Comedy is concerned, this deadening corruption is by no means invariably entertaining; and in many pieces, in which fools of quality give the tone, for example in the *Chevalier a la mode de Dancourt*, the picture of complete moral dissoluteness which, although true, is nevertheless both unpoetical and unnatural, is productive not merely of *ennui*, but of the most decided repugnance and disgust.

From the number of writers to whom this charge chiefly applies, we must in justice except Destouches and Marivaux, fruitful or at least diligent comic writers, the former in verse and the latter in prose. They acquired considerable distinction among their contemporaries in the first half of the eighteenth century, but on the stage few of their works survived either of them. Destouches was a moderate, tame, and well-meaning author, who applied himself with all his powers to the composition of regular comedies, which were always drawn out to the length of five acts, and in which there is nothing laughable, with the exception of the vivacity displayed in virtue of their situation, by Lisette and her lover Frontin, or Pasquin. He was in no danger, from any excess of frolicsome petulance, of falling from the dignified tone of the supposed high comic into the familiarity of farce, which the French hold in such contempt. With moderate talents, without humour, and almost without vivacity, neither ingenious in invention, nor possessed of a deep insight into the human mind and human affairs, he has in some of his productions, *Le Glorieux*, *Le Philosophe Marie*, and especially *L'Indecis*, shewn with great credit to himself what true and unpretending diligence is by itself capable of effecting. Other pieces, for instance, *L'Ingrat* and *L'Homme Singulier*, are complete failures, and enable us to see that a poet who considers *Tartuffe* and *The Misanthrope* as the highest objects of imitation, (and with Destouches this was evidently the case,) has only another step to take to lose sight of the comic art altogether. These two works of Moliere have not been friendly beacons to his followers, but false lights to their ruin. Whenever a comic poet in his preface worships *The Misanthrope* as a model, I can immediately foretell the result of his labours. He will sacrifice every thing like the gladsome inspiration of fun and all truly poetical amusement, for the dull and formal seriousness of prosaic life, and for prosaical applications stamped with the respectable name of morals.

That Marivaux is a mannerist is so universally acknowledged in France, that the peculiar term of *marivaudage* has been invented for his mannerism. But this is at least his own, and at first sight by no means unpleasing. Delicacy of mind cannot be denied to Marivaux, only it is coupled with a certain littleness. We have stated it to be the most refined species of the comic of observation, when a peculiarity or property shows itself most conspicuously at the very time its possessor has the least suspicion of it, or is most studious to conceal it. Marivaux has applied this to the passions; and *naivete* in the involuntary disclosure of emotions certainly belongs to the domain of Comedy. But then this *naivete* is prepared by him with too much art, appears too solicitous for our applause, and, we may almost say, seems too well pleased with it himself. It is like children in the game of hide and seek, they cannot stay quiet in their corner, but keep popping out their heads, if they are not immediately discovered; nay, sometimes, which is still worse, it is like the squinting over a fan held up from affected modesty. In Marivaux we always see his aim from the very beginning, and all our attention is directed to discovering the way by which he is to lead us to it. This would be a skilful mode of composing, if it did not degenerate into the insignificant and the superficial. Petty inclinations are strengthened by petty motives, exposed to petty probations, and brought by petty steps nearer and nearer to a petty conclusion. The whole generally turns on a declaration of love, and all sorts of clandestine means are tried to elicit it, or every kind of slight allusion is hazarded to hasten it. Marivaux has neither painted characters, nor contrived intrigues. The whole plot generally turns on an unpronounced word, which is always at the tongue's end, and which is frequently kept back in a pretty arbitrary manner. He is so uniform in the motives that he employs, that when we have read one of his pieces with a tolerable degree of attention we know all of them. However, we must still rank him above the herd of stiff imitators; something is to be learned even from him, for he possessed a peculiar though a very limited view of the essence of Comedy.

Two other single works are named as master-pieces in the regular Comedy in verse, belonging to two writers who here perhaps have taken more pains, but in other departments have given a freer scope to their natural talent: the *Metromanie* of Piron and the *Mechant* of Gresset. The *Metromanie* is not written without humorous inspiration. In the young man possessed with a passion for poetry, Piron intended in some measure to paint himself; but as we always go tenderly to work in the ridicule of ourselves, together with the amiable weakness in question, he endows his hero with talents, magnanimity, and a good heart. But this tender reserve is not peculiarly favourable for comic strength. As to the *Mechant*, it is one of those gloomy comedies which might be rapturously hailed by a Timon as serving to confirm his aversion to human society, but which, on social and cheerful minds, can only give rise to the most painful impression. Why paint a dark and odious disposition which, devoid of all human sympathy, feeds its vanity in a cold contempt and derision of everything, and solely occupies itself in aimless detraction? Why exhibit such a moral deformity, which could hardly be tolerated even in Tragedy, for the mere purpose of producing domestic discontent and petty embarrassments?

Yet, according to the decision of the French critics, these three comedies, the *Glorieux*, the *Metromanie*, and the *Mechant*, are all that the eighteenth century can oppose to Moliere. We should be disposed to rank the *Le Vieux Bachelier* of Collin d'Harleville much higher; but for judging this true picture of manners there is no scale afforded in the works of Moliere, and it can only be compared with those of Terence. We have here the utmost refinement and accuracy of characterization, most felicitously combined with an able plot, which keeps on the stretch and rivets our attention, while a certain mildness of sentiment is diffused over the whole.

I purpose now to make a few observations on the secondary species of the *Opera*, *Operettes*, and *Vaudevilles*, and shall conclude with a view of the present condition of the French stage with reference to the histrionic art.

In the serious, heroic, or rather the ideal *opera*, if we may so express ourselves, we can only mention one poet of the age of Louis XIV., Quinault--who is now little read, but yet deserving of high praise. As a tragic poet, in the early period of his career, he was satirized by Boileau; but he was afterwards highly successful in another species, the musical drama. Mazarin had introduced into France a taste for the Italian opera; Louis was also desirous of rivalling or surpassing foreign countries in the external magnificence of the drama, in decoration, machinery, music, and dancing; these were all to be employed in the celebration of the court festivals; and accordingly Moliere was employed to write gay, and Quinault serious operas, to the music of Lulli. I am not sufficiently versed in the earlier literature of the Italian opera to be able to speak with accuracy, but I suspect that here also Quinault laboured more after Spanish than Italian models; and more particularly, that he derived from the Fiestas of Calderon the general form of his operas, and their frequently allegorical preludes which are often to be found in them. It is true, poetical ornament is much more sparingly dealt out, as the whole is necessarily shortened for the sake of the music, and the very nature of the French language and versification is incompatible with the splendid magnificence, the luxurious fulness, displayed by Calderon. But the operas of Quinault are, in their easy progress, truly fanciful; and the serious opera cannot, in my opinion, be stripped of the charm of the marvellous without becoming at length wearisome. So far

Quinault appears to me to have taken a much better road towards the true vocation of particular departments of art, than that on which Metastasio travelled long after him. The latter has admirably provided for the wants of a melodious music expressive solely of feeling; but where does he furnish the least food for the imagination? On the other hand, I am not so sure that Quinault is justly entitled to praise for sacrificing, in compliance with the taste of his countrymen, everything like comic intermixture. He has been censured for an occasional play on language in the expression of feeling. But is it just to exact the severity of the tragical cothurnus in light works of this description? Why should not Poetry also be allowed her arabesque? No person can be more an enemy to mannerism than I am; but to censure it aright, we ought first to understand the degree of nature and truth which we have a right to expect from each species, and what is alone compatible with it. The verses of Quinault have no other *naivete* and simplicity than those of the madrigal; and though they occasionally fall into the luscious, at other times they express a languishing tenderness with gracefulness and a soft melody. The opera ought to resemble the enchanted gardens of Armida, of which Quinault says,

Dans ces lieux enchantes la volupte preside.

We ought only to be awaked out of the voluptuous dreams of feeling to enjoy the magical illusions of fancy. When once we have come to imagine, instead of real men, beings whose only language is song, it is but a very short step to represent to ourselves creatures whose only occupation is love; that feeling which hovers between the sensible and intellectual world; and the first invention becomes natural again by means of the second.

Quinault has had no successors. How far below his, both in point of invention and of execution, are the French operas of the present day! The heroic and tragic have been required in a department where they cannot produce their proper effect. Instead of handling with fanciful freedom mythological materials or subjects taken from chivalrous or pastoral romances, they have after the manner of Tragedy chained themselves down to history, and by means of their heavy seriousness, and the pedantry of their rules, they have so managed matters, that Dulness with leaden sceptre presides over the opera. The deficiencies of their music, the unfitness of the French language for composition in a style anything higher than that of the most simple national melodies, the unaccented and arbitrary nature of their recitative, the bawling bravura of the singers, must be left to the animadversions of musical critics.

With pretensions far lower, the *Comic Opera* or *Operette* approaches much more nearly to perfection. With respect to the composition, it may and indeed ought to assume only a national tone. The transition from song to speech, without any musical accompaniment or heightening, which was censured by Rousseau as an unsuitable mixture of two distinct modes of composition, may be displeasing to the ear; but it has unquestionably produced an advantageous effect on the structure of the pieces. In the recitatives, which generally are not half understood, and seldom listened to with any degree of attention, a plot which is even moderately complicated cannot be developed with due clearness. Hence in the Italian *opera buffa*, the action is altogether neglected; and along with its grotesque caricatures, it is distinguished for uniform situations, which admit not of dramatic progress. But the comic opera of the French, although from the space occupied by the music it is unsusceptible of any very perfect dramatic development, is still calculated to produce a considerable stage effect, and speaks pleasingly to the imagination. The poets have not here been prevented by the constraint of rules from following out their theatrical views. Hence these fleeting productions are in no wise deficient in the rapidity, life, and amusement, which are frequently wanting in the more correct dramatic works of the French. The distinguished favour which the *operettes* of a Favart, a Sedaine and later poets, of whom some are still alive, always meet with in Germany, (where foreign literature has long lost its commanding influence, and where the national taste has pronounced so strongly against French Tragedy,) is by no means to be placed to the account of the music; it is in reality owing to their poetical merit. To cite only one example out of many, I do not hesitate to declare the whole series of scenes in *Raoul Sire de Crequy*, where the children of the drunken turnkey set the prisoner at liberty, a master-piece of theatrical painting. How much were it to be wished that the Tragedy of the French, and even their Comedy in court-dress, had but a little of this truth of circumstance, this vivid presence, and power of arresting the attention. In several *operettes*, for instance in a *Richard Coeur de Lion* and a *Nina*, the traces of the romantic spirit are not to be mistaken.

The *vaudeville* is but a variation of the comic opera. The essential difference is that it dispenses with composition, by which the comic opera forms a musical whole, as the songs are set to well-known popular airs. The incessant skipping from the song to the dialogue, often after a few scrapes of the violin and a few words, with the accumulation of airs mostly common, but frequently also in a style altogether different from the poetry, drives an ear accustomed to Italian music to despair. If we can once make up our minds to bear with this, we shall not unfrequently be richly recompensed in comic drollery; even in the choice of a melody, and the allusion to the common and well-known words, there is often a display of wit. In earlier times writers of higher pretensions, a Le Sage and a

Piron have laboured in the department of the *vaudeville*, and even for *marionettes*. The wits who now dedicate themselves to this species are little known out of Paris, but this gives them no great concern. It not unfrequently happens that several of them join together, that the fruit of their common talents may be sooner brought to light. The parody of new theatrical pieces, the anecdotes of the day, which form the common talk among all the idlers of the capital, must furnish them with subjects in working up which little delay can be brooked. These *vaudevilles* are like the gnats that buzz about in a summer evening; they often sting, but they fly merrily about so long as the sun of opportunity shines upon them. A piece like the *Despair of Jocrisse*, which, after a lapse of years, may be still occasionally brought out, passes justly among the ephemeral productions for a classical work that has gained the crown of immortality. We must, however, see it acted by Brunet, whose face is almost a mask, and who is nearly as inexhaustible in the part of the simpleton as Puncinello is in his.

From a consideration of the sportive secondary species, formed out of a mixture of the comic with the affecting, in which authors and spectators give themselves up without reserve to their natural inclinations, it appears to me evident, that as comic wit with the Italians consists in grotesque mimicry or buffoonery, and with the English in humour, with the French it consists in good-natured gaiety. Among the lower orders especially this property is everywhere visible, where it has not been supplanted by the artifice of corruption.

With respect to the present condition of Dramatic Art in France, every thing depends on the endeavours to introduce the theatrical liberties of other countries, or mixed species of the drama. The hope of producing any thing truly new in the two species which are alone admitted to be regular, of excelling the works already produced, of filling up the old frames with richer pictures, becomes more and more distant every day. A new work seldom obtains a decided approbation; and, even at best, this approbation only lasts till it has been found out that the work is only a new preparation of their old classical productions.

We have passed over several things relating to these endeavours, that we may deliver together all the observations which we have to make on the subject. The attacks hitherto made against the French forms of art, first by De la Motte, and afterwards by Diderot and Mercier, have been like voices in the wilderness. It could not be otherwise, as the principles on which these writers proceeded were in reality destructive, not merely of the conventional forms, but of all poetical forms whatever, and as none of them showed themselves capable of suitably supporting their doctrine by their own example, even when they were in the right they contrived, nevertheless, by a false application, to be in the wrong.

The most remarkable among them is Diderot, whom Lessing calls the best critic of the French. In opposition to this opinion I should be disposed to affirm that he was no critic at all. I will not lay any stress on his mistaking the object of poetry and the fine arts, which he considered to be merely moral: a man may be a critic without being a theorist. But a man cannot be a critic without being thoroughly acquainted with the conditions, means, and styles of an art; and here the nature of Diderot's studies and acquirements renders his critical capabilities extremely questionable. This ingenious sophist deals out his blows with such boisterous haste in the province of criticism, that the half of them are thrown away. The true and the false, the old and the new, the essential and the unimportant, are so mixed up together, that the highest praise we can bestow upon him is, that he is worthy of the labour of disentangling them. What he wished to accomplish had either been accomplished, though not in France, or did not deserve to be accomplished, or was altogether impracticable. His attack on the formality and holiday primness of the dramatic probabilities, of the excessive symmetry of the French versification, declamation, and mode of acting, was just; but, at the same time, he objected to all theatrical elevation, and refused to allow to the characters anything like a perfect mode of communicating what was passing within them. He nowhere assigns the reason why he held versification as not suitable, or prose as more suitable, to familiar tragedy; this has been extended by others, and among the rest, unfortunately, by Lessing, to every species of the drama; but the ground for it evidently rests on nothing but the mistaken principles of illusion and nature, to which we have more than once adverted. [Footnote: I have stated and refuted them in a treatise *On the Relation of the Fine Arts to Nature* in the fifth number of the periodical work *Prometheus*, published by Leo von Seckendorf.] And if he gives an undue preference to the sentimental drama and the familiar tragedy, species valuable in themselves, and susceptible of a truly poetic treatment; was not this on account of the application? The main thing, according to him, is not character and situations, but ranks of life and family relations, that spectators in similar ranks and relations may lay the example to heart. But this would put an end to everything like true enjoyment in art. Diderot recommended that the composition should have this direction, with the very view which, in the case of a historical tragedy founded on the events of their own times, met with the disapprobation of the Athenians, and subjected its author Phrynichus to their displeasure [Footnote: See page 72.]. The view of a fire by night may, from the wonderful effect produced by the combination of flames and darkness, fill the unconcerned spectator with delight; but when our neighbour's house is burning,--*jam oreximus ardet Ucalegon*--we shall hardly be disposed to see the affair in such a picturesque light.

It is clear that Diderot was induced to take in his sail as he made way with his own dramatic attempts. He displayed the greatest boldness in an offensive publication of his youth, in which he wished to overturn the entire dramatic system of the French; he was less daring in the dialogues which accompany the *Fils Naturel*, and he showed the greatest moderation in the treatise appended to the *Pere de Famille*. He carried his hostility a great deal too far with respect to the forms and the objects of the dramatic art. But in other respects he has not gone far enough: in his view of the Unities of Place and Time, and the mixture of seriousness and mirth, he has shown himself infected with the prejudices of his nation.

The two pieces above mentioned, which obtained an unmerited reputation on their first appearance, have long since received their due appreciation. On the *Fils Naturel* Lessing has pronounced a severe sentence, without, however, censuring the scandalous plagiarism from Goldoni. But the *Pere de Famille* he calls an excellent piece, but has forgotten, however, to assign any grounds for his opinion. Its defective plot and want of connexion have been well exposed by La Harpe. The execution of both pieces exhibits the utmost mannerism: the characters, which are anything but natural, become from their frigid prating about virtue in the most hypocritical style, and the tears which they are perpetually shedding, altogether intolerable. We Germans may justly say, *Hinc illae lacrymae!* hence the unnecessary tears with which our stage has ever since been overflowed. The custom which has grown up of giving long and circumstantial directions respecting the action, and which we owe also to Diderot, has been of the greatest detriment to dramatic eloquence. In this way the poet gives, as it were, an order on the player, instead of paying out of his own purse. [Footnote: I remember to have read the following direction in a German drama, which is not worse than many others:--"He flashes lightning at him with his eyes (*Er blitzt ihn mit den Augen an*) and goes off."] All good dramatists have uniformly had the action in some degree present to their minds; but if the actor requires instruction on the subject, he will hardly possess the talent of following it up with the suitable gestures. The speeches should be so framed that an intelligent actor could hardly fail to give them the proper action.

It will he admitted, that long before Diderot there were serious family pictures, affecting dramas, and familial tragedies, much better than any which he was capable of executing. Voltaire, who could never rightly succeed in Comedy, gave in his *Enfant Prodigue* and *Nanine* a mixture of comic scenes and affecting situations, the latter of which are deserving of high praise. The affecting drama had been before attempted in France by La Chaussee. All this was in verse: and why not? Of the familiar tragedy (with the very same moral direction for which Diderot contended) several examples have been produced on the English stage: and one of them, *Beverley, or the Gamester*, is translated into French. The period of sentimentality was of some use to the affecting or sentimental drama; but the familiar tragedy was never very successful in France, where they were too much attached to brilliancy and pomp. The *Melanie* of La Harpe (to whom the stage of the present day owes *Philoctete*, the most faithful imitation of a Grecian piece) abounds with those painful impressions which form the rock this species may be said to split upon. The piece may perhaps be well adapted to enlighten the conscience of a father who has determined to force his daughter to enter a cloister; but to other spectators it can only be painful.

Notwithstanding the opposition which Diderot experienced, he was however the founder of a sort of school of which the most distinguished names are Beaumarchais and Mercier. The former wrote only two pieces in the spirit of his predecessor--*Eugenie*, and *La Mere Coupable*; and they display the very same faults. His acquaintance with Spain and the Spanish theatre led him to bring something new on the stage in the way of the piece of intrigue, a species which had long been neglected. These works were more distinguished by witty sallies than by humour of character; but their greatest attraction consisted in the allusions to his own career as an author. The plot of the *Barber of Seville* is rather trite; the *Marriage of Figaro* is planned with much more art, but the manners which it portrays are loose; and it is also censurable in a poetical point of view, on account of the number of foreign excrescences with which it is loaded. In both French characters are exhibited under the disguise of a Spanish costume, which, however, is very ill observed [Footnote: The numerous sins of Beaumarchais against the Spanish manners and observances, are pointed out by De la Huerta in the introduction to his *Teatro Espanol*.]. The extraordinary applause which these pieces met with would lead to the conclusion, that the French public do not hold the comedy of *intrigue* in such low estimation as it is by the critics: but the means by which Beaumarchais pleased were certainly, in part it least, foreign to art.

The attempt of Ducis to make his countrymen acquainted with Shakspeare by modelling a few of his tragedies according to the French rules, cannot be accounted an enlargement of their theatre. We perceive here and there indeed the "torn members of the poet"--*disjecta membra poetae*; but the whole is so constrained, disfigured, and, from the simple fulness of the original, tortured and twisted into such miserable intricacy, that even when the language is retained word for word, it ceases to convey its genuine meaning. The crowd which these tragedies attracted, especially from their affording an unusual room to the inimitable Talma for the display of his art, must be looked upon as no slight symptom of the people's dissatisfaction with their old works, and the want of others more powerfully agitating.

As the Parisian theatres are at present tied down to certain kinds, and as poetry has here a point of contact with the police, the numerous mixed and new attempts are for the most part banished to the subordinate theatres. Of these new attempts the *Melo-dramas* constitute a principal part. A statistical writer of the theatre informs us, that for a number of years back the new productions in Tragedy and regular Comedy have been fewest, and that the melo-dramas have in number exceeded all the others put together. They do not mean by melo-drama, as we do, a drama in which the pauses are filled up by monologue with instrumental music, but where actions in any wise wonderful, adventurous, or even sensuous, are exhibited in emphatic prose with suitable decorations and dresses. Advantage might be taken of this prevailing inclination to furnish a better description of entertainment: since most of the melo-dramas are unfortunately rude even to insipidity, and resemble abortive attempts at the romantic.

In the sphere of dramatic literature the labours of a Le Mercier are undoubtedly deserving of the critic's attention. This able man endeavours to break through the prescribed limits in every possible way, and is so passionately fond of his art that nothing can deter him from it; although almost every new attempt which he makes converts the pit into a regular field of battle. [Footnote: Since these Lectures were held, such a tumult arose in the theatre at Paris on the representation of his *Christopher Columbus*, that several of the champions of Boileau came off with bruised heads and broken shins. They were in the right to fight like desperadoes; for if this piece had succeeded, it would have been all over with the consecrated Unities and good taste in the separation of the heroic and the low. The first act takes place in the house of Columbus, the second at the court of Isabella, the third and last on shipboard near the New World. The object of the poet was to show that the man in whom any grand idea originates is everywhere opposed and thwarted by the limited and common-place views of other men; but that the strength of his enthusiasm enables him to overcome all obstacles. In his own house, and among his acquaintances, Columbus is considered as insane; at court he obtains with difficulty a lukewarm support; in his own vessel a mutiny is on the point of breaking out, when the wished-for land is discovered, and the piece ends with the exclamation of "Land, land!" All this is conceived and planned very skilfully; but in the execution, however, there are numerous defects. In another piece not yet acted nor printed, called *La Journee des Dupes*, which I heard the author read, he has painted with historical truth, both in regard to circumstances and the spirit of the age, a well-known but unsuccessful court-cabal against Cardinal Richelieu. It is a political comedy, in which the rag-gatherer and the king express themselves in language suitable to their stations. The poet has, with the greatest ingenuity, shown the manner in which trivial causes assist or impede the execution of a great political design, the dissimulation practised by political personages towards others, and even towards themselves, and the different tones which they assume according to circumstances; in a word, he has exhibited the whole inward aspect of the game of politics.]

From all this we may infer, that the inclinations of the French public, when they forget the duties they have imbibed from Boileau's *Art of Poetry*, are not quite so hostile to the dramatic liberties of other nations as might be supposed, and that the old and narrow system is chiefly upheld by a superstitious attachment to traditional opinions.

The histrionic art, particularly in high comedy and tragedy, has been long carried in France to great perfection. In external dignity, quickness, correctness of memory, and in a wonderful degree of propriety and elegance in the delivery of verse, the best French actors are hardly to be surpassed. Their efforts to please are incredible: every moment they pass on the stage is a valuable opportunity, of which they must avail themselves. The extremely fastidious taste of a Paris pit, and the wholesome severity of the journalists, excite in them a spirit of incessant emulation; and the circumstance of acting a number of classical works, which for generations have been in the possession of the stage, contributes also greatly to their excellence in their art. As the spectators have these works nearly by heart, their whole attention may be directed to the acting, and every faulty syllable meets in this way with immediate detection and reprobation.

In high comedy the social refinement of the nation affords great advantages to their actors. But with respect to tragical composition, the art of the actor should also accommodate itself to the spirit of the poetry. I am inclined to doubt, however, whether this is the case with the French actors, and whether the authors of the tragedies, especially those of the age of Louis XIV. would altogether recognise themselves in the mode in which these compositions are at present represented.

The tragic imitation and recitation of the French oscillate between two opposite extremes, the first of which is occasioned by the prevailing tone of the piece, while the second seems rather to be at variance with it,--between measured formality and extravagant boisterousness. The first might formerly preponderate, but the balance is now on the other side.

Let us hear Voltaire's description of the manner in which, in the time of Louis XIV., Augustus delivered his discourse to Cinna and Maximus. Augustus entered with the step of a braggadocio, his head covered with a four-cornered peruque, which hung down to his girdle; the peruque was stuck full of laurel leaves, and above this he wore a large hat with a double row of red feathers. He seated himself on a huge fauteuil, two steps high, Cinna and Maximus on two low chairs; and the pompous declamation fully corresponded to the ostentatious manner in which he made his appearance. As at that time, and even long afterwards, tragedies were acted in a court-dress of the newest fashion, with large cravats, swords, and hats, no other movements were practicable but such as were allowable in an antechamber, or, at most, a slight waving of the hand; and it was even considered a bold theatrical attempt, when, in the last scene of *Polyeucte*, Severus entered with his hat on his head for the purpose of accusing Felix of treachery, and the latter listened to him with his hat under his arm.

However, there were even early examples of an extravagance of an opposite description. In the *Mariamne* of Mairet, an older poet than Corneille, the player who acted Herod, roared himself to death. This may, indeed, be called "out-heroding Herod!" When Voltaire was instructing an actress in some tragic part, she said to him, "Were I to play in this manner, sir, they would say the devil was in me."--"Very right," answered Voltaire, "an actress ought to have the devil in her." This expression proves, at least, no very keen sense for that dignity and sweetness which in an ideal composition, such as the French Tragedy pretends to be, ought never to be lost sight of, even in the wildest whirlwind of passion.

I found occasionally, even in the action of the very best players of the present day, sudden leaps from the measured solemnity in recitation and gesticulation which the general tone of the composition required, to a boisterousness of passion absolutely convulsive, without any due preparation or softening by intervening gradations. They are led to this by a sort of obscure feeling, that the conventional forms of poetry generally impede the movements of nature; when the poet any where leaves them at liberty, they then indemnify themselves for the former constraint, and load, as it were, this rare moment of abandonment with the whole amount of life and animation which had been kept back, and which ought to have been equally diffused over the whole. Hence their convulsive and obstreperous violence. In bravura they take care not to be deficient; but they frequently lose sight of the true spirit of the composition. In general, (with the single exception of the great Talma,) they consider their parts as a sort of mosaic work of brilliant passages, and they rather endeavour to make the most of each separate passage, independently of the rest, than to go back to the invisible central point of the character, and to consider every expression of it as an emanation from that point. They are always afraid of underdoing their parts; and hence they are worse qualified for reserved action, for eloquent silence, where, under an appearance of outward tranquillity, the most hidden emotions of the mind are betrayed. However, this is a part which is seldom imposed on them by their poets; and if the cause of such excessive violence in the expression of passion is not to be found in the works themselves, they at all events occasion the actor to lay greater stress on superficial brilliancy than on a profound knowledge of character [Footnote: See a treatise of M. Von Humboldt the elder, in Goethe's *Propylaen*, on the French acting, equally distinguished for a refined and solid spirit of observation.].

LECTURE XXII.

Comparison of the English and Spanish Theatres--Spirit of the Romantic Drama--Shakspeare--His age and the circumstances of his Life.

In conformity with the plan which we laid down at the first, we shall now proceed to treat of the English and Spanish theatres. We have been, on various occasions, compelled in passing to allude cursorily, sometimes to the one and sometimes to the other, partly for the sake of placing, by means of contrast, many ideas in a clearer light, and partly on account of the influence which these stages have had on the theatres of other countries. Both the English and Spaniards possess a very rich dramatic literature, both have had a number of prolific and highly talented dramatists, among whom even the least admired and celebrated, considered as a whole, display uncommon aptitude for dramatic animation, and insight into the essence of theatrical effect. The history of their theatres has no connexion with that of the Italians and French, for they developed themselves wholly out of the abundance of their own intrinsic energy, without any foreign influence: the attempts to bring them back to an imitation of the ancients, or even of the French, have either been attended with no success, or not been made till a late period in the decay of the drama. The formation of these two stages, again, is equally independent of each other; the Spanish poets were altogether unacquainted with the English; and in the older and most important period of the English theatre I could discover no trace of any knowledge of Spanish plays, (though their novels and romances were certainly known,) and it was not till the time of Charles II. that translations from Calderon first made their appearance.

So many things among men have been handed down from century to century and from nation to nation, and the human mind is in general so slow to invent, that originality in any department of mental exertion is everywhere a rare phenomenon. We are desirous of seeing the result of the efforts of inventive geniuses when, regardless of what in the same line has elsewhere been carried to a high degree of perfection, they set to work in good earnest to invent altogether for themselves; when they lay the foundation of the new edifice on uncovered ground, and draw all the preparations, all the building materials, from their own resources. We participate, in some measure, in the joy of success, when we see them advance rapidly from their first helplessness and need to a finished mastery in their art. The history of the Grecian theatre would afford us this cheering prospect could we witness its rudest beginnings, which were not preserved, for they were not even committed to writing; but it is easy, when we compare together Aeschylus and Sophocles, to form some idea of the preceding period. The Greeks neither inherited nor borrowed their dramatic art from any other people; it was original and native, and for that very reason was it able to produce a living and powerful effect. But it ended with the period when Greeks imitated Greeks; namely, when the Alexandrian poets began learnedly and critically to compose dramas after the model of the great tragic writers. The reverse of this was the case with the Romans: they received the form and substance of their dramas from the Greeks; they never attempted to act according to their own discretion, and to express their own way of thinking; and hence they occupy so insignificant a place in the history of dramatic art. Among the nations of modern Europe, the English and Spaniards alone (for the German stage is but forming), possess as yet a theatre entirely original and national, which, in its own peculiar shape, has arrived at maturity.

Those critics who consider the authority of the ancients as models to be such, that in poetry, as in all the other arts, there can be no safety out of the pale of imitation, affirm, that as the nations in question have not followed this course, they have brought nothing but irregular works on the stage, which, though they may possess occasional passages of splendour and beauty, must yet, as a whole, be for ever reprobated as barbarous, and wanting in form. We have already, in the introductory part of these Lectures, stated our sentiments generally on this way of thinking; but we must now examine the subject somewhat more closely.

If the assertion be well founded, all that distinguishes the works of the greatest English and Spanish dramatists, a Shakspeare and a Calderon, must rank them far below the ancients; they could in no wise be of importance for theory, and would at most appear remarkable, on the assumption that the obstinacy of these nations in refusing to comply with the rules, may have afforded a more ample field to the poets, to display their native originality, though at the expense of art. But even this assumption, on a closer examination, appears extremely questionable. The poetic spirit requires to be limited, that it may move with a becoming liberty, within its proper precincts, as has been felt by all nations on the first invention of metre; it must act according to laws derivable from its own essence, otherwise its strength will evaporate in boundless vacuity.

The works of genius cannot therefore be permitted to be without form; but of this there is no danger. However, that we may answer this objection of want of form, we must understand the exact meaning of the term form, since most critics, and more especially those who insist on a stiff regularity, interpret it merely in a mechanical, and not in an organical sense. Form is mechanical when, through external force, it is imparted to any material merely as an accidental addition without reference to its quality; as, for example, when we give a particular shape to a soft mass that it may retain the same after its induration. Organical form, again, is innate; it unfolds itself from within, and acquires its determination contemporaneously with the perfect development of the germ. We everywhere discover such forms in nature throughout the whole range of living powers, from the crystallization of salts and minerals to plants and flowers, and from these again to the human body. In the fine arts, as well as in the domain of nature--the supreme artist, all genuine forms are organical, that is, determined by the quality of the work. In a word, the form is nothing but a significant exterior, the speaking physiognomy of each thing, which, as long as it is not disfigured by any destructive accident, gives a true evidence of its hidden essence.

Hence it is evident that the spirit of poetry, which, though imperishable, migrates, as it were, through different bodies, must, so often as it is newly born in the human race, mould to itself, out of the nutrimental substance of an altered age, a body of a different conformation. The forms vary with the direction taken by the poetical sense; and when we give to the new kinds of poetry the old names, and judge of them according to the ideas conveyed by these names, the application which we make of the authority of classical antiquity is altogether unjustifiable. No one should be tried before a tribunal to which he is not amenable. We may safely admit, that the most of the English and Spanish dramatic works are neither tragedies nor comedies in the sense of the ancients: they are romantic dramas. That the stage of a people who, in its foundation and formation, neither knew nor wished to know anything of foreign models, will possess many peculiarities; and not only deviate from, but even exhibit a striking contrast to, the theatres of other nations who had a common model for imitation before their eyes, is easily supposable, and we should only be astonished were it otherwise. But when in two nations, differing so widely as the English and Spanish, in physical, moral, political, and religious respects, the theatres (which, without being known to each other, arose about the same time,) possess, along with external and internal diversities, the most striking features of affinity, the attention even of the most thoughtless cannot but be turned to this phenomenon; and the conjecture will naturally occur, that the same, or, at least, a kindred principle must have prevailed in the development of both. This comparison, however, of the English and Spanish theatre, in their common contrast with every dramatic literature which has grown up out of an imitation of the ancients, has, so far as we know, never yet been attempted. Could we raise from the dead a countryman, contemporary, and intelligent admirer of Shakspeare, and another of Calderon, and introduce to their acquaintance the works of the poet to which in life they were strangers, they would both, without doubt, considering the subject rather from a national than a general point of view, enter with difficulty into the above idea, and have many objections to urge against it. But here a reconciling criticism [Footnote: This appropriate expression was, if we mistake not, first used by M. Adam Muller in his *Lectures on German Science and Literature*. If, however, he gives himself out for the inventor of the thing itself, he is, to use the softest word, in error. Long before him other Germans had endeavoured to reconcile the contrarieties of taste of different ages and nations, and to pay due homage to all genuine poetry and art. Between good and bad, it is true, no reconciliation is possible.] must step in; and this, perhaps, may be best exercised by a German, who is free from the national peculiarities of either Englishmen or Spaniards, yet by inclination friendly to both, and prevented by no jealousy from acknowledging the greatness which has been earlier exhibited in other countries than in his own.

The similarity of the English and Spanish theatres does not consist merely in the bold neglect of the Unities of Place and Time, and in the commixture of comic and tragic elements: that they were unwilling or unable to comply with the rules and with right reason, (in the meaning of certain critics these terms are equivalent,) may be considered as an evidence of merely negative properties. The ground of the resemblance lies far deeper, in the inmost substance of the fictions, and in the essential relations, through which every deviation of form, becomes a true requisite, which, together with its validity, has also its significance. What they have in common with each other is the spirit of the romantic poetry, giving utterance to itself in a dramatic shape. However, to explain ourselves with due precision, the Spanish theatre, in our opinion, down to its decline and fall in the commencement of the eighteenth century, is almost entirely romantic; the English is completely so in Shakspeare alone, its founder and greatest master: in later poets the romantic principle appears more or less degenerated, or is no longer perceivable, although the march of dramatic composition introduced by virtue of it has been, outwardly at least, pretty generally retained. The manner in which the different ways of thinking of the two nations, one a northern and the other a southern, have been expressed; the former endowed with a gloomy, the latter with a glowing imagination; the one nation possessed of a scrutinizing seriousness disposed to withdraw within themselves, the other impelled outwardly by the violence of passion; the mode in which all this has been accomplished will be most satisfactorily explained at the close of this section, when we come to institute a parallel between Shakspeare and Calderon, the only two poets who are entitled to be called great.

Of the origin and essence of the romantic I treated in my first Lecture, and I shall here, therefore, merely briefly mention the subject. The ancient art and poetry rigorously separate things which are dissimilar; the romantic delights in indissoluble mixtures; all contrarieties: nature and art, poetry and prose, seriousness and mirth, recollection and anticipation, spirituality and sensuality, terrestrial and celestial, life and death, are by it blended together in the most intimate combination. As the oldest lawgivers delivered their mandatory instructions and prescriptions in measured melodies; as this is fabulously ascribed to Orpheus, the first softener of the yet untamed race of mortals; in like manner the whole of the ancient poetry and art is, as it were, a *rhythmical nomos* (law), an harmonious promulgation of the permanently established legislation of a world submitted to a beautiful order, and reflecting in itself the eternal images of things. Romantic poetry, on the other hand, is the expression of the secret attraction to a chaos which lies concealed in the very bosom of the ordered universe, and is perpetually striving after new and marvellous births; the life-giving spirit of primal love broods here anew on the face of the waters. The former is more simple, clear, and like to nature in the self-existent perfection of her separate works; the latter, notwithstanding its fragmentary appearance, approaches more to the secret of the universe. For Conception can only comprise each object separately, but nothing in truth can ever exist separately and by itself; Feeling perceives all in all at one and the same time. Respecting the two species of poetry with which we are here principally occupied, we compared the ancient Tragedy to a group in sculpture: the figures corresponding to the characters, and their grouping to the action; and to these two in both productions of art is the consideration exclusively directed, as being all that is properly exhibited. But the romantic drama must be viewed as a large picture, where not merely figure and motion are exhibited in larger, richer groups, but where even all that surrounds the figures must also be portrayed; where we see not merely the nearest objects, but are indulged with the prospect of a considerable distance; and all this under a magical light, which assists in giving to the impression the particular character desired.

Such a picture must be bounded less perfectly and less distinctly, than the group; for it is like a fragment cut out of the optic scene of the world. However the painter, by the setting of his foreground, by throwing the whole of his light into the centre, and by other means of fixing the point of view, will learn that he must neither wander beyond the composition, nor omit any thing within it.

In the representation of figure, Painting cannot compete with Sculpture, since the former can only exhibit it by a deception and from a single point of view; but, on the other hand, it communicates more life to its imitations, by colours which in a picture are made to imitate the lightest shades of mental expression in the countenance. The look, which can be given only very imperfectly by Sculpture, enables us to read much deeper in the mind, and to perceive its lightest movements. Its peculiar charm, in short, consists in this, that it enables us to see in bodily objects what is least corporeal, namely, light and air.

The very same description of beauties are peculiar to the romantic drama. It does not (like the Old Tragedy) separate seriousness and the action, in a rigid manner, from among the whole ingredients of life; it embraces at once the whole of the chequered drama of life with all its circumstances; and while it seems only to represent subjects brought accidentally together, it satisfies the unconscious requisitions of fancy, buries us in reflections on the inexpressible signification of the objects which we view blended by order, nearness and distance, light and colour, into one harmonious whole; and thus lends, as it were, a soul to the prospect before us.

The change of time and of place, (supposing its influence on the mind to be included in the picture; and that it comes to the aid of the theatrical perspective, with reference to what is indicated in the distance, or half-concealed by intervening objects;) the contrast of sport and earnest (supposing that in degree and kind they bear a proportion to each other;) finally, the mixture of the dialogical and the lyrical elements, (by which the poet is enabled, more or less perfectly, to transform his personages into poetical beings:) these, in my opinion, are not mere licenses, but true beauties in the romantic drama. In all these points, and in many others also, the English and Spanish works, which are pre-eminently worthy of this title of Romantic, fully resemble each other, however different they may be in other respects.

Of the two we shall first notice the English theatre, because it arrived earlier at maturity than the Spanish. In both we must occupy ourselves almost exclusively with a single artist, with Shakspeare in the one and Calderon in the other; but not in the same order with each, for Shakspeare stands first and earliest among the English; any remarks we may have to make on earlier or contemporary antiquities of the English stage may be made in a review of his history. But Calderon had many predecessors; he is at once the summit and the close nearly of dramatic art in Spain.

The wish to speak with the brevity which the limits of my plan demand, of a poet to the study of whom I have devoted many years of my life, places me in no little embarrassment. I know not where to begin; for I should never be able to end, were I to say all that I have felt and thought on the perusal of his works. With the poet as with the man, a more than ordinary intimacy prevents us, perhaps, from putting ourselves in the place of those who are first forming an acquaintance with him: we are too familiar with his most striking peculiarities, to be able to pronounce upon the first impression which they are calculated to make on others. On the other hand, we ought to possess, and to have the power of communicating, more correct ideas of his mode of procedure, of his concealed or less obvious views, and of the meaning and import of his labours, than others whose acquaintance with him is more limited.

Shakspeare is the pride of his nation. A late poet has, with propriety, called him "the genius of the British isles." He was the idol of his contemporaries: during the interval indeed of puritanical fanaticism, which broke out in the next generation, and rigorously proscribed all liberal arts and literature, and during the reign of the Second Charles, when his works were either not acted at all, or if so, very much changed and disfigured, his fame was awhile obscured, only to shine forth again about the beginning of the last century with more than its original brightness; and since then it has but increased in lustre with the course of time; and for centuries to come, (I speak it with the greatest confidence,) it will, like an Alpine *avalanche*, continue to gather strength at every moment of its progress. Of the future extension of his fame, the enthusiasm with which he was naturalized in Germany, the moment that he was known, is a significant earnest. In the South of Europe, [Footnote: This difficulty extends also to France; for it must not be supposed that a literal translation can ever be a faithful one. Mrs. Montague has done enough to prove how wretchedly, even Voltaire, in his rhymeless Alexandrines, has translated a few passages from *Hamlet* and the first act of *Julius Caesar*.] his language, and the great difficulty of translating him with fidelity, will be, perhaps, an invincible obstacle to his general diffusion. In England, the greatest actors vie with each other in the impersonation of his characters; the printers in splendid editions of his works; and the painters in transferring his scenes to the canvas. Like Dante, Shakspeare has received the perhaps indispensable but still cumbersome honour of being treated like a classical author of antiquity. The oldest editions have been carefully collated, and where the readings seemed corrupt, many corrections have been suggested; and the whole literature of his age has been drawn forth from the oblivion to which it had been consigned, for the sole purpose of explaining the phrases, and illustrating the allusions of Shakspeare. Commentators have succeeded one another in such number, that their labours alone, with the critical controversies to which they have given rise, constitute of themselves no inconsiderable library. These labours deserve both our praise and gratitude; and more especially the historical investigations into the sources from which Shakspeare drew the materials of his plays, and also into the previous and contemporary state of the English stage, and other kindred subjects of inquiry. With respect, however, to their merely philological criticisms, I am frequently compelled to differ from the commentators; and where, too, considering him simply as a poet, they endeavour to enter into his views and to decide upon his merits, I must separate myself from them entirely. I have hardly ever found either truth or profundity in their remarks; and these critics seem to me to be but stammering interpreters of the general and almost idolatrous admiration of his countrymen. There may be people in England who entertain the same views of them with myself, at least it is a well-known fact that a satirical poet has represented Shakspeare, under the hands of his commentators, by Actaeon worried to death by his own dogs; and, following up the story of Ovid, designated a female writer on the great poet as the snarling Lycisca.

We shall endeavour, in the first place, to remove some of these false views, in order to clear the way for our own homage, that we may thereupon offer it the more freely without let or hindrance.

From all the accounts of Shakspeare which have come down to us, it is clear that his contemporaries knew well the treasure they possessed in him; and that they felt and understood him better than most of those who succeeded him. In those days a work was generally ushered into the world with Commendatory Verses; and one of these, prefixed to an early edition of Shakspeare, by an unknown author, contains some of the most beautiful and happy lines that ever were applied to any poet [Footnote: It begins with the words: *A mind reflecting ages past*, and is subscribed, I.M.S.]. An idea, however, soon became prevalent that Shakspeare was a rude and wild genius, who poured forth at random, and without aim or object, his unconnected compositions. Ben Jonson, a younger contemporary and rival of Shakspeare, who laboured in the sweat of his brow, but with no great success, to expel the romantic drama from the English stage, and to form it on the model of the ancients, gave it as his opinion that Shakspeare did not blot enough, and that as he did not possess much school-learning, he owed more to nature than to art. The learned, and sometimes rather pedantic Milton was also of this opinion, when he says,

Our sweetest Shakspeare, fancy's child,
Warbles his native wood-notes wild.

Yet it is highly honourable to Milton, that the sweetness of Shakspeare, the quality which of all others has been least allowed, was felt and acknowledged by him. The modern editors, both in their prefaces, which may be considered as so many rhetorical exercises in praise of the poet, and in their remarks on separate passages, go still farther. Judging them by principles which are not applicable to them, not only do they admit the irregularity of his pieces, but on occasions they accuse him of bombast, of a confused, ungrammatical, and conceited mode of writing, and even of the most contemptible buffoonery. Pope asserts that he wrote both better and worse than any other man. All the scenes and passages which did not square with the littleness of his own taste, he wished to place to the account of interpolating players; and he was in the right road, had his opinion been taken, of giving us a miserable dole of a mangled Shakspeare. It is, therefore, not to be wondered at if foreigners, with the exception of the Germans latterly, have, in their ignorance of him, even improved upon these opinions. [Footnote: Lessing was the first to speak of Shakspeare in a becoming tone; but he said unfortunately a great deal too little of him, as in the time when he wrote the *Dramaturgie* this poet had not yet appeared on our stage. Since that time he has been more particularly noticed by Herder in the *Blutter von deutscher Art und Kunst*; Goethe, in *Wilhelm Meister*; and Tieck, in Letters on Shakspeare (*Poetisches Journal*, 1800), which break off, however, almost at the commencement.]. They speak in general of Shakspeare's plays as monstrous productions, which could only have been given to the world by a disordered imagination in a barbarous age; and Voltaire crowns the whole with more than usual assurance, when he observes that *Hamlet*, the profound master-piece of the philosophical poet, "seems the work of a drunken savage." That foreigners, and in particular Frenchmen, who ordinarily speak the most strange language of antiquity and the middle ages, as if cannibalism had only been put an end to in Europe by Louis XIV. should entertain this opinion of Shakspeare, might be pardonable; but that Englishmen should join in calumniating that glorious epoch of their history, [Footnote: The English work with which foreigners of every country are perhaps best acquainted is Hume's *History*; and there we have a most unjustifiable account both of Shakspeare and his age. "Born in a *rude age*, and educated in the lowest manner, without any instruction either *from the world* or from books." How could a man of Hume's acuteness suppose for a moment that a poet, whose characters display such an intimate acquaintance with life, who, as an actor and manager of a theatre, must have come in contact with all descriptions of individuals, had no instruction from the world? But this is not the worst; he goes even so far as to say, "a reasonable propriety of thought he cannot for any time uphold." This is nearly as offensive as Voltaire's "drunken savage."--TRANS.] which laid the foundation of their national greatness, is incomprehensible. Shakspeare flourished and wrote in the last half of the reign of Queen Elizabeth and first half of that of James I.; and, consequently, under monarchs who were learned themselves, and held literature in honour. The policy of modern Europe, by which the relations of its different states have been so variously interwoven with each other, commenced a century before. The cause of the Protestants was decided by the accession of Elizabeth to the throne; and the attachment to the ancient belief cannot therefore be urged as a proof of the prevailing darkness. Such was the zeal for the study of the ancients, that even court ladies, and the queen herself, were acquainted with Latin and Greek, and taught even to speak the former; a degree of knowledge which we should in vain seek for in the courts of Europe at the present day. The trade and navigation which the English carried on with all the four quarters of the world, made them acquainted with the customs and mental productions of other nations; and it would appear that they were then more indulgent to foreign manners than they are in the present day. Italy had already produced all nearly that still distinguishes her literature, and in England translations in verse were diligently, and even successfully, executed from the Italian. Spanish literature also was not unknown, for it is certain that *Don Quixote* was read in England soon after its first appearance. Bacon, the founder of modern experimental philosophy, and of whom it may be said, that he carried in his pocket all that even in this eighteenth century merits the name of philosophy, was a contemporary of Shakspeare. His fame, as a writer, did not, indeed, break forth into its glory till after his death; but what a number of ideas must have been in circulation before such an author could arise! Many branches of human knowledge have, since that time, been more extensively cultivated, but such branches as are totally unproductive to poetry: chemistry, mechanics, manufactures, and rural and political economy, will never enable a man to become a poet. I have elsewhere [Footnote: In my Lectures on the *Spirit of the Age*.] examined into the pretensions of modern enlightenment, as it is called, which looks with such contempt on all preceding ages; I have shown that at bottom it is all little, superficial, and unsubstantial. The pride of what has been called the existing maturity of human intensity, has come to a miserable end; and the structures erected by those pedagogues of the human race have fallen to pieces like the baby-houses of children.

With regard to the tone of society in Shakspeare's day, it is necessary to remark that there is a wide difference between true mental cultivation and what is called polish. That artificial polish which puts an end to every thing like free original communication, and subjects all intercourse to the insipid uniformity of certain rules, was undoubtedly wholly unknown to the age of Shakspeare, as in a great measure it still is at the present day in England. It possessed, on the other hand, a fulness of healthy vigour, which showed itself always with boldness, and sometimes also with petulance. The spirit of chivalry was not yet wholly extinct, and a queen, who was far more jealous in exacting homage to her sex than to her throne, and who, with her determination, wisdom, and magnanimity, was in fact, well qualified to inspire the minds of her subjects with an ardent enthusiasm, inflamed that spirit to the noblest love of glory and renown. The feudal independence also still survived in some measure; the nobility vied with each other in splendour of dress and number of retinue, and every great lord had a sort of small court of his own. The distinction of ranks was as yet strongly marked: a state of things ardently to be desired by the dramatic poet. In conversation they took pleasure in quick and unexpected answers; and the witty sally passed rapidly like a ball from mouth to mouth, till the merry game could no longer be kept up. This, and the abuse of the play on words, (of which King James was himself very fond, and we need not therefore wonder at the universality of the mode,) may, doubtless, be considered as instances of a bad taste; but to take them for symptoms of rudeness and barbarity, is not less absurd than to infer the poverty of a people from their luxurious extravagance. These strained repartees are frequently employed by Shakspeare, with the view of painting the actual tone of the society in his day; it does not, however, follow, that they met with his approbation; on the contrary, it clearly appears that he held them in derision. Hamlet says, in the scene with the Gravedigger, "By the Lord, Horatio, these three years I have taken note of it: the age is grown so picked, that the toe of the peasant comes so near the heel of the courtier, he galls his kibe." And Lorenzo, in the *Merchant of Venice*, alluding to Launcelot:

O dear discretion, how his words are suited!
The fool hath planted in his memory
An army of good words: and I do know
A many fools, that stand in better place,
Garnish'd like him, that for a tricksy word.
Defy the matter.

Besides, Shakspeare, in a thousand places, lays great and marked stress on correct and refined tone of society, and lashes every deviation from it, whether of boorishness or affected foppery; not only does he give admirable discourses on it, but he represents it in all its shades and modifications by rank, age, or sex. What foundation is there, then, for the alleged barbarity of his age? Its offences against propriety? But if this is to be admitted as a test, then the ages of Pericles and Augustus must also be described as rude and uncultivated; for Aristophanes and Horace, who both were considered as models of urbanity, display, at times, the coarsest indelicacy. On this subject, the diversity in the moral feeling of ages depends on other causes. Shakspeare, it is true, sometimes introduces us to improper company; at others, he suffers ambiguous expressions to escape in the presence of women, and even from women themselves. This species of petulance was probably not then unusual. He certainly did not indulge in it merely to please the multitude, for in many of his pieces there is not the slightest trace of this sort to be found: and in what virgin purity are many of his female parts worked out! When we see the liberties taken by other dramatic poets in England in his time, and even much later, we must account him comparatively chaste and moral. Neither must we overlook certain circumstances in the existing state of the theatre. The female parts were not acted by women, but by boys; and no person of the fair sex appeared in the theatre without a mask. Under such a carnival disguise, much might be heard by them, and much might be ventured to be said in their presence, which in other circumstances would have been absolutely improper. It is certainly to be wished that decency should be observed on all public occasions, and consequently also on the stage. But even in this it is possible to go too far. That carping censoriousness which scents out impurity in every bold sally, is, at best, but an ambiguous criterion of purity of morals; and beneath this hypocritical guise there often lurks the consciousness of an impure imagination. The determination to tolerate nothing which has the least reference to the sensual relation between the sexes, may be carried to a pitch extremely oppressive to a dramatic poet, and highly prejudicial to the boldness and freedom of his compositions. If such considerations were to be attended to, many of the happiest parts of Shakspeare's plays, for example, in *Measure for Measure*, and *All's Well that Ends Well*, which, nevertheless, are handled with a due regard to decency, must be set aside as sinning against this would-be propriety.

Had no other monument of the age of Elizabeth come down to us than the works of Shakspeare, I should, from them alone, have formed the most favourable idea of its state of social culture and enlightenment. When those who look through such strange spectacles as to see nothing in them but rudeness and barbarity cannot deny what I have now historically proved, they are usually driven to this last resource, and demand, "What has Shakspeare to do with the mental culture of his age? He had no share in it. Born in an inferior rank, ignorant and uneducated, he passed his life in low society, and laboured to please a vulgar audience for his bread, without ever dreaming of fame or posterity."

In all this there is not a single word of truth, though it has been repeated a thousand times. It is true we know very little of the poet's life; and what we do know consists for the most part of raked-up and chiefly suspicious anecdotes, of such a description nearly as those which are told at inns to inquisitive strangers, who visit the birthplace or neighbourhood of a celebrated man. Within a very recent period some original documents have been brought to light, and among them his will, which give us a peep into his family concerns. It betrays more than ordinary deficiency of critical acumen in Shakspeare's commentators, that none of them, so far as we know, have ever thought of availing themselves of his sonnets for tracing the circumstances of his life. These sonnets paint most unequivocally the actual situation and sentiments of the poet; they make us acquainted with the passions of the man; they even contain remarkable confessions of his youthful errors. Shakspeare's father was a man of property, whose ancestors had held the office of alderman and bailiff in Stratford, and in a diploma from the Heralds' Office for the renewal or confirmation of his coat of arms, he is styled *gentleman*. Our poet, the oldest son but third child, could not, it is true, receive an academical education, as he married when hardly eighteen, probably from mere family considerations. This retired and unnoticed life he continued to lead but a few years; and he was either enticed to London from wearisomeness of his situation, or banished from home, as it is said, in consequence of his irregularities. There he assumed the profession of a player, which he considered at first as a degradation, principally, perhaps, because of the wild excesses [Footnote: In one of his sonnets he says:

O, for my sake do you with fortune chide,
The guilty goddess of my harmless deeds,
That did not better for my life provide,
Than public means which public manners breeds.

And in the following:--

Your love and pity doth the impression fill,
Which *vulgar scandal* stamp'd upon my brow.] into which he was seduced by the example of his comrades. It is extremely probable, that the poetical fame which in the progress of his career he afterwards acquired, greatly contributed to ennoble the stage, and to bring the player's profession into better repute. Even at a very early age he endeavoured to distinguish himself as a poet in other walks than those of the stage, as is proved by his juvenile poems of *Adonis* and *Lucrece*. He quickly rose to be a sharer or joint proprietor, and also manager of the theatre for which he wrote. That he was not admitted to the society of persons of distinction is altogether incredible. Not to mention many others, he found a liberal friend and kind patron in the Earl of Southampton, the friend of the unfortunate Essex. His pieces were not only the delight of the great public, but also in great favour at court: the two monarchs under whose reigns he wrote were, according to the testimony of a contemporary, quite "taken" with him [Footnote: Ben Jonson:--

And make those flights upon the banks of Thames,
That so did take Eliza and our James!]. Many were acted at court; and Elizabeth appears herself to have commanded the writing of more than one to be acted at her court festivals. King James, it is well known, honoured Shakspeare so far as to write to him with his own hand. All this looks very unlike either contempt or banishment into the obscurity of a low circle. By his labours as a poet, player, and stage-manager, Shakspeare acquired a considerable property, which, in the last years of his too short life, he enjoyed in his native town in retirement and in the society of a beloved daughter. Immediately after his death a monument was erected over his grave, which may be considered sumptuous for those times.

In the midst of such brilliant success, and with such distinguished proofs of respect and honour from his contemporaries, it would be singular indeed if Shakspeare, notwithstanding the modesty of a great mind, which he certainly possessed in a peculiar degree, should never have dreamed of posthumous fame. As a profound thinker he had pretty accurately taken the measure of the circle of human capabilities, and he could say to himself with confidence, that many of his productions would not easily be surpassed. What foundation then is there for the contrary assertion, which would degrade the immortal artist to the situation of a daily labourer for a rude multitude?--Merely this, that he himself published no edition of his whole works. We do not reflect that a poet, always accustomed to labour immediately for the stage, who has often enjoyed the triumph of overpowering assembled crowds of spectators, and drawing from them the most tumultuous applause, who the while was not dependent on the caprice of crotchety stage directors, but left to his own discretion to select and determine the mode of theatrical representation, naturally cares much less for the closet of the solitary reader. During the first formation of a national theatre, more especially, we find frequent examples of such indifference. Of the almost innumerable pieces of Lope de Vega, many undoubtedly were never printed, and are consequently lost; and Cervantes did not print his earlier dramas, though he certainly boasts of them as meritorious works. As Shakspeare, on his retiring from the theatre, left his manuscripts behind with his fellow-managers, he may have relied on theatrical tradition for handing them down to posterity, which would indeed have been sufficient for that purpose if the closing of the theatres, under the tyrannical intolerance of the Puritans, had not interrupted the natural order of things. We know, besides, that the poets used then to sell the exclusive copyright of their pieces to the theatre [Footnote: This is perhaps not uncommon still in some countries. The Venetian Director Medebach, for whose company many of Goldoni's Comedies were composed, claimed an exclusive right to them.--TRANS.]: it is therefore not improbable that the right of property in his unprinted pieces was no longer vested in Shakspeare, or had not at least yet reverted to him. His fellow-managers entered on the publication seven years after his death (which probably cut short his own intention,) as it would appear on their own account and for their own advantage.

LECTURE XXIII.

Ignorance or Learning of Shakspeare--Costume as observed by Shakspeare, and how far necessary, or may be dispensed with in the Drama--Shakspeare the greatest drawer of Character--Vindication of the genuineness of his pathos--Play on words--Moral delicacy–Irony--Mixture of the Tragic and Comic--The part of the Fool or Clown--Shakspeare's Language and Versification.

Our poet's want of scholarship has been the subject of endless controversy, and yet it is surely a very easy matter to decide. Shakspeare was poor in dead school-cram, but he possessed a rich treasury of living and intuitive knowledge. He knew a little Latin, and even something of Greek, though it may be not enough to read with ease the writers in the original. With modern languages also, the French and Italian, he had, perhaps, but a superficial acquaintance. The general direction of his mind was not to the collection of words but of facts. With English books, whether original or translated, he was extensively acquainted: we may safely affirm that he had read all that his native language and literature then contained that could be of any use to him in his poetical avocations. He was sufficiently intimate with mythology to employ it, in the only manner he could wish, in the way of symbolical ornament. He had formed a correct notion of the spirit of Ancient History, and more particularly of that of the Romans; and the history of his own country was familiar to him even in detail. Fortunately for him it had not as yet been treated in a diplomatic and pragmatic spirit, but merely in the chronicle-style; in other words, it had not yet assumed the appearance of dry investigations respecting the development of political relations, diplomatic negotiations, finances, &c., but exhibited a visible image of the life and movement of an age prolific of great deeds. Shakspeare, moreover, was a nice observer of nature; he knew the technical language of mechanics and artisans; he seems to have been well travelled in the interior of his own country, while of others he inquired diligently of travelled navigators respecting their peculiarity of climate and customs. He thus became accurately acquainted with all the popular usages, opinions, and traditions which could be of use in poetry.

The proofs of his ignorance, on which the greatest stress is laid, are a few geographical blunders and anachronisms. Because in a comedy founded on an earlier tale, he makes ships visit Bohemia, he has been the subject of much laughter. But I conceive that we should be very unjust towards him, were we to conclude that he did not, as well as ourselves, possess the useful but by no means difficult knowledge that Bohemia is nowhere bounded by the sea. He could never, in that case, have looked into a map of Germany, who yet describes elsewhere, with great accuracy, the maps of both Indies, together with the discoveries of the latest navigators. [Footnote: *Twelfth Night, or What You Will*--Act iii. scene ii.] In such matters Shakspeare is only faithful to the details of the domestic stories. In the novels on which he worked, he avoided disturbing the associations of his audience, to whom they were known, by novelties--the correction of errors in secondary and unimportant particulars. The more wonderful the story, the more it ranged in a purely poetical region, which he transfers at will to an indefinite distance. These plays, whatever names they bear, take place in the true land of romance, and in the very century of wonderful love stories. He knew well that in the forest of Ardennes there were neither the lions and serpents of the Torrid Zone, nor the shepherdesses of Arcadia: but he transferred both to it, [Footnote: *As You Like It.*] because the design and import of his picture required them. Here he considered himself entitled to take the greatest liberties. He had not to do with a hair-splitting, hypercritical age like ours, which is always seeking in poetry for something else than poetry; his audience entered the theatre, not to learn true chronology, geography, and natural history, but to witness a vivid exhibition. I will undertake to prove that Shakspeare's anachronisms are, for the most part, committed of set purpose and deliberately. It was frequently of importance to him to move the exhibited subject out of the background of time, and bring it quite near us. Hence in *Hamlet*, though avowedly an old Northern story, there runs a tone of modish society, and in every respect the costume of the most recent period. Without those circumstantialities it would not have been allowable to make a philosophical inquirer of Hamlet, on which trait, however, the meaning of the whole is made to rest. On that account he mentions his education at a university, though, in the age of the true Hamlet of history, universities were not in existence. He makes him study at Wittenberg, and no selection of a place could have been more suitable. The name was very popular: the story of *Dr. Faustus of Wittenberg* had made it well known; it was of particular celebrity in protestant England, as Luther had taught and written there shortly before, and the very name must have immediately suggested the idea of freedom in thinking. I cannot oven consider it an anachronism that Richard the Third should speak of Macchiavel. The word is here used altogether proverbially: the contents, at least, of the book entitled *Of the Prince (Del Principe,)* have been in existence ever since the existence of tyrants; Macchiavel was merely the first to commit them to writing.

That Shakspeare has accurately hit the essential costume, namely, the spirit of ages and nations, is at least acknowledged generally by the English critics; but many sins against external costume may be easily remarked. But here it is necessary to bear in mind that the Roman pieces were acted upon the stage of that day in the European dress. This was, it is true, still grand and splendid, not so silly and tasteless as it became towards the end of the seventeenth century. (Brutus and Cassius appeared in the Spanish cloak; they wore, quite contrary to the Roman custom, the sword by their side in time of peace, and, according to the testimony of an eye witness, [Footnote: In one of the commendatory poems in the first folio edition:

And on the stage at *half sword parley* were
Brutus and Cassius.] it was, in the dialogue where Brutus stimulates Cassius to the conspiracy, drawn, as if involuntarily, half out of the sheath.) This does in no way agree with our way of thinking: we are not content without the toga. The present, perhaps, is not an inappropriate place for a few general observations on costume, considered with reference to art. It has never been more accurately observed than in the present day; art has become a slop-shop for pedantic antiquities. This is because we live in a learned and critical, but by no means poetical age. The ancients before us used, when they had to represent the religions of other nations, which deviated very much from their own, to bring them into conformity with the Greek mythology. In Sculpture, again, the same dress, namely, the Phrygian, was adopted, once for all, for every barbaric tribe. Not that they did not know that there were as many different dresses as nations; but in art they merely wished to acknowledge the great contrast between barbarian and civilized: and this, they thought, was rendered most strikingly apparent in the Phrygian garb. The earlier Christian painters represent the Saviour, the Virgin Mary, the Patriarchs, and the Apostles in an ideal dress; but the subordinate actors or spectators of the action, in the dresses of their own nation and age. Here they were guided by a correct feeling: the mysterious and sacred ought to be kept at an awe-inspiring distance, but the human cannot be rightly understood if seen without its usual accompaniments. In the middle ages all heroical stories of antiquity, from Theseus and Achilles down to Alexander, were metamorphosed into true tales of chivalry. What was related to themselves spoke alone an intelligible language to them; of differences and distinctions they did not care to know. In an old manuscript of the *Iliad*, I saw a miniature illumination representing Hector's funeral procession, where the coffin is hung with noble coats of arms, and carried into a Gothic church. It is easy to make merry with this piece of simplicity, but a reflecting mind will see the subject in a very different light. A powerful consciousness of the universal validity and the solid permanency of their own manner of being, an undoubting conviction that it has always so been and will ever continue so to be in the world: these feelings of our ancestors were symptoms of a fresh fulness of life; they were the marrow of action in reality as well as in fiction. Their plain and affectionate attachment to every thing around them, handed down from

their fathers, is by no means to be confounded with the obstreperous conceit of ages of mannerism, who, out of vanity, introduce the fleeting modes and fashion of the day into art, because to them everything like noble simplicity seems boorish and rude. The latter impropriety is now abolished: but, on the other hand, our poets and artists, if they would hope for our approbation, must, like servants, wear the livery of distant centuries and foreign nations. We are everywhere at home except at home. We do ourselves the justice to allow that the present mode of dressing, forms of politeness, &c., are altogether unpoetical, and art is therefore obliged to beg, as an alms, a poetical costume from the antiquaries. To that simple way of thinking, which is merely attentive to the inward truth of the composition, without stumbling at anachronisms, or other external inconsistencies, we cannot, alas! now return; but we must envy the poets to whom it offered itself; it allowed them a great breadth and freedom in the handling of their subject.

Many things in Shakspeare must be judged of according to the above principles, respecting the difference between the essential and the merely learned costume. They will also in their measure admit of an application to Calderon.

So much with respect to the spirit of the age in which Shakspeare lived, and his peculiar mental culture and knowledge. To me he appears a profound artist, and not a blind and wildly luxuriant genius. I consider, generally speaking, all that has been said on the subject a mere fable, a blind and extravagant error. In other arts the assertion refutes itself; for in them acquired knowledge is an indispensable condition of clever execution. But even in such poets, as are usually given out as careless pupils of nature, devoid of art or school discipline, I have always found, on a nearer consideration of the works of real excellence they may have produced, even a high cultivation of the mental powers, practice in art, and views both worthy in themselves and maturely considered. This applies to Homer as well as to Dante. The activity of genius is, it is true, natural to it, and, in a certain sense, unconscious; and, consequently, the person who possesses it is not always at the moment able to render an account of the course which he may have pursued; but it by no means follows, that the thinking power had not a great share in it. It is from the very rapidity and certainty of the mental process, from the utmost clearness of understanding, that thinking in a poet is not perceived as something abstracted, does not wear the appearance of reflex meditation. That notion of poetical inspiration, which many lyrical poets have brought into circulation, as if they were not in their senses, and like Pythia, when possessed by the divinity, delivered oracles unintelligible to themselves --this notion, (a mere lyrical invention,) is least of all applicable to dramatic composition, one of the most thoughtful productions of the human mind. It is admitted that Shakspeare has reflected, and deeply reflected, on character and passion, on the progress of events and human destinies, on the human constitution, on all the things and relations of the world; this is an admission which must be made, for one alone of thousands of his maxims would be a sufficient refutation of whoever should attempt to deny it. So that it was only for the structure of his own pieces that he had no thought to spare? This he left to the dominion of chance, which blew together the atoms of Epicurus. But supposing that, devoid of any higher ambition to approve himself to judicious critics and posterity, and wanting in that love of art which longs for self-satisfaction in the perfection of its works, he had merely laboured to please the unlettered crowd; still this very object alone and the pursuit of theatrical effect, would have led him to bestow attention to the structure and adherence of his pieces. For does not the impression of a drama depend in an especial manner on the relation of the parts to each other? And, however beautiful a scene may be in itself, if yet it be at variance with what the spectators have been led to expect in its particular place, so as to destroy the interest which they had hitherto felt, will it not be at once reprobated by all who possess plain common sense, and give themselves up to nature? The comic intermixtures may be considered merely as a sort of interlude, designed to relieve the straining of the mind after the stretch of the more serious parts, so long as no better purpose can be found in them; but in the progress of the main action, in the concatenation of the events, the poet must, if possible, display even more expenditure of thought than in the composition of individual character and situations, otherwise he would be like the conductor of a puppet-show who has entangled his wires, so that the puppets receive from their mechanism quite different movements from those which he actually intended.

The English critics are unanimous in their praise of the truth and uniform consistency of his characters, of his heartrending pathos, and his comic wit. Moreover, they extol the beauty and sublimity of his separate descriptions, images, and expressions. This last is the most superficial and cheap mode of criticising works of art. Johnson compares him who should endeavour to recommend this poet by passages unconnectedly torn from his works, to the pedant in Hierocles, who exhibited a brick as a sample of his house. And yet how little, and how very unsatisfactorily does he himself speak of the pieces considered as a whole! Let any man, for instance, bring together the short characters which he gives at the close of each play, and see if the aggregate will amount to that sum of admiration which he himself, at his outset, has stated as the correct standard for the appreciation of the poet. It was, generally speaking, the prevailing tendency of the time which preceded our own, (and which has showed itself particularly in physical science,) to consider everything having life as a mere accumulation of dead parts, to separate what exists only in connexion and cannot otherwise be conceived, instead of penetrating to the central point and viewing all the parts as so many irradiations from it. Hence nothing is so rare as a critic who can elevate himself to the comprehensive contemplation of a work of art. Shakspeare's compositions, from the very depth of purpose displayed in them, have been especially liable to the misfortune of being misunderstood. Besides, this prosaic species of criticism requires always that the poetic form should he applied to the details of execution; but when the plan of the piece is concerned, it never looks for more than the logical connexion of causes and effects, or some partial and trite moral by way of application; and all that cannot be reconciled therewith is declared superfluous, or even a pernicious appendage. On these principles we must even strike out from the Greek tragedies most of the choral songs, which also contribute nothing to the development of the action, but are merely an harmonious echo of the impressions the poet aims at conveying. In this they altogether mistake the rights of poetry and the nature of the romantic drama, which, for the very reason that it is and ought to be picturesque, requires richer accompaniments and contrasts for its main groups. In all Art and Poetry, but more especially in the romantic, the Fancy lays claims to be considered as an independent mental power governed according to its own laws.

In an essay on *Romeo and Juliet*, [Footnote: In the first volume of *Charakteristiken und Kritiken*, published by my brother and myself.] written a number of years ago, I went through the whole of the scenes in their order, and demonstrated the inward necessity of each with reference to the whole; I showed why such a particular circle of characters and relations was placed around the two lovers; I explained the signification of the mirth here and there scattered, and justified the use of the occasional heightening given to the poetical colours. From all this it seemed to follow unquestionably, that with the exception of a few witticisms, now become unintelligible or foreign to the present taste, (imitations of the tone of society of that day,) nothing could be taken away, nothing added, nothing otherwise arranged, without mutilating and disfiguring the perfect work. I would readily undertake to do the same for all the pieces of Shakspeare's maturer years, but to do this would require a separate book. Here I am reduced to confine my observations to the tracing his great designs with a rapid pencil; but still I must previously be allowed to deliver my sentiments in a general manner on the subject of his most eminent peculiarities.

Shakspeare's knowledge of mankind has become proverbial: in this his superiority is so great, that he has justly been called the master of the human heart. A readiness to remark the mind's fainter and involuntary utterances, and the power to express with certainty the meaning of these signs, as determined by experience and reflection, constitutes "the observer of men;" but tacitly to draw from these still further conclusions, and to arrange the separate observations according to grounds of probability, into a just and valid combination, this, it may be said, is to know men. The distinguishing property of the dramatic poet who is great in characterization, is something altogether different here, and which, (take it which way we will,) either includes in it this readiness and this acuteness, or dispenses with both. It is the capability of transporting himself so completely into every situation, even the most unusual, that he is enabled, as plenipotentiary of the whole human race, without particular instructions for each separate case, to act and speak in the name of every individual. It is the power of endowing the creatures of his imagination with such self-existent energy, that they afterwards act in each conjuncture according to general laws of nature: the poet, in his dreams, institutes, as it were, experiments which are received with as much authority as if they had been made on waking objects. The inconceivable element herein, and what moreover can never be learned, is, that the characters appear neither to do nor to say any thing on the spectator's account merely; and yet that the poet simply, by means of the exhibition, and without any subsidiary explanation, communicates to his audience the gift of looking into the inmost recesses of their minds. Hence Goethe has ingeniously compared Shakspeare's characters to watches with crystalline plates and cases, which, while they point out the hours as correctly as other watches, enable us at the same time to perceive the inward springs whereby all this is accomplished.

Nothing, however, is more foreign to Shakspeare than a certain anatomical style of exhibition, which laboriously enumerates all the motives by which a man is determined to act in this or that particular manner. This rage of supplying motives, the mania of so many modern historians, might be carried at length to an extent which would abolish every thing like individuality, and resolve all character into nothing but the effect of foreign or external, influences whereas we know that it often announces itself most decidedly in earliest infancy. After all, a man acts so because he is so. And what each man is, that Shakspeare reveals to us most immediately: he demands and obtains our belief, even for what is singular and deviates from the ordinary course of nature. Never perhaps was there so comprehensive a talent for characterization as Shakspeare. It not only grasps every diversity of rank, age, and sex, down to the lispings of infancy; not only do the king and the beggar, the hero and the pickpocket, the sage and the idiot, speak and act with equal truthfulness; not only does he transport himself to distant ages and foreign nations, and portray with the greatest accuracy (a few apparent violations of costume excepted) the spirit of the ancient Romans, of the French in the wars with the English, of the English themselves during a great part of their history, of the Southern Europeans (in the serious part of many comedies), the cultivated society of the day, and the rude barbarism of a Norman fore-time; his human characters have not only such depth and individuality that they do not admit of being classed under common names, and are inexhaustible even in conception: no, this Prometheus not merely forms men, he opens the gates of the magical world of spirits, calls up the midnight ghost, exhibits before us the witches with their unhallowed rites, peoples the air with sportive fairies and sylphs; and these beings, though existing only in the imagination, nevertheless possess such truth and consistency, that even with such misshapen abortions as Caliban, he extorts the assenting conviction, that were there such beings they would so conduct themselves. In a word, as he carries a bold and pregnant fancy into the kingdom of nature, on the other hand, he carries nature into the regions of fancy, which lie beyond the confines of reality. We are lost in astonishment at the close intimacy he brings us into with the extraordinary, the wonderful, and the unheard-of.

Pope and Johnson appear strangely to contradict each other, when the first says, "all the characters of Shakspeare are individuals," and the second, "they are species." And yet perhaps these opinions may admit of reconciliation. Pope's expression is unquestionably the more correct. A character which should be merely a personification of a naked general idea could neither exhibit any great depth nor any great variety. The names of genera and species are well known to be merely auxiliaries for the understanding, that we may embrace the infinite variety of nature in a certain order. The characters which Shakspeare has so thoroughly delineated have undoubtedly a number of individual peculiarities, but at the same time they possess a significance which is not applicable to them alone: they generally supply materials for a profound theory of their most prominent and distinguishing property. But even with the above correction, this opinion must still have its limitations. Characterization is merely one ingredient of the dramatic art, and not dramatic poetry itself. It would be improper in the extreme, if the poet were to draw our attention to superfluous traits of character, at a time when it ought to be his endeavour to produce other impressions. Whenever the musical or the fanciful preponderates, the characteristical necessarily falls into the background. Hence many of the figures of Shakspeare exhibit merely external designations, determined by the place which they occupy in the whole: they are like secondary persons in a public procession, to whose physiognomy we seldom pay much attention; their only importance is derived from the solemnity of their dress and the duty in which they are engaged. Shakspeare's messengers, for instance, are for the most part mere messengers, and yet not common, but poetical messengers: the messages which they have to bring is the soul which suggests to them their language. Other voices, too, are merely raised to pour forth these as melodious lamentations or rejoicings, or to dwell in reflection on what has taken place; and in a serious drama without chorus this must always be more or less the case, if we would not have it prosaical.

If Shakspeare deserves our admiration for his characters, he is equally deserving of it for his exhibition of passion, taking this word in its widest signification, as including every mental condition, every tone, from indifference or familiar mirth to the wildest rage and despair. He gives us the history of minds; he lays open to us, in a single word, a whole series of their anterior states. His passions do not stand at the same height, from first to last, as is the case with so many tragic poets, who, in the language of Lessing, are thorough masters of the legal style of love. He paints, with inimitable veracity, the gradual advance from the first origin; "he gives," as Lessing says, "a living picture of all the slight and secret artifices by which a feeling steals into our souls, of all the imperceptible advantages which it there gains, of all the stratagems by which it makes every other passion subservient to itself, till it becomes the sole tyrant of our desires and our aversions." Of all the poets, perhaps, he alone has portrayed the mental diseases, melancholy, delirium, lunacy, with such inexpressible and, in every respect, definite truth, that the physician may enrich his observations from them in the same manner as from real cases.

And yet Johnson has objected to Shakspeare that his pathos is not always natural and free from affectation. There are, it is true, passages, though comparatively speaking very few, where his poetry exceeds the bounds of actual dialogue, where a too soaring imagination, a too luxuriant wit, rendered a complete dramatic forgetfulness of himself impossible. With this exception, the censure originated in a fanciless way of thinking, to which everything appears unnatural that does not consort with its own tame insipidity. Hence an idea has been formed of simple and natural pathos, which consists in exclamations destitute of imagery and nowise elevated above every-day life. But energetical passions electrify all the mental powers, and will consequently, in highly-favoured natures, give utterance to themselves in ingenious and figurative expressions. It has been often remarked that indignation makes a man witty; and as despair occasionally breaks out into laughter, it may sometimes also give vent to itself in antithetical comparisons.

Besides, the rights of the poetical form have not been duly weighed. Shakspeare, who was always sure of his power to excite, when he wished, sufficiently powerful emotions, has occasionally, by indulging in a freer play of fancy, purposely tempered the impressions when too painful, and immediately introduced a musical softening of our sympathy. [Footnote: A contemporary of the poet, the author of the already-noticed poem, (subscribed I. M. S.,) tenderly felt this while he says--

Yet so to temper passion, that our ears
Take pleasure in their pain, and eyes in tears
Both smile and weep.] He had not those rude ideas of his art which many moderns seem to have, as if the poet, like the clown in the proverb, must strike twice on the same place. An ancient rhetorician delivered a caution against dwelling too long on the excitation of pity; for nothing, he said, dries so soon as tears; and Shakspeare acted conformably to this ingenious maxim without having learned it. The paradoxical assertion of Johnson that "Shakspeare had a greater talent for comedy than tragedy, and that in the latter he has frequently displayed an affected tone," is scarcely deserving of lengthy notice. For its refutation, it is unnecessary to appeal to the great tragical compositions of the poet, which, for overpowering effect, leave far behind them almost everything that the stage has seen besides; a few of their less celebrated scenes would be quite sufficient. What to many readers might lend an appearance of truth to this assertion are the verbal witticisms, that playing upon words, which Shakspeare not unfrequently introduces into serious and sublime passages, and even into those also of a peculiarly pathetic nature.

I have already stated the point of view in which we ought to consider this sportive play upon words. I shall here, therefore, merely deliver a few observations respecting the playing upon words in general, and its poetical use. A thorough investigation would lead us too far from our subject, and too deeply into considerations on the essence of language, and its relation to poetry, or rhyme, &c.

There is in the human mind a desire that language should exhibit the object which it denotes, sensibly, by its very sound, which may be traced even as far back as in the first origin of poetry. As, in the shape in which language comes down to us, this is seldom perceptibly the case, an imagination which has been powerfully excited is fond of laying hold of any congruity in sound which may accidentally offer itself, that by such means he may, for the nonce, restore the lost resemblance between the word and the thing. For example, How common was it and is it to seek in the name of a person, however arbitrarily bestowed, a reference to his qualities and fortunes,--to convert it purposely into a significant name. Those who cry out against the play upon words as an unnatural and affected invention, only betray their own ignorance of original nature. A great fondness for it is always evinced among children, as well as with nations of simple manners, among whom correct ideas of the derivation and affinity of words have not yet been developed, and do not, consequently, stand in the way of this caprice. In Homer we find several examples of it; the Books of Moses, the oldest written memorial of the primitive world, are, as is well known, full of them. On the other hand, poets of a very cultivated taste, like Petrarch, or orators, like Cicero, have delighted in them. Whoever, in *Richard the Second*, is disgusted with the affecting play of words of the dying John of Gaunt on his own name, should remember that the same thing occurs in the *Ajax* of Sophocles. We do not mean to say that all playing upon words is on all occasions to be justified. This must depend on the disposition of mind, whether it will admit of such a play of fancy, and whether the sallies, comparisons, and allusions, which lie at the bottom of them, possess internal solidity. Yet we must not proceed upon the principle of trying how the thought appears after it is deprived of the resemblance in sound, any more than we are to endeavour tc feel the charm of rhymed versification after depriving it of its rhyme. The laws of good taste on this subject must, moreover, vary with the quality of the languages. In those which possess a great number of homonymes, that is, words possessing the same, or nearly the same, sound, though quite different in their derivation and signification, it is almost more difficult to avoid, than to fall on such a verbal play. It has, however, been feared, lest a door might be opened to puerile witticism, if they were not rigorously proscribed. But I cannot, for my part, find that Shakspeare had such an invincible and immoderate passion for this verbal witticism. It is true, he sometimes makes a most lavish use of this figure; at others, he has employed it very sparingly; and at times (for example, in *Macbeth*), I do not believe a vestige of it is to be found. Hence, in respect to the use or the rejection of the play upon words, he must have been guided by the measure of the objects, and the different style in which they required to be treated, and probably have followed here, as in every thing else, principles which, fairly examined, will bear a strict examination.

The objection that Shakspeare wounds our feelings by the open display of the most disgusting moral odiousness, unmercifully harrows up the mind, and tortures even our eyes by the exhibition of the most insupportable and hateful spectacles, is one of greater and graver importance. He has, in fact, never varnished over wild and blood-thirsty passions with a pleasing exterior--never clothed crime and want of principle with a false show of greatness of soul; and in that respect he is every way deserving of praise. Twice he has portrayed downright villains, and the masterly way in which he has contrived to elude impressions of too painful a nature may be seen in Iago and Richard the Third. I allow that the reading, and still more the sight, of some of his pieces, is not advisable to weak nerves, any more than was the *Eumenides* of Aeschylus; but is the poet, who can only reach an important object by a bold and hazardous daring, to be checked by considerations for such persons? If the effeminacy of the present day is to serve as a general standard of what tragical composition may properly exhibit to human nature, we shall be forced to set very narrow limits indeed to art, and the hope of anything like powerful effect must at once and for ever be renounced. If we wish to have a grand purpose, we must also wish to have the grand means, and our nerves ought in some measure to accommodate themselves to painful impressions, if, by way of requital, our mind is thereby elevated and strengthened. The constant reference to a petty and puny race must cripple the boldness of the poet. Fortunately for his art, Shakspeare lived in an age extremely susceptible of noble and tender impressions, but which had yet inherited enough of the firmness of a vigorous olden time, not to shrink with dismay from every strong and forcible painting. We have lived to see tragedies of which the catastrophe consists in the swoon of an enamoured princess: if Shakspeare falls occasionally into the opposite extreme, it is a noble error, originating in the fulness of a gigantic strength. And this tragical Titan, who storms the heavens and threatens to tear the world from off its hinges, who, more terrible than Aeschylus, makes our hair to stand on end, and congeals our blood with horror, possessed at the same time the insinuating loveliness of the sweetest poesy; he toys with love like a child, and his songs die away on the ear like melting sighs. He unites in his soul the utmost elevation and the utmost depth; and the most opposite and even apparently irreconcilable properties subsist in him peaceably together. The world of spirits and nature have laid all their treasures at his feet: in strength a demi-god, in profundity of view a prophet, in all-seeing wisdom a guardian spirit of a higher order, he lowers himself to mortals as if unconscious of his superiority, and is as open and unassuming as a child.

If the delineation of all his characters, separately considered, is inimitably bold and correct, he surpasses even himself in so combining and contrasting them, that they serve to bring out each other's peculiarities. This is the very perfection of dramatic characterization: for we can never estimate a man's true worth if we consider him altogether abstractedly by himself; we must see him in his relations with others; and it is here that most dramatic poets are deficient. Shakspeare makes each of his principal characters the glass in which the others are reflected, and by like means enables us to discover what could not be immediately revealed to us. What in others is most profound, is with him but surface. Ill-advised should we be were we always to take men's declarations respecting themselves and others for sterling coin. Ambiguity of design with much propriety he makes to overflow with the most praiseworthy principles; and sage maxims are not unfrequently put in the mouth of stupidity, to show how easily such common-place truisms may be acquired. Nobody ever painted so truthfully as he has done the facility of self-deception, the half self-conscious hypocrisy towards ourselves, with which even noble minds attempt to disguise the almost inevitable influence of selfish motives in human nature. This secret irony of the characterization commands admiration as the profound abyss of acuteness and sagacity; but it is the grave of enthusiasm. We arrive at it only after we have had the misfortune to see human nature through and through; and when no choice remains but to adopt the melancholy truth, that "no virtue or greatness is altogether pure and genuine," or the dangerous error that "the highest perfection is attainable." Here we therefore may perceive in the poet himself, notwithstanding his power to excite the most fervent emotions, a certain cool indifference, but still the indifference of a superior mind, which has run through the whole sphere of human existence and survived feeling.

The irony in Shakspeare has not merely a reference to the separate characters, but frequently to the whole of the action. Most poets who pourtray human events in a narrative or dramatic form take themselves a part, and exact from their readers a blind approbation or condemnation of whatever side they choose to support or oppose. The more zealous this rhetoric is, the more certainly it fails of its effect. In every case we are conscious that the subject itself is not brought immediately before us, but that we view it through the medium of a different way of thinking. When, however, by a dexterous manoeuvre, the poet allows us an occasional glance at the less brilliant reverse of the medal, then he makes, as it were, a sort of secret understanding with the select circle of the more intelligent of his readers or spectators; he shows them that he had previously seen and admitted the validity of their tacit objections; that he himself is not tied down to the represented subject, but soars freely above it; and that, if he chose, he could unrelentingly annihilate the beautiful and irresistibly attractive scenes which his magic pen has produced. No doubt, wherever the proper tragic enters every thing like irony immediately ceases; but from the avowed raillery of Comedy, to the point where the subjection of mortal beings to an inevitable destiny demands the highest degree of seriousness, there are a multitude of human relations which unquestionably may be considered in an ironical view, without confounding the eternal line of separation between good and evil. This purpose is answered by the comic characters and scenes which are interwoven with the serious parts in most of those pieces of Shakspeare where romantic fables or historical events are made the subject of a noble and elevating exhibition. Frequently an intentional parody of the serious part is not to be mistaken in them; at other times the connexion is more arbitrary and loose, and the more so the more marvellous the invention of the whole, and the more entirely it is become a light revelling of the fancy. The comic intervals everywhere serve to prevent the pastime from being converted into a business, to preserve the mind in the possession of its serenity, and to keep off that gloomy and inert seriousness which so easily steals upon the sentimental, but not tragical, drama. Most assuredly Shakspeare did not intend thereby, in defiance to his own better judgment, to humour the taste of the multitude: for in various pieces, and throughout considerable portions of others, and especially when the catastrophe is approaching, and the mind consequently is more on the stretch and no longer likely to give heed to any amusement which would distract their attention, he has abstained from all such comic intermixtures. It was also an object with him, that the clowns or buffoons should not occupy a more important place than that which he had assigned them: he expressly condemns the extemporizing with which they love to enlarge their parts [Footnote: In Hamlet's directions to the players. Act iii, sc. 2.]. Johnson founds the justification of the species of drama in which seriousness and mirth admixed, on this, that in real life the vulgar is found close to the sublime, that the merry and the sad usually accompany and succeed one another. But it does not follow that because both are found together, therefore they must not be separable in the compositions of art. The observation is in other respects just, and this circumstance invests the poet with a power to adopt this procedure, because every thing in the drama must be regulated by the conditions of theatrical probability; but the mixture of such dissimilar, and apparently contradictory, ingredients, in the same works, can only be justifiable on principles reconcilable with the views of art, which I have already described. In the dramas of Shakspeare the comic scenes are the antechamber of the poetry, where the servants remain; these prosaic attendants must not raise their voices so high as to deafen the speakers in the presence-chamber; however, in those intervals when the ideal society has retired they deserve to be listened to; their bold raillery, their presumption of mockery, may afford many an insight into the situation and circumstances of their masters.

Shakspeare's comic talent is equally wonderful with that which he has shown in the pathetic and tragic: it stands on an equal elevation, and possesses equal extent and profundity; in all that I have hitherto said, I only wished to guard against admitting that the former preponderated. He is highly inventive in comic situations and motives: it will be hardly possible to show whence he has taken any of them, whereas, in the serious part of his dramas, he has generally laid hold of some well-known story. His comic characterization is equally true, various, and profound, with his serious. So little is he disposed to caricature, that rather, it may be said, many of his traits are almost too nice and delicate for the stage, that they can only be made available by a great actor, and fully understood by an acute audience. Not only has he delineated many kinds of folly, but even of sheer stupidity has he contrived to give a most diverting and entertaining picture. There is also in his pieces a peculiar species of the farcical, which apparently seems to be introduced more arbitrarily, but which, however, is founded on imitation of some actual custom. This is the introduction of the merry-maker, the fool with his cap and bells, and motley dress, called more commonly in England *Clown*, who appears in several comedies, though not in all, but of the tragedies in *Lear* alone, and who generally merely exercises his wit in conversation with the principal persons, though he is also sometimes incorporated into the action. In those times it was not only usual for princes to have their court fools, but many distinguished families, among their other retainers, kept such an exhilarating housemate as a good antidote against the insipidity and wearisomeness of ordinary life, and as a welcome interruption of established formalities. Great statesmen, and even ecclesiastics, did not consider it beneath their dignity to recruit and solace themselves after important business with the conversation of their fools; the celebrated Sir Thomas More had his fool painted along with himself by Holbein. Shakspeare appears to have lived immediately before the time when the custom began to be abolished; in the English comic authors who succeeded him the clown is no longer to be found. The dismissal of the fool has been extolled as a proof of refinement; and our honest forefathers have been pitied for taking delight in such a coarse and farcical amusement. For my part, I am rather disposed to believe, that the practice was dropped from the difficulty in finding fools able to do full justice to their parts: [Footnote: See Hamlet's praise of Yorick. In *The Twelfth Night*, Viola says:--

This fellow is wise enough to play the fool,
And to do that well craves a kind of wit;
He must observe their mood on whom he jests,
The quality of the persons, and the time;
And like the haggard, check at every feather
That comes before his eye. This is a practice
As full of labour as a wise man's art:
For folly that he wisely shows if fit,
But wise mens' folly fall'n quite taints their wit.--AUTHOR.

The passages from Shakspeare, in the original work, are given from the author's masterly translation. We may be allowed, however, to observe that the last line--

"Doch wozu ist des Weisen Thorheit nutz?"

literally, *Of what use is the folly of the wise?*--does not convey the exact meaning of Shakespeare.--TRANS.] on the other hand, reason, with all its conceit of itself, has become too timid to tolerate such bold irony; it is always careful lest the mantle of its gravity should be disturbed in any of its folds; and rather than allow a privileged place to folly beside itself, it has unconsciously assumed the part of the ridiculous; but, alas! a heavy and cheerless ridicule. [Footnote: "Since the little wit that fools have was silenced, the little foolery that wise men have makes a greater show."--*As You Like It*. Act i., sc. 2.] It would be easy to make a collection of the excellent sallies and biting sarcasms which have been preserved of celebrated court fools. It is well known that they frequently told such truths to princes as are never now told to them. [Footnote: Charles the Bold, of Burgundy, is known to have frequently boasted that he wished to rival Hannibal as the greatest general of all ages. After his defeat at Granson, his fool accompanied him in his hurried flight, and exclaimed, "Ah, your Grace, they have for once Hanniballed us!" If the Duke had given an ear to this warning raillery, he would not so soon afterwards have come to a disgraceful end.] Shakspeare's fools, along with somewhat of an overstraining for wit, which cannot altogether be avoided when wit becomes a separate profession, have for the most part an incomparable humour, and an infinite abundance of intellect, enough indeed to supply a whole host of ordinary wise men.

I have still a few observations to make on the diction and versification of our poet. The language is here and there somewhat obsolete, but on the whole much less so than in most of the contemporary writers, a sufficient proof of the goodness of his choice. Prose had as yet been but little cultivated, as the learned generally wrote in Latin: a favourable circumstance for the dramatic poet; for what has he to do with the scientific language of books? He had not only read, but studied the earlier English poets; but he drew his language immediately from life itself, and he possessed a masterly skill in blending the dialogical element with the highest poetical elevation. I know not what certain critics mean, when they say that Shakspeare is frequently ungrammatical. To make good their assertion, they must prove that similar constructions never occur in his contemporaries, the direct contrary of which can, however, be easily shown. In no language is every thing determined on principle; much is always left to the caprice of custom, and if this has since changed, is the poet to be made answerable for it? The English language had not then attained to that correct insipidity which has been introduced into the more recent literature of the country, to the prejudice, perhaps, of its originality. As a field when first brought under the plough produces, along with the fruitful shoots, many luxuriant weeds, so the poetical diction of the day ran occasionally into extravagance, but an extravagance originating in the exuberance of its vigour. We may still perceive traces of awkwardness, but nowhere of a laboured and spiritless display of art. In general Shakspeare's style yet remains the very best model, both in the vigorous and sublime, and the pleasing and tender. In his sphere he has exhausted all the means and appliances of language. On all he has impressed the stamp of his mighty spirit. His images and figures, in their unsought, nay, uncapricious singularity, have often a sweetness altogether peculiar. He becomes occasionally obscure from too great fondness for compressed brevity; but still, the labour of poring over Shakspeare's lines will invariably meet an ample requital.

The verse in all his plays is generally the rhymeless Iambic of ten or eleven syllables, occasionally only intermixed with rhymes, but more frequently alternating with prose. No one piece is written entirely in prose; for even in those which approach the most to the pure Comedy, there is always something added which gives them a more poetical hue than usually belongs to this species. Many scenes are wholly in prose, in others verse and prose succeed each other alternately. This can only appear an impropriety in the eyes of those who are accustomed to consider the lines of a drama like so many soldiers drawn up rank and file on a parade, with the same uniform, arms, and accoutrements, so that when we see one or two we may represent to ourselves thousands as being every way like them.

In the use of verse and prose Shakspeare observes very nice distinctions according to the ranks of the speakers, but still more according to their characters and disposition of mind. A noble language, elevated above the usual tone, is only suitable to a certain decorum of manners, which is thrown over both vices and virtues, and which does not even wholly disappear amidst the violence of passion. If this is not exclusively possessed by the higher ranks, it still, however, belongs naturally more to them than to the lower; and therefore in Shakspeare dignity and familiarity of language, poetry, and prose, are in this manner distributed among the characters. Hence his tradesmen, peasants, soldiers, sailors, servants, but more especially his fools and clowns, speak almost without exception, in the tone of their actual life. However, inward dignity of sentiment, wherever it is possessed, invariably displays itself with a nobleness of its own, and stands not in need, for that end, of the artificial elegancies of education and custom; it is a universal right of man, of the highest as well as the lowest; and hence also, in Shakspeare, the nobility of nature and morality is ennobled above the artificial nobility of society. Not unfrequently also he makes the very same persons express themselves at times in the sublimest language, and at others in the lowest; and this inequality is in like manner founded in truth. Extraordinary situations, which intensely occupy the head and throw mighty passions into play, give elevation and tension to the soul: it collects together all its powers, and exhibits an unusual energy, both in its operations and in its communications by language. On the other hand, even the greatest men have their moments of remissness, when to a certain degree they forget the dignity of their character in unreserved relaxation. This very tone of mind is necessary before they can receive amusement from the jokes of others, or what surely cannot dishonour even a hero, from passing jokes themselves. Let any person, for example, go carefully through the part of Hamlet. How bold and powerful the language of his poetry when he conjures the ghost of his father, when he spurs himself on to the bloody deed, when he thunders into the soul of his mother! How he lowers his tone down to that of common life, when he has to do with persons whose station demands from him such a line of conduct;

when he makes game of Polonius and the courtiers, instructs the player, and even enters into the jokes of the grave-digger. Of all the poet's serious leading characters there is none so rich in wit and humour as Hamlet; hence he it is of all of them that makes the greatest use of the familiar style. Others, again, never do fall into it; either because they are constantly surrounded by the pomp of rank, or because a uniform seriousness is natural to them; or, in short, because through the whole piece they are under the dominion of a passion, calculated to excite, and not, like the sorrow of Hamlet, to depress the mind. The choice of the one form or the other is everywhere so appropriate, and so much founded in the nature of the thing, that I will venture to assert, even where the poet in the very same speech makes the speaker leave prose for poetry, or the converse, this could not be altered without danger of injuring or destroying some beauty or other. The blank verse has this advantage, that its tone may be elevated or lowered; it admits of approximation to the familiar style of conversation, and never forms such an abrupt contrast as that, for example, between plain prose and the rhyming Alexandrines.

Shakspeare's Iambics are sometimes highly harmonious and full sounding; always varied and suitable to the subject, at one time distinguished by ease and rapidity, at another they move along with ponderous energy. They never fall out of the dialogical character, which may always be traced even in the continued discourses of individuals, excepting when the latter run into the lyrical. They are a complete model of the dramatic use of this species of verse, which, in English, since Milton, has been also used in epic poetry; but in the latter it has assumed a quite different turn. Even the irregularities of Shakspeare's versification are expressive; a verse broken off, or a sudden change of rhythmus, coincides with some pause in the progress of the thought, or the entrance of another mental disposition. As a proof that he purposely violated the mechanical rules, from a conviction that too symmetrical a versification does not suit with the drama, and on the stage has in the long run a tendency to lull the spectators asleep, we may observe that his earlier pieces are the most diligently versified, and that in the later works, when through practice he must have acquired a greater facility, we find the strongest deviations from the regular structure of the verse. As it served with him merely to make the poetical elevation perceptible, he therefore claimed the utmost possible freedom in the use of it.

The views or suggestions of feeling by which he was guided in the use of rhyme may likewise be traced with almost equal certainty. Not unfrequently scenes, or even single speeches, close with a few rhyming lines, for the purpose of more strongly marking the division, and of giving it more rounding. This was injudiciously imitated by the English tragic poets of a later date; they suddenly elevated the tone in the rhymed lines, as if the person began all at once to speak in another language. The practice was welcomed by the actors from its serving as a signal for clapping when they made their exit. In Shakspeare, on the other hand, the transitions are more easy: all changes of forms are brought about insensibly, and as if of themselves. Moreover, he is generally fond of heightening a series of ingenious and antithetical sayings by the use of rhyme. We find other passages in continued rhyme, where solemnity and theatrical pomp were suitable, as, for instance, in the mask, [Footnote: I shall take the opportunity of saying a few words respecting this species of drama when I come to speak of Ben Jonson.] as it is called, *The Tempest*, and in the play introduced in *Hamlet*. Of other pieces, for instance, the *Midsummer Night's Dream*, and *Romeo and Juliet*, the rhymes form a considerable part; either because he may have wished to give them a glowing colour, or because the characters appropriately utter in a more musical tone their complaints or suits of love. In these cases he has even introduced rhymed strophes, which approach to the form of the sonnet, then usual in England. The assertion of Malone, that Shakspeare in his youth was fond of rhyme, but that he afterwards rejected it, is sufficiently refuted by his own chronology of the poet's works. In some of the earliest, for instance, in the Second and Third Part of *Henry the Sixth*, there are hardly any rhymes; in what is stated to be his last piece, *The Twelfth Night, or What You Will*, and in *Macbeth*, which is proved to have been composed under the reign of King James, we find them in no inconsiderable number. Even in the secondary matters of form Shakspeare was not guided by humour and accident, but, like a genuine artist, acted invariably on good and solid grounds. This we might also show of the kinds of verse which he least frequently used; for instance, if the rhyming verses of seven and eight syllables, were we not afraid of dwelling too long on merely technical peculiarities.

In England the manner of handling rhyming verse, and the opinion as to its harmony and elegance, have, in the course of two centuries, undergone a much greater change than is the case with the rhymeless Iambic or blank verse. In the former, Dryden and Pope have become models; these writers have communicated the utmost smoothing to rhyme, but they have also tied it down to a harmonious uniformity. A foreigner, to whom antiquated and new are the same, may perhaps feel with greater freedom the advantages of the more ancient manner. Certain it is, the rhyme of the present day, from the too great confinement of the couplet, is unfit for the drama. We must not estimate the rhyme of Shakspeare by the mode of subsequent times, but by a comparison with his contemporaries or with Spenser. The comparison will, without doubt, turn out to his advantage. Spenser is often diffuse; Shakspeare, though sometimes hard, is always brief and vigorous. He has more frequently been induced by the rhyme to leave out something necessary than to insert anything superfluous. Many of his rhymes, however, are faultless: ingenious with attractive ease, and rich without false brilliancy. The songs interspersed (those, I mean, of the poet himself) are generally sweetly playful and altogether musical; in imagination, while we merely read them, we hear their melody.

The whole of Shakspeare's productions bear the certain stamp of his original genius, but yet no writer was ever farther removed from every thing like a mannerism derived from habit or personal peculiarities. Rather is he, such is the diversity of tone and colour, which varies according to the quality of his subjects he assumes, a very Proteus. Each of his compositions is like a world of its own, moving in its own sphere. They are works of art, finished in one pervading style, which revealed the freedom and judicious choice of their author. If the formation of a work throughout, even in its minutest parts, in conformity with a leading idea; if the domination of one animating spirit over all the means of execution, deserves the name of correctness (and this, excepting in matters of grammar, is the only proper sense of the term); we shall then, after allowing to Shakspeare all the higher qualities which demand our admiration, be also compelled, in most cases, to concede to him the title of a correct poet.

It would be in the highest degree instructive to follow, if we could, in his career step by step, an author who at once founded and carried his art to perfection, and to go through his works in the order of time. But, with the exception of a few fixed points, which at length have been obtained, all the necessary materials for this are still wanting. The diligent Malone has, indeed, made an attempt to arrange the plays of Shakspeare in chronological order; but he himself only gives out the result of his labours for hypothetical, and it could not possibly be attended with complete success, since he excluded from his inquiry a considerable number of pieces which have been ascribed to the poet, though rejected as spurious by all the editors since Rowe, but which, in my opinion, must, if not wholly, at least in great measure be attributed to him. [Footnote: Were this book destined immediately for an English public, I should not have hazarded an opinion like this at variance with that which is generally received, without supporting it by proofs. The inquiry, however, is too extensive for our present limits, and I have therefore reserved it for a separate treatise. Besides at the present moment, while I am putting the last hand to my Lectures, no collection of English books but my own is accessible to me. The latter I should have enlarged with a view to this object, if the interruption of intercourse with England had not rendered it impossible to procure any other than the most common English books. On this point, therefore, I must request indulgence. In an Appendix to this Lecture I shall merely make a few cursory observations.]

LECTURE XXIV.

Criticisms on Shakspeare's Comedies.

The best and easiest mode of reviewing Shakspeare's dramas will be to arrange them in classes. This, it must be owned, is merely a makeshift: several critics have declared that all Shakspeare's pieces substantially belong to the same species, although sometimes one ingredient, sometimes another, the musical or the characteristical, the invention of the wonderful or the imitation of the real, the pathetic or the comic, seriousness or irony, may preponderate in the mixture. Shakspeare himself, it would appear, did but laugh at the petty endeavours of critics to find out divisions and subdivisions of species, and to hedge in what had been so separated with the most anxious care; thus the pedantic Polonius in *Hamlet* commends the players, for their knowledge of "tragedy, comedy, history, pastoral, pastoral-comical, historical-pastoral, tragical-historical, tragical-comical, historical-pastoral, scene-undividable, or poem unlimited." On another occasion he ridicules the limitation of Tragedy to an unfortunate catastrophe:

"And tragical, my noble lord, it is;
For Pyramus therein doth kill himself."

However the division into Comedies, Tragedies, and Historical Dramas, according to the usual practice, may in some measure be adopted, if we do not lose sight of the transitions and affinities. The subjects of the comedies are generally taken from novels: they are romantic love tales; none are altogether confined to the sphere of common or domestic relations: all of them possess poetical ornament, some of them run into the wonderful or the pathetic. With these two of his most famous tragedies are connected by an immediate link, *Romeo and Juliet* and *Othello*; both true novels, and composed on the same principles. In many of the historical plays a considerable space is occupied by the comic characters and scenes; others are serious throughout, and leave behind a tragical impression. The essential circumstance by which they are distinguished is, that the plot bears reference to a poetical and national interest. This is not equally the case in *Hamlet*, *Lear*, and *Macbeth*; and therefore it is that we do not include these tragedies among the historical pieces, though the first is founded on an old northern, the second on a national tradition; and the third comes even within the era of Scottish history, after it ceased to be fabulous.

Among the comedies, *The Two Gentlemen of Verona*, *The Taming of the*

Shrew, and *The Comedy of Errors*, bear many traces of an early origin. *The Two Gentlemen of Verona* paints the irresolution of love, and its infidelity to friendship, pleasantly enough, but in some degree superficially, we might almost say with the levity of mind which a passion suddenly entertained, and as suddenly given up, presupposes. The faithless lover is at last, on account of a very ambiguous repentance, forgiven without much difficulty by his first mistress; for the more serious part, the premeditated flight of the daughter of a Prince, the capture of her father along with herself by a band of robbers, of which one of the Two Gentlemen, the betrayed and banished friend, has been against his will elected captain: for all this a peaceful solution is soon found. It is as if the course of the world was obliged to accommodate itself to a transient youthful caprice, called love. Julia, who accompanies her faithless lover in the disguise of a page, is, as it were, a light sketch of the tender female figures of a Viola and an Imogen, who, in the latter pieces of Shakspeare, leave their home in similar disguises on love adventures, and to whom a peculiar charm is communicated by the display of the most virginly modesty in their hazardous and problematical situation.

The Comedy of Errors is the subject of the *Menaechmi* of Plautus, entirely recast and enriched with new developments: of all the works of Shakspeare this is the only example of imitation of, or borrowing from, the ancients. To the two twin brothers of the same name are added two slaves, also twins, impossible to be distinguished from each other, and of the same name. The improbability becomes by this means doubled: but when once we have lent ourselves to the first, which certainly borders on the incredible, we shall not perhaps be disposed to cavil at the second; and if the spectator is to be entertained by mere perplexities they cannot be too much varied. In such pieces we must, to give to the senses at least an appearance of truth, always pre-suppose that the parts by which the misunderstandings are occasioned are played with masks, and this the poet no doubt observed. I cannot acquiesce in the censure that the discovery is too long deferred: so long as novelty and interest are possessed by the perplexing incidents, there is no need to be in dread of wearisomeness. And this is really the case here: matters are carried so far that one of the two brothers is first arrested for debt, then confined as a lunatic, and the other is forced to take refuge in a sanctuary to save his life. In a subject of this description it is impossible to steer clear of all sorts of low circumstances, abusive language, and blows; Shakspeare has however endeavoured to ennoble it in every possible way. A couple of scenes, dedicated to jealousy and love, interrupt the course of perplexities which are solely occasioned by the illusion of the external senses. A greater solemnity is given to the discovery, from the Prince presiding, and from the re-union of the long separated parents of the twins who are still alive. The exposition, by which the spectators are previously instructed while the characters themselves are still involved in ignorance, and which Plautus artlessly conveys in a prologue, is here masterly introduced in an affecting narrative by the father. In short, this is perhaps the best of all written or possible Menaechmi; and if the piece be inferior in worth to other pieces of Shakspeare, it is merely because nothing more could be made of the materials.

The Taming of the Shrew has the air of an Italian comedy; and indeed the love intrigue, which constitutes the main part of it, is derived mediately or immediately from a piece of Ariosto. The characters and passions are lightly sketched; the intrigue is introduced without much preparation, and in its rapid progress impeded by no sort of difficulties; while, in the manner in which Petruchio, though previously cautioned as to Katherine, still encounters the risks in marrying her, and contrives to tame her--in all this the character and peculiar humour of the English are distinctly visible. The colours are laid on somewhat coarsely, but the ground is good. That the obstinacy of a young and untamed girl, possessed of none of the attractions of her sex, and neither supported by bodily nor mental strength, must soon yield to the still rougher and more capricious but assumed self-will of a man: such a lesson can only be taught on the stage with all the perspicuity of a proverb.

The prelude is still more remarkable than the play itself: a drunken tinker, removed in his sleep to a palace, where he is deceived into the belief of being a nobleman. The invention, however, is not Shakspeare's. Holberg has handled the same subject in a masterly manner, and with inimitable truth; but he has spun it out to five acts, for which such material is hardly sufficient. He probably did not borrow from the English dramatist, but like him took the hint from a popular story. There are several comic motives of this description, which go back to a very remote age, without ever becoming antiquated. Here, as well as everywhere else, Shakspeare has proved himself a great poet: the whole is merely a slight sketch, but in elegance and delicate propriety it will hardly ever be excelled. Neither has he overlooked the irony which the subject naturally suggested: the great lord, who is driven by idleness and ennui to deceive a poor drunkard, can make no better use of his situation than the latter, who every moment relapses into his vulgar habits. The last half of this prelude, that in which the tinker, in his new state, again drinks himself out of his senses, and is transformed in his sleep into his former condition, is from some accident or other, lost. It ought to have followed at the end of the larger piece. The occasional remarks of the tinker, during the course of the representation of the comedy, might have been improvisatory, but it is hardly credible that Shakspeare should have trusted to the momentary suggestions of the players, whom he did not hold in high estimation, the conclusion, however short, of a work which he had so carefully commenced. Moreover, the only circumstance which connects the play with the prelude, is, that it belongs to the new life of the supposed nobleman to have plays acted in his castle by strolling actors. This invention of introducing spectators on the stage, who contribute to the entertainment, has been very wittily used by later English poets.

Love's Labour Lost is also numbered among the pieces of his youth. It is a humorsome display of frolic; a whole cornucopia of the most vivacious jokes is emptied into it. Youth is certainly perceivable in the lavish superfluity of labour in the execution: the unbroken succession of plays on words, and sallies of every description, hardly leave the spectator time to breathe; the sparkles of wit fly about in such profusion, that they resemble a blaze of fireworks; while the dialogue, for the most part, is in the same hurried style in which the passing masks at a carnival attempt to banter each other. The young king of Navarre, with three of his courtiers, has made a vow to pass three years in rigid retirement, and devote them to the study of wisdom; for that purpose he has banished all female society from his court, and imposed a penalty on the intercourse with women. But scarcely has he, in a pompous harangue, worthy of the most heroic achievements, announced this determination, when the daughter of the king of France appears at his court, in the name of her old and bed-ridden father, to demand the restitution of a province which he held in pledge. Compelled to give her audience, he falls immediately in love with her. Matters fare no better with his companions, who on their parts renew an old acquaintance with the princess's attendants. Each, in heart, is already false to his vow, without knowing that the wish is shared by his associates; they overhear one another, as they in turn confide their sorrows in a love-ditty to the solitary forest: every one jeers and confounds the one who follows him. Biron, who from the beginning was the most satirical among them, at last steps forth, and rallies the king and the two others, till the discovery of a love-letter forces him also to hang down his head. He extricates himself and his companions from their dilemma by ridiculing the folly of the broken vow, and, after a noble eulogy on women, invites them to swear new allegiance to the colours of love. This scene is inimitable, and the crowning beauty of the whole. The manner in which they afterwards prosecute their love-suits in masks and disguise, and in which they are tricked and laughed at by the ladies, who are also masked and disguised, is, perhaps, spun out too long. It may be thought, too, that the poet, when he suddenly announces the death of the king of France, and makes the princess postpone her answer to the young prince's serious advances till the expiration of the period of her mourning, and impose, besides, a heavy penance on him for his levity, drops the proper comic tone. But the tone of raillery, which prevails throughout the piece, made it hardly possible to bring about a more satisfactory conclusion: after such extravagance, the characters could not return to sobriety, except under the presence of some foreign influence. The grotesque figures of Don Armado, a pompous fantastic Spaniard, a couple of pedants, and a clown, who between whiles contribute to the entertainment, are the creation of a whimsical imagination, and well adapted as foils for the wit of so vivacious a society.

All's Well that Ends Well, *Much Ado about Nothing*, *Measure for Measure*, and *The Merchant of Venice*, bear, in so far, a resemblance to each other, that, along with the main plot, which turns on important relations decisive of nothing less than the happiness or misery of life, and therefore is calculated to make a powerful impression on the moral feeling, the poet, with the skill of a practised artist, has contrived to combine a number of cheerful accompaniments. Not, however, that the poet seems both to allow full scope to the serious impressions: he merely adds a due counterpoise to them in the entertainment which he supplies for the imagination and the understanding. He has furnished the story with all the separate features which are necessary to give to it the appearance of a real, though extraordinary, event. But he never falls into the lachrymose tone of the sentimental drama, nor into the bitterness of those dramas which have a moral direction, and which are really nothing but moral invectives dramatized. Compassion, anxiety, and dissatisfaction become too oppressive when they are too long dwelt on, and when the whole of a work is given up to them exclusively. Shakspeare always finds means to transport us from the confinement of social institutions or pretensions, where men do but shut out the light and air from each other, into the open space, even before we ourselves are conscious of our want.

All's Well that Ends Well is the old story of a young maiden whose love looked much higher than her station. She obtains her lover in marriage from the hand of the King as a reward for curing him of a hopeless and lingering disease, by means of a hereditary arcanum of her father, who had been in his lifetime a celebrated physician. The young man despises her virtue and beauty; concludes the marriage only in appearance, and seeks in the dangers of war, deliverance from a domestic happiness which wounds his pride. By faithful endurance and an innocent fraud, she fulfils the apparently impossible conditions on which the Count had promised to acknowledge her as his wife. Love appears here in humble guise: the wooing is on the woman's side; it is striving, unaided by a reciprocal inclination, to overcome the prejudices of birth. But as soon as Helena is united to the Count by a sacred bond, though by him considered an oppressive chain, her error becomes her virtue.--She affects us by her patient suffering: the moment in which she appears to most advantage is when she accuses herself as the persecutor of her inflexible husband, and, under the pretext of a pilgrimage to atone for her error, privately leaves the house of her mother-in-law. Johnson expresses a cordial aversion for Count Bertram, and regrets that he should be allowed to come off at last with no other punishment than a temporary shame, nay, even be rewarded with the unmerited possession of a virtuous wife. But has Shakspeare ever attempted to soften the impression made by his unfeeling pride and light-hearted perversity? He has but given him the good qualities of a soldier. And does not the poet paint the true way of the world, which never makes much of man's injustice to woman, if so-called family honour is preserved? Bertram's sole justification is, that by the exercise of arbitrary power, the King thought proper to constrain him, in a matter of such delicacy and private right as the choice of a wife. Besides, this story, as well as that of Grissel and many similar ones, is intended to prove that woman's truth and patience will at last triumph over man's abuse of his superior power, while other novels and *fabliaux* are, on the other hand, true satires on woman's inconsistency and cunning. In this piece old age is painted with rare favour: the plain honesty of the King, the good-natured impetuosity of old Lafeu, the maternal indulgence of the Countess to Helena's passion for her son, seem all as it were to vie with each other in endeavours to overcome the arrogance of the young Count. The style of the whole is more sententious than imaginative: the glowing colours of fancy could not with propriety have been employed on such a subject. In the passages where the humiliating rejection of the poor Helena is most painfully affecting, the cowardly Parolles steps in to the relief of the spectator. The mystification by which his pretended valour and his shameless slanders are unmasked must be ranked among the most comic scenes that ever were invented: they contain matter enough for an excellent comedy, if Shakspeare were not always rich even to profusion. Falstaff has thrown Parolles into the shade, otherwise among the poet's comic characters he would have been still more famous.

The main plot in *Much Ado about Nothing* is the same with the story of *Ariodante and Ginevra* in Ariosto; the secondary circumstances and development are no doubt very different. The mode in which the innocent Hero before the altar at the moment of the wedding, and in the presence of her family and many witnesses, is put to shame by a most degrading charge, false indeed, yet clothed with every appearance of truth, is a grand piece of theatrical effect in the true and justifiable sense. The impression would have been too tragical had not Shakspeare carefully softened it in order to prepare for a fortunate catastrophe. The discovery of the plot against Hero has been already partly made, though not by the persons interested; and the poet has contrived, by means of the blundering simplicity of a couple of constables and watchmen, to convert the arrest and the examination of the guilty individuals into scenes full of the most delightful amusement. There is also a second piece of theatrical effect not inferior to the first, where Claudio, now convinced of his error, and in obedience to the penance laid on his fault, thinking to give his hand to a relation of his injured bride, whom he supposes dead, discovers on her unmasking, Hero herself. The extraordinary success of this play in Shakspeare's own day, and even since in England, is, however, to be ascribed more particularly to the parts of Benedict and Beatrice, two humoursome beings, who incessantly attack each other with all the resources of raillery. Avowed rebels to love, they are both entangled in its net by a merry plot of their friends to make them believe that each is the object of the secret passion of the other. Some one or other, not over-stocked with penetration has objected to the same artifice being twice used in entrapping them; the drollery, however, lies in the very symmetry of the deception. Their friends attribute the whole effect to their own device; but the exclusive direction of their raillery against each other is in itself a proof of a growing inclination. Their witty vivacity does not even abandon them in the avowal of love; and their behaviour only assumes a serious appearance for the purpose of defending the slandered Hero. This is exceedingly well imagined; the lovers of jesting must fix a point beyond which they are not to indulge in their humour, if they would not be mistaken for buffoons by trade.

In *Measure for Measure* Shakspeare was compelled, by the nature of the subject, to make his poetry more familiar with criminal justice than is usual with him. All kinds of proceedings connected with the subject, all sorts of active or passive persons, pass in review before us: the hypocritical Lord Deputy, the compassionate Provost, and the hard-hearted Hangman; a young man of quality who is to suffer for the seduction of his mistress before marriage, loose wretches brought in by the police, nay, even a hardened criminal, whom even the preparations for his execution cannot awaken out of his callousness. But yet, notwithstanding this agitating truthfulness, how tender and mild is the pervading tone of the picture! The piece takes improperly its name from punishment; the true significance of the whole is the triumph of mercy over strict justice; no man being himself so free from errors as to be entitled to deal it out to his equals. The most beautiful embellishment of the composition is the character of Isabella, who, on the point of taking the veil, is yet prevailed upon by sisterly affection to tread again the perplexing ways of the world, while, amid the general corruption, the heavenly purity of her mind is not even stained with one unholy thought: in the humble robes of the novice she is a very angel of light. When the cold and stern Angelo, heretofore of unblemished reputation, whom the Duke has commissioned, during his pretended absence, to restrain, by a rigid administration of the laws, the excesses of dissolute immorality, is even himself tempted by the virgin charms of Isabella, supplicating for the pardon of her brother Claudio, condemned to death for a youthful indiscretion; when at first, in timid and obscure language, he insinuates, but at last impudently avouches his readiness to grant Claudio's life to the sacrifice of her honour; when Isabella repulses his offer with a noble scorn; in her account of the interview to her brother, when the latter at first applauds her conduct, but at length, overcome by the fear of death, strives to persuade her to consent to dishonour;--in these masterly scenes, Shakspeare has sounded the depths of the human heart. The interest here reposes altogether on the represented action; curiosity contributes nothing to our delight, for the Duke, in the disguise of a Monk, is always present to watch over his dangerous representative, and to avert every evil which could possibly be apprehended; we look to him with confidence for a happy result. The Duke acts the part of the Monk naturally, even to deception; he unites in his person the wisdom of the priest and the prince. Only in his wisdom he is too fond of round-about ways; his vanity is flattered with acting invisibly like an earthly providence; he takes more pleasure in overhearing his subjects than governing them in the customary way of princes. As he ultimately extends a free pardon to all the guilty, we do not see how his original purpose, in committing the execution of the laws to other hands, of restoring their strictness, has in any wise been accomplished. The poet might have had this irony in view, that of the numberless slanders of the Duke, told him by the petulant Lucio, in ignorance of the person whom he is addressing, that at least which regarded his singularities and whims was not wholly without foundation. It is deserving of remark, that Shakspeare, amidst the rancour of religious parties, takes a delight in painting the condition of a monk, and always represents his influence as beneficial. We find in him none of the black and knavish monks, which an enthusiasm for Protestantism, rather than poetical inspiration, has suggested to some of our modern poets. Shakspeare merely gives his monks an inclination to busy themselves in the affairs of others, after renouncing the world for themselves; with respect, however, to pious frauds, he does not represent them as very conscientious. Such are the parts acted by the monk in *Romeo and Juliet*, and another in *Much Ado about Nothing*, and even by the Duke, whom, contrary to the well-known proverb, the cowl seems really to make a monk.

The *Merchant of Venice* is one of Shakspeare's most perfect works: popular to an extraordinary degree, and calculated to produce the most powerful effect on the stage, and at the same time a wonder of ingenuity and art for the reflecting critic. Shylock, the Jew, is one of the inimitable masterpieces of characterization which are to be found only in Shakspeare. It is easy for both poet and player to exhibit a caricature of national sentiments, modes of speaking, and gestures. Shylock, however, is everything but a common Jew: he possesses a strongly-marked and original individuality, and yet we perceive a light touch of Judaism in everything he says or does. We almost fancy we can hear a light whisper of the Jewish accent even in the written words, such as we sometimes still find in the higher classes, notwithstanding their social refinement. In tranquil moments, all that is foreign to the European blood and Christian sentiments is less perceptible, but in passion the national stamp comes out more strongly marked. All these inimitable niceties the finished art of a great actor can alone properly express. Shylock is a man of information, in his own way, even a thinker, only he has not discovered the region where human feelings dwell; his morality is founded on the disbelief in goodness and magnanimity. The desire to avenge the wrongs and indignities heaped upon his nation is, after avarice, his strongest spring of action. His hate is naturally directed chiefly against those Christians who are actuated by truly Christian sentiments: a disinterested love of our neighbour seems to him the most unrelenting persecution of the Jews. The letter of the law is his idol; he refuses to lend an ear to the voice of mercy, which, from the mouth of Portia, speaks to him with heavenly eloquence: he insists on rigid and inflexible justice, and at last it recoils on his own head. Thus he becomes a symbol of the general history of his unfortunate nation. The melancholy and self-sacrificing magnanimity of Antonio is affectingly sublime. Like a princely merchant, he is surrounded with a whole train of noble friends. The contrast which this forms to the selfish cruelty of the usurer Shylock was necessary to redeem the honour of human nature. The danger which almost to the close of the fourth act, hangs over Antonio, and which the imagination is almost afraid to approach, would fill the mind with too painful anxiety, if the poet did not also provide for its recreation and diversion. This is effected in an especial manner by the scenes at Portia's country-seat, which transport the spectator into quite another world. And yet they are closely connected with the main business by the chain of cause and effect: Bassanio's preparations for his courtship are the cause of Antonio's subscribing the dangerous bond; and Portia again, by the counsel and advice of her uncle, a famous lawyer, effects the safety of her lover's friend. But the relations of the dramatic composition are the while admirably observed in yet another respect. The trial between Shylock and Antonio is indeed recorded as being a real event, still, for all that, it must ever remain an unheard-of and singular case. Shakspeare has therefore associated it with a love intrigue not less extraordinary: the one consequently is rendered natural and probable by means of the other. A rich, beautiful and clever heiress, who can only be won by the solving the riddle--the locked caskets--the foreign princes, who come to try the venture--all this powerfully excites the imagination with the splendour of an olden tale of marvels. The two scenes in which, first the Prince of Morocco, in the language of Eastern hyperbole, and then the self-conceited Prince of Arragon, make their choice among the caskets, serve merely to raise our curiosity, and give employment to our wits; but on the third, where the two lovers stand trembling before the inevitable choice, which in one moment must unite or separate them for ever, Shakspeare has lavished all the charms of feeling--all the magic of poesy. We share in the rapture of Portia and Bassanio at the fortunate choice: we easily conceive why they are so fond of each other, for they are both most deserving of love. The judgment scene, with which the fourth act is occupied, is in itself a perfect drama, concentrating in itself the interest of the whole. The knot is now untied, and according to the common ideas of theatrical satisfaction, the curtain ought to drop. But the poet was unwilling to dismiss his audience with the gloomy impressions which Antonio's acquittal, effected with so much difficulty, and contrary to all expectation, and the condemnation of Shylock, were calculated to leave behind them; he has therefore added the fifth act by way of a musical afterlude in the piece itself. The episode of Jessica, the fugitive daughter of the Jew, in whom Shakspeare has contrived to throw a veil of sweetness over the national features, and the artifice by which Portia and her companion are enabled to rally their newly-married husbands, supply him with the necessary materials. The scene opens with the playful prattling of two lovers in a summer evening; it is followed by soft music, and a rapturous eulogy on this powerful disposer of the human mind and the world; the principal characters then make their appearance, and after a simulated quarrel, which is gracefully maintained, the whole end with the most exhilarating mirth.

As You Like It is a piece of an entirely different description. It would be difficult to bring the contents within the compass of an ordinary narrative; nothing takes place, or rather what is done is not so essential as what is said; even what may be called the *denouement* is brought about pretty arbitrarily. Whoever can perceive nothing but what can as it were be counted on the fingers, will hardly be disposed to allow that it has any plan at all. Banishment and flight have assembled together, in the forest of Arden, a strange band: a Duke dethroned by his brother, who, with the faithful companions of his misfortune, lives in the wilds on the produce of the chase; two disguised Princesses, who love each other with a sisterly affection; a witty court fool; lastly, the native inhabitants of the forest, ideal and natural shepherds and shepherdesses. These lightly-sketched figures form a motley and diversified train; we see always the shady dark-green landscape in the background, and breathe in imagination the fresh air of the forest. The hours are here measured by no clocks, no regulated recurrence of duty or of toil: they flow on unnumbered by voluntary occupation or fanciful idleness, to which, according to his humour or disposition, every one yields himself, and this unrestrained freedom compensates them all for the lost conveniences of life. One throws himself down in solitary meditation under a tree, and indulges in melancholy reflections on the changes of fortune, the falsehood of the world, and the self-inflicted torments of social life; others make the woods resound with social and festive songs, to the accompaniment of their hunting-horns. Selfishness, envy, and ambition, have been left behind in the city; of all the human passions, love alone has found an entrance into this wilderness, where it dictates the same language alike to the simple shepherd and the chivalrous youth, who hangs his love-ditty to a tree. A prudish shepherdess falls at first sight in love with Rosalind, disguised in men's apparel; the latter sharply reproaches her with her severity to her poor lover, and the pain of refusal, which she feels from experience in her own case, disposes her at length to compassion and requital. The fool carries his philosophical contempt of external show, and his raillery of the illusion of love so far, that he purposely seeks out the ugliest and simplest country wench for a mistress. Throughout the whole picture, it seems to be the poet's design to show that to call forth the poetry which has its indwelling in nature and the human mind, nothing is wanted but to throw off all artificial constraint, and restore both to mind and nature their original liberty. In the very progress of the piece, the dreamy carelessness of such an existence is sensibly expressed: it is even alluded to by Shakspeare in the title. Whoever affects to be displeased, if in this romantic forest the ceremonial of dramatic art is not duly observed, ought in justice to be delivered over to the wise fool, to be led gently out of it to some prosaical region.

The Twelfth Night, or What you Will, unites the entertainment of an intrigue, contrived with great ingenuity, to a rich fund of comic characters and situations, and the beauteous colours of an ethereal poetry. In most of his plays, Shakspeare treats love more as an affair of the imagination than the heart; but here he has taken particular care to remind us that, in his language, the same word, *fancy*, signified both fancy and love. The love of the music-enraptured Duke for Olivia is not merely a fancy, but an imagination; Viola appears at first to fall arbitrarily in love with the Duke, whom she serves as a page, although she afterwards touches the tenderest strings of feeling; the proud Olivia is captivated by the modest and insinuating messenger of the Duke, in whom she is far from suspecting a disguised rival, and at last, by a second deception, takes the brother for the sister. To these, which I might call ideal follies, a contrast is formed by the naked absurdities to which the entertaining tricks of the ludicrous persons of the piece give rise, under the pretext also of love: the silly and profligate Knight's awkward courtship of Olivia, and her declaration of love to Viola; the imagination of the pedantic steward Malvolio, that his mistress is secretly in love with him, which carries him so far that he is at last shut up as a lunatic, and visited by the clown in the dress of a priest. These scenes are admirably conceived, and as significant as they are laughable. If this were really, as is asserted, Shakspeare's latest work, he must have enjoyed to the last the same youthful elasticity of mind, and have carried with him to the grave the undiminished fulness of his talents.

The Merry Wives of Windsor, though properly a comedy in the usual acceptation of the word, we shall pass over at present, till we come to speak of *Henry the Fourth*, that we may give our opinion of the character of Falstaff in connexion.

The Midsummer Night's Dream and *The Tempest*, may be in so far compared together that in both the influence of a wonderful world of spirits is interwoven with the turmoil of human passions and with the farcical adventures of folly. *The Midsummer Night's Dream* is certainly an earlier production; but *The Tempest*, according to all appearance, was written in Shakspeare's later days: hence most critics, on the supposition that the poet must have continued to improve with increasing maturity of mind, have honoured the last piece with a marked preference. I cannot, however, altogether concur with them: the internal merit of these two works are, in my opinion, pretty nearly balanced, and a predilection for the one or the other can only be governed by personal taste. In profound and original characterization the superiority of *The Tempest* is obvious: as a whole we must always admire the masterly skill which he has here displayed in the economy of his means, and the dexterity with which he has disguised his preparations,--the scaffoldings for the wonderful aerial structure. In *The Midsummer Night's Dream*, on the other hand, there flows a luxuriant vein of the boldest and most fantastical invention; the most extraordinary combination of the most dissimilar ingredients seems to have been brought about without effort by some ingenious and lucky accident, and the colours are of such clear transparency that we think the whole of the variegated fabric may be blown away with a breath. The fairy world here described resembles those elegant pieces of arabesque, where little genii with butterfly wings rise, half embodied, above the flower-cups. Twilight, moonshine, dew, and spring perfumes, are the element of these tender spirits; they assist nature in embroidering her carpet with green leaves, many-coloured flowers, and glittering insects; in the human world they do but make sport childishly and waywardly with their beneficent or noxious influences. Their most violent rage dissolves in good-natured raillery; their passions, stripped of all earthly matter, are merely an ideal dream. To correspond with this, the loves of mortals are painted as a poetical enchantment, which, by a contrary enchantment, may be immediately suspended, and then renewed again. The different parts of the plot; the wedding of Theseus and Hippolyta, Oberon and Titania's quarrel, the flight of the two pair of lovers, and the theatrical manoeuvres of the mechanics, are so lightly and happily interwoven that they seem necessary to each other for the formation, of a whole. Oberon is desirous of relieving the lovers from their perplexities, but greatly adds to them through the mistakes of his minister, till he at last comes really to the aid of their fruitless amorous pain, their inconstancy and jealousy, and restores fidelity to its old rights. The extremes of fanciful and vulgar are united when the enchanted Titania awakes and falls in love with a coarse mechanic with an ass's head, who represents, or rather disfigures, the part of a tragical lover. The droll wonder of Bottom's transformation is merely the translation of a metaphor in its literal sense; but in his behaviour during the tender homage of the Fairy Queen we have an amusing proof how much the consciousness of such a head-dress heightens the effect of his usual folly. Theseus and Hippolyta are, as it were, a splendid frame for the picture; they take no part in the action, but surround it with a stately pomp. The discourse of the hero and his Amazon, as they course through the forest with their noisy hunting-train, works upon the imagination like the fresh breath of morning, before which the shapes of night disappear. Pyramus and Thisbe is not unmeaningly chosen as the grotesque play within the play; it is exactly like the pathetic part of the piece, a secret meeting of two lovers in the forest, and their separation by an unfortunate accident, and closes the whole with the most amusing parody.

The Tempest has little action or progressive movement; the union of Ferdinand and Miranda is settled at their first interview, and Prospero merely throws apparent obstacles in their way; the shipwrecked band go leisurely about the island; the attempts of Sebastian and Antonio on the life of the King of Naples, and the plot of Caliban and the drunken sailors against Prospero, are nothing but a feint, for we foresee that they will be completely frustrated by the magical skill of the latter; nothing remains therefore but the punishment of the guilty by dreadful sights which harrow up their consciences, and then the discovery and final reconciliation. Yet this want of movement is so admirably concealed by the most varied display of the fascinations of poetry, and the exhilaration of mirth, the details of the execution are so very attractive, that it requires no small degree of attention to perceive that the *denouement* is, in some degree, anticipated in the exposition. The history of the loves of Ferdinand and Miranda, developed in a few short scenes, is enchantingly beautiful: an affecting union of chivalrous magnanimity on the one part, and on the other of the virgin openness of a heart which, brought up far from the world on an uninhabited island, has never learned to disguise its innocent movements. The wisdom of the princely hermit Prospero has a magical and mysterious air; the disagreeable impression left by the black falsehood of the two usurpers is softened by the honest gossipping of the old and faithful Gonzalo; Trinculo and Stephano, two good-for-nothing drunkards, find a worthy associate in Caliban; and Ariel hovers sweetly over the whole as the personified genius of the wonderful fable.

Caliban has become a by-word as the strange creation of a poetical imagination. A mixture of gnome and savage, half daemon, half brute, in his behaviour we perceive at once the traces of his native disposition, and the influence of Prospero's education. The latter could only unfold his understanding, without, in the slightest degree, taming his rooted malignity: it is as if the use of reason and human speech were communicated to an awkward ape. In inclination Caliban is maliciously cowardly, false, and base; and yet he is essentially different from the vulgar knaves of a civilized world, as portrayed occasionally by Shakspeare. He is rude, but not vulgar; he never falls into the prosaic and low familiarity of his drunken associates, for he is, in his way, a poetical being; he always speaks in verse. He has picked up every thing dissonant and thorny in language to compose out of it a vocabulary of his own; and of the whole variety of nature, the hateful, repulsive, and pettily deformed, have alone been impressed on his imagination. The magical world of spirits, which the staff of Prospero has assembled on the island, casts merely a faint reflection into his mind, as a ray of light which falls into a dark cave, incapable of communicating to it either heat or illumination, serves merely to set in motion the poisonous vapours. The delineation of this monster is throughout inconceivably consistent and profound, and, notwithstanding its hatefulness, by no means hurtful to our feelings, as the honour of human nature is left untouched.

In the zephyr-like Ariel the image of air is not to be mistaken, his name even bears an allusion to it; as, on the other hand Caliban signifies the heavy element of earth. Yet they are neither of them simple, allegorical personifications but beings individually determined. In general we find in *The Midsummer Night's Dream*, in *The Tempest*, in the magical part of *Macbeth*, and wherever Shakspeare avails himself of the popular belief in the invisible presence of spirits, and the possibility of coming in contact with them, a profound view of the inward life of nature and her mysterious springs, which, it is true, can never be altogether unknown to the genuine poet, as poetry is altogether incompatible with mechanical physics, but which few have possessed in an equal degree with Dante and himself.

The Winter's Tale is as appropriately named as *The Midsummer Night's Dream*. It is one of those tales which are peculiarly calculated to beguile the dreary leisure of a long winter evening, and are even attractive and intelligible to childhood, while animated by fervent truth in the delineation of character and passion, and invested with the embellishments of poetry lowering itself, as it were, to the simplicity of the subject, they transport even manhood back to the golden age of imagination. The calculation of probabilities has nothing to do with such wonderful and fleeting adventures, when all end at last in universal joy;

and, accordingly, Shakspeare has here taken the greatest license of anachronisms and geographical errors; not to mention other incongruities, he opens a free navigation between Sicily and Bohemia, makes Giulio Romano the contemporary of the Delphic oracle. The piece divides itself in some degree into two plays. Leontes becomes suddenly jealous of his royal bosom-friend Polyxenes, who is on a visit to his court; makes an attempt on his life, from which Polyxenes only saves himself by a clandestine flight;--Hermione, suspected of infidelity, is thrown into prison, and the daughter which she there brings into the world is exposed on a remote coast;--the accused Queen, declared innocent by the oracle, on learning that her infant son has pined to death on her account, falls down in a swoon, and is mourned as dead by her husband, who becomes sensible, when too late, of his error: all this makes up the three first acts. The last two are separated from these by a chasm of sixteen years; but the foregoing tragical catastrophe was only apparent, and this serves to connect the two parts. The Princess, who has been exposed on the coast of Polyxenes's kingdom, grows up among low shepherds; but her tender beauty, her noble manners, and elevation of sentiment, bespeak her descent; the Crown Prince Florizel, in the course of his hawking, falls in with her, becomes enamoured, and courts her in the disguise of a shepherd; at a rural entertainment Polyxenes discovers their attachment, and breaks out into a violent rage; the two lovers seek refuge from his persecutions at the court of Leontes in Sicily, where the discovery and general reconciliation take place. Lastly, when Leontes beholds, as he imagines, the statue of his lost wife, it descends from the niche: it is she herself, the still living Hermione, who has kept herself so long concealed; and the piece ends with universal rejoicing. The jealousy of Leontes is not, like that of Othello, developed through all its causes, symptoms and variations; it is brought forward at once full grown and mature, and is portrayed as a distempered frenzy. It is a passion whose effects the spectator is more concerned with than with its origin, and which does not produce the catastrophe, but merely ties the knot of the piece. In fact, the poet might perhaps have wished slightly to indicate that Hermione, though virtuous, was too warm in her efforts to please Polyxenes; and it appears as if this germ of inclination first attained its proper maturity in their children. Nothing can be more fresh and youthful, nothing at once so ideally pastoral and princely as the love of Florizel and Perdita; of the prince, whom love converts into a voluntary shepherd; and the princess, who betrays her exalted origin without knowing it, and in whose hands nosegays become crowns. Shakspeare has never hesitated to place ideal poetry side by side of the most vulgar prose: and in the world of reality also this is generally the case. Perdita's foster-father and his son are both made simple boors, that we may the more distinctly see how all that ennobles her belongs only to herself. Autolycus, the merry pedlar and pickpocket, so inimitably portrayed, is necessary to complete the rustic feast, which Perdita on her part seems to render meet for an assemblage of gods in disguise.

Cymbeline is also one of Shakspeare's most wonderful compositions. He has here combined a novel of Boccacio's with traditionary tales of the ancient Britons reaching back to the times of the first Roman Emperors, and he has contrived, by the most gentle transitions, to blend together into one harmonious whole the social manners of the newest times with olden heroic deeds, and even with appearances of the gods.

In the character of Imogen no one feature of female excellence is omitted: her chaste tenderness, her softness, and her virgin pride, her boundless resignation, and her magnanimity towards her mistaken husband, by whom she is unjustly persecuted, her adventures in disguise, her apparent death, and her recovery, form altogether a picture equally tender and affecting. The two Princes, Guiderius and Arviragus, both educated in the wilds, form a noble contrast to Miranda and Perdita. Shakspeare is fond of showing the superiority of the natural over the artificial. Over the art which enriches nature, he somewhere says, there is a higher art created by nature herself. [Footnote: The passage in Shakspeare here quoted, taken with the context, will not bear the construction of the author. The whole runs thus:--

Yet nature is made better by no mean,
But nature makes that mean: so, o'er that art
Which you say adds to nature, is an art
That nature makes. You see, sweet maid, we marry
A gentler scion to the wildest stock;
And make conceive a bark of baser kind
By bud of nobler race: this is an art
Which does mend nature, change it rather; but
The art itself is nature.

Winter's Tale, Act iv. sc. 3.

Shakspeare does not here mean to institute a comparison between the relative excellency of that which is innate and that which we owe to instruction; but merely says, that the instruction or art is itself a part of nature. The speech is addressed by Polyxenes to Perdita, to persuade her that the changes effected in the appearance of flowers by the art of the gardener are not to be accounted unnatural; and the expression of *making conceive a bark of baser kind by bud of nobler race* (i.e., engrafting), would rather lead to the inference, that the mind derived its chief value from the influence of culture.--TRANS.] As Miranda's unconscious and unstudied sweetness is more pleasing than those charms which endeavour to captivate us by the brilliant embellishments of a refined cultivation, so in these two youths, to whom the chase has given vigour and hardihood, but who are ignorant of their high destination, and have been brought up apart from human society, we are equally enchanted by a *naive* heroism which leads them to anticipate and to dream of deeds of valour, till an occasion is offered which they are irresistibly compelled to embrace. When Imogen comes in disguise to their cave; when, with all the innocence of childhood, Guiderius and Arviragus form an impassioned friendship for the tender boy, in whom they neither suspect a female nor their own sister; when, on their return from the chase, they find her dead, then "sing her to the ground," and cover the grave with flowers:--these scenes might give to the most deadened imagination a new life for poetry. If a tragical event is only apparent, in such case, whether the spectators are already aware of it or ought merely to suspect it, Shakspeare always knows how to mitigate the impression without weakening it: he makes the mourning musical, that it may gain in solemnity what it loses in seriousness. With respect to the other parts, the wise and vigorous Belarius, who after long living as a hermit again becomes a hero, is a venerable figure; the Italian Iachimo's ready dissimulation and quick presence of mind is quite suitable to the bold treachery which he plays; Cymbeline, the father of Imogen, and even her husband Posthumus, during the first half of the piece, are somewhat sacrificed, but this could not be otherwise; the false and wicked Queen is merely an instrument of the plot; she and her stupid son Cloton (the only comic part in the piece) whose rude arrogance is portrayed with much humour, are, before the conclusion, got rid of by merited punishment. As for the heroical part of the fable, the war between the Romans and Britons, which brings on the denouement, the poet in the extent of his plan had so little room to spare, that he merely endeavours to represent it as a mute procession. But to the last scene, where all the numerous threads of the knot are untied, he has again given its full development, that he might collect together into one focus the scattered impressions of the whole. This example and many others are a sufficient refutation of Johnson's assertion, that Shakspeare usually hurries over the conclusion of his pieces. Rather does he, from a desire to satisfy the feelings, introduce a great deal which, so far as the understanding of the *denouement* requires, might in a strict sense be justly spared: our modern spectators are much more impatient to see the curtain drop, when there is nothing more to be determined, than those of his day could have been.

LECTURE XXV.

Criticisms on Shakspeare's Tragedies.

Romeo and Juliet, and *Othello*, differ from most of the pieces which we have hitherto examined, neither in the ingredients of the composition, nor in the manner of treating them: it is merely the direction of the whole that gives them the stamp of Tragedy. *Romeo and Juliet* is a picture of love and its pitiable fate, in a world whose atmosphere is too sharp for this the tenderest blossom of human life. Two beings created for each other feel mutual love at the first glance; every consideration disappears before the irresistible impulse to live in one another; under circumstances hostile in the highest degree to their union, they unite themselves by a secret marriage, relying simply on the protection of an invisible power. Untoward incidents following in rapid succession, their heroic constancy is within a few days put to the proof, till, forcibly separated from each other, by a voluntary death they are united in the grave to meet again in another world. All this is to be found in the beautiful story which Shakspeare has not invented, and which, however simply told, will always excite a tender sympathy: but it was reserved for Shakspeare to join in one ideal picture purity of heart with warmth of imagination; sweetness and dignity of manners with passionate intensity of feeling. Under his handling, it has become a glorious song of praise on that inexpressible feeling which ennobles the soul and gives to it its highest sublimity, and which elevates even the senses into soul, while at the same time it is a melancholy elegy on its inherent and imparted frailty; it is at once the apotheosis and the obsequies of love. It appears here a heavenly spark, that, as it descends to the earth, is converted into the lightning flash, which almost in the same moment sets on fire and consumes the mortal being on whom it lights. All that is most intoxicating in the odour of a southern spring,--all that is languishing in the song of the nightingale, or voluptuous in the first opening of the rose, all alike breathe forth from this poem. But even more rapidly than the earliest blossoms of youth and beauty decay, does it from the first timidly-bold declaration and modest return of love hurry on to the most unlimited passion, to an irrevocable union; and then hastens, amidst alternating storms of rapture and despair, to the fate of the two lovers, who yet appear enviable in their hard lot, for their love survives them, and by their death they have obtained an endless triumph over every separating power. The sweetest and the bitterest love and hatred, festive rejoicings and dark forebodings, tender embraces and sepulchral horrors, the fulness of life and self-annihilation, are here all brought close to each other; and yet these contrasts are so blended into a unity of impression, that the echo which the whole leaves behind in the mind resembles a single but endless sigh.

The excellent dramatic arrangement, the significance of every character in its place, the judicious selection of all the circumstances, even the most minute, have already been dwelt upon in detail. I shall only request attention to a trait which may serve for an example of the distance to which Shakspeare goes back to lay the preparatory foundation. The most striking and perhaps incredible circumstance in the whole story is the liquor given by the Monk to Julia, by which she for a number of hours not merely sleeps, but fully resembles a corpse, without however receiving the least injury. How does the poet dispose us to believe that Father Lorenzo possesses such a secret?--At his first appearance he exhibits him in a garden, where he is collecting herbs and descanting on their wonderful virtues. The discourse of the pious old man is full of deep meaning: he sees everywhere in nature emblems of the moral world; the same wisdom with which he looks through her has also made him master of the human heart. In this manner a circumstance of an ungrateful appearance, has become the source of a great beauty.

If *Romeo and Juliet* shines with the colours of the dawn of morning, but a dawn whose purple clouds already announce the thunder of a sultry day, *Othello* is, on the other hand, a strongly shaded picture: we might call it a tragical Rembrandt. What a fortunate mistake that the Moor (under which name in the original novel, a baptized Saracen of the Northern coast of Africa was unquestionably meant), has been made by Shakspeare in every respect a negro! We recognize in Othello the wild nature of that glowing zone which generates the most ravenous beasts of prey and the most deadly poisons, tamed only in appearance by the desire of fame, by foreign laws of honour, and by nobler and milder manners. His jealousy is not the jealousy of the heart, which is compatible with the tenderest feeling and adoration of the beloved object; it is of that sensual kind which, in burning climes, has given birth to the disgraceful confinement of women and many other unnatural usages. A drop of this poison flows in his veins, and sets his whole blood in the wildest ferment. The Moor *seems* noble, frank, confiding, grateful for the love shown him; and he is all this, and, moreover, a hero who spurns at danger, a worthy leader of an army, a faithful servant of the state; but the mere physical force of passion puts to flight in one moment all his acquired and mere habitual virtues, and gives the upper hand to the savage over the moral man. This tyranny of the blood over the will betrays itself even in the expression of his desire of revenge upon Cassio. In his repentance, a genuine tenderness for his murdered wife, and in the presence of the damning evidence of his deed, the painful feeling of annihilated honour at last bursts forth; and in the midst of these painful emotions he assails himself with the rage wherewith a despot punishes a runaway slave. He suffers as a double man; at once in the higher and the lower sphere into which his being was divided.--While the Moor bears the nightly colour of suspicion and deceit only on his visage, Iago is black within. He haunts Othello like his evil genius, and with his light (and therefore the more dangerous,) insinuations, he leaves him no rest; it is as if by means of an unfortunate affinity, founded however in nature, this influence was by necessity more powerful over him than the voice of his good angel Desdemona. A more artful villain than this Iago was never portrayed; he spreads his nets with a skill which nothing can escape. The repugnance inspired by his aims becomes tolerable from the attention of the spectators being directed to his means: these furnish endless employment to the understanding. Cool, discontented, and morose, arrogant where he dare be so, but humble and insinuating when it suits his purposes, he is a complete master in the art of dissimulation; accessible only to selfish emotions, he is thoroughly skilled in rousing the passions of others, and of availing himself of every opening which they give him: he is as excellent an observer of men as any one can be who is unacquainted with higher motives of action from his own experience; there is always some truth in his malicious observations on them. He does not merely pretend an obdurate incredulity as to the virtue of women, he actually entertains it; and this, too, falls in with his whole way of thinking, and makes him the more fit for the execution of his purpose. As in every thing he sees merely the hateful side, he dissolves in the rudest manner the charm which the imagination casts over the relation between the two sexes: he does so for the purpose of revolting Othello's senses, whose heart otherwise might easily have convinced him of Desdemona's innocence. This must serve as an excuse for the numerous expressions in the speeches of Iago from which modesty shrinks. If Shakespeare had written in our days he would not perhaps have dared to hazard them; and yet this must certainly have greatly injured the truth of his picture. Desdemona is a sacrifice without blemish. She is not, it is true, a high ideal representation of sweetness and enthusiastic passion like Juliet; full of simplicity, softness, and humility, and so innocent, that she can hardly form to herself an idea of the possibility of infidelity, she seems calculated to make the most yielding and tenderest of wives. The female propensity wholly to resign itself to a foreign destiny has led her into the only fault of her life, that of marrying without her father's consent. Her choice seems wrong; and yet she has been gained over to Othello by that which induces the female to honour in man her protector and guide,--admiration of his determined heroism, and compassion for the sufferings which he had undergone. With great art it is so contrived, that from the very circumstance that the possibility of a suspicion of her own purity of motive never once enters her mind, she is the less reserved in her solicitations for Cassio, and thereby does but heighten more and more the jealousy of Othello. To throw out still more clearly the angelic purity of Desdemona, Shakspeare has in Emilia associated with her a companion of doubtful virtue. From the sinful levity of this woman it is also conceivable that she should not confess the abstraction of the handkerchief when Othello violently demands it back: this would otherwise be the circumstance in the whole piece the most difficult to justify. Cassio is portrayed exactly as he ought to be to excite suspicion without actual guilt,--amiable and nobly disposed, but easily seduced. The public events of the first two acts show us Othello in his most glorious aspect, as the support of Venice and the terror of the Turks: they serve to withdraw the story from the mere domestic circle, just as this is done in *Romeo and Juliet* by the dissensions between the houses of Montague and Capulet. No eloquence is capable of painting the overwhelming force of the catastrophe in *Othello*,--the pressure of feelings which measure out in a moment the abysses of eternity.

Hamlet is singular in its kind: a tragedy of thought inspired by continual and never-satisfied meditation on human destiny and the dark perplexity of the events of this world, and calculated to call forth the very same meditation in the minds of the spectators. This enigmatical work resembles those irrational equations in which a fraction of unknown magnitude always remains, that will in no way admit of solution. Much has been said, much written, on this piece, and yet no thinking head who anew expresses himself on it, will (in his view of the connexion and the signification of all the parts) entirely coincide with his predecessors. What naturally most astonishes us, is the fact that with such hidden purposes, with a foundation laid in such unfathomable depth, the whole should, at a first view, exhibit an extremely popular appearance. The dread appearance of the Ghost takes possession of the mind and the imagination almost at the very commencement; then the play within the play, in which, as in a glass, we see reflected the crime, whose fruitlessly attempted punishment constitutes the subject-matter of the piece; the alarm with which it fills the King; Hamlet's pretended and Ophelia's real madness; her death and burial; the meeting of Hamlet and Laertes at her grave; their combat, and the grand determination; lastly, the appearance of the young hero Fortinbras, who, with warlike pomp, pays the last honours to an extinct family of kings; the interspersion of comic characteristic scenes with Polonius, the courtiers, and the grave-diggers, which have all of them their signification,--all this fills the stage with an animated and varied movement. The only circumstance from which this piece might be judged to be less theatrical than other tragedies of Shakspeare is, that in the last scenes the main action either stands still or appears to retrograde. This, however, was inevitable, and lay in the nature of the subject. The whole is intended to show that a calculating consideration, which exhausts all the relations and possible consequences of a deed, must cripple the power of acting; as Hamlet himself expresses it:--

And thus the native hue of resolution
Is sicklied o'er with the pale cast of thought;
And enterprises of great pith and moment,
With this regard, their currents turn awry,
And lose the name of action.

With respect to Hamlet's character: I cannot, as I understand the poet's views, pronounce altogether so favourable a sentence upon it as Goethe does. He is, it is true, of a highly cultivated mind, a prince of royal manners, endowed with the finest sense of propriety, susceptible of noble ambition, and open in the highest degree to an enthusiastic admiration of that excellence in others of which he himself is deficient. He acts the part of madness with unrivalled power, convincing the persons who are sent to examine into his supposed loss of reason, merely by telling them unwelcome truths, and rallying them with the most caustic wit. But in the resolutions which he so often embraces and always leaves unexecuted, his weakness is too apparent: he does himself only justice when he implies that there is no greater dissimilarity than between himself and Hercules. He is not solely impelled by necessity to artifice and dissimulation, he has a natural inclination for crooked ways; he is a hypocrite towards himself; his far-fetched scruples are often mere pretexts to cover his want of determination: thoughts, as he says on a different occasion, which have

----but one part wisdom
And ever three parts coward.-----

He has been chiefly condemned both for his harshness in repulsing the love of Ophelia, which he himself had cherished, and for his insensibility at her death. But he is too much overwhelmed with his own sorrow to have any compassion to spare for others; besides his outward indifference gives us by no means the measure of his internal perturbation. On the other hand, we evidently perceive in him a malicious joy, when he has succeeded in getting rid of his enemies, more through necessity and accident, which alone are able to impel him to quick and decisive measures, than by the merit of his own courage, as he himself confesses after the murder of Polonius, and with respect to Rosencrantz and Guildenstern. Hamlet has no firm belief either in himself or in anything else: from expressions of religious confidence he passes over to sceptical doubts; he believes in the Ghost of his father as long as he sees it, but as soon as it has disappeared, it appears to him almost in the light of a deception. [Footnote: It has been censured as a contradiction, that Hamlet in the soliloquy on self-murder should say,

  The undiscover'd country, from whose bourn
  No traveller returns-----

For was not the Ghost a returned traveller? Shakspeare, however, purposely wished to show, that Hamlet could not fix himself in any conviction of any kind whatever.] He has even gone so far as to say, "there is nothing either good or bad, but thinking makes it so;" with him the poet loses himself here in labyrinths of thought, in which neither end nor beginning is discoverable. The stars themselves, from the course of events, afford no answer to the question so urgently proposed to them. A voice from another world, commissioned it would appear, by heaven, demands vengeance for a monstrous enormity, and the demand remains without effect; the criminals are at last punished, but, as it were, by an accidental blow, and not in the solemn way requisite to convey to the world a warning example of justice; irresolute foresight, cunning treachery, and impetuous rage, hurry on to a common destruction; the less guilty and the innocent are equally involved in the general ruin. The destiny of humanity is there exhibited as a gigantic Sphinx, which threatens to precipitate into the abyss of scepticism all who are unable to solve her dreadful enigmas.

As one example of the many niceties of Shakspeare which have never been understood, I may allude to the style in which the player's speech about Hecuba is conceived. It has been the subject of much controversy among the commentators, whether this was borrowed by Shakspeare from himself or from another, and whether, in the praise of the piece of which it is supposed to be a part, he was speaking seriously, or merely meant to ridicule the tragical bombast of his contemporaries. It seems never to have occurred to them that this speech must not be judged of by itself, but in connexion with the place where it is introduced. To distinguish it in the play itself as dramatic poetry, it was necessary that it should rise above the dignified poetry of the former in the same proportion that generally theatrical elevation soars above simple nature. Hence Shakspeare has composed the play in Hamlet altogether in sententious rhymes full of antitheses. But this solemn and measured tone did not suit a speech in which violent emotion ought to prevail, and the poet had no other expedient than the one of which he made choice: overcharging the pathos. The language of the speech in question is certainly falsely emphatical; but yet this fault is so mixed up with true grandeur, that a player practised in artificially calling forth in himself the emotion he is imitating, may certainly be carried away by it. Besides, it will hardly be believed that Shakspeare knew so little of his art, as not to be aware that a tragedy in which Aeneas had to make a lengthy epic relation of a transaction that happened so long before as the destruction of Troy, could neither be dramatical nor theatrical.

Of *Macbeth* I have already spoken once in passing, and who could exhaust the praises of this sublime work? Since *The Eumenides* of Aeschylus, nothing so grand and terrible has ever been written. The witches are not, it is true, divine Eumenides, and are not intended to be: they are ignoble and vulgar instruments of hell. A German poet, therefore, very ill understood their meaning, when he transformed them into mongrel beings, a mixture of fates, furies, and enchantresses, and clothed them with tragic dignity. Let no man venture to lay hand on Shakspeare's works thinking to improve anything essential: he will be sure to punish himself. The bad is radically odious, and to endeavour in any manner to ennoble it, is to violate the laws of propriety. Hence, in my opinion, Dante, and even Tasso, have been much more successful in their portraiture of daemons than Milton. Whether the age of Shakspeare still believed in ghosts and witches, is a matter of perfect indifference for the justification of the use which in *Hamlet* and *Macbeth* he has made of pre-existing traditions.

No superstition can be widely diffused without having a foundation in human nature: on this the poet builds; he calls up from their hidden abysses that dread of the unknown, that presage of a dark side of nature, and a world of spirits, which philosophy now imagines it has altogether exploded. In this manner he is in some degree both the portrayer and the philosopher of superstition; that is, not the philosopher who denies and turns it into ridicule, but, what is still more difficult, who distinctly exhibits its origin in apparently irrational and yet natural opinions. But when he ventures to make arbitrary changes in these popular traditions, he altogether forfeits his right to them, and merely holds up his own idle fancies to our ridicule. Shakspeare's picture of the witches is truly magical: in the short scenes where they enter, he has created for them a peculiar language, which, although composed of the usual elements, still seems to be a collection of formulae of incantation. The sound of the words, the accumulation of rhymes, and the rhythmus of the verse, form, as it were, the hollow music of a dreary witch-dance. He has been abused for using the names of disgusting objects; but he who fancies the kettle of the witches can be made effective with agreeable aromatics, is as wise as those who desire that hell should sincerely and honestly give good advice. These repulsive things, from which the imagination shrinks, are here emblems of the hostile powers which operate in nature; and the repugnance of our senses is outweighed by the mental horror. With one another the witches discourse like women of the very lowest class; for this was the class to which witches were ordinarily supposed to belong: when, however, they address Macbeth they assume a loftier tone: their predictions, which they either themselves pronounce, or allow their apparitions to deliver, have all the obscure brevity, the majestic solemnity of oracles.

We here see that the witches are merely instruments; they are governed by an invisible spirit, or the operation of such great and dreadful events would be above their sphere. With what intent did Shakspeare assign the same place to them in his play, which they occupy in the history of Macbeth as related in the old chronicles? A monstrous crime is committed: Duncan, a venerable old man, and the best of kings, is, in defenceless sleep, under the hospitable roof, murdered by his subject, whom he has loaded with honours and rewards. Natural motives alone seem inadequate, or the perpetrator must have been portrayed as a hardened villain. Shakspeare wished to exhibit a more sublime picture: an ambitious but noble hero, yielding to a deep-laid hellish temptation; and in whom all the crimes to which, in order to secure the fruits of his first crime, he is impelled by necessity, cannot altogether eradicate the stamp of native heroism. He has, therefore, given a threefold division to the guilt of that crime. The first idea comes from that being whose whole activity is guided by a lust of wickedness. The weird sisters surprise Macbeth in the moment of intoxication of victory, when his love of glory has been gratified; they cheat his eyes by exhibiting to him as the work of fate what in reality can only be accomplished by his own deed, and gain credence for all their words by the immediate fulfilment of the first prediction. The opportunity of murdering the King immediately offers; the wife of Macbeth conjures him not to let it slip; she urges him on with a fiery eloquence, which has at command all those sophisms that serve to throw a false splendour over crime. Little more than the mere execution falls to the share of Macbeth; he is driven into it, as it were, in a tumult of fascination. Repentance immediately follows, nay, even precedes the deed, and the stings of conscience leave him rest neither night nor day. But he is now fairly entangled in the snares of hell; truly frightful is it to behold that same Macbeth, who once as a warrior could spurn at death, now that he dreads the prospect of the life to come [Footnote: We'd jump the life to come.], clinging with growing anxiety to his earthly existence the more miserable it becomes, and pitilessly removing out of the way whatever to his dark and suspicious mind seems to threaten danger. However much we may abhor his actions, we cannot altogether refuse to compassionate the state of his mind; we lament the ruin of so many noble qualities, and even in his last defence we are compelled to admire the struggle of a brave will with a cowardly conscience. We might believe that we witness in this tragedy the over-ruling destiny of the ancients represented in perfect accordance with their ideas: the whole originates in a supernatural influence, to which the subsequent events seem inevitably linked. Moreover, we even find here the same ambiguous oracles which, by their literal fulfilment, deceive those who confide in them. Yet it may be easily shown that the poet has, in his work, displayed more enlightened views. He wishes to show that the conflict of good and evil in this world can only take place by the permission of Providence, which converts the curse that individual mortals draw down on their heads into a blessing to others. An accurate scale is followed in the retaliation. Lady Macbeth, who of all the human participators in the king's murder is the most guilty, is thrown by the terrors of her conscience into a state of incurable bodily and mental disease; she dies, unlamented by her husband, with all the symptoms of reprobation. Macbeth is still found worthy to die the death of a hero on the field of battle. The noble Macduff is allowed the satisfaction of saving his country by punishing with his own hand the tyrant who had murdered his wife and children. Banquo, by an early death, atones for the ambitious curiosity which prompted the wish to know his glorious descendants, as he thereby has roused Macbeth's jealousy; but he preserved his mind pure from the evil suggestions of the witches: his name is blessed in his race, destined to enjoy for a long succession of ages that royal dignity which Macbeth could only hold for his own life. In the progress of the action, this piece is altogether the reverse of *Hamlet*: it strides forward with amazing rapidity, from the first catastrophe (for Duncan's murder may be called a catastrophe) to the last. "Thought, and done!" is the general motto; for as Macbeth says,

The flighty purpose never is o'ertook,
Unless the deed go with it.

In every feature we see an energetic heroic age, in the hardy North which steels every nerve. The precise duration of the action cannot be ascertained,--years perhaps, according to the story; but we know that to the imagination the most crowded time appears always the shortest. Here we can hardly conceive how so very much could ever have been compressed into so narrow a space; not merely external events,--the very inmost recesses in the minds of the dramatic personages are laid open to us. It is as if the drags were taken from the wheels of time, and they rolled along without interruption in their descent. Nothing can equal this picture in its power to excite terror. We need only allude to the circumstances attending the murder of Duncan, the dagger that hovers before the eyes of Macbeth, the vision of Banquo at the feast, the madness of Lady Macbeth; what can possibly be said on the subject that will not rather weaken the impression they naturally leave? Such scenes stand alone, and are to be found only in this poet; otherwise the tragic muse might exchange her mask for the *head of Medusa*.

I wish merely to point out as a secondary circumstance the prudent dexterity of Shakspeare, who could still contrive to flatter a king by a work in every part of whose plan nevertheless the poetical views are evident. James the First drew his lineage from Banquo; he was the first who united the threefold sceptre of England, Scotland, and Ireland: this is foreshown in the magical vision, when a long series of glorious successors is promised to Banquo. Even the gift of the English kings to heal certain maladies by the touch, which James pretended to have inherited from Edward [Footnote: The naming of Edward the Confessor gives us at the same time the epoch in which these historically accredited transactions are made to take place. The ruins of Macbeth's palace are yet standing at Inverness; the present Earls of Fife are the descendants of the valiant Macduff, and down to the union of Scotland with England they were in the enjoyment of peculiar privileges for their services to the crown.] the Confessor, and on which he set a great value, is brought in very naturally.--With such occasional matters we may well allow ourselves to be pleased without fearing from them any danger to poetry: by similar allusions Aeschylus endeavoured to recommend the Areopagus to his fellow-citizens, and Sophocles to celebrate the glory of Athens.

As in *Macbeth* terror reaches its utmost height, in *King Lear* the science of compassion is exhausted. The principal characters here are not those who act, but those who suffer. We have not in this, as in most tragedies, the picture of a calamity in which the sudden blows of fate seem still to honour the head which they strike, and where the loss is always accompanied by some flattering consolation in the memory of the former possession; but a fall from the highest elevation into the deepest abyss of misery, where humanity is stripped of all external and internal advantages, and given up a prey to naked helplessness. The threefold dignity of a king, an old man, and a father, is dishonoured by the cruel ingratitude of his unnatural daughters; the old Lear, who out of a foolish tenderness has given away every thing, is driven out to the world a wandering beggar; the childish imbecility to which he was fast advancing changes into the wildest insanity, and when he is rescued from the disgraceful destitution to which he was abandoned, it is too late: the kind consolations of filial care and attention and of true friendship are now lost on him; his bodily and mental powers are destroyed beyond all hope of recovery, and all that now remains to him of life is the capability of loving and suffering beyond measure. What a picture we have in the meeting of Lear and Edgar in a tempestuous night and in a wretched hovel! The youthful Edgar has, by the wicked arts of his brother, and through his father's blindness, fallen, as the old Lear, from the rank to which his birth entitled him; and, as the only means of escaping further persecution, is reduced to assume the disguise of a beggar tormented by evil spirits. The King's fool, notwithstanding the voluntary degradation which is implied in his situation, is, after Kent, Lear's most faithful associate, his wisest counsellor. This good-hearted fool clothes reason with the livery of his motley garb; the high-born beggar acts the part of insanity; and both, were they even in reality what they seem, would still be enviable in comparison with the King, who feels that the violence of his grief threatens to overpower his reason. The meeting of Edgar with the blinded Gloster is equally heart-rending; nothing can be more affecting than to see the ejected son become the father's guide, and the good angel, who under the disguise of insanity, saves him by an ingenious and pious fraud from the horror and despair of self-murder. But who can possibly enumerate all the different combinations and situations by which our minds are here as it were stormed by the poet? Respecting the structure of the whole I will only make one observation. The story of Lear and his daughters was left by Shakspeare exactly as he found it in a fabulous tradition, with all the features characteristical of the simplicity of old times. But in that tradition there is not the slightest trace of the story of Gloster and his sons, which was derived by Shakspeare from another source. The incorporation of the two stories has been censured as destructive of the unity of action. But whatever contributes to the intrigue or the *denouement* must always possess unity. And with what ingenuity and skill are the two main parts of the composition dovetailed into one another! The pity felt by Gloster for the fate of Lear becomes the means which enables his son Edmund to effect his complete destruction, and affords the outcast Edgar an opportunity of being the saviour of his father. On the other hand, Edmund is active in the cause of Regan and Gonerill, and the criminal passion which they both entertain for him induces them to execute justice on each other and on themselves. The laws of the drama have therefore been sufficiently complied with; but that is the least: it is the very combination which constitutes the sublime beauty of the work. The two cases resembles each other in the main: an infatuated father is blind towards his well-disposed child, and the unnatural children, whom he prefers, requite him by the ruin of all his happiness. But all the circumstances are so different, that these stories, while they each make a correspondent impression on the heart, form a complete contrast for the imagination. Were Lear alone to suffer from his daughters, the impression would be limited to the powerful compassion felt by us for his private misfortune. But two such unheard-of examples taking place at the same time have the appearance of a great commotion in the moral world: the picture becomes gigantic, and fills us with such alarm as we should entertain at the idea that the heavenly bodies might one day fall from their appointed orbits. To save in some degree the honour of human nature, Shakspeare never wishes his spectators to forget that the story takes place in a dreary and barbarous age: he lays particular stress on the circumstance that the Britons of that day were still heathens, although he has not made all the remaining circumstances to coincide learnedly with the time which he has chosen. From this point of view we must judge of many coarsenesses in expression and manners; for instance, the immodest manner in which Gloster acknowledges his bastard, Kent's quarrel with the Steward, and more especially the cruelty personally inflicted on Gloster by the Duke of Cornwall. Even the virtue of the honest Kent bears the stamp of an iron age, in which the good and the bad display the same uncontrollable energy. Great qualities have not been superfluously assigned to the King; the poet could command our sympathy for his situation, without concealing what he had done to bring himself into it. Lear is choleric, overbearing, and almost childish from age, when he drives out his youngest daughter because she will not join in the hypocritical exaggerations of her sisters. But he has a warm and affectionate heart, which is susceptible of the most fervent gratitude; and even rays of a high and kingly disposition burst forth from the eclipse of his understanding. Of Cordelia's heavenly beauty of soul, painted in so few words, I will not venture to speak; she can only be named in the same breath with Antigone. Her death has been thought too cruel; and in England the piece is in acting so far altered that she remains victorious and happy. I must own, I cannot conceive what ideas of art and dramatic connexion those persons have who suppose that we can at pleasure tack a double conclusion to a tragedy; a melancholy one for hard-hearted spectators, and a happy one for souls of a softer mould. After surviving so many sufferings, Lear can only die; and what more truly tragic end for him than to die from grief for the death of Cordelia? and if he is also to be saved and to pass the remainder of his days in happiness, the whole loses its signification. According to Shakspeare's plan the guilty, it is true, are all punished, for wickedness destroys itself; but the virtues that would bring help and succour are everywhere too late, or overmatched by the cunning activity of malice. The persons of this drama have only such a faint belief in Providence as heathens may be supposed to have; and the poet here wishes to show us that this belief requires a wider range than the dark pilgrimage on earth to be established in full extent.

LECTURE XXVI.

Criticisms on Shakspeare's Historical Dramas.

The five tragedies of which I have just spoken are deservedly the most celebrated of all the works of Shakspeare. In the three last, more especially, we have a display of a loftiness of genius which may almost be said to surpass the powers of human nature: the mind is as much lost in the contemplation of all the heights and depths of these works as our feelings are overpowered by the first impression which they produce. Of his historical plays, however, some possess a high degree of tragical perfection, and all are distinguished by peculiar excellencies.

In the three Roman pieces, *Coriolanus*, *Julius Caesar*, and *Antony and Cleopatra*, the moderation with which Shakspeare excludes foreign appendages and arbitrary suppositions, and yet fully satisfies the wants of the stage, is particularly deserving of admiration. These plays are the very thing itself; and under the apparent artlessness of adhering closely to history as he found it, an uncommon degree of art is concealed. Of every historical transaction Shakspeare knows how to seize the true poetical point of view, and to give unity and rounding to a series of events detached from the immeasurable extent of history without in any degree changing them. The public life of ancient Rome is called up from its grave, and exhibited before our eyes with the utmost grandeur and freedom of the dramatic form, and the heroes of Plutarch are ennobled by the most eloquent poetry.

In *Coriolanus* we have more comic intermixtures than in the others, as the many-headed multitude plays here a considerable part; and when Shakspeare portrays the blind movements of the people in a mass, he almost always gives himself up to his merry humour. To the plebeians, whose folly is certainly sufficiently conspicuous already, the original old satirist Menenius is added by way of abundance. Droll scenes arise of a description altogether peculiar, and which are compatible only with such a political drama; for instance, when Coriolanus, to obtain the consulate, must solicit the lower order of citizens whom he holds in contempt for their cowardice in war, but cannot so far master his haughty disposition as to assume the customary humility, and yet extorts from them their votes.

I have already shown [Footnote: Page 240.] that the piece of *Julius Caesar*, to complete the action, requires to be continued to the fall of Brutus and Cassius. Caesar is not the hero of the piece, but Brutus. The amiable beauty of this character, his feeling and patriotic heroism, are portrayed with peculiar care. Yet the poet has pointed out with great nicety the superiority of Cassius over Brutus in independent volition and discernment in judging of human affairs; that the latter from the purity of his mind and his conscientious love of justice, is unfit to be the head of a party in a state entirely corrupted; and that these very faults give an unfortunate turn to the cause of the conspirators. In the part of Caesar several ostentatious speeches have been censured as unsuitable. But as he never appears in action, we have no other measure of his greatness than the impression which he makes upon the rest of the characters, and his peculiar confidence in himself. In this Caesar was by no means deficient, as we learn from history and his own writings; but he displayed it more in the easy ridicule of his enemies than in pompous discourses. The theatrical effect of this play is injured by a partial falling off of the last two acts compared with the preceding in external splendour and rapidity. The first appearance of Caesar in festal robes, when the music stops, and all are silent whenever he opens his mouth, and when the few words which he utters are received as oracles, is truly magnificent; the conspiracy is a true conspiracy, which in stolen interviews and in the dead of night prepares the blow which is to be struck in open day, and which is to change the constitution of the world;--the confused thronging before the murder of Caesar, the general agitation even of the perpetrators after the deed, are all portrayed with most masterly skill; with the funeral procession and the speech of Antony the effect reaches its utmost height. Caesar's shade is more powerful to avenge his fall than he himself was to guard against it. After the overthrow of the external splendour and greatness of the conqueror and ruler of the world, the intrinsic grandeur of character of Brutus and Cassius is all that remain to fill the stage and occupy the minds of the spectators: suitably to their name, as the last of the Romans, they stand there, in some degree alone; and the forming a great and hazardous determination is more powerfully calculated to excite our expectation, than the supporting the consequences of the deed with heroic firmness.

Antony and Cleopatra may, in some measure, be considered as a continuation of *Julius Caesar*: the two principal characters of *Antony and Augustus* are equally sustained in both pieces. *Antony and Cleopatra*, is a play of great extent; the progress is less simple than in *Julius Caesar*. The fulness and variety of political and warlike events, to which the union of the three divisions of the Roman world under one master necessarily gave rise, were perhaps too great to admit of being clearly exhibited in one dramatic picture. In this consists the great difficulty of the historical drama:--it must be a crowded extract, and a living development of history;--the difficulty, however, has generally been successfully overcome by Shakspeare. But now many things, which are transacted in the background, are here merely alluded to, in a manner which supposes an intimate acquaintance with the history; but a work of art should contain, within itself, every thing necessary for its being fully understood. Many persons of historical importance are merely introduced in passing; the preparatory and concurring circumstances are not sufficiently collected into masses to avoid distracting our attention. The principal personages, however, are most emphatically distinguished by lineament and colouring, and powerfully arrest the imagination. In Antony we observe a mixture of great qualities, weaknesses, and vices; violent ambition and ebullitions of magnanimity; we see him now sinking into luxurious enjoyment and then nobly ashamed of his own aberrations,--manning himself to resolutions not unworthy of himself, which are always shipwrecked against the seductions of an artful woman. It is Hercules in the chains of Omphale, drawn from the fabulous heroic ages into history, and invested with the Roman costume. The seductive arts of Cleopatra are in no respect veiled over; she is an ambiguous being made up of royal pride, female vanity, luxury, inconstancy, and true attachment. Although the mutual passion of herself and Antony is without moral dignity, it still excites our sympathy as an insurmountable fascination:--they seem formed for each other, and Cleopatra is as remarkable for her seductive charms as Antony for the splendour of his deeds. As they die for each other, we forgive them for having lived for each other. The open and lavish character of Antony is admirably contrasted with the heartless littleness of Octavius, whom Shakspeare seems to have completely seen through, without allowing himself to be led astray by the fortune and the fame of Augustus.

Timon of Athens, and *Troilus and Cressida*, are not historical plays; but we cannot properly call them either tragedies or comedies. By the selection of the materials from antiquity they have some affinity to the Roman pieces, and hence I have hitherto abstained from mentioning them.

Timon of Athens, of all the works of Shakspeare, possesses most the character of satire:--a laughing satire in the picture of the parasites and flatterers, and Juvenalian in the bitterness of Timon's imprecations on the ingratitude of a false world. The story is very simply treated, and is definitely divided into large masses:--in the first act the joyous life of Timon, his noble and hospitable extravagance, and around him the throng of suitors of every description; in the second and third acts his embarrassment, and the trial which he is thereby reduced to make of his supposed friends, who all desert him in the hour of need;--in the fourth and fifth acts, Timon's flight to the woods, his misanthropical melancholy, and his death. The only thing which may be called an episode is the banishment of Alcibiades, and his return by force of arms. However, they are both examples of ingratitude,--the one of a state towards its defender, and the other of private friends to their benefactor. As the merits of the General towards his fellow-citizens suppose more strength of character than those of the generous prodigal, their respective behaviours are not less different; Timon frets himself to death, Alcibiades regains his lost dignity by force. If the poet very properly sides with Timon against the common practice of the world, he is, on the other hand, by no means disposed to spare Timon. Timon was a fool in his generosity; in his discontent he is a madman: he is every where wanting in the wisdom which enables a man in all things to observe the due measure. Although the truth of his extravagant feelings is proved by his death, and though when he digs up a treasure he spurns the wealth which seems to tempt him, we yet see distinctly enough that the vanity of wishing to be singular, in both the parts that he plays, had some share in his liberal self-forgetfulness, as well as in his anchoritical seclusion. This is particularly evident in the incomparable scene where the cynic Apemantus visits Timon in the wilderness. They have a sort of competition with each other in their trade of misanthropy: the Cynic reproaches the impoverished Timon with having been merely driven by necessity to take to the way of living which he himself had long been following of his free choice, and Timon cannot bear the thought of being merely an imitator of the Cynic. In such a subject as this the due effect could only be produced by an accumulation of similar features, still, in the variety of the shades, an amazing degree of understanding has been displayed by Shakspeare. What a powerfully diversified concert of flatteries and of empty testimonies of devotedness! It is highly amusing to see the suitors, whom the ruined circumstances of their patron had dispersed, immediately flock to him again when they learn that he has been revisited by fortune. On the other hand, in the speeches of Timon, after he is undeceived, all hostile figures of speech are exhausted,--it is a dictionary of eloquent imprecations.

Troilus and Cressida is the only play of Shakspeare which he allowed to be printed without being previously represented. It seems as if he here for once wished, without caring for theatrical effect, to satisfy the nicety of his peculiar wit, and the inclination to a certain guile, if I may say so, in the characterization. The whole is one continued irony of that crown of all heroic tales, the tale of Troy. The contemptible nature of the origin of the Trojan war, the laziness and discord with which it was carried on, so that the siege was made to last ten years, are only placed in clearer light by the noble descriptions, the sage and ingenious maxims with which the work overflows, and the high ideas which the heroes entertain of themselves and each other. Agamemnon's stately behaviour, Menelaus' irritation, Nestor's experience, Ulysses' cunning, are all productive of no effect; when they have at last arranged a single combat between the coarse braggart Ajax and Hector, the latter will not fight in good earnest, as Ajax is his cousin. Achilles is treated worst: after having long stretched himself out in arrogant idleness, and passed his time in the company of Thersites the buffoon, he falls upon Hector at a moment when he is defenceless, and kills him by means of his myrmidons. In all this let no man conceive that any indignity was intended to the venerable Homer. Shakspeare had not the *Iliad* before him, but the chivalrous romances of the Trojan war derived from *Dares Phrygius*. From this source also he took the love-intrigue of *Troilus and Cressida*, a story at one time so popular in England, that the name of Troilus had become proverbial for faithful and ill-requited love, and Cressida for female falsehood. The name of the agent between them, Pandarus, has even been adopted into the English language to signify those personages (*panders*) who dedicate themselves to similar services for inexperienced persons of both sexes. The endless contrivances of the courteous Pandarus to bring the two lovers together, who do not stand in need of him, as Cressida requires no seduction, are comic in the extreme. The manner in which this treacherous beauty excites while she refuses, and converts the virgin modesty which she pretends, into a means of seductive allurement, is portrayed in colours extremely elegant, though certainly somewhat voluptuous. Troilus, the pattern of lovers, looks patiently on, while his mistress enters into an intrigue with Diomed. No doubt, he swears that he will be revenged; but notwithstanding his violence in the fight next day, he does no harm to any one, and ends with only high-sounding threats. In a word, in this heroic comedy, where, from traditional fame, and the pomp of poetry, every thing seems to lay claim to admiration, Shakspeare did not wish that any room should be left, except, perhaps, in the character of Hector, for esteem and sympathy; but in this double meaning of the picture, he has afforded us the most choice entertainment.

The dramas derived from the English history, ten in number, form one of the most valuable of Shakspeare's works, and partly the fruit of his maturest age. I say advisedly *one* of his works, for the poet evidently intended them to form one great whole. It is, as it were, an historical heroic poem in the dramatic form, of which the separate plays constitute the rhapsodies. The principal features of the events are exhibited with such fidelity; their causes, and even their secret springs, are placed in such a clear light, that we may attain from them a knowledge of history in all its truth, while the living picture makes an impression on the imagination which can never be effaced. But this series of dramas is intended as the vehicle of a much higher and much more general instruction; it furnishes examples of the political course of the world, applicable to all times. This mirror of kings should be the manual of young princes; from it they may learn the intrinsic dignity of their hereditary vocation, but they will also learn from it the difficulties of their situation, the dangers of usurpation, the inevitable fall of tyranny, which buries itself under its attempts to obtain a firmer foundation; lastly, the ruinous consequences of the weaknesses, errors, and crimes of kings, for whole nations, and many subsequent generations. Eight of these plays, from *Richard the Second* to *Richard the Third*, are linked together in an uninterrupted succession, and embrace a most eventful period of nearly a century of English history. The events portrayed in them not only follow one another, but they are linked together in the closest and most exact connexion; and the cycle of revolts, parties, civil and foreign wars, which began with the deposition of Richard II., first ends with the accession of Henry VII. to the throne. The careless rule of the first of these monarchs, and his injudicious treatment of his own relations, drew upon him the rebellion of Bolingbroke; his dethronement, however, was, in point of form, altogether unjust, and in no case could Bolingbroke be considered the rightful heir to the crown. This shrewd founder of the House of Lancaster never as Henry IV. enjoyed in peace the fruits of his usurpation: his turbulent Barons, the same who aided him in ascending the throne, allowed him not a moment's repose upon it. On the other hand, he was jealous of the brilliant qualities of his son, and this distrust, more than any really low inclination, induced the Prince, that he might avoid every appearance of ambition, to give himself up to dissolute society. These two circumstances form the subject-matter of the two parts of *Henry the Fourth*; the enterprises of the discontented make up the serious, and the wild youthful frolics of the heir-apparent supply the comic scenes. When this warlike Prince ascended the throne under the name of Henry V., he was determined to assert his ambiguous title; he considered foreign conquests as the best means of guarding against internal disturbances, and this gave rise to the glorious, but more ruinous than profitable, war with France, which Shakspeare has celebrated in the drama of *Henry the Fifth*. The early death of this king, the long legal minority of Henry VI., and his perpetual minority in the art of government, brought the greatest troubles on England. The dissensions of the Regents, and the consequently wretched administration, occasioned the loss of the French conquests and there arose a bold candidate for the crown, whose title was indisputable, if the prescription of three governments may not be assumed to confer legitimacy on usurpation. Such was the origin of the wars between the Houses of York and Lancaster, which desolated the kingdom for a number of years, and ended with the victory of the House of York. All this Shakspeare has represented in the three parts of *Henry the Sixth*. Edward IV. shortened his life by excesses, and did not long enjoy the throne purchased at the expense of so many cruel deeds. His brother Richard, who had a great share in the elevation of the House of York, was not contented with the regency, and his ambition paved himself a way to the throne through treachery and violence; but his gloomy tyranny made him the object of the people's hatred, and at length drew on him the destruction which he merited. He was conquered by a descendant of the royal house unstained by the guilt of the civil wars, and what might seem defective in his title was made good by the merit of freeing his country from a monster. With the accession of Henry VII. to the throne, a new epoch of English history begins: the curse seemed at length to be expiated, and the long series of usurpations, revolts, and civil wars, occasioned by the levity with which the Second Richard sported away his crown, was now brought to a termination.

Such is the evident connexion of these eight plays with each other, but they were not, however, composed in chronological order. According to all appearance, the four last were first written; this is certain, indeed, with respect to the three parts of *Henry the Sixth*; and *Richard the Third* is not only from its subject a continuation of these, but is also composed in the same style. Shakspeare then went back to *Richard the Second*, and with the most careful art connected the second series with the first. The trilogies of the ancients have already given us an example of the possibility of forming a perfect dramatic whole, which shall yet contain allusions to something which goes before, and follows it. In like manner the most of these plays end with a very definite division in the history: *Richard the Second*, with the murder of that King; *the Second Part of Henry the Fourth*, with the accession of his son to the throne; *Henry the Fifth*, with the conclusion of peace with France; *the First Part of Henry the Sixth*, also, with a treaty of Peace; the third, with the murder of Henry, and Edward's elevation to the throne; *Richard the Third*, with his overthrow and death. *The First Part of Henry the Fourth*, and *the Second of Henry the Sixth*, are rounded off in a less satisfactory manner. The revolt of the nobles was only half quelled by the overthrow of Percy, and it is therefore continued through the following part of the piece. The victory of York at St. Alban's could as little be considered a decisive event, in the war of the two houses. Shakspeare has fallen into this dramatic imperfection, if we may so call it, for the sake of advantages of much more importance. The picture of the civil war was too great and too rich in dreadful events for a single drama, and yet the uninterrupted series of events offered no more convenient resting-place. The government of Henry IV. might certainly have been comprehended in one piece, but it possesses too little tragical interest, and too little historical splendour, to be attractive, if handled in a serious manner throughout: hence Shakspeare has given to the comic characters belonging to the retinue of Prince Henry, the freest development, and the half of the space is occupied by this constant interlude between the political events.

The two other historical plays taken from the English history are chronologically separate from this series: King John reigned nearly two centuries before Richard II., and between Richard III. and Henry VIII. comes the long reign of Henry VII., which Shakspeare justly passed over as unsusceptible of dramatic interest. However, these two plays may in some measure be considered as the Prologue and the Epilogue to the other eight. In *King John*, all the political and national motives which play so great a part in the following pieces are already indicated: wars and treaties with France; a usurpation, and the tyrannical actions which it draws after it; the influence of the clergy, the factions of the nobles. *Henry the Eighth* again shows us the transition to another age; the policy of modern Europe, a refined court-life under a voluptuous monarch, the dangerous situation of favourites, who, after having assisted in effecting the fall of others, are themselves precipitated from power; in a word, despotism under a milder form, but not less unjust and cruel. By the prophecies on the birth of Elizabeth, Shakspeare has in some degree brought his great poem on English history down to his own time, as far at least as such recent events could be yet handled with security. He composed probably the two plays of *King John* [Footnote: I mean the piece with this title in the collection of his works. There is an older *King John*, in two parts, of which the former is a re-cast:--perhaps a juvenile work of Shakspeare, though not hitherto acknowledged as such by the English critics. See the disquisition appended to this Lecture.] and *Henry the Eighth* at a later period, as an addition to the others.

In *King John* the political and warlike events are dressed out with solemn pomp, for the very reason that they possess but little of true grandeur. The falsehood and selfishness of the monarch speak in the style of a manifesto. Conventional dignity is most indispensable where personal dignity is wanting. The bastard Faulconbridge is the witty interpreter of this language: he ridicules the secret springs of politics, without disapproving of them, for he owns that he is endeavouring to make his fortune by similar means, and wishes rather to belong to the deceivers than the deceived, for in his view of the world there is no other choice. His litigation with his brother respecting the succession of his pretended father, by which he effects his acknowledgment at court as natural son of the most chivalrous king of England, Richard Coeur de Lion, forms a very entertaining and original prelude in the play itself. When, amidst so many disguises of real sentiments, and so much insincerity of expression, the poet shows us human nature without a veil, and allows us to take deep views of the inmost recesses of the mind, the impression produced is only the more deep and powerful. The short scene in which John urges Hubert to put out of the way Arthur, his young rival for the possession of the throne, is superlatively masterly: the cautious criminal hardly ventures to say to himself what he wishes the other to do. The young and amiable prince becomes a sacrifice of unprincipled ambition: his fate excites the warmest sympathy. When Hubert, about to put out his eyes with the hot iron, is softened by his prayers, our compassion would be almost overwhelming, were it not sweetened by the winning innocence of Arthur's childish speeches. Constance's maternal despair on her son's imprisonment is also of the highest beauty; and even the last moments of John--an unjust and feeble prince, whom we can neither respect nor admire--are yet so portrayed as to extinguish our displeasure with him, and fill us with serious considerations on the arbitrary deeds and the inevitable fate of mortals.

In *Richard the Second*, Shakspeare exhibits a noble kingly nature, at first obscured by levity and the errors of an unbridled youth, and afterwards purified by misfortune, and rendered by it more highly and splendidly illustrious. When he has lost the love and reverence of his subjects, and is on the point of losing also his throne, he then feels with a bitter enthusiasm the high vocation of the kingly dignity and its transcendental rights, independent of personal merit or changeable institutions. When the earthly crown is fallen from his head, he first appears a king whose innate nobility no humiliation can annihilate. This is felt by a poor groom: he is shocked that his master's favourite horse should have carried the proud Bolingbroke to his coronation; he visits the captive king in prison, and shames the desertion of the great. The political incident of the deposition is sketched with extraordinary knowledge of the world;--the ebb of fortune, on the one hand, and on the other, the swelling tide, which carries every thing along with it. While Bolingbroke acts as a king, and his adherents behave towards him as if he really were so, he still continues to give out that he has come with an armed band merely to demand his birthright and the removal of abuses. The usurpation has been long completed, before the word is pronounced and the thing publicly avowed. The old John of Gaunt is a model of chivalrous honour: he stands there like a pillar of the olden time which he has outlived. His son, Henry IV., was altogether unlike him: his character is admirably sustained throughout the three pieces in which he appears. We see in it that mixture of hardness, moderation, and prudence, which, in fact, enabled him to secure the possession of the throne which he had violently usurped; but without openness, without true cordiality, and incapable of noble ebullitions, he was so little able to render his government beloved, that the deposed Richard was even wished back again.

The first part of *Henry the Fourth* is particularly brilliant in the serious scenes, from the contrast between two young heroes, Prince Henry and Percy (with the characteristical name of Hotspur.) All the amiability and attractiveness is certainly on the side of the prince: however familiar he makes himself with bad company, we can never mistake him for one of them: the ignoble does indeed touch, but it does not contaminate him; and his wildest freaks appear merely as witty tricks, by which his restless mind sought to burst through the inactivity to which he was constrained, for on the first occasion which wakes him out of his unruly levity he distinguishes himself without effort in the most chivalrous guise. Percy's boisterous valour is not without a mixture of rude manners, arrogance, and boyish obstinacy; but these errors, which prepare for him an early death, cannot disfigure the majestic image of his noble youth; we are carried away by his fiery spirit at the very moment we would most censure it. Shakspeare has admirably shown why so formidable a revolt against an unpopular and really an illegitimate prince was not attended with success: Glendower's superstitious fancies respecting himself, the effeminacy of the young Mortimer, the ungovernable disposition of Percy, who will listen to no prudent counsel, the irresolution of his older friends, the want of unity of plan and motive, are all characterized by delicate but unmistakable traits. After Percy has departed from the scene, the splendour of the enterprise is, it is true, at an end; there remain none but the subordinate participators in the revolts, who are reduced by Henry IV., more by policy than by warlike achievements. To overcome this dearth of matter, Shakspeare was in the second part obliged to employ great art, as he never allowed himself to adorn history with more arbitrary embellishments than the dramatic form rendered indispensable. The piece is opened by confused rumours from the field of battle; the powerful impression produced by Percy's fall, whose name and reputation were peculiarly adapted to be the watchword of a bold enterprise, make him in some degree an acting personage after his death. The last acts are occupied with the dying king's remorse of conscience, his uneasiness at the behaviour of the prince, and lastly, the clearing up of the misunderstanding between father and son, which make up several most affecting scenes. All this, however, would still be inadequate to fill the stage, if the serious events were not interrupted by a comedy which runs through both parts of the play, which is enriched from time to time with new figures, and which first comes to its catastrophe at the conclusion of the whole, namely, when Henry V., immediately after ascending the throne, banishes to a proper distance the companions of his youthful excesses, who had promised to themselves a rich harvest from his kingly favour.

Falstaff is the crown of Shakspeare's comic invention. He has, without exhausting himself, continued this character throughout three plays, and exhibited him in every variety of situation; the figure is drawn so definitely and individually, that even to the mere reader it conveys the clear impression of personal acquaintance. Falstaff is the most agreeable and entertaining knave that ever was portrayed. His contemptible qualities are not disguised: old, lecherous, and dissolute; corpulent beyond measure, and always intent upon cherishing his body with eating, drinking, and sleeping; constantly in debt, and anything but conscientious in his choice of means by which money is to be raised; a cowardly soldier, and a lying braggart; a flatterer of his friends before their face, and a satirist behind their backs; and yet we are never disgusted with him. We see that his tender care of himself is without any mixture of malice towards others; he will only not be disturbed in the pleasant repose of his sensuality, and this he obtains through the activity of his understanding. Always on the alert, and good-humoured, ever ready to crack jokes on others, and to enter into those of which he is himself the subject, so that he justly boasts he is not only witty himself, but the cause of wit in others, he is an admirable companion for youthful idleness and levity. Under a helpless exterior, he conceals an extremely acute mind; he has always at command some dexterous turn whenever any of his free jokes begin to give displeasure; he is shrewd in his distinctions, between those whose favour he has to win and those over whom he may assume a familiar authority. He is so convinced that the part which he plays can only pass under the cloak of wit, that even when alone he is never altogether serious, but gives the drollest colouring to his love-intrigues, his intercourse with others, and to his own sensual philosophy. Witness his inimitable soliloquies on honour, on the influence of wine on bravery, his descriptions of the beggarly vagabonds whom he enlisted, of Justice Shallow, &c. Falstaff has about him a whole court of amusing caricatures, who by turns make their appearance, without ever throwing him into the shade. The adventure in which the Prince, under the disguise of a robber, compels him to give up the spoil which he had just taken; the scene where the two act the part of the King and the Prince; Falstaff's behaviour in the field, his mode of raising recruits, his patronage of Justice Shallow, which afterwards takes such an unfortunate turn:--all this forms a series of characteristic scenes of the most original description, full of pleasantry, and replete with nice and ingenious observation, such as could only find a place in a historical play like the present.

Several of the comic parts of *Henry the Fourth*, are continued in *The Merry Wives of Windsor*. This piece is said to have been composed by Shakspeare, in compliance with the request of Queen Elizabeth, [Footnote: We know with certainty, that it was acted before the Queen. Many local descriptions of Windsor and its neighbourhood, and an allusion in which the Order of the Garter is very poetically celebrated, make it credible that the play was destined to be first represented on the occasion of some festival of the Order at the palace of Windsor, where the Knights of the Garter have their hall of meeting.] who admired the character of Falstaff, and wished to see him exhibited once more, and in love. In love, properly speaking, Falstaff could not be; but for other purposes he could pretend to be so, and at all events imagine that he was the object of love. In the present piece accordingly he pays his court, as a favoured Knight, to two married ladies, who lay their heads together and agree to listen apparently to his addresses, for the sake of making him the butt of their just ridicule. The whole plan of the intrigue is therefore derived from the ordinary circle of Comedy, but yet richly and artificially interwoven with another love affair. The circumstance which has been so much admired in Moliere's *School of Women*, that a jealous individual should be made the constant confidant of his rival's progress, had previously been introduced into this play, and certainly with much more probability. I would not, however, be understood as maintaining that it was the original invention of Shakspeare: it is one of those circumstances which must almost be considered as part of the common stock of Comedy, and everything depends on the delicacy and humour with which it is used. That Falstaff should fall so repeatedly into the snare gives us a less favourable opinion of his shrewdness than the foregoing pieces had led us to form; still it will not be thought improbable, if once we admit the probability of the first infatuation on which the whole piece is founded, namely, that he can believe himself qualified to inspire a passion. This leads him, notwithstanding his age, his corpulency, and his dislike of personal inconveniences and dangers, to venture on an enterprise which requires the boldness and activity of youth; and the situations occasioned by this infatuation are droll beyond all description. Of all Shakspeare's pieces, this approaches the nearest to the species of pure Comedy: it is exclusively confined to the English manners of the day, and to the domestic relations; the characters are almost all comic, and the dialogue, with the exception of a couple of short love scenes, is written in prose. But we see that it was a point of principle with Shakspeare to make none of his compositions a mere imitation of the prosaic world, and to strip them of all poetical decoration: accordingly he has elevated the conclusion of the comedy by a wonderful intermixture, which suited the place where it was probably first represented. A popular superstition is made the means of a fanciful mystification [Footnote: This word is French; but it has lately been adopted by some English writers.--TRANS.] of Falstaff; disguised as the Ghost of a Hunter who, with ragged horns, wanders about in the woods of Windsor, he is to wait for his frolicsome mistress; in this plight he is surprised by a chorus of boys and girls disguised like fairies, who, agreeably to the popular belief, are holding their midnight dances, and who sing a merry song as they pinch and torture him. This is the last affront put upon poor Falstaff; and with this contrivance the conclusion of the second love affair is made in a most ingenious manner to depend.

King Henry the Fifth is manifestly Shakspeare's favourite hero in English history: he paints him as endowed with every chivalrous and kingly virtue; open, sincere, affable, yet, as a sort of reminiscence of his youth, still disposed to innocent raillery, in the intervals between his perilous but glorious achievements. However, to represent on the stage his whole history subsequent to his accession to the throne, was attended with great difficulty. The conquests in France were the only distinguished event of his reign; and war is an epic rather than a dramatic object. For wherever men act in masses against each other, the appearance of chance can never wholly be avoided; whereas it is the business of the drama to exhibit to us those determinations which, with a certain necessity, issue from the reciprocal relations of different individuals, their characters and passions. In several of the Greek tragedies, it is true, combats and battles are exhibited, that is, the preparations for them and their results; and in historical plays war, as the *ultima ratio regum*, cannot altogether be excluded. Still, if we would have dramatic interest, war must only be the means by which something else is accomplished, and not the last aim and substance of the whole. For instance, in *Macbeth*, the battles which are announced at the very beginning merely serve to heighten the glory of Macbeth and to fire his ambition; and the combats which take place towards the conclusion, before the eyes of the spectator, bring on the destruction of the tyrant. It is the very same in the Roman pieces, in the most of those taken from English history, and, in short, wherever Shakspeare has introduced war in a dramatic combination. With great insight into the essence of his art, he never paints the fortune of war as a blind deity who sometimes favours one and sometimes another; without going into the details of the art of war, (though sometimes he even ventures on this), he allows us to anticipate the result from the qualities of the general, and their influence on the minds of the soldiers; sometimes, without claiming our belief for miracles, he yet exhibits the issue in the light of a higher volition: the consciousness of a just cause and reliance on the protection of Heaven give courage to the one party, while the presage of a curse hanging over their undertaking weighs down the other. [Footnote: Aeschylus, with equal wisdom, in the uniformly warlike tragedy of the *Seven before Thebes*, has given to the Theban chiefs foresight, determination, and presence of mind; to their adversaries, arrogant audacity. Hence all the combats, excepting that between Eteocles and Polynices, turn out in favour of the former. The paternal curse, and the blindness to which it gives rise, carry headlong the two brothers to the unnatural strife in which they both fall by the hands of each other.--See page 91.] In *Henry the Fifth*, no opportunity was afforded Shakspeare of adopting the last-mentioned course, namely, rendering the issue of the war dramatic; but he has skilfully availed himself of the first.--Before the battle of Agincourt he paints in the most lively colours the light-minded impatience of the French leaders for the moment of battle, which to them seemed infallibly the moment of victory; on the other hand, he paints the uneasiness of the English King and his army in their desperate situation, coupled with their firm determination, if they must fall, at least to fall with honour. He applies this as a general contrast between the French and English national characters; a contrast which betrays a partiality for his own nation, certainly excusable in a poet, especially when he is backed with such a glorious document as that of the memorable battle in question.

He has surrounded the general events of the war with a fulness of individual, characteristic, and even sometimes comic features. A heavy Scotchman, a hot Irishman, a well-meaning, honourable, but pedantic Welchman, all speaking in their peculiar dialects, are intended to show us that the warlike genius of Henry did not merely carry the English with him, but also the other natives of the two islands, who were either not yet fully united or in no degree subject to him. Several good-for-nothing associates of Falstaff among the dregs of the army either afford an opportunity for proving Henry's strictness of discipline, or are sent home in disgrace. But all this variety still seemed to the poet insufficient to animate a play of which the subject was a conquest, and nothing but a conquest. He has, therefore, tacked a prologue (in the technical language of that day a *chorus*) to the beginning of each act. These prologues, which unite epic pomp and solemnity with lyrical sublimity, and among which the description of the two camps before the battle of Agincourt forms a most admirable night-piece, are intended to keep the spectators constantly in mind, that the peculiar grandeur of the actions described cannot be developed on a narrow stage, and that they must, therefore, supply, from their own imaginations, the deficiencies of the representation. As the matter was not properly dramatic, Shakspeare chose to wander in the form also beyond the bounds of the species, and to sing, as a poetical herald, what he could not represent to the eye, rather than to cripple the progress of the action by putting long descriptions in the mouths of the dramatic personages. The confession of the poet that "four or five most vile and ragged foils, right ill disposed, can only disgrace the name of Agincourt," (a scruple which he has overlooked in the occasion of many other great battles, and among others of that of Philippi,) brings us here naturally to the question how far, generally speaking, it may be suitable and advisable to represent wars and battles on the stage. The Greeks have uniformly renounced them: as in the whole of their theatrical system they proceeded on ideas of grandeur and dignity, a feeble and petty imitation of the unattainable would have appeared insupportable in their eyes. With them, consequently, all fighting was merely recounted. The principle of the romantic dramatists was altogether different: their wonderful pictures were infinitely larger than their theatrical means of visible execution; they were every where obliged to count on the willing imagination of the spectators, and consequently they also relied on them in this point. It is certainly laughable enough that a handful of awkward warriors in mock armour, by means of two or three swords, with which we clearly see they take especial care not to do the slightest injury to one another, should decide the fate of mighty kingdoms. But the opposite extreme is still much worse. If we in reality succeed in exhibiting the tumult of a great battle, the storming of a fort, and the like, in a manner any way calculated to deceive the eye, the power of these sensible impressions is so great that they render the spectator incapable of bestowing that attention which a poetical work of art demands; and thus the essential is sacrificed to the accessory. We have learned from experience, that whenever cavalry combats are introduced the men soon become secondary personages beside the four-footed players [Footnote: The Greeks, it is true, brought horses on the tragic stage, but only in solemn processions, not in the wild disorder of a fight. Agamemnon and Pallas, in Aeschylus, make their appearance drawn in a chariot with four horses. But their theatres were built on a scale very different from ours.]. Fortunately, in Shakspeare's time, the art of converting the yielding boards of the theatre into a riding course had not yet been invented. He tells the spectators in the first prologue in *Henry the Fifth*:--

Think, when we talk of horses, that you see them
Printing their proud hoofs in the receiving earth.

When Richard the Third utters the famous exclamation,--

A horse! a horse! my kingdom for a horse!

it is no doubt inconsistent to see him both before and afterwards constantly fighting on foot. It is however better, perhaps, that the poet and player should by overpowering impressions dispose us to forget this, than by literal exactness to expose themselves to external interruptions. With all the disadvantages which I have mentioned, Shakspeare and several Spanish poets have contrived to derive such great beauties from the immediate representation of war, that I cannot bring myself to wish they had abstained from it. A theatrical manager of the present day will have a middle course to follow: his art must, in an especial manner, be directed to make what he shows us appear only as separate groups of an immense picture, which cannot be taken in at once by the eye; he must convince the spectators that the main action takes place behind the stage; and for this purpose he has easy means at his command in the nearer or more remote sound of warlike music and the din of arms.

However much Shakspeare celebrates the French conquest of Henry, still he has not omitted to hint, after his way, the secret springs of this undertaking. Henry was in want of foreign war to secure himself on the throne; the clergy also wished to keep him employed abroad, and made an offer of rich contributions to prevent the passing of a law which would have deprived them of the half of their revenues. His learned bishops consequently are as ready to prove to him his indisputable right to the crown of France, as he is to allow his conscience to be tranquillized by them. They prove that the Salic law is not, and never was, applicable to France; and the matter is treated in a more succinct and convincing manner than such subjects usually are in manifestoes. After his renowned battles,

Henry wished to secure his conquests by marriage with a French princess; all that has reference to this is intended for irony in the play. The fruit of this union, from which two nations promised to themselves such happiness in future, was the weak and feeble Henry VI., under whom every thing was so miserably lost. It must not, therefore, be imagined that it was without the knowledge and will of the poet that a heroic drama turns out a comedy in his hands, and ends in the manner of Comedy with a marriage of convenience.

The three parts of *Henry the Sixth*, as I have already remarked, were composed much earlier than the preceding pieces. Shakspeare's choice fell first on this period of English history, so full of misery and horrors of every kind, because the pathetic is naturally more suitable than the characteristic to a young poet's mind. We do not yet find here the whole maturity of his genius, yet certainly its whole strength. Careless as to the apparent unconnectedness of contemporary events, he bestows little attention on preparation and development: all the figures follow in rapid succession, and announce themselves emphatically for what we ought to take them; from scenes where the effect is sufficiently agitating to form the catastrophe of a less extensive plan, the poet perpetually hurries us on to catastrophes still more dreadful. The First Part contains only the first forming of the parties of the White and Red Rose, under which blooming ensigns such bloody deeds were afterwards perpetrated; the varying results of the war in France principally fill the stage. The wonderful saviour of her country, Joan of Arc, is portrayed by Shakspeare with an Englishman's prejudices: yet he at first leaves it doubtful whether she has not in reality a heavenly mission; she appears in the pure glory of virgin heroism; by her supernatural eloquence (and this circumstance is of the poet's invention) she wins over the Duke of Burgundy to the French cause; afterwards, corrupted by vanity and luxury, she has recourse to hellish fiends, and comes to a miserable end. To her is opposed Talbot, a rough iron warrior, who moves us the more powerfully as, in the moment when he is threatened with inevitable death, all his care is tenderly directed to save his son, who performs his first deeds of arms under his eye. After Talbot has in vain sacrificed himself, and the Maid of Orleans has fallen into the hands of the English, the French provinces are completely lost by an impolitic marriage; and with this the piece ends. The conversation between the aged Mortimer in prison, and Richard Plantagenet, afterwards Duke of York, contains an exposition of the claims of the latter to the throne: considered by itself it is a beautiful tragic elegy.

In the Second Part, the events more particularly prominent are the murder of the honest Protector, Gloster, and its consequences; the death of Cardinal Beaufort; the parting of the Queen from her favourite Suffolk, and his death by the hand of savage pirates; then the insurrection of Jack Cade under an assumed name, and at the instigation of the Duke of York. The short scene where Cardinal Beaufort, who is tormented by his conscience on account of the murder of Gloster, is visited on his death-bed by Henry VI. is sublime beyond all praise. Can any other poet be named who has drawn aside the curtain of eternity at the close of this life with such overpowering and awful effect? And yet it is not mere horror with which the mind is filled, but solemn emotion; a blessing and a curse stand side by side; the pious King is an image of the heavenly mercy which, even in the sinner's last moments, labours to enter into his soul. The adulterous passion of Queen Margaret and Suffolk is invested with tragical dignity and all low and ignoble ideas carefully kept out of sight. Without attempting to gloss over the crime of which both are guilty, without seeking to remove our disapprobation of this criminal love, he still, by the magic force of expression, contrives to excite in us a sympathy with their sorrow. In the insurrection of Cade he has delineated the conduct of a popular demagogue, the fearful ludicrousness of the anarchical tumult of the people, with such convincing truth, that one would believe he was an eye-witness of many of the events of our age, which, from ignorance of history, have been considered as without example.

The civil war only begins in the Second Part; in the Third it is unfolded in its full destructive fury. The picture becomes gloomier and gloomier; and seems at last to be painted rather with blood than with colours. With horror we behold fury giving birth to fury, vengeance to vengeance, and see that when all the bonds of human society are violently torn asunder, even noble matrons became hardened to cruelty. The most bitter contempt is the portion of the unfortunate; no one affords to his enemy that pity which he will himself shortly stand in need of. With all party is family, country, and religion, the only spring of action. As York, whose ambition is coupled with noble qualities, prematurely perishes, the object of the whole contest is now either to support an imbecile king, or to place on the throne a luxurious monarch, who shortens the dear-bought possession by the gratification of an insatiable voluptuousness. For this the celebrated and magnanimous Warwick spends his chivalrous life; Clifford revenges the death of his father with blood-thirsty filial love; and Richard, for the elevation of his brother, practises those dark deeds by which he is soon after to pave the way to his own greatness. In the midst of the general misery, of which he has been the innocent cause, King Henry appears like the powerless image of a saint, in whose wonder-working influence no man any longer believes: he can but sigh and weep over the enormities which he witnesses. In his simplicity, however, the gift of prophecy is lent to this pious king: in the moment of his death, at the close of this great tragedy, he prophesies a still more dreadful tragedy with which futurity is pregnant, as much distinguished for the poisonous wiles of cold-blooded wickedness as the former for deeds of savage fury.

The part of Richard III. has become highly celebrated in England from its having been filled by excellent performers, and this has naturally had an influence on the admiration of the piece itself, for many readers of Shakspeare stand in want of good interpreters of the poet to understand him properly. This admiration is certainly in every respect well founded, though I cannot help thinking there is an injustice in considering the three parts of *Henry the Sixth* as of little value compared with *Richard the Third.* These four plays were undoubtedly composed in succession, as is proved by the style and the spirit in the handling of the subject: the last is definitely announced in the one which precedes it, and is also full of references to it: the same views run through the series; in a word, the whole make together only one single work. Even the deep characterization of Richard is by no means the exclusive property of the piece which bears his name: his character is very distinctly drawn in the two last parts of *Henry the Sixth*; nay, even his first speeches lead us already to form the most unfavourable anticipations of his future conduct. He lowers obliquely like a dark thundercloud on the horizon, which gradually approaches nearer and nearer, and first pours out the devastating elements with which it is charged when it hangs over the heads of mortals. Two of Richard's most significant soliloquies which enable us to draw the most important conclusions with regard to his mental temperament, are to be found in *The Last Part of Henry the Sixth.* As to the value and the justice of the actions to which passion impels us, we may be blind, but wickedness cannot mistake its own nature; Richard, as well as Iago, is a villain with full consciousness. That they should say this in so many words, is not perhaps in human nature: but the poet has the right in soliloquies to lend a voice to the most hidden thoughts, otherwise the form of the monologue would, generally speaking, be censurable. [Footnote: What, however, happens in so many tragedies, where a person is made to avow himself a villain to his confidants, is most decidedly unnatural. He will, indeed, announce his way of thinking, not, however, under damning names, but as something that is understood of itself, and is equally approved of by others.] Richard's deformity is the expression of his internal malice, and perhaps in part the effect of it: for where is the ugliness that would not be softened by benevolence and openness? He, however, considers it as an iniquitous neglect of nature, which justifies him in taking his revenge on that human society from which it is the means of excluding him. Hence these sublime lines:

And this word love, which graybeards call divine.
Be resident in men like one another,
And not in me. I am myself alone.

Wickedness is nothing but selfishness designedly unconscientious; however it can never do altogether without the form at least of morality, as this is the law of all thinking beings,--it must seek to found its depraved way of acting on something like principles. Although Richard is thoroughly acquainted with the blackness of his mind and his hellish mission, he yet endeavours to justify this to himself by a sophism: the happiness of being beloved is denied to him; what then remains to him but the happiness of ruling? All that stands in the way of this must be removed. This envy of the enjoyment of love is so much the more natural in Richard, as his brother Edward, who besides preceded him in the possession of the crown, was distinguished by the nobleness and beauty of his figure, and was an almost irresistible conqueror of female hearts. Notwithstanding his pretended renunciation, Richard places his chief vanity in being able to please and win over the women, if not by his figure at least by his insinuating discourse. Shakspeare here shows us, with his accustomed acuteness of observation, that human nature, even when it is altogether decided in goodness or wickedness, is still subject to petty infirmities. Richard's favourite amusement is to ridicule others, and he possesses an eminent satirical wit. He entertains at bottom a contempt for all mankind: for he is confident of his ability to deceive them, whether as his instruments or his adversaries. In hypocrisy he is particularly fond of using religious forms, as if actuated by a desire of profaning in the service of hell the religion whose blessings he had inwardly abjured.

So much for the main features of Richard's character. The play named after him embraces also the latter part of the reign of Edward IV., in the whole a period of eight years. It exhibits all the machinations by which Richard obtained the throne, and the deeds which he perpetrated to secure himself in its possession, which lasted however but two years. Shakspeare intended that terror rather than compassion should prevail throughout this tragedy: he has rather avoided than sought the pathetic scenes which he had at command. Of all the sacrifices to Richard's lust of power, Clarence alone is put to death on the stage: his dream excites a deep horror, and proves the omnipotence of the poet's fancy: his conversation with the murderers is powerfully agitating; but the earlier crimes of Clarence merited death, although not from his brother's hand. The most innocent and unspotted sacrifices are the two princes: we see but little of them, and their murder is merely related. Anne disappears without our learning any thing farther respecting her: in marrying the murderer of her husband, she had shown a weakness almost incredible. The parts of Lord Rivers, and other friends of the queen, are of too secondary a nature to excite a powerful sympathy; Hastings, from his triumph at the fall of his friend, forfeits all title to compassion; Buckingham is the satellite of the tyrant, who is afterwards consigned by him to the axe of the executioner. In the background the widowed Queen Margaret appears as the fury of the past, who invokes a curse on the future: every calamity, which her enemies draw down on each other, is a cordial to her revengeful heart. Other female voices join, from time to time, in the lamentations and imprecations. But Richard is the soul or rather the daemon, of the whole tragedy. He fulfils the promise which he formerly made of leading the murderous Macchiavel to school. Notwithstanding the uniform aversion with which he inspires us, he still engages us in the greatest variety of ways by his profound skill in dissimulation, his wit, his prudence, his presence of mind, his quick activity, and his valour. He fights at last against Richmond like a desperado, and dies the honourable death of a hero on the field of battle. Shakspeare could not change this historical issue, and yet it is by no means satisfactory to our moral feelings, as Lessing, when speaking of a German play on the same subject, has very judiciously remarked. How has Shakspeare solved this difficulty? By a wonderful invention he opens a prospect into the other world, and shows us Richard in his last moments already branded with the stamp of reprobation. We see Richard and Richmond in the night before the battle sleeping in their tents; the spirits of the murdered victims of the tyrant ascend in succession, and pour out their curses against him, and their blessings on his adversary. These apparitions are properly but the dreams of the two generals represented visibly. It is no doubt contrary to probability that their tents should only be separated by so small a space; but Shakspeare could reckon on poetical spectators who were ready to take the breadth of the stage for the distance between two hostile camps, if for such indulgence they were to be recompensed by beauties of so sublime a nature as this series of spectres and Richard's awakening soliloquy. The catastrophe of *Richard the Third* is, in respect of the external events, very like that of *Macbeth*: we have only to compare the thorough difference of handling them to be convinced that Shakspeare has most accurately observed poetical justice in the genuine sense of the word, that is, as signifying the revelation of an invisible blessing or curse which hangs over human sentiments and actions.

Although the last four pieces of the historical series paint later events, yet the plays of *Henry the Fourth and Fifth* have, in tone and costume, a much more modern appearance. This is partly owing to the number of comic scenes; for the comic must always be founded not only in national, but also in contemporary manners. Shakspeare, however, seems also to have had the same design in the serious part. Bloody revolutions and devastations of civil war appear to posterity as a relapse into an earlier and more uncultivated condition of society, or they are in reality accompanied by such a relapse into unbridled savageness. If therefore the propensity of a young poetical mind to remove its object to a wonderful distance has had an influence on the style in which *Henry the Sixth* and *Richard the Third* are conceived, Shakspeare has been rightly guided by his instinct. As it is peculiar to the heroic poem to paint the races of men in times past as colossal in strength of body and resolution, so in these plays, the voices of a Talbot, a Warwick, a Clifford, and others, so ring on our ear that we imagine we hear the clanging trumpets of foreign or of civil war. The contest of the Houses of York and Lancaster was the last outbreak of feudal independence; it was the cause of the great and not of the people, who were only dragged into the struggle by the former. Afterwards the part was swallowed up in the whole, and no longer could any one be, like Warwick, a maker of kings. Shakspeare was as profound a historian as a poet; when we compare his *Henry the Eighth* with the preceding pieces, we see distinctly that the English nation during the long, peaceable, and economical reign of Henry VII., whether from the exhaustion which was the fruit of the civil wars, or from more general European influences, had made a sudden transition from the powerful confusion of the middle age, to the regular tameness of modern times. *Henry the Eighth* has, therefore, somewhat of a prosaic appearance; for Shakspeare, artist-like, adapted himself always to the quality of his materials. If others of his works, both in elevation of fancy and in energy of pathos and character, tower far above this, we have here on the other hand occasion to admire his nice powers of discrimination and his perfect knowledge of courts and the world. What tact was requisite to represent before the eyes of the queen [Footnote: It is quite clear that *Henry the Eighth* was written while Elizabeth was still alive. We know that Ben Jonson, in the reign of King James, brought the piece again on the stage with additional pomp, and took the liberty of making several changes and additions. Without doubt, the prophecy respecting James the First is due to Ben Jonson: it would only have displeased Elizabeth, and is so ill introduced that we at once recognize in it a foreign interpolation.] subjects of such a delicate nature, and in which she was personally so nearly concerned, without doing violence to the truth! He has unmasked the tyrannical king, and to the intelligent observer exhibited him such as he was actually: haughty and obstinate, voluptuous and unfeeling, extravagant in conferring favours, and revengeful under the pretext of justice; and yet the picture is so dexterously handled that a daughter might take it for favourable. The legitimacy of Elizabeth's birth depended on the invalidity of Henry's first marriage, and Shakspeare has placed the proceedings respecting his separation from Catharine of Arragon in a very doubtful light. We see clearly that Henry's scruples of conscience are no other than the beauty of Anne Boleyn. Catharine is, properly speaking, the heroine of the piece; she excites the warmest sympathy by her virtues, her defenceless misery, her mild but firm opposition, and her dignified resignation. After her, the fall of Cardinal Wolsey constitutes the principal part of the business. Henry's whole reign was not adapted for dramatic poetry. It would have merely been a repetition of the same scenes: the repudiation, or the execution of his wives, and the disgrace of his most estimable ministers, which was usually soon followed by death. Of all that distinguished Henry's life Shakspeare has given us sufficient specimens. But as, properly speaking, there is no division in the history where he breaks off, we must excuse him if he gives us a flattering compliment of the great Elizabeth for a fortunate catastrophe. The piece ends with the general joy at the birth of that princess, and with prophecies of the happiness which she was afterwards to enjoy or to diffuse. It was only by such a turn that the hazardous freedom of thought in the rest of the composition could have passed with impunity: Shakspeare was not certainly himself deceived respecting this theatrical delusion. The true conclusion is the death of Catharine, which under a feeling of this kind, he has placed earlier than was conformable to history. I have now gone through all the unquestionably genuine works of Shakspeare. I have carefully abstained from all indefinite eulogies, which merely serve to prove a disproportion betwixt the feeling and the capability of expressing it. To many the above observations will appear too diffuse for the object and plan of these Lectures; to others they will perhaps seem unsatisfactory. I shall be satisfied if they place those readers who are not yet familiar with the poet in the right point of view, and pave the way for a solid knowledge, and if they recall to the minds of intelligent critics some of those thoughts which have occurred to themselves.

APPENDIX

Respecting the Pieces said to be falsely attributed to Shakspeare.

The commentators of Shakspeare, in their attempts to deprive him of parts of his works, or even of whole pieces, have for the most part displayed very little of a true critical spirit. Pope, as is well known, was strongly disposed to reject whole scenes as interpolations by the players; but his opinion was not much listened to. However, Steevens acceded to the opinion of Pope, as to the apparition of the ghosts and of Jupiter, in *Cymbeline*, while Posthumus is sleeping in the dungeon. But Posthumus finds on waking a tablet on his breast, with a prophecy on which the *denouement* of the piece depends. Is it to be imagined that Shakspeare would require of his spectators the belief in a wonder without a visible cause? Can Posthumus have got this tablet with the prophecy by dreaming? But these gentlemen do not descend to this objection. The verses which the apparitions deliver do not appear to them good enough to be Shakspeare's. I imagine I can discover why the poet has not given them more of the splendour of diction. It is the aged parents and brothers of Posthumus, who, from concern for his fate, return from the world below: ought they not consequently to speak the language of a more simple olden time, and their voices, too, ought they not also to seem a feeble sound of wailing, when contrasted with the thundering oracular language of Jupiter? For this reason Shakspeare chose a syllabic measure which was very common before his time, but which was then going out of fashion, though it still continued to be frequently used, especially in translations of the classical poets. In some such manner might the shades express themselves in the then existing translations of Homer and Virgil. The speech of Jupiter is, on the other hand, majestic, and in form and style bears a complete resemblance to Shakspeare's sonnets. Nothing but incapacity to appreciate the views of the poet, and the perspective observed by him, could lead them to stumble at this passage.

Pope would willingly have declared the *Winter's Tale* spurious, one of the noblest creations of the equally bold and lovely fancy of Shakspeare. Why? I suppose on account of the ship coming to Bohemia, and of the chasm of sixteen years between the third and fourth acts, which Time as a prologue entreats us to overleap.

The Three Parts of Henry the Sixth are now at length admitted to be Shakspeare's. Theobald, Warburton, and lastly Farmer, affirmed that they were not Shakspeare's. In this case, we might well ask them to point out the other works of the unknown author, who was capable of inventing, among many others, the noble death-scenes of Talbot, Suffolk, Beaufort, and York. The assertion is so ridiculous, that in this case *Richard the Third* might also not be Shakspeare's, as it is linked in the most immediate manner to the three other pieces, both by the subject, and the spirit and style of handling.

All the editors, with the exception of Capell, are unanimous in rejecting *Titus Andronicus* as unworthy of Shakspeare, though they always allow it to be printed with the other pieces, as the scape-goat, as it were, of their abusive criticism. The correct method in such an investigation is first to examine into the external grounds, evidences, &c., and to weigh their value; and then to adduce the internal reasons derived from the quality of the work. The critics of Shakspeare follow a course directly the reverse of this; they set out with a preconceived opinion against a piece, and seek, in justification of this opinion, to render the historical ground suspicious, and to set them aside. Now *Titus Andronicus* is to be found in the first folio edition of Shakspeare's works, which it is known was published by Heminge and Condell, for many years his friends and fellow-managers of the same theatre. Is it possible to persuade ourselves that they would not have known if a piece in their repertory did or did not really belong to Shakspeare? And are we to lay to the charge of these honourable men an intentional fraud in this single case, when we know that they did not show themselves so very desirous of scraping everything together which went by the name of Shakspeare, but, as it appears, merely gave those plays of which they had manuscripts in hand? Yet the following circumstance is still stronger. George Meres, a contemporary and admirer of Shakspeare, in an enumeration of his works, mentions *Titus Andronicus*, in the year 1598. Meres was personally acquainted with the poet, and so very intimately, that the latter read over to him his sonnets before they were printed. I cannot conceive that all the critical scepticism in the world would ever be able to get over such a testimony.

This tragedy, it is true, is framed according to a false idea of the tragic, which by an accumulation of cruelties and enormities, degenerates into the horrible, and yet leaves no deep impression behind: the story of Tereus and Philomela is heightened and overcharged under other names, and mixed up with the repast of Atreus and Thyestes, and many other incidents. In detail there is no want of beautiful lines, bold images, nay, even features which betray the peculiar conception of Shakspeare. Among these we may reckon the joy of the treacherous Moor at the blackness and ugliness of his adulterous offspring; and in the compassion of Titus Andronicus, grown childish through grief, for a fly which had been struck dead, while his rage afterwards, when he imagines he discovers in it his black enemy, we recognize the future poet of *Lear*. Are the critics afraid that Shakspeare's fame would be injured, were it established that in his early youth he ushered into the world a feeble and immature work? Was Rome the less the conqueror of the world, because Remus could leap over its first walls? Let any one place himself in Shakspeare's situation at the commencement of his career. He found only a few indifferent models, and yet these met with the most favourable reception, because in the novelty of an art, men are never difficult to please, before their taste has been made fastidious by choice and abundance. Must not this situation have had its influence on him before he learned to make higher demands on himself, and by digging deeper in his own mind, discovered the rich veins of noble metal that ran there? It is even highly probable that he must have made several failures before he succeeded in getting into the right path. Genius is in a certain sense infallible, and has nothing to learn; but art is to be learned, and must be acquired by practice and experience. In Shakspeare's acknowledged works we find hardly any traces of his apprenticeship, and yet apprenticeship he certainly had. This every artist must have, and especially in a period where he has not before him the examples of a school already formed. I consider it as extremely probable that Shakspeare began to write for the theatre at a much earlier period than the one which is generally stated, namely, after the year 1590. It appears that, as early as the year 1584, when only twenty years of age, he had left his paternal home and repaired to London. Can we imagine that such an active head would remain idle for six whole years without making any attempt to emerge by his talents from an uncongenial situation? That in the dedication of the poem of *Venus and Adonis* he calls it "the first heir of his invention," proves nothing against the supposition. It was the first which he printed; he might have composed it at an earlier period; perhaps, also, in this term, "heirs of his invention," he did not indulge theatrical labours, especially as they then conferred but little to his literary dignity. The earlier Shakspeare began to compose for the theatre, the less are we enabled to consider the immaturity and imperfection of a work a proof of its spuriousness in opposition to historical evidence, if only we can discern in it prominent features of his mind. Several of the works rejected as spurious, may still have been produced in the period betwixt *Titus Andronicus*, and the earliest of the acknowledged pieces.

At last, in two supplementary volumes, Steevens published seven pieces ascribed to Shakspeare. It is to be remarked, that they all appeared in print in Shakspeare's life-time, with his name prefixed at full length. They are the following:--

1. *Lochrine.* The proofs of the genuineness of this piece are not altogether unambiguous; the grounds for doubt, on the other hand, are entitled to attention. However, this question is immediately connected with that respecting *Titus Andronicus*, and must with it be resolved in the affirmative or negative.

2. *Pericles, Prince of Tyre.* This piece was acknowledged by Dryden to be a work, but a youthful work of Shakspeare's. It is most undoubtedly his, and it has been admitted into several late editions of his works. The supposed imperfections originate in the circumstance, that Shakspeare here handled a childish and extravagant romance of the old poet Gower, and was unwilling to drag the subject out of its proper sphere. Hence he even introduces Gower himself, and makes him deliver a prologue in his own antiquated language and versification. This power of assuming so foreign a manner is at least no proof of helplessness.

3. *The London Prodigal.* If we are not mistaken, Lessing pronounced this piece to be Shakspeare's, and wished to bring it on the German stage.

4. *The Puritan; or The Widow of Wailing Street.* One of my literary friends, intimately acquainted with Shakspeare, was of opinion that the poet must have wished for once to write a play in the style of Ben Jonson, and that in this way we must account for the difference between the present piece and his usual manner. To follow out this idea, however, would lead to a long and very nice critical investigation.

5. *Thomas Lord Cromwell.*

6. *Sir John Oldcastle.*--First part.

7. *A Yorkshire Tragedy.*

The three last pieces are not only unquestionably Shakspeare's, but in my opinion they deserve to be classed among his best and maturest works. Steevens at last admits, in some degree, that they, as well as the rest, except *Lochrine*, are Shakspeare's, but he speaks of all of them with great contempt, as worthless productions. His condemnatory sentence is not, however, in the slightest degree convincing, nor is it supported by much critical acumen. I should like to see how such a critic would, of his own natural suggestion, have decided on Shakspeare's acknowledged master-pieces, and how much he would have thought of praising in them, had not the public opinion already imposed on him the duty of admiration. *Thomas Lord Cromwell* and *Sir John Oldcastle* are biographical dramas, and in this species they are models: the first, by its subject, attaches itself to *Henry the Eighth*, and the second to *Henry the Fifth*. The second part of *Sir John Oldcastle* is wanting; I know not whether a copy of the old edition has been discovered in England, or whether it is lost. *The Yorkshire Tragedy* is a tragedy in one act, a dramatised tale of murder: the tragical effect is overpowering, and it is extremely important to see how poetically Shakspeare could handle such a subject.

Still farther, there have been ascribed to him, 1st. *The Merry Devil of Edmonton*, a comedy in one act, printed in Dodsley's Collection of Old Plays. This has, certainly, some appearance in its favour. It contains a merry landlord, who bears great similarity to the one in *The Merry Wives of Windsor*. However, at all events, though a clever, it is but a hasty sketch. 2nd. *The Arraignment of Paris*. 3rd. *The Birth of Merlin*. 4th. *Edward the Third*. 5th. *The Fair Em*. (Emma). 6th. *Mucedorus*. 7th. *Arden of Feversham*. I have never seen any of these, and cannot therefore say anything respecting them. From the passages cited, I am led to conjecture that the subject of *Mucedorus* is the popular story of Valentine and Orson: a beautiful subject which Lope de Vega has also taken for a play. *Arden of Feversham* is said to be a tragedy on the story of a man from whom the poet descended by the mother's side. This circumstance, if the quality of the piece be not too directly at variance with its supposed authorship, would afford an additional probability in its favour. For such motives were not without their influence on Shakspeare: thus he treated with a manifest partiality, Henry VII., who had bestowed lands on his forefathers for services performed by them.

Of Shakspeare's share in *The Two Noble Cousins*, it will be the time to speak when I come to mention Fletcher's works.

It would be very instructive, if it could be proved that several earlier attempts of works, afterwards re-written, proceeded from himself, and not from an unknown author. We should thus be best enabled to trace his development as an artist. Of the older *King John*, in two parts, (printed by Steevens among six old plays,) this might probably be made out. That he sometimes returned to an old piece is certain. With respect to *Hamlet*, for instance, it is well known, that it was very gradually formed by him to its present perfect state.

Whoever takes from Shakspeare a play early ascribed to him, and confessedly belonging to his time, is certainly bound to answer, with some degree of probability, this question: who then wrote it? Shakspeare's competitors in the dramatic walk are pretty well known, and if those of them who have even acquired a considerable reputation, a Lilly, a Marlow, a Heywood, are still very far below him, we can hardly imagine that the author of a work, which rises so high beyond theirs, could have remained unknown.

LECTURE XXVII.

Two periods of the English Theatre: the first the most important--The first conformation of the Stage, and its advantages--State of the Histrionic Art in Shakspeare's time--Antiquities of Dramatic Literature-- Lilly, Marlow, Heywood--Ben Jonson--Criticism of his Works--Masques-- Beaumont and Fletcher--General characterization of these Poets, and remarks on some of their Pieces--Massinger and other contemporaries of Charles the First.

The great master of whom we have spoken in the preceding Lecture, forms so singular an exception to the whole history of art, that we are compelled to assign a particular place to him. He owed hardly anything to his predecessors, and he has had the greatest influence on his successors: but no man has yet learned from him his secret. For two whole centuries, during which his countrymen have diligently employed themselves in the cultivation of every branch of science and art, according to their own confession, he has not only never yet been surpassed, but has left every dramatic poet at a great distance behind him.

In the sketch of a history of the English theatre which I am now to give, I shall be frequently obliged to return to Shakspeare. The dramatic literature of the English is very rich; they can boast of a large number of dramatic poets, who possessed in an eminent degree the talent of original characterization, and the knowledge of theatrical effect. Their hands were not shackled by prejudices, by arbitrary rules, and by the anxious observance of so-called proprieties. There has never been in England an academical court of taste; in art, as in life, every man there gives his voice for what best pleases him, or what is most suitable to his nature. Notwithstanding this liberty, their writers have not, however, been able to escape the influence either of varying modes, or of the spirit of different ages.

We shall here remain true to our principle of merely dwelling at length on what we consider as the highest efforts of poetry, and of taking brief views of all that occupies but the second or third place.

The antiquities of the English theatre have been sufficiently illustrated by the English writers, and especially by Malone. The earliest dramatic attempts were here as well as elsewhere Mysteries and Moralities. However it would seem that in these productions the English distinguished themselves at an earlier period than other nations. In the History of the

Council of Constance it is recorded that the English prelates, in one of the intervals between the sittings, entertained their brethren with a spiritual play in Latin, such as the latter were either entirely unacquainted with, or at least in such perfection, (as perfection was understood by the simple ideas of art of those times). The beginning of a theatre, properly so called, cannot, however, be placed farther back than the reign of Elizabeth. John Heywood, the buffoon of Henry VIII. is considered as the oldest comic writer: the single *Interlude* under his name, published in Dodsley's collection, is in fact merely a dialogue, and not a drama. But *Gammer Gurton's Needle*, which was first acted about the year 1560, certainly deserves the name of a comedy. However antiquated in language and versification, it possesses unequivocal merit in the low comic. The whole plot turns on a lost needle, the search for which is pursued with the utmost assiduity: the poverty of the persons of the drama, which this supposes, and the whole of their domestic condition, is very amusingly portrayed, and the part of a cunning beggar especially is drawn with much humour. The coarse comic of this piece bears a resemblance to that of the *Avocat Patelin*; yet the English play has not, like the French, been honoured with a revival on the stage in a new shape.

The history of the English theatre divides itself naturally into two periods. The first begins nearly with the accession of Elizabeth, and extends to about the end of the reign of Charles I., when the Puritans gained the ascendency, and effected the prohibition of all plays whatsoever. The closing of the theatres lasted thirteen years; and they were not again opened till the restoration of Charles II. This interruption, the change which had taken place in the mean time on the general way of thinking and in manners, and lastly, the influence of the French literature which was then flourishing, gave quite a different character to the plays subsequently written. The works of the older school were indeed in part sought out, but the school itself was extinct. I apply the term of a "school" to the dramatical poets of the first aera, in the same sense as it is taken in art, for with all their personal differences we may still perceive on the whole a common character in their productions. Independently of the language or contemporary allusions, we should never be disposed to take a play of that school, though ignorant of its author, and the date of its production, for a work of the more modern period. The latter period admits of many subdivisions, but with these, however, we may dispense. The talents of the authors, and the taste of the public, have fluctuated in every possible way; foreign influence has gained more and more the ascendency, and (to express myself without circumlocution,) the English theatre has in its progress become more and more destitute of character and independence. For a critic, who everywhere seeks originality, troubling himself little about what has arisen from the following or the avoiding of imitation, the dramatic poets of the first period are by far the most important, although, with the exception of Shakspeare, they may be reproached with great defects and extravagances, and although many of the moderns are distinguished for a more careful polish.

There are times when the human mind all at once makes gigantic strides in an art previously almost unknown, as if during its long sleep it had been collecting strength for the effort. The age of Elizabeth was in England such an epoch for dramatic poetry. This queen, during her long reign, witnessed the first infantine attempts of the English theatre, and its most masterly productions. Shakspeare had a lively feeling of this general and rapid development of qualities not before called into exercise; in one of his sonnets he calls his age, *these time-lettering days*. The predilection for the theatre was so great, that in a period of sixty years, under this and the following reign, seventeen play-houses were built or fitted up in London, whereas the capital of the present day, with twice the population, [Footnote: The author might almost have said six times.--TRANS.] is satisfied with two. No doubt they did not act every day, and several of these theatres were very small, and probably not much better fitted up than Marionette booths. However, they served to call forth the fertility of those writers who possessed, or supposed that they possessed, dramatic talents; for every theatre must have had its peculiar repertory, as the pieces were either not printed at all, or at least not till long after their composition, and as a single theatrical company was in the exclusive possession of the manuscripts. However many of feeble and lame productions might have been called forth, still it was impossible that such an extensive competition should not have been advantageous. Of all the different species of poetry the dramatic is the only one in which experience is necessary: and the failure of others is, for the man of talents, an experiment at their expense. Moreover, the exercise of this art requires vigorous determination, to which the great artist is often the least inclined, as in the execution he finds the greatest difficulty in satisfying himself; while, on the other hand, his greatest enjoyment consists in embodying in his own mind the beloved creation of his imagination. It is therefore fortunate for him when the bolder forwardness of those who, with trifling means, venture on this difficult career stimulates him to put fresh hand to the work. Further, it is of importance to the dramatic poet to be connected immediately with the stage, that he may either himself guide it, or learn to accommodate himself to its wants; and the dramatic poets of that day were, for the most part, also players. The theatre still made small claims to literature, and it thus escaped the pedantry of scholastic learning. There were as yet no periodical writings which, as the instrument of cabal, could mislead opinion. Of jealousies, indeed, and bickerings among the authors there was no want: this, however, was more a source of amusement than of displeasure to the public, who decided without prejudice or partiality according to the amount of entertainment. The poets and players, as well as the spectators, possessed in general the most essential requisite of success: a true love for the business. This was the more unquestionable, as the theatrical art was not then surrounded with all those foreign ornaments and inventions of luxury which serve to distract the attention and corrupt the sense, but made its appearance in the most modest, and we may well say in the most humble shape. For the admirers of Shakspeare it must be an object of curiosity to know what was the appearance of the theatre in which his works were first performed. We have an engraving of the play-house of which he was manager, and which, from the symbol of a Hercules supplying the place of Atlas, was called the Globe: it is a massive structure destitute of architectural ornaments, and almost without windows in the outward walls. The pit was open to the sky, and the acting was by day-light; the scene had no other decoration than wrought tapestry, which hung at some distance from the walls, and left space for several entrances. In the back-ground of the stage there was a second stage raised above it, a sort of balcony, which served for various purposes, and according to circumstances signified all manner of things. The players appeared, excepting on a few rare occasions, in the dress of their time, or at most distinguished by higher feathers on their hats and roses on their shoes. The chief means of disguise were false hair and beards, and occasionally also masks. The female parts were played by boys so long as their voice allowed it. Two companies of actors in London consisted entirely of boys, namely, the choir of the Queen's Chapel and that of St. Paul's. Betwixt the acts it was not customary to have music, but in the pieces themselves marches, dances, solo songs, and the like, were introduced on fitting occasions, and trumpet flourishes at the entrance of great personages. In the more early time it was usual to represent the action before it was spoken, in silent pantomime (*dumb show*) between each act, allegorically or even without any disguise, to give a definite direction to the expectation. Shakspeare has observed this practice in the play in *Hamlet*.

By the present lavish appliance of every theatrical accessory;--of architecture, lighting, music, the illusion of decorations changing in a moment as if by enchantment, machinery and costume;--by all this, we are now so completely spoiled, that this earlier meagreness of stage decoration will in no wise satisfy us. Much, however, might be urged in favour of such a constitution of the theatre. Where the spectators are not allured by any splendid accessories, they will be the more difficult to please in the main thing, namely, the excellence of the dramatic composition, and its embodying by delivery and action. When perfection is not attainable in external decoration, the critic will rather altogether overlook it than be disturbed by its deficiencies and tastelessness. And how seldom has perfection been here attained! It is about a century and a half since attention began to be paid to the observance of costume on the European stage; what with this view has been accomplished has always appeared excellent to the multitude, and yet, to judge from the engravings which sometimes accompany the printed plays, and from every other evidence, it is plain that it was always characterized by puerility and mannerism, and that in none the endeavours to assume a foreign or antique appearance, could shake themselves free of the fashions of the time. A sort of hoop was long considered as an indispensable appendage of a hero; the long peruques and *fontanges*, or topknots, kept their ground in heroical tragedy as long as in real life; afterwards it would have been considered as barbarous to appear without powdered and frizzled hair; on this was placed a helmet with variegated feathers; a taffeta scarf fluttered over the gilt paper coat of mail; and the Achilles or Alexander was then completely mounted. We have now at last returned to a purer taste, and in some great theatres the costume is actually observed in a learned and severe style. We owe this principally to the antiquarian reform in the arts of design, and the approximation of the female dress to the Grecian; for the actresses were always the most inveterate in retaining on the stage those fashions by which they turned their charms to account in society. However, even yet there are very few players who know how to wear a Grecian purple mantle, or a toga, in a natural and becoming manner; and who, in moments of passion, do not seem to be unduly occupied with holding and tossing about their drapery.

Our system of decoration was properly invented for the opera, to which it is also in reality best adapted. It has several unavoidable defects; others which certainly may be, but seldom are avoided. Among the inevitable defects I reckon the breaking of the lines in the side scenes from every point of view except one; the disproportion between the size of the player when he appears in the background, and the objects as diminished in the perspective; the unfavourable lighting from below and behind; the contrast between the painted and the actual lights and shades; the impossibility of narrowing the stage at pleasure, so that the inside of a palace and a hut have the same length and breadth, &c. The errors which may be avoided are, want of simplicity and of great and reposing masses; overloading the scenery with superfluous and distracting objects, either from the painter being desirous of showing his strength in perspective, or not knowing how otherwise to fill up the space; an architecture full of mannerism, often altogether unconnected, nay, even at variance with possibility, coloured in a motley manner which resembles no species of stone in the world. Most scene-painters owe their success entirely to the spectator's ignorance of the arts of design; I have often seen a whole pit enchanted with a decoration from which the eye of skill must have turned away with disgust, and in whose place a plain green wall would have been infinitely better. A vitiated taste for splendour of decoration and magnificence of dress, has rendered the arrangement of the theatre a complicated and expensive business, whence it frequently happens that the main requisites, good pieces and good players, are considered as secondary matters; but this is an inconvenience which it is here unnecessary to mention.

Although the earlier English stage had properly no decorations, we must allow, however, that it was not altogether destitute of machinery: without it, it is almost impossible to conceive how several pieces, for instance, *Macbeth*, *The Tempest*, and others, could ever be represented. The celebrated architect, Inigo Jones, who lived in the reign of James the First, put in motion very complicated and artificial machines for the decoration of the Masques of Ben Jonson which were acted at court.

With the Spanish theatre at the time of its formation, it was the same as with the English, and when the stage had remained a moment empty, and other persons came in by another entrance, a change of scene was to be supposed though none was visible; and this circumstance had the most favourable influence on the form of the dramas. The poet was not obliged to consult the scene-painter to know what could or what could not be represented; nor to calculate whether the store of decorations on hand were sufficient, or new ones would be requisite: he was not driven to impose restraint on the action as to change of times and places, but represented it entirely as it would naturally have taken place: [Footnote: Capell, an intelligent commentator on Shakspeare, unjustly underrated by the others, has placed the advantages in this respect in the clearest light, in an observation on *Antony and Cleopatra*. It emboldened the poet, when the truth of the action required it, to plan scenes which the most skilful mechanist and scene-painter could scarcely exhibit to the eye; as for instance, in a Spanish play where sea-fights occur.] he left to the imagination to fill up the intervals agreeably to the speeches, and to conceive all the surrounding circumstances. This call on the fancy to supply the deficiencies supposes, indeed, not merely benevolent, but also intelligent spectators of a poetical tone of mind. That is the true illusion, when the spectators are so completely carried away by the impressions of the poetry and the acting, that they overlook the secondary matters, and forget the whole of the remaining objects around them. To lie morosely on the watch to detect every circumstance that may violate an apparent reality which, strictly speaking, can never be attained, is in fact a proof of inertness of imagination and an incapacity for mental illusion. This prosaical incredulity may be carried so far as to render it utterly impossible for the theatrical artists, who in every constitution of the theatre require many indulgences, to amuse the spectators by their productions; and thus they are, in the end, the enemies of their own enjoyment.

We now complain, and with justice, that in the acting of Shakspeare's pieces the too frequent change of scenes occasions an interruption. But the poet is here perfectly blameless. It ought to be known that the English plays of that time, as well as the Spanish, were printed without any mention of the scene and its changes. In Shakspeare the modern editors have inserted the scenical directions; and in doing so, they have proceeded with the most pedantic accuracy. Whoever has the management of the representation of a piece of Shakspeare's may, without any hesitation, strike out at once all such changes of scene as the following:-"Another room in the palace, another street, another part of the field of battle," &c. By these means alone, in most cases, the change of decorations will be reduced to a very moderate number.

Of the actor's art on a theatre which possessed so little external splendour as the old English, those who are in the habit of judging of the man from his dress will not be inclined to entertain a very favourable idea. I am induced, however, from this very circumstance, to draw quite a contrary conclusion: the want of attractions of an accessory nature renders it the more necessary to be careful in essentials. Several Englishmen [Footnote: See a Dialogue prefixed to the 11th volume of Dodsley's *Old Plays*.] have given it as their opinion, that the players of the first epoch were in all likelihood greatly superior to those of the second, at least with the exception of Garrick; and if we had no other proof, the quality of Shakspeare's pieces renders this extremely probable. That most of his principal characters require a great player is self-evident; the elevated and compressed style of his poetry cannot be understood without the most energetic and flexible delivery; besides, he often supposes between the speeches a mute action of great difficulty, for which he gives no directions. A poet who labours only and immediately for the stage will not rely for his main effect on traits which he must beforehand know will be lost in the representation from the unskilfulness of his interpreters. Shakspeare consequently would have been driven to lower the tone of his dramatic art, if he had not possessed excellent theatrical coadjutors. Of these, some have descended by name and fame even to our times. As for Shakspeare himself, since we are not fond of allowing any one man to possess two great talents in an equal degree, it has been assumed on very questionable grounds, that he was but an indifferent actor. [Footnote: No certain account has yet been obtained of any principal part played by Shakspeare in his own pieces. In *Hamlet* he played the Ghost; certainly a very important part, if we consider that from the failure in it, the whole piece runs a risk of appearing ridiculous. A writer of his time says in a satirical pamphlet, that the Ghost whined in a pitiful manner; and it has been concluded from this that

Shakspeare was a bad player. What logic! On the restoration of the theatre under Charles II., a desire was felt of collecting traditions and information respecting the former period. Lowin, the original Hamlet, instructed Betterton as to the proper conception of the character. There was still alive a brother of Shakspeare, a decrepid old man, who had never had any literary cultivation, and whose memory was impaired by age. From him they could extract nothing, but that he had sometimes visited his brother in town, and once saw him play an old man with grey hair and beard. From the above description it was concluded that this must have been the faithful servant Adam in *As You Like It*, also a second-rate part. In most of Shakspeare's pieces we have not the slightest knowledge of the manner in which the parts were distributed. In two of Ben Jonson's pieces we see Shakspeare's name among the principal actors.] Hamlet's instructions, however, to the players prove at least that he was an excellent judge of acting. We know that correctness of conception and judgment are not always coupled with the power of execution; Shakspeare, however, possessed a very important and too frequently neglected requisite for serious acting, a beautiful and noble countenance. Neither is it probable that he could have been the manager of the most respectable theatre, had he not himself possessed the talent both of acting and guiding the histrionic talents of others. Ben Jonson, though a meritorious poet, could not even obtain the situation of a player, as he did not possess the requisite qualifications. From the passage cited from *Hamlet*, from the burlesque tragedy of the mechanics in the *Midsummer Night's Dream*, and many other passages, it is evident that there was then an inundation of bad players, who fell into all the aberrations from propriety which offend at the present day, but the public, it would appear, knew well how to distinguish good and bad acting, and would not be easily satisfied. [Footnote: In this respect, the following simile in *Richard the Second* is deserving of attention:--

As in a theatre the eyes of men,
After a well-graced actor leaves the stage,
Are idly bent on him that enters next,
Thinking his prattle to be tedious, &c.]

A thorough critical knowledge of the antiquities of the English theatre can only he obtained in England; the old editions of the pieces which belong to the earlier period are even there extremely rare, and in foreign libraries they are never to be met with; the modern collectors have merely been able to give a few specimens, and not the whole store. It would be highly important to see together all the plays which were undoubtedly in existence before Shakspeare entered on his career, that we might be able to decide with certainty how much of the dramatic art it was possible for him to learn from others. The year of the appearance of a piece on the stage is generally, however, difficult to ascertain, as it was often not printed till long afterwards. If in the labours of Shakspeare's contemporaries, even the older who continued to write at the same time with himself, we can discover resemblances to his style and traces of his art, still it will always remain doubtful whether we are to consider these as the feeble model, or the imperfect imitation. Shakspeare appears to have had all the flexibility of mind, and all the modesty of Raphael, who, also, without ever being an imitator and becoming unfaithful to his sublime and tranquil genius, applied to his own advantage all the improvements of his competitors.

A few feeble attempts to introduce the form of the antique tragedy with choruses, &c., were at an early period made, and praised, without producing any effect. They, like most of the attempts of the moderns in this way, serve to prove how strange were the spectacles through which the old poets were viewed; for it is hardly to be conceived how unlike they are to the Greek tragedies, not merely in merit (for that we may easily suppose), but even in those external circumstances which may be the most easily seized and imitated. *Ferrex and Porrex, or the Tragedy of Gorboduc*, is most frequently cited, which was the production of a nobleman [Footnote: Thomas Sackville, Lord Buckhurst, conjointly with Norton.--F.D.], in the first part of the reign of Elizabeth. Pope bestows high praise on this piece, on account of its regularity, and laments that the contemporary poets did not follow in the same track; for thus he thought a classical theatre might have been formed in England. This opinion only proves that Pope (who, however, passes for a perfect judge of poetry,) had not even an idea of the first elements of Dramatic Art. Nothing can be more spiritless and inanimate, nor more drawling and monotonous in the language and the versification, than this *Ferrex and Porrex*; and although the Unities of Place and Time are in no way observed, and a number of events are crowded into it, yet the scene is wholly destitute of movement: all that happens is previously announced by endless consultations, and afterwards stated in equally endless narratives. *Mustapha*, another unsuccessful work of a kindred description, and also by a great lord, [Footnote: Grevile, Lord Broke.] is a tedious web of all sorts of political subtleties; the choruses in particular are true treatises. However, of the innumerable maxims in rhyme, there are many which might well have a place in the later pieces of Corneille. Kyd, one of the predecessors of Ben Jonson, and mentioned by him in terms of praise, handled the *Cornelia* of Garnier. This may be called receiving an imitation of the ancients from the third or fourth hand.

The first serious piece calculated for popular effect is *The Spanish Tragedy* [by Thomas Kyd], so called from the scene of the story, and not from its being borrowed from a Spanish writer. It kept possession of the stage for a tolerable length of time, though it was often the subject of the ridicule and the parodies of succeeding poets. It usually happens that the public do not easily give up a predilection formed in their first warm susceptibility for the impressions of an art yet unknown to them, even after they have long been acquainted with better, nay, with excellent works. This piece is certainly full of puerilities; the author has ventured on the picture of violent situations and passions without suspecting his own want of power; the catastrophe, more especially, which in horror is intended to outstrip everything conceivable, is very sillily introduced, and produces merely a ludicrous effect. The whole is like the drawings of children, without the observance of proportion, and without steadiness of hand. With a great deal of bombast, the tone of the dialogue, however, has something natural, nay, even familiar, and in the change of scenes we perceive a light movement, which in some degree will account for the general applause received by this immature production.

Lilly and Marlow deserve to be noticed among the predecessors of Shakspeare. Lilly was a scholar, and laboured to introduce a stilted elegance into English prose, and in the tone of dialogue, with such success, that for a period he was the fashionable writer, and the court ladies even formed their conversation after the model of his *Euphues*. His comedy in prose, *Campaspe*, is a warning example of the impossibility of ever constructing, out of mere anecdotes and epigrammatic sallies, anything like a dramatic whole. The author was a learned witling, but in no respect a poet.

Marlow possessed more real talent, and was in a better way. He has handled the history of Edward the Second with very little of art, it is true, but with a certain truth and simplicity, so that in many scenes he does not fail to produce a pathetic effect. His verses are flowing, but without energy: how Ben Jonson could come to use the expression "*Marlow's mighty line*," is more than I can conceive. Shakspeare could neither learn nor derive anything from the luscious manner of Lilly: but in Marlow's *Edward the Second* I certainly imagine that I can discover the feebler model of the earliest historical pieces of Shakspeare.

Of the old comedies in Dodsley's collection, *The Pinner of Wakefielde*, and *Grim, the Collier of Croydon*, seem alone to belong to a period before Shakspeare. Both are not without merit, in the manner of Marionette pieces; in the first, a popular tradition, and in the second, a merry legend, is handled with hearty joviality.

I have dwelt longer on the beginnings of the English theatre, than from their internal worth they deserve, because it has been affirmed recently in England that Shakspeare shows more affinity to the works of his contemporaries now sunk in oblivion than people have hitherto been usually disposed to believe. We are as little to wonder at certain outward resemblances, as at the similarity of the dresses in portraits of the same period. In a more limited sense, however, we apply the word resemblance exclusively to the relation of those features which express the spirit and the mind. Moreover, such plays alone can be admitted to be a satisfactory proof of an assertion of this kind as are ascertained to have been written before the commencement of Shakspeare's career; for in the works of his younger contemporaries, a Decker, Marston, Webster, and others, something of a resemblance may be very naturally accounted for: distinct traces of imitation of Shakspeare are sufficiently abundant. Their imitation was, however, merely confined to external appearance and separate peculiarities; these writers, without the virtues of their model, possess in reality all the faults which senseless critics have falsely censured in Shakspeare.

A sentence somewhat more favourable is merited by Chapman, the translator of Homer, and Thomas Heywood, if we may judge of them from the single specimens of their works in Dodsley's collection. Chapman has handled the well-known story of the Ephesian matron, under the title of *The Widow's Tears*, not without comic talent. Heywood's *Woman Killed with Kindness* is a familiar tragedy: so early may we find examples of this species, which has been given out for new. It is the story of a wife tenderly beloved by her husband, and seduced by a man whom he had loaded with benefits; her sin is discovered, and the severest resolution which her husband can bring himself to form is to remove her from him, without proclaiming her dishonour; she repents, and grieves to death in bitter repentence. A due gradation is not observed in the seduction, but the last scenes are truly agitating. A distinct avowal of a moral aim is, perhaps, essential to the familiar tragedy; or rather, by means of such an aim, a picture of human destinies, whether afflicting kings or private families, is drawn from the ideal sphere into the prosaic world. But when once we admit the title of this subordinate species, we shall find that the demands of morality and the dramatic art coincide, and that the utmost severity of moral principles leads again to poetical elevation. The aspect of that false repentance which merely seeks exemption from punishment, is painful; repentance, as the pain arising from the irreparable forfeiture of innocence, is susceptible of a truly tragic portraiture. Let only the play in question receive a happy conclusion, such as in a well-known piece [Footnote: The author alludes to Kotzebue's play of *Menschenhass und Reue--(The Stranger)*.--TRANS.] has, notwithstanding this painful feeling, been so generally applauded in the present day--viz., the reconciliation of the husband and wife, not on the death-bed of the repentant sinner, but in sound mind and body, and the renewal of the marriage; and it will then be found that it has not merely lost its moral, but also its poetical impression.

In other respects, this piece of Heywood is very inartistic, and carelessly finished: instead of duly developing the main action, the author distracts our attention by a second intrigue, which can hardly be said to have the slightest connection with the other. At this we need hardly be astonished, for Heywood was both a player and an excessively prolific author. Two hundred and twenty pieces were, he says, written entirely, or for the greatest part, by himself; and he was so careless respecting these productions, which were probably thrown off without any great labour, that he had lost the manuscript of the most of them, and only twenty-five remained for publication through the press.

All the above authors, and many others beside, whatever applause they obtained in their life-time, have been unsuccessful in transmitting a living memorial of their works to posterity. Of Shakspeare's younger contemporaries and competitors, few have attained this distinction; and of these Ben Jonson, Beaumont and Fletcher, and Massinger, are the chief.

Ben Jonson found in Shakspeare a ready encourager of his talents. His first piece, imperfect in many respects, *Every Man in his Humour*, was by Shakspeare's intervention brought out on the stage; *Sejanus* was even retouched by him, and in both he undertook a principal character. This hospitable reception on the part of that great man, who was far above every thing like jealousy and petty rivalry, met with a very ungrateful return. Jonson assumed a superiority over Shakspeare on account of his school learning, the only point in which he really had an advantage; he introduced all sorts of biting allusions into his pieces and prologues, and reprobated more especially those magical flights of fancy, the peculiar heritage of Shakspeare, as contrary to genuine taste. In his excuse we must plead, that he was not born under a happy star: his pieces were either altogether unsuccessful, or, compared with the astonishing popularity of Shakspeare's, they obtained but a small share of applause; moreover, he was incessantly attacked, both on the stage and elsewhere, by his rivals, as a disgraceful pedant, who pretended to know every thing better than themselves, and with all manner of satires: all this rendered him extremely irritable and uneven of temper. He possessed in reality a very solid understanding; he was conscious that in the exercise of his art he displayed zeal and earnestness: that Nature had denied him grace, a quality which no labour can acquire, he could not indeed suspect. He thought every man may boast of his assiduity, as Lessing says on a similar occasion. After several failures on the stage, he formed the resolution to declare of his pieces in the outset that they were good, and that if they should not please, this could only proceed from the stupidity of the multitude. The epigraph on one of his unsuccessful pieces with which he committed it to the press, is highly amusing: "As it was never acted, but most negligently played by some, the King's servants, and more squeamishly beheld and censured by others, the King's subjects."

Jonson was a critical poet in the good and the bad sense of the word. He endeavoured to form an exact estimate of what he had on every occasion to perform; hence he succeeded best in that species of the drama which makes the principal demand on the understanding and with little call on the imagination and feeling,--the comedy of character. He introduced nothing into his works which critical dissection should not be able to extract again, as his confidence in it was such, that he conceived it exhausted every thing which pleases and charms us in poetry. He was not aware that, in the chemical retort of the critic, what is most valuable, the volatile living spirit of a poem, evaporates. His pieces are in general deficient in soul, in that nameless something which never ceases to attract and enchant us, even because it is indefinable. In the lyrical pieces, his Masques, we feel the want of a certain mental music of imagery and intonation, which the most accurate observation of difficult measures cannot give. He is everywhere deficient in those excellencies which, unsought, flow from the poet's pen, and which no artist, who purposely hunts for them, can ever hope to find. We must not quarrel with him, however, for entertaining a high opinion of his own works; since, whatever merits they have, he owed like acquired moral properties altogether to himself. The production of them was attended with labour, and unfortunately it is also a labour to read them. They resemble solid and regular, edifices, before which, however, the clumsy scaffolding still remains, to interrupt and prevent us from viewing the architecture with ease, and receiving from it a harmonious impression.

We have of Jonson two tragical attempts, and a number of comedies and masques.

He could have risen to the dignity of the tragic tone, but, for the pathetic, he had not the smallest turn. As he incessantly preaches up the imitation of the ancients, (and he had, we cannot deny, a learned acquaintance with their works,) it is astonishing to observe how much his two tragedies differ, both in substance and form, from the Greek tragedy. From this example we see the influence which the prevailing tone of an age, and the course already pursued in any art, necessarily have upon even the most independent minds. In the historical extent given by Jonson to his *Sejanus* and *Cataline*, unity of time and place were entirely out of the question; and both pieces are crowded with a multitude of secondary persons, such as are never to be found in a Greek tragedy. In *Cataline*, the prologue is spoken by the spirit of Sylla, and it bears a good deal of resemblance to that of Tantalus, in the *Atreus and Thyestes* of Seneca;

to the end of each act an instructive moralizing chorus is appended, without being duly introduced or connected with the whole. This is the extent of the resemblance to the ancients; in other respects, the form of Shakspeare's historical dramas is adhered to, but without their romantic charm. We cannot with certainty say, whether or not Jonson had the Roman pieces of Shakspeare before him: it is probable that he had in *Cataline* at least; but, at all events, he has not learned from him the art of being true to history, and yet satisfying the demands of poetry. In Jonson's hands, the subject continues history, without becoming poetry; the political events which he has described have more the appearance of a business than an action. *Cataline* and *Sejanus* are solid dramatic studies after Sallust and Cicero, after Tacitus, Suetonius, Juvenal, and others; and that is the best which we can say of them. In *Cataline*, which upon the whole is preferable to *Sejanus*, he is also to be blamed for not having blended the dissimilarity of the masses. The first act possesses most elevation, though it disgusts us from its want of moderation: we see a secret assembly of conspirators, and nature appears to answer the furious inspiration of wickedness by dreadful signs. The second act, which paints the intrigues and loves of depraved women, by means of which the conspiracy was brought to light, treads closely on comedy; the last three acts contain a history in dialogue, developed with much good sense, but little poetical elevation. It is to be lamented that Jonson gave only his own text of *Sejanus* without communicating Shakspeare's alterations. We should have been curious to know the means by which he might have attempted to give animation to the monotony of the piece without changing its plan, and how far his genius could adapt itself to another's conceptions.

After these attempts, Jonson took his leave of the Tragic Muse, and in reality his talents were far better suited to Comedy, and that too merely the Comedy of Character. His characterization, however, is more marked with serious satire than playful ridicule: the later Roman satirists, rather than the comic authors, were his models. Nature had denied him that light and easy raillery which plays harmlessly round every thing, and which seems to be the mere effusion of gaiety, but which is so much the more philosophic, as it is not the vehicle of any definite doctrine, but merely the expression of a general irony. There is more of a spirit of observation than of fancy in the comic inventions of Jonson. From this cause his pieces are also defective in point of intrigue. He was a strong advocate for the purity of the species, was unwilling to make use of any romantic motives, and he never had recourse to a novel for the subject of his plots. But his contrivances for the entangling and disentangling his plot are often improbable and forced, without gaining over the imagination by their attractive boldness. Even where he had contrived a happy plot, he took so much room for the delineation of the characters, that we often lose sight of the intrigue altogether, and the action lags with heavy pace. Occasionally he reminds us of those over-accurate portrait painters, who, to insure a likeness, think they must copy every mark of the small-pox, every carbuncle or freckle. Frequently he has been suspected of having, in the delineation of particular characters, had real persons in his eye, while, at the same time, he has been reproached with making his characters mere personifications of general ideas; and, however inconsistent with each other these reproaches may appear, they are neither of them, however, without some foundation. He possessed a methodical head; consequently, where he had once conceived a character in its leading idea, he followed it out with the utmost rigour; whatever, having no reference to this leading idea, served merely to give individual animation, appeared to him in the light of a digression. Hence his names are, for the most part, expressive even to an unpleasant degree of distinctness: and, to add to our satiety, he not unfrequently tacks explanatory descriptions to the dramatis personae. On the other hand, he acted upon the principle, that the comic writer must exhibit real life, with a minute and petty accuracy. Generally he succeeded in seizing the manners of his own age and nation: in itself this was deserving of praise; but even here he confined himself too much to external peculiarities, to the singularities and affectations of the modish tone which were then called humours, and which from their nature are as transient as dresses. Hence a great part of his comic very soon became obsolete, and as early as the re-opening of the theatre under Charles II., no actors could be found who were capable of doing justice to such caricatures. Local colours like these can only be preserved from fading by the most complete seasoning with wit. This is what Shakspeare has effected. Compare, for instance, his Osric, in *Hamlet*, with Fastidius Brisk, in Jonson's *Every Man out of his Humour*: both are portraitures of the insipid affectation of a courtier of the day; but Osric, although he speaks his own peculiar language, will remain to the end of time an exact and intelligible image of foppish folly, whereas Fastidius is merely a portrait in a dress no longer in fashion, and nothing more. However, Jonson has not always fallen into this error; his Captain Bobadil, for example, in *Every Man in his Humour*, a beggarly and cowardly adventurer, who passes himself off with young and simple people for a Hector, is, it is true, far from being as amusing and original as Pistol; but he also, notwithstanding the change of manners, still remains a model in his way, and he has been imitated by English writers of comedy in after times.

In the piece I have just named, the first work of Jonson, the action is extremely feeble and insignificant. In the following, *Every Man out of his Humour*, he has gone still farther astray, in seeking the comic effect merely in caricatured traits, without any interest of situation: it is a rhapsody of ludicrous scenes without connexion and progress. The

Bartholomew Fair, also, is nothing but a coarse *Bambocciate*, in which no more connexion is to be found than usually exists in the hubbub, the noise, the quarrelling, and thefts, which attend upon such amusements of the populace. Vulgar delight is too naturally portrayed; the part of the Puritan, however, is deserving of distinction: his casuistical consultation, whether he ought to eat a sucking-pig according to the custom of the fair, and his lecture afterwards against puppet-shows as a heathen idolatry, are inimitable, and full of the most biting salt of comedy. Ben Jonson did not then foresee that, before the lapse of one generation, the Puritans would be sufficiently powerful to take a very severe revenge on his art, on account of similar railleries.

In so far as plot is concerned, the greatest praise is merited by *Volpone, The Alchemist*, and *Epicoene, or the Silent Woman.* In *Volpone* Jonson for once has entered into Italian manners, without, however, taking an ideal view of them. The leading idea is admirable, and for the most part worked out with masterly skill. Towards the end, however, the whole turns too much on swindling and villany, which necessarily call for the interference of criminal justice, and the piece, from the punishment of the guilty, has everything but a merry conclusion. In the *Alchemist*, both the deceivers and deceived supply a fund of entertainment, only the author enters too deeply into the learning of alchemy. Of an unintelligible jargon very short specimens at most ought to be given in comedy, and it is best that they should also have a secondary signification, of which the person who uses the mysterious language should not himself be aware; when carried to too great a length, the use of them occasions as much weariness as the writings themselves which served as a model. In *The Devil's an Ass* the poet has failed to draw due advantage from a fanciful invention with which he opens, but which indeed was not his own; and our expectation, after being once deceived, causes us to remain dissatisfied with other scenes however excellently comic.

Of all Jonson's pieces there is hardly one which, as it stands, would please on the stage in the present day, even as most of them failed to please in his own time; extracts from them, however, could hardly fail to be successful. In general, much might be borrowed from him, and much might be learned both from his merits and defects. His characters are, for the most part, solidly and judiciously drawn; what he most fails in, is the art of setting them off by the contrast of situations. He has seldom planned his scenes so successfully in this respect as in *Every Man in his Humour*, where the jealous merchant is called off to an important business, when his wife is in expectation of a visit of which he is suspicious, and when he is anxious to station his servant as a sentinel, without however confiding his secret to him, because, above all things he dreads the discovery of his own jealousy. This scene is a master-piece, and if Jonson had always so composed, we must have been obliged to rank him among the first of comic writers.

Merely lest we should be charged with an omission do we mention *The Masques*: allegorical, occasional pieces, chiefly designed for court festivals, and decorated with machinery, masked dresses, dancing, and singing. This secondary species died again nearly with Jonson himself; the only subsequent production in this way of any fame is the *Comus* of Milton. When allegory is confined to mere personification, it must infallibly turn out very frigid in a play; the action itself must be allegorical, and in this respect there are many ingenious inventions, but the Spanish poets have almost alone furnished us with successful examples of it. The peculiarity of Jonson's *Masques* most deserving of remark seems to me to be the anti-masque, as they are called, which the poet himself sometimes attaches to his own invention, and generally allows to precede the serious act. As the ideal flatteries, for whose sake the gods have been brought down from Olympus, are but too apt to fall into mawkishness, this antidote on such occasions is certainly deserving of commendation.

Ben Jonson, who in all his pieces took a mechanical view of art, bore a farther resemblance to the master of a handicraft in taking an apprentice. He had a servant of the name of Broome, who formed himself as a theatrical writer from the conversation and instructions of his master, and brought comedies on the stage with applause.

Beaumont and Fletcher are always named together, as if they had been two inseparable poets, whose works were all planned and executed in common. This idea, however, is not altogether correct. We know, indeed, but little of the circumstances of their lives: this much however is known, that Beaumont died very young; and that Fletcher survived his younger friend ten years, and was so unremittingly active in his career as a dramatic poet, that several of his plays were first brought on the stage after his death, and some which he left unfinished were completed by another hand. The pieces collected under both names amount to upwards of fifty; and of this number it is probable that the half must be considered as the work of Fletcher alone. Beaumont and Fletcher's works did not make their appearance until a short time after the death of the latter; the publishers have not given themselves the trouble to distinguish critically the share which belonged to each, and still less to afford us any information respecting the diversity of their talents. Some of their contemporaries have attributed boldness of imagination to Fletcher, and a mature judgment to his friend: the former, according to their opinion, was the inventive genius; the latter, the directing and moderating critic. But this account rests on no foundation. It is now impossible to distinguish with certainty the hand of each; nor would the knowledge repay the labour. All the pieces ascribed to them, whether they proceed from one alone or from both, are composed in the same spirit and in the same manner. Hence it is probable that it was not so much the need of supplying the deficiencies of each other, as the great resemblance of their way of thinking, which induced them to continue so long and so inseparably united.

Beaumont and Fletcher began their career in the lifetime of Shakspeare: Beaumont even died before him, and Fletcher only survived him nine years. From some allusions in the way of parody, we may conclude that they entertained no very extravagant admiration of their great predecessor; from whom, nevertheless, they both learned much, and unquestionably borrowed many of their thoughts. In the whole form of their plays they followed his example, regardless of the different principles of Ben Jonson and of the imitation of the ancients. Like him they drew from novels and romances; they combined pathetic and burlesque scenes in the same play, and, by the concatenation of the incidents, endeavoured to excite the impression of the extraordinary and the wonderful. A wish to surpass Shakspeare in this species is often evident enough; contemporary eulogists, indeed, have no hesitation in ranking Shakspeare far below them, and assert that the English stage was first brought to perfection by Beaumont and Fletcher. And, in reality, Shakspeare's fame was in some degree eclipsed by them in the generation which immediately succeeded, and in the time of Charles II. they still enjoyed greater popularity: the progress of time, however, has restored all three to their due places. As on the stage the highest excellence will wear out by frequent repetition, and novelty always possesses a great charm, the dramatic art is, consequently, much influenced by fashion; it is more than other branches of literature and the fine arts exposed to the danger of passing rapidly from a grand and simple style to dazzling and superficial mannerism.

Beaumont and Fletcher were in fact men of the most distinguished talents; they scarcely wanted anything more than a profounder seriousness of mind, and that artistic sagacity which everywhere observes a due measure, to rank beside the greatest dramatic poets of all nations. They possessed extraordinary fecundity and flexibility of mind, and a facility which however too often degenerated into carelessness. The highest perfection they have hardly ever attained; and I should have little hesitation in affirming that they had not even an idea of it: however, on several occasions they have approached quite close to it. And why was it denied them to take this last step? Because with them poetry was not an inward devotion of the feeling and imagination, but a means to obtain brilliant results. Their first object was effect, which the great artist can hardly fail of attaining if he is determined above all things to satisfy himself.

They were not like the most of their predecessors, players, [Footnote: In the privilege granted by James I. to the royal players, a *Laurence Fletcher* is named along with Shakspeare as manager of the company. The poet's name was John Fletcher. Perhaps the former might be his brother or near relation.] but they lived in the neighbourhood of the theatre, were in constant intercourse with it, and possessed a perfect understanding of theatrical matters. They were also thoroughly acquainted with their contemporaries; but they found it more convenient to lower themselves to the taste of the public than to follow the example of Shakspeare, who elevated the public to himself. They lived in a vigorous age, which more willingly pardoned extravagancies of every description than feeblenesss and frigidity. They therefore never allowed themselves to be restrained by poetical or moral considerations; and in this confidence they found their account: they resemble in some measure somnambulists, who with closed eyes pass safely through the greatest dangers. Even when they undertake what is most depraved they handle it with a certain felicity. In the commencement of a degeneracy in the dramatic art, the spectators first lose the capability of judging of a play as a whole; hence Beaumont and Fletcher bestow very little attention on harmony of composition and the observance of due proportion between all the different parts. They not unfrequently lose sight of a happily framed plot, and appear almost to forget it; they bring something else forward equally capable of affording pleasure and entertainment, but without preparation, and in the particular place where it occurs without propriety. They always excite curiosity, frequently compassion--they hurry us along with them; they succeed better, however, in exciting than in gratifying our expectation. So long as we are reading them we feel ourselves keenly interested; but they leave very few imperishable impressions behind. They are least successful in their tragic attempts, because their feeling is not sufficiently drawn from the depths of human nature, and because they bestowed too little attention on the general consideration of human destinies: they succeed much better in Comedy, and in those serious and pathetic pictures which occupy a middle place betwixt Comedy and Tragedy. Their characters are often arbitrarily drawn, and, when it suits the momentary wants of the poet, become even untrue to themselves; in external matters they are tolerably in keeping. Beaumont and Fletcher employ the whole strength of their talents in pictures of passion; but they enter little into the secret history of the heart; they pass over the first emotions and the gradual heightening of a feeling; they seize it, as it were, in its highest maturity, and then develope its symptoms with the most overpowering illusion, though with an exaggerated strength and fulness. But though its expression does not always possess the strictest truth, nevertheless it still appears natural, every thing has free motion; nothing is laboriously constrained or far-fetched, however striking it may sometimes appear. In their dialogue they have completely succeeded in uniting the familiar tone of real conversation and the appearance of momentary suggestion with poetical elevation. They even run into that popular affectation of the natural which has ensured such great success to some dramatic poets of our own time; but as the latter sought it in the absence of all elevation of fancy, they could not help falling into insipidity. Beaumont and Fletcher generally couple nature with fancy; they succeed in giving an extraordinary appearance to what is common, and thus preserve a certain fallacious image of the ideal. The morality of these writers is ambiguous. Not that they failed in strong colours to contrast greatness of soul and goodness with baseness and wickedness, or did not usually conclude with the disgrace and punishment of the latter, but an ostentatious generosity is often favourably exhibited in lieu of duty and justice. Every thing good and excellent in their pictures arises more from transient ebullition than fixed principle; they seem to place the virtues in the blood; and close beside them impulses of merely a selfish and instinctive nature hold up their heads, as if they were of nobler origin. There is an incurable vulgar side of human nature which, when he cannot help but show it, the poet should never handle without a certain bashfulness; but instead of this Beaumont and Fletcher throw no veil whatever over nature. They express every thing bluntly in words; they make the spectator the unwilling confidant of all that more noble minds endeavour even to hide from themselves. The indecencies in which these poets indulged themselves go beyond conception. Licentiousness of language is the least evil; many scenes, nay, even whole plots, are so contrived that the very idea, not to mention the beholding of them, is a gross insult to modesty. Aristophanes is a bold mouth-piece of sensuality; but like the Grecian statuaries in the figures of satyrs, &c., he banishes them into the animal kingdom to which they wholly belong; and judging him by the morality of his times, he is much less offensive. But Beaumont and Fletcher hold up to view the impure and nauseous colours of vice in quite a different sphere; their compositions resemble the sheet, in the vision of the Apostle, full of pure and impure animals. This was the universal tendency of the dramatic poets under James and Charles I. They seem as if they purposely wished to justify the assertion of the Puritans, that theatres were so many schools of seduction and chapels of the Devil.

To those who merely read for amusement and general cultivation, we can only recommend the works of Beaumont and Fletcher with some limitation [Footnote: Hence I cannot approve of the undertaking, which has been recently commenced, of translating them into German. They are not at all adapted for our great public, and whoever makes a particular study of dramatic poetry will have little difficulty in finding his way to the originals.]. For the practical artist, however, and the critical judge of dramatic poetry, an infinite deal may be learned from them; as well from their merits as their extravagancies. A minute dissection of one of their works, for which we have not here the necessary space, would serve to place this in the clearest light. With regard to representation, these pieces had, in their day, this advantage, that they did not require such great actors to fill the principal characters as Shakspeare's plays did. In order to bring them on the stage in our days, it would be necessary to re-cast most of them; which might be done with some of them by omitting, moderating, and purging various passages [Footnote: So far as I know only one play has yet been brought on the German theatre, namely, *Rule a Wife and have a Wife*, re-written by Schroder under the title of *Stille Wasser sind tief* (Still Waters run deep) which, when well acted, has always been uncommonly well received.].

The Two Noble Kinsmen is deserving of more particular mention, as it is the joint production of Shakspeare and Fletcher. I see no ground for calling this in question; the piece, it is true, did not make its appearance till after the death of both; but what could be the motive with the editor or printer for any deception, as Fletcher's name was at the time in as great, at least, if not greater celebrity than Shakspeare's? Were it the sole production of Fletcher, it would, undoubtedly, have to be ranked as the best of his serious and heroic pieces. However, it would be unfair to a writer of talent to take from him a work simply because it seems too good for him. Might not Fletcher, who in his thoughts and images not unfrequently shows an affinity to Shakspeare, have for once had the good fortune to approach closer to him than usual? It would still be more dangerous to rest on the similarity of separate passages to others in Shakspeare. This might rather arise from imitation. I rely therefore entirely on the historical statement, which, probably, originated in a tradition of the players. There are connoisseurs, who, in the pictures of Raphael, (which, as is well know, were not always wholly executed by himself,) take upon them to determine what parts were painted by Francesco Penni, or Giulio Romano, or some other scholar. I wish them success with the nicety of their discrimination; they are at least secure from contradiction, as we have no certain information on the subject. I would only remind these connoisseurs, that Giulio Romano was himself deceived by a copy from Raphael of Andrea del Sarto's, and that, too, with regard to a figure which he had himself assisted in painting. The case in point is, however, a much more complicated problem in criticism. The design of Raphael's figures was at least his own, and the execution only was distributed in part among his scholars. But to find out how much of *The Two Noble Kinsmen* may belong to Shakspeare, we must not only be able to tell the difference of hands in the execution, but also to determine the influence of Shakspeare on the plan of the whole. When, however, he once joined another poet in the production of a work, he must also have accommodated himself, in a certain degree, to his views, and renounced the prerogative of unfolding his inmost peculiarity. Amidst so many grounds for doubting, if I might be allowed to hazard an opinion, I should say, that I think I can perceive the mind of Shakspeare in a certain ideal purity, which distinguishes this piece from all others of Fletcher's, and in the conscientious fidelity with which the story adheres to that of Chaucer's *Palamon and Arcite*. In the style Shakspeare's hand is at first discoverable in a brevity and fulness of thought bordering on obscurity; in the colour of the expression, almost all the poets of that time bear a strong resemblance to each other. The first acts are most carefully laboured; afterwards the piece is drawn out to too great a length and in an epic manner; the dramatic law of quickening the action towards the conclusion, is not sufficiently observed. The part of the jailor's daughter, whose insanity is artlessly conducted in pure monologues, is certainly not Shakspeare's; for, in that case, we must suppose him to have had an intention of arrogantly imitating his own Ophelia.

Moreover, it was then a very general custom for two or even three poets to join together in the production of one play. Besides the constant example of Beaumont and Fletcher, we have many others. The consultations, respecting the plan, were generally held at merry meetings in taverns. Upon one of these occasions it happened that one in a poetical intoxication calling out, "I will undertake to kill the king!" was immediately taken into custody as a traitor, till the misunderstanding was cleared up. This mode of composing may answer very well in the lighter species of the drama, which require to be animated by social wit. With regard to theatrical effect, four eyes may, in general, see better than two, and mutual objections may be of use in finding out the most suitable means. But the highest poetical inspiration is much more eremitical than communicative; for it always seeks to express something which sets language at defiance, which, therefore, can only be weakened and dissipated by detached words, and can only be attained by the common impression of the complete work, whose idea is hovering before it.

The Knight of the Burning Pestle, of Beaumont and Fletcher, is an incomparable work and singular in its kind. It is a parody of the chivalry romances; the thought is borrowed from *Don Quixote*, but the imitation is handled with freedom, and so particularly applied to Spenser's *Fairy Queen*, that it may pass for a second invention. But the peculiarly ingenious novelty of the piece consists in the combination of the irony of a chimerical abuse of poetry with another irony exactly the contrary, of the incapacity to comprehend any fable, and the dramatic form more particularly. A grocer and his wife come as spectators to the theatre: they are discontented with the piece which has just been announced; they demand a play in honour of the corporation, and Ralph, their apprentice, is to act a principal part in it. Their humour is complied with; but still they are not satisfied, make their remarks on every thing, and incessantly address themselves to the players. Ben Jonson had already exhibited imaginary spectators, but they were either benevolent expounders or awkward censurers of the poet's views: consequently, they always conducted his, the poet's, own cause. But the grocer and his wife represent a whole genus, namely, those unpoetical spectators, who are destitute of a feeling for art. The illusion with them becomes a passive error; the subject represented has on them all the effect of reality, they accordingly resign themselves to the impression of each moment, and take part for or against the persons of the drama. On the other hand, they show themselves insensible to all genuine illusion, that is, of entering vividly into the spirit of the fable: for them Ralph, however heroically and chivalrously he may conduct himself, is always Ralph their apprentice; and in the whim of the moment they take upon them to demand scenes which are quite inconsistent with the plan of the piece that has been commenced. In short, the views and demands with which poets are often oppressed by a prosaical public are very cleverly and amusingly personified in these caricatures of spectators.

The Faithful Shepherdess, a pastoral, is highly extolled by some English critics, as it is without doubt finished with great care, in rhymed, and partly, in lyrical verses. Fletcher wished also to be classical for once, and did violence to his natural talent. Perhaps he had the intention of surpassing Shakspeare's *Midsummer Night's Dream*; but the composition which he has ushered into the world is as heavy as that of the other was easy and aerial. The piece is overcharged with mythology and rural painting, is untheatrical, and so far from pourtraying the genuine ideality of a pastoral world, it even contains the greatest vulgarities. We might rather call it an immodest eulogy of chastity. I am willing to hope that Fletcher was unacquainted with the *Pastor Fido* of Guarini, for otherwise his failure would admit of less justification.

We are in want of space to speak in detail of the remaining works of Beaumont and Fletcher, although they might be made the subject of many instructive observations. On the whole, we may say of these writers that they have built a splendid palace, but merely in the suburbs of poetry, while Shakspeare has his royal residence in the very centre point of the capital.

The fame of Massinger has been lately revived by an edition of his works. Some literary men wish to rank him above Beaumont and Fletcher, as if he had approached more closely to the excellence of Shakspeare. I cannot see it. He appears to me to bear the greatest resemblance to Beaumont and Fletcher in the plan of the pieces, in the tone of manners, and even in the language and negligences of versification. I would not undertake to decide, from internal symptoms, whether a play belonged to Massinger, or Beaumont and Fletcher. This applies also to the other contemporaries; for instance, to Shirley, of whose pieces two are stated to have crept into the works ascribed to the two last-named poets. There was (as already said) at this time in England a school of dramatic art, a school of which Shakspeare was the invisible and too often unacknowledged head; for Ben Jonson remained almost without successors. It is a characteristic of what is called manner in art to efface the features of personal originality, and to make the productions of various artists bear a resemblance to each other; and from manner no dramatic poet of this age, who succeeded Shakspeare, can be pronounced altogether free. When, however, we compare their works with those of the succeeding age, we perceive between them something about the same relation as between the paintings of the school of Michel Angelo and those of the last half of the seventeenth and the first half of the eighteenth century. Both are tainted with manner; but the manner of the former bears the trace of a sublime origin in the first ages; in the latter, all is little, affected, empty, and superficial. I repeat it: in a general history of the dramatic art, the first period of the English theatre is the only one of importance. The plays of the least known writers of that time, (I venture to affirm this, though I am far from being acquainted with all of them) are more instructive for theory, and more remarkable, than the most celebrated of all the succeeding times.

LECTURE XXVIII.

Closing of the Stage by the Puritans--Revival of the Stage under Charles the Second--Depravity of Taste and Morals--Dryden, Otway, and others-- Characterization of the Comic Poets from Wycherley and Congreve to the middle of the eighteenth century--Tragedies of the same Period--Rowe-- Addison's *Cato*--Later Pieces--Familiar Tragedy: Lillo--Garrick-- Latest state.

In this condition nearly the theatre remained under the reign of Charles I. down to the year 1647, when the invectives of the Puritans (who had long murmured at the theatre, and at last thundered loudly against it,) were changed into laws. To act, or even to be a spectator of plays was prohibited under a severe penalty. A civil war followed, and the extraordinary circumstance here happened, that the players, (who, in general, do not concern themselves much about forms of government, and whose whole care is usually devoted to the peaceable entertainment of their follow-citizens,) compelled by want, joined that political party the interests of which were intimately connected with their own existence. Almost all of them entered the army of the King, many perished for the good cause, the survivors returned to London and continued to exercise their art in secret. Out of the ruins of all the former companies of actors, one alone was formed, which occasionally, though with very great caution, gave representations at the country seats of the great, in the vicinity of London. For among the other singularities to which the violence of those times gave rise, it was considered a proof of attachment to the old constitution to be fond of plays, and to reward and harbour those who acted them in private houses.

Fortunately the Puritans did not so well understand the importance of a censorship as the Governments of our day, or the yet unprinted dramatic productions of the preceding age could not have issued from the press, by which means many of them would have been irrecoverably lost. These gloomy fanatics were such enemies of all that was beautiful, that they not only persecuted every liberal mental entertainment, calculated in any manner to adorn life, and more especially the drama, as being a public worship of Baal, but they even shut their ears to church music, as a demoniacal howling. If their ascendency had been maintained much longer, England must infallibly have been plunged in an irremediable barbarity. The oppression of the drama continued down to the year 1660, when the free exercise of all arts returned with Charles II.

The influence which the government of this monarch had on the manners and spirit of the time, and the natural reaction against the principles previously dominant, are sufficiently well known. As the Puritans had brought republican principles and religious zeal into universal odium, so this light-minded monarch seemed expressly born to sport away all respect for the kingly dignity. England was inundated with foreign follies and vices in his train. The court set the fashion of the most undisguised immorality, and its example was the more contagious, the more people imagined that they could only show their zeal for the new order of things by an extravagant way of thinking and living. The fanaticism of the republicans had been associated with strictness of manners, nothing therefore could be more easy and agreeable than to obtain the character of royalists, by the extravagant indulgence of all lawful and unlawful pleasures. Nowhere was the age of Louis XIV. imitated with greater depravity. But the prevailing gallantry of the court of France had its reserve and a certain delicacy of feeling; they sinned (if I may so speak) with some degree of dignity, and no man ventured to attack what was honourable, however at variance with it his own actions might be. The English played a part which was altogether unnatural to them: they gave themselves up heavily to levity; they everywhere confounded the coarsest licentiousness with free mental vivacity, and did not perceive that the kind of grace which is still compatible with depravity, disappears with the last veil which it throws off.

We can easily conceive the turn which, under such auspices, the new formation of taste must have taken. There existed no real knowledge of the fine arts, which were favoured merely like other foreign fashions and inventions of luxury. The age neither felt a true want of poetry, nor had any relish for it: in it they merely wished for a light and brilliant entertainment. The theatre, which in its former simplicity had attracted the spectators solely by the excellence of the dramatic works and the skill of the actors, was now furnished out with all the appliances with which we are at this day familiar; but what it gained in external decoration, it lost in internal worth.

To Sir William Davenant, the English theatre, on its revival after the interruption which we have so often mentioned, owes its new institution, if this term may be here used. He introduced the Italian system of decoration, the *costume*, as it was then well or ill understood, the opera music, and in general the use of the orchestra. For this undertaking Charles II. had furnished him with extensive privileges. Davenant was a sort of adventurer and wit; in every way worthy of the royal favour; to enjoy which, dignity of character was never a necessary requisite. He set himself to work in every way that a rich theatrical repertory may render necessary; he made alterations of old pieces, and also wrote himself plays, operas, prologues, &c. But of all his writings nothing has escaped a merited oblivion.

Dryden soon became and long remained the hero of the stage. This man, from his influence in fixing the laws of versification and poetical language, especially in rhyme, has acquired a reputation altogether disproportionate to his true merit. We shall not here inquire whether his translations of the Latin poets are not manneristical paraphrases, whether his political allegories (now that party interest is dead) can be read without the greatest weariness; but confine ourselves to his plays, which considered relatively to his great reputation, are incredibly bad. Dryden had a gift of flowing and easy versification; the knowledge which he possessed was considerable, but undigested; and all this was coupled with the talent of giving a certain appearance of novelty to what however was borrowed from all quarters; his serviceable muse was the resource of an irregular life. He had besides an immeasurable vanity; he frequently disguises it under humble prologues; on other occasions he speaks out boldly and confidently, avowing his opinion that he has done better than Shakspeare, Fletcher, and Jonson (whom he places nearly on the same level); all the merit of this he is, however, willing to ascribe to the refinement and advances of the age. The age indeed! as if that of Elizabeth compared with the one in which Dryden lived, were not in every respect "Hyperion to a Satyr!" Dryden played also the part of the critic: he furnished his pieces richly with prefaces and treatises on dramatic poetry, in which he chatters most confusedly about the genius of Shakspeare and Fletcher, and about the entirely opposite example of Corneille; of the original boldness of the British stage, and of the rules of Aristotle and Horace.--He imagined that he had invented a new species, namely the Heroic Drama; as if Tragedy had not from its very nature been always heroical! If we are, however, to seek for a heroic drama which is not peculiarly tragic, we shall find it among the Spaniards, who had long possessed it in the greatest perfection. From the uncommon facility of rhyming which Dryden possessed, it cost him little labour to compose the most of his serious pieces entirely in rhyme. With the English, the rhymed verse of ten syllables supplies the place of the Alexandrine; it has more freedom in its pauses, but on the other hand it wants the alternation of male and female rhymes; it proceeds in pairs exactly like the French Alexandrine, and in point of syllabic measure it is still more uniformly symmetrical. It therefore unavoidably communicates a great stiffness to the dialogue. The manner of the older English poets before them, who generally used blank verse, and only occasionally introduced rhymes, was infinitely preferable. But, since then, on the other hand, rhyme has come to be too exclusively rejected.

Dryden's plans are improbable, even to silliness; the incidents are all thrown out without forethought; the most wonderful theatrical strokes fall incessantly from the clouds. He cannot be said to have drawn a single character; for there is not a spark of nature in his dramatic personages. Passions, criminal and magnanimous sentiments, flow with indifferent levity from their lips, without ever having dwelt in the heart: their chief delight is in heroical boasting. The tone of expression is by turns flat or madly bombastical; not unfrequently both at the same time: in short, this poet resembles a man who walks upon stilts in a morass. His wit is displayed in far-fetched sophistries; his imagination in long-spun similies, awkwardly introduced. All these faults have been ridiculed by the Duke of Buckingham in his comedy of *The Rehearsal*. Dryden was meant under the name of Bayes, though some features are taken from Davenant and other contemporary writers. The vehicle of this critical satire might have been more artificial and diversified; the matter, however is admirable, and the separate parodies are very amusing and ingenious. The taste for this depraved manner was, however, too prevalent to be restrained by the efforts of so witty a critic, who was at the same time a grandee of the kingdom.

Otway and Lee were younger competitors of Dryden in tragedy. Otway lived in poverty, and died young; under more favourable circumstances greater things perhaps would have been done by him. His first pieces in rhyme are imitations of Dryden's manner; he also imitated the *Berenice* of Racine. Two of his pieces in blank verse have kept possession of the stage--*The Orphan* and *Venice Preserved.* These tragedies are far from being good; but there is matter in them, especially in the last; and amidst much empty declamation there are some truly pathetic passages. How little Otway understood the true rules of composition may be inferred from this, that he has taken the half of the scenes of his *Caius Marius* verbally, or with disfiguring changes, from the *Romeo and Juliet* of Shakspeare. Nothing more incongruous can well he conceived, than such an episode in Roman manners, and in a historical drama. This impudent plagiarism is in no manner justified by his confessing it.

Dryden altered pieces of Shakspeare; for then, and even long afterwards, every person thought himself qualified for this task. He also wrote comedies; but Wycherley and Congreve were the first to acquire a name in this species of composition. The mixed romantic drama was now laid entirely aside; all was either tragedy or comedy. The history of each of these species will therefore admit of being separately handled--if, indeed, that can be correctly said to have a history where we can perceive no progressive development, but mere standing still, or even retrograding, and an inconstant fluctuation in all directions. However, the English, under Charles II. and Queen Anne, and down to the middle of the eighteenth century, had a series of comic writers, who may be all considered as belonging to one common class; for the only considerable diversity among them arises merely from an external circumstance, the varying tone of manners.

I have elsewhere in these Lectures shown that elegance of form is of the greatest importance in Comedy, as from the want of care in this respect it is apt to degenerate into a mere prosaical imitation of reality, and thereby to forfeit its pretensions to rank as either poetry or art. It is exactly, however, in the form, that the English comedies are most negligent. In the first place, they are written entirely in prose. It has been well remarked by an English critic, that the banishment of verse from Comedy had even a prejudicial influence on versification in Tragedy. The older dramatists could elevate or lower the tone of their Iambics at pleasure; from the exclusion of this verse from familiar dialogue, it has become more pompous and inflexible. Shakspeare's comic scenes, it is true, are also written, for the most part, in prose; but in the Mixed Comedy, which has a serious, wonderful, or pathetic side, the prose, mixed with the elevated language of verse, serves to mark the contrast between vulgar and ideal sentiments; it is a positive means of exhibition. Continued prose in Comedy is nothing but the natural language, on which the poet has failed to employ his skill to refine and smoothe it down, while apparently he seems the more careful to give an accurate imitation of it: it is that prose which Moliere's Bourgeois Gentilhomme has been speaking his whole lifetime without suspecting it.

Moreover, the English comic poets tie themselves down too little to the unity of place. I have on various occasions declared that I consider change of scene even a requisite, whenever a drama is to possess historical extent or the magic of romance. But in the comedy of common life the case is somewhat altogether different. I am convinced that it would almost always have had a beneficial influence on the conduct of the action in the English plays, if their authors had, in this respect, subjected themselves to stricter laws.

The lively trickery of the Italian masks has always found a more unfavourable reception in England than in France. The fool or clown in Shakspeare's comedies is far more of an ironical humorist than a mimical buffoon. Intrigue in real life is foreign to the Northern nations, both from the virtues and the defects of their character; they have too much openness of disposition, and too little acuteness and nicety of understanding. It is remarkable that, with greater violence of passion, the Southern nations possess, nevertheless, in a much higher degree the talent of dissembling. In the North, life is wholly founded on mutual confidence. Hence, in the drama, the spectators, from being less practised in intrigue, are less inclined to be delighted with concealment of views and their success by bold artifice, and with the presence of mind which, in unexpected events of an untoward nature, readily extricates its possessor from embarrassment. However, there may be an intrigue in Comedy, in the dramatic sense, though none of the persons carry on what is properly called intrigue. Still it is in the entangling and disentangling their plots that the English comic writers are least deserving of praise. Their plans are defective in unity. From this reproach I have, I conceive, sufficiently exculpated Shakspeare; it is rather merited by many of Fletcher's pieces. When, indeed, the imagination has a share in the composition, then it is far from being as necessary that all should be accurately connected together by cause and effect, as when the whole is framed and held together exclusively by the understanding. The existence of a double or even triple intrigue in many modern English comedies has been acknowledged even by English critics themselves. [Footnote: Among others, by the anonymous author of a clever letter to Garrick, prefixed to Coxeter's edition of *Massinger's Works*, who says--"What with their plots, and double plots, and counter-plots, and under-plots, the mind is as much perplexed to piece out the story as to put together the disjointed parts of an ancient drama."] The inventions to which they have recourse are often everything but probable, without charming us by their happy novelty; they are chiefly deficient, however, in perspicuity and easy development. Most English comedies are much too long. The authors overload their composition with characters: and we can see no reason why they should not have divided them into several pieces. It is as if we were to compel to travel in the same stage-coach a greater number of persons, all strangers to each other, than there is properly room for; the journey becomes more inconvenient, and the entertainment not a whit more lively.

The great merit of the English comic poets of this period consists in the delineation of character; yet though many have certainly shown much talent, I cannot ascribe to any a peculiar genius for characterization. Even in this department the older poets (not only Shakspeare, for that may easily be supposed, but even Fletcher and Jonson) are superior to them. The moderns seldom possess the faculty of seizing the most hidden and involuntary emotions, and giving a comic expression to them; they generally draw merely the natural or assumed surface of men. Moreover, the same circumstance which in France, after Moliere's time, was attended with such prejudicial effects, came here also into play. The comic muse, instead of becoming familiar with life in the middle and lower ranks (her proper sphere), assumed an air of distinction: she squeezed herself into courts, and endeavoured to snatch a resemblance of the *beau monde*. It was now no longer an English national, but a London comedy. The whole turns almost exclusively on fashionable love-suits and fashionable raillery; the love-affairs are either disgusting or insipid, and the raillery is always puerile and destitute of wit. These comic writers may have accurately hit the tone of their time; in this they did their duty;

but they have reared a lamentable memorial of their age. In few periods has taste in the fine arts been at such a low ebb as about the close of the seventeenth and during the first half of the eighteenth century. The political machine kept its course; wars, negotiations, and changes of states, give to this age a certain historical splendour; but the comic poets and portrait-painters have revealed to us the secret of its pitifulness--the former in their copies of the dresses, and the latter in the imitation of the social tone. I am convinced that if we could now listen to the conversation of the *beau monde* of that day, it would appear to us as pettily affected and full of tasteless pretension, as the hoops, the towering head-dresses and high-heeled shoes of the women, and the huge perukes, cravats, wide sleeves, and ribbon-knots of the men. [Footnote: When I make good or bad taste in dress an infallible criterion of social elegance or deformity, this must be limited to the age in which the fashion came up; for it may sometimes be very difficult to overturn a wretched fashion even when, in other things, a better taste has long prevailed. The dresses of the ancients were more simple, and consequently less subject to change of fashion; and the male dress, in particular, was almost unchangeable. However, even from the dresses alone, as we see them in the remains of antiquity, we may form a pretty accurate judgment of the character of the Egyptians, the Greeks, and the Romans. In the female portrait-busts of the time of the later Roman emperors, we often find the head-dresses extremely tasteless; nay, even busts with peruques which may be taken off, probably for the purpose of changing them, as the originals themselves did.]

The last, and not the least defect of the English comedies is their offensiveness. I may sum up the whole in one word by saying, that after all we know of the licentiousness of manners under Charles II., we are still lost in astonishment at the audacious ribaldry of Wycherley and Congreve. Decency is not merely violated in the grossest manner in single speeches, and frequently in the whole plot; but in the character of the rake, the fashionable debauchee, a moral scepticism is directly preached up, and marriage is the constant subject of their ridicule. Beaumont and Fletcher portrayed an irregular but vigorous nature: nothing, however, can be more repulsive than rude depravity coupled with claims to higher refinement. Under Queen Anne manners became again more decorous; and this may easily be traced in the comedies: in the series of English comic poets, Wycherley, Congreve, Farquhar, Vanbrugh, Steele, Cibber, &c., we may perceive something like a gradation from the most unblushing indecency to a tolerable degree of modesty. However, the example of the predecessors has had more than a due influence on the successors. From prescriptive fame pieces keep possession of the stage such as no man in the present day durst venture to bring out. It is a remarkable phenomenon, the causes of which are deserving of inquiry, that the English nation, in the last half of the eighteenth century, passed all at once from the most opposite way of thinking, to an almost over-scrupulous strictness of manners in social conversation, in romances and plays, and in the plastic arts.

Some writers have said of Congreve that he had too much wit for a comic poet. These people must have rather a strange notion of wit. The truth is, that Congreve and the other writers above mentioned possess in general much less comic than epigrammatic wit. The latter often degenerates into a laborious straining for wit. Steele's dialogue, for example, puts us too much in mind of the letters in the *Spectator*. Farquhar's plots seem to me to be the most ingenious of all.

The latest period of English Comedy begins nearly with Colman. Since that time the morals have been irreproachable, and much has been done in the way of refined and original characterization; the form, however, has on the whole remained the same, and in that respect I do not think the English comedies at all models.

Tragedy has been often attempted in England in the eighteenth century, but a genius of the first rank has never made his appearance. They laid aside the manner of Dryden, however, and that at least was an improvement. Rowe was an honest admirer of Shakspeare, and his modest reverence for this superior genius was rewarded by a return to nature and truth. The traces of imitation are not to be mistaken: the part of Gloster in *Jane Shore* is even directly borrowed from *Richard the Third*. Rowe did not possess boldness and vigour, but was not without sweetness and feeling; he could excite the softer emotions, and hence in his *Fair Penitent*, *Jane Shore*, and *Lady Jane Gray*, he has successfully chosen female heroines and their weaknesses for his subjects.

Addison possessed an elegant mind, but he was by no means a poet. He undertook to purify the English Tragedy, by bringing it into a compliance with the supposed rules of good taste. We might have expected from a judge of the ancients, that he would have endeavoured to approach the Greek models. Whether he had any such intention I know not, but certain it is that he has produced nothing but a tragedy after the French model. *Cato* is a feeble and frigid piece, almost destitute of action, without one truly overpowering moment. Addison has so narrowed a great and heroic picture by his timid manner of treating it, that he could not, without foreign intermixture, even fill up the frame. Hence, he had recourse to the traditional love intrigues; if we count well, we shall find in this piece no fewer than six persons in love: Cato's two sons, Marcia and Lucia, Juba and Sempronius. The good Cato cannot, therefore, as a provident father of a family, avoid arranging two marriages at the close. With the exception of Sempronius, the villain of the piece, the lovers are one and all somewhat silly. Cato, who ought to be the soul of the whole, is hardly ever shown to us in action; nothing remains for him but to admire himself and to die. It might be thought that the stoical determination of suicide, without struggle and without passion, is not a fortunate subject; but correctly speaking, no subjects are unfortunate, every thing depends on correctly apprehending them. Addison has been induced, by a wretched regard to Unity of Place, to leave out Caesar, the only worthy contrast to Cato; and, in this respect even Metastasio has managed matters better. The language is pure and simple, but without vigour; the rhymeless Iambic gives more freedom to the dialogue, and an air somewhat less conventional than it has in the French tragedies; but in vigorous eloquence, Cato remains far behind them.

Addison took his measures well; he placed all the great and small critics, with Pope at their head, the whole militia of good taste under arms, that he might excite a high expectation of the piece which he had produced with so much labour. *Cato* was universally praised, as a work without an equal. And on what foundation do these boundless praises rest? On regularity of form? This had been already observed by the French poets for nearly a century, and notwithstanding its constraints they had often attained a much stronger pathetic effect. Or on the political sentiments? But in a single dialogue between Brutus and Cassius in Shakspeare there is more of a Roman way of thinking and republican energy than in all *Cato*.

I doubt whether this piece could ever have produced a powerful impression, but its reputation has certainly had a prejudicial influence on Tragedy in England. The example of *Cato*, and the translation of French tragedies, which became every day more frequent, could not, it is true, render universal the belief in the infallibility of the rules; but they were held in sufficient consideration to disturb the conscience of the dramatic poets, who consequently were extremely timid in availing themselves of the prerogatives they inherited from Shakspeare. On the other hand, these prerogatives were at the same time problems; it requires no ordinary degree of skill to arrange, with simplicity and perspicuity, such great masses as Shakspeare uses to bring together: more of drawing and perspective are required for an extensive fresco painting, than for a small oil picture. In renouncing the intermixture of comic scenes when they no longer understood their ironical aim, they did perfectly right: Southern still attempted them in his *Oroonoko*, but in his hands they exhibit a wretched appearance. With the general knowledge and admiration of the ancients which existed in England, we might have looked for some attempt at a true imitation of the Greek Tragedy; no such imitation has, however, made its appearance; in the choice and handling of their materials they show an undoubted affinity to the French. Some poets of celebrity in other departments of poetry, Young, Thomson, Glover, have written tragedies, but no one of them has displayed any true tragical talent.

They have now and then had recourse to familiar tragedy to assist the barrenness of imagination; but the moral aim, which must exclusively prevail in this species, is a true extinguisher of genuine poetical inspiration. They have, therefore, been satisfied with a few attempts. The *Merchant of London*, and *The Gamester*, are the only plays in this way which have attained any great reputation. *George Barnwell* is remarkable from having been praised by Diderot and Lessing, as a model for imitation. This error could only have escaped from Lessing in the keenness of his hostility to the French conventional tone. For in truth it is necessary to keep Lillo's honest views constantly in mind, to prevent us from finding *George Barnwell* as laughable as it is certainly trivial. Whoever possesses so little, or rather, no knowledge of men and of the world, ought not to set up for a public lecturer on morals. We might draw a very different conclusion from this piece, from that which the author had in view, namely, that to prevent young people from entertaining a violent passion, and being led at last to steal and murder, for the first wretch who spreads her snares for them, (which they of course cannot possibly avoid,) we ought, at an early period, to make them acquainted with the true character of courtezans. Besides, I cannot approve of not making the gallows visible before the last scene; such a piece ought always to be acted with a place of execution in the background. With respect to the edification to be drawn from a drama of this kind, I should prefer the histories of malefactors, which in England are usually printed at executions; they contain, at least, real facts, instead of awkward fictions.

Garrick's appearance forms an epoch in the history of the English theatre, as he chiefly dedicated his talents to the great characters of Shakspeare, and built his own fame on the growing admiration for this poet. Before his time, Shakspeare had only been brought on the stage in mutilated and disfigured alterations. Garrick returned on the whole to the true originals, though he still allowed himself to make some very unfortunate changes. It appears to me that the only excusable alteration of Shakspeare is, to leave out a few things not in conformity to the taste of the time. Garrick was undoubtedly a great actor. Whether he always conceived the parts of Shakspeare in the sense of the poet, I, from the very circumstances stated in the eulogies on his acting, should be inclined to doubt. He excited, however, a noble emulation to represent worthily the great national poet; this has ever since been the highest aim of actors, and even at present the stage can boast of men whose histrionic talents are deservedly famous.

But why has this revival of the admiration of Shakspeare remained unproductive for dramatic poetry? Because he has been too much the subject of astonishment, as an unapproachable genius who owed everything to nature and nothing to art. His success, it is thought, is without example, and can never be repeated; nay, it is even forbidden to venture into the same region. Had he been considered more from an artistic point of view, it would have led to an endeavour to understand the principles which he followed in his practice, and an attempt to master them. A meteor appears, disappears, and leaves no trace behind; the course of a heavenly body, however, ought to be delineated by the astronomer, for the sake of investigating more accurately the laws of general mechanics.

I am not sufficiently acquainted with the latest dramatic productions of the English, to enter into a minute account of them. That the dramatic art and the public taste are, however, in a wretched state of decline, may, I think, be safely inferred from the following circumstance. Some years ago, several German plays found their way to the English stage; plays, which, it is true, are with us the favourites of the multitude, but which are not considered by the intelligent as forming a part of our literature, and in which distinguished actors are almost ashamed of earning applause. These pieces have met with extraordinary favour in England; they have, properly speaking, as the Italians say, *fatto furore*, though indeed the critics did not fail to declaim against their immorality, veiled over by sentimental hypocrisy. From the poverty of our dramatic literature, the admission of such abominations into Germany may be easily comprehended; but what can be alleged in favour of this depravity of taste in a nation like the English, which possesses such treasures, and which must therefore descend from such an elevation? Certain writers are nothing in themselves; they are merely symptoms of the disease of their age; and were we to judge from them, there is but too much reason to fear that, in England, an effeminate sentimentality in private life is more frequent, than from the astonishing political greatness and energy of the nation we should be led to suppose.

May the romantic drama and the grand historical drama, those truly native species, be again speedily revived, and may Shakspeare find such worthy imitators as some of those whom Germany has to produce!

LECTURE XXIX.

Spanish Theatre--Its three Periods: Cervantes, Lope de Vega, Calderon-- Spirit of the Spanish Poetry in general--Influence of the National History on it--Form, and various species of the Spanish Drama--Decline since the beginning of the eighteenth century.

The riches of the Spanish stage have become proverbial, and it has been more or less the custom of the Italian, French, and English dramatists, to draw from this source, and generally without acknowledgment. I have often, in the preceding Lectures, had occasion to notice this fact; it was incompatible, however, with my purpose, to give an enumeration of all that has been so borrowed, for it would have assumed rather a bulky appearance, and without great labour it could not have been rendered complete. What has been taken from the most celebrated Spanish poets might be easily pointed out; but the writers of the second and third rank have been equally laid under contribution, and their works are not easily met with out of Spain. Ingenious boldness, joined to easy clearness of intrigue, is so exclusively peculiar to the Spanish dramatists, that whenever I find these in a work, I consider myself justified in suspecting a Spanish origin, even though the circumstance may have been unknown to the author himself, who drew his plagiarism from a nearer source. [Footnote: Thus for example, *The Servant of two Masters*, of Goldoni, a piece highly distinguished above his others for the most amusing intrigue, passes for an original. A learned Spaniard has assured me, that he knows it to be a Spanish invention. Perhaps Goldoni had here merely an older Italian imitation before him.]

From the political preponderance of Spain in the sixteenth century, a knowledge of its language became widely diffused throughout Europe. Even in the first half of the seventeenth century, many traces are to be found of an acquaintance with Spanish literature in France, Italy, England, and Germany; since that time, however, the study of it had every where fallen into neglect, till of late some zeal for it has been again excited in Germany. In France they have no other idea of the Spanish theatre, than what can be formed from the translations of Linguet. These again have been rendered into German, and their number has been increased by others, in no respect better, derived immediately from the originals. The translators have, however, confined themselves almost exclusively to the department of comedies of intrigue, and though all the Spanish plays with the exception of a few *Entremeses*, *Saynetes*, and those of a very late period, are versified, they have turned the whole into prose, and even considered themselves entitled to praise for having carefully removed every thing like poetical ornament. After such a mode of proceeding nothing but the material scaffolding of the original could remain; the beautiful colouring must have disappeared together with the form of execution. That translators who could show such a total want of judgment as to poetical excellences would not choose the best pieces of the store, may be easily supposed. The species in question, though in the invention of innumerable intrigues, of such a kind as the theatrical literature of all other countries can produce but few examples of it, it certainly shows astonishing acuteness, is, nevertheless, by no means the most valuable part of the Spanish theatre, which displays a much greater brilliancy in the handling of wonderful, mythological, or historical subjects.

The selection published by De la Huerta in sixteen small volumes, under the title of *Teatro Hespanol*, with introductions giving an account of the authors of the pieces and the different species, will not afford, even to one conversant with the language, a very extensive acquaintance with the Spanish theatre. His collection is limited almost exclusively to the department of comedies in modern manners, and he has not admitted into it any of the pieces of an earlier period, composed by Lope de Vega, or his predecessors. Blankenburg and Bouterwek [Footnote: The former, in his annotations on *Sulzers Theorie der schonen Kunste*, the latter in his *Geschichte der Spanischen Poesie*.] among ourselves have laboured to throw light on the earlier history of the Spanish theatre, before it acquired its proper shape and attained literary dignity,--a subject involved in much obscurity. But even at an after period, an immense number of works were written for the stage which never appeared in print, and which are either now lost or only exist in manuscript; while, on the other hand, there is hardly an instance of a piece being printed without having first been brought on the stage. A correct and complete history of the Spanish theatre, therefore, can only be executed in Spain. The notices of the German writers above-mentioned, are however of use, though not free from errors; their opinions of the poetical merit of the several pieces, and the general view which they have taken, appear to me exceedingly objectionable.

The first advances of Dramatic Art in Spain were made in the last half of the sixteenth century; and with the end of the seventeenth it ceased to flourish. In the eighteenth, after the War of the Succession, (which seems to have had a very prejudicial influence on the Spanish literature in general,) very little can be mentioned which does not display extravagance, decay, the retention of old observances without meaning, or a tame imitation of foreign productions. The Spanish literari of the last generation frequently boast of their old national poets, the people entertain a strong attachment to them, and in Mexico, as well as Madrid, their pieces are always represented with impassioned applause.

The various epochs in the formation of the Spanish theatre may be designated by the names of three of its most famous authors, Cervantes, Lope de Vega, and Calderon.

The earliest and most valuable information and opinions on this subject are to be found in the writings of Cervantes; chiefly in *Don Quixote* (in the dialogue with the Canon), in the Preface to his later plays, and in the *Journey to Parnassus*. He has also in various other places thrown out occasional remarks on the subject. He had witnessed in his youth the commencement of the dramatic art in Spain; the poetical poverty of which, as well as the meagreness of the theatrical decorations, are very humorously described by him. He was justified in looking upon himself as one of the founders of this art; for before he gained immortal fame by his *Don Quixote* he had diligently laboured for the stage, and from twenty to thirty pieces (so negligently does he speak of them) from his pen had been acted with applause. On this account, however, he made no very high claims, nor after they had fulfilled their momentary destination did he allow any of them to be printed; and it was only lately that two of these earlier labours were for the first time published. One of these plays, probably Cervantes' first, *The Way of Living in Algiers* (*El Trato de Argel*), still bears traces of the infancy of the art in the preponderance of narrative, in the general meagreness, and in the want of prominency in the figures and situations. The other, however, *The Destruction of Numantia*, has altogether the elevation of the tragical cothurnus; and, from its unconscious and unlaboured approximation to antique grandeur and purity, forms a remarkable phenomenon in the history of modern poetry. The idea of destiny prevails in it throughout; the allegorical figures which enter between the acts supply nearly, though in a different way, the place of the chorus in the Greek tragedies; they guide the reflection and propitiate the feeling. A great deed of heroism is accomplished; the extremity of suffering is endured with constancy; but it is the deed and the suffering of a whole nation whose individual members, it may almost be said, appear but as examples of the general fortitude and magnanimity, while the Roman heroes seem merely the instruments of fate. There is, if I may so speak, a sort of Spartan pathos in this piece: every single and personal consideration is swallowed up in the feeling of patriotism; and by allusions to the warlike fame of his nation in modern times, the poet has contrived to connect the ancient history with the interests of his own day.

Lope de Vega appeared, and soon became the sole monarch of the stage; Cervantes was unable to compete with him; yet he was unwilling altogether to abandon a claim founded on earlier success; and shortly before his death, in the year 1615, he printed eight plays and an equal number of smaller interludes, as he had failed in his attempts to get them brought on the stage. They have generally been considered greatly inferior to his other prose and poetical works; their modern editor is even of opinion that they were meant as parodies and satires on the vitiated taste of the time: but to find this hypothesis ridiculous, we have only to read them without any such prepossession. Had Cervantes entertained such a design, he would certainly have accomplished it in a very different way in one piece, and also in a manner both highly amusing and not liable to misconception. No, they were intended as pieces in the manner of Lope: contrary to his own convictions, Cervantes has here endeavoured, by a display of greater variety, of wonderful plots, and theatrical effect to comply with the taste of his contemporaries. It would appear from them that he considered a superficial composition as the main requisite for applause; his own, at least, is for the most part, extremely loose and ill-connected, and we have no examples in his prose works of a similar degree of negligence. Hence, as he partly renounced his peculiar excellences, we need not be astonished that he did not succeed in surpassing Lope in his own walk. Two, however, of these pieces, *The Christian Slaves in Algiers (Los Banos de Argel)*, an alteration of the piece before-mentioned, and *The Labyrinth of Love*, are, in their whole plot, deserving of great praise, while all of them contain so many beautiful and ingenious traits, that when we consider them by themselves, and without comparing them with the *Destruction of Numantia*, we feel disposed to look on the opinion entertained pretty generally by the Spanish critics as a mere prejudice. But on the other hand, when we compare them with Lope's pieces, or bear in mind the higher excellences to which Calderon had accustomed the public, this opinion will appear to admit of conditional justification. We may, on the whole, allow that the mind of this poet was most inclined to the epic, (taking the word in its more extensive signification, for the narrative form of composition); and that the light and gentle manner in which he delights to move the mind is not well suited to the making the most of every moment, and to the rapid compression which are required on the theatre. But when we, on the other hand, view the energetical pathos in *The Destruction of Numantia*, we are constrained almost to consider it as merely accidental that Cervantes did not devote himself wholly to this species of writing, and find room in it for the complete development of his inventive mind.

The sentence pronounced by Cervantes on the dramas of his later contemporaries is one of the neglected voices which, from time to time, in Spain have been raised, insisting on the imitation of the ancient classics, while the national taste had decidedly declared in favour of the romantic drama in its boldest form. On this subject Cervantes, from causes which we may easily comprehend, was not altogether impartial. Lope de Vega had followed him as a dramatic writer, and by his greater fertility and the effective brilliancy of his pieces, had driven him from the stage; a circumstance which ought certainly to be taken into account in explaining the discontent of Cervantes in his advanced age with the direction of the public taste and the constitution of the theatre. It would appear, too, that in his poetical mind there was a certain prosaical corner in which there still lurked a disposition to reject the wonderful, and the bold play of fancy, as contrary to probability and nature. On the authority of the ancients he recommended a stricter separation of the several kinds of the drama; whereas the romantic art endeavours, in its productions, as he himself had done in his romances and novels, to blend all the elements of poetry; and he censured with great severity, as real offences against propriety, the rapid changes of time and place. It is remarkable that Lope himself was unacquainted with his own rights, and confessed that he wrote his pieces, contrary to the rules with which he was well acquainted, merely for the sake of pleasing the multitude. That this object entered prominently into his consideration is certainly true; still he remains one of the most extraordinary of all the popular and favourite theatrical writers that ever lived, and well deserves to be called in all seriousness by his rival and adversary, Cervantes, a wonder of nature.

The pieces of Lope de Vega, numerous beyond all belief, have partly never been printed; while of those that have, a complete collection is seldom to be found, except in Spain. Many pieces are probably falsely ascribed to him; an abuse of which Calderon also complains. I know not whether Lope himself ever gave a list of the pieces actually composed by him; indeed he could hardly at last have remembered the whole of them. However, by reading a few, we shall advance pretty far towards an acquaintance with this poet; nor need we be much afraid lest we should have failed to peruse the most excellent, as in his separate productions he does not surprise us by any elevated flight nor by laying open the whole unfathomable depths of his mind. This prolific writer, at one time too much idolized, at another too much depreciated, appears here undoubtedly in the most advantageous light, as the theatre was the best school for the correction of his three great errors, want of connexion, diffuseness, and an unnecessary parade of learning. In some of his pieces, especially the historical ones, founded on old romances or traditional tales, for instance, *King Wamba*, *The Youthful Tricks of Bernardo del Carpio*, *The Battlements of Toro*, &c., there prevails a certain rudeness of painting, which, however, is not altogether without character, and seems to have been purposely chosen to suit the subjects: in others, which portray the manners of his own time, as for instance, *The Lively Fair One of Toledo*, *The Fair deformed*, we may observe a highly cultivated social tone. All of them contain, besides truly interesting situations, a number of inimitable jokes; and there are, perhaps, very few of them which would not, if skilfully treated and adapted to our stages, produce a great effect in the present day. Their chief defects are, a profusion of injudicious invention, and negligence in the execution. They resemble the groups which an ingenious sketcher scrawls on paper without any preparation, and without even taking the necessary time; in which, notwithstanding this hasty negligence every line is full of life and significance. Besides the want of careful finish, the works of Lope are deficient in depth, and also in those more delicate allusions which constitute the peculiar mysteries of the art.

If the Spanish theatre had not advanced farther, if it had possessed only the works of Lope and the more eminent of his contemporaries, as Guillen de Castro, Montalban, Molina, Matos-Fragoso, &c., we should have to praise it, rather for grandeur of design and for promising subjects than for matured perfection. But Don Pedro Calderon de la Barca now made his appearance, a writer as prolific and diligent as Lope, and a poet of a very different kind,--a poet if ever any man deserved that name. The "wonder of nature," the enthusiastic popularity, and the sovereignty of the stage were renewed in a much higher degree. The years of Calderon [Footnote: Born in 1601.] keep nearly equal pace with those of the seventeeth century; he was consequently sixteen when Cervantes, and thirty-five when Lope died, whom he survived nearly half a century. According to his biographer's account, Calderon wrote more than a hundred and twenty plays, more than a hundred spiritual allegorical acts (*Autos*), a hundred merry interludes or *Saynetes* [Footnote: This account is perhaps somewhat rhetorical. The most complete, and in every respect the best edition of the plays, that of Apontes, contains only a hundred and eight pieces. At the request of a great Lord, Calderon, shortly before his death, gave a list of his genuine works. He names a hundred and eleven plays; but among them there are considerably more than three which are not to be found in the collection of Apontes. Some of them may, indeed, be concealed under other titles, as, for instance, the piece, which Calderon himself calls, *El Tuzani de la Alpujarra*, is named in the collection, *Amar despues de la Muerte*. Others are unquestionably omitted, for instance, a *Don Quixote*, which I should be particularly desirous of seeing. We may infer from many circumstances that Calderon had a great respect for Cervantes. The collection of the *Autos sacramentales* contains only seventy-two, and of these several are not mentioned by Calderon. And yet he lays the greatest stress on these; wholly devoted to religion, he had become in his age more indifferent towards the temporal plays of his muse, although he did not reject them, and still continued to add to the number. It might well be with him as with an excessively wealthy man, who, in a general computation, is apt to forget many of the items of his capital. I have never yet been able to see any of the *Saynetes* of Calderon; I cannot even find an account whether or not they have been ever collected and printed.] besides a number of poems which were not dramatical. As from his fourteenth to his eighty-first year, that in which he died, he continued to produce dramatic works, they spread over a great space, and we may therefore suppose that he did not write with the same haste as Lope; he had sufficient leisure to consider his plans maturely, which, without doubt, he has done. In the execution, he could not fail from his extensive practice to acquire great readiness.

In this almost incalculable exuberance of production, we find nothing thrown out at random; all is finished in masterly perfection, agreeably to established and consistent principles, and with the most profound artistic views. This cannot be denied even by those who would confound the pure and high style of the romantic drama with mannerism, and consider these bold flights of poetry, on the extreme boundaries of the conceivable, as aberrations in art. For Calderon has every where converted that into matter what passed with his predecessors for form;--nothing less than the noblest and most exquisite excellence could satisfy him. And this is why he repeats himself in many expressions, images, comparisons, nay, even in many plays of situation; for he was too rich to be under the necessity of borrowing from himself, much less from others. The effect on the stage is with Calderon the first and last thing; but this consideration, which is generally felt by others as a restraint, is with him a positive end. I know of no dramatist equally skilled in converting effect into poetry, who is at once so sensibly vigorous and so ethereal.

His dramas divide themselves into four principal classes: compositions on sacred subjects taken from scripture and legends; historical; mythological, or founded upon other fictitious materials; and finally, pictures of social life in modern manners.

The pieces founded on the history of his own country are historical only in the more limited acceptation. The earlier periods of Spanish history have often been felt and portrayed by Calderon with the greatest truth; but, in general, he had too decided, I might almost say, too burning a predilection for his own nation, to enter into the peculiarities of another; at best he could have portrayed what verges towards the sun, the South and the East; but classical antiquity, as well as the North of Europe, were altogether foreign to his conception. Materials of this description he has therefore taken in a perfectly fanciful sense: generally the Greek mythology became in his hands a delightful tale, and the Roman history a majestic hyperbole.

His sacred compositions must, however, in some degree, be ranked as historical; for although surrounded with rich fiction, as is always the case in Calderon, they nevertheless in general express the character of Biblical or legendary story with great fidelity. They are distinguished, however, from the other historical pieces by the frequent prominency of a significant allegory, and by the religious enthusiasm with which the poet, in the spiritual acts designed for the celebration of the festival of Corpus Christi, the *Autos* exhibits the universe as it were, under an allegorical representation in the purple flames of love. In this last class he was most admired by his contemporaries, and here also he himself set the highest value on his labours. But without having read, at least, one of them in a truly poetical translation, my auditors could not form the slightest idea of them; while the due consideration of these *Autos* would demand a difficult investigation into the admissibility of allegory into dramatical composition. I shall therefore confine myself to those of his dramas which are no allegorical. The characterization of these I shall be very far from exhausting; I can merely exhibit a few of their more general features.

Of the great multitude of ingenious and acute writers, who were then tempted by the dazzling splendour of the theatrical career to write for the stage, the greater part were mere imitators of Calderon; a few only deserve to be named along with him, as Don Agustin Moreto, Don Franzisco de Roxas, Don Antonio de Solis, the acute and eloquent historian of the conquest of Mexico, &c. The dramatic literature of the Spaniards can even boast of a royal poet, Philip IV., the great patron and admirer [Footnote: This monarch seems, in reality, to have had a relish for the peculiar excellence of his favourite poet, whom he considered as the brightest ornament of his court. He was so prepossessed in favour of the national drama, that he forbade the introduction into Spain of the Italian opera, which was then in general favour at the different European courts: an example which deserves to be held up to the German Princes, who have hitherto, from indifference towards every thing national, and partiality for every thing foreign, done all in their power to discourage the German poets.] of Calderon, to whom several anonymous pieces, with the epigraph *de un ingenio de esta corte*, are ascribed. All the writers of that day wrote in a kindred spirit; they formed a true school of art. Many of them have peculiar excellences, but Calderon in boldness, fulness, and profundity, soars beyond them all; in him the romantic drama of the Spaniards attained the summit of perfection.

We shall endeavour to give a feeble idea of the spirit and form of these compositions, which differ so widely from every other European production. For this purpose, however, we must enter in some measure into the character of the Spanish poetry in general, and those historical circumstances by which it has been determined.

The beginnings of the Spanish poetry are extremely simple: its two fundamental forms were the romaunt and the song, and in these original national melodies we everywhere fancy we hear the accompaniment of the guitar. The romaunt, which is half Arabian in its origin, was at first a simple heroic tale; afterwards it became a very artificial species, adapted to various uses, but in which the picturesque ingredient always predominated even to the most brilliant luxuriance of colouring. The song again, almost destitute of imagery, expressed tender feelings in ingenious turns; it extends its sportiveness to the very limits where the self-meditation, which endeavours to transfuse an inexpressible disposition of mind into thought, wings again the thought to dreamlike intimations. The forms of the song were diversified by the introduction into poetry of what in music is effected by variation. The rich properties of the Spanish language however could not fully develop themselves in these species of poetry, which were rather tender and infantine than elevated. Hence towards the beginning of the sixteenth century they adapted the more comprehensive forms of Italian poetry, *Ottave Terzine*, *Canzoni*, *Sonetti*; and the Castilian language, the proudest daughter of the Latin, was then first enabled to display her whole power in dignity, beautiful boldness, and splendour of imagery. The Spanish with its guttural sounds, and frequent termination with consonants, is less soft than the Italian; but its tones are, if possible, more fuller and deeper, and fill the ear with a pure metallic resonance. It had not altogether lost the rough strength and heartiness of the Gothic, when Oriental intermixtures gave it a wonderful degree of sublimity, and elevated its poetry, intoxicated as it were with aromatic fragrances, far above all the scrupulous moderation of the sober West.

The stream of poetical inspiration, swelled by every proud consciousness, increased with the growing fame in arms of this once so free and heroic nation. The Spaniards played a glorious part in the events of the middle ages, a part but too much forgotten by the envious ingratitude of modern times. They were then the forlorn out-posts of Europe; they lay on their Pyrenean peninsula as in a camp, exposed without foreign assistance to the incessant eruptions of the Arabians, but always ready for renewed conflicts. The founding of their Christian kingdom, through centuries of conflicts, from the time when the descendants of the Goths driven before the Moors into the mountains of the North first left their protecting shelter for the war of freedom and independence, down to the complete expulsion of the Arabian invaders, was one long adventure of chivalry; nay, the preservation of Christianity itself in the face of so powerful a foe seems the wondrous work of more than mortal guidance. Accustomed to fight at the same time for liberty and religion, the Spaniard clung to his faith with a fiery zeal, as an acquisition purchased by the costly expenditure of noble blood. These consolations of a holy worship were to him the rewards of heroic exertion; in every church he saw as it were a trophy of his forefathers' bravery. Ready to shed the last drop of his blood in the cause of his God and his King; tenderly sensitive of his honour; proud, yet humble in the presence of all that is sacred and holy; serious, temperate, and modest was the old Castilian: and yet forsooth some are found to scoff at a noble and a loyal race because even at the plough they were lothe to lay aside the beloved sword, the instrument of their high vocation of patriotism and liberty.

This love of war, and spirit of enterprise, which so many circumstances had thus served to keep alive among their subjects, the monarchs of Spain made use of, at the close of the fifteenth and throughout the sixteenth century, in an attempt to obtain universal monarchy; and while the arms of the Spaniard were thus employed to effect the subjugation of other nations, he was himself deprived of his own political freedom. The faithless and tyrannical policy of Philip II. has unmeritedly drawn down on the whole nation the hatred of foreigners. In Italy, Macchiavelism was not confined to the Princes and Republican leaders; it was the universal character; all ranks were infected with the same love of artifice and fraud. But in Spain it must be laid to the charge of the Government alone, and even the religious persecutions in that country seldom or never proceeded from the outbreakings of a universal popular fury. The Spaniard never presumed to question the conduct of his spiritual and worldly superiors, and carried on their wars of aggression and ambition with the same fidelity and bravery which he had formerly displayed in his own wars of self-defence and patriotism. Personal glory, and a mistaken religious zeal, blinded him with respect to the justice of his cause. Enterprises before unexampled, were eagerly undertaken, and successfully achieved; a newly discovered world beyond the ocean was conquered by a handful of bold adventurers; individual instances of cruelty and avarice may have stained the splendour of resolute heroism, but the mass of the nation was uninfected by its contagion. Nowhere did the spirit of chivalry so long outlive its political existence as in Spain. Long after the internal prosperity, as well as the foreign influence of the nation, had fatally declined under the ruinous errors of the Second Philip, this spirit propagated itself even to the most flourishing period of their literature, and plainly imprinted upon it an indelible stamp. Here, in all their dazzling features, but associated with far higher mental culture, the middle ages were, as it were, renewed--those times when princes and nobles loved to indite the lays of love and bravery, and when, with hearts devoted equally to their lady-love and the Holy Sepulchre, knights joyfully exposed themselves to the dangers and hardships of pilgrimage to the Land of Promise, and when even a lion-hearted king touched the lute to tender sounds of amorous lamentation. The poets of Spain were not, as in most other countries of Europe, courtiers or scholars, or engaged in some peaceful art or other; of noble birth for the most part, they also led a warlike life. The union of the sword and the pen, and the exercise of arms and the nobler mental arts, was their watch-word. Garcilaso, one of the founders of Spanish poetry under Charles V., was a descendant of the Yncas of Peru, and in Africa, still accompanied by his agreeable muse, fell before the walls of Tunis: Camoens, the Portuguese, sailed as a soldier to the remotest Indies, in the track of the glorious Adventurer whose discoveries he celebrated: Don Alonso de Ercilla composed his *Araucana* in the midst of warfare with revolted savages, in a tent at the foot of the Cordilleras, or in wildernesses yet untrodden by men, or in a storm-tossed vessel on the restless ocean; Cervantes purchased, with the loss of an arm, and a long slavery in Algiers, the honour of having fought, as a common soldier, in the battle of Lepanto, under the illustrious John of Austria; Lope de Vega, among other adventures, survived the misfortunes of the Invincible Armada; Calderon served several campaigns in Flanders and in Italy, and discharged the warlike duties of a knight of Santiago until he entered holy orders, and thus gave external evidence that religion was the ruling motive of his life.

If a feeling of religion, a loyal heroism, honour, and love, be the foundation of romantic poetry, it could not fail to attain to its highest development in Spain, where its birth and growth were cherished by the most friendly auspices. The fancy of the Spaniards, like their active powers, was bold and venturesome; no mental adventure seemed too hazardous for it to essay. The popular predilection for surpassing marvels had already shown itself in its chivalrous romaunts. And so they wished also to see the wonderful on the stage; when, therefore, their poets, standing on the lofty eminence of a highly polished state of art and society, gave it the requisite form, breathed into it a musical soul, and refined its beautiful hues and fragrance from all corporeal grossness, there arose, from the very contrast of the matter and the form, an irresistible fascination. Amid the harmony of the most varied metre, the elegance of fanciful allusions, and that splendour of imagery and simile which no other language than their own could hope to furnish, combined with inventions ever new, and almost always pre-eminently ingenious, the spectators perceived in imagination a faint refulgence of the former greatness of their nation which had measured the whole world with its victories. The most distant zones were called upon to contribute, for the gratification of the mother country, the treasures of fancy as well as of nature, and on the dominions of this poetry, as on that of Charles V., the sun may truly be said never to set.

Even those plays of Calderon which, cast in modern manners, descend the most to the tone of common life, still fascinate us by a sort of fanciful magic, and cannot be considered in the same light with the ordinary run of comedies. Of those of Shakspeare, we have seen that they are always composed of two dissimilar elements: the comic, which, in so far as comic imitation requires the observance of local conditions, is true to English manners; and the romantic, which, as the native soil was not sufficiently poetical for it, is invariably transplanted to a foreign scene. In Spain, on the other hand, the national costume of that day still admitted of an ideal exhibition. This would not indeed have been possible, had Calderon introduced us into the interior of domestic life, where want and habit generally reduce all things to every-day narrowness. His comedies, like those of the ancients, end with marriages; but how different is all that precedes! With them the most immoral means are set in motion for the gratification of sensual passions and selfish views, human beings with their mental powers stand opposed to each other as mere physical beings, endeavouring to spy out and to expose their mutual weaknesses. Calderon, it is true, also represents to us his principal characters of both sexes carried away by the first ebullitions of youth, and in its unwavering pursuit of the honours and pleasures of life; but the aim after which they strive, and in the prosecution of which every thing else kicks the beam, is never in their minds confounded with any other good. Honour, love, and jealousy, are uniformly the motives out of which, by their dangerous but noble conflict, the plot arises, and is not purposely complicated by knavish trickery and deception. Honour is always an ideal principle; for it rests, as I have elsewhere shown, on that higher morality which consecrates principles without regard to consequences. It may sink down to a mere conventional observance of social opinions or prejudices, to a mere instrument of vanity, but even when so disfigured we may still recognize in it some faint feature of a sublime idea. I know no apter symbol of tender sensibility of honour as portrayed by Calderon, than the fable of the ermine, which is said to prize so highly the whiteness of its fur, that rather than stain it in flight, it at once yields itself up to the hunters and death. This sense of honour is equally powerful in the female characters; it rules over love, which is only allowed a place beside it, but not above it. According to the sentiments of Calderon's dramas, the honour of woman consists in loving only one man of pure and spotless honour, and loving him with perfect purity, free from all ambiguous homage which encroaches too closely on the severe dignity of woman. Love requires inviolable secrecy till a lawful union permits it to be publicly declared. This secrecy secures it from the poisonous intermixture of vanity, which might plume itself with pretensions or boasts of a confessed preference; it gives it the appearance of a vow, which from its mystery is the more sacredly observed. This morality does not, it is true, condemn cunning and dissimulation if employed in the cause of love, and in so far as the rights of honour may be said to be infringed; but nevertheless the most delicate consideration is observed in the conflict with other duties,--with the obligations, for instance, of friendship. Moreover, a power of jealousy, always alive and often breaking out into fearful violence,--not, like that of the East, a jealousy of possession,--but one watchful of the slightest emotions of the heart and its most imperceptible demonstrations serves to ennoble love, as this feeling, whenever it is not absolutely exclusive, ceases to be itself. The perplexity to which the mental conflict of all these motives gives rise, frequently ends in nothing, and in such cases the catastrophe is truly comic; sometimes, however, it takes a tragic turn, and then honour becomes a hostile destiny for all who cannot satisfy its requisitions without sacrificing either their happiness or their innocence.

These are the dramas of a higher kind, which by foreigners are called Pieces of Intrigue, but by Spaniards, from the dress in which they are acted, Comedies of Cloak and Sword (*Comedias de Capa y Espada*). They have commonly no other burlesque part than that of the merry valet, known by the name of the *Gracioso*. This valet serves chiefly to parody the ideal motives from which his master acts, and this he frequently does with much wit and grace. Seldom is he with his artifices employed as an efficient lever in establishing the intrigue, in which we rather admire the wit of accident than of contrivance. Other pieces are called *Comedias de figuron*; all the figures, with one exception, are usually the same as those in the former class, and this one is always drawn in caricature, and occupies a prominent place in the composition. To many of Calderon's dramas we cannot refuse the name of pieces of character, although we cannot look for very delicate characterization from the poets of a nation in which vehemence of passion and exaltation of fancy neither leave sufficient leisure nor sufficient coolness for prying observation.

Another class of his pieces is called by Calderon himself festal dramas (*fiestas*). They were destined for representation at court on solemn occasions; and though they require the theatrical pomp of frequent change of decoration and visible wonders, and though music also is often introduced into them, still we may call them poetical operas, that is, dramas which, by the mere splendour of poetry, perform what in the opera can only be attained by the machinery, the music, and the dancing. Here the poet gives himself wholly up to the boldest flights of fancy, and his creations hardly seem to touch the earth.

The mind of Calderon, however, is most distinctly expressed in the pieces on religious subjects. Love he paints merely in its most general features; he but speaks her technical poetical language. Religion is his peculiar love, the heart of his heart. For religion alone he excites the most overpowering emotions, which penetrate into the inmost recesses of the soul. He did not wish, it would seem, to do the same for mere worldly events. However turbid they may be in themselves to him, such is the religious medium through which he views them, they are all cleared up and perfectly bright. Blessed man! he had escaped from the wild labyrinths of doubt into the stronghold of belief; from thence, with undisturbed tranquillity of soul, he beheld and portrayed the storms of the world; to him human life was no longer a dark riddle. Even his tears reflect the image of heaven, like dew-drops on a flower in the sun. His poetry, whatever its apparent object, is a never-ending hymn of joy on the majesty of the creation; he celebrates the productions of nature and human art with an astonishment always joyful and always new, as if he saw them for the first time in an unworn festal splendour. It is the first awaking of Adam, and an eloquence withal, a skill of expression, and a thorough insight into the most mysterious affinities of nature, such as high mental culture and mature contemplation can alone bestow. When he compares the most remote objects, the greatest and the smallest, stars and flowers, the sense of all his metaphors is the mutual attraction subsisting between created things by virtue of their common origin, and this delightful harmony and unity of the world again is merely a refulgence of the eternal all-embracing love.

Calderon was still flourishing at the time when other countries of Europe began to manifest a strong inclination for that mannerism of taste in the arts, and those prosaic views in literature, which in the eighteenth century obtained such universal dominion. He is consequently to be considered as the last summit of romantic poetry. All its magnificence is lavished in his writings, as in fireworks the most brilliant and rarest combinations of colours, the most dazzling of fiery showers and circles are usually reserved for the last explosion.

The Spanish theatre continued for nearly a century after Calderon to be cultivated in the same spirit. All, however, that was produced in that period is but an echo of previous productions, and nothing new and truly peculiar appeared such as deserves to be named after Calderon. After him a great barrenness is perceptible. Now and then attempts were made to produce regular tragedies, that is to say, after the French model. Even the declamatory drama of Diderot found imitators. I remember reading a Spanish play, which had for its object the abolition of the torture. The exhilaration to be expected from such a work may be easily conceived. A few Spaniards, apostates from the old national taste, extol highly the prosaical and moral dramas of Moratin; but we see no reason for seeking in Spain what we have as good, or, more correctly speaking, equally bad at home. The theatrical audience has for the most part preserved itself tolerably exempt from all such foreign influences; a few years ago when a *bel esprit* undertook to reduce a justly admired piece of Moreto (*El Pareceido en la Corte*,) to a conformity with the three unities, the pit at Madrid were thrown into such a commotion that the players could only appease them by announcing the piece for the next day in its genuine shape.

When in any country external circumstances, such, for instance, as the influence of the clergy, the oppression of the censorship, and even the jealous vigilance of the people in the maintenance of their old national customs, oppose the introduction of what in neighbouring states passes for a progress in mental culture, it frequently happens that clever description of heads will feel an undue longing for the forbidden fruit, and first begin to admire some artistic depravity, when it has elsewhere ceased to be fashionable. In particular ages certain mental maladies are so universally epidemic that a nation can never be secure from infection till it has been innoculated with it. With respect, however, to the fatal enlightenment of the last generation, the Spaniards it would appear have come off with the chicken-pox, while in the features of other nations the disfiguring variolous scars are but too visible. Living nearly in an insular situation, Spaniards have slept through the eighteenth century, and how in the main could they have applied their time better? Should the Spanish poetry ever again awake in old Europe, or in the New World, it would certainly have a step to make, from instinct to consciousness. What the Spaniards have hitherto loved from innate inclination, they must learn to reverence on clear principles, and, undismayed at the criticism to which it has in the mean time been exposed, proceed to fresh creations in the spirit of their greatest poets.

LECTURE XXX.

Origin of the German Theatre--Hans Sachs--Gryphius--The age of Gottsched-- Wretched Imitation of the French--Lessing, Goethe, and Schiller--Review of their Works--Their influence on Chivalrous Dramas, Affecting Dramas, and Family Pictures--Prospect for Futurity.

In its cultivated state, the German theatre is much younger than any of those of which we hare already spoken, and we are not therefore to wonder if the store of our literature in valuable original works, in this department, is also much more scanty.

Little more than half a century ago, German literature was in point of talent at the very lowest ebb; at that time, however, greater exertions first began to be made, and the Germans have since advanced with gigantic strides. And if Dramatic Art has not been cultivated with the same success, and I may add with the same zeal, as other branches, the cause must perhaps be attributed to a number of unfavourable circumstances rather than to any want of talents.

The rude beginnings of the stage are with us as old as with other countries [Footnote: The first mention of the mysteries or religious representations in Germany, with which I am acquainted, is to be found in the *Eulenspiegel*. In the 13th History, we may see this merry, but somewhat disgusting trick, of the celebrated buffoon: "How Eulenspiegel made a play in the Easter fair, in which the priest and his maid-servant fought with the boors." Eulenspiegel is stated to have lived towards the middle of the fourteenth century, but the book cannot be placed farther back than the beginning of the fifteenth.]. The oldest drama which we have in manuscript is the production of one Hans Rosenpluet, a native of Nuremberg, about the middle of the fifteenth century. He was followed by two fruitful writers born in the same imperial city, Hans Sachs and Ayrer. Among the works of Hans Sachs we find, besides merry carnival plays, a great multitude of tragedies, comedies, histories both spiritual and temporal, where the prologue and epilogue are always spoken by the herald. The latter, it appears, were all acted without any theatrical apparatus, not by players, but by respectable citizens, as an allowable relaxation for the mind. The carnival plays are somewhat coarse, but not unfrequently extremely droll, as the jokes in general are; they often run out into the wildest farce, and, inspired by mirth and drollery, leave far behind the narrow bounds of the world of reality. In all these plays the composition is respectable, and without round-about goes at once to the point: all the characters, from God the Father downwards, state at once in the clearest terms what they have at heart, and the reasons which have caused them to make their appearance; they resemble those figures in old pictures who have written labels placed in their mouths, to aid the defective expression of the attitudes. In form they approach most nearly to what was elsewhere called Moralities; allegorical personages are frequent in them. These sketches of a dramatic art yet in its infancy, are feebly but not falsely drawn; and if only we had continued to proceed in the same path, we should have produced something better and more characteristic than the fruits of the seventeenth century.

In the first half of this century, poetry left the sphere of common life, to which it had so long been confined, and fell into the hands of the learned. Opiz, who may be considered as the founder of its modern form, translated several tragedies from the ancients into verse, and composed pastoral operas after the manner of the Italians; but I know not whether he wrote anything expressly for the stage. He was followed by Andreas Gryphius, who may be styled our first dramatic writer. He possessed a certain extent of erudition in his particular department, as is proved by several of his imitations and translations; a piece from the French, one from the Italian, a tragedy from the Flemish of Vondel; lastly, a farce called *Peter Squenz*, an extension of the burlesque tragedy of *Pyramus and Thisbe*, in *The Midsummer Night's Dream* of Shakspeare. The latter was then almost unknown beyond his own island; the learned Morhof, who wrote in the last half of the seventeenth century, confesses that he had never seen Shakspeare's works, though he was very well acquainted with Ben Jonson. Even about the middle of the last century, a writer of repute in his days, and not without merit, has in one of his treatises instituted a comparison between Shakspeare and Andreas Gryphius, the whole resemblance consisting in this, that Gryphius, like Shakspeare, was also fond of calling up the spirits of the departed. He seems rather to have had Vondel, the Fleming, before his eyes, a writer still highly celebrated by his countrymen, and universally called by them, the great Vondel, while Gryphius himself has been consigned to oblivion. Unfortunately the metre in Gryphius's plays is the Alexandrine; the form, however, is not so confined as that of the French at an after period; the scene sometimes changes, and the interludes, partly musical, partly allegorical, bear some resemblance to the English masques. In other respects, Gryphius possessed little theatrical skill, and I do not even know if his pieces were ever actually brought out on the stage. The tragedies of Lohenstein, who in his day may be styled the Marino of our literature, in their structure resemble those of Gryphius; but, not to mention their other faults, they are of such an immeasurable length as to set all ideas of representation at defiance.

The pitiful condition of the theatre in Germany at the end of the seventeenth and during the first third part of the eighteenth century, wherever there was any other stage than that of puppet-shows and mountebanks, corresponded exactly to that of the other branches of our literature. We have a standard for this wretchedness, in the fact that Gottsched actually once passed for the restorer of our literature; Gottsched, whose writings resemble the watery beverage, which was then usually recommended to convalescent patients, from an idea that they could bear nothing stronger, which, however, did but still more enfeeble their stomachs. Gottsched, among his other labours, composed a great deal for the theatre; connected with a certain Madam Neuber, who was at the head of a company of players in Leipsic, he discarded Punch (Hanswurst), whom they buried solemnly with great triumph. I can easily conceive that the extemporaneous part of *Punch*, of which we may even yet form some notion from the puppet-shows, was not always very skilfully filled up, and that many platitudes were occasionally uttered by him; but still, on the whole, Punch had certainly more sense in his little finger than Gottsched in his whole body. Punch, as an allegorical personage, is immortal; and however strong the belief in his death may be, in some grave office-bearer or other he still pops up unexpectedly upon us almost every day.

Gottsched and his school now inundated the German theatre, which, under the influence of these insipid and diffuse translations from the French, was hereafter to become regular. Heads of a better description began to labour for the stage; but, instead of bringing forth really original works, they contented themselves with producing wretched imitations; and the reputation of the French theatre was so great, that from it was borrowed the most contemptible mannerism no less than the fruits of a better taste. Thus, for example, Gellert still composed pastoral plays after bad French models, in which shepherds and shepherdesses, with rose-red and apple-green ribands, uttered all manner of insipid compliments to one another.

Besides the versions of French comedies, others, translated from the Danish of Holberg, were acted with great applause. This writer has certainly great merit. His pictures of manners possess great local truth; his exhibitions of depravity, folly, and stupidity, are searching and complete; in strength of comic motives and situations he is not defective; only he does not show much invention in his intrigues. The execution runs out too much into breadth. The Danes speak in the highest terms of the delicacy of his jokes in their own language; but to our present taste the vulgarity of his tone is revolting, though in the low sphere in which he moves, and amidst incessant storms of cudgellings, it may be natural enough. Attempts have lately been made to revive his works, but seldom with any great success. As his principal merit consists in his characterization, which certainly borders somewhat on caricature, he requires good comic actors to represent him with advantage.

A few plays of that time, in the manners of our own country, by Gellert and Elias Schlegel, are not without merit; only they have this error, that in drawing folly and stupidity the same wearisomeness has crept into their picture which is inseparable from them in real life.

In tragedies, properly so called, after French models, the first who were in any degree successful were Elias Schlegel, and afterwards Cronegk and Weisse. I know not whether their labours, if translated into good French verse, would then appear as frigid as they now do in German. It is insufferable to us to read verses of an ell long, in which the style seldom rises above watery prose; for a true poetic language was not formed in German until a subsequent period. The Alexandrine, which in no language can be a good metre, is doubly stiff and heavy in ours. Long after our poetry had again begun to take a higher flight, Gotter, in his translation of French tragedies, made the last attempt to ennoble the Alexandrine and procure its re-admission into Tragedy, and, it appears to me, proved by his example that we must for ever renounce the idea. It serves admirably, however, for a parody of the stilted style of false tragical emphasis; its use, too, is much to be recommended in some kinds of Comedy, especially in small afterpieces. Those earlier tragedies, after the French model, notwithstanding the uncommon applause they met with in their day, show how little hope there is of any progress of art in the way of slavish imitation. Even a form, narrow in itself, when it has been established under the influence of a national way of thinking, has still some significance; but when it is blindly taken on trust in other countries, it becomes altogether a Spanish mantle.

Thus bad translations of French comedies, with pieces from Holberg, and afterwards from Goldoni, and with a few imitations of a public nature, and without any peculiar spirit, constituted the whole repertory of our stage, till at last Lessing, Goethe, and Schiller, successively appeared and redeemed the German theatre from its long-continued mediocrity.

Lessing, indeed, in his early dramatic labours, did homage to the spirit of his age. His youthful comedies are rather insignificant; they do not already announce the great mind who was afterwards to form an epoch in so many departments of literature. He sketched several tragedies after the French rules, and executed several scenes in Alexandrines, but has succeeded with none: it would appear that he had not the requisite facility for so difficult a metre. Even his *Miss Sara Sampson* is a familiar tragedy in the lachrymose and creeping style, in which we evidently see that he had *George Barnwell* before his eyes as a model. In the year 1767, his connexion with a company of actors in Hamburgh, and the editorship of a periodical paper dedicated to theatrical criticism, gave him an opportunity of considering more closely into the nature and requisitions of theatrical composition. In this paper he displayed much wit and acuteness; his bold, nay, (considering the opinions then prevalent,) his hazardous attacks were especially successful in overthrowing the usurpation of French taste in Tragedy. With such success were his labours attended, that, shortly after the publication of his *Dramaturgie*, translations of French tragedies, and German tragedies modelled after them, disappeared altogether from the stage. He was the first who spoke with warmth of Shakspeare, and paved the way for his reception in Germany. But his lingering faith in Aristotle, with the influence which Diderot's writings had had on him, produced a strange compound in his theory of the dramatic art. He did not understand the rights of poetical imitation, and demanded not only in dialogue, but everywhere else also, a naked copy of nature, just as if this were in general allowable, or even possible in the fine arts. His attack on the Alexandrine was just, but, on the other hand, he wished to, and was only too successful in abolishing all versification: for it is to this that we must impute the incredible deficiency of our actors in getting by heart and delivering verse. Even yet they cannot habituate themselves to it. He was thus also indirectly the cause of the insipid affectation of nature of our Dramatic writers, which a general use of versification would, in some degree, have restrained.

Lessing, by his own confession, was no poet, and the few dramas which he produced in his riper years were the slow result of great labour. *Minna van Barnhelm* is a true comedy of the refined class; in point of form it holds a middle place between the French and English style; the spirit of the invention, however, and the social tone portrayed in it, are peculiarly German. Every thing is even locally determined; and the allusions to the memorable events of the Seven Years War contributed not a little to the extraordinary success which this comedy obtained at the time. In the serious part the expression of feeling is not free from affectation, and the difficulties of the two lovers are carried even to a painful height. The comic secondary figures are drawn with much drollery and humour, and bear a genuine German stamp.

Emilia Galotti was still more admired than *Minna von Barnhelm*, but hardly, I think, with justice. Its plan, perhaps, has been better considered, and worked out with still greater diligence; but *Minna von Barnhelm* answers better to the genuine idea of Comedy than *Emilia Galotti* to that of Tragedy. Lessing's theory of the Dramatic Art would, it is easily conceived, have much less of prejudicial influence on a demi-prosaic species than upon one which must inevitably sink when it does not take the highest flight. He was now too well acquainted with the world to fall again into the drawling, lachrymose, and sermonizing tone which prevails in his *Miss Sara Sampson* throughout. On the other hand, his sound sense, notwithstanding all his admiration of Diderot, preserved him from his declamatory and emphatical style, which owes its chief effect to breaks and marks of interrogation. But as in the dialogue he resolutely rejected all poetical elevation, he did not escape this fault without falling into another. He introduced into Tragedy the cool and close observation of Comedy; in *Emilia Galotti* the passions are rather acutely and wittily characterized than eloquently expressed. Under a belief that the drama is most powerful when it exhibits faithful copies of what we know, and comes nearest home to ourselves, he has disguised, under fictitious names, modern European circumstances, and the manners of the day, an event imperishably recorded in the history of the world, a famous deed of the rough old Roman virtue--the murder of Virginia by her father. Virginia is converted into a Countess Galotti, Virginius into Count Odoardo, an Italian prince takes the place of Appius Claudius, and a chamberlain that of the unblushing minister of his lusts, &c. It is not properly a familiar tragedy, but a court tragedy in the conversational tone, to which in some parts the sword of state and the hat under the arm as essentially belong as to many French tragedies. Lessing wished to transplant into the renownless circle of the principality of Massa Carara the violent injustice of the Decemvir's inevitable tyranny; but as by taking a few steps we can extricate ourselves from so petty a territory, so, after a slight consideration, we can easily escape from the assumption so laboriously planned by the poet; on which, however, the necessity of the catastrophe wholly rests. The visible care with which he has assigned a motive for every thing, invites to a closer examination, in which we are little likely to be interrupted by any of the magical illusions of imagination: and in such examination the want of internal connectedness cannot escape detection, however much of thought and reflection the outward structure of a drama may display.

It is singular enough, that of all the dramatical works of Lessing, the last, *Nathan der Weise*, which he wrote when his zeal for the improvement of the German theatre had nearly cooled, and, as he says, merely with a view to laugh at theologists, should be the most conformable to the genuine rules of art. A remarkable tale of Boccacio is wrought up with a number of inventions, which, however wonderful, are yet not improbable, if the circumstances of the times are considered; the fictitious persons are grouped round a real and famous character, the great Saladin, who is drawn with historical truth; the crusades in the background, the scene at Jerusalem, the meeting of persons of various nations and religions on this Oriental soil,--all this gives to the work a romantic air, and with the thoughts, foreign to the age in question, which for the sake of his philosophical views the poet has interspersed, forms a contrast somewhat hazardous indeed, but yet exceedingly attractive. The form is freer and more comprehensive than in Lessing's other pieces; it is very nearly that of a drama of Shakspeare. He has also returned here to the use of versification, which he had formerly rejected; not indeed of the Alexandrine, for the discarding of which from the serious drama we are in every respect indebted to him, but the rhymeless Iambic. The verses in *Nathan* are indeed often harsh and carelessly laboured, but truly dialogical; and the advantageous influence of versification becomes at once apparent upon comparing the tone of the present piece with the prose of the others. Had not the development of the truths which Lessing had particularly at heart demanded so much of repose, had there been more of rapid motion in the action, the piece would certainly have pleased also on the stage. That Lessing, with all his independence of mind, was still in his dramatical principles influenced in some measure by the general inclination and tastes of his age, I infer from this, that the imitators of *Nathan* were very few as compared with those of *Emilia Galotti*. Among the striking imitations of the latter style, I will merely mention the *Julius van Tarent*.

Engel must be regarded as a disciple of Lessing. His small after-pieces in the manner of Lessing are perfectly insignificant; but his treatise on imitation (*Mimik*) shows the point to which the theory of his master leads. This book contains many useful observations on the first elements of the language of gesture: the grand error of the author is, that he considered it a complete system of mimicry or imitation, though it only treats of the expression of the passions, and does not contain a syllable on the subject of exhibition of character. Moreover, in his histrionic art he has not given a place to the ideas of tragic comic; and it may easily be supposed that he rejects ideality of every kind [Footnote: Among other strange things Engel says, that as the language of Euripides, the latest, and in his opinion the most perfect of the Greek tragedians has less elevation than that of his predecessors, it is probable that, had the Greeks carried Tragedy to further perfection, they would have proceeded a step farther: the next step forward would have been to discard verse altogether. So totally ignorant was Engel of the spirit of Grecian art. This approach to the tone of common life, which certainly may be traced in Euripides, is the very indication of the decline and impending fall of Tragedy: but even in Comedy the Greeks never could bring themselves to make use of prose.], and merely requires a bare copy of nature.

The nearer I draw to the present times the more I wish to be general in my observations, and to avoid entering into a minute criticism of works of living writers with part of whom I have been, or still am, in relations of personal friendship or hostility. Of the dramatic career, however, of Goethe and Schiller, two writers of whom our nation is justly proud, and whose intimate society has frequently enabled me to correct and enlarge my own ideas of art, I may speak with the frankness that is worthy of their great and disinterested labours. The errors which, under the influence of erroneous principles, they at first gave rise to, are either already, or soon will be, sunk in oblivion, even because from their very mistakes they contrived to advance towards greater purity and perfectness; their works will live, and in them, to say the least, we have the foundation of a dramatic school at once essentially German, and governed by genuine principles of art.

Scarcely had Goethe, in his *Werther*, published as it were a declaration of the rights of feeling in opposition to the tyranny of social relations, when, by the example which he set in *Gotz von Berlichingen*, he protested against the arbitrary rules which had hitherto fettered dramatic poetry. In this play we see not an imitation of Shakspeare, but the inspiration excited in a kindred mind by a creative genius. In the dialogue, he put in practice Lessing's principles of nature, only with greater boldness; for in it he rejected not only versification and all embellishments, but also disregarded the laws of written language to a degree of licence which had never been ventured upon before. He avoided all poetical circumlocutions; the picture was to be the very thing itself; and thus he sounded in our ears the tone of a remote age in a degree illusory enough for those at least who had never learned from historical monuments the very language in which our ancestors themselves spoke. Most movingly has he expressed the old German cordiality: the situations which are sketched with a few rapid strokes are irresistibly powerful; the whole conveys a great historical meaning, for it represents the conflict between a departing and a coming age; between a century of rude but vigorous independence, and one of political tameness. In this composition the poet never seems to have had an eye to its representation on the stage; rather does he appear, in his youthful arrogance, to have scorned it for its insufficiency.

It seems, in general, to have been the grand object of Goethe to express his genius in his works, and to give new poetical animation to his age; as to form, he was indifferent about it, though, for the most part, he preferred the dramatic. At the same time he was a warm friend of the theatre, and sometimes condescended even to comply with its demands as settled by custom and the existing taste; as, for instance, in his *Clavigo*, a familiar tragedy in Lessing's manner. Besides other defects of this piece, the fifth act does not correspond with the rest. In the four first acts Goethe adhered pretty closely to the story of Beaumarchais, but he invented the catastrophe; and when we observe that it strongly reminds the reader of Ophelia's burial, and the meeting of Hamlet and Laertes at her grave, we have said enough to convey an idea how strong a contrast it forms to the tone and colouring of the rest. In *Stella* Goethe has taken nearly the same liberty with the story of Count von Gleichen which Lessing did with that of *Virginia*, but his labours were still more unsuccessful; the trait of the times of the Crusades on which he founded his play is affecting, true-hearted, and even edifying; but *Stella* can only flatter the sentimentality of superficial feeling.

At a later period he endeavoured to effect a reconciliation between his own views of art and the common dramatic forms, even the very lowest, in all of which almost he has made at least a single attempt. In *Iphigenia*, he attempted to express the spirit of Ancient Tragedy, according to his conceptions of it, with regard especially to repose, perspicuity, and ideality. With the same simplicity, flexibility, and noble elegance, he composed his *Tasso*, in which he has availed himself of an historical anecdote to embody in a general significance the contrast between a court and a poet's life. *Egmont* again is a romantic and historical drama, the style of which steers a middle course between his first manner in *Gotz*, and the form of Shakspeare. *Erwin und Elmire* and *Claudine von Villabella*, if I may say so, are ideal operettes, which breathe so lightly and airily that, with the accompaniments of music and acting, they would be in danger of becoming heavy and prosaic; in these pieces the noble and sustained style of the dialogue in *Tasso* is diversified with the most tender songs. *Jery und Bately* is a charming natural picture of Swiss manners, and in the spirit and form of the best French operettes; *Scherz List und Bache* again is a true *opera buffa*, full of Italian *Lazzi. Die Mitschuldigen* is a comedy of common life in rhyme, and after the French rules. Goethe carried his condescension so far that he even wrote a continuation of an after-piece of Florian's; and his taste was so impartial that he even translated several of Voltaire's tragedies for the German stage. Goethe's words and rhythm no doubt have always golden resonance, but still we cannot praise these pieces as successful translations; and indeed it would be matter of regret if that had succeeded which ought never to have been attempted. To banish these unprofitable productions from the German soil, it is not necessary to call in the aid of Lessing's *Dramaturgie*; Goethe's own masterly parody on French Tragedy in some scenes of *Esther*, will do this much more amusingly and effectually.

Der Triumph der Empfindsamkeit (The Triumph of Sensibility) is a highly ingenious satire of Goethe's own imitators, and inclines to the arbitrary comic, and the fancifully symbolical of Aristophanes, but a modest Aristophanes in good company and at court. At a much earlier period Goethe had, in some of his merry tales and carnival plays, completely appropriated the manner of our honest Hans Sachs.

In all these transformations we distinctly recognize the same free and powerful poetical spirit, to which we may safely apply the Homeric lines on Proteus:

All' aetoi protista leon genet' aeugeneios--
Pineto d' aegron aedor, kai dendreon uphipertaelon.
Odyss. lib. iv

A lion now, he curls a surgy mane;
Here from our strict embrace a stream he glides,
And last, sublime his stately growth he rears,
A tree, and well-dissembled foliage wears.--POPE.

[Footnote: I have here quoted the translation of Pope, though nothing can well be more vapid and more unlike the original, which is literally, "First, he became a lion with a huge mane--and then flowing water; and a tree with lofty foliage."--It would not, perhaps, be advisable to recur to our earliest mode of classical translation, line for line, and nearly word for word; but when German Literature shall be better known in England, it will be seen from the masterly versions of Voss and Schlegel, that without diluting by idle epithets one line into three, as in the above example, it is still possible to combine fidelity with spirit. The German translation quoted by Mr. Schlegel runs,

Erstlich ward er ein Leu mit furchterlich rollender Mahne,
Floss dann als Wasser dahin, und rauscht' als Baum in den Wolken.
--TRANS.]

To the youthful epoch belongs his *Faust*, a work which was early planned, though not published till a late period, and which even in its latest shape is still a fragment, and from its very nature perhaps must always remain so. It is hard to say whether we are here more lost in astonishment at the heights which the poet frequently reaches, or seized with giddiness at the depths which he lays open to our sight. But this is not the place to express the whole of our admiration of this labyrinthine and boundless work, the peculiar creation of Goethe; we hare merely to consider it in a dramatic point of view. The marvellous popular story of Faustus is a subject peculiarly adapted for the stage; and the Marionette play, from which Goethe, after Lessing [Footnote: Lessing has borrowed the only scene of his sketch which he has published, (Faustus summoning the evil spirits in order to select the nimblest for his servant,) from the old piece which bears the showy title: *Infelix Prudentia, or Doctor Joannes Faustus*. In England Marlow had long ago written a *Faustus*, but unfortunately it is not printed in Dodsley's Collection.], took the first idea of a drama, satisfies our expectation even in the meagre scenes and sorry words of ignorant puppet-showmen. Goethe's work, which in some points adheres closely to the tradition, but leaves it entirely in others, purposely runs out in all directions beyond the dimensions of the theatre. In many scenes the action stands quite still, and they consist wholly of long soliloquies, or conversations, delineating Faustus' internal conditions and dispositions, and the development of his reflections on the insufficiency of human knowledge, and the unsatisfactory lot of human nature; other scenes, though in themselves extremely ingenious and significant, nevertheless, in regard to the progress of the action, possess an accidental appearance; many again, while they are in the conception theatrically effective, are but slightly sketched,--rhapsodical fragments without beginning or end, in which the poet opens for a moment a surprising prospect, and then immediately drops the curtain again: whereas in the truly dramatic poem, intended to carry the spectators along with it, the separate parts must be fashioned after the figure of the whole, so that we may say, each scene may have its exposition, its intrigue, and winding up. Some scenes, full of the highest energy and overpowering pathos, for example, the murder of Valentine, and Margaret and Faustus in the dungeon, prove that the poet was a complete master of stage effect, and that he merely sacrificed it for the sake of more comprehensive views. He makes frequent demands on the imagination of his readers; nay, he compels them, by way of background for his flying groups, to supply immense moveable pictures, and such as no theatrical art is capable of bringing before the eye. To represent the *Faustus* of Goethe, we must possess Faustus' magic staff, and his formulas of conjuration. And yet with all this unsuitableness for outward representation, very much may be learned from this wonderful work, with regard both to plan and execution. In a prologue, which was probably composed at a later period, the poet explains how, if true to his genius, he could not accommodate himself to the demands of a mixed multitude of spectators, and writes in some measure a farewell letter to the theatre.

All must allow that Goethe possesses dramatic talent in a very high degree, but not indeed much theatrical talent. He is much more anxious to effect his object by tender development than by rapid external motion; even the mild grace of his harmonious mind prevented him from aiming at strong demagogic effect. *Iphigenia in Taurus* possesses, it is true, more affinity to the Greek spirit than perhaps any other work of the moderns composed before Goethe's; but is not so much an ancient tragedy as a reflected image of one, a musical echo: the violent catastrophes of the latter appear here in the distance only as recollections, and all is softly dissolved within the mind. The deepest and most moving pathos is to be found in *Egmont*, but in the conclusion this tragedy also is removed from the external world into the domain of an ideal soul-music.

That with this direction of his poetical career to the purest expression of his inspired imagining, without regard to any other object, and with the universality of his artistic studies, Goethe should not have had that decided influence on the shape of our theatre which, if he had chosen to dedicate himself exclusively and immediately to it, he might have exercised, is easily conceivable.

In the mean time, shortly after Goethe's first appearance, the attempt had been made to bring Shakspeare on our stage. The effort was a great and extraordinary one. Actors still alive acquired their first laurels in this wholly novel kind of exhibition, and Schroder, perhaps, in some of the most celebrated tragic and comic parts, attained to the same perfection for which Garrick had been idolized. As a whole, however, no one piece appeared in a very perfect shape; most of them were in heavy prose translations, and frequently mere extracts, with disfiguring alterations, were exhibited. The separate characters and situations had been hit to a certain degree of success, but the sense of his composition was often missed.

In this state of things Schiller made his appearance, a man endowed with all the qualifications necessary to produce at once a strong effect on the multitude, and on nobler minds. He composed his earliest works while very young, and unacquainted with that world which he attempted to paint; and although a genius independent and boldly daring, he was nevertheless influenced in various ways by the models which he saw in the already mentioned pieces of Lessing, by the earlier labours of Goethe, and in Shakspeare, so far as he could understand him without an acquaintance with the original.

In this way were produced the works of his youth:--*Die Rauber*, *Cabale und Liebe*, and *Fiesco*. The first, wild and horrible as it was, produced so powerful an effect as even to turn the heads of youthful enthusiasts. The defective imitation here of Shakspeare is not to be mistaken: Francis Moor is a prosaical Richard III., ennobled by none of the properties which in the latter mingle admiration with aversion. *Cabale und Liebe* can hardly affect us by its extravagant sentimentality, but it tortures us by the most painful impressions. *Fiesco* is in design the most perverted, in effect the feeblest.

So noble a mind could not long persevere in such mistaken courses, though they gained him applauses which might have rendered the continuance of his blindness excusable. He had in his own case experienced the dangers of an undisciplined spirit and an ungovernable defiance of all constraining authority, and therefore, with incredible diligence and a sort of passion, he gave himself up to artistic discipline. The work which marks this new epoch is *Don Carlos*. In parts we observe a greater depth in the delineation of character; yet the old and tumid extravagance is not altogether lost, but merely clothed with choicer forms. In the situations there is much of pathetic power, the plot is complicated even to epigrammatic subtlety; but of such value in the eyes of the poet were his dearly purchased reflections on human nature and social institutions, that, instead of expressing them by the progress of the action, he exhibited them with circumstantial fulness, and made his characters philosophize more or less on themselves and others, and by that means swelled his work to a size quite incompatible with theatrical limits.

Historical and philosophical studies seemed now, to the ultimate profit of his art, to have seduced the poet for a time from his poetical career, to which he returned with a riper mind, enriched with varied knowledge, and truly enlightened at last with respect to his own aims and means. He now applied himself exclusively to Historical Tragedy, and endeavoured, by divesting himself of his personality, to rise to a truly objective representation. In *Wallenstein* he has adhered so conscientiously to historical truth, that he could not wholly master his materials, an event of no great historical extent is spun out into two plays, with prologue in some degree didactical. In form he has closely followed Shakspeare; only that he might not make too large a demand on the imagination of the spectators, he has endeavoured to confine the changes of place and time within narrower limits. He also tied himself down to a more sustained observance of tragical dignity, and has brought forward no persons of mean condition, or at least did not allow them to speak in their natural tone, and banished into the prelude the mere people, here represented by the army, though Shakspeare introduced them with such vividness and truth into the very midst of the great public events. The loves of Thekla and Max Piccolomini form, it is true, properly an episode, and bear the stamp of an age very different from that depicted in the rest of the work; but it affords an opportunity for the most affecting scenes, and is conceived with equal tenderness and dignity.

Maria Stuart is planned and executed with more artistic skill, and also with greater depth and breadth. All is wisely weighed; we may censure particular parts as offensive: the quarrel for instance, between the two Queens, the wild fury of Mortimer's passion, &c.; but it is hardly possible to take any thing away without involving the whole in confusion. The piece cannot fail of effect; the last moments of Mary are truly worthy of a queen; religious impressions are employed with becoming earnestness; only from the care, perhaps superfluous, to exercise, after Mary's death, poetical justice on Elizabeth, the spectator is dismissed rather cooled and indifferent.

With such a wonderful subject as the *Maid of Orleans*, Schiller thought himself entitled to take greater liberties. The plot is looser; the scene with Montgomery, an epic intermixture, is at variance with the general tone; in the singular and inconceivable appearance of the black knight, the object of the poet is ambiguous; in the character of Talbot, and many other parts, Schiller has entered into an unsuccessful competition with Shakspeare; and I know not but the colouring employed, which is not so brilliant as might be imagined, is an equivalent for the severer pathos which has been sacrificed to it. The history of the *Maid of Orleans*, even to its details, is generally known; her high mission was believed by herself and generally by her contemporaries, and produced the most extraordinary effects. The marvel might, therefore, have been represented by the poet, even though the sceptical spirit of his contemporaries should have deterred him from giving it out for real; and the real ignominious martyrdom of this betrayed and abandoned heroine would have agitated us more deeply than the gaudy and rose-coloured one which, in contradiction to history, Schiller has invented for her. Shakspeare's picture, though partial from national prejudice, still possesses much more historical truth and profundity. However, the German piece will ever remain as a generous attempt to vindicate the honour of a name deformed by impudent ridicule; and its dazzling effect, strengthened by the rich ornateness of the language, deservedly gained for it on the stage the most eminent success.

Least of all am I disposed to approve of the principles which Schiller followed in *The Bride of Messina*, and which he openly avows in his preface. The examination of them, however, would lead me too far into the province of theory. It was intended to be a tragedy, at once ancient in its form, but romantic in substance. A story altogether fictitious is kept in a costume so indefinite and so devoid of all intrinsic probability, that the picture is neither truly ideal nor truly natural, neither mythological nor historical. The romantic poetry seeks indeed to blend together the most remote objects, but it cannot admit of combining incompatible things; the way of thinking of the people represented cannot be at once Pagan and Christian. I will not complain of him for borrowing openly as he has done; the whole is principally composed of two ingredients, the story of Eteocles and Polynices, who, notwithstanding the mediation of their mother Jocaste, contend for the sole possession of the throne, and of the brothers, in the *Zwillingen van Klinger*, and in *Julius von Tarent*, impelled to fratricide by rivalry in love. In the introduction of the choruses also, though they possess much lyrical sublimity and many beauties, the spirit of the ancients has been totally mistaken; as each of the hostile brothers has a chorus attached to his, the one contending against the other, they both cease to be a true chorus; that is, the voice of human sympathy and contemplation elevated above all personal considerations.

Schiller's last work, *Wilhelm Tell*, is, in my opinion, also his best. Here he has returned to the poetry of history; the manner in which he has handled his subject, is true, cordial, and when we consider Schiller's ignorance of Swiss nature and manners, wonderful in point of local truth. It is true he had here a noble source to draw from in the speaking pictures of the immortal John Muller. This soul-kindling picture of old German manners, piety, and true heroism, might have merited, as a solemn celebration of Swiss freedom, five hundred years after its foundation, to have been exhibited, in view of Tell's chapel on the banks of the lake of Lucerne, in the open air, and with the Alps for a background.

Schiller was carried off by an untimely death in the fulness of mental maturity; up to the last moment his health, which had long been undermined, was made to yield to his powerful will, and completely exhausted in the pursuit of most praiseworthy objects. How much might he not have still performed had he lived to dedicate himself exclusively to the theatre, and with every work attained a higher mastery in his art! He was, in the genuine sense of the word, a virtuous artist; with parity of mind he worshipped the true and the beautiful, and to his indefatigable, efforts to attain them his own existence was the sacrifice; he was, moreover, far removed from that petty self-love and jealousy but too common even among artists of excellence.

Great original minds in Germany have always been followed by a host of imitators, and hence both Goethe and Schiller have been the occasion, without any fault of theirs, of a number of defective and degenerate productions being brought on our stage.

Gotz van Berlichingen was followed by quite a flood of chivalrous plays, in which there was nothing historical but the names and other external circumstances, nothing chivalrous but the helmets, bucklers, and swords, and nothing of old German honesty but the supposed rudeness: the sentiments were as modern as they were vulgar. From chivalry-pieces they became true cavalry-pieces, which certainly deserved to be acted by horses rather than by men. To all those who in some measure appeal to the imagination by superficial allusions to former times, may be applied what I said of one of the most admired of them:

Mit Harsthornern, und Burgen, uud Harnischen, pranget Johanna;
Traun! mir gefiele das Stuck, waren nicht Worte dabey.

[Footnote:
With trumpets, and donjons, and helmets, Johanna parades it.
It would certainly please were but the words all away.--ED.]

The next place in the public favour has been held by the *Family Picture* and the *Affecting Drama*, two secondary species. From the charge of encouraging these both by precept and example Lessing, Goethe, and Schiller (the two last by their earliest compositions *Stella*, *Glavigo*, *Die Geschwister*, *Cabale und Liebe*), cannot be acquitted. I will name no one, but merely suppose that two writers of some talent and theatrical knowledge had dedicated themselves to these species, that they had both mistaken the essence of dramatic poetry, and laid down to themselves a pretended moral aim; but that the one saw morality under the narrow guise of economy, and the other in that of sensibility: what sort of fruits would thus be put forth, and how would the applause of the multitude finally decide between these two competitors?

The family picture is intended to portray the every-day course of the middle ranks of society. The extraordinary events which are produced by intrigue are consequently banished from it: to cover this want of motion, the writer has recourse to a characterization wholly individual, and capable of receiving vividness from a practised player, but attaches itself to external peculiarities just as a bad portrait-painter endeavours to attain a resemblance by noticing every pit of small-pox and wart, and peculiar dress and cravat-tie: the motives and situations are sometimes humorous and droll, but never truly diverting, as the serious and prosaical aim which is always kept in view completely prevents this. The rapid determinations of Comedy generally end before the family life begins, by which all is fixed in every-day habits. To make economy poetical is impossible: the dramatic family painter will be able to say as little of a fortunate and tranquil domestic establishment, as the historian can of a state in possession of external and internal tranquillity. He is therefore driven to interest us by painting with painful accuracy the torments and the penury of domestic life--chagrins experienced in the honest exercise of duty, in the education of children, interminable dissensions between husband and wife, the bad conduct of servants, and, above all things, the cares of earning a daily subsistence. The spectators understand these pictures but too well, for every man knows where the shoe pinches; it may be very salutary for them to have, in presence of the stage, to run over weekly in thought the relation between their expenditure and income; but surely they will hardly derive from it elevation of mind or recreation, for they do but find again on the stage the very same thing which they have at home from morning to night.

The sentimental poet, again, contrives to lighten their heart. His general doctrine amounts properly to this, that what is called a good heart atones for all errors and extravagances, and that, with respect to virtue, we are not to insist so strictly on principles. Do but allow, he seems to say to his spectators, free scope to your natural impulses; see how well it becomes my *naive* girls, when they voluntarily and without reserve confess every thing. If he only knows how to corrupt by means of effeminate emotions--rather sensual than moral, but at the close contrives, by the introduction of some generous benefactor, who showers out his liberality with open hands, to make all things pretty even, he then marvellously delights the vitiated hearts of his audience: they feel as if they had themselves done noble actions, without, however, putting their hands in their own pockets--all is drawn from the purse of the generous poet. In the long run, therefore, the affecting species can hardly fail to gain a victory over the economical; and this has actually been the case in Germany. But what in these dramas is painted to us not only as natural and allowable, but even as moral and dignified, is strange beyond all thought, and the seduction, consequently, is much more dangerous than that of the licentious Comedy, for this very reason, that it does not disgust us by external indecency, but steals into unguarded minds, and selects the most sacred names for a disguise.

The poetical as well as moral decline of taste in our time has been attended with this consequence, that the most popular writers for the stage, regardless of the opinion of good judges, and of true repute, seek only for momentary applause; while others, who have both higher aims, keep both the former in view, cannot prevail on themselves to comply with the demands of the multitude, and when they do compose dramatically, have no regard to the stage. Hence they are defective in the theatrical part of art, which can only be attained in perfection by practice and experience.

The repertory of our stage, therefore, exhibits, in its miserable wealth, a motley assemblage of chivalrous pieces, family pictures, and sentimental dramas, which are occasionally, though seldom, varied by works in a grander and higher style by Shakspeare and Schiller. In this state of things, translations and imitations of foreign novelties, and especially of the French after-pieces and operettes, are indispensable. From the worthlessness of the separate works, nothing but the fleeting charm of novelty is sought for in theatrical entertainment, to the great injury of the histrionic art, as a number of insignificant parts must be got by heart in the most hurried manner, to be immediately forgotten [Footnote: To this must be added, by way of rendering the vulgarity of our theatre almost incurable, the radically depraved disposition of every thing having any reference to the theatre. The companies of actors ought to be under the management of intelligent judges and persons practised in the dramatic art, and not themselves players. Engel presided for a time over the Berlin theatre, and eye-witnesses universally assert that he succeeded in giving it a great elevation. What Goethe has effected in the management of the theatre of Weimar, in a small town, and with small means, is known to all good theatrical judges in Germany. Rare talents he can neither create nor reward, but he accustoms the actors to order and discipline, to which they are generally altogether disinclined, and thereby gives to his representations a unity and harmony which we do not witness on larger theatres, where every individual plays as his own fancy prompts him. The little correctness with which their parts are got by heart, and the imperfection of their oral delivery, I have elsewhere censured. I have heard verses mutilated by a celebrated player in a manner which would at Paris be considered unpardonable in a beginner. It is a fact, that in a certain theatre, when they were under the melancholy necessity of representing a piece in verse they wrote out the parts as prose, that the players might not be disturbed in their darling but stupid affectation of nature, by observation of the quantity. How many "periwig-pated fellows" (as Shakspeare called such people), must we suffer, who imagine they are affording the public an enjoyment, when they straddle along the boards with their awkward persons, considering the words which the poet has given them to repeat merely as a necessary evil. Our players are less anxious to please than the French. By the creation of standing national theatres as they are called, by which in several capitals people suppose that they have accomplished wonders, and are likely to improve the histrionic art, they have on the contrary put a complete end to all competition. They bestow on the players exclusive privileges--they secure their salaries for life; having now nothing to dread from more accomplished rivals, and being independent of the fluctuating favour of the spectators, the only concern of the actors is to enjoy their places, like so many benefices, in the most convenient manner. Hence the national theatres have become true hospitals for languor and laziness. The question of Hamlet with respect to the players--"Do they grow rusty?" will never become obsolete; it must, alas! be always answered in the affirmative. The actor, from the ambiguous position in which he lives (which, in the nature of things, cannot well be altered), must possess a certain extravagant enthusiasm for his art, if he is to gain any extraordinary repute. He cannot be too passionately alive to noisy applause, reputation, and every brilliant reward which may crown his efforts to please. The present moment is his kingdom, time is his most dangerous enemy, as there is nothing durable in his exhibition. Whenever he is filled with the tradesman-like anxiety of securing a moderate maintenance for himself, his wife, and children, there is an end of all improvement. We do not mean to say that the old age of deserving artists ought not to be provided for. But to those players who from age, illness, or other accidents, have lost their qualifications for acting, we ought to give pensions to induce them to leave off instead of continuing to play. In general, we ought not to put it into the heads of the players that they are such important and indispensable personages. Nothing is more rare than a truly great player; but nothing is more common than the qualifications for filling characters in the manner we generally see them filled; of this we may be convinced in every amateur theatre among tolerably educated people. Finally, the relation which subsists with us between the managers of theatres and writers, is also as detrimental as possible. In France and England, the author of a piece has a certain share of the profits of each representation; this procures for him a permanent income, whenever any of his pieces are so successful as to keep their place on the theatre. Again, if the piece is unsuccessful, he receives nothing. In Germany, the managers of theatres pay a certain sum beforehand, and at their own risk, for the manuscripts which they receive. They may thus be very considerable losers; and on the other hand, if the piece is extraordinarily successful, the author is not suitably rewarded.

The Author is under a mistake with respect to the reward which falls to the share of the dramatic writer in England. He has not a part of the profits of each representation. If the play runs three nights, it brings him in as much as if it were to run three thousand nights.--TRANS.] The labours of the poets who do not write immediately for the theatre take every variety of direction: in this, as in other departments, may be observed the ferment of ideas that has brought on our literature in foreign countries the reproach of a chaotic anarchy, in which, however, the striving after a higher aim as yet unreached is sufficiently visible.

The more profound study of Aesthetics has among the Germans, by nature a speculative rather than a practical people, led to this consequence, that works of art, and tragedies more especially, have been executed on abstract theories, more or less misunderstood. It was natural that these tragedies should produce no effect on the theatre; nay, they are, in general, unsuited for representation, and wholly devoid of any inner principle of life.

Others again, with true feeling for it, have, as it were, appropriated the very spirit of the ancient tragedians, and sought for the most suitable means of accommodating the simple and pure forms of ancient art to the present constitution of our stage.

Men truly distinguished for their talents have attached themselves to the romantic drama, but in it they have generally adopted a latitude which is not really allowable, except in a romance, wholly disregarding the compression which the dramatic form necessarily requires. Or they have seized only the musically fanciful and picturesquely sportive side of the Spanish dramas, without their thorough keeping, their energetical power, and their theatrical effect.

What path shall we now enter? Shall we endeavour to accustom ourselves again to the French form of Tragedy, which has been so long banished?

Repeated experience of it has proved that, however modified in the translation and representation, for even in the hands of a Goethe or a Schiller some modification is indispensable, it can never be very successful. The genuine imitation of Greek Tragedy has far more affinity to our national ways of thinking; but it is beyond the comprehension of the multitude, and, like the contemplation of ancient statues, can never be more than an acquired artistic enjoyment for a few highly cultivated minds.

In Comedy, Lessing has already pointed out the difficulty of introducing national manners which are not provincial, inasmuch as with us the tone of social life is not modelled after a common central standard. If we wish pure comedies, I would strongly recommend the use of rhyme; with the more artificial form they might, perhaps, gradually assume also a peculiarity of substance.

To me, however, it appears that this is not the most urgent want: let us first bring to perfection the serious and higher species, in a manner worthy of the German character. Now here, it appears to me, that our taste inclines altogether to the romantic. What most attracts the multitude in our half-sentimental, half-humorous dramas, which one moment transport us to Peru, and the next to Kamschatka, and soon after into the times of chivalry, while the sentiments are all modern and lachrymose, is invariably a certain sprinkling of the romantic, which we recognize even in the most insipid magical operas. The true significance of this species was lost with us before it was properly found; the fancy has passed with the inventors of such chimeras, and the views of the plays are sometimes wiser than those of their authors. In a hundred play-bills the name "romantic" is profaned, by being lavished on rude and monstrous abortions; let us therefore be permitted to elevate it, by criticism and history, again to its true import. We have lately endeavoured in many ways to revive the remains of our old national poetry. These may afford the poet a foundation for the wonderful festival-play; but the most dignified species of the romantic is the historical.

In this field the most glorious laurels may yet be reaped by dramatic poets who are willing to emulate Goethe and Schiller. Only let our historical drama be in reality and thoroughly national; let it not attach itself to the life and adventures of single knights and petty princes, who exercised no influence on the fortunes of the whole nation. Let it, at the same time, be truly historical, drawn from a profound knowledge, and transporting us back to the great olden time. In this mirror let the poet enable us to see, while we take deep shame to ourselves for what we are, what the Germans were in former times, and what they must again be. Let him impress it strongly on our hearts, that, if we do not consider the lessons of history better than we have hitherto done, we Germans--we, formerly the greatest and most illustrious nation of Europe, whose freely-elected prince was willingly acknowledged the head of all Christendom--are in danger of disappearing altogether from the list of independent nations. The higher ranks, by their predilection for foreign manners, by their fondness for exotic literature, which, transplanted from its natural climate into hot-houses, can only yield a miserable fruit, have long alienated themselves from the body of the people; still longer, even for three centuries, at least, has internal dissension wasted our noblest energies in civil wars, whose ruinous consequences are now first beginning to disclose themselves. May all who have an opportunity of influencing the public mind exert themselves to extinguish at last the old misunderstandings, and to rally, as round a consecrated banner, all the well-disposed objects of reverence, which, unfortunately, have been too long deserted, but by faithful attachment to which our forefathers acquired so much happiness and renown, and to let them feel their indestructible unity as Germans! What a glorious picture is furnished by our history, from the most remote times, the wars with the Romans, down to the establishment of the German Empire! Then the chivalrous and brilliant era of the House of Hohenstaufen! and lastly, of greater political importance, and more nearly concerning ourselves, the House of Hapsburg, with its many princes and heroes. What a field for a poet, who, like Shakspeare, could discern the poetical aspect of the great events of the world! But, alas, so little interest do we Germans take in events truly important to our nation, that its greatest achievements still lack even a fitting historical record.

Made in United States
Troutdale, OR
09/29/2024

23237261R00256